Ron Blue • Dr. Justin M Henegar, CFP®, ChFC®, CRPC®

Biblical Financial Planning:
A Biblical Worldview
of Personal Finance

Pearson Education, Inc., 330 Hudson Street, New York, New York 10013
A Pearson Education Company
www.pearsoned.com

Printed in the United States of America

1 16

000200010271959740

RM/KE

ISBN 10: 1-323-39112-6
ISBN 13: 978-1-323-39112-9

Brief Contents

Contents

Chapter 11: **Home Buying Decisions**   **251**

Chapter 12: **Auto Decisions**   **277**

The Big Ideas

Chapter 1–Biblical worldview works for financial decision making at all times in every circumstance for everyone.

Chapter 2—God owns it all, therefore I am a steward.

Chapter 3—Having an eternal perspective allows me to be content whatever the circumstances.

Chapter 4—Asking how much is enough is a question that everyone must answer.

Chapter 5—Every goal is a faith goal.

Our decisions are made based on our best known alternatives.

Chapter 6—Belief drives financial behaviors.

Chapter 7—Understanding where you are in the financial life cycle may encourage you; you are not alone.

Chapter 8—Spend less than you earn because every success in your financial life depends on this habit; Financial priorities are simultaneous, not sequential.

Chapter 9—Avoid the use of debt because debt always mortgages the future.

Chapter 10—Build short-term savings because the unexpected will occur.

Chapter 11—Purchasing a home or a car are privileges, not rights.

Chapter 12—A car will not make you, but it may break you.

Chapter 13—We should pay taxes with gratitude because they are symptomatic of God's provision (income).

Chapter 14—Employee benefits creates a foundation in which to build your financial plan.

Chapter 15—Set long term goals because there is always a trade-off between the short term and the long term.

Chapter 16—Giving generously will break the power of money.

Chapter 17—Pass wisdom before wealth.

Chapter 18—We are to be obedient to those over us as they are ordained by God.

Chapter 19—Listen and accept godly advice from godly advisors

Preface

I remember it as if it were yesterday. I had started a financial planning practice in 1979 dedicated to helping Christians plan and manage their money well so that they could maximize their giving. It was about 18 months later when Judy and I took three very generous couples on a vision trip to Kenya. We had traveled about four hours outside of Nairobi and were visiting with a local pastor. While sitting on a slight hillside, having tea, and looking down at his one-room mud hut, I asked him, "What was the greatest barrier to the spread of the gospel in that part of the world?" I expected him to say something such as transportation, communication, money, tribalism, etc. His answer, however, was, "Materialism!" I, probably like you, would have never ever expected that answer as I always associated materialism with America and the accumulation of things. To further understand, I questioned, "What do you mean?" His response was, "If a man has a mud, hut he wants a stone hut; if he has a thatched roof, he wants a metal roof; if he has one cow, he wants two cows; if he has one acre, he wants two acres." It was then that I realized that materialism was a disease of the heart and had nothing to do with money or where you lived.

Since that time almost 35 years ago, I have had the privilege of helping build a financial planning practice which today serves more than 7,000 clients in 15 locations. I have also had the privilege of training over 1,000 professional financial advisors of many disciplines on how to give the highest level of financial advice, all beginning with what God has to say about money and money management. I have written several books relative to personal biblical financial decision making and have been on countless radio shows answering questions. I have learned and observed many things. Most significant is that money decisions are always symptomatic of a belief system. To say it another way, my money mindset drives all of my financial decision making, and a mindset is a matter of choice. By definition, it is what I choose to set my mind on. Dallas Willard has said, "The ultimate freedom we have as human beings is the ability to select what we will allow or require our minds to dwell upon."

In our culture today, there are three goals which drive financial decision making that people are most likely to set their minds on: how much does it take to be successful, significant, and/or secure? It is easy to believe that more money or possessions will answer that question when in reality it has very little to do with money and everything to do with a mindset. God's word has more to say about money than any other subject, including prayer, heaven, and hell. Knowing our heart, He told us that if our treasure is in earthly possessions, we are doomed to rot and pass away. The answer to "How much is enough?" is always found, as the African pastor so explained it, in my heart.

Money is one of the tools that God has given me to help me get to where He wants me to go. He has designed me uniquely, gifted me uniquely, and called me uniquely.

My experience is that when we have an eternal perspective, follow God's principles of money management, and seek His wisdom, the end result is a life of contentment because everything is in its proper perspective. God's principles will never change; they are always relevant; and they are always right.

This textbook is unique and is far more than a financial literacy book. It is a book that will equip you for a lifetime of making wise financial decisions. Everything in it begins with a biblical worldview worked out in the day-to-day financial decisions and issues that you will face as you go through life. These principles apply whether you are married or single, young or old, male or female, educated to the highest levels or not. It contains all of the financial literacy that you will ever need and then provides a practical "how to" from a biblical worldview.

Dr. Justin Henegar has taken my 40 plus years as a practicing financial advisor giving biblically consistent advice, and combined it with his considerable knowledge of research and experience related to personal finance. Justin brings over a decade of experience in the financial services industry in addition to his years of teaching topics in personal finance. He has made my professional experience academically pure and relevant.

Discipleship Moments and Reflections

We hope that this text accomplishes two main points. First and foremost, we hope that throughout this text you can see how important our handling of God's resources in our lives is to our Father in Heaven. Second, we hope that the information found in this textbook helps change your heart as it relates to the way you think, feel, and act about money. You see, it is not just a matter of knowing the laws, it is a matter of our heart. We see time and time again that the Pharisees knew the law, understood the law, and followed the law to the letter of the law. What they did not see was that it is not the law that is important, it is our understanding that we need the law, we need a savior. For we have all sinned and have fallen short of God's expectations. This text will hopefully give you an appropriate biblical perspective on handling God's resources, but there comes a time that we all will need support. Because of this, we have created *Discipleship Moments and Reflections* throughout each chapter. The goal of these sections is to take a brief moment, reflect on the content presented in each short section, and then reach out to your prayer and accountability partner. If you do not have someone that you hold yourself accountable too, we would strongly encourage you to find someone to be this accountability partner for you. We need to have biblically minded individuals that can help us avoid temptation, keep us in the word, and support us through scripture reading and prayer. These brief *Discipleship Moments and Reflections* are designed to help change our heart, not just our thinking. Additionally, these *Discipleship Moments and Reflections* may be used in discussion forums as a means to apply the material personally to students' lives. May God bless you abundantly as you seek to understand His view of your money and possessions.

Ron's Corner

There have been many that have contributed to the body of knowledge as it relates to this idea of biblical financial principles or biblical financial planning. Ron Blue is one of those individuals. Ron has written many books and presented at conferences all over the world regarding biblical wisdom relating to money and money management. He was instrumental in the founding of the National Christian Foundation; started multiple different financial services firms; is the founder of Kingdom Advisors, a non-profit organization that helps financial professionals integrate biblical wisdom into their practice; and finally has partnered with Indiana Wesleyan University to create the Ron Blue Institute for Financial Planning. Needless to say, Ron Blue has laid the framework for continued scholarly work in this robust field of biblical financial planning. Therefore, we have added sections throughout each chapter titled "Ron's Corner" where Ron has provided personal snippets of his testimony, ideas, and practical experience as it relates to topics relevant to each section. We hope these are a blessing to you as they were to us as we were putting this textbook together.

Acknowledgements

When taking on a project such as writing a textbook, the end always seems so far in the distance. However, when the journey is taken with a great group of colleagues, the time and distance are far less noticeable. As we hope to get across, this project was established for the sole purpose of giving God all the glory He deserves. By establishing this as our foundation, we pray that the information is presented in a way that helps guide students to begin to see money the way God does and in the midst of this, begin to change the way they think, act, and communicate about money and money management. All this wouldn't be possible with the leading and guidance of our Lord Jesus Christ, whom all things were created through and all things were created for. It is to Him who receives all honor and praise.

There were almost countless individuals that have provided support, guidance, feedback, and editing as it relates to this project. Although we may not be able to identify everyone, know that the Lord knows who you are should we miss an appropriate acknowledgement.

We like to thank all the support from the Ron Blue Institute team who has been so instrumental in guiding and directing this project: Larry, Beth, and Michael. We can't say enough about the feedback and editing from Beth Sheaffer for her diligence in helping put many of the pieces together, Jay Kujawski who helped create many of our supplemental teaching aids, and Michael Blue who helped to make sure we were always on point and focused as well as supplying us with appropriate estate planning documents for the Case Study. Michael, thanks for everything! Larry, your continued support and uplifting nature went far beyond and came in handy more than you are probably aware. Thank you all.

We also like to thank the many contributors and editors who provided feedback in the early stages of this project. Thank you Dr. Matthew Mize for providing us with a robust tax return that will allow students to see the realities of taxes and to Russ Denstorff, of Denstorff Insurance, who helped us with various insurance policies used within our Case Study. Russ, we greatly appreciate your outside help. A big thank you to Camelot Portfolios and Ryan Zeeb and Matthew Moses who helped us with putting together investment accounts for our Case Study. Thank you for such a quick turnaround. Dr. Wayne Schmidt, thank you for eloquently drafting a message of salvation for our readers who may not have experienced the love and peace of Christ in their own life. We pray your words will have a profound impact on the students who are engaged in this textbook. We also want to pay special homage to Dr. Kelly Rush for her support in helping guide and direct the Case Study questions as well as helping to edit and providing feedback to the Case Study overall. We couldn't have done this without her time and commitment.

We also want to acknowledge many of you who provided feedback, questions, comments, insights, and other valuable information as we were putting this together: Nathan Harness, Russell James, Anita Dale, Eric Reid,

Kurt Cornfield, Shane Enete, and Eveline Lewis. Thank you for your time and effort to support this vision of fully integrating biblical wisdom in personal finance. Your insights and feedback were invaluable.

We want to also thank our publisher, Pearson Publishing, for the many meetings we had in putting this project together. Their team was extremely prompt and wonderful to work with during formatting, editing, and drafting. Thank you to Tony Belfora, Ruth Moore, Christina Battista, Jill Garrett, Rasheite Calhoun, Shalon Anderson, Micah Cox, and the entire Pearson staff for the support and guidance they gave in this project.

I would like to thank God for the opportunity He has laid before me to be involved in such an amazing group of people. Thanks to Ron Blue for his amazing insights and development of content over the past 40 years of his professional life. Thank you RBI team for the support you have given me this past year in putting this together. I want to thank my parents, Charles and Tina, for their love and support. I am so grateful for both of you. Finally, I couldn't have done this without the love and support from my wife, Lexi, and our 6 children. I love you all: Jaylyn, Jaxon, Ellie, Adley, Cora, and Brynlee!! Thank you and God bless you.

Chapter 1

Biblical Worldview

Courtesy of duncanandison/Fotolia.

BIG IDEA:
A biblical worldview works for financial decision making at all times in every circumstance for everyone.

LEARNING OUTCOMES

- Explain what it means to have a biblical worldview

- Explain the worldviews of naturalism, moral relativism, multiculturalism, pragmatism, and utopianism

- List the three main sources to reference when making biblical decisions

- List the four fundamental biblical principles of money and money management

Introduction

Financial planning has its roots in many modern disciplines, including economics, psychology, finance, and strategic resource management. When looking at personal finance, one can view different aspects of financial planning through these various lenses to gain a deeper understanding of the concepts involved (i.e., financial literacy) and then use those concepts in practical applications. Unfortunately, to date, few in the academic world have sought to understand financial planning from the wisdom and guidance of God's word, where He has preserved and protected his revelation for everybody through the power of the Holy Spirit. **1 Timothy 3:16**: "All scripture is God-breathed, and is useful in teaching, rebuking, correcting, and training in righteousness." Therefore, if one wants to handle money in alignment with God's word, it is necessary to seek out what God has to say about money and money management. To understand what God's word says about money and money management, it is important to understand what the difference between a biblical worldview and a non-Christian worldview is. This chapter looks at what a worldview is and then defines our Christian/biblical worldview. This section sets up the paradigm for how we believe Christians should view and manage money.

WHAT IS A BIBLICAL WORLDVIEW?

Worldview The ultimate core beliefs that make up one's convictions about one's self and the world in which one lives.

A **worldview** is the foundation and basis from which individuals make all of their decisions. Worldview can be defined as one's ultimate core beliefs that make up one's convictions about one's self and the world in which one lives. *Merriam-Webster's* provides a broader definition, which is "the way someone thinks about the world." In this idea of worldview, it should then be the driving force behind the way each person runs his or her life. Barna (2005) has done some extensive research on worldview and has articulated a description of the beliefs of those who adhere to a biblical worldview. According to Barna, those with a biblical worldview hold to the following eight beliefs extrapolated from the Bible (Reprinted from www.barna.org, 2005, by permission of The Barna Group.):

1. Absolute moral truth exists.
2. Moral truth is found in the Holy Scriptures (Bible).
3. The Bible is accurate (inerrant) in all of the principles it teaches.
4. External spiritual salvation cannot be earned.
5. Jesus (God's only begotten son) lived a perfect and sinless life on earth.
6. Those in Christ are commanded to share the Gospel message to the world.
7. Satan is a living force and not just a symbol of evil and seeks to draw people away from God.
8. God is the all-knowing (omniscience), all powerful (omnipotent) maker of the universe who still rules His creation today.

In its research, Barna (2005) found that roughly 5% of adults hold to this biblical worldview. Barna also notes that even within the church there are differences in worldviews. Barna found that only 8% of Protestants held to the aforementioned biblical worldview, and only 0.5% of Catholics held to a biblical worldview.

OTHER WORLDVIEWS

Chuck Colson is another Christian writer who has done significant research and writing about the idea of a biblical worldview. In the book *How Now Shall We Live?*, Colson and Pearcey (2004) present four fundamental questions that they believe all people answer at some point:

Naturalism The idea that nature has existed from the beginning and the world in which we live can and does explain everything.

Moral relativism The idea that in a naturalistic worldview, moral laws are created by those who exist in society.

Multiculturalism The idea that all cultures are all equal and acceptable and are derived from their historical and continual evolution through their experiences.

Pragmatism The idea that what is thought to work is thought to be best.

1. Where did I come from?
2. Why is there sin in the world?
3. Is there an answer to the sin issue?
4. What is my purpose?

Colson and Pearcey point out that many worldviews exist, and although not exhaustive, they provide a brief overview of several non-Christian worldviews that fall under what is referred to as a naturalism. **Naturalism** is this idea that nature has existed from the beginning (i.e., no Creator), and the world in which we live can and does explain everything. Several philosophies fall under this broad category, which we will just briefly mention here. **Moral relativism** is the idea that in a naturalistic worldview, moral laws are created by those who exist in one's society. **Multiculturalism** provides the idea that all cultures are equal and acceptable and are derived from their history and continually evolve through their experiences. **Pragmatism** stems from the idea that what is thought to work is thought to be best—in other words, if it's not broken, don't fix it. Finally, **utopianism** revolves around the construct that all humans are mostly good and that through the right governance (social structure) we can live in a perfect society. This list is far from inclusive of all possible worldviews but provides a glimpse into how many non-Christians view the world.

Colson and Pearcey (2004) conclude that the biblical worldview provides the only set of beliefs that will allow us not only to answer the four fundamental questions just listed, but also allow us to live our lives consistently in accordance with answers to these questions.

Ken Boa is another renowned author and speaker who has spent significant time in researching and understanding different worldviews. Through his work, Ken Boa has concluded that everyone has a worldview, yet most do not know or realize what it is. Refer to Table 1.1, which outlines Boa's conceptualization of three different types of worldviews. Boa postulates that most of those who do possess a worldview have not spent any amount of time reflecting on and contemplating the implications of that view. Finally, Boa concludes, in agreement with Colson and Pearcey (2004), that the biblical worldview is the only view that can *rationally* be lived out.

Table 1.1 Boa's Three Worldviews

Worldview	Origin	Purpose	Destiny
Theism (Personal)	Personal Creator	Relationships (Other-Centered)	Unbounded Relational Life
Transcendentalism (Spiritual)	Impersonal Agency (Energy)	Self-Actualization	Absorption (Spiritual Annihilation)
Naturalism (Material)	Impersonal plus Time plus Chance	Survival Autonomy	Physical Annihilation

Ron's Corner

My personal convictions and worldview encompass the following beliefs:

1. My worldview is my ultimate core belief, and as a Christian, I believe in a personal Creator who created me to be in relationships with others for all eternity.

2. My life is an empowered, other-centered life that requires my radical obedience to our Lord and Savior.

3. I know that God always has my best interest at heart, and ultimately it is all about God and not me.

4. Everything I do while living on earth has an eternal consequence.

Courtesy of daniilantiq2010/Fotolia.

DISCIPLESHIP MOMENT AND REFLECTION

Take some time to think through your personal convictions and reflect on the previous section on worldviews. Discuss the implications with your accountability and prayer partner.

Biblical wisdom The quality of having experience, knowledge, and good judgment that is derived from knowing, understanding, and accepting the Scriptures as truth.

Omniscience The phrase that describes God's knowledge and understanding. The fact that God knows all things.

Omnipresence The phrase that describes God's perspective. The fact that God is everywhere.

Omnipotence The phrase that describes God's experience. That fact that God has unlimited power.

Now that we have an understanding of a biblical worldview and its belief that the Bible is inerrant and that there is an all-knowing and all-powerful God who has provided a way for us to enter into a relationship with Him, Jesus Christ, we can now look to the Scriptures for how our worldview and ultimately our views about money and money management should be fleshed out. As we look through the Word of God, we find biblical wisdom that is timeless, transcendent, accurate, universal, and practical. **Biblical wisdom** is defined as the quality of having experience, knowledge, and good judgment that is derived from knowing, understanding, and accepting the Scriptures as truth. As we saw in the previous section, the naturalistic worldview relies on human understanding and wisdom as a means of understanding life, whereas the biblical worldview relies on the wisdom of God as communicated to us in the Bible. With a biblical worldview, we must rely on God's wisdom, which is based on God's knowledge and understanding (**omniscience**), God's perspective (**omnipresence**), and God's experience (**omnipotence**).

God's word says the fear of the Lord is the beginning of wisdom (Proverbs 9:10). Having an understanding of this fear and a desire to apply a biblical worldview to money and money management requires us to look to the Lord in reverence and realize that He is God and we are not, and understand that all of life is about God and His Glory and His Purpose, not all about us. We also know that the Lord gives wisdom, that from His mouth comes knowledge and wisdom (Proverbs 2:6). We must search and seek through the Scriptures to find and know the truths that are outlined there for us.

OUR SOURCES OF BIBLICAL WISDOM

There exist three main sources that we can look to for biblical wisdom when making all of our decisions. First and foremost, we should seek the Scriptures.

As we saw at the beginning of this chapter, 1 Timothy 3:16–17 provides us Paul's words in relation to knowing and using scripture:

> All Scripture is God-breathed and is useful for teaching, rebuking, correcting, and training in righteousness so that the servant of God may be equipped for every good work.

Paul's words were written before the collection of the New Testament into the books we know them as today, and therefore he was primarily referring to the Old Testament books as being inspired by God. His logic and argument follow the New Testament as well, and as a result, one with a biblical worldview must acknowledge that all of the Bible (Old and New Testament) is inspired by God and, as such, is infallible.

The next source from which we can seek biblical wisdom is God's Holy Spirit. After Jesus was crucified and walking among His disciples, discussing with them that He would be departing, some became obviously concerned of knowing their way (John 14:5). Thomas asks, "Lord, we do not know where You are going, how do we know the way?" Jesus responds (John 14:16–17), "I will ask the Father, and He will give you another Helper, that He may be with you forever; that is the Spirit of truth whom the world cannot receive, because it does not see Him or know Him, but you know Him because He abides with you and will be in you."

We see later, in John 16:13, that "when He, the Spirit of truth, comes, He will guide you into all the truth. He will not speak on His own; He will speak only what He hears, and He will tell you what is yet to come."

The final source from which we can seek biblical wisdom is in the wise counsel of other believers in Christ. We find support for this in Paul's writing to the Corinthians, 1 Corinthians 12:7: "But to each other one is given the manifestation of the Spirit for the common good."

We also find many verses in Proverbs that support this idea of seeking others with a biblical worldview as we begin to make decisions:

Proverbs 15:22 "Plans fail for lack of counsel, but with many advisers they succeed."

Proverbs 12:15 "The way of a fool is right in his own eyes; but he that seeks counsel is wise."

Proverbs 19:20 "Hear counsel, and receive instruction, that thou mayest be wise in the latter end."

When one relies on the proper sources of biblical wisdom, instead of making things up as one goes, the result is confidence, peace of mind, eternal perspective, and a focus on God's agenda. A decision that is based on Scripture, the Holy Spirit, and counsel from other Christians is one in which a person may have supreme confidence and the utmost belief in its accuracy. That is not to say that everything will always work out in a way that the world would acknowledge as good or in a way that results in us becoming more comfortable, but it is to say that it will always work out for that person's ultimate good. Simply stated, biblical wisdom leads to our eternal good and our immediate peace of mind.

Ron's Corner

My personal convictions in relation to biblical wisdom are as follows:

1. Biblical wisdom is transcendent.

2. Biblical wisdom comes from the Holy Spirit.

3. Biblical wisdom is available to the believer who asks in faith.

4. The integration of biblical wisdom and professional advice is the exclusive purview of the Christian professional advisor.

5. The integration of biblical wisdom and professional advice is a value proposition that the rest of the financial services world cannot match.

WISDOM MANIFESTED THROUGH PRINCIPLES

Principle A fundamental truth or proposition that serves as the foundation for a system of belief or behavior or for a chain of reasoning.

We have already defined *biblical wisdom* as having experience, knowledge, and good judgment that is derived from knowing and understanding the Scriptures. According to our biblical worldview, the Scriptures provides us this wisdom, which is understood through a variety of principles that are given in God's word. The term **principle** is defined by the *Oxford Dictionary* as "a fundamental truth or proposition that serves as the foundation for a system of belief or behavior or for a chain of reasoning."

In their work on biblical financial principles and their application, Damazio and Brott (2005) outlined over 90 different principles relating to money and possessions. Although there are too many to list in context, we will cover four fundamental principles that will help us define our path as we dive further into the world of biblical

Courtesy of Peter Atkins/Fotolia.

financial planning. Let us look at the Parable of the Talents, provided to us by Jesus while he was teaching in the synagogue. Matthew 25:14–30:

> For it will be like a man going on a journey, who called his servants and entrusted to them his property. To one he gave five talents, to another two, to another one, to each according to his ability. Then he went away. He who had received the five talents went at once and traded with them, and he made five talents more. So also he who had the two talents made two talents more. But he who had received the one talent went and dug in the ground and hid his master's money. Now after a long time the master of those servants came and settled accounts with them. And he who had received the five talents came forward, bringing five talents more, saying, "Master, you delivered to me five talents; here I have made five talents more." His master said to him, "Well done, good and faithful servant. You have been faithful over a little; I will set you over much. Enter into the joy of your master." And he also who had the two talents came forward, saying, "Master, you delivered to me two talents; here I have made two talents more." His master said to him, "Well done, good and faithful servant. You have been faithful over a little; I will set you over much. Enter into the joy of your master." He also who had received the one talent came forward, saying, "Master, I knew you to be a hard man, reaping where you did not sow, and gathering where you scattered no seed, so I was afraid, and I went and hid your talent in the ground. Here you have what is yours." But his master answered him, "You wicked and slothful servant! You knew that I reap where I have not sown and gather where I scattered no seed? Then you ought to have invested my money with the bankers, and at my coming I should have received what was my own with interest. So take the talent from him and give it to him who has the ten talents. For to everyone who has will more be given, and he will have an abundance. But from the one who has not, even what he has will be taken away. And cast the worthless servant into the outer darkness. In that place there will be weeping and gnashing of teeth."

This will not be an exhaustive commentary on this passage of Scripture, but rather we will use this passage as a framework to develop four fundamental biblical principles of money and money management, or financial stewardship: (1) God owns it all, (2) we are in a growth process, (3) the amount is not important, and (4) faith requires us to act.

God Owns It All

The most fundamental and significant difference between a biblical worldview and a secular worldview as it relates to money and money management is the difference in understanding who actually owns one's earthly possessions. **Possessions** can be defined as an item(s) of property belonging to someone. It is evident in the Scripture passage just excerpted that the master in this parable owns the money and gives it to his servants. One might suggest that few Christians would argue with the principle that God owns it all, and yet few would follow that principle. The principle that God owns it all leads to three revolutionary implications.

First of all, God has the right to whatever He wants, whenever He wants it. It is all His because an owner has **rights**, which are legal and contractual agreements of freedom of entitlement. Our place falls within that of a steward, which is a position that has **responsibilities**, a state of having a duty to deal with something or have control over something, not rights. The term *steward* can be defined in a wide variety

Possessions Items of property belonging to someone.

Rights Legal and contractual agreements of freedom of entitlement.

Responsibilities A state of having a duty to deal with something or have control over something.

Stewardship The activities or job of protecting and being responsible for something.

of ways, and throughout this textbook, we will see this idea of stewardship broken down into various subcomponents. Largely, **stewardship** refers to the activities or job of protecting and being responsible for something. As you might infer, a steward does not actually have ownership of what he or she is responsible for. As a steward, one may receive some benefits while meeting his or her responsibilities, but the owner retains ownership.

Review: Financial implications of knowing and understanding that God owns it all:

1. God has the right to whatever He wants, whenever He wants it.
2. Every spending decisions is a spiritual decision.
3. Wise stewardship is an indicator of spiritual health.

Ron's Corner

One of the reasons my hair turned gray early in life is because I taught five teenagers to drive. When my oldest child reached driving age, she was very eager to use my car, and as her father, I entrusted my car to her. There was never any question that I could take back my car at any time for any reason. She had responsibilities. I maintained all the rights. But I, as the owner, gave her a great benefit by entrusting her with the car's use, and she returned that benefit with responsible use and care of the car. In the same way, every single possession that I have comes from someone else—God. I literally possess much but own nothing. God benefits me by sharing His property with me. I have a responsibility to Him to use it in a way that blesses and glorifies Him.

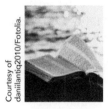

Courtesy of daniilantiq2010/Fotolia.

DISCIPLESHIP MOMENT AND REFLECTION

If you own your own home, take a walk around your property to get a feel for the reality of this principle. Go barefoot if weather permits. Reflect on how long that dirt has been there and how long it will continue to be there. Then ask yourself if you really own it or whether you merely possess it. You may have the title to it in your fireproof file cabinet, but that title reflects your right to possess it temporarily, not forever. Only God literally owns it forever. Take a moment to contact your prayer and accountability partner and proclaim to him or her that everything belongs to God and that you understand that all possessions you manage are to be used for God's glory.

The ultimate truth about God's ownership of financial resources is in the Bible in Haggai 2:8. God says, "The silver is mine and the gold is mine, says the Lord of hosts."

Review: Take a few minutes and look up the following verses in the Appendix. Pray through each of those and you allow the Holy Spirit to teach you.

1 Chronicles 29:13–14	Isaiah 66:1–2	2 Kings 19:15
Exodus 9:20–22	Acts 7:49–50	Nehemiah 9:6

Jeremiah 27:5	Job 12:9–10	Daniel 4:17
Hebrews 1:10	Psalm 89:11	John 19:11
Acts 17:24	Psalm 95: 3, 5	Revelation 4:11

Let me paraphrase this verse to say, first, God owns it all, and second, through his Word, He has given written instructions regarding the proper attitudes and decisions regarding money and its management.

If you really believe that God owns all your resources, two things will happen. First, you will treat each financial decision as something important to God because you are handling His resources. And second, you will certainly have less anxiety regarding money because rather than being an owner of financial resources, you are a manager, trustee, or steward of someone else's resources. Therefore, whether you have a little or a lot becomes unimportant to you. That's true contentment and will be discussed in more detail in Chapter 3.

The first implication of believing that God owns it all is that when you lose any possession, for whatever reason, you may struggle emotionally, but your mind and spirit have not the slightest question as to *the right of God to take whatever He wants, whenever He wants it*. Really believing this also frees you to give generously of God's resources to God's purposes and His people. All that you have belongs to Him.

Notice in the parable excerpted earlier (Matthew 25:14–30) how much leeway the master gave the stewards. He did not set any limits or state any restrictions. The second implication of God owning it all is that not only is a giving decision a spiritual decision, but *every spending decision is a spiritual decision*. There is nothing more spiritual than buying a car, taking a vacation, buying food, paying off debt, paying taxes, and so on. These are all responsible uses of His resources. He owns all that we have. He does not say we must use it all in one way, say, as an offering. He does not say we must use it all the same way each time. He gives us resources to provide for us, benefit us, and reach the world for Christ. Many God-glorifying responsible uses fit into these broad categories.

Think about the freedom of knowing that if God owns it all—and He does—He must have some thoughts about how He wants us to use His property. The Bible reveals many specific guidelines as to how the Owner wants His property used. As a steward, I have a great deal of latitude, but I am still responsible to the Owner. Someday, I will give an accounting of how I used His property.

The third implication of the truth that God owns it all is that *wise stewardship is an indicator of spiritual health.* Your checkbook reveals all that you really believe about stewardship. Your life story could be written from your checkbook. It reflects your goals, priorities, convictions, relationships, and even the use of your time. A person who has been a Christian for even a short while can fake prayer, Bible study, evangelism, and going to church, but that person cannot fake what his or her checkbook reveals. Maybe that is why so many of us are so secretive about our personal finances. Even within accountability groups, where people share many intimate struggles, it is rare that anyone shares information about how much (or how little) they give.

We Are in a Growth Process

In reading the Scriptures, we cannot escape the truths that our time on earth is temporary (James 4:14) and is to be used for our Lord. While one continues to grow and mature in one's relationship with Christ, God uses money and material possessions in one's earthly life during this growth process as *a tool, a test,* and *a testimony.*

Money as a Tool

Money and material possessions are effective tools that God uses to help each of us grow in our spiritual journey, but also as a means by which we meet our basic needs. We see this in Scripture repeatedly, specifically:

> **Philippians 4:19**: "And my God will supply every need of yours according to his riches in glory in Christ Jesus."

> **2 Corinthians 9:8–11**: "And God is able to make all grace abound to you, so that having all sufficiency in all things at all times, you may abound in every good work. As it is written, 'he has distributed freely, he has given to the poor; his righteousness endures forever.' He who supplies seed to the sower and bread for food will supply and multiply your seed for sowing and increase the harvest of your righteousness. You will be enriched in every way to be generous in every way, which through us will produce thanksgiving to God."

> **2 Peter 1:3**: "His divine power has granted to us all things that pertain to life and godliness, through the knowledge of him who called us to his own glory and excellence. . ."

> **Matthew 6:31–34**: "Therefore do not be anxious, saying, 'What shall we eat?' or 'What shall we drink?' or 'What shall we wear?' For the Gentiles seek after all these things, and your heavenly Father knows that you need them all. But seek first the kingdom of God and his righteousness, and all these things will be added to you. Therefore do not be anxious about tomorrow, for tomorrow will be anxious for itself. Sufficient for the day is its own trouble."

It is important, however, to keep in mind that when we are using God's resources as a means to make a decision, we need to seek God's counsel and ask, "God, what do You want me to learn?"

Ron's Corner

My role as a counselor has been to help people discover what God would have them learn, either from the situation of their abundance or from the situation of their apparent lack of financial resources. God is not trying to frustrate us. He is trying to get our attention, and money is a great attention-getter.

Money as a Test

> "So if you have not been trustworthy in handling worldly wealth, who will trust you with true riches? And if you have not been trustworthy with someone else's property, who will give you property of your own?" (Luke 16:11–12)

We may not understand it, but we do know that somehow our eternal position and reward are determined irrevocably by our faithfulness in handling property that has been entrusted to us by God. And not only that, but this verse and others indicate that God trusts the true riches of knowing and understanding Him more to those who show their resolute commitment to Him in tangible ways, such as letting go of money or relationships.

Further evidence that money is a means of a test can be found in the following verses:

1 Timothy 6:17–19—"As for the rich in this present age, charge them not to be haughty, nor to set their hopes on the uncertainty of riches, but on God, who richly provides us with everything to enjoy. They are to do good, to be rich in good works, to be generous and ready to share, thus storing up treasure for themselves as a good foundation for the future, so that they may take hold of that which is truly life."

Proverbs 3:9—"Honor the Lord with your wealth and with the first fruits of all your produce."

Romans 15:26–27—"For Macedonia and Achaia have been pleased to make some contribution for the poor among the saints at Jerusalem. For they were pleased to do it, and indeed they owe it to them. For if the Gentiles have come to share in their spiritual blessings, they ought also to be of service to them in material blessings."

Money as a Testimony

We have already looked at the fact that we are called to be salt and light in Matthew 5:13–16. Believing that God can utilize our use of His resources as a testimony to the world, my attitude as a Christian toward wealth becomes the testimony. My attitude when He withholds a desire is also a testimony. My verbal praise when He arranges and allows financial blessings—or prevents my undoing—is also a testimony.

The following story of Alan Barnhart and his family highlights a life that demonstrates what happens when people understand that money is a tool, a test, and a testimony.

This story was written by Liz Essley Whyte of *Philanthropy Magazine* (originally published spring 2014).

Alan Barnhart and his brother Eric owned a $250 million company. Owned. Past tense. Because they gave it away.

Alan and Eric Barnhart

Alan Barnhart was 25 and planning to go into business with his brother. An evangelical Christian, he wondered what Scripture had to say about the profits he hoped to make. So he combed the Bible for whatever advice it had to offer about money. That's when he came across verses like this:

"The love of money is a root of all kinds of evil. . ."
"Do not lay up for yourselves treasures on earth. . ."
"It is hard for a rich man to enter the kingdom of heaven. . ."

No matter where he turned, it seemed to him that Scripture was sending a very clear warning: Money can be dangerous. "I read all these verses, and I thought: 'I want to be good in business, and I'm competitive,'" Barnhart says. "But I didn't want to make a lot of money if doing so would damage my life. And I could see where it really could."

So Alan and his brother Eric decided to do something unusual: They vowed to cap their income, earning no more than the middle-class members of their Memphis, Tennessee, Sunday school class did, and give much of their company's profits to charity. In their first year of business, they gave away $50,000—more than Alan's salary.

Now, nearly 30 years later, the results are even more tremendous: The Barnharts oversee a $250 million crane and rigging company, and they've donated nearly $100 million of its profits to charity. Moreover, in 2007 they decided to go even further. They gave the entire company away. Though they still run its daily operations, the National Christian Foundation (NCF) now owns Barnhart Crane & Rigging. The brothers will never reap its accrued value; they kept none of it.

"That's one of the things that make Alan and Eric so rare: they decided to give it all away," says NCF president David Wills. "That was their wealth. They didn't have three other companies. That was it."

Simple Living

Alan Barnhart is a modest man, with a soft Tennessee drawl. He wears jeans and cotton oxfords to work. He started giving interviews about his philanthropy only after others convinced him to do so.

"'Don't let the left hand know what the right hand is doing.' For the first 15 years that was our thinking," Barnhart says. But "people challenged us, [saying] what's happened to your company is pretty unusual. . . . God has done amazing things through your company, and you need to tell people all that you've done with what God's done."

He is quick to emphasize that his salary cap was not a vow of poverty. "We have vehicles and air conditioning. It was not a Mother Teresa lifestyle."

To make sure they stuck to their limit, the Barnharts told their associates at the company about their income pledge, enlisting others to hold them to their promise. He

and his brother allowed themselves cost-of-living adjustments, and salary increases when children were born. Alan has six children; Eric has five. Alan and his wife Katherine are the Barnhart family spokespeople, while Eric is the brainy, quiet engineer, friends say.

One of the best things about their lifestyle choice, Alan says, is that his children did not grow up wealthy. "There's great benefits to a kid to hear the word 'no,' and the theology of the Rolling Stones: 'You don't always get what you want,'" he says. The Barnhart kids didn't get trips to Disney World, or even treats at the grocery store. Instead their parents took them to developing countries to see the wells, churches, and farms their gifts had enabled. "It wasn't about things. It wasn't about money. It wasn't about wanting. I taught them the joy of giving early. I taught them the joy of contentment," Katherine says.

And the Barnharts taught their children about God. They speak of Him often. "It is God who has led us in this, and it is He who multiplied us," states Katherine. Though donors of many religious—and non-religious—backgrounds give generously, and interpretations of Scripture's teaching on wealth differ, the Barnharts stand out in their willingness to act on what they believe God has called them to.

Profit with a Purpose

Using business skills to serve God through "constructive work" and "ministry funding" is at the heart of the purpose statement posted on the Barnharts' company website. The brothers' attempt to directly harness capitalist plentitude to do spiritual work is further explained in one of the company's "core values," which proclaims: "Profit with a Purpose—We will attempt to make a profit and will invest the profit to expand the company and to meet the needs of people (physically, mentally, spiritually)."

In practice, about 50 percent of all company earnings are donated immediately to charity. The other 50 percent are used to grow the business. The firm has been run that way since the beginning.

And the Barnharts don't even allow themselves the luxury of choosing where their company's gifts should go. A group of 55 employees and spouses decides where to distribute half of the money made every year by Barnhart Crane & Rigging. Each employee in the group—which is dubbed GROVE, God's Resources Operating Very Effectively—develops a relationship with one or two grant recipients, researching their effectiveness and vetting their requests. Under NCF ownership the group will continue to give away company earnings.

Alan and Eric did something unusual: They vowed to cap their income, earning no more than the middle-class members of their Sunday school class did, and give much of their profits to charity.

Katherine says the group actively searches for the best people addressing a problem, rather than giving money only to groups with powerful fundraising arms. GROVE volunteers take small grant requests to a six-member committee for approval; requests for more than $100,000 go before a 12-member board that meets quarterly. Most of the donations boost international development and Christian ministry in Africa, the Middle East, India, and southeast Asia, where the group sees needs larger than those at home. "That's where God is really working," says Joye Allen, GROVE administrator. The group focuses its giving on five causes: Christian evangelism, church planting, Christian discipleship, leadership training, and ministering to the poor.

GROVE's biggest grants—millions of dollars' worth—have gone to Hope International, which provides microfinance in the developing world; the Seed Company, a Bible translation group; and Strategic Resources Group, an umbrella organization for Christian ministries in the Middle East. Though the bulk of its giving is overseas, the group has also given domestically, to places like Repairing the Breach, which works with youth in rundown Memphis neighborhoods, and Citizens for Community Values, which helps women escape the sex trade.

The profits headed toward charity are not funneled through a corporate foundation or invested for future giving. The Barnharts want to put their dollars to work for God right away. "We want to get the money and invest it in other people as quickly as possible. We see a higher return in investments in people than we do in investment instruments," Alan says.

Giving It All Away

The Barnhart brothers had given away millions in annual profits when, in 2006, they approached Wills with a big question: How do we give away our entire company? Many successful businessmen leave their private companies to their foundations when they die, but doing so while still living is unusual, even in the philanthropic world. So National Christian Foundation staff got to work on figuring out how to accomplish what the Barnharts requested.

In 2007, the Barnharts got what they wanted: They put 99 percent of their business ownership interests, in the form of non-voting stock, into a charitable trust under the National Christian Foundation. In 2012 they gave the remaining 1 percent to a second charitable trust that gives NCF the beneficial interest and ultimate ownership but allows the family to retain operating control by serving as trustee. NCF sought, and received, special approval from the IRS for the arrangement.

Wills credits the Barnharts' deep convictions for the unusual gift. "They actually don't believe that they own their company anyway. It wasn't theirs; it was God's. They were just taking care of it for him," Wills says. "When they gave away their company, it didn't change their life at all, Alan will say. It significantly changed their balance sheet, but it didn't change their lives."

Not Alone

The Barnharts are not alone in giving away their source of income. The National Christian Foundation has developed a specialty in working with entrepreneurs who want to donate businesses, parts of businesses, or other assets—which helps account for the foundation's explosive growth. NCF grew from a two-person operation three decades ago to the 19th biggest American recipient of private gifts, topping Harvard, Yale, and the American Heart Association in 2012. The foundation has received about $1 billion worth of companies since it started facilitating that type of giving in 2002, Wills says.

NCF isn't the only foundation that is channeling entrepreneurial gifts to charity. The Greater Houston Community Foundation owns about 12 percent of local businessman Leo Linbeck III's construction, real estate, health care, and education firm, Aquinas Companies, which earns $500 million in annual revenues. The plan, Linbeck says, is to transfer more and more of the company to a supporting organization of the foundation. By the time he dies, if not before, he wants the foundation to own it all, though the Linbeck family will still steer the firm and run its day-to-day operations.

For Linbeck, the choice to give away his company came down to one principle: stewardship. He wanted to work to benefit others, and did not want his family to feel entitled to wealth. Yet he thought a for-profit business was the best way to help people. "From an overall societal benefit standpoint, there's a whole lot more benefit that comes out of for-profit businesses than philanthropic contributions," he says.

In addition to gradually shifting the ownership of Aquinas to the community foundation, Linbeck also funnels 10 percent of its annual profits to GHCF, reinvesting the other 90 percent in business operations. Linbeck, a devout Catholic, calls that a tithe. His idea of stewardship, he says,

Has God worked a financial miracle for you? Do not discount it as coincidence. Do not forget it years down the road when you have more affluence. Remember, rest, and revel in His answered prayer over financial matters, just do not let resentment creep in when things do not go your way in human terms. This is teaching time. This is testimony time. Have you failed in your use of God's money? What was your response to His "No"? What is your verbal witness of His involvement in your life? Do not let your first failure keep you so defeated that you talk yourself into failing again. Confess it, receive His mercy, and move on. You will have another chance tomorrow. Remember that growth is a process, not a once-for-all-then-done approach. Jesus wants children who rely on Him and students who listen to Him, not grown-up graduates who do not need Him anymore.

The Amount Is Not Important

When you look back at on the parable in the first part of this chapter (Matthew 25:14–30), notice that the commendation for the first two servants is exactly the same. Both were reminded that they had been faithful with a few things, and both were promised something as a reward. You can draw the conclusion that the amount you have is unimportant, but how you handle what you have been entrusted with is very important. We can see this idea that the amount is not important when Paul writes in Philippians 4:11–12:

> I am not saying this because I am in need, for I have learned to be content whatever the circumstances. I know what it is to be in need, and I know what it is to have plenty. I have learned the secret of being content in any and every situation, whether well fed or hungry, whether living in plenty or in want.

Take a moment to look back at the parable of the talents. What do you notice regarding the response from the master to the unfaithful servant? Before he was sent to hell and darkness, he was ordered to give his portion to the one who already had the most. Why was it not given or shared with the other commended servant? They both doubled their shares. They both received the same commendation.

Perhaps the master felt he could manage more and wanted to bless him for the risk undertaken. One can only speculate as to why the master did this, but it doesn't really matter. It is His money (Jeremiah 27:5). He can do what He wants to do with it. We do not need to know, and we do not have a right to know. It was His to begin with and His to decide what to do with. That is a life-changing thought.

How much energy and time do we waste trying to figure God out when He just wants us to be faithful? Why do some people in this world have more than others? We do not know, and it is not fruitful to speculate about it. We can only be accountable for what God has given us. I am not a fruit inspector. There is only One who will determine if everyone has received what is fair. Most do not ask, "Why do some have less than me?" We should be thankful for what we have.

Ron's Corner

There is much controversy today about whether an American Christian is more spiritual by accumulating much (God's "blessing") or by giving it all away (God's "martyr"). I believe that both are extremes and not reflective of what God says. He neither condemns wealth nor commends poverty, or vice versa. The principle found in Scripture is that He owns it all. Therefore, whatever He chooses to entrust you with, hold with an open hand, allowing Him to entrust you with more if He so chooses, or allowing Him to take whatever He wants. It is all His. That is the attitude He wants you to develop, and whatever you have, little or much, your attitude should remain the same.

Faith Requires Action

The lazy and wicked servant knew he had his master's money. Simply knowing He owns it all is not enough. The wicked slave knew better, *but* he did nothing. Many of us know what we ought to do, but we disobey or delay. We have emotional faith and/or intellectual faith, but not volitional faith. We know *but. . .*

We may know deep down what God would have us do, but we are so bombarded with worldly input, which seems to be acceptable, that we are paralyzed. Take a look at the story of Zacchaeus as portrayed in Luke's gospel (Luke 19:1–10). Notice what Zacchaeus did when he was transformed:

> He entered Jericho and was passing through. And behold, there was a man named Zacchaeus. He was a chief tax collector and was rich. And he was seeking to see who Jesus was, but on account of the crowd he could not, because he was small in stature. So he ran on ahead and climbed up into a sycamore tree to see him, for he was about to pass that way. And when Jesus came to the place, he looked up and said to him, "Zacchaeus, hurry and come down, for I must stay at your house today." So he hurried and came down and received him joyfully. And when they saw it, they all grumbled, "He has gone in to be the guest of a man who is a sinner." And Zacchaeus stood and said to the Lord, "Behold, Lord, the half of my goods I give to the poor. And if I have defrauded anyone of anything, I restore it fourfold." And Jesus said to him, "Today salvation has come to this house, since he also is a son of Abraham. For the Son of Man came to seek and to save the lost."

We take no action because of the fear of making a mistake, biblically or financially. We see this tax collector and assume that his collection practices were probably not honorable. Yet, we see that his faith was lived out by his actions in giving back to the poor (half of his goods) and anyone he had defrauded (four times what he took). Unlike Zacchaeus's response, we respond by doing only what we feel good about. Living by our feelings rather than "the truth" can be very dangerous. "Jesus answered, 'I am the way and the truth and the life. No one comes to the Father except through me'" (John 14:6). We need to respond more like Zacchaeus and turn our faith into action. After all, *faith* is an action verb.

SUMMARY

As we seek to understand the world of money that surrounds us, we first need to know the worldview in which we see our lives. Obviously, throughout this text, a biblical worldview is the standpoint, but it is important to know the viewpoints of those secular worldviews that also exist. Your worldview is what drives how you think and act and, ultimately, which decisions you choose. We know that God is everywhere, knows everything, and is all-powerful, and the fear of the Lord is the beginning of all wisdom (Proverbs 9:10). We find that we can use three main sources for seeking biblical wisdom: (1) the Holy Scriptures, (2) the Holy Spirit, and (3) other Godly believers who are seeking and yearning after God. The Holy Scriptures provide us with principles, or fundamental truths, that we need to know and understand prior to falling deeper into cultural traps. Four of these fundamental principles are (1) God owns it all, (2) we are in a growth process in our faith, (3) the amount of money is not important, and (4) faith requires us to act. Once we understand the idea that God owns everything, then we begin to move away from actions as owners to actions as stewards, which we will cover in the next chapter.

SUMMARY REVIEW QUESTIONS

1. Define the concept of a worldview. Why is one's worldview so important?

2. According to Barna (2005), what are the eight beliefs that make up a biblical worldview?

3. What are the four fundamental questions that all people strive to answer?

4. Describe three different worldviews that oppose the biblical worldview. How do they differ in answering the four fundamental questions of life?

5. In your own words, why do you think fear of the Lord is the beginning of wisdom (Proverbs 9:10)?

6. Explain how the three main sources of biblical wisdom can help you make decisions.

7. Explain what 1 Timothy 3:16–17 means in our own understanding.

8. What are principles? How do we use principles?

9. What are the four principles revealed in the Parable of the Talents (Matthew 25:14–30)?

10. Describe the differences between rights and responsibilities. Who has rights and who has responsibilities?

Case Study Analysis

Bob and Debbie have planned an evening to visit with their associate pastor, Steve, who was a financial advisor prior to entering the ministry. It is mid-November, and as they think through paying for Christmas, they feel they need to get some biblical counsel in relation to their finances.

Steve was a financial advisor for a national brokerage firm for 15 years, received his CFP® designation in 2007, and decided during the recession of 2008–2009 to answer the call to full-time ministry. Steve took evening seminary classes and completed his seminary degree in 2013. He has worked full time at Lovington Community Church as an associate pastor of ministry and stewardship. Steve regularly meets with members of the congregation for discussion of matters related to personal finances.

During the first meeting, the conversation with Steve revolves around the idea of developing a solid understanding of their worldview. Steve knows the general background of Bob and Debbie because they have been members of Lovington Community Church for about 5 years. Steve reviewed the balance sheet and their completed Financial Values Questionnaire, which was given to them by their financial advisor, James Miller, a local independent financial advisor in the Lovington area. James has been in the business for about 8 years (he took over the business from his dad, who retired) but is not a professing Christian. The conversation about religious beliefs has never come up in annual meetings with James.

As a result of the first meeting with Steve, Bob and Debbie realize that they have a lot of thinking to do in relation to their worldview and their personal finances. Use the Case Study, as well as the chapter material, to answer the following questions as they relate to Bob and Debbie's situation.

Assignment

Answer the following questions:

1. What impact does a biblical worldview have on a person's financial decisions?

2. How do other worldviews (for example, moral relativism, naturalism, or utopianism) influence the way a person makes financial decisions?

3. In what ways have Bob and Debbie made decisions inconsistent with a biblical worldview?

4. Who (or what) has influenced Bob and Debbie in their personal financial decisions?

5. In what ways is money a tool for Bob and Debbie?

6. In what ways is money a test for Bob and Debbie?

7. Think of the different individuals presented in the Parable of the Talents. Whom is Bob most similar to? Whom does Debbie have the most in common with? Explain.

8. At this point in Bob and Debbie's growth process, what testimony do Bob and Debbie have to share as in relation to their finances?

9. In the past, what has held Bob and Debbie back from taking action in their financial planning?

DEFINITIONS

Biblical wisdom (p. 4)

Moral relativism (p. 2)

Multiculturalism (p. 2)

Naturalism (p. 2)

Omnipotence (p. 4)

Omnipresence (p. 4)

Omniscience (p. 4)

Possessions (p. 6)

Pragmatism (p. 2)

Principle (p. 5)

Responsibilities (p. 6)

Rights (p. 6)

Stewardship (p. 7)

Utopianism (p. 3)

Worldview (p. 2)

SCRIPTURE VERSES (ESV)

1 Timothy 3:16–17—All Scripture is breathed out by God and profitable for teaching, for reproof, for correction, and training in righteousness, that the man of God may be complete, equipped for every good work.

Romans 3:10—As it is written: "None is righteous, no, not one."

Proverbs 9:10—The fear of the Lord is the beginning of wisdom, and the knowledge of the Holy One is insight.

Proverbs 2:6—For the Lord gives wisdom, from his mouth come knowledge and wisdom.

John 14:5—Thomas said to him, "Lord, we do not know where you are going, how can we know the way?"

John 14:16–17—And I will ask the Father, and he will give you another Helper, to be with you forever, even the Spirit of Truth, whom the world cannot receive, because it neither sees him nor knows him. You know him, for he dwells with you and will be in you.

John 16:13—When the Spirit of Truth comes, he will guide you into all truth, for he will not speak on his own authority, but whatever he hears he will speak, and he will declare to you the things that are to come.

Proverbs 15:22—Without counsel plans fail, but with many advisers they succeed.

Proverbs 12:15—The way of a fool is right in his own eyes, but a wise man listens to advice.

Proverbs 19:20—Listen to advice and accept instruction, that you may gain wisdom in the future.

1 Chronicles 29:13–14—And now we thank you, our God, and praise your glorious name. But who am I, and what is my people, that we should be able thus to offer willingly? For all things come from you, and of your own have we given you.

Exodus 9:20–22—"Then whoever feared the word of the Lord among the servants of Pharaoh hurried his slaves and his livestock into the houses, but whoever did not pay attention to the word of the Lord left his slaves and his livestock in the field. Then the Lord said to Moses, 'Stretch out your hand toward heaven, so that there may be hail in all the land of Egypt, on man and beast and every plant of the field, in the land of Egypt.

Isaiah 66:1–2—Thus says the Lord: "Heaven is my throne, and the earth is my footstool; what is the house that you would build for me, and what is the place of my rest? All these things my hand has made, and so all these things came to be, declares the Lord. But this is the one to whom I will look: he who is humble and contrite in spirit and trembles at my word."

Acts 7:49–50—Heaven is my throne, and the earth is my footstool. What kind of house will you build for me, says the Lord, or what is the place of my rest? Did not my hand make all these things?

2 Kings 19:15—And Hezekiah prayed before the Lord and said: "O Lord, the God of Israel, enthroned above the cherubim, you are the God, you alone, of all the kingdoms of the earth, you have made heaven and earth."

Nehemiah 9:6—You are the Lord, you alone. You have made heaven, the heaven of heavens, with all your host, the earth and all that is on it, the seas and all that is in them; and you preserve all of them, and the host of heaven worships you.

Jeremiah 27:5—It is I who by my great power and my outstretched arm have made the earth, with the men and animals that are on the earth, and I give it to whomever it seems right to me.

Hebrews 1:10—And, "You, Lord, laid the foundation of the earth in the beginning, and the heavens are the work of your hands;"

Acts 17:24—The God who made the world and everything in it, begin Lord of heaven and earth, does no live in temples made by man. . .

Job 12:9–10—Who among all these does not know that the hand of the Lord has done this? In his hand is the life of every living thing and the breadth of all mankind.

Psalm 89:11—The heavens are yours; the earth is also yours; the world and all that is in it, you have founded them.

Psalm 95:3—For the Lord is the great God, and a great King above all gods.

Psalm 95:5—The sea is his, for he made it, and his hands formed the dry land.

Daniel 4:17—The sentence is by the decree of the watchers, the decision by the word of the holy ones, to the end that the living may know that the Most High rules the kingdom of men and gives it to whom he will and sets over it the lowliest of men.

John 19:11—Jesus answered him, "You would have no authority over me at all unless it had been given you from above. Therefore he who delivered me over to you has the greater sin."

Revelation 4:11—"Worthy are you, our Lord our God, to receive glory and honor and power, for you created all things, and by your will they existed and were created."

James 4:14—yet you do not know what tomorrow will bring. What is your life? For you are a mist that appears for a little time and then vanishes.

Philippians 4:11–12—Not that I am speaking of being in need, for I have learned in whatever situation I am to be content. I know how to be brought low, and I know how to abound. In any and every circumstance, I have learned the secret of facing plenty and hunger, abundance and need.

Philippians 4:19—And may God supply every need of yours according to his riches in glory in Christ Jesus.

2 Corinthians 9:8–11—And God is able to make all grace abound to you, so that having all sufficiency in all things at all times, you may abound in every good work. As it is written, "he has distributed freely, he has given to the poor; his righteousness endures forever." He who supplies seed to the sower and bread for food will supply and multiply your seed for sowing and increase the harvest of you righteousness. You will be enriched in every way to be generous in every way, which through us will produce thanksgiving to God.

2 Peter 1:3—His divine power has granted to us all things that pertain to life and godliness, through the knowledge of him who called us to his own glory and excellence. . .

Matthew 6:31–34—Therefore do not be anxious, saying, "What shall we eat?" or "What shall we drink?" or "What shall we wear?" For the Gentiles seek after all these things, and your heavenly Father knows that you need them all. But seek first the kingdom of God and his righteousness, and all these things will be added to you. Therefore do not be anxious about tomorrow, for tomorrow will be anxious for itself. Sufficient for the day is its own trouble.

1 Timothy 6:17–19—As for the rich in this present age, charge them not to be haughty, nor to set their hopes on the uncertainty of riches, but on God, who richly provides us with everything to enjoy. They are to do good, to be rich in good works, to be generous and ready to share, thus storing up treasure for themselves as a good foundation for the future, so that they may take hold of that which is truly life.

Proverbs 3:9—Honor the Lord with your wealth and with the first fruits of all your produce.

Romans 15:26–27—For Macedonia and Achaia have been pleased to make some contribution for the poor among the saints at Jerusalem. For they were pleased to do it, and indeed they owe it to them. For if the Gentiles have come to share in their spiritual blessings, they ought also to be of service to them in material blessings.

Matthew 5:13–16—You are the salt of the earth, but if salt has lost its taste, how shall its saltiness be restored? It is no longer good for anything except to be thrown out and trampled under people's feet. You are the light of the world. A city set on a hill cannot be hidden. Nor do people light a lamp and put it under a basket, but on a stand, and it gives light to all in the house. In the same way, let your light shine before others, so that they may see your good works and give glory to your Father who is in heaven.

Luke 19:1–10—He entered Jericho and was passing through. And behold, there was a man named Zacchaeus. He was a chief tax collector and was rich. And he was seeking to see who Jesus was, but on account of the crowd he could not, because he was small in stature. So he ran on ahead and climbed up into a sycamore tree to see him, for he was about to pass that way. And when Jesus came to the place, he looked up and said to him, "Zacchaeus, hurry and come down, for I must stay at your house today." So he hurried and came down and received him joyfully. And when they saw it, they all grumbled, "He has gone in to be the guest of a man who is a sinner." And Zacchaeus stood and said to the Lord, "Behold, Lord, the half of my goods I give to the poor. And if I have defrauded anyone of anything, I restore it fourfold." And Jesus said to him, "Today salvation has come to this house, since he also is a son of Abraham. For the Son of Man came to seek and to save the lost."

ADDITIONAL READINGS ON DEVELOPING A CHRISTIAN WORLDVIEW

Beckwith, F. J., Craig, W. L., & Moreland, J. P. (Eds.). (2004). *To everyone an answer: A case for the Christian worldview*. Downers Grove, IL: InterVarsity Press.

Boa, K. D., & Bowman Jr., R. M. (2005). *Faith has its reasons: An integrative approach to defending Christianity* (2nd ed.). Colorado Springs, CO: Navpress.

Campbell, J., & McGrath, G. J. (2006). *New dictionary of Christian apologetics*. Leicester, England: Inter-Varsity Press.

Copan, P. (2001). *That's just your interpretation: Responding to skeptics who challenge your faith*. Grand Rapids, MI: Baker Book House.

Corduan, W. (1997). *No doubt about it: The case for Christianity*. Nashville, TN: Broadman & Holman Publishers.

Craig, W. L. (1984). *Reasonable faith: Christian truth and apologetics*. Wheaton, IL: Crossway Books.

Dembski, W. A., & Licona, M. R. (Eds.). (2010). *Evidence for God: 50 arguments for faith from the Bible, history, philosophy, and science*. Grand Rapids, MI: Baker Books.

Feser, E. (2008). *The last superstition: A refutation of the new atheism*. South Bend, IN: St. Augustine's Press.

Geisler, N. L. (1999). *Baker encyclopedia of Christian apologetics*. Grand Rapids, MI: Baker Books.

Geisler, N. L., & Hoffman, P. K. (2001). *Why I am a Christian: Leading thinkers explain why they believe*. Grand Rapids, MI: Baker Books.

Geisler, N. L., & Meister, C. (Eds.). (2007). *Reasons for faith: Making a case for the Christian faith*. Wheaton, IL: Crossway.

Geisler, N. L., & Turek, F. (2004). *I don't have enough faith to be an atheist*. Wheaton, IL: Crossway Books.

Hindson, E., & Canner, E. (Eds.). (2008). *The popular encyclopedia of apologetics: Surveying the evidence for the truth of Christianity*. Eugene, OR: Harvest House Publishers, 2008.

Kreeft, P. (2008). *Between heaven and hell: A dialog somewhere beyond death with John F. Kennedy, C. S. Lewis, and Aldous Huxley*. Downers Grove, IL: Inter-Varsity Press.

Lewis, C. S. (1943). *Mere Christianity: What one must believe to be a Christian*. New York, NY: Macmillan Publishing.

Little, P. E. (1968). *Know why you believe: A clear affirmation of the reasonableness of the Christian faith*. Downers Grove, IL: Inter-Varsity Press.

McDowell, J. (1999). *The new evidence that demands a verdict*. Nashville, TN: Thomas Nelson Publishers.

Meister, C. V. (2006). *Building belief: Constructing faith from the ground up*. Grand Rapids, MI: Baker Books.

Moreland, J. P. (1987). *Scaling the secular city: A defense of Christianity*. Grand Rapids, MI: Baker Book House.

Nash, R. H. (1984). *The gospel and the Greeks*. Grand Rapids, MI: Zondervan/Probe.

Pearcey, N. (2004). *Total truth: Liberating Christianity from its cultural captivity*. Wheaton, IL: Crossway Books.

Sproul, R. C., Gerstner, J., & Lindsley, A. (1984). *Classical apologetics: A rational defense of the Christian faith and a critique of presuppositional apologetics*. Grand Rapids, MI: Academie Books.

Strobel, L. (2000). *The case for faith: A journalist investigates the toughest objections to Christianity*. Grand Rapids, MI: Zondervan Publishing House.

GOSPEL MESSAGE

God is generous.

The biblical account of His generosity begins with the Paradise He created in Eden and concludes with the Paradise He is preparing for eternity. Scriptures make clear that His generosity is for our enjoyment.[1] God not only invites our enjoyment, but commands our engagement as stewards in what He has so generously provided. God's first communication with the human race involved stewardship.[2] Human beings have been created with the capacity to manage what belongs to God, with a mandate from God to steward it well.

A steward is someone who manages something that belongs to another. God entrusts time, money, and abilities to us, and we're accountable for the way we manage them. With any arena of stewardship, there is opportunity for either wise use or abuse.

The first temptation[3] stirs pride within humanity to believe they own everything and can utilize it for the fulfillment of their desires. Ever since, people have been trading the blessed life that results from proper stewardship for the mirage of selfishness and control that comes from thinking that what they have originated with them and belongs to them.

The brokenness and sinfulness of humanity have had devastating impacts globally and individually. The personal guilt and accompanying shame create a need for transformation deeper than behavior modification.

Using financial terms to describe our spiritual reality, we are bankrupt. We have a debt to be forgiven and have a need for a fresh investment.

Once again, God is generous . . . and He is gracious. His grace provides both the freedom and the power to choose Him and the salvation He makes available through His Son, Jesus Christ. He does not determine our choice for or against Him, but makes it possible for us to acknowledge our spiritual bankruptcy, ask for His forgiveness of our sin, and receive His gracious gift of new life.[4]

Have You Experienced His Gracious Gift of Personal Salvation?

Once we receive His transformational gift, His grace continues to empower us to grow and change. Who we've been doesn't need to determine who we become. We are no longer bound to "the way I've always been." We can break patterns from our household of origin or our own personal past track record, creating new habits that deepen us spiritually and lead to true success financially.

Money is important to God—it reveals what has captured our hearts and dominates our values.[5] Our use of money is a tangible expression of what we treasure and serve.

God invites us to receive true riches and join Him in living generously. More than an invitation, He issues a command that grants deep fulfillment to all who receive it: ". . . not to be arrogant nor to put their hope in wealth, which is so uncertain, but to put their hope in God, who richly provides everything for our enjoyment. Command them to do good, to be rich in good deeds, and to be generous and willing to share. In this way they will lay up treasure for themselves as a firm foundation for the coming age, so that they may take hold of the life that is truly life."[6]

Courtesy of alswart/Fotolia.

[1] 1 Timothy 6:17
[2] Genesis 1:28
[3] Genesis 3

[4] Ephesians 2:8–9
[5] Matthew 6:19–24
[6] 1 Timothy 6:17–19

Chapter 2

Financial Stewardship

Courtesy of Monkey Business/Fotolia.

BIG IDEA:
God owns everything; therefore, we are stewards of His resources.

LEARNING OUTCOMES

- Define the term *fiduciary*, and describe its history
- Describe the idea of stewardship
- List and describe five indicators of stewardship

The foundation established in the first chapter sets the paradigm for this chapter and the rest of the book. As Christians, we need to understand first and foremost that God owns everything. He owns your possessions, He owns your money, and He owns your life. God owns everything because He created all things. So, where does that leave us? Perhaps you're wondering, *What about all the stuff I have—if God owns it, then what am I doing with it?* Great question. This chapter discusses what we are to do with the "stuff" we have. We will look at two concepts, one from a secular standpoint and the other from a biblical standpoint. These two concepts, however, lead us to the same conclusions: We have responsibilities (as discussed in Chapter 1), and someone else (in the biblical context, God) has rights. These two positions will overlap in many areas; they are *fiduciary* and *steward*.

FIDUCIARY

Fiduciary One that is entrusted with the responsibilities to act and care on someone's behalf and that the actions taken serve the best interest of the owner(s).

A fiduciary is a unique relationship between two parties in which one party, the fiduciary, is required to consider the other party's position as superior to his or her own. In other words, the fiduciary must elevate the other party's interests over his or her own. This relationship is most commonly seen in a trustee/beneficiary relationship. According to *Merriam-Webster's*, the term *fiduciary* is defined as (1) one who holds a fiduciary relation or acts in a fiduciary capacity, (2) relating to or involving trust (such as the trust between a customer and a professional). A **fiduciary** is one who is entrusted with the responsibility to act and care on someone else's (the owner's) behalf and serve the best interest of the owner. In other words, the actions taken by a fiduciary need to best serve the interest of the owner rather than the interest of the person who is responsible for making the decisions. Over the past few years, financial regulators have become increasingly interested in implementing and monitoring this idea of fiduciary responsibility.

HISTORY OF FIDUCIARY

The following is a brief outline of the history of U.S. fiduciary standards dating back to the mid-1970s. This chronology of events was outlined by the Security Industry and Financial Markets Association (SIFMA) in 2015:

1974: The Employee Retirement Income Security Act (ERISA) is passed into law.

1978: The Department of Labor is given the responsibility to interpret the fiduciary requirements found in Title 1 of ERISA.

The 1974 ERISA laws were introduced as the retirement landscape began to transition from a **pension**-based **defined benefit retirement program**, a source of funds that an employer puts away on behalf of employees to later pay out to employees when they retire from the company, to an employee-driven **defined contribution program**, which implemented two significant changes: (1) Employers were no longer responsible for the investment decisions of plan assets (money invested on behalf of the employees), and (2) employees were now responsible for making contributions on their own behalf to fund their retirement years. Due to this change, lawmakers wanted to make sure that the plans offered to employees protected employees from those who managed their retirement dollars. As a result, the necessity for defined fiduciary standards emerged. The following is an excerpt from the 1974 ERISA law that outlines this very idea:

> The Employee Retirement Income Security Act (ERISA) protects your plan's assets by requiring that those persons or entities who exercise discretionary control or authority over plan management or plan assets, have discretionary authority or responsibility for the administration of a plan, or provide investment advice to a plan for compensation or have any authority or responsibility to do so are subject to fiduciary responsibilities. Plan fiduciaries include, for example, plan trustees, plan administrators, and members of a plan's investment committee.

> The primary responsibility of fiduciaries is to run the plan solely in the interest of participants and beneficiaries and for the exclusive purpose of providing benefits and paying plan expenses. Fiduciaries must act prudently and must diversify the plan's investments in order to minimize the risk of large losses. In addition, they must follow the terms of plan documents to the extent that the plan terms are consistent with ERISA. They also must avoid conflicts of interest. In other words, they may not engage in transactions on behalf of the plan that benefit parties related to the plan, such as other fiduciaries, services providers, or the plan sponsor. (http://www.dol.gov/dol/topic/health-plans/fiduciaryresp.htm).

Pension A company offered retirement program where a company contributes dollars to fund employees' later retirement from the company.

Defined benefit retirement program A source of funds that an employer puts away on behalf of employees to later pay out to the employee when they retire from the company. See also *pension*.

Defined contribution program An employee funded account used as a source to fund one's future retirement.

Courtesy of anyaberkut/Fotolia.

At this point in time (1978), the concept of fiduciaries, as related to the financial services industry, was relatively isolated to those who managed these new defined contribution, or employee-funded, accounts. Roughly 30 years later, we see a renewed vigor behind the importance of this idea of fiduciary responsibility as a reaction to various financial industry scandals, such as those involving Bernie Madoff and Allen Stanford, to name a few.

Bernie Madoff, in full **Bernard Lawrence Madoff** (born April 29, 1938, Queens, N.Y., U.S.), American hedge-fund investment manager and former chairman of the NASDAQ (National Association of Securities Dealers Automated Quotations) stock market. He was best known for operating history's largest Ponzi scheme, a financial swindle in which early investors are repaid with money acquired from later investors rather than from actual investment income.

Madoff grew up in the predominantly Jewish neighbourhood of Laurelton in Queens, N.Y. After spending his freshman year at the University of Alabama, he earned a degree (1960) in political science from Hofstra University, Hempstead, N.Y. He studied law briefly at Brooklyn Law School before founding (1960) Bernard L. Madoff Investment Securities with his wife, Ruth, who worked on Wall Street after earning a degree in psychology from Queens College, City University of New York. Madoff's specialty was so-called penny stocks—very low-priced shares that traded on the over-the-counter (OTC) market, the predecessor to the NASDAQ exchange. Madoff served as a NASDAQ director for three one-year terms.

Madoff cultivated close friendships with wealthy, influential businessmen in New York City and Palm Beach, Fla., signed them as investors, paid them handsome returns, and used their positive recommendations to attract more investors. He also burnished his reputation by developing relationships with financial regulators. He exploited an air of exclusivity to attract serious, moneyed investors; not everyone was accepted into his funds, and it became a mark of prestige to be admitted as a Madoff investor. Investigators later posited that Madoff's pyramid, or Ponzi, scheme, originated in the early 1980s. As more investors joined, their money was used to fund payouts to existing investors—as well as fee payments to Madoff's firm and, allegedly, to his family and friends.

Some skeptical individuals concluded that his promised investment returns (10 percent annually, in both up and down markets) were not credible and questioned why the firm's auditor was a small storefront operation with few employees. In 2001 Barron's financial magazine published an article that cast doubt on Madoff's integrity, and financial analyst Harry Markopolos repeatedly presented the Securities and Exchange Commission (SEC) with evidence, notably a detailed investigation, "The World's Largest Hedge Fund Is a Fraud," in 2005. Still, the SEC took no actions against Madoff; large accounting firms such as PricewaterhouseCoopers, KPMG, and BDO Seidman reported no signs of irregularities in their financial reviews; and JPMorgan Chase bank ignored possible signs of money-laundering activities in Madoff's multimillion-dollar Chase bank account. In fact, the Chase account was used to transfer funds to London-based Madoff Securities International Ltd., which some said existed solely to convey an appearance of investing in British and other European securities. No one knew that the supposed trades were not taking place, because, as a broker-dealer, Madoff's firm was permitted to book its own trades. Madoff's employees reportedly were instructed to generate false trading records and bogus monthly investor statements.

The scheme's longevity was made possible largely through "feeder funds"—management funds that bundled moneys from other investors, poured the pooled investments into Madoff Securities for management, and thereby earned fees in the millions of dollars; individual investors often had no idea that their money was entrusted to Madoff. When Madoff's operations collapsed in December 2008 amid the global economic crisis, he reportedly admitted the dimensions of the scam to members of his family. The feeder funds collapsed, and losses were reported by such international banks as Banco Santander of Spain, BNP Paribas in France, and Britain's HSBC, often because of the huge loans that they had made to investors who were wiped out and unable to repay the debt.

In March 2009 Madoff pleaded guilty to fraud, money laundering, and other crimes associated with running the Ponzi scheme. Madoff's accountant, David G. Friehling, was also charged in March with securities fraud. The thousands of people and numerous charitable foundations who had invested with Madoff, directly or indirectly through feeder funds, thus spent the early months of 2009 assessing their often huge financial losses. U.S. federal investigators continued to pursue suspects, including some other members of the Madoff family. Estimates of losses ranged from $50 billion to $65 billion, but investigators acknowledged that locating the missing funds might prove to be impossible. In June 2009 federal judge Denny Chin gave Madoff the maximum sentence of up to 150 years in prison.

Full text from the below site:

Bernie Madoff. (2016). In Encyclopaedia Britannica. Retrieved from http://www.britannica.com/biography/Bernie-Madoff

Allen Stanford, the fallen Texan billionaire and one time king of cricket, has been sentenced to 110 years in jail for defrauding investors of $7bn. He was also ordered to pay back $5.9bn—a symbolic gesture as the fraudster is now penniless.

The Texan tycoon's bizarre and lengthy trial came to its conclusion in Houston after both Stanford and victims had addressed the court.

Showing no contrition, Stanford, 62 and dressed in green prison fatigues, told the court: "If I live the rest of my life in prison, I will always be at peace with the way I conducted myself in business."

He accused the prosecution of "Gestapo" tactics and said they had ruined a legitimate business. "I'm not a thief," he said. "I never defrauded anyone."

In court one of his victims, Angela Shaw, told the judge: "Allen Stanford has stolen more than billions of dollars. He took our lives as we knew them." She said some 28,000 people had lost money in the scam. Shaw asked for other victims in the court to stand and half the gallery rose to their feet, according to court reports.

Prosecutors said Stanford had treated his victims like "roadkill." They had asked for a prison sentence spanning more than two centuries, calling him a "ruthless predator" who stole from investors "simply to satisfy his own greed and vanity."

After a jury convicted Stanford in March on 13 of 14 fraud-related counts, prosecutors called on US district judge David Hittner to sentence Stanford to 230 years in prison, the maximum sentence for all his convictions.

Stanford has been in jail since his arrest in June 2009 and his lawyers asked for a maximum of 44 months, a sentence he could complete within about eight months because of the time he has already served. The trial was delayed after Stanford's defence team claimed their client had lost his memory following a vicious prison beating following a dispute over a telephone call.

The 6ft 4in Texan was arrested three years ago after the police tracked him down to a modest townhouse in Fredericksburg, Virginia, owned by one of his girlfriends.

After it became clear his business empire was on the point of collapse, Stanford had been attempting to flee to Antigua. The Caribbean island was his second home. He was known as Sir Allen there and was one of the largest landowners with business interests including the local cricket ground, newspapers and restaurants. He had spent much of his time there on his 112ft motor yacht, Sea Eagle Bikini.

Abandoned by his mother as a child, Stanford had grown up poor in the tiny town of Mexia, Texas. After an early career in gyms failed to pan out he moved into finance, eventually building Stanford International Bank into a global investment firm with offices from Caracas to Zurich.

The money bought him power and influence. He was said to be close to the Bush family. In Washington, he and his executives gave over $1.8m to Democrat and Republican politicians. President Barack Obama received $4,600 for his 2008 election campaign.

It also allowed him to buy his way into the heart of the cricket establishment. Stanford developed a love of the game in Antigua. In 2008 the august England and Wales Cricket Board signed a five-year deal with him for a series of matches between England and an all-star West Indies team.

The billionaire announced the deal in typically flamboyant style, arriving at Lord's cricket ground in a black helicopter and posing for photographs with a perspex case containing $20m in cash.

But according to the prosecution all this wealth belonged to someone else. Stanford's lavish lifestyle was financed by investors who bought certificates of deposit, or CDs, from his bank. But instead of investing the cash, he spent it.

One unanswered mystery is how he got away with it for so long. US diplomats had warned government officials not to be seen or photographed with Stanford three years before his arrest.

"Embassy officers do not reach out to Stanford because of the allegations of bribery and money-laundering. The ambassador managed to stay out of any one-on-one photos with Stanford during the breakfast," a government official wrote in a cable obtained by Wikileaks.

White collar crime expert attorney Andrew Stoltmann said it was a fair sentence and in line with the 150 years that Bernard Madoff received for his massive Ponzi scheme. "There is no doubt he is a crook. But this case leaves a lot of people with egg on their faces. The regulators should have spotted this guy years ago and they didn't do anything until they came under pressure after Madoff."

Stoltmann said far larger amounts of money had been lost by Wall Street bankers but that no one had prosecuted them. "They went after the fly in the ointment," he said.

Taken in full from:

http://www.theguardian.com/world/2012/jun/14/allen-stanford-jailed-110-years

Courtesy of danilantiq2010/Fotolia.

Securities and Exchange Commission (SEC)
A regulatory body created under the Securities Act of 1933 to oversee the protection of investors, maintain fair, orderly, and efficient markets, and facilitate capital formation.

Broker dealers An individual or company that engages in the business of buying and selling marketable securities for its own account and the accounts of others.

Investment advisors An individual or company that makes investment recommendations through both direct and indirect methods of communication to their audience.

DISCIPLESHIP MOMENT AND REFLECTION

Take a few moments and read the brief stories of Bernie Madoff and Allen Stanford. Then review the following verses. Talk to your prayer partner and accountability partner about ways you can protect yourself from falling into these traps. (Proverbs 11:2, Proverbs 16:5, Proverbs 29:23, Proverbs 16:18, Galatians 6:3, Proverbs 27:2, Proverbs 26:12, James 4:6, Jeremiah 9:23, Philippians 2:3)

2010: Legislators passed the Dodd–Frank Wall Street Reform and Consumer Protection Act, commonly known as the Dodd–Frank Act. Section 913 of this legislation requires the **Securities and Exchange Commission (SEC)**, which is the regulatory body created under the Securities Act of 1933, to "oversee the protection of investors, maintain fair, orderly, and efficient markets, and facilitate capital formation" (SEC.gov), and to review new proposals that will broaden the scope of fiduciary responsibilities to brokers and other financial advisors providing personalized investment advice.

January 2011: The SEC releases a staff study recommending a uniform fiduciary standard of conduct for **broker dealers**, individuals or companies that engage in the business of buying and selling marketable securities for their own accounts and the accounts of others, and **investment advisors**, individuals or companies that make investment recommendations through both direct and indirect methods of communication to their audience.

February 2011–August 2015: Over the course of these 4 years, the SEC, the Department of Labor, and the securities industry (represented by SIFMA) debated multiple components of these laws, including how to redefine the term *fiduciary* and the responsibilities of those fiduciaries, and have yet to come to an agreement.

STEWARDSHIP: A BIBLICAL PERSPECTIVE

Fortunately, God has given us directions as to our fiduciary responsibilities with His resources in His preserved and protected word. Remember, God owns it all. He has complete and unhindered rights of His possessions, and God has given us responsibilities with respect to those possessions. As we previously examined, a fiduciary is one who is entrusted with the responsibilities to act on someone else's behalf and whose actions must serve the best interest of that owner. As Christians, we have the responsibility to act as fiduciaries of God's resources; however, the more common term used by Christians is *steward*. Although very similar to the definition of a fiduciary, the definition of a steward carries a bit of a different connotation.

According to *Merriam-Webster's*, the general definition of *steward* encompasses the following:

1. One employed in a large household or estate to manage domestic concerns (as the supervision of servants, collection of rents, and keeping of accounts)
2. One charged with overseeing: shop steward, union steward
3. A fiscal agent
4. An employee on a ship, airplane, bus, or train who manages the provisioning of food and attends passengers

5. One appointed to supervise the provision and distribution of food and drink in an institution

6. One who actively directs affairs: manager

Steward One who oversees the management and care of another's affairs.

Based on this definition, a **steward** can aptly be described as one who oversees the management and care of another's affairs. One must keep in mind that the concept of stewardship applies to lots of different areas of one's life, not just money. Stewardship applies to our time and how we use it for the benefit of another, to our talents and how our skill set allows us to benefit others, to our money and how we spend it on behalf of another, and to our true relationships and how our interactions benefit others. In Christian circles, we use the terms *steward* and *stewardship* quite often. When used in the context of the church, *steward* is usually intended to mean someone who handles money wisely and gives regularly to the church. Actually, the Bible does not use the word *steward* for this meaning. If you look in a concordance for the English Standard Version (ESV) of the Bible, you only find a few uses of the word *steward*. All of those uses are in the typical context of an employee working for an employer or serving food or drink. There are only four uses of the word *steward* in the New Testament, according to the ESV translation (Blomberg, 2013). These can be found in the following verses:

1 Corinthians 9:17—"For if I do this of my own will, I have a reward, but if not of my own will, I am still entrusted with a stewardship."

Ephesians 3:2—"assuming that you have heard of the stewardship of God's grace that was given to me for you"

Colossians 1:25—"of which I became a minister according to the stewardship from God that was given to me for you, to make the word of God fully known"

1 Timothy 1:4—"nor to devote themselves to myths and endless genealogies, which promote speculations rather than the stewardship from God that is by faith."

Biblical stewardship The use of God-given gifts and resources (time, talent, treasure, and true relationships) for the accomplishment of God-given goals and objectives.

Throughout the Bible, however, the concept of stewardship is pervasive. The recurring idea is that God owns it all and that we are managers for a temporary period. All we have is from God's hand. He entrusts us with it. Throughout this textbook, our working definition of **biblical stewardship** is the use of God-given gifts and resources (time, talent, treasure, truth, relationships) for the accomplishment of God-given goals and objectives.

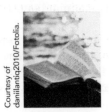

Courtesy of daniilantiq2010/Fotolia.

DISCIPLESHIP MOMENT AND REFLECTION

Review the following verses, reflect, and pray that the Holy Spirit will provide you with insight into the practical application of these verses to your life. What areas of your life do you need to reassess and alter to become a better steward?

Time	Treasure	True Relationships
Genesis 1:28	2 Corinthians 9:6-7	1 Peter 4:10
Luke 12:42-46	Luke 16:11	1 Corinthians 4:1–21
		Titus 1:7

Talents
Colossians 3:23
Proverb 16:3

Although we do not want to minimize our roles as stewards in all areas of our lives, we will specifically focus on financial stewardship, which consists of our "treasure." **Financial stewardship** can be defined as the use of both money and possessions to achieve and accomplish God's will.

Ron's Corner

Whatever He's given me, I'm using it for His goals and objectives. I'm trying to accomplish what He's asked me to by using what He's given me. You could change the previous definition of *biblical stewardship* to define success the same way. I want to someday hear Him say, "Well done, good and faithful servant."

What Does a Good Steward Look Like?

Richard Niebuhr, a 21st-century theologian, has been attributed with saying, "Stewardship is everything we do after we accept Christ." This idea suggests that once individuals become Christians, their lives will reflect their understanding that we are called to give all of our time, talent, treasure, and true relationships in order to accomplish God-given goals and objectives. We, as Christians, guided by the Holy Scriptures, all do it right then! Unfortunately, this is not the case. According to Blomberg (2013), the amount of giving per member of the at-large American church as a percentage of income, both for general budget needs as well as spending on special programs for the poor and needy, has declined over the past century. Since the 1920s, when giving was around 4% of annual income, we have seen interesting fluctuations. In 1942, giving hit a low of 1.5%, but then it steadily climbed back up to 3% by the 1960s. Over the next few decades and into the present age, we have seen giving steadily decline back to roughly 2% of earned income. Additionally, a study by Smith, Emerson, and Snell (2008) found that 20% of "strong" or "very strong" donors accounted for 80% of the giving, whereas 10% of those labeled in the same category did not give anything at all.

Recently, the pastor of a large evangelical organization sought to understand what a major donor usually looks like. What he found was that if individuals *look* like they can give large sums of money by the homes in which they live, the cars they drive, and so on, chances are very likely that they are actually *unable* or *unwilling* to give significantly. Outward looks can be deceiving.

So what, then, are characteristics of a steward? There are five main components that make up a good steward. These indicators come from years of experience, anecdotal heuristics, and Scripture. The five indicators are (1) proportionate giving; (2) controlled, debt-free lifestyle; (3) taxes paid with integrity and thanksgiving; (4) financial goals set as a family; and (5) accountability.

Indicators of Stewardship

1. Proportionate Giving

    Many church attenders have asked about (or in some cases debated) the biblical requirements of giving. Must Christians still give a tithe, or 10%, of their income? Is that the minimum or the maximum? Is it based on gross pay or net pay? Must the tithe go only to the church, or can it include other para-church ministries? How do I tithe from increases of net worth and not just income? If the tithe is required, why does Jesus not command it specifically?

There are answers to these questions, but sometimes we miss the overall point. Giving should be based on one's income and should increase as one's income increases. Proportionate giving is measurable. We see this as Paul writes to the Corinthians:

> 2 Corinthians 8:3—"For they gave according to their means, as I can testify, and beyond their means, of their own accord."

This idea presented by Paul can help provide a framework for how giving should be in proportion to means. We will cover giving in more detail in later chapters. The point here, though, is that as a steward, one's giving needs to be aligned properly with one's income. One way to evaluate one's giving and income is to take out one's previous income tax returns. The data you find will be objective and not subjective. People tend to think they give more than they do.

Ron's Corner

Everybody deducts everything they can for charitable giving—and perhaps a bit more. I used to prepare tax returns. The common conversation was usually something like this, "Well, how much charitable giving was there for us to deduct?"

The client would often respond, "Well, how much did I do last year?"

"Exactly $1,000," the tax preparers says.

"Oh, I did more than that this year, increase it by $500."

That was pretty common. So, if your tax return has your giving and your income data, how do you measure up? Test yourself over the past few years. What's the trend of your giving? Are you showing this indicator of good stewardship?

---

2. Controlled Lifestyle

A second characteristic of good stewards is a controlled **lifestyle**, which can be simply be defined as the decisions one makes that encompass one's way of life. As a preview to our later discussion on decision making, one's lifestyle is made up of choices, and there are no independent choices. In fact, you will always be in a position of having a finite income and unlimited or infinite choices for how to spend that income. Therefore, lifestyle is a matter of choice, and each spending decision made begins to define this "way of life." Many people with high income (e.g., athletes, doctors, business owners) also have high spending patterns. Their choices of spending are what make up their lifestyles.

There are athletes, doctors, and businesspeople with very high income, and yet we find that many spend beyond what they earn (through the use of credit/debt). This understanding actually was conceptualized through the work of several economists, including Milton Friedman and his work on the permanent income hypothesis. Friedman took the foundation of existing consumptive theories and expanded the idea to include future income. Under this theory, Friedman suggested that people will spend or consume based on their perspective of future earnings. In the case of athletes, doctors, and business owners, many perceive that their future income will either remain consistently high for an extended period of time or that their income will continue on an upward trend. Spending is based on monthly income; unfortunately, our purchases can be larger than our monthly income, which leads to borrowing and committing to continual debt payments that can cause a spiral into an out-of-control lifestyle. If something unexpected occurs and there are obligations that must be repaid, this can begin a downward spiral. It should be noted that someone's status of being in debt does not necessarily indicate that he or she is not a good steward; however, the individual should be moving toward a debt-free lifestyle.

DISCIPLESHIP MOMENT AND REFLECTION

Answer the following lifestyle question: If God called you into full-time ministry tomorrow, could you go? Or are you in bondage to your lifestyle? Take some time to evaluate how your lifestyle is a reflection of your decision making. What changes in your decisions need to be made to begin to eliminate your debt bondage? Talk to your accountability and prayer partner about your decisions.

Here is an example of this idea of living an uncontrolled lifestyle. A board member of a not-for-profit organization was involved in the hiring process for a senior leadership position. The committee had identified a talented professional who was passionate about serving the Lord. He was in the latter years of his career. He really wanted to get out of the rat race of his profession and work in what he called a "life-changing organization." As the board tried to finalize the job arrangements, this professional finally declined. Despite his desire to work for the nonprofit organization, he was making $450,000 a year as an attorney and did not think he could live on less. Because of his present commitments—he had a couple of homes, expensive hobbies, memberships, and so forth—he felt he could not accept the offer because of the lower salary.

Understand that it is not wrong to have nice things, a vacation home, or a high salary, nor is it implied that one should work in a Christian ministry over the marketplace. Rather, seek prayer and perhaps ask yourself whether your lifestyle would allow you to go full time into Christian work. We need to be unencumbered by the things of this world. Debt is not the only encumbrance, but it is often symptomatic of maintaining a lifestyle beyond your means.

3. Taxes Paid with Integrity and Thanksgiving

   Generally, most citizens dislike paying taxes. Oh, sure, one may try to muster up some patriotic feelings to ease the displeasure. As Arthur Godfrey said, "I'm proud to be paying taxes in the United States. The only thing is—I could be just as proud for half the money."

   It is quite a shift to pay the correct amount of taxes with thanksgiving. The thanksgiving part gets you. Certainly, any of us can find disagreement with the spending decisions of a large and complex government. But this book is not suggesting anyone should say "thanks" to the government as much as it is suggesting that everyone should say "thanks" to God.

   We will go over taxes in depth in a later chapter, but know that if one is paying more income taxes, most of the increase is due to making more money. No one pays out 100% of his or her income in income taxes. One is taxed on a percentage far less than 100%. So, if you have been blessed with property or income and have planned for your taxes well, the taxes you pay are symptomatic of God's provision. Again, paying taxes is a result of God's provision in your life. Because all we have comes from Him, thanksgiving should be our attitude rather than curses when paying that property tax bill in the fall, the income tax amount on April 15, or the quarterly estimated income tax payment. We can remind ourselves by thanking the Lord as we write our tax checks: "Thank you, Lord. Thank you for blessing me in this particular way, so that I can even do this."

More information will be provided about how taxes are calculated in later chapters, but we would like to address the idea that nobody should render unto Caesar any more than he requires. Knowing and understanding how taxes are calculated and being aware of legitimate ways to minimize taxes can be a characteristic of a good steward. The Bible commands us to pay taxes to those in authority. The availability of money to pay the tax *and* the attitude of gratitude are both indicators of stewardship.

4. Financial Goals Set as a Family

    Many have heard, and research has identified, that money is one of the most commonly cited reasons for marital problems (Albrect, 1979; Madden & Janoff-Bulman, 1981), or at least a component of arguments that lead to conflicts (Oggins, 2003). Research has found a vast array of causes that lead to marital conflict, which include budgeting practices (Lawrence, Thomasson, Wozniak, & Prawitz, 1993) and spending behaviors (Rick, Small, & Finkel, 2009). In other words, many conflicts relate back to how couples desire to allocate their resources within the household. In their study on the determinants of money arguments between spouses, Britt, Huston, and Durband (2010) found that communication was the strongest predictor of money arguments, even greater than availability of resources (i.e., how money is budgeted) and how power is distributed among the members of household (i.e., who brings the most money home, what type of job each spouse has, etc.). In essence, communication is foundational in relationships, and specifically as it relates to the way we individually think and act around money and how our past experiences influence our beliefs about money. These past experiences and beliefs are and will undoubtedly be different than the beliefs of one's spouse. It is crucial to understand that there will be differences between spouses and to talk through those differences prior to them escalating out of control. The following is a list of questions that are good conversation starters for any married couple desiring to have conversations that relate to money.

Questions for Understanding Your Spouse's View of Money

1. What is your earliest memory of money?
2. How would you describe your parents' use of money?
3. In what ways did you receive money when growing up (allowance, work, etc.)?
4. How important is money as it relates to accomplishing your life goals?
5. What would you like to do with our kids relating to teaching them about money, and what aspects are the same as or different from the way you were raised?
6. Describe a time when you spent money and regretted that decision.

Courtesy of danilantiq2010/Fotolia.

DISCIPLESHIP MOMENT AND REFLECTION

Take some time to come up with a list of questions you would like to ask about the way your spouse or the person you are in a relationship with thinks about money. You can use the questions listed here as a starting point. Get to know the person's thoughts and feelings about money. Find out where you agree and disagree. Talk to your accountability and prayer partner about the conversation, and pray together to see where the Holy Spirit leads you to go.

There may be other questions you have in relation to the way your spouse thinks about money, so feel free to ask. The goal is to communicate and set goals around using money and developing good spending habits. Working and praying through setting goals is where the benefit lies, not just in the end goals. Keep in mind that the husband and wife talking together, thinking together, praying together, and planning together is the ultimate goal. It's good to have goals, but if a goal requires one spouse to work extra to earn extra income or put too much into a retirement plan instead of giving, then that couple may be sacrificing in other areas, such as family time, health, or the other spouse working less outside the home. Set family goals first, then set the financial goals. The financial goals should be a subset of the family goals, not the driver of the family goals.

5. Accountability

    Accountability is scriptural—iron sharpens iron, carry one another's burdens, seek wise counsel, and so on. When it comes to financial matters, are you accountable to anybody? This is one reason this book integrates "Discipleship Moments and Reflection" sections throughout each chapter. It is important that you have an accountability and prayer partner whom you can turn to in times of need.

Ron's Corner

You may be surprised to know that I've used a financial advisor for years. When I was involved with my financial planning firm, we required every staff member to have a financial advisor. I still do. It's not because I don't understand how to plan—in fact, he uses my material and the programs that I had developed to give me advice.

The reason I use an advisor is because I need somebody in my life to ask me questions like, "Why are you doing that? Why are you buying a vacation property? Why are you getting another car now?"

Here's a recent example of how it works. I had bought a 2001 luxury car, a really nice car. But it now had nearly 100,000 miles on it and didn't look or smell like a new car anymore. So, as it approached 100,000 miles, I thought maybe it was time to get a new car. However, I had written several financial books in the 1980s and had researched all of the buying and leasing options, and I came to the conclusion that the cheapest car is the one that you already have. No exceptions. But that was 20 years ago, I thought. Surely things had changed.

I called Layne, my advisor, who incidentally is five "generations" down from me, in terms of training. That is, I trained an advisor who later trained an advisor, and so on, in the firm. I said, "Layne, I'm sure the rules have changed. Judy has her own business now. Perhaps it'd be better to buy a new car and use it in the business. Would you look at it?"

He called me back a couple of days later and said, "Ron, the rules still apply. The cheapest car you will ever have is the car you presently have." My own words hit me in the head like a boomerang. So now I understand—if I'm going to get a new car, it's strictly an ego decision. I can't justify it as a wise financial decision. But I needed him to challenge me on that.

(As a "P.S." to this car story: It wasn't but a few days after my discussion with Layne when a car pulled out in front of me. I hit it broadside—very hard. After realizing that nobody was hurt, my first thought was "YES! God's provision. I can smell that new car now!" The wrecker towing my car in stated the obvious: "It's totaled."

The response from the collision center and the auto insurance center, however, was that they never "total" that type of car. So, they spent thousands of dollars repairing my car, and I am still driving this older, repaired car. God does have a sense of humor!)

Courtesy of B-C-designs/Fotolia.

Everyone needs accountability. Even if one knows all the rules, one sometimes needs someone to say no and explain why. Another reason for an advisor is for your spouse. Chances are that he or she may outlive you. Your spouse is always a good sounding board; however, your spouse may not be the best accountability person. As a husband or wife, you are inclined to want to please your spouse and make him or her happy. Unfortunately, this can lead to collectively making poor financial decisions. This is where an objective third party (your financial advisor) can listen to both of you and help you through financial decisions that have or could become emotional decisions and not spiritual decisions.

SUMMARY

This chapter focused on the idea that those who belong to Christ become biblical stewards, managers of God's resources. We saw how the corporate role of acting as a manager over other people's possessions, known as a fiduciary, has become a more pressing issue in recent years. We defined the concepts of a steward, the process of acting as a steward (stewardship), as well as a subcomponent of stewardship: financial stewardship. Finally, we focused our attention on the five indicators of good stewardship, namely: (1) proportionate giving, (2) a controlled lifestyle, (3) paying taxes with integrity and thanksgiving, (4) setting goals as a family, and (5) being held accountable.

SUMMARY REVIEW QUESTIONS

1. Define *fiduciary*.

2. What makes a person a fiduciary?

3. Outline the timeline leading to the establishment of a fiduciary.

4. What financial regulation created the idea of a fiduciary?

5. What legislation has pushed for expanding the concept of fiduciary?

6. Define *steward*.

7. What makes a person a steward?

8. What are the different areas of stewardship? Provide verses that support each area.

9. Explain in your own words each of the five indicators of a steward:
   a. Proportionate giving
   b. Controlled lifestyle
   c. Paying taxes with integrity and thanksgiving
   d. Setting financial goals as a family
   e. Being held accountable

10. In your own words, what differentiates a fiduciary from a steward? Can you come up with other examples that match this type of relationship?

Case Study Analysis

After what seemed like hours, Bob and Debbie left the meeting with Steve, a bit confused. They went to Steve to discuss their finances and spent an hour and a half talking about the way they viewed the world. As they entered their car, Bob said, "Well, that felt like a complete waste of time. I don't really know what our thoughts about God and the way we see the world has anything to do with creating a budget. Are we sure we want to continue to pursue these meetings with Steve?" Debbie sat quietly with the folder Steve gave them as they left. Bob started back up again, "We are already millionaires; I really don't feel like we are doing anything wrong. We are in the top 1% in terms of wealth in the nation. We probably have more money saved in retirement than Steve does!"

Debbie finally responded, "Bob, let's just see what God is trying to teach us with all of this. Let's do this: Laurianne just mentioned to me that Rebecca and Michael have been dying to see this new movie and asked if Chloe and Clara wanted to go. We will have the girls go with them to the movie and we can go over this 'homework' that Steve wanted us to complete."

The next night, as Clara and Chloe left for Laurianne's house, Bob and Debbie sat in their sunroom overlooking the small lake in the back of their house. As they opened the folder, there were a couple of sentences at the top of the first page followed by several blank pages. The instructions read:

The definition of financial stewardship is the use of money and possessions to achieve and accomplish God's will. Use the space between each question to write down your answer. You will need your balance sheet as a reference. We will discuss your responses at our next meeting.

There were only three questions:

1. How are your assets being used to achieve and accomplish God's will?
2. How did your liabilities seek to achieve and accomplish God's will?
3. How will your net worth achieve and accomplish God's will?

Bob and Debbie both looked at each other, and one could feel the tension. Previous communication about money never seemed to end well. In many cases, Bob would dominate the conversation, and Debbie would leave the room feeling that her views were not being considered. Debbie always let Bob handle the money, and she wouldn't ever say anything, but she definitely felt uneasy as to where they were.

Debbie, in a soft, low voice, said, "Bob, if we are going to do this, we need to allow each of us to talk through our own thoughts and ideas."

Bob just looked at Debbie and sighed. "Fine," he responded.

Looking at these questions from the viewpoint of Bob and Debbie, provide an answer for Steve for each question. Think about what you would do in this situation, and feel free to answer as if you were Bob and Debbie.

Use the Case Study, as well as the chapter material, to answer the following questions as they relate to Bob and Debbie's situation:

Questions

1. In what aspects of Bob's life does he serve as a fiduciary/steward?
2. In what aspects of Debbie's life does she serve as a steward?
3. What percentage of Bob and Debbie's income is being tithed to their local church? Are they typical for an American family or atypical? Explain.
4. What evidence is there that Bob and Debbie's lifestyle and spending patterns are influenced by their level of income and not a controlled lifestyle?
5. As Bob and Debbie begin to identify who might be a source of accountability in terms of their finances, what are some advantages/disadvantages of Steve playing that role for the couple? What are some of the advantages/disadvantages to their current financial advisor, James, playing that role?

DEFINITIONS

Biblical stewardship (p. 28)

Broker dealers (p. 27)

Defined benefit retirement
program (p. 24)

Defined contribution
program (p. 24)

Fiduciary (p. 23)

Financial stewardship (p. 28)

Investment advisors (p. 27)

Lifestyle (p. 30)

Pension (p. 24)

Securities and Exchange
Commission (SEC) (p. 27)

Steward (p. 28)

SCRIPTURE VERSES (ESV)

Proverbs 11:2—When pride comes, then comes disgrace, but with the humble is wisdom.

Proverbs 16:5—Everyone who is arrogant in heart is an abomination to the Lord; be assured, he will not go unpunished.

Proverbs 29:23—One's pride will bring him low, but he who is lowly in spirit will obtain honor.

Proverbs 16:18—Pride goes before destruction, and a haughty spirit before a fall.

Galatians 6:3—For if anyone thinks he is something, when he is nothing, he deceives himself.

Proverbs 27:2—Let another praise you, and not your own mouth; a stranger, and not your own lips.

Proverbs 26:12—Do you see a man who is wise in his own eyes? There is more hope for a fool than for him.

James 4:6—But he gives more grace. Therefore it says, "God opposes the proud, but gives grace to the humble."

Jeremiah 9:23—Thus says the Lord: "Let not the wise man boast in his wisdom, let not the mighty man boast in his might, let not the rich man boast in his riches. . . .

Philippians 2:3—Do nothing from rivalry or conceit, but in humility count others more significant than yourselves.

1 Corinthians 4:1–21—This is how one should regard us, as servants of Christ and stewards of the mysteries of God. Moreover, it is required of stewards that they be found trustworthy. But with me it is a very small thing that I should be judged by you or by any human court. In fact, I do not even judge myself. For I am not aware of anything against myself, but I am not thereby acquitted. It is the Lord who judges me. Therefore do not pronounce judgment before the time, before the Lord comes, who will bring to light the things now hidden in darkness and will disclose the purposes of the heart. Then each one will receive his commendation from God. . . .

Luke 12:42–46—And the Lord said, "Who then is the faithful and wise manager, whom his master will set over his household, to give them their portion of food at the proper time? Blessed is that servant whom his master will find so doing when he comes. Truly, I say to you, he will set him over all his possessions. But if that servant says to himself, 'My master is delayed in coming', and begins to beat the male and female servants, and to eat and drink and get drunk, the master of that servant will come on a day when he does not expect him and at an hour he does not know, and will cut him in pieces and put him with the unfaithful.

Titus 1:7—For an overseer, as God's steward, must be above reproach. He must not be arrogant or quick-tempered or a drunkard or violent or greedy for gain,

Proverbs 16:3—Commit your work to the Lord, and your plans will be established.

Luke 16:11—If then you have not been faithful in the unrighteous wealth, who will entrust to you the true riches?

Colossians 3:23—Whatever you do, work heartily, as for the Lord and not for men,

1 Peter 4:10—As each has received a gift, use it to serve one another, as good stewards of God's varied grace:

Genesis 1:28—And God blessed them. And God said to them, "Be fruitful and multiply and fill the earth and subdue it and have dominion over the fish of the sea and over the birds of the heavens and over every living thing that moves on the earth."

2 Corinthians 9:6-7—The point is this: whoever sows sparingly will also reap sparingly, and whoever sows bountifully will also reap bountifully. Each one must give as he has decided in his heart, not reluctantly or under compulsion, for God loves a cheerful giver.

1 Corinthians 9:17—For if I do this of my own will, I have a reward, but if not of my own will, I am still entrusted with a stewardship

Ephesians 3:2—assuming that you have heard of the stewardship of God's grace that was given to me for you,

Colossians 1:25—of which I became a minister according to the stewardship from God that was given to me for you, to make the word of God fully known,

1 Timothy 1:4—nor to devote themselves to myths and endless genealogies, which promote speculations rather than the stewardship from God that is by faith.

2 Corinthians 8:3—For they gave according to their means, as I can testify, and beyond their means, of their own accord.

ADDITIONAL READINGS

Block, P. (1993). *Stewardship: Choosing service over self-interest.* San Francisco, CA: Berrett-Koehler Publishers.

Christopher, J. C. (2008). *Not your parents' offering plate: A new vision for financial stewardship.* Nashville, TN: Abingdon Press.

Curtis, G. (2012). *The stewardship of wealth: Successful private wealth management for investors and their advisors.* New York, NY: John Wiley & Sons.

Davis, J. H., Schoorman, F. D., & Donaldson, L. (1997). Toward a stewardship theory of management. *Academy of Management Review, 22*(1), 20–47.

Donaldson, L., & Davis, J. H. (1991). Stewardship theory or agency theory: CEO governance and shareholder returns. *Australian Journal of Management, 16*(1), 49–64.

Fox, M. A., & Hamilton, R. T. (1994). Ownership and diversification: Agency theory or stewardship theory. *Journal of Management Studies, 31*(1), 69–81.

Ireland, D. J. (1992). *Stewardship and the kingdom of God: An historical, exegetical, and contextual study of the parable of the unjust steward in Luke 16: 1–13* (Vol. 70). Leiden, Netherlands: Brill.

Jeavons, T. H. (1994). Stewardship revisited: Secular and sacred views of governance and management. *Nonprofit and Voluntary Sector Quarterly, 23*(2), 107–122.

Martin, A. (1991). *Biblical stewardship.* Neptune, NJ: Loizeaux Brothers.

Muth, M. M., & Donaldson, L. (1998). Stewardship theory and board structure: A contingency approach. *Corporate Governance, 6*(1), 5–28.

Spears, L. C. (1998). *Insights on leadership: Service, stewardship, spirit, and servant-leadership.* New York, NY: John Wiley & Sons.

Taft, J. G., & Ellis, C. D. (2012). *Stewardship: Lessons learned from the lost culture of Wall Street.* New York, NY: John Wiley & Sons.

REFERENCES

Albrecht, S. L. (1979). Correlates of marital happiness among the remarried. *Journal of Marriage and the Family,* 857–867.

Blomberg, C. (2013). *Christians in an age of wealth: A biblical theology of stewardship.* Grand Rapids, MI: Zondervan.

Britt, S. L., Huston, S., & Durband, D. B. (2010). The determinants of money arguments between spouses. *Journal of Financial Therapy, 1*(1), 7.

Keynes, J. M. (2006). *General theory of employment, interest and money.* New Delhi, India: Atlantic Publishers & Dist.

Lawrence, F. C., Thomasson, R. H., Wozniak, P. J., & Prawitz, A. D. (1993). Factors relating to spousal financial arguments. *Financial Counseling and Planning, 4,* 85–93.

Madden, M. E., & Janoff-Bulman, R. (1981). Blame, control, and marital satisfaction: Wives' attributions for conflict in marriage. *Journal of Marriage and the Family,* 663–674.

Oggins, J. (2003). Topics of marital disagreement among African-American and Euro-American newlyweds. *Psychological Reports, 92*(2), 419–425.

Rick, S. I., Small, D. A., & Finkel, E. J. (2011). Fatal (fiscal) attraction: Spendthrifts and tightwads in marriage. *Journal of Marketing Research, 48*(2), 228–237.

Smith, C., Emerson, M. O., & Snell, P. (2008). *Passing the plate: Why American Christians don't give away more money.* New York, NY: Oxford University Press.

Chapter 3

Contentment

Courtesy of duncanandison/Fotolia.

BIG IDEA:
Having an eternal perspective allows me to be content.

LEARNING OUTCOMES

- List three foundational verses that help define what contentment is and looks like lived out

- Define *contentment* and *sustainment*

- Explain three reasons why people are generally not content

- List and describe four ways in which peace of mind is obtained

- List several possible financial idols

- Recognize the difference between prosperity and posterity

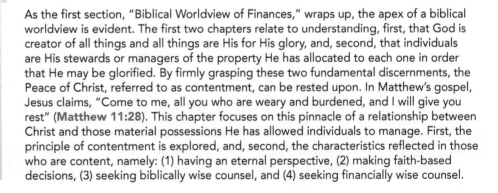

As the first section, "Biblical Worldview of Finances," wraps up, the apex of a biblical worldview is evident. The first two chapters relate to understanding, first, that God is creator of all things and all things are His for His glory, and, second, that individuals are His stewards or managers of the property He has allocated to each one in order that He may be glorified. By firmly grasping these two fundamental discernments, the Peace of Christ, referred to as contentment, can be rested upon. In Matthew's gospel, Jesus claims, "Come to me, all you who are weary and burdened, and I will give you rest" (**Matthew 11:28**). This chapter focuses on this pinnacle of a relationship between Christ and those material possessions He has allowed individuals to manage. First, the principle of contentment is explored, and, second, the characteristics reflected in those who are content, namely: (1) having an eternal perspective, (2) making faith-based decisions, (3) seeking biblically wise counsel, and (4) seeking financially wise counsel.

Ron's Corner

For years I said that "financial freedom" is what we should try to experience. I published a pamphlet called the "Keys to Financial Freedom." I wrote articles on how to experience financial freedom. In summary, I taught that the pinnacle of doing well financially, giving cheerfully, managing debt, and so on was financial freedom.

My thought process was along these lines: If a person was not a "slave to the lender," but recognized that God owned it all and had the right view of money, then he or she was free—he or she wasn't caught up in the bondage of materialism.

I don't believe any of this teaching was wrong. But I believe the Lord has been showing me a greater vision and a deeper understanding of what we're aiming for. As I've been reflecting on this book, I've reviewed previous writings, and the Lord has shown me personally that contentment is the aim and result.

BIBLICAL FOUNDATIONS FOR CONTENTMENT

There are three foundational verses that help define what contentment is and what it looks like when lived out.

> Philippians 4:10–13—I rejoice in the Lord greatly that now at length you have revived your concern for me. You were indeed concerned for me, but you had no opportunity. Not that I am speaking of being in need, for I have learned in whatever situation I am to be content. I know how to be brought low, and I know how to abound. In any and every circumstance, I have learned the secret of facing plenty and hunger, abundance and need. I can do all things through Him who strengthens me.

> Luke 11:2–4 (The Lord's Prayer)—And he said to them, "When you pray, say: 'Father, hallowed be your name. Your kingdom come. Give us each day our daily bread, and forgive us our sins, for we ourselves forgive everyone who is indebted to us. And lead us not into temptation.'"

> Hebrews 13:5—Keep your life free from the love of money, and be content with what you have, for he has said, "I will never leave you nor forsake you."

Looking at these three verses, contentment comes with one main theme: dependence on Christ. The apostle Paul was content because he relied on Christ, Jesus told His followers to pray for their daily bread (not to pray for tomorrow's bread), and the writer of Hebrews confirms this by letting his readers know that all individuals can be content with what they have when they depend on Christ, who "will never leave nor forsake us."

The secular definition of contentment might be aptly described as a state of being happy or satisfied. For the purpose of this text, we define contentment a bit more narrowly. **Contentment** is a state of being completely satisfied by a dependence on God's provision for an individual's sustainment. **Sustainment**, or the act of being sustained, are the actions required to meet a person's daily needs in order to live.

Contentment is being satisfied with one's circumstances, not complaining, not craving something else, and having a mind at peace. David Jeremiah, senior pastor of Shadow Mountain Community Church, provided his definition of contentment. He says it has three aspects:

Contentment A state of being in which we are completely satisfied by our dependence on God's provision for our sustainment.

Sustainment The act of being sustained; the required actions in order to meet our daily needs so that we may live.

- Looking back without regret
- Looking at the present without envy
- Looking to the future without fear

Based on David Jeremiah's definition, contentment has nothing to do with money. A person may have a lot or a little money and still miss the whole point of contentment. Individuals often complain whether they have a little or a lot. They can be covetous just as easily with a lot of money as with a little. They can still experience regret, envy, and fear.

There does seem to be a correlation, however, with contentment and money. The idea of contentment has been associated too closely with the idea of financial independence—someone who has built up enough assets or income stream to work when they want, vacation where they want, and buy what they want. A person can be financially independent without being content. Conversely, a person can be content without being financially independent.

Besides avoiding the potential confusion between contentment and financial independence, the focus should be on contentment because that is the word the Bible uses. Take a few minutes to review the following verses:

1 Timothy 6:6-11   Luke 12:15
Matthew 6:30–33   Philippians 4:19

Courtesy of danilantiq2010/Fotolia.

DISCIPLESHIP MOMENT AND REFLECTION

Take a few minutes to review the scriptures just listed. As you review the verses, what common thread do you see in these verses? Do you have a true sense of contentment in your life? Pray through each of these verses and talk to your accountability and prayer partner on where the Holy Spirit is leading you.

Why People Are Generally Not Content

Research has been conducted that provides insight into the reasons why, in general, people are not content. Although many reasons exist, three explanations have been offered by way of research (Klontz, Sullivan, Seay, & Canale, 2015), as described next.

Money Ambivalence

Ambivalence The exhibition of both positive and negative thoughts regarding something or someone, leading to some sort of psychological discomfort.

Developed in part by Klontz and Britt (2012), the concept of money ambivalence involves having opposing dichotomous feelings about money. **Ambivalence** is defined as exhibiting both positive and negative thoughts regarding something or someone, leading to psychological discomfort. Many Christians seek to keep their desires in balance with biblical theology; however, when opportunities to meet those desires are presented, they may act differently. They don't want to become materialistic, yet they seem to desire materialism. The struggle leads to ambivalence.

Relative Deprivation

Relative deprivation A theory suggesting that individuals do not look at their own realities, but rather base reality on comparison with others around them.

The second suggested reason for a lack of contentment comes from the idea of relative deprivation. In its simplest form, the theory of **relative deprivation** suggests that individuals do not look at their own realities, but rather make comparisons with others around them. In other words, people compare their level of satisfaction within the social groups in which they belong. Students, for example, can be included in a wide variety of groups, including fraternities, school clubs, and residential halls. Under this idea of relative deprivation, students will base their feeling of success in relation to and in comparison with others within these groups.

Financial Envy

Envy An unpleasant, often painful emotion characterized by feelings of inferiority, hostility, and resentment produced by an awareness of another person or groups of people who enjoy a desired possession, position, attribute, or quality of being.

It is clear that people struggle with a push/pull relationship with money and may constantly compare themselves with others in the same social group. These situations can thus lead us to financial envy. Smith and Kim (2007) defined **envy** as "an unpleasant, often painful emotion characterized by feelings of inferiority, hostility, and resentment produced by an awareness of another person or group of person's who enjoy a desired possession, position, attribute, or quality of being" (p. 1). In his work on envy, Festinger (1954) suggested that envy is more prevalent when others share the same or similar characteristics or attributes. For example, if one of your classmates had a father who was a policeman (and perhaps your dad was a policeman in the city in which you lived) and this classmate drove a brand new Lexus and you drove a used Ford, you may be inclined to experience more envy than if that classmate's father was a chief executive officer of a large company.

Courtesy of daniilantiq2010/Fotolia.

HOW TO BE FINANCIALLY CONTENT

Is financial contentment really possible in today's society—a society where people are constantly bombarded with limitless options and are constantly told that they will not be happy unless they have the latest innovation, the newest technology, or the biggest-screen TV?

Wise King Solomon wrote, "He who loves money will not be satisfied with money, nor he who loves abundance with its income. This too is vanity" (Ecclesiastes 5:10). Contentment is a learned response. The apostle Paul stated this very clearly: "Not that I speak from want; for I have learned to be content in whatever circumstances I am. I know how to get along with humble means, and I also know how to live in prosperity; in any and every circumstance I have learned the secret of being filled and going hungry, both of having abundance and suffering need" (Philippians 4:11–12).

The secret to which Paul was alluding was a result of learning to think correctly about money and God. Contentment is learning to see money as God sees it and nothing more. It is also learning to see God for who He is. He is like the bedrock of contentment. Major Ian Thomas says: "All you need is what you have; what you have is what He is; you cannot have more; and you do not need to have less."

Ron's Corner

Only when I realize He is sovereign and providentially in control of my earthly lot (my vocation and income) can I truly be content. Only when I learn to trust Him can I have contentment. Only when I realize that the Creator God of the universe loves me and has my best interests at heart can I be content.

Contentment really is a spiritual issue; it's not an amount-of-money issue. God is always there and never changes. He is consistent and stable. He can be trusted. But the same cannot be said about money. Proverbs 23:4–5 speaks to this when it says, "Do not weary yourself to gain wealth, cease from your consideration of it. When you set your eyes on it, it is gone. For wealth certainly makes itself wings, like an eagle that flies toward the heavens." How content can a person be in something that flies away?

No financial principle can have a greater impact on a life or lead to freedom more than this truth: *Money is not the key to contentment!* Contentment has everything to do with a relationship with God and nothing to do with money. Once individuals are free from the love of money and the pursuit of it, they can have a lot or a little and be content all the same. At that point they have learned the secret to contentment. It's not just the rich and high-income who struggle with contentment. Many families struggling to make ends meet struggle with contentment because they think the only thing they are lacking to be content is enough money.

WHAT DOES "FINANCIAL CONTENTMENT" LOOK LIKE?

The starting point for financial contentment is simply living within one's income. How individuals handle what God has given them will reveal whether they have financial contentment or not. One example is that of a business man who earned in excess of $600,000 a year. Unfortunately, instead of being content and at peace, he was miserable; he had financial pressures because he was spending $100,000 more than he was making. The key to contentment in one's finances is not the amount one makes, but rather a willingness to live within that amount.

Ron's Corner

Recently when I spoke to a group of men, I asked how many of them were making twice what they were making 10 years ago. Every hand in the audience went up. I then asked them how they would respond if, 10 years ago, they were asked, "Would you be content if you were making twice what you're making now?" Here again they all answered positively.

But when I asked them if they were in fact content now, they said no. The point is, their income had doubled, but they had not learned to live within that income. Therefore, they were not content. I have found in my counseling that living within one's income is an indicator of contentment.

Financial contentment has less to do with money and more to do with our attitudes, belief systems, and decisions. Financial contentment brings peace of mind. Despite the commercials of financial service companies, financial security is not the same as financial peace of mind. Both may help to move a person further along toward financial contentment. But it's possible to have financial security without financial peace of mind. Peace of mind is obtained by having the following:

- Eternal perspective
- Faith-based decisions
- Biblically wise counsel
- Financially wise counsel

Eternal Perspective

Having an eternal **perspective**, a point of view or attitude toward something, helps a person deal with the earthly up and downs, stock market highs and lows, and getting new stuff and having stuff break. Author Beth Moore says, "All that will matter in eternity is the glory that came to God as a result of my life. I will be most blessed when God is most glorified." If a person is concerned about God being glorified, then he or she is less concerned about hoarding, giving the kids the best stuff, being comfortable, seeking a life of leisure, or keeping up with the neighbors.

The Bible speaks to the brevity of a person's life:

> Come now, you who say, "Today or tomorrow we will go to such and such a city, spend a year there, buy and sell, and make a profit," whereas you do not know what will happen tomorrow. For what is your life? It is even a vapor that appears for a little time and then vanishes away. Instead you ought to say, "If the Lord wills, we shall live and do this or that." (James 4:13–15)

Recall the theory of relative deprivation, in which individuals view their circumstances in relation to others in their same social circles. Research has found that this deception shortens a person's perspective from a longer term to a shorter term. Callan, Shead, and Olsen (2011) found a link between relative deprivation and a preference for more immediate and smaller rewards at the expense of larger, delayed rewards. This might suggest that a person is willing to give up eternal rewards for earthly temporal satisfaction. The story of the rich young ruler provides a perfect illustration of this concept:

> And as he was setting out on his journey, a man ran up and knelt before him and asked him, "Good Teacher, what must I do to inherit eternal life?" And Jesus said to him, "Why do you call me good? No one is good except God alone. You know the commandments: 'Do not murder, Do not commit adultery, Do not steal, Do not bear false witness, Do not defraud, Honor your father and mother.'" And he said to him, "Teacher, all these I have kept from my youth." And Jesus, looking at him, loved him, and said to him, "You lack one thing: go, sell all that you have and give to the poor, and you will have treasure in heaven; and come, follow me." Disheartened by the saying, he went away sorrowful, for he had great possessions. (Mark 10:17–22)

Faith-Based Decisions

Faith, defined by the writer of Hebrews, is the assurance of things hoped for, the conviction of things not seen (Hebrews 11:1). If individuals are exhibiting faith, then they are pleasing God. If they are pleasing God, then it's easier for them to be content with their physical and financial position. For, "without faith it is impossible to please Him. For he who comes to God must believe that He is, and that He is a rewarder of those who diligently seek Him" (Hebrews 11:6).

As individuals think through their financial decisions, they don't always know the outcomes. Part of contentment, though, is not allowing the potential outcomes to hinder the glory God deserves. Should you need reminding of how God is glorified by faithfulness, read back through the following scriptures of the following faith servants:

> Abraham and Isaac—Genesis 22
>
> Moses and the Red Sea—Exodus 14
>
> Joshua and the Battle of Jericho—Joshua 6

Biblically Wise Counsel

If individuals rely on the movies, advertising, fashion trends, Hollywood celebrities, or the gang at work for their guidance and counsel, then they will not be content. They begin to experience envy or even relative deprivation. But seek first God's Kingdom and His counsel through His word. The Bible compares the result of earthly wisdom and heavenly wisdom:

> For where envy and self-seeking exist, confusion and every evil thing are there. But the wisdom that is from above is first pure, then peaceable, gentle, willing to yield, full of mercy and good fruits, without partiality and without hypocrisy. (James 3:16–17)

> All scripture is given by inspiration of God and is profitable for doctrine, for reproof, for correction, for instruction in righteousness, that the man of God may be complete, thoroughly equipped for every good work. (2 Timothy 3:16)

Financially Wise Counsel

Keep in mind the three sources of biblical wisdom: (1) the Scriptures, (2) the Holy Spirit, and (3) biblically minded individuals. These three sources should be used as decisions are made, especially financial decisions. The Bible gives instruction to seek counsel, and believers should be looking to their church staff and pastors as well as those who are consistently in God's word for advice and guidance in their lives.

EXPERIENCING FINANCIAL CONTENTMENT

One of the most obvious examples of contentment comes from watching a sleeping baby. Everyone has heard the saying, "sleep like a baby." A baby experiences a certain amount of peace and tranquility that adults often no longer experience. Many things cause individuals to be worried or anxious. But babies are motivated by a few basic needs, and after those needs are met, they have very little to worry about. They can rest in total peace.

Contentment comes when money and financial decisions do not control a person's thoughts. In other words, contentment comes with an attitude about money that is totally free from worry and anxiety caused by any possible use or misuse of money; therefore, content individuals can sleep like a baby.

One common misconception people believe is that if they had just a little more money, then they would be content. The truth is, however, that no amount of money is ever enough to provide contentment.

Several prominent examples of this misconception exist. When asked, "How much is enough?" John D. Rockefeller responded, "Just a little bit more." Howard Hughes was one of the world's wealthiest men at the time of his death, and yet he had a fearful and anxiety-ridden existence during the last years of his life. He was certainly not a picture of one who was financially free.

In order to experience true freedom from the love of money, as well as freedom from money worries, four things are required: First, a person must have a proper belief system regarding money (i.e., a biblical worldview). Second, a person needs a money management system that works for his or her family. Third, a person needs a decision-making process for money decisions. Fourth, the ultimate key to being content, is that a person must give the resources God has entrusted to him or her back to God.

The U.S. culture's perspective is as follows:

- Culture encourages individuals to spend all that they make. (It says, "Keep the economy going!")
- Culture aggressively teaches discontentment. (It says, "You deserve a break.") This is opposite of what God wants. He wants individuals to learn to be content.
- Culture attaches self-worth to net worth. (It says, "You are winning the game because of what you own.")

"Too many people spend money that they don't have to buy things they don't need to impress people they don't like." (Will Rogers)

Financial Idols

Further, the question must be asked: Is there discontentment with God that draws a person to find contentment in the stuff of this world?

One of the Ten Commandments is not to have any idols in your life. Individuals are not to worship any other form of god. This seems like one of the easier commandments to obey—compared to not lying, not coveting, or honoring your parents. After all, there are no longer wooden carved images or poles on a mountain like those described in the Old Testament.

Consider the following Scripture verse, where we find parallels with today:

They rejected His laws and the covenant he had made with their ancestors and they despised all His warnings. They worshiped worthless idols and became worthless themselves. (2 Kings 17:15)

The Lord reminds us that we are drawn to what we worship. A similar verse in Matthew 6:21 says, "Where your treasure is, there your heart will be also." That really is the same thought. What a person treasures will ultimately capture his or her heart and mind, so that treasure is what a person thinks about, worries about, plans around, and spends time on.

Today, it is tempting to think about and spend time on financial idols. Here are examples of financial idols:

- Your house and its fair market value
- Income stream from your career
- Your retirement plan account value
- Certificates of deposit

- Pension plan
- Health insurance coverage
- Cars, trucks, and boats
- Value of your business
- Jewelry
- Clothes
- School your kids go to

Interestingly, the verse in Matthew doesn't say, "Don't have any treasures." In fact, it says to store up treasures in heaven. People are commanded to treasure, to value, and to worship. So, then, the issue is not that they have treasure, but what the treasure is. Whatever people treasure, worship, and value will determine the focus of their hearts and lives. To become more Christ-like, the Lord must be treasured, worshipped, and valued.

Ron's Corner

The challenge to my heart and mind is to focus my thoughts, my heart, my intentions—my whole being—on treasuring and worshiping my Lord and Savior. By doing so, my life has value, purpose, and meaning, and, more importantly, eternal significance. My challenge to you is to think about what you're worshiping: Is it a worthless financial idol or a treasure of eternal significance?

Courtesy of daniilantiq2010/Fotolia.

DISCIPLESHIP MOMENT AND REFLECTION

What financial idols are in your life? Take a look at the previous list, or consider others that may come to mind. Write these down and seek guidance on how you can remove them from your worship. Talk to your accountability and prayer partner about your decisions, and have your partner help you by being holding you accountable.

PROSPERITY OR POSTERITY?

Prosperity State of being prosperous; financially successful.

Posterity Relating to all future generations of people.

Except for two letters, the words *prosperity* and *posterity* are exactly the same. They sound so much alike, and yet are so different in what they mean. Although most people have probably not stopped to think about the meaning of these two words, everyone is in pursuit of one or the other. **Prosperity** is the state of being prosperous or having success, usually related to money, whereas **posterity** refers to all future generations of people. The way a person lives clearly demonstrates which of these two words is being pursued.

Each individual places hope in something—something of value, profit, gain, or reward. Hope keeps an individual's motivation alive. It incites people to action. A person will never be motivated and thus disciplined to do anything unless he or she has hope. The key, then, is *where that hope is placed.*

The Bible makes it plain that prosperity, material goods, houses, buildings, and so forth will not last. Stop and think about that for a minute. The high-rise office building a person works in each day, the mighty fortress home he has built to go home to, the estate she has amassed . . . none of it will last.

It is interesting, on the other hand, that a person can be prosperous and successful if the right things are pursued. Prosperity is succeeding in advancing in wealth or any good. It is making good progress in anything desirable. In evaluating this definition of prosperity, one finds that wealth, materialism, houses, boats, and so forth are really not the essence of the definition. Prosperity occurs when someone is making progress in the pursuit and accomplishment of a desired end.

Ron's Corner

In counseling couples, I've observed a great difference between people motivated by prosperity and those motivated by posterity. However, those motivated by prosperity are usually driven by a mistaken concept of posterity! Most Americans (Christians included) have defined prosperity as health, wealth, and materialism. As a result, they miss the true meaning. They subtly order their lives in the pursuit of things that God's word tells us will not last. If I misplace my hope in material things, and then apply all my motivation to attaining those things, I will find at the end of my life that I have missed the boat.

This is vividly expressed in Psalm 49, which points out the plight of so many who have placed their hope in prosperity rather than in the things that God says are important. Psalm 49:11, 12, 17–20 tells that a man's

> inner thought is that their houses are forever, and their dwelling places to all generations; they have called their lands [and buildings!] after their own names. But man in his pomp will not endure. . . When [man] dies he will carry nothing away; his glory will not descend after him. Though while he lives he congratulates himself—and though men praise you when you do well for yourself—He shall go to the generations of his fathers. . . Man in his pomp, yet without understanding, is like the beasts that perish.

Joshua 1:8 is so true when it says, "This Book of the law shall not depart from your mouth, but you shall meditate on it day and night, so that you may be careful to do according to all that is written in it; for then you will make your way prosperous, and then you will have success." One can be prosperous and successful, but only if he or she is doing what God says is important. That, then, leads to the second word: posterity.

As has already been defined, posterity is simply the descendants of the future generations. This, of course, includes a person's children, but it also implies other people whom the person affects for eternity. Psalm 37 says the righteous man will have posterity, but the posterity of the wicked will be cut off. In other words, if a person's focus is not on developing a godly posterity, then he or she will leave nothing of significance to mark for the generations that come after.

Clearly, one is prosperous and successful as he or she makes progress in developing and enhancing a godly posterity. What a travesty to pursue prosperity at the exclusion of posterity. After all, prosperity is not true wealth.

What will it be for you? Will you be motivated to spend your time pursuing prosperity as defined by materialism—which will not last—or will you pursue a godly posterity, and thus be truly prosperous?

RICH OR POOR: WHAT'S YOUR PERSPECTIVE?

Take a minute to read through the following story:

> One day a father of a wealthy family took his son on a trip to the country with the firm purpose of showing his son how poor people can be. They spent a couple of days and nights on the farm of what would be considered a very poor family. On their return from the trip, the father asked his son, "How was the trip?"
>
> "It was great, Dad."
>
> "Did you see how poor people can be?" the father asked.
>
> "Oh yeah," said the son.
>
> "So what did you learn from the trip?" asked the father.
>
> The son answered: "I saw that we have one dog and they have four. We have a pool that reaches to the middle of our garden and they have a creek that has no end. We have imported lanterns in our garden and they have stars at night. Our patio reaches to the front yard and they have the whole horizon.
>
> "We have a small piece of land to live on and they have fields that go beyond sight. We buy our food but they grow theirs. We have walls around our property to protect us, but they have their friends to protect them."
>
> With this, the boy's father was speechless.
>
> Then his son added, "Thanks, Dad, for showing me how poor we are."

Too many times people forget what they have and concentrate on what they don't have. What is one person's worthless object is another's prize possession. It's all based on perspective. Give thanks to God for all the bounty He has provided, instead of worrying about wanting more. Take joy in all He has given—and be content with that.

SUMMARY

This chapter is the pinnacle of personal finance, the ultimate goal of which is contentment. Unfortunately, contentment can be elusive for many people. Three seminal Scripture verses (Philippians 4:10–13; Luke 11:2–4; Hebrews 13:5) outline what contentment is. Contentment is defined as the state of being in which a person is completely satisfied by depending on God's provision for daily sustainment. Next, three main psychological behaviors that keep a person from being content were discussed: money ambivalence, relative deprivation, and financial envy. What is found, however, is that money is not the key to contentment. Rather, there are four main components that help cultivate an attitude of contentment: (1) having an eternal perspective, (2) making faith-based decisions, (3) seeking biblically wise counsel, and (4) seeking financially wise counsel. A list of financial idols was provided in order to evaluate how prosperity and posterity should align. Finally, a simple story that demonstrated a biblical perspective on being content was offered.

SUMMARY REVIEW QUESTIONS

1. What are the three foundational Scripture verses that discuss what contentment is?

2. Define *contentment* and *sustainment*.

3. Explain money ambivalence. Give an example of ambivalence.

4. Explain relative deprivation.

5. Explain financial envy.

6. How is contentment a learned response?

7. Explain why contentment is not a money issue.

8. Describe the four components that help deliver peace of mind in relation to money.

9. How is the U.S. culture's perspective different from the biblical perspective in relation to money?

10. Define *prosperity* and *posterity*. How are they connected?

Case Study Analysis

Bob and Debbie began to get really busy and had to push back meetings with Steve multiple times. Roughly 6 weeks had passed since the time Bob and Debbie sat down at their table and completed the questions Steve asked them to complete about their view of stewardship.

Sean came home from New Mexico State for Christmas break and seemed to only talk about joining a fraternity that he has heard is the best fraternity to be in and associate with for those wanting to pursue medical school. There is lots of money affiliated with the fraternity, and many doctors who were fraternity members come back and socialize with the up-and-coming students. Chloe and Clara both had year-end programs to prepare for. Chloe had a volleyball tournament that took Bob and Debbie all over the state. Chloe's team ended up placing third at the state championship, which was a huge accomplishment. Bob and Debbie had even thought about getting Chloe a car for all of her hard work, and because she now has her driver's license. Clara has been quietly hinting that she wants her own horse for Christmas after working in the Christmas pageant at the Freedom Riders Camp, the handicapped children's horseback riding facility where she works. Clara has such a compassionate heart.

Now Christmas is over, and, as usual, Bob and Debbie feel strapped again, a feeling that occurs every year around January. Bob calls it the Christmas Trough, where the realization occurs that the stuff bought for Christmas now has to be paid for. This is what really brought Bob and Debbie back to the reality that they need to continue to see Steve, regardless of the fact that Bob really doesn't think all this spiritual stuff is necessary to get their finances in order.

On January 18, Bob and Debbie finally meet with Steve again. After some talk about Christmas celebrations, Steve began to lead into the focus for the meeting.

"Bob, how do you and Debbie feel now, after Christmas?" Steve asked.

"Steve, I tend to say this every year—it's the feeling of the 'Christmas Trough'. We always seem to get this feeling every year that we overspent and now have to pay it all off. This year we decided to pay to get Sean into a fraternity, and it will cost us roughly $1500 per month to cover his housing costs and fraternity fees—but it was so important to him so that he will have a better opportunity to

get connected with doctors who are fraternity brothers. Apparently, it's the fraternity with the most significant connection to doctors in the area. Then, we committed to taking Chloe to look at cars on her birthday in about a month. We didn't go too much into how much we were planning on spending, but the look on her face when we told her that we would buy her a new car was worth it all. Finally, Debbie and I decided to get Clara a horse, which she can keep at the riding camp where she works. That means we will have to give her an allowance to pay for the feed, vet bills, and shoeing. She couldn't wait. We are talking with a horse trainer next week. We are probably looking at $5,000 for the horse.

"All that said, we love our kids so much and want to provide for them the way we were never provided for. We want our kids to experience life and not feel like they are struggling. So here we are. We know we need help to figure out how to pay for all that we have just committed to."

Steve sat and listened to all Bob talked about. When Bob was done, Steve got up from the couch and looked in his desk for five sheets of paper. "Bob, I would like you and Debbie to do one more exercise before we get into the nitty gritty of your finances. I would like you two and the kids—I feel like they are all old enough—to take this Financial Contentment Survey. This will help me determine where everyone stands so that as we finish going through each one of the sections we plan to cover, we can assess how content you are. I believe that contentment is the ultimate goal Christ has for us. When we are content, we are relying on God's grace and mercy and have complete and utmost dependence on Christ to provide for what we need."

Steve handed Bob the few pages.

"Can you get everyone to complete these surveys by next week, although I am only concerned with the outcomes of yours for right now? Let's plan on meeting again next Tuesday. Does that sound okay?"

Bob shrugged. "Steve, I don't really see what all this has to do with getting some guidance on our finances."

Steve replied instantly, "Bob, I can understand that this maybe unorthodox, but I assure you that there is a reason behind it all. What I need from you and Debbie is a commitment to complete the entire process. Can you do that?"

Bob replied hesitantly, "Steve, I am going to trust that you know what you are doing. All right, I guess we'll see you next week."

Review the Financial Contentment Survey in the Appendix of the textbook to see the types of questions asked of Bob and Debbie.

Use the Case Study following Chapter 19, as well as the chapter material, to answer the following questions as they relate to Bob and Debbie's situation:

Questions

1. What evidence is there that Bob, Debbie, and their children lack contentment?

2. In what ways are Bob and Debbie exhibiting ambivalence toward their finances?

3. In what ways does Sean exhibit relative deprivation?

4. What financial idols do Bob and Debbie have in their lives?

5. In what ways are Bob and Debbie modeling the pursuit of prosperity to their children?

6. In what ways are Bob and Debbie modeling the pursuit of posterity to their children?

DEFINITIONS

SCRIPTURE VERSES (ESV)

Matthew 11:38—Come to me, all you who are weary and burdened, and I will give you rest.

Philippians 4:10–13—I rejoice in the Lord greatly that now at length you have revived your concern for me. You were indeed concerned for me, but you had no opportunity. Not that I am speaking of being in need, for I have learned in whatever situation I am to be content. I know how to be brought low, and I know how to abound. In any and every circumstance, I have learned the secret of facing plenty and hunger, abundance and need. I can do all things through him who strengthens me.

Luke 11:2–4 (The Lord's Prayer)—And he said to them, "When you pray, say: 'Father, hallowed be your name. Your kingdom come. Give us each day our daily bread, and forgive us our sins, for we ourselves forgive everyone who is indebted to us. And lead us not into temptation.'"

Hebrews 13:5—Keep your life free from love of money, and be content with what you have, for he has said, "I will never leave you nor forsake you."

1 Timothy 6:6–11—Now there is great gain in godliness with contentment, for we brought nothing into the world, and we cannot take anything out of the world. But if we have food and clothing, with these we will be content. But those who desire to be rich fall into temptation, into a snare, into many senseless and harmful desires that plunge people into ruin and destruction. For the love of money is a root of all kinds of evils. It is through this craving that some have wandered away from the faith and pierced themselves with many pangs.

Matthew 6:30–33—But if God so clothes the grass of the field, which today is alive and tomorrow is thrown into the oven, will he not much more clothe you, O you of little faith? Therefore do not be anxious, saying, "What shall we eat?" or "What shall we drink?" or "What shall we wear?'" For the Gentiles seek after all these things, and your heavenly Father knows that you need them all. But seek first the kingdom of God and his righteousness, and all these things will be added to you.

Luke 12:15—And he said to them, "Take care, and be on your guard against all covetousness, for one's life does not consist in the abundance of his possessions."

Philippians 4:19—And my God will supply every need of yours according to his riches in glory in Christ Jesus.

Philippians 4:11–12—Not that I am speaking of being in need, for I have learned in whatever situation I am to be content. I know how to be brought low, and I know how to abound. In any and every circumstance, I have learned the secret of facing plenty and hunger, abundance and need.

Ecclesiastes 5:10—He who loves money will not be satisfied with money, nor he who loves wealth with his income; this also is vanity.

Genesis 22—After these things God tested Abraham and said to him, "Abraham!" And he said, "Here I am." He said, "Take your son, your only son Isaac, whom you love, and go to the land of Moriah, and offer him there as a burnt offering on one of the mountains of which I shall tell you." So Abraham rose early in the morning, saddled his donkey, and took two of his young men with him, and his son Isaac. And he cut the wood for the burnt offering and arose and went to the place of which God had told him. On the third day Abraham lifted up his eyes and saw the place from afar. Then Abraham said to his young men, "Stay here with the donkey; I and the boy will go over there and worship and come again to you." And Abraham took the wood of the burnt offering and laid it on Isaac his son. And he took in his hand the fire and the knife. So they went both of them together. And Isaac said to his father Abraham, "My father!" And he said, "Here I am, my son." He said, "Behold, the fire and the wood, but where is the lamb for a burnt offering?" Abraham said, "God will provide for himself the lamb for a burnt offering, my son." So they went both of them together.

When they came to the place of which God had told him, Abraham built the altar there and laid the wood in order and bound Isaac his son and laid him on the altar, on top of the wood. Then Abraham reached out his hand and took the knife to slaughter his son. But the angel of the Lord called to him from heaven and said, "Abraham, Abraham!" And he said, "Here I am." He said, "Do not lay your hand on the boy or do anything to him, for now I know that you fear God, seeing you have not withheld your son, your only son, from me." And Abraham lifted up his eyes and looked, and behold, behind him was a ram, caught in a thicket by his horns. And Abraham went and took the ram and offered it up as a burnt offering instead of his son. So Abraham called the name of that place, "The Lord will provide"as it is said to this day, "On the mount of the Lord it shall be provided."

And the angel of the Lord called to Abraham a second time from heaven and said, "By myself I have sworn, declares the Lord, because you have done this and have not withheld your son, your only son, I will surely bless you, and I will surely multiply your offspring as the stars of heaven and as the sand that is on the seashore. And your offspring shall possess the gate of his enemies, and in your offspring shall all the nations of the earth be blessed, because you have obeyed my voice." So Abraham returned to his young men, and they arose and went together to Beersheba. And Abraham lived at Beersheba.

Now after these things it was told to Abraham, "Behold, Milcah also has borne children to your brother Nahor: Uz his firstborn, Buz his brother, Kemuel the father of Aram, Chesed, Hazo, Pildash, Jidlaph, and Bethuel." (Bethuel fathered Rebekah.) These eight Milcah bore to Nahor, Abraham's brother. Moreover, his concubine, whose name was Reumah, bore Tebah, Gaham, Tahash, and Maacah.

Exodus 14—Then the Lord said to Moses, "Tell the people of Israel to turn back and encamp in front of Pi-hahiroth, between Migdol and the sea, in front of Baal-zephon; you shall encamp facing it, by the sea. For Pharaoh will say of the people of Israel, 'They are wandering in the land; the wilderness has shut them in.' And I will harden Pharaoh's heart, and he will pursue them, and I will get glory over Pharaoh and all his host, and the Egyptians shall know that I am the Lord." And they did so.

When the king of Egypt was told that the people had fled, the mind of Pharaoh and his servants was changed toward the people, and they said, "What is this we have done, that we have let Israel go from serving us?" So he made ready his chariot and took his army with him, and took six hundred chosen chariots and all the other chariots of Egypt with officers over all of them. And the Lord hardened the heart of Pharaoh king of Egypt, and he pursued the people of Israel while the people of Israel were going out defiantly. The Egyptians pursued them, all Pharaoh's horses and chariots and his horsemen and his army, and overtook them encamped at the sea, by Pi-hahiroth, in front of Baal-zephon.

When Pharaoh drew near, the people of Israel lifted up their eyes, and behold, the Egyptians were marching after them, and they feared greatly. And the people of Israel cried out to the Lord. They said to Moses, "Is it because there are no graves in Egypt that you have taken us away to die in the wilderness? What have you done to us in bringing us out of Egypt? Is not this what we said to you in Egypt: 'Leave us alone that we may serve the Egyptians'? For it would have been better for us to serve the Egyptians than to die in the wilderness." And Moses said to the people, "Fear not, stand firm, and see the salvation of the Lord, which he will work for you today. For the Egyptians whom you see today, you shall never see again. The Lord will fight for you, and you have only to be silent."

The Lord said to Moses, "Why do you cry to me? Tell the people of Israel to go forward. Lift up your staff, and stretch out your hand over the sea and divide it, that the people of Israel may go through the sea on dry ground. And I will harden the hearts of the Egyptians so that they shall go in after them, and I will get glory over Pharaoh and all his host, his chariots, and his horsemen. And the Egyptians shall know that I am the Lord, when I have gotten glory over Pharaoh, his chariots, and his horsemen."

Then the angel of God who was going before the host of Israel moved and went behind them, and the pillar of cloud moved from before them and stood behind them, coming between the host of Egypt and the host of Israel. And there was the cloud and the darkness. And it lit up the night without one coming near the other all night.

Then Moses stretched out his hand over the sea, and the Lord drove the sea back by a strong east wind all night and made the sea dry land, and the waters were divided. And the people of Israel went into the midst of the sea on dry ground, the waters being a wall to them on their right hand and on their left. The Egyptians pursued and went in after them into the midst of the sea, all Pharaoh's horses, his chariots, and his horsemen. And in the morning watch the Lord in the pillar of fire and of cloud looked down on the Egyptian forces and threw the Egyptian forces into a panic, clogging their chariot wheels so that they drove heavily. And the Egyptians said, "Let us flee from before Israel, for the Lord fights for them against the Egyptians."

Then the Lord said to Moses, "Stretch out your hand over the sea that the water may come back upon the Egyptians, upon their chariots, and upon their horsemen." So Moses stretched out his hand over the sea, and the sea returned to its normal course when the morning appeared. And as the Egyptians fled into it, the Lord threw the Egyptians into the midst of the sea. The waters returned and covered the chariots and the horsemen; of all the host of Pharaoh that had followed them into the sea, not one of them remained. But the people of Israel walked on dry ground through the sea, the waters being a wall to them on their right hand and on their left.

Thus the Lord saved Israel that day from the hand of the Egyptians, and Israel saw the Egyptians dead on the seashore. Israel saw the great power that the Lord used against the Egyptians, so the people feared the Lord, and they believed in the Lord and in his servant Moses.

Joshua 6—Now Jericho was shut up inside and outside because of the people of Israel. None went out, and none came in. And the Lord said to Joshua, "See, I have given Jericho into your hand, with its king and mighty men of valor. You shall march around the city, all the men of war going around the city once. Thus shall you do for six days. Seven priests shall bear seven trumpets of rams' horns before the ark. On the seventh day you shall march around the city seven times, and the priests shall blow the trumpets. And when they make a long blast with the ram's horn, when you hear the sound of the trumpet, then all the people shall shout with a great shout, and the wall of the city will fall down flat, and the people shall go up, everyone straight before him." So Joshua the son of Nun called the priests and said to them, "Take up the Ark of the Covenant and let seven priests bear seven trumpets of rams' horns before the ark of the Lord." And he said to the people, "Go forward. March around the city and let the armed men pass on before the ark of the Lord."

And just as Joshua had commanded the people, the seven priests bearing the seven trumpets of rams' horns before the Lord went forward, blowing the trumpets, with the ark of the covenant of the Lord following them. The armed men were walking before the priests who were blowing the trumpets, and the rear guard was walking after the ark, while the trumpets blew continually. But Joshua commanded the people, "You shall not shout or make your voice heard, neither shall any word go out of your mouth, until the day I tell you to shout. Then you shall shout." So he caused the ark of the Lord to circle the city, going about it once. And they came into the camp and spent the night in the camp.

Then Joshua rose early in the morning, and the priests took up the ark of the Lord. And the seven priests bearing the seven trumpets of rams' horns before the ark of the Lord walked on, and they blew the trumpets continually. And the armed men were walking before

them, and the rear guard was walking after the ark of the Lord, while the trumpets blew continually. And the second day they marched around the city once, and returned into the camp. So they did for six days.

On the seventh day they rose early, at the dawn of day, and marched around the city in the same manner seven times. It was only on that day that they marched around the city seven times. And at the seventh time, when the priests had blown the trumpets, Joshua said to the people, "Shout, for the Lord has given you the city. And the city and all that is within it shall be devoted to the Lord for destruction. Only Rahab the prostitute and all who are with her in her house shall live, because she hid the messengers whom we sent. But you, keep yourselves from the things devoted to destruction, lest when you have devoted them you take any of the devoted things and make the camp of Israel a thing for destruction and bring trouble upon it. But all silver and gold, and every vessel of bronze and iron, are holy to the Lord; they shall go into the treasury of the Lord." So the people shouted, and the trumpets were blown. As soon as the people heard the sound of the trumpet, the people shouted a great shout, and the wall fell down flat, so that the people went up into the city, every man straight before him, and they captured the city. Then they devoted all in the city to destruction, both men and women, young and old, oxen, sheep, and donkeys, with the edge of the sword.

But to the two men who had spied out the land, Joshua said, "Go into the prostitute's house and bring out from there the woman and all who belong to her, as you swore to her." So the young men who had been spies went in and brought out Rahab and her father and mother and brothers and all who belonged to her. And they brought all her relatives and put them outside the camp of Israel. And they burned the city with fire, and everything in it. Only the silver and gold, and the vessels of bronze and of iron, they put into the treasury of the house of the Lord. But Rahab the prostitute and her father's household and all who belonged to her, Joshua saved alive. And she has lived in Israel to this day, because she hid the messengers whom Joshua sent to spy out Jericho.

Joshua laid an oath on them at that time, saying, "Cursed before the Lord be the man who rises up and rebuilds this city, Jericho.

"At the cost of his firstborn shall he
    lay its foundation,
and at the cost of his youngest son
    shall he set up its gates."

So the Lord was with Joshua, and his fame was in all the land.

2 Kings 17:15—They despised his statutes and his covenant that he made with their fathers and the warnings that he gave them. They went after false idols and became false, and they followed the nations that were around them, concerning whom the Lord had commanded them that they should not do like them.

Matthew 6:21— For where your treasure is, there your heart will be also.

Psalm 49—Hear this, all peoples!
  Give ear, all inhabitants of the world,
both low and high,
  rich and poor together!
My mouth shall speak wisdom;
  the meditation of my heart shall be understanding.

I will incline my ear to a proverb;
  I will solve my riddle to the music of the lyre.

Why should I fear in times of trouble,
  when the iniquity of those who cheat me
    surrounds me,
those who trust in their wealth
  and boast of the abundance of their riches?
Truly no man can ransom another,
  or give to God the price of his life,
for the ransom of their life is costly
  and can never suffice,
that he should live on forever
  and never see the pit.

For he sees that even the wise die;
  the fool and the stupid alike must perish
  and leave their wealth to others.
Their graves are their homes forever,
  their dwelling places to all generations,
  though they called lands by their own names.
Man in his pomp will not remain;
  he is like the beasts that perish.

This is the path of those who have foolish confidence;
  yet after them people approve of their boast

Selah

Like sheep they are appointed for Sheol;
  death shall be their shepherd,
and the upright shall rule over them in the morning.
  Their form shall be consumed in Sheol, with no
    place to dwell.
But God will ransom my soul from the power of Sheol,
  for he will receive me. Selah

Be not afraid when a man becomes rich,
  when the glory of his house increases.
For when he dies he will carry nothing away;
  his glory will not go down after him.
For though, while he lives, he counts himself blessed
  —and though you get praise when you do well
    for yourself—
his soul will go to the generation of his fathers,
  who will never again see light.
Man in his pomp yet without understanding is like
  the beasts that perish.

ADDITIONAL READINGS

Allestree, R., & Pakington, L. D. C. (1841). *The art of contentment* (Vol. 17). J. Burns.

Burroughs, J. (2001). *Rare jewel of Christian Contentment*. Mulberry, IN: Sovereign Grace Publishers.

Chidvilasananda, G. (1999). *Courage and Contentment: A collection of talks on spiritual life*. South Fallsburg, NY: Syda Foundation.

Galbraith, C., Jenkin, G., Davis, P., Coope, P., & Tatau, T. T. (1992). *The culture of contentment*.

John, J. (2011). *The happiness secret: finding true contentment*. London, England: Hachette.

Johnson, R. A., & Ruhl, J. M. (2009). *Contentment*. New York, NY: Harper Collins.

Lykken, D. (2000). *Happiness: The nature and nurture of joy and contentment*. New York, NY: Picador.

Paquette, J. (2015). *Real happiness: Proven paths for contentment, peace and well-being*. Eau Claire, WI: PESI Publishing & Media.

Root, E. T. (1890). Contentment and fellowship: Or Paul's teachings regarding property. *The Old and New Testament Student*, 286–294.

Swenson, R. A. (2004). *Margin: Restoring emotional, physical, financial, and time reserves to overloaded lives* (Vol. 69). NavPress.

Swenson, R. A. (2014). *Contentment: The secret to a lasting calm*. Tyndale House.

Warren, N. C. (1997). *Finding contentment: When momentary happiness just isn't enough*. Thomas Nelson Publishers.

Watson, T. (1988). *The art of divine contentment: An exposition of Philippians 4: 11*. CCEL.

REFERENCES

Callan, M. J., Shead, N. W., & Olson, J. M. (2011). Personal relative deprivation, delay discounting, and gambling. *Journal of Personality and Social Psychology, 101*(5), 955.

Festinger, L. (1954). A theory of social comparison processes. *Human Relations, 7*(2), 117–140.

Klontz, B. T., & Britt, S. L. (2012). How clients' money scripts predict their financial behaviors. *Journal of Financial Planning, 25*(11), 33–43.

Klontz, B. T., Sullivan, P., Seay, M. C., & Canale, A. (2015). The wealthy: A financial psychological profile. *Consulting Psychology Journal: Practice and Research, 67*(2), 127.

Smith, R. H., & Kim, S. H. (2007). Comprehending envy. *Psychological Bulletin, 133*(1), 46.

THE FOUR USES OF MONEY

No matter how you view the unlimited alternatives on which to spend your income, there are really only four uses of money. These four uses may help you focus more intently when making plans and setting budgets.

- Live (lifestyle choices)
- Give
- Owe (debt and taxes)
- Grow (saving and investing)

Every spending decision will fit into one of these four uses, or categories. As simple as these four categories are, the challenge comes from determining how much to allocate to each of them. I can't give you exact amounts, and the Bible doesn't give a direct commandment for any of these (yes, not even giving)—although it gives us many principles and guidelines about each one of these four areas. This is where our definition of financial planning comes into play—allocating those limited financial resources.

To determine what God would have you do in balancing your priorities requires the discipline of spending time with Him. No one other person, including financial planners, can tell you how to prioritize your spending. Why? God has entrusted those resources to you to manage (but not own) rather than to someone else; only you are accountable for managing the use of God's resources entrusted to you.

How your money is allocated among the categories is a function of two factors: the commitments you already have and your priorities. For example, your family size will create certain lifestyle commitments that will probably be different from those of others. If you are single and do not have any dependents, your commitments will be different than if you are married and have several children. Ultimately, priorities dictate the use of one's remaining resources.

Courtesy of daniilantiq2010/Fotolia.

DISCIPLESHIP MOMENT AND REFLECTION

Make two columns on a piece of paper. In the first column, write commitments you have; in the second column, write down your priorities. As you look at the sheet, what thoughts come to mind? Are your priorities aligned with your commitments? Are there any commitments that are blocking you from your priorities? Talk to your accountability and prayer partner after your reflection. Pray that the Holy Spirit will help you begin to balance and align these two columns.

As Christians, we must believe that God provides for our needs, yet we are still called to work (Genesis 2:15). Unfortunately, there is not always a direct correlation between how hard we work and how much we make. Scripture makes it clear that we are to work, but the income we make is in God's hands, and He will meet our needs. Psalm 127:2 tells us, "It is vain for you to rise up early, to retire late, and to eat the bread of painful labors; for He gives to His beloved even in his sleep."

The apostle Paul writes, "Whatever you do, do your work heartily, as for the Lord rather than for men" (Colossians 3:23). Tremendous freedom results when one accepts the fact that it's one's responsibility to work heartily and to trust God for His provision (i.e., income), and then to live within that God-given income.

Commandments Rules, typically given to us by God through His word.

The Bible offers four basic **commandments**, or rules, typically given to us by God through His word, for the use of the income God provides to the individual or family.

First, we are commanded to give. "Honor the Lord from your wealth, and from the first of all your produce" (**Proverbs 3:9**). Paul adds, "On the first day of every week let each one of you put aside and save, as he may prosper, that no collections be made when I come" (**1 Corinthians 16:2**).

Second, we are commanded to pay taxes. **Romans 13:7** says, "Render to all what is due them: tax to whom tax is due; custom to whom custom; fear to whom fear; honor to whom honor." Jesus Himself also gave us insight on this command when He said, "Render to Caesar the things that are Caesar's; and to God the things that are God's" (**Matthew 22:21**).

Third, we are commanded to pay our debts. **Psalm 37:21** says, "The wicked borrows and does not pay back, but the righteous is gracious and gives." Not paying our debts responsibly makes us no better than the wicked.

Fourth, we are commanded to provide for our family's needs. "But if anyone does not provide for his own, and especially for those of his household, he has denied the faith and is worse than an unbeliever" (**1 Timothy 5:8**).

These commandments clearly indicate that God provides my income, and He has determined what is the appropriate income for each person. But I am then responsible to prioritize the use of this income to obey His commands to live (provide for myself and my family), give (give back to God and His kingdom), owe (pay my debts and taxes), and grow (set aside money for the future).

For many, however, we are not appropriately allocating to each of these areas. Unfortunately, we have a tendency to overallocate resources toward the live category, which then forces less resources to the others. Remember, we only have a set amount of money that we earn but an unlimited number of ways that our earned income can be spent. You may have thought, or perhaps heard someone say, "I'd like to give, but by the time I pay my taxes, repay my debts, and provide for my family, there's just not enough left over to give."

We should believe that God can be fully trusted to give us the income we need in order to obey His commands for the use of our money.

TRYING TO CONTROL THE LIFESTYLE CATEGORY

Consumptive To use or consume something.

Productive To yield or result in something more.

Of the four uses of money, two are **consumptive**, defined as to use or consume, and two are **productive**, defined as yielding more or resulting in something more. Paying for our lifestyle choices, debt repayment, and taxes are all consumptive in nature (the live and owe categories); when the money is spent, it is gone forever. Saving and giving (the give and grow categories) are both productive in nature. These two uses will yield more to use in the future.

Courtesy of daniilantiq2010/Fotolia.

DISCIPLESHIP MOMENT AND REFLECTION

Take a few moments and reflect on this concept of consumptive versus productive uses of money. How would your life be different if you used your money in more productive ways (yielding more or resulting in more) than consumptive? Talk to your accountability and prayer partner about ways you can become more productive in your financial decision making.

The live use is the sum total of all financial spending not related to the other three uses of money. It's typically the most significant use of money for most families, but it should not absorb so much of the available dollars that too little is left for our productive uses. The live use typically drives debt decisions; in other words, it's what causes the decision to incur debt. Also, it's always an after-tax amount.

As we previously explained, **contentment** is a state of being in which we are completely satisfied by our dependence on God's provision for our sustainment. The word *satisfied* is probably the most important word in that definition. Being satisfied is a choice, not a function of lifestyle. Yes, we are commanded to "provide" for our family, but one can never accumulate enough to protect the family's lifestyle against all contingencies. There is a difference between provision and protection, and that difference is usually determined by the heart's attitude toward God as a result of the money we are accumulating or spending. Learning to be content within the lifestyle God has chosen for you should be accepted with joy.

The following are seven strategies that will help guide you in controlling your lifestyle spending. Each of these seven strategies is listed and then supported by a Scripture reference. Each Scripture reference can also be found at the end of the chapter.

1. **Prayerfully seek God's direction regarding your lifestyle:** Before we start making decisions, specifically as they relate to finances, prayer should be our first step. Allow the Holy Spirit to direct your thoughts and feelings. Seek God's truth through His Spirit.

   "Trust in the LORD with all your heart and do not lean on your own understanding. In all your ways acknowledge Him, and He will make your paths straight." (Proverbs 3:5–6)

2. **Learn to be content:** Contentment is not an easy task. All have sinned (Romans 3:23), and no one is righteous (Romans 3:10), so it is not in our nature to be content. However, we can learn to be content and satisfied with God's provision. This is one of the important reasons that we strongly encourage you to have an accountability and prayer partner.

   "I have learned to be content in whatever circumstances I am." (Philippians 4:11)

3. **Learn to avoid coveting:** As we outlined in point 2, being content is a learned skill and with it comes the requirement to not look on what others have with envy and thoughts of jealousy. When we truly understand that everything is God's and He can allocate what is His in any way, then it is much easier for us to overcome jealousy and envy of other's possessions.

   "You shall not covet your neighbor's house; you shall not covet your neighbor's wife or his male servant or his female servant or his ox or his donkey or anything that belongs to your neighbor." (Exodus 20:17)

4. **Do not determine your lifestyle by comparing it to those of others:** As you may recall, in Chapter 2 we looked at relative deprivation, the suggestion that we compare our social standing in comparison to others in the same social class. This is very similar to item 3 coveting, so be mindful not to judge yourself against the standards of your social class.

   "Do not love the world nor the things in the world. If anyone loves the world, the love of the Father is not in him. For all that is in the world, the lust of the flesh and the lust of the eyes and the boastful pride of life, is not from the Father, but is from the world. The world is passing away, and also its lusts; but the one who does the will of God lives forever." (1 John 2:15–17)

5. **Freely enjoy whatever you spend in the "spirit":** If you have inherited wealth, you don't have to feel undue guilt. God chose you to be born there. Or, if you're living a life as God desires and have saved for items, don't feel guilty about buying a new couch or going on a vacation.

    "For everything created by God is good, and nothing is to be rejected if it is received with gratitude." (1 Timothy 4:4).

6. **Make an effort to live more simply:** Remember that money is broken up into four uses, and two of those are consumptive, producing little results. Living more simply may afford you the ability to put more money into productive uses such as saving and investing.

    "Make it your ambition to lead a quiet life and attend to your own business and work with your hands, just as we commanded you, so that you will behave properly toward outsiders and not be in any need." (1 Thessalonians 4:11–12)

7. **Do not be conformed to this world:** Consumers are constantly bombarded with advertisements for products and services. Be mindful of the media surrounding you and the ways you may be influenced by what you see and hear.

    "And do not be conformed to this world, but be transformed by the renewing of your mind, so that you may prove what the will of God is, that which is good and acceptable and perfect." (Romans 12:2)

WHAT ABOUT THE LONG-TERM?

We have looked at the five principles of money management and reviewed briefly the four uses of money. One of the five principles is to save for the long term, and the application of that within the four uses of money is in the grow category (saving and investing). We want to lay the groundwork here as well for the items covered later in Chapter 15, "Setting Long-Term Goals." There are really just six ways that one's long term savings can be used:

- Financial independence
- Debt elimination
- Starting a business
- Family needs (college education, dependent care)
- Lifestyle choices (second homes, cars, travel)
- Maximized giving

In the short term, there are four uses of money. When there is a surplus, or margin, your net worth grows. As your net worth grows, you can use the accumulated assets to meet your long-term goals.

Figure 4.1 shows how the short-term cash management uses are bridged together by use in the grow category to integrate one's long-term goals.

Figure 4.1

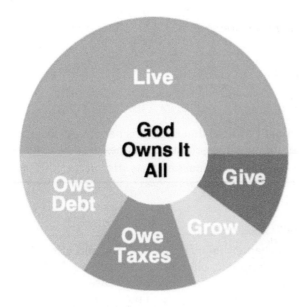

Live, Give, Owe, Grow

Live:
- Balancing provision and protection (God's protection, my responsibility to provide)
- How much is enough?

Give:
- Giving breaks the power of money

Owe:
- Debt always mortgages the future
- I owe taxes, but they are symptomatic of God's provision

Grow:
- Growing margin is the only way to meet long term goals

Five Money Management Principles:
- Spend less than you earn
- Give generously
- Avoid debt
- Build cash flow margin
- Set long term goals

Integrated Planning

Visually, you can see how the four short-term uses of money are connected to the way long-term money can be used. As you put together the four uses and six long-term goals, you can begin to integrate these notions and build a process. This process is the "plan" part of financial planning. Here's an outline of this four-step process:

Step 1: Summarize your present situation.

Step 2: Establish your financial goals.

Step 3: Plan to increase your cash flow margin.

Step 4: Control your cash flow.

As you review the diagram in Figure 4.1, there are three very important implications. The first is that there are *no independent financial decisions*. Think of your finances like a pie chart. When you eat a piece, it is gone and cannot be eaten by anyone else. If you make a decision to use financial resources in any one area, by definition, you have chosen not to use those same resources in the other areas. This means that if you choose to set aside money for college education or financial independence, you no longer have that money available to spend on giving, lifestyle desires, debt repayment, and the like. By the same token, if you decide to spend money on lifestyle desires, you no longer have those same resources available for any other short-term or long-term goals.

The second implication, when looking at the diagram, is that the more long term your perspective is, the better the possibility of your making a good financial decision now. Recall that two of the short-term uses of money are consumptive and two are productive. Once money is used on consumption, it is gone forever.

The third implication of this diagram is the *lifetime nature of financial decisions*. This implication ties the first two implications together. As we understand that there are no independent financial decisions, we see that what is spent in the short term cannot be used in the long term.

Ron's Corner

I like to remind those whom I counsel that decisions determine destiny. Once a decision is made either to save or spend, it determines to some extent one's financial destiny.

WHY HAVE A FINANCIAL PLAN?

As defined earlier in this chapter, financial planning is allocating limited financial resources among various unlimited alternatives. When we know what financial resources we have, or will have, and have planned to use them to accomplish specific goals and objectives, our lives become much more orderly, and we sense greater contentment. There are three main reasons to build a financial plan. First, it takes you through a process of thinking through the plan; second, it builds family/spousal communication; and third, it serves as the foundation from which to make decisions.

TAKING YOU THROUGH A PROCESS

The purpose of building a plan is not the result or outcome that is achieved, but rather the process that we go through to reach that outcome. Dwight D. Eisenhower once said, "Plans are nothing, but planning is everything." The process of planning allows us to think through our goals, identify obstacles, and identify alternatives.

Ron's Corner

Many people are like the person who starts on a trip, yet has no idea how long he has to take the trip, let alone where he is going. The likely result is that he gets nowhere. The same happens with people who manage their finances with no discernable plan. They are paralyzed with indecision; consequently, they fulfill the statistic once published by the Social Security Board that says only 2% of Americans achieve financial independence by age 65.

BUILDING FAMILY/SPOUSAL COMMUNICATION

Another significant reason for developing a personal financial plan is that it offers a basis for family or spousal communication. When couples or families work through the process of building a financial plan, they must collectively agree on their financial goals. Research, as well as our own experience, affirms that money plays a significant role in disagreements within relationships. By crafting a plan together and agreeing on the process as well as the outcomes, many disagreements about money are likely to be minimized, if not eliminated altogether.

SERVES AS A GUIDE FOR FINANCIAL DECISIONS

Finally, a financial plan serves as a guide for making financial decisions. Because of the plan, many financial decisions are made in advance. For example, if the plan calls for the establishment and funding of an individual retirement account (IRA), then the money allocated toward that account (perhaps the maximum, which is $6000/year) has been committed to that objective and is not available for any other use, regardless of how attractive the alternative use might appear to be. Because this decision was agreed upon by both spouses, there should be no debate or disagreement later over potential alternatives. In other words, a financial plan brings order rather than confusion.

In developing a personal financial plan, realize that you are *beginning a process* rather than *concluding a project*. Financial planning should be continuous because of changing circumstances, goals, priorities, and commitments. By using a financial plan to make good financial decisions, you bring balance into your life and have time for relationships—which really matter more in life than your net worth.

Courtesy of daniilantiq2010/Fotolia.

DISCIPLESHIP MOMENT AND REFLECTION

Think back on the three main reasons for creating a financial plan. It takes you through a process of thinking through the plan, it establishes communication between spouses and family members, and it serves as a guide for financial decisions. How have you implemented a financial plan? What are the obstacles for you to begin the process? Talk to your accountability and prayer partner regarding your thoughts and feelings toward creating a financial plan.

HOW MUCH IS ENOUGH?

If there was just one question relating to personal finances, this would be it: How much is enough? Solving or answering this question is what drives most financial decisions we make. This question leads into multiple other questions:

- How much is enough for retirement?
- How much do I spend on my lifestyle?
- How much do I give away?
- How much should I be earning?
- How much do I give to my kids?
- How much until I am financially independent?

Keep in mind that the answer to any of these questions is not strictly financial. More important than a dollar amount is attitude—for someone who desires more and more, no amount will ever satisfy.

WHY SHOULD I ANSWER THIS, AND WHY IS THIS QUESTION SO HARD TO ANSWER?

Hope Knowing what is not seen but believing it to exist.

Hoarding Difficulty in discarding something or lack of control in accumulating possessions.

There are two good reasons for defining how much is enough: to give hope and avoid hoarding. **Hope** is defined as the feeling that what is wanted can be had or that events will turn out for the best. For those who are still accumulating because they have not yet achieved their goal of "enough," answering that question with a dollar amount will give them hope. Then, accumulating "enough" will avoid **hoarding**, defined as difficulty in discarding something or lack of control in accumulating possessions, by knowing when you have enough and have reached your goals.

The question, "How much is enough?" implies a definite answer in dollar terms. However, the exact amount depends on the needs and goals of the individual or couple answering the question. And, by the way, there are two ways to accumulate enough: One is to *accumulate more* and the other is to *desire less*.

Here are two things to consider as you answer this question. First, if you have not yet accumulated enough, develop a plan to get there, outlining the specific steps you need to take now to start you on the path to your goal. Second, if you have defined how much is enough and you have accumulated more than your goal, consider giving the excess away. This decision may be difficult to make because of the uncertainty of the future, but remember that for the Christian, the future is eternally secure. As the Bible says, you will be storing lasting treasures in heaven, rather than on earth. Earthly treasures will not last eternally—although they could last longer than you will.

Desiring less is another option that will help you accumulate "enough." For example, if you had originally planned to buy a new car every 10 years from the time you are 30 until you are 60, then your plan will allocate resources to that goal. That goal will not be met until there are sufficient resources to buy those four vehicles. However, instead of accumulating enough to fund those four cars, you may choose to not "desire" those new cars and instead buy a used car every 12 years and move more of your savings to another category. In other words, you are desiring less and will not require as much to accumulate enough.

Everyone can answer the question as to how much is enough, although many choose not to. It will differ for every family and is a number that should be determined prayerfully. That answer will change periodically over time as circumstances change.

How do you increase your wealth over time in order to meet your "enough" goals? The beginning step is simple: Spend less than you earn and do it for a long time. As the Bible says, "He who gathers money little by little makes it grow" (Proverbs 13:11).

We discussed the "live" category as one of the uses of money previously in this chapter. The level of lifestyle a person maintains is one of the primary determinants of "How much is enough?"

Financial independence When one's income and assets are sufficient to meet short-term and long-term objectives.

If a couple knows their ongoing short-range objectives, then they can calculate how large an investment fund they need to become financially independent. **Financial independence** refers to having income and assets that are sufficient to meet short- and long-term objectives. By defining and quantifying your long-term goals, you will have answered the question, "How much is enough?" Once this question is answered, the end goals have been established and you now know "how much is enough"—you now know where the finish lines are.

The process in defining and quantifying your goals is simple:

1. Quantify each long-term goal as of today.

2. Determine how much has been accumulated to date toward the accomplishment of each goal.

3. Determine the difference between the amount accumulated; this is either the overaccumulation or the shortfall.

4. The shortfall divided by the number of years until the need must be met will give the average amount per year that must be accumulated to accomplish that specific goal.

Let's go through each step to help you understand how this works.

The first step is to determine the "number" needed to be achieved for that goal. So after you calculate several time-value-of-money problems (discussed in a later chapter in great detail), you should have the dollar figure you need in order to achieve your goals. The most prominent goal that you will hear about is how much you need in your retirement in order to sustain your desired lifestyle while in retirement. Determining this retirement dollar and the dollars needed for your other goals and objectives is step 1.

Once we know how much we need, we need to determine how much we already have set aside toward those goals. This will be an ongoing process because our "beginning" number will constantly be increasing. The next step is then to determine the difference between what we need and where we are trying to get to. Finally, we can take the number we need in order to reach our goals and divide it by the number of years we have until we want to accomplish those goals. We can take it one step further and divide the annual number by 12 to see what we need to put away or save each month rather than each year. Keep in mind that this is a process that will need to be recalculated regularly because your current balances will continue to grow and your time to reach your goals will be going down. Let's look at an example.

Say you started supporting yourself at age 20, and for the next 40 years you always spent $1,000 less than you earned and invested that $1,000 each year in an investment earning at least 12.5% interest. At age 60 you would have an investment fund of $1,000,000 (ignoring the tax implications). *The interest rate for this example is arbitrary and will vary based on actual annual investment performance.*

If you didn't catch the math, you might be surprised to see that $1,000 per year for 40 years would actually only be $40,000. How, then, do you get $1,000,000? That's nearly 25 times what was put aside. Exactly! This is called compounding. **Compounding** occurs when interest you earn on an original investment earns additional interest, which then earns interest, and so on, until the money is withdrawn from the account. As you can see, there are two important factors in compounding: the **interest rate,** which is the rate at which your money earns interest, and the amount of time the money is left to earn interest. The earlier you start and the more you earn in interest, the less you need to start with.

Compounding The process by which interest from savings earns additional interest and continues to do so until the money is withdrawn.

Interest rate The rate at which money earns interest.

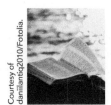

DISCIPLESHIP MOMENT AND REFLECTION

Take a few minutes to determine what your number is; in other words, what's enough for you? We strongly encourage you to pray about this number, talk to your spouse or significant other, and then talk through this with your accountability and prayer partner. Make sure you can articulate why this is the number.

Ron's Corner

> I strongly believe that you can't accumulate enough to feel financially secure, significant, or successful. A person's wealth is only a measurement of God's provision, not a measurement of your significance to God.

TWO MORE HARD QUESTIONS

Unfortunately, we can't stop by answering the previous question, "How much is enough?" Two subquestions need to be thought through as well:

- Will I ever have enough?
- Will it continue to be enough?

Once you have spent time going through your analysis and coming up with your number, you may begin to ask yourself the question, "Will I ever achieve that number?" This question will probably affect individuals differently. If you are 21 years old and have just finished your undergraduate degree and secured a new job, your answer may be more optimistic than that of a 55-year-old father of four who is getting ready to have three of his kids in college. We follow up the question, "Will I ever have enough?" with "Will it continue to be enough?" Life has a tendency to throw curveballs. Questions thus arise, such as: Is there any economic threat out there? Terrorism? Health? Inflation? Real estate downturn? Stock market downturn? Interest rates? Cost of medical care? Will I need to support my parents and kids at the same time? All of these questions will lead us to ask ourselves, "Will this amount last me?"

These questions are constantly in our subconscious, and therefore we all deal with them somehow in our decision making. Our decisions then make us fall into one of two traps. The first trap is to hoard everything, and the second trap is to do everything you can do to get the most you can. Voddie Baucham, former senior pastor at Grace Baptist Church in Spring, Texas, once said that we have the mind-set to "Get all we can, can all we get, then sit on the can!"

The reason these questions are important is because there are uncertainties in the world. Here's a summary on the worldly perspective of wealth and accumulation:

- My money is necessary for my protection.
- Money makes us anxious.
- I need to store and save all I can.
- There is never enough time to get all I need.
- I just need to keep accumulating.
- What I have is all mine.

How, then, can we help think about our money from a biblical perspective? One answer to this question can be answered by one word: Give. So, how much do you give, then? An important verse illustrating the concept of "How much is enough to give?" is Luke 6:38: "Give, and it will be given to you, pressed down, shaken together they will pour into your lap. By your standard of measure it will be measured unto you."

Jesus never defines what "it" is, whether it's your time, your love, your relationships, or your money, but He says, "the quantity of what God will pour into your lap is generous." But it has cost you something—and you get to see the standard of how much is given back for you to steward. This is not a name-it-and-claim-it verse; it's about moving your treasure to heaven, like Jesus says in Matthew 6:19–20. The key is that you need to ask yourself the questions, "Am I in the act of regular giving now, and am I setting a limit on how much I will give in my lifetime?"

As the Ron's Corner feature illustrates, the question of how much is enough isn't meant for you to assume that you must sell everything and join a monastery.

Ron's Corner

A ministry invited me to speak on a cruise—I liked to say with a feigned suffering look that God called me to the "cruise ministry." During my seminar, I focused on this question: "How much is enough?" A prosperous owner of a demolition business from California attended the seminar. Afterward, he told me that God had used that question to reveal to him that he had more than enough. The businessman concluded after hearing me speak that he should sell his business.

I asked him, "Well, then what are you going to do?"

He replied, "I may go full time into Christian ministry."

As we visited further and I learned more about him, I ventured, "You know, I think God has given you the gift of making money. Why don't you develop a giving plan?"

He and his wife developed a goal to give away $1 billion dollars in their lifetime. That's right—no misprint. That number had a "b." This was in the 1980s, when a billion was even more than it is today.

During this time, California was booming, his business was growing, many competitors were entering into his market, and he was making a lot of money. He felt he had more than enough cash. I suggested that he take the available cash flow generated by the business and pay off all his debt. As was common in the demolition and excavation industry, he had borrowed to buy his heavy equipment. He paid off his debt despite this advice being against the conventional wisdom of using debt for leverage to buy more equipment.

Soon after, California went through a severe recession—more severe than in the rest of the country. The state had been through a boom and was going through a bust. The businessman's competitors all went out of business when they couldn't make the payments on their debt. He bought the competitors out and picked up their equipment for pennies on the dollar. He essentially had a monopoly in the western part of the United States.

You may remember the San Francisco earthquake in 1988 that occurred during the Oakland–San Francisco World Series baseball game. I happened to be in this gentleman's home in California when the earthquake hit. His equipment showed up quickly to the damaged area—he was the only demolition and clean-up company in town. He made millions from that earthquake.

A few years later when a major earthquake hit southern California, he was still the main demolition company in the area.

He gave away millions when he owned the company. He later sold it for a significant sum of money and gave away most of it. He and his wife are still working toward their billion-dollar giving goal.

No one could see the result coming, but it started with the question, "How much is enough?"

As baby boomers are beginning to retire, they are asking the question, "How much is enough for retirement?" But I think we can ask similar questions with a deeper meaning and application: How much is enough for me in light of God's desire to reach the world?

What are my finish lines? As we close this chapter on how much is enough, I want to summarize the key points by reminding you of what's important to know with conviction and what's important to do.

SUMMARY

This chapter provides the broad scope in which we look at our finances. We find that there are only five principles of money management, and those principles lead us to four uses. The five principles are:

- Spend less than you earn.
- Avoid the use of debt.
- Maintain liquidity (or emergency savings).
- Set long-term goals.
- Give generously.

These principles lead us to the four uses of money:

- Live
- Give
- Owe
- Grow

Once we understand how money is used, we must turn to answering the question, "How much is enough?" Our answers change over time, and it's important to put "enough" in hard dollars. However, we need to avoid the trap that the idea of enough will lead us to feel secure, significant, or successful, because it will not. We need to be in constant prayer regarding our long-term goals and work through these questions of "How much . . ." with our families.

I will end this chapter with several scripture verses:

But if anyone does not provide for his own, and especially for those of his household, he has denied the faith, and is worse than an unbeliever. (1 Timothy 5:8)

Unless the Lord builds the house, they labor in vain who build it; unless the Lord guards the city, the watchman keeps awake in vain. It is vain for you to rise up early, to retire late, to eat the bread of painful labors; for He gives to His beloved even in his sleep. (Psalm 127:1–2)

Do not weary yourself to gain wealth, cease from your consideration of it. When you set your eyes on it, it is gone. For wealth certainly makes itself wings, like an eagle that flies toward the heavens. (Proverbs 23:4–5)

. . . And from everyone who has been given much, much shall be required; and to whom they entrusted much, of him they will ask all the more. (Luke 12:48)

Moreover, when God gives any man wealth and possessions, and enables him to enjoy them, to accept his lot and be happy in his work—this is a gift of God. (Ecclesiastes 5:19)

Do not store up for yourselves treasures on earth, where moth and rust destroy, and where thieves break in and steal. But store up for yourselves treasures in heaven, where moth and rust do not destroy, and where thieves do not break in and steal. For where your treasure is, there your heart will be also. (Matthew 6:19–21)

SUMMARY REVIEW QUESTIONS

1. How would you define financial planning?

2. List the five principles of financial planning. Explain each principle.

3. What are the four uses of money?

4. What are four directives (commands) that outline how we should spend our money? Provide Scripture references to support each command.

5. What is the difference between consumptive use of money and productive use of money? Give an example of each.

6. List the seven strategies outlined in the chapter that guide our lifestyle choices.

7. List and explain the six long-term uses of money.

8. How do you incorporate the four uses of money and then add the six uses of long-term savings/investing?

9. Explain the following phrase: There are no independent financial decisions.

10. What are three implications of our spending decisions?

11. Why is it important to put together a financial plan?

12. What are the two ways to accumulate "enough"? Which do you feel is a better option?

13. What happens when we have sufficient income and assets to reach our goals?

14. What four simple steps can you take to define and quantify your goals?

15. Explain how compounding works. What are the two most critical factors in compounding?

16. What other two questions are vital for us to consider, beyond "How much is enough?"

17. How does the secular world view wealth?

Case Study Analysis

Bob and Debbie were wrapping up their evening meal and were heading off on a walk around the lake behind their house. Chloe headed to Mike's Café, a local coffee bar where many of the school kids would sit around the tables and text everyone who wasn't there. Bob and Debbie could never figure that one out. Clara, with almost the upmost in precision, went to her favorite rocking chair in her room and read. That's probably the reason she won the writing contest last year.

As Bob and Debbie began walking, Bob asked, "Honey, what did you think of that financial contentment survey?"

"Well, it really got me thinking about what we spend our money on and wondering if we will ever be content," Debbie responded.

Bob pondered Debbie's words for a few minutes, then said, "Honey, I think we need to sit down with Steve again soon. My perspective has changed over these past few months, and I think it's time to start fresh. What do you think?"

Debbie smiled. "I agree!"

As Bob and Debbie walked into their next meeting, Steve took one look at Bob and noticed a different look on his face. Previously, his look gave signs of disagreement and aloofness, whereas now Bob's look was that of determination, one might even say passion.

"Bob and Debbie, it's good to see you again. I appreciate the way that you both are sticking with the process and being faithful to see it through to the end. I can tell something is different today, isn't it?"

Bob replied, "The Holy Spirit has really been working in me lately, especially after taking that financial contentment survey and realizing that I would never be content on the path we were on."

"I'm glad you recognized that, and know that I have you and Debbie on my prayer list, so let's just thank God for our blessings."

After they prayed, Steve began to talk through three main components of financial planning. Steve articulated the five principles of money management: We need to spend less than we earn, avoid the use of debt, build margin or liquidity in our finances, save for the long term, and give generously. Steve then provided Bob and Debbie a brief outline of the four uses of money: live, give, owe, and grow.

"It really is so simple," Bob commented.

"The principles of money management and the use of money are very simple." Steve replied. "Unfortunately, determining the answer to 'How much is enough?' is not quite as simple and is your next assignment. Once you determine how much is enough, then we can begin to use our tools and applications to solve the Rubik's cube so that everything lines up."

Bob and Debbie looked at each other and smiled. "We're all in!" Bob said.

Use the Case Study, as well as the chapter material, to answer the following questions as they relate to Bob and Debbie's situation:

Questions

1. Give some examples of how Bob and Debbie have allowed happenstance to control their financial planning in the past.

2. Identify specific examples of where Bob and Debbie's money goes each month in relation to the four uses of money: live, give, owe, and grow. How do the examples you identified reflect Bob and Debbie's commitments and priorities?

3. In what ways have Bob and Debbie made short-sighted financial decisions in the past?

4. What long-term goals do Bob and Debbie have that need attention in their current financial plan?

5. In what ways might Bob and Debbie benefit from developing a financial plan?

6. What evidence is there that Bob and Debbie have suffered from hoarding in the past?

DEFINITIONS

Commandments (p. 64)   **Decisions** (p. 62)   **Hope** (p. 70)

Compounding (p. 71)   **Financial independence** (p. 70)   **Interest rate** (p. 71)

Consumptive (p. 64)   **Financial planning** (p. 62)   **Productive** (p. 64)

Contentment (p. 65)   **Hoarding** (p. 70)

SCRIPTURE VERSES (ESV)

Psalm 127:1–2—"Unless the Lord builds the house, those who build it labor in vain. Unless the Lord watches over the city, the watchman stays awake in vain. It is in vain that you rise up early and go late to rest, eating the bread of anxious toil; for he gives to his beloved sleep."

Colossians 3:23—"Whatever you do, work heartily, as for the Lord and not for men"

Proverbs 3:9—"Honor the Lord with your wealth and with the first fruits of all your produce;"

Genesis 2:15—"The Lord God took the man and put him in the garden of Eden to work it and keep it."

1 Corinthians 16:2—"On the first day of every week, each of you is to put something aside and store it up, as he may prosper, so that there will be no collecting when I come."

Romans 13:7—"Pay to all what is owed to them: taxes to whom taxes are owed, revenue to whom revenue is owed, respect to whom respect is owed, honor to whom honor is owed."

Matthew 22:21—They said, "Caesar's." Then he said to them, "Therefore render to Caesar the things that are Caesar's, and to God the things that are God's."

Psalm 37:21—"The wicked borrows but does not pay back, but the righteous is generous and gives;"

1 Timothy 5:8—"But if anyone does not provide for his relatives, and especially for members of his household, he has denied the faith and is worse than an unbeliever."

Proverbs 3:5-6—"Trust in the Lord with all your heart, and do not lean on your own understanding. In all your ways acknowledge him, and he will make straight your paths."

Philippians 4:11—"Not that I am speaking of being in need, for I have learned in whatever situation I am to be content."

Exodus 20:17—"You shall not covet your neighbor's house; you shall not covet your neighbor's wife, or his male servant, or his female servant, or his ox, or his donkey, or anything that is your neighbor's."

1 John 2:15–17—"Do not love the world or the things in the world. If anyone loves the world, the love of the Father is not in him. For all that is in the world—the desires of the flesh and the desires of the eyes and pride of life is not from the Father but is from the world. And the world is passing away along with its desires, but whoever does the will of God abides forever."

1 Timothy 4:4—"For everything created by God is good, and nothing is to be rejected if it is received with thanksgiving."

1 Thessalonians 4:11–12—"And to aspire to live quietly, and to mind your own affairs, and to work with your hands, as we instructed you, so that you may walk properly before outsiders and be dependent on no one."

Romans 12:2—"Do not be conformed to this world, but be transformed by the renewal of your mind, that by testing you may discern what is the will of God, what is good and acceptable and perfect."

Proverbs 13:11—"Wealth gained hastily will dwindle, but whoever gathers little by little will increase it."

Luke 6:38—"Give, and it will be given to you. Good measure, pressed down, shaken together, running over, will be put into your lap. For with the measure you use it will be measured back to you."

Matthew 6:19–21—"Do not lay up for yourselves treasures on earth, where moth and rust destroy and where thieves break in and steal, but lay up for yourselves treasures in heaven, where neither moth nor rust destroys and where thieves do not break in and steal. For where your treasure is, there your heart will be also.

Proverbs 23:4–5—"Do not toil to acquire wealth; be discerning enough to desist. When your eyes light on it, it is gone, for suddenly it sprouts wings, flying like an eagle toward heaven."

Luke 12:48—"But the one who did not know, and did what deserved a beating, will receive a light beating. Everyone to whom much was given, of him much will be required, and from him to whom they entrusted much, they will demand the more."

Ecclesiastes 5:19—"Everyone also to whom God has given wealth and possessions and power to enjoy them, and to accept his lot and rejoice in his toil—this is the gift of God."

Hebrews 11:1—"Now faith is the assurance of things hoped for, the conviction of things not seen."

ADDITIONAL READINGS

Alcorn, R. (2003). Money, possessions, and eternity. Tyndale House Publishing, Inc.

Course, G. S. B. (2002). by Dick Towner and John Tofilon.

Fitch, A. M. (1987). *What the Bible says about money*. College Press Publishing Company.

Godwin, D. D. (1990). Family financial management. *Family Relations*, 221–228.

Hill, M. (2008). *Biblical financial wisdom*. Retrieved from http://lulu.com

Joyner R. D. (1997). *The Bible-based family: A plan for economic empowerment*. Beckham House.

Katz, R., & Katz, J. (2006). *Money came by the house the other day: A guide to Christian financial planning and stories of stewardship*. DC Press.

Lamb, M. L. (1992). Theology and money: "Rationality, religion, and economics." *The American Behavioral Scientist*, 35(6), 735.

LaPorter, D. B., & LaPorter, A. B. (2006). *Biblical strategies to financial freedom*. BookSurge Publishing.

McPherson, J. S. (2014). *Leaving Laodicea: A Christian's guide to wealth management*. McPherson Consulting.

Schut, M., & McKibben, B. (2009). *Simpler living, compassionate life: A Christian perspective*. Church Publishing, Inc.

Chapter 5

Goal Setting and Decision Making

Courtesy of duncanandison/Fotolia.

BIG IDEA:
Every goal is a faith goal.

BIG IDEA:
Our decisions are made based on our best known alternatives.

LEARNING OUTCOMES

- Define *goals* and *goal setting*
- Describe a faith financial goal
- Understand the mistakes to avoid and benefits provided when setting financial goals
- Describe the three mistakes people tend to make when making decisions
- Define a SMART goal
- List and describe the seven barriers to good decision making
- List and describe the 10 steps to the criteria-based decision model

In his national bestseller *The 7 Habits of Highly Effective People*, Stephen Covey (2014) outlines his research by providing seven behaviors that people who have demonstrated success exemplify. The second habit that Covey describes is to "Begin with the End in Mind." In other words, you need to think about where you want to end up prior to starting. This concept can easily be described as goal setting.

There's been vast amount of research on goal setting. For example, Locke (1996) found that goal setting increases planning processes, and Rothkopf and Billington (1979) suggested that having goals sets both cognitive and behavioral attention toward goal achievement. Research concludes that "goal setting increases commitment, motivation, energy, and persistence toward goals" (Johnson, Garrison, Hernez-Broome, Fleenor, & Steed, 2012, p. 555).

Goal A desired future outcome or expectation.

Goal setting Determining what future outcome or expectation is to be desired.

A **goal** is defined as a desired future outcome or expectation. An example of a goal might be to save $10,000 by the completion of your degree program. **Goal setting**, then, is determining what future outcome or expectation you desire. In our previous example, goal setting includes the process of developing the rationale behind why we set the $10,000 goal. The amount of $10,000 may come from the hope to buy a car, to use it as a down payment on a house, or some other use.

Defining a goal and then verbally articulating why and how that goal was obtained (goal setting) can be made simple and easily accomplished. Despite the relatively simple process of goal setting, many do not ever set goals or ever achieve their goals. The most common time for goal setting is the beginning of each year. Many refer to these goals as New Year's resolutions. These resolutions tend to follow culturally relevant topics, such as goals to lose weight, further one's education, pay off a bill or credit card, and so forth. Despite many people setting New Year's resolutions each year, most people do not intentionally and prayerfully set goals, and even if they do, they do not typically write them down. Why don't people write their goals down? The answers can range from a fear of failure to concern that it takes a great deal of time, lack of knowledge of how to set goals, belief that setting goals is not living by faith, or a lack of understanding of what goals to set. Locke and Latham (2002) compiled research over the last 35 years on the theory of goal setting and task motivation. They acknowledged three significant findings: (1) the relationship between goals and performance is strongest when people commit to their goals, (2) public commitment enhances goal commitment, and (3) because tasks and goals require higher-level skills prior to automation of behaviors, goal effects will be dependent on the ability to discover appropriate goal-obtainment strategies.

The focus throughout the rest of this goal-setting section will be to assist in discovering these "goal-obtaining strategies," specifically as they relate to our finances. First, we will look at our goals through a biblical lens.

WHAT IS A FAITH FINANCIAL GOAL?

Biblical stewardship The use of God-given gifts and resources (time, talent, treasure, truth, relationships, etc.) for the accomplishment of God-given goals and objectives.

Faith The assurance of things hoped for; the conviction of things not seen (**Hebrews 11:1**).

Recall that **biblical stewardship** is defined as the use of God-given gifts and resources (time, talent, treasure, truth, relationships, etc.) for the accomplishment of God-given goals and objectives. Focus on that final part of the definition: *God-given goals/objectives*.

When there is an understanding that goals are "God-given," then there is an element of faith that must be involved. Therefore, we can refer to many of our goals as faith goals. **Faith** as defined in the book of Hebrews is the assurance of things hoped for, the conviction of things not seen. When faith and goals come together, there is a future outcome that is uncertain, yet one we strive through our convictions to achieve. We have been given the Holy Spirit to help us along our path as we strive to achieve our faith goals. A faith goal, then, is an objective toward which God wants us to move.

The convergence of faith and goal setting is evident when answering the question, "How much is enough?" Determining the answer to this question (i.e., the goal) is the result of setting a faith-based goal. Questions such as "How much do you want to give away?" or "What will you do after this career?" lead us to rely on our faith. Our goals however, are not left for God to complete on his own. Remember that faith requires action. There is our part, and then there is God's part; however, God has a right to change it all. An example of this is found in **Proverbs 16:1–3**:

> The plans of the heart belong to man, but the answer of the tongue is from the LORD. All the ways of a man are clean in his own sight, but the LORD weighs the motives. Commit your works to the LORD and your plans will be established.

God's Part

God can do far more than we know and is not limited by our present resources. The idea of God doing His part of the goal is emphasized in the Book of Ephesians:

> Now to Him who is able to do immeasurably more than all we ask or imagine, according to His power that is at work within us . . . (Ephesians 3:20)

Our Part

First, don't focus on past experiences:

> Do not remember the former things. Nor consider the things of old. Behold, I will do a new thing. Now it shall spring forth: Shall you not know it? I will even make a road in the wilderness, and rivers in the desert. (Isaiah 43:18–19)

Next, do not only focus on your present resources or limitations. Do you remember the story of Abraham and Sarah in the Bible? God was going to bless them with a child, but they only looked at their present situation:

> And the Lord said to Abraham, "why did Sarah laugh, saying, 'Shall I surely bear a child since I am old?' "Is anything too hard for the Lord? At the appointed time I will return to you according to the time of life, and Sarah shall have a son." (Genesis 18:13–14)

But then in the book of Ephesians, the Bible tells us that we are to do our part:

> Look carefully then how you walk! Live purposefully and worthily and accurately, not as the unwise and witless, but as wise—sensible, intelligent people; making the very most of the time—buying up each opportunity—because the days are evil. Therefore do not be vague and thoughtless and foolish, but understanding and firmly grasping what the will of the Lord is. (Ephesians 5:15–17)

These passages may appear to be contradictory at first, but there's a combination needed of faith and practicality. Rather than being opposite ideas, they work together. Understand what God can do, and then make it work with sensible plans. God is not an impractical God. He wants me to understand who He is and what He can do, and then work that out in my life. The consequence is that He gets the glory. If it's God's goal in the first place, then He gets the glory. It's His goal in my life.

We will establish plans, but we should submit those back to the Lord. He answers, weighs motives, and establishes plans. God is more interested in faith developing than anything else. God can use the process of financial planning and goal setting to build one's faith. Keep in mind that the process is more important than the end result. A faith financial goal is always a statement of faith and is one of the primary ways that we can see the hand of God work. Goals should be made measurable, documented, and reviewed on at least an annual basis.

SETTING FAITH FINANCIAL GOALS

There are several components to setting faith financial goals; however, before we explain those, it is important to understand something. When setting goals, we need to know that God can change it all. Remember, God is the owner of all things, including our possessions and our time. So before you get too attached to the goals you outline throughout this chapter, know and understand that God is omniscient and you are not. Allow Him to move and make changes knowing that He is a loving God looking out for what's best for each of His children.

The first step to setting faith goals is to seek God's direction through reading, studying, and praying through Scripture. As you seek God's wisdom, the Holy Spirit can begin to lead you to thoughts, feelings, or impressions. As you feel led, write down your impressions, perhaps in a journal or the margin of your Bible. The next step in this process is to take your recorded impressions and turn them into measurable and objective action items. During this step, you are writing down specific goals. A good format in which to write these goals is as follows: I believe God would have me _____. Recall Locke and Latham's (2002) research suggesting that you make your commitments public. Although you may not go show these action items to anyone, you should commit them back to the Lord. Finally, you are now ready to take action. Get moving.

Setting goals is not a process of ignoring God and relying on self. You should focus on what God directs you to do.

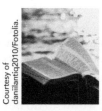

Courtesy of daniilantiq2010/Fotolia.

DISCIPLESHIP MOMENT AND REFLECTION

Take a few minutes and begin to think about your goal-setting process. As you prepare, set some time to get in God's word (keeping a journal close by) and pray through Scripture as you begin to prepare your goals. Talk through your impressions, thoughts, and ideas with your accountability and prayer partner. Be intentional and start to write down your measurable goals.

Ron's Corner

I've prayed before, "God, I want your goal, and don't let me be limited by my own thinking or past experiences or what the world tells me I can or can't do."

STARTING QUESTIONS

As you begin to set your faith financial goals, here are some questions that may help get you started toward those God-given goals and objectives:

1. [If you are married] What does my spouse think about this goal?
2. What is the motive behind this goal—my glory or God's glory?
3. What would God think about this goal?
4. What am I most concerned about in the next 6 to 12 months?
5. What am I most concerned about in the next 1 to 5 years?
6. Am I comfortable with my level of charitable giving?

7. Am I paying too much in taxes?

8. Are my living expenses too high or too low?

9. Are most of my goals focused on lifestyle rather than other short-term uses of money?

10. Do I have peace of mind with my short-term financial decision making?

11. Are there some potential financial events that cause me fear?

12. Am I comfortable with my debt level?

13. Am I making progress toward my prior goals?

14. Is my investment portfolio moving me toward accomplishing my goals?

15. What am I most concerned about in the long term?

16. [If you are married] Have I addressed my spouse's spoken or unspoken concerns?

17. Do I have peace of mind with my long-term financial decision making?

GOAL SETTING: MISTAKES TO AVOID IN SETTING GOALS

As you begin your goal-setting process, several obstacles should be understood in order to maximize the effectiveness of your goals. In this section, we describe the various mistakes.

Mistake 1: Not Having Any Specific Goals

Many successful businesspeople are goal oriented. Unfortunately, once success has become apparent, most people need to make a conscious decision to create new goals. For example, let's say that you finish your degree and decide to start a business. Your goal is to make $1,000,000 in revenue in your first 5 years. Come year 4, you realize that you have accomplished your goal and are exceeding $1,000,000 in revenue. Do you stop and reevaluate your goals and create new ones? Or do you relax, knowing that you have accomplished what you set out to do? The process of goal setting must be an ongoing task, and once a goal is achieved, then it is time to consider possible new goals.

If you don't know where you're going, you'll never know when you have arrived, nor will you know how to get there. So, it is important to know where you are going. For mental health alone, goals help you to have a better self-image because you know where you are going; then when you get there, you have a sense of achievement.

Mistake 2: Spouse Incongruity

Each person usually has his or her own set of goals and aspirations, and rarely do those goals always coincide with the goals of that person's spouse. As one might imagine, if both spouses have a different set of goals or perhaps a different path to achieve those goals, conflict will be inevitable. There are several ways to help create spousal congruity within the goal-setting process. One of the most effective ways is to be proactive and make specific plans to set goals together. One way to do this is through a goal-setting retreat or family meeting. The end of this chapter provides an agenda that you may use to walk through this process of goal setting for each spouse/family member to agree to.

Mistake 3: Not Quantifying Your Goals

When it comes to personal finances, many people articulate their goals in unmeasurable ways. When people are asked what their goals are, the following responses are unfortunately very common:

- I want to retire.
- I want to finish my degree in Computer Science.
- I want to make sure my kids are taken care of.
- I want to save money for my kids' college eduction.
- I want to support my parents.
- I want to have a good job.

These are all wonderful aspirations; unfortunately, they lack one thing: specificity. In order for you to know if you have ever achieved a goal, it needs to be measurable. The **SMART** method is a great way to remember how goals should be expressed. SMART is an acronym with the following meaning:

SMART Characteristics of goals: specific, measurable, attainable, realistic, and timely.

S—Specific

M—Measurable

A—Attainable

R—Realistic

T—Time-bound

Each of these characteristics needs to be expressed for goals be obtainable and for you to know when you have obtained your goals. Without these components, you cannot determine if you have ever reached your goal.

Ron's Corner

Someone recently sent me an e-mail with the anonymous quote, "A dream is just a dream. A goal is just a dream with a deadline and a plan." It's not a goal until it's measurable. At best it is a good intention. Set goals, write them in sand, and see God at work.

Mistake 4: Basing Goals on Fear Rather than Faith

Many goals, unfortunately, are established on the basis of fear rather than faith. So often goals are set as a result of listening to what others have to say rather than listening to God. If God has entrusted certain resources to you, do you think He is concerned about how they are allocated? Of course He is. That is why He has given us the Bible for direction, as well as wise counsel from mature believers. He gives us the Holy Spirit to guide and direct us. A faith goal comes from God. I can literally say, "This is what God would have me do with His resources." Knowing that can remove all fear.

For example, many people fear an economic collapse. Based on that fear, what type of goals do those people tend to set to avoid an economic collapse? Perhaps it's investing, or buying a farm in the country, or stocking up on food. On the other hand, God says, "I have given you those resources." Our question should therefore be, "God, what would you have me do with those resources?" The goals for each person may be entirely different; or they might be the same. However, the basis of setting them is the critical issue. If the goal comes from God and God's Word, then it's a faith goal. If it came from some fear or panic and you just assume it's the right thing to do, then it's a mistake.

THE RESULTS OF FAITH GOAL SETTING

Thomas Lifson (2004) wrote a brief article on the process by which George W. Bush sought to set goals. Lifson wrote:

> A second broad and important lesson the President learned at Harvard Business School is to embrace a finite number of strategic goals, and to make each one of those goals serve as many desirable ends as possible. The truism of this lesson is that if everything is a priority, then nothing is a priority. If you can't focus on everything, then you need to be able to focus on those few goals which will have the broadest impact, leading to a future capacity to attain other desirable ends. No exact number of goals is the limit, but three is an awfully good number to aim at. Those goals should be mutually consistent, so that the step-by-step accomplishment of each one aids in the achievement of the others. (Lifson, 2004, p. 1)

This brief synopsis establishes the case for setting fewer, but more far-reaching goals, which can have a big impact in your life. This is especially true with respect to faith goals. As you set goals for your life, you will see that they provide the following benefits:

- They provide direction and purpose.
- They help to crystallize thinking.
- They provide personal motivation.
- They are a statement of God's will.

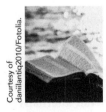

Courtesy of daniilantiq2010/Fotolia.

DISCIPLESHIP MOMENT AND REFLECTION

Take this time to set some SMART goals, keeping the list of goals to three important and significant goals. If you are married, make sure they are mutually acceptable to your spouse. Write them down and share them with your accountability and prayer partner.

Ron's Corner

My mom was self-appointed to carry the worrying responsibilities of our family. If worrying needed to be done, she was the one to do it. I once told her that psychologists estimated that 90% of things a person worries about never happen. Her response? "See. That proves that worrying works."

I often called her when I was traveling out of the country. I forgot to do that once when traveling to Africa. Upon returning to the United States, I called her. After hearing I was in Africa, she gave a classic line, "You should have called me because I could have worried!"

As is often the case, second-guessing and doubting accompanied my mom's worrying tendency. We teased her that she had the gift of hindsight because she frequently said, "You should have known." She often worried about and second-guessed decisions she made and ones my dad made. The ability to make sound, confident decisions without regret and anxiety is an important skill. I think wise decision making is a skill that is best developed through a process.

Matrix A collection of columns and rows that produce varying outcomes based on the rules applied to those columns and rows.

Once you have established your SMART faith goals, the next stage is to understand how to make decisions that will enable you to achieve those goals. The remaining part of this chapter focuses on decision making. The decision-making process is explained through the use of what is referred to as a decision-making matrix. A **matrix** is nothing more than a collection of columns and rows that produce varying outcomes based on the rules applied to those columns and rows.

Although a decision-making matrix will be explained and utilized, there are still inherent issues with decision making—specifically, fear. There are two reasons for this: First, decisions always deal with the future. Therefore, you are dealing with unknown events and consequences, so you are always at risk of making a mistake. Second, because decisions are always future-oriented, you never have all the information you need.

As a consequence, people tend to make three mistakes when making decisions:

1. Making decisions on an intuitive basis; that is, deciding strictly on the basis of how one feels about it.

2. Gathering the opinions of others and therefore falling prey to the devices and feelings of those who are not at risk in making the decision.

3. Falling into the "binary trap," or thinking that you only have two alternatives to consider—to do or not to do whatever it is you are considering. Because you only have two alternatives, your decision can never be any better than those two alternatives. However, in fact, there may be other, better alternatives.

The late Peter Drucker, famed management consultant, stated astutely:

A decision is a judgment . . . a choice among alternatives. Rarely is the choice between right or wrong, but rather the best choice between almost right and probably wrong.

Courtesy of maxpetrov/Fotolia.

In order to avoid falling into the "probably wrong" choice of decisions, you must have a process for making decisions. This is particularly important for those decisions that, in turn, determine other aspects of your life—such as buying a home, choosing a school for your children, accepting a job, selecting a college, or deciding what car to buy. Those decisions are obviously of greater consequence than deciding what to order at a restaurant or what clothes to buy. An established process can make decision making less fear driven because you will work through certain steps to determine objectives and consider alternatives. This process gives you a chance at a much better, and certainly a much better-informed, decision.

THE SEVEN BARRIERS TO GOOD DECISION MAKING

The ability to make sound, confident decisions without regret and anxiety is an important skill. Before we outline the matrix process for decision making, there are barriers to decision making that need to be identified and understood. These barriers are (1) time, (2) raw data versus relevant information, (3) poor process in decision making, (4) lack of decision-making experience and skill, (5) answering the wrong question, (6) making decisions in God's name, and (7) falling into emotional traps. Each of these barriers is described in more detail in this section, along with a principle that seeks to overcome that barrier.

- **Time:** When your time is limited, when you face a deadline, or when someone else involved is rushed, your decisions are rarely the best ones. On some occasions, we simply perceive we have little time, when in fact we have more time available. For example, a salesman at the car lot pressuring you, the time period of a sale, or the urgent schedule of your life leads you to think something must be done now for later convenience.

Regarding lack of time, you have time for everything God wants you to do. Notice I did not say you have time for "everything," but everything God desires you to do. Jesus died after only around three years of public ministry. There were still people who were not healed, people who had not heard Him teach, and people who had not believed. But Jesus was able to say that He had finished the work God had for Him to do.

- **Raw Data versus Relevant Information:** Information is important in making decisions, but we can be overwhelmed by it. Too much information can cause "paralysis by analysis." Especially today with the vast amount of information available through the Internet, we can have lots of data, but not relevant information. It is critical to decipher not only what information is relevant but also the trustworthiness of the sources by which the information was obtained.

Learn how to sift relevant information from large quantities of raw data. Apply an effective and robust process that will help you avoid the barriers. When looking up details about consumer products, you may find product reviews, customer testimonials, and so forth. It is important to know the source of the information and what makes that source reliable in providing such information.

- **Poor Process:** Throwing darts, rolling dice, or doing what your parents did—these are processes, but poor ones, when making decisions. Some people gather recommendations from friends and then vote. Others make a decision and then go ask friends or counselors for affirmation, which is known as confirmation bias. When asking for the affirmation, they color the decision, or the factors in the decision, to tilt the listener to their chosen decision.

Practice the process and develop the needed skills to become a consummate decision maker (Proverbs 22:29). Focus on the question, *not* the answer—while you're at it, focus on the right question.

- **Lack of Experience and Skill:** If you have let your spouse or your parents make decisions for you, then your lack of experience and skill is also a barrier. Proper decision making is an important skill to have. Keep in mind that everything you do is nothing more than a compilation of decisions. If you have had people make decisions for you in the past, start small.

- **Answering the Wrong Question:** At times, poor decisions are the result of addressing the wrong issue or answering the wrong question. There are times when we naturally substitute an "easier" question that is different from the one we are trying to make. For example, when thinking about buying a car, the questions that should be asked is, "What is the best way to meet my transportation need?" Unfortunately, many of us will jump to a different question, "Can I afford a $300 car payment?" You can see that by answering the latter question, we put ourselves in a different frame of mind when deciding on our transportation question.

- **Making Your Decisions in God's Name:** Just because we tack on the phrase "This is God's will" doesn't mean our decisions were proper. God's ways of doing things are not our usual ways. I am reminded of a few verses in the book of Isaiah:

> "Woe to the rebellious children," declares the LORD, "Who execute a plan, but not Mine, And make an alliance, but not of My Spirit." (Isaiah 30:1)

> "For my thoughts are not your thoughts, neither are your ways, my ways," declares the Lord. (Isaiah 55:8)

God wants to be involved in your decision making. Seek God's will on any given decision, not just yours. See decision making as a team sport between you and God. God's involvement in your decision making can come in the form of reading Scripture, praying, responding to the Holy Spirit's guidance, and listening to counselors. Beware of the emotional/psychological traps in decision making. Don't make key decisions at weak emotional moments.

God's involvement in your decisions needs to be first and foremost. Review the following verses under each heading:

Scripture

- Psalm 119:105
- Psalm 19

Prayer

- Psalm 32:8
- Isaiah 59:1–2
- 1 Peter 3:7

Holy Spirit
- Galatians 5:22–23

Mature Counselors
- 1 Kings 12

- **Falling into Emotional Traps:** Our emotions can sometimes get the better of our logic and rationale. Here are five common emotional traps:
  - **Flying by the Seat of Your Pants:** This trap is that something just feels right. Fortunately, trained pilots go by instruments. It's easy to be disoriented in the air, so pilots learn to fly by instruments, not by gut or intuition or by the seat of their pants. We are to follow and rely on our "instrument": God's word.
  - **Underestimating the Influence of Personality . . . Yours!** Personality tests and surveys are helpful in understanding your particular disposition. Overall, no personality disposition is better than another. All types have uniqueness and usefulness. With that disclaimer being said (so as not to offend anyone), some personality types are not naturally conducive to good decision making. In other words, they may have to work harder.

Ron's Corner

I've used the four personality types from a commonly used personality inventory called DISC to illustrate the tendencies of each regarding decision making:

D—Decisive/Fast
FIRE, READY, AIM

I—Spontaneous
FIRE, FIRE, FIRE

S—Conferring/Methodical
READY, AIM, FIRE

C—Deliberate/Detailed/Cautious
READY, READY, READY

- **Moving Too Fast—Jumping to Conclusions:** It's natural for first impressions to last. Too often, though, we rely too much on initial impressions. We may jump to a conclusion that this situation will be like the last, somewhat similar situation or that a certain person will be like as similar person we have encountered. Daniel Kahneman (2011), winner of the Nobel Prize in Economics, in his book *Thinking Fast and Slow*, wrote

  > Jumping to conclusions is efficient if the conclusions are likely to be correct and the costs of an occasional mistake are acceptable, and if the jump saves much time and effort. Jumping to conclusions is risky when the situation is unfamiliar, the stakes are high, and there is no time to collect more information. (p. 79)

- **Overconfidence:** After some success in an area or after several good decisions, it's tempting to think you'll always have similar success. Overconfidence can trick you into thinking you don't need to analyze, pray, or work through a process. Generally, people overestimate how much they know about the world in which we live and thus underestimate the role of God's hand in various outcomes.

Knowing overconfidence is a bias; take time to pray through each decision. God's will, through the Holy Spirit, provides you the guidance you seek.

- **Groupthink:** Groupthink is the momentum a group can build that stymies critical thinking or the vocalizing of dissenting voices. This line of thinking is that if the votes in the group tally in favor, then it must be the right decision. When the 12 spies from Israel went to check out the land promised to them by God, 10 were in agreement that they could not overcome those in the land. Caleb and Joshua were the two who said God had instructed the Israelites and had promised them this land. But they were outvoted. The other 10 and the entire nation of Israel regretted that decision for the next 40 years.

As this example demonstrates, when decisions need to be made, it is best to have everyone write down their suggestions prior to any group discussion because group discussions can heavily influence your initial decisions.

Here are the right financial questions to ask with decision making:

- What do you think God would have you do? If you ask the question in this way, what are the number of alternatives? Limitless. If you just ask about what you should do, then you're limited to your alternatives.
- What is the best use of this money?

Now that the barriers to decision making have been addressed, we now present a criteria-based decision model that can be used as a guide to the decision-making process. Remember, this is a process—you should repeat these steps for decisions you need to make.

CRITERIA-BASED DECISION MODEL

Step 1: Pray (James 1:5–6).

Step 2: Define your decision—what's the question?
Many times, your decision statement will have the words *choose* or *select* and *best* in it.

Write this step at the top of your matrix. You can use Figure 5.1 as a template. As you complete this step, it is important that you write out the decision. Confirm that what you wrote down is actually the decision you are making. Focus on the question and not on the answers at this point. A few questions to ask yourself may include:

- What is the heart of the matter?
- Am I addressing the core issue or just a component of the issue?
- Am I looking at this from a long-term or short-term perspective?
- How many alternatives do I really have?

Enter in the decision you are evaluating below:
What college major should I pursue?

Step 3: Clarify your objectives—what are the decision criteria?

Criteria can be defined as the principles or standards by which something can be decided. Therefore, the criteria are the standards by which you will make your decision. These are all of the components that will influence your decision. These will be broad in nature originally and will ultimately need to be refined throughout the process. For example, when selecting a college major, you may set the following as broad criteria:

- Job availability
- Earning potential
- Ease of completion
- Family pressures
- Most attractive building on campus
- Time for outside activities

And there may be many more. This is the step where you need to identify the criteria on which you will base your decision. Write each criterion down, even if you think it is a small thing. For example, if you don't quite get along with your roommate and he or she is pursuing a certain major, you probably need to add the criterion of "being happy while in class or lab" or something similar.

Once the broad criteria are set, you need to begin to make each of these measurable, or deepen the criteria. Here is an example of how this can be accomplished for the previous list regarding choice of college major:

- Job availability: Looking for at least five different careers my degree will allow
- Earning potential: Starting salary of at least $50,000 per year
- Ease of completion: Not to exceed 5 hours of homework per week
- Family pressures: Eliminate Mom and Dad's "You should've . . ." talks
- Most attractive building on campus: Want clean restrooms!
- Time for outside activities: Get involved with a fraternity/sorority and still play recreational tennis

Step 4: Prioritize your objectives—what are the nonnegotiables? What are the trade-offs?

This step may be the hardest as you seek to differentiate needs versus wants. Out of the criteria listed in step 3, what are the "must-haves" and what are criteria you just want?

Your must-haves are considered *nonnegotiable* to your decision, and *no other alternative* will be acceptable. If an alternative identified in the next step does not meet one of your nonnegotiable criteria, then you should throw it out. Your "want" criteria are all of your criteria that do not fall into the nonnegotiable category. You can usually evaluate these criteria using a scale (1–10) and then compare each with the other "want" criteria. During this step, select one of the "want" criteria and use this as your baseline, giving it a score of 5. Next, compare each other "want" criterion to that baseline and give it a rank as it relates to the baseline. If it is more important than your baseline, then give it a higher value, and vice versa.

List "Must-Haves" in the spaces below:

Must Haves

1. Fit my major with my Christian values
2. Be in agreement with my parents.
3.

List "want to haves" in the spaces below:

Want to Haves

1. Be able to make $50,000 starting salary
2. Attractive Campus
3. Good sports program (football)
4. Want at least 4 jobs that fit my major
5.
6.
7.

Step 5: Identify your alternatives.
Once all the criteria have been given a rank, the next step is to determine alternatives. Be cautious not to fall into the binary decision trap (i.e., limiting your consideration to only two options, such as either take a bus or buy a car). Being creative can come in handy. Feel free to ask those around you to come up with alternatives as well. Past experiences can help you see through your own blindness when seeking alternatives. Place the alternatives at the top of your matrix.

List alternatives in the spaces below:

Alternatives

Business and Entrepreneurship

Finance

Liberal Arts

Communication and Public Speaking

Architecture

Pre-Med

Step 6: Evaluate your alternatives—what are the facts?
The alternatives are then compared to each criterion you established in step 3 and prioritized in step 4. Analyze each alternative against the "must-have" criteria. If any alternative fails to meet any of your must-haves, then it is eliminated as an alternative. Next, evaluate the alternatives against the "wants." Keep in mind that you are evaluating alternatives based on the criteria, not against other alternatives. Go back to the scale procedure and determine on a scale of 1 to 10 how each alternative measures up with each criterion.

Compare your "must haves" with your alternatives. If the alternative is in agreement with the "must have," select YES from the dropdown. If it is not in agreement, select NO. If you are not sure, select UNCERTAIN.

Must Haves	Business and Entrepreneurship	Finance	Liberal Arts	Communication and Public Speaking	Architecture	Business and Entrepreneurship
Fit my major with my Christian values	YES	YES	YES	YES	YES	UNCERTAIN
Be in agreement with my parents	YES	YES	UNCERTAIN	YES	YES	YES

Compare your "want to haves" with your alternatives and score them from 1-10 (10 being best) based on how well the alternative meets the "want to have."

Want to Haves	Business and Entrepreneurship	Finance	Liberal Arts	Communication and Public Speaking	Architecture	Pre-Med
Be able to make $50,000 starting salary	8	10	5	6	10	4
Attractive building on campus	5	8	4	7	10	5
Top program according to US News	4	4	8	10	8	6
At least 4 different career options	9	6	7	7	3	3

Step 7: Make a preliminary decision.
This next step takes some basic math, so don't get too nervous. Each criterion has been given a rank (step 4). In the previous step, you should have ranked each alternative against each criterion. Now, take each alternative criterion number and multiply it by the rank you have given each criterion. Next, add up each alternative (column in your matrix) to get a total for each alternative. This will quantitatively give you what your decision should be, based on your own objective and subjective measures.

		Alternatives											
Criteria	Priorities	Business and Entrepreneurship		Finance		Liberal Arts		Communication and Public Speaking		Architecture		Pre-Med	
Must Haves													
Fit my major with my Christian values	Must Have	■		■		■		■		■		UNCERTAIN	
Be in agreement with my parents	Must Have	■		■		UNCERTAIN		■		■		■	
	Must Have												
	Must Have												
Want to Haves	Priorities												
Be able to make $50,000 starting salary	10	8	80	10	100	5	50	6	60	10	100	4	40
Attractive building on campus	6	5	30	8	48	4	24	7	42	10	60	5	30
Top program according to US News	8	4	32	4	32	8	64	10	80	8	64	6	48
At least 4 different career options	8	9	72	6	48	7	56	7	56	3	24	3	24

Step 8: Assess the risk—what could go wrong here?
We don't stop there. The next step is to ask yourself the following questions:

- What is the worst that can happen if I choose this option?
- How likely is that worst-case scenario to happen?
- Am I okay with that risk?

Step 9: Make the final decision.
It's officially time to take action and move forward. This is now the time to inform the appropriate people of your decision as well as to determine what the next step will be and when you need to take that step. In our example, you may need to schedule a meeting with an academic advisor to inform the advisor of your college major.

Step 10: Test the decision.
The best way to test your decision is to put it back up against Scripture and let the Holy Spirit lead you. Here are several biblical tests that you can use to evaluate your decision with guidance from Scripture:

Name	Scripture	Application
God's Glory	Isaiah 43:7; 1 Corinthians 10:31	Ask, "Is my decision serving God's glory and honor?"
God's Wisdom	James 1:5; Psalm 32:8	Ask for God's wisdom.
Wise Counsel	Proverbs 1:5; Proverbs 15:27	Review your decision with spiritually mature Christians.
Your Preference	Psalm 37:4; Philippians 2:13	After a time of prayer and listening, does the decision reflect your desires?
Your Peace	Colossians 3:15; Philippians 4:7	Wait at least 24 hours, then, through prayer, evaluate whether you feel confident and peaceful about your decision.

Ron's Corner

Our family has used the matrix presented in this chapter for various decisions. Our kids have used it for college or career options. As an example, our younger son faced a difficult decision about college. He had the fortunate distinction of receiving scholarship offers from various colleges to play tennis. Having been raised on this decision-making process, his matrix included five colleges and 15 criteria ranging from the school's academic reputation to the strength of the tennis coach to how pretty the girls on campus were. We were glad he gave the school's academic strength a higher value than the number of pretty girls he saw. Nevertheless, they were his objectives, not ours, that counted! In his first year, however, he began to doubt. His experience provides another reason for writing down the factors involved in the decision. After attending his chosen college for 6 months, he was ready to leave. He retrieved his decision-making matrix to look back at why he went there in the first place, and he realized that it was still the best choice. He was able to remember why he made the decision. He ended up with a successful college career there, making All-American in tennis, being accepted into law school, and meeting the wonderful woman who agreed to become his wife.

The multistep matrix of the criteria-based decision model has these benefits:

- Maximizes objectivity/minimizes bias
- Effectively sifts relevant data from the trivial
- Is scalable
- Structures thinking
- Makes thinking visible
- Facilitates the participation of others
- Increases confidence for implementation

SUMMARY

This chapter focused on two vital components relating to our finances: goal setting and decision making. These two constructs of financial planning will help to guide you throughout your life in all areas, not just financial areas. Goals are defined as desired outcomes or expectations, and goal setting is the process to determine what future outcome or expectation is to be desired. God needs to be the center of our goals, and because of this notion, our goals are actually faith goals. In order to set faith goals, one must stay in the Word and in prayer with God. As we set out to set our goals, we need to be mindful of several mistakes we can make: (1) not having any specific goals, (2) not being in unity with our spouse, (3) not quantifying the goals, and (4) basing our goals on fear rather than faith. Goals provide direction and purpose, help formalize our thinking, provide personal motivations, and should solidify us toward God's will. Goals must also be specific, measurable, attainable, realistic, and time-bound (the SMART method).

A process for decision making using the matrix concept was described. Seven barriers were identified that inhibit us from making God-centered decisions: (1) lack of time, (2) raw data versus relevant information, (3) poor process in decision making, (4) lack of experience in decision making, (5) answering the wrong questions, (6) making decisions in God's name with our own motives, and (7) falling into emotional traps. Once those barriers are identified, we can follow the 10-step criteria-based decision model. The first step is to pray through the decision, followed by defining what the decision is (step 2). The third step is to clarify and articulate the criteria, and then in the fourth step prioritize those criteria in a ranking order. After we rank our criteria, we identify the alternatives (step 5) and evaluate the alternatives for each criterion (step 6). Once each alternative is evaluated, we can make our preliminary decision (step 7) and assess what the risks would be with making that decision (step 8). Once a preliminary decision has been tested against the risks, we should go forward with that decision by determining the next steps (step 9). Finally, our decisions can be measured or tested against Scripture (step 10).

SUMMARY REVIEW QUESTIONS

1. According to the text, when is the most common time people set goals? Why?

2. What are several reasons people don't write down their goals?

3. Describe both God's part and our own part in the goal-creation process. Provide Bible verses for support.

4. List and explain the five goal-setting mistakes.

5. What does SMART stand for in reference to goals?

6. What are the four benefits that goal setting can provide?

7. What are the two reasons decision making can cause fear?

8. What are three common mistakes people make when making decisions?

9. Describe the seven barriers to good decision making.

10. Explain each of the 10 steps to the criteria-based decision model.

11. Outline the five tests that can be used to validate your decision. Use Scripture references to support your answer.

12. What are the seven benefits to using the criteria-based decision model in your decision-making process?

Case Study Analysis

Bob sat pensively at his desk, lost in thought, chewing on his pencil. He couldn't stop thinking about this idea of "What is enough?" presented by Pastor Steve, but at the same time now had another dilemma to deal with. Sheets from a yellow pad were scattered across his desk. It was after 10:00 p.m. on Thursday evening and he has been at work on his thoughts for over an hour. Actually, "work" was not a good term for what he has been doing: thinking, fretting, doubting, scheming . . . all were better descriptions of his late night endeavors than "working."

He has attempted to spend some time in the Word when he first entered his study earlier that evening. But he found himself too unsettled and distracted from his dinner interaction with Debbie to focus his attention on Scripture. Prayer proved even more difficult. He remembered that there was something in the Bible that said if you were crossways in the chute with your wife, your prayers would be hindered. That certainly seemed to be the case tonight.

Bob began to reflect on the events leading up to this point. It had started off as such a great week. Receiving a $40,000 inheritance check from the estate of his dad's sister was a total surprise to both him and Debbie. They had only met her once nearly 15 years ago on a vacation trip through upper New York. She passed away over a year ago and had never been close to Bob's side of the family. For all practical purposes, aside from that 45-minute visit for coffee, Bob and Debbie have had no contact with this woman. They had no idea she was wealthy enough to even have an estate.

Despite the pleasant surprise, what appeared at first to be a windfall seemed to be turning into a whirlpool of problems! And, if tonight were any indication, by tomorrow they would be sinking even deeper.

Over dinner, Chloe, their 16-year old daughter, with all the force her melodramatic mind could muster, challenged Bob and Debbie's commitment to good parenting. Bob was so angry with Chloe's outburst that he could hardly remember the points of her message, but something along the lines of "you are ruining my life" seem to be a good summary.

Chloe has been pressuring Bob and Debbie about getting a new car. "All" of her friends have been driving new cars and she is the "only one" at her school without a car. Not being able to drive to meet her volleyball teammates and friends was starting to weigh on Chloe's "reputation" at school. Tonight was a big hang out at the Mike's coffee shop and Bob and Debbie seemed to no longer be "eligible" to drop her off. That just isn't cool anymore.

Chloe has been looking online for various cars and has always talked about having an Audi A3 Convertible. She loves Audi because the logo looks like a Volleyball floating through the air. Chloe's recent discovery was a 2014 certified pre-owned A3 at Lovington Auto sales for $25,000 with only 9800 miles on it. She just couldn't let it go.

Even if they invested Aunt Sara's money in the car, Bob was not convinced that Chloe was ready for such a car and was thinking more along the lines of a $6,000–$8,000 domestic car. She has demonstrated to be a cautious driver, but Bob is more concerned about the "other people" that may damage the car. Debbie is also hesitant about the car situation but seldom takes Chloe on in head-to-head conflict, particularly when tempers are flaring. She generally leaves that to Bob, as she did tonight. As a consequence, Bob took the brunt of Chloe's wrath.

Prior to the sudden episode regarding the car, Bob was excitedly sharing with Debbie Gary Garfield's offer concerning the initial public offering (IPO) of a promising stock. "It's a sure bet," Bob explained. "You know Gary. He is one of the brightest and most successful brokers on Wall Street. We will get at least a 500% return within 18 months. This could be the answer to a lot of our financial goals."

"It's a bet all right," Debbie responded. "It's a big gamble. And you are right, I do know Gary. He is the poster child for the 'eat, drink, and be merry' club. With his lifestyle he has to be successful. Alimony to two ex-wives is no small matter."

"He may not be a saint, but he is a genius when it comes to money. Remember in grad school when I invested $1000 with him? I had $3500 by the end of summer. That paid my tuition for fall quarter."

Debbie had never thought highly of Gary. Gary and Bob had been fraternity brothers in college and remained close friends for years afterwards. However, because of distance, the relation had cooled a bit over the past few years, much of that fueled by Bob's newfound faith in Christ and a change in priorities. Going out for a couple of beers just wasn't an enjoyable night's entertainment anymore.

After Chloe stomped out of the dining room, Debbie stared into her coffee and Bob toyed with a piece of cheesecake for which he had lost his appetite. Debbie gathered her thoughts first. "Bob, I know she is upset, she will get over it. A used car is a good idea. We both know that Chloe doesn't demonstrate the discipline to maintain such a nice car and keep it out of an accident." Bob, still playing with his cheesecake, nodded absently.

Debbie continued, "I am sorry if I hurt your feelings with Gary, but he has not demonstrated mature behavior since I first met him over 20 years ago. I believe risking the entire amount on that investment idea is unwise." Bob shook his head thinking, she is so predictable. Debbie is, by Bob's standards, very conservative and looked at risk from a much different vantage point. Bob is decisive, a risk taker, optimistic, and spontaneous. (Debbie would often correct him when describing himself as "spontaneous"—she would say more "impulsive").

Debbie, on the other hand, is risk-averse, conservative, and in control of things. If she had to come up with a t-shirt slogan it would be something like, "Better Safe than Sorry," or "Caution is the Better Part of Valor." In this respect, Bob and Debbie could not be more different. They always felt that "Opposites Attract!"

Again, Debbie ventured into the conversation. "Bob, we need to look at this gift as an opportunity to make an investment that will bring longer-term benefits. This last week you reminded me of the importance of paying off some of our debt, to include the credit cards and any car loans we have. Since we have been in discussion with Steve regarding developing our financial plan, it might be best to pay off debt versus saving or spending it."

Bob interjected, "Using the money that way is like minimizing the loss versus maximizing the profit. If we invest this money with Gary, we have the potential to make a tremendous impact on our financial goals. We need to have an investment mindset. We need to use this money to make more money."

"If you want to invest, let's consider using the money for the kitchen. Remodeling the kitchen gives us the possibility of staying in this house or, if we elect to move, selling at a premium greater than the investment because of the improvements. Our realtor said that for every dollar we invest in that kitchen, we will get $4 in return on the selling price. What could be a better investment than that? That's a sure thing in contrast to that IPA thing of Gary's."

"It's an IPO," responded Bob. "And it is not such a long shot. It certainly would have a higher return than a kitchen!"

"Well, it's clear that we are not of like mind on this," Debbie responded. "We need to pray about this. We have learned too many times the hard way, that if we are not in agreement on a major decision, it inevitably won't work." she paused, thinking for a moment: "How do we know what God wants us to do with this money?"

Bob stared back, perplexed, confused, and very much up in the air about how to answer that question. "I need to go call Mom and Dad," Bob said as she began to clear the table. "I talked to Mom yesterday, and although Dad is getting stronger after his heart attack, she can sense he is growing frailer. I know that we have talked about having the resources to support them, but I never guessed that it might be so imminent. That is one more issue we need to work through."

At this point Bob sat in his study and began contemplating the issues. He had collected a number of papers that argued for one direction or another for this newfound wealth all the while thinking about this "How much is enough?" question for him and his family. He shook his head, musing how calm it had been prior to the arrival of Aunt Sara's attorney. On top of the stack of papers was one more unsettling issue in this decision. Saturday morning Bob had mentioned the windfall to Pastor McElrath after the church service. Bob and Debbie had attended Lovington Community Church for 5 years and really felt a call to become more involved this past year. Bob had long wanted to make a serious personal commitment to get more involved in church life but never really felt he could let go of his ego. Debbie, on the other hand, begun hosting a small group in their home on Tuesday evenings.

However, the McElrath letter arrived this morning and he was feeling a bit like Hezekiah after he shared the wealth of the Temple with the Babylonian ministers. Loose lips sink good intentions about surprise inheritance, mused Bob.

Bob has wrestled with the alternatives and wants to resolve the use of this inheritance tonight because he and Debbie have an upcoming meeting with Steve soon. Although Steve is aware they have received the check, Bob has not had an opportunity to share with him the growing conflicts over its use. As Bob begins to straighten his desk, he wonders if he should delay the meeting with Steve until he and Debbie can find some middle ground and resolve the differences between them.

Instructions

Part 1:

Take Bob and Debbie's situation with this inheritance of $40,000 and go through the decision making process as if you were making the decision. Using the information for the four situations (located at the end of the Case Study) complete the Criteria Based Decision Model template and be prepared to talk through each step of the process.

Part 2:

Use the Case Study, as well as the chapter material to answer the following questions as they relate to Bob and Debbie's situation.

Questions

1. What past experiences is Bob focusing on that may be interfering with the couple's ability to set a faith financial goal in relation to the inheritance check they just received?

2. What present resources/limitations is Debbie focusing on that may be interfering with the couple's ability to set a faith financial goal in relation to the inheritance check they just received?

3. In what ways are Bob and Debbie making some of the common mistakes that become obstacles to setting goals?

4. In regard to the four personality types that Ron illustrated with the DISC acrostic, what personality does Bob seem to be demonstrating? What personality type does Debbie seem to be demonstrating?

Mini Case Study 1: Chloe's Car Option

Courtesy of sun_orbiter/Fotolia.

Courtesy of Gudellaphoto/Fotolia.

Dear Chloe,

Your interest in our incredible selection of automobiles is of most importance to us here at Lovington Auto Sales. Per your inquiry through our online car finder, I have found exactly what I think you are looking for. Above you will find pictures of the vehicle which matches your requirements.

- Audi A3 Convertible

- 9,800 Miles

- $25,000

- Extras: Remote keyless entry, leather seats, bluetooth entertainment system w/touchscreen navigation, and safety features.

Please feel free to contact me with any further questions or concerns that you may have about this vehicle. I am committed to getting you the car that fits your needs and desires. This is a really fun car and I think you are truly going to enjoy every chance you get to drive it.

Sincerely,

Craig Lightfoot
Lovington Auto Sales—Inquiry Specialist
5000 Jackson Boulevard
(936) 555-8889
Lovington, NM 11112

Mini Case Study 2: Investment Offer

PAXTON PARTNERS
1600 AVENUE OF THE AMERICUS
NEW YORK, NEW YORK 10020
January 12, 2016

Bob Smith
1000 Residential Lane
Lovington, NM 11111

Dear Bob,

How's your ole' scruffy neck? I'm looking forward to coming to Atlanta; it's about time we got one of those 22-ounce T-bones at Chops. That is, if you're still man enough to wrestle one of those dudes to the ground.

Bob, on a more serious note I want to share a very, very unique opportunity. One of my key clients in the bio-genetics field has just retained Merrill Lynch as their lead advisors on an IPO. Because of our relationship, even though we are a very small player in this type of market, we will be part of a syndicate and as a result have been allocated a reasonable number of shares to market to our client base. The biggest challenge is that the minimum needs to be $200,000. Because of my work on the overall structure of the deal and some of the underlying strategy I have been given two allotments and permission to pool one of them, allowing a few individuals to invest at less than the $200,000. I am extending a one-time offer to my five closest friends to come in for $40,000 each on GOTech IPO, which will be rolling out sometime in the next six to eight weeks.

Visit their website at www.gotech.com. You will find a series of press releases and articles out of both the Bio-Medical and Business Press giving the background on this company, but I am estimating that at the bare minimum you will receive a five-to-one return on your money within 18 months. This stock is so hot it is smoking, and you can take that to the bank.

Time is of the essence. I need to hear back from you sometime in the next week to let me know if this would be of any interest. Regardless, the offer on the steak goes.

Looking forward from hearing you.

Your buddy,

Gary Garfield

Mini Case Study 3: Kitchen Proposal

PROPOSAL AND CONTRACT
THIS AGREEMENT IS BETWEEN:

Kitchens Extraordinaire
Contractor's License Number: 34567cxb78yf221
Contractor's Address: 2345 Excelsior Avenue, Decatur, GA 30365
Contractor's Telephone: 404-988-0002 Fax: 404-661-8000

AND

Owner's Name: Bob and Debbie Smith
Owner's Address: 1000 Residential Lane
Lovington, NM 1111
Owner's Telephone: 936-233-1234

DESCRIPTION OF PROJECT (including materials and equipment to be used or installed): Kitchen Remodel—
Walls, Cabinets, Floors, Plumbing, and Fixtures

Phase I:
Walls, flooring, window side cabinets, center console and plumbing. See schematics
and plans for list of materials and layout $36,000

Phase II:
Connecting breakfast nook walls, flooring, and den-side cabinets $16, 750

Phase III:
Pantry, built in china cabinets, connecting deck doors, sub-zero refrigerator $23,600

Contractor will furnish all labor, materials and equipment to construct in a good workmanlike manner.

TIME FOR COMPLETION: The work (Phase I) to be performed by Contractor pursuant to this Agreement shall
be commenced within 60 days from this date or approximately on June 15 and shall be substantially completed
within 60 days or approximately on August 26. Commencement of work shall be defined as (briefly describe type
of work representing commencement):

Contractor's failure to substantially commence work without lawful excuse, within twenty (20) days from the
date specified above is a violation of the Contractor's License Law.

PAYMENT: Owner agrees to pay Contractor a total cash price of $36,000 for Phase I DOWN PAYMENT $8000
returned with this signed contract PAYMENT SCHEDULE TO BE AS FOLLOWS:
- Down Payment—Phase One—With signed contract
- Remainder/Phase I at completion on or about August 26
- Phases II and III will be scheduled at the convenience of owners—Price adjustments re: material, appliances, etc.
  will be reflected, if necessary, at that time

RELEASE: Upon satisfactory payment being made for any portion of the work performed, the contractor shall, prior to any further payment being made, furnish to the person contracting for the home improvement or swimming pool a full and unconditional release from any claim or mechanic's lien for that portion of the work for which payment has been made.

The contract price shall be adjusted upward or downward based on actual amounts rather than estimated amounts herein.

Owner's Signature _____ Date _____

Contractor's Signature _____ Date _____

Mini Case Study 4: Church Request

Lovington Community Church
1600 Saxon Avenue
Lovington, NM 11112
www.lovingtoncc.org

January 12, 2016

Bob and Debbie Smith
1000 Residential Lane
Lovington, NM 11111

Dear Bob and Debbie,

Taking God's Word to the World

I enjoyed our time this past Saturday morning. You have certainly made a significant contribution to this church over the past few years and I am particularly encouraged to see younger men look to you, Bob Smith, and a number of the older "saints" of the church for leadership and inspiration. Don't get me wrong, I am not calling you old, just older than some of these young bucks we've got nipping at our heels.

Bob, the purpose of this letter is to share with you a very important need, one with which you're well-acquainted and to encourage you and Laura about praying to take a serious and significant step of faith and leadership to address this need. You know we are beginning to build the Children's Christian Education Center in the adjacent property of First Church. With increasing numbers of young families joining our Sunday school, facilities are "pressed down, shaken together, and running over!" We must do something soon if we are going to continue to see the growth both in the numbers of attendees and ministry impact. These children are our future!

This next month I am going to begin challenging the congregation to support this building expansion. From a budget perspective we need to raise almost $2,000,000 and in light of the expansion we moved through three or four years ago this will be a sacrifice to our church. To that end I am asking fifteen key couples in the congregation to take a critical first step with lead gifts to stimulate this most important initiative. In every case, I am asking these couples to invest $25,000. I am anticipating a positive answer from each one of you and with this amount in hand, we can go to the congregation next month with the message that 20% of the cost of this building has already been donated by key leaders throughout the church because of their vision and to encourage the rest of us to step up to the plate sacrificially.

You know that I wouldn't ask this if I did not feel it was critically important to the future of our church and the vision to which God has called us. Secondly, after much prayer concerning the fifteen couples I should encourage to participate, I am clear that you should be one of those challenged to stand in the gap with us. Please pray about this, knowing that I asked humbly but with great seriousness. I'd like to talk to you sometime this next weekend to see how you and Laura feel concerning God's leading on this most important matter. In the meantime blessings on you. I look forward to talking to you soon.

In Christ,

Senior Pastor George McElrath

Figure 5.1

Alternatives

Criteria	Priorities	Retirement Account		Matham		Kitchen		Reserve: Parent Care		Equity Debt		Church		IPO	
Must-Haves	Priorities														
Biblical Support	Must Have	Yes		Yes		Yes		Yes		Yes		Yes		UNCERTAIN	
Bill Oliver Will (FP) agree	Must Have	Yes		UNCERTAIN		Yes		Yes		Yes		UNCERTAIN		UNCERTAIN	
	Must Have														
	Must Have														
Want-to-Haves	Priorities														
Honor Crown Commitment	10	10	100	10	100	10	100	10	100	10	100	10	100	5	50
Maximize Liquidity	6	5	30					7	42	10	60				
In Financial Plan	8	8	64	2	16	5	40	6	48	7	56	1	8	1	8
Unity re: decision	8	7	56	2	16	6	48	8	64	7	56	2	16	3	24
Maximize ROI	7	8	56	2	14	6	42	2	14	8	56			6	42
Totals		306		146		230		268		328		124		124	

DEFINITIONS

Biblical stewardship   (p. 82)   **Goal**   (p. 82)   **Matrix**   (p. 88)

Criteria   (p. 93)   **Goal setting**   (p. 82)   **SMART**   (p. 86)

Faith   (p. 82)

SCRIPTURE VERSES (ESV)

Isaiah 43:18-19—Do not remember the former things. Nor consider the things of old. Behold, I will do a new thing, Now it shall spring forth: Shall you not know it? I will even make a road in the wilderness, and rivers in the desert.

Proverbs 16:1–3—The plans of the heart belong to man, but the answer of the tongue is from the LORD. All the ways of a man are clean in his own sight, but the LORD weighs the motives. Commit your works to the LORD and your plans will be established."

Genesis 18:13–14—And the Lord said to Abraham, "why did Sarah laugh, saying, 'Shall I surely bear a child since I am old?' "Is anything too hard for the Lord? At the appointed time I will return to you according to the time of life, and Sarah shall have a son."

Ephesians 3:20—Now to Him who is able to do immeasurably more than all we ask or imagine, according to His power that is at work within us . . .

Ephesians 5:15–17—Look carefully then how you walk! Live purposefully and worthily and accurately, not as the unwise and witless, but as wise—sensible, intelligent people; making the very most of the time—buying up each opportunity—because the days are evil. Therefore do not be vague and thoughtless and foolish, but understanding and firmly grasping what the will of the Lord is.

Isaiah 30:1—"Woe to the rebellious children," declares the LORD, "Who execute a plan, but not Mine, and make an alliance, but not of My Spirit"

Isiah 55:8—"For my thoughts are not your thoughts, neither are your ways, my ways," declares the Lord.

Proverbs 22:29—Do you see a man skillful in his work? He will stand before kings; he will not stand before obscure men.

Psalm 119:105—Your word is a lamp to my feet and a light to my path.

Psalm 19—The heavens declare the glory of God, and the sky above proclaims his handiwork. Day to day pours out speech, and night to night reveals knowledge.

There is no speech, nor are there words, whose voice is not heard. Their voice goes out through all the earth, and their words to the end of the world. In them he has set a tent for the sun, which comes out like a bridegroom leaving his chamber, and, like a strong man, runs its course with joy. Its rising is from the end of the heavens, and its circuit to the end of them, and there is nothing hidden from its heat. The law of the Lord is perfect, reviving the soul; the testimony of the Lord is sure, making wise the simple the precepts of the Lord are right, rejoicing the heart; the commandment of the Lord is pure, enlightening the eyes the fear of the Lord is clean, enduring forever; the rules of the Lord are true, and righteous altogether. More to be desired are they than gold, even much fine gold; sweeter also than honey and drippings of the honeycomb. Moreover, by them is your servant warned; in keeping them there is great reward. Who can discern his errors? Declare me innocent from hidden faults. Keep back your servant also from presumptuous sins; let them not have dominion over me. Then I shall be blameless, and innocent of great transgression. Let the words of my mouth and the meditation of my heart be acceptable in your sight, O Lord, my rock and my redeemer.

Psalm 32:8—I will instruct you and teach you in the way you should go; I will counsel you with my eye upon you.

Isaiah 59:1–2—Behold, the LORD's hand is not shortened, that it cannot save, or his ear dull, that it cannot hear; but your iniquities have made a separation between you and your God, and your sins have hidden his face from you so that he does not hear.

1 Peter 3:7—Likewise, husbands, live with your wives in an understanding way, showing honor to the woman as the weaker vessel, since they are heirs with you of the grace of life, so that your prayers may not be hindered.

Galatians 5:22–23—But the fruit of the Spirit is love, joy, peace, patience, kindness, goodness, faithfulness, gentleness, self-control; against such things there is no law.

1 Kings 12—Rehoboam went to Shechem, for all Israel had come to Shechem to make him king. And as soon as Jeroboam the son of Nebat heard of it (for he was still in Egypt, where he had fled from King Solomon), then Jeroboam returned from Egypt. And they sent and called him, and Jeroboam and all the assembly of Israel came and said to Rehoboam, "Your father made our yoke heavy. Now therefore lighten the hard service of your father and his heavy yoke on us, and we will serve you." He said to them, "Go away for three days, then come again to me." So the people went away.

Then King Rehoboam took counsel with the old men, who had stood before Solomon his father while he was yet alive, saying, "How do you advise me to answer this people?" And they said to him, "If you will be a servant to this people today and serve them, and speak good words to them when you answer them, then they will be your servants forever." But he abandoned the counsel that the old men gave him and took counsel with the young men who had grown up with him and stood before him. And he said to them, "What do you advise that we answer this people who have said to me, 'Lighten the yoke that your father put on us'?" And the young men who had grown up with him said to him, "Thus shall you speak to this people who said to you, 'Your father made our yoke heavy, but you lighten it for us,' thus shall you say to them, 'My little finger is thicker than my father's thighs. And now, whereas my father laid on you a heavy yoke, I will add to your yoke. My father disciplined you with whips, but I will discipline you with scorpions.'"

So Jeroboam and all the people came to Rehoboam the third day, as the king said, "Come to me again the third day." And the king answered the people harshly, and forsaking the counsel that the old men had given him, he spoke to them according to the counsel of the young men, saying, "My father made your yoke heavy, but I will add to your yoke. My father disciplined you with whips, but I will discipline you with scorpions." So the king did not listen to the people, for it was a turn of affairs brought about by the Lord that he might fulfill his word, which the Lord spoke by Ahijah the Shilonite to Jeroboam the son of Nebat.

And when all Israel saw that the king did not listen to them, the people answered the king, "What portion do we have in David? We have no inheritance in the son of Jesse. To your tents, O Israel! Look now to your own house, David." So Israel went to their tents. But Rehoboam reigned over the people of Israel who lived in the cities of Judah. Then King Rehoboam sent Adoram, who was taskmaster over the forced labor, and all Israel stoned him to death with stones. And King Rehoboam hurried to mount his chariot to flee to Jerusalem. So Israel has been in rebellion against the house of David to this day. And when all Israel heard that Jeroboam had returned, they sent and called him to the assembly and made him king over all Israel. There was none that followed the house of David but the tribe of Judah only.

When Rehoboam came to Jerusalem, he assembled all the house of Judah and the tribe of Benjamin, 180,000 chosen warriors, to fight against the house of Israel, to restore the kingdom to Rehoboam the son of Solomon. But the word of God came to Shemaiah the man of God: "Say to Rehoboam the son of Solomon, king of Judah, and to all the house of Judah and Benjamin, and to the rest of the people, 'Thus says the Lord, You shall not go up or fight against your relatives the people of Israel. Every man return to his home, for this thing is from me.'" So they listened to the word of the Lord and went home again, according to the word of the Lord.

Then Jeroboam built Shechem in the hill country of Ephraim and lived there. And he went out from there and built Penuel. And Jeroboam said in his heart, "Now the kingdom will turn back to the house of David. If this people go up to offer sacrifices in the temple of the Lord at Jerusalem, then the heart of this people will turn again to their lord, to Rehoboam king of Judah, and they will kill me and return to Rehoboam king of Judah." So the king took counsel and made two calves of gold. And he said to the people, "You have gone up to Jerusalem long enough. Behold your gods, O Israel, who brought you up out of the land of Egypt." And he set one in Bethel, and the other he put in Dan. Then this thing became a sin, for the people went as far as Dan to be before one. He also made temples on high places and appointed priests from among all the people, who were not of the Levites. And Jeroboam appointed a feast on the fifteenth day of the eighth month like the feast that was in Judah, and he offered sacrifices on the altar. So he did in Bethel, sacrificing to the calves that he made. And he placed in Bethel the priests of the high places that he had made. He went up to the altar that he had made in Bethel on the fifteenth day in the eighth month, in the month that he had devised from his own heart. And he instituted a feast for the people of Israel and went up to the altar to make offerings.

James 1:5–6—If any of you lacks wisdom, let him ask God, who gives generously to all without reproach, and it will be given him. But let him ask in faith, with no doubting, for the one who doubts is like a wave of the sea that is driven and tossed by the wind.

ADDITIONAL READINGS

Elliot, A. J., & Harackiewicz, J. M. (1994). Goal setting, achievement orientation, and intrinsic motivation: A mediational analysis. *Journal of Personality and social psychology, 66*(5), 968.

Erez, M. (1977). Feedback: A necessary condition for the goal setting-performance relationship. *Journal of Applied Psychology, 62*(5), 624.

Friesen, G. (2004). *Decision making and the will of God.* Multnomah.

Gallagher, T. M. (2009). *Discerning the will of God: An Ignatian guide to Christian decision making.* Crossroad Publishing Company.

Galotti, K. M. (2005). *Making decisions that matter: How people face important life choices.* Psychology Press.

Isen, A. M., & Means, B. (1983). The influence of positive affect on decision-making strategy. *Social Cognition, 2*(1), 18–31.

Johnson, L. T. (2011). *Scripture and discernment: Decision making in the church.* Abingdon Press.

Latham, G. P., & Locke, E. A. (1991). Self-regulation through goal setting. *Organizational behavior and human decision processes, 50*(2), 212–247.

Liebert, E. (2008). *The way of discernment: Spiritual practices for decision making.* Louisville, KY: Westminster John Knox Press.

Locke, E. A. (1996). Motivation through conscious goal setting. *Applied and Preventive Psychology, 5*(2), 117–124.

Locke, E. A., & Latham, G. P. (1990). *A theory of goal setting & task performance.* Prentice-Hall, Inc.

Locke, E. A., & Latham, G. P. (2002). Building a practically useful theory of goal setting and task motivation: A 35-year odyssey. *American Psychologist, 57*(9), 705.

Locke, E. A., & Latham, G. P. (2006). New directions in goal-setting theory. *Current Directions in Psychological Science, 15*(5), 265–268.

Loewenstein, G., & Lerner, J. S. (2003). The role of affect in decision making. In R. Davidson, K. Scherer, & H. Goldsmith (Eds.), *Handbook of affective science* (pp. 619–642). New York, NY: Oxford University Press.

March, J. G. (1994). *Primer on decision making: How decisions happen.* Simon and Schuster.

Schauer, F. (1991). *Playing by the rules: A philosophical examination of rule-based decision-making in law and in life.* New York, NY: Oxford University Press.

Shiv, B., & Fedorikhin, A. (1999). Heart and mind in conflict: The interplay of affect and cognition in consumer decision making. *Journal of Consumer Research, 26*(3), 278–292.

TerKeurst, L. (2012). *Unglued: Making wise choices in the midst of raw emotions.* Zondervan.

Zimmerman, B. J., Bandura, A., & Martinez-Pons, M. (1992). Self-motivation for academic attainment: The role of self-efficacy beliefs and personal goal setting. *American Educational Research Journal, 29*(3), 663–676.

REFERENCES

Covey, S. R. (2014). *The 7 habits of highly effective families.* London, England: St. Martin's Press.

Johnson, S. K., Garrison, L. L., Hernez-Broome, G., Fleenor, J. W., & Steed, J. L. (2012). Go for the goal(s): Relationship between goal setting and transfer of training following leadership development. *Academy of Management Learning & Education, 11*(4), 555–569. doi:10.5465/amle.2010.0149

Kahneman, D. (2011). *Thinking, fast and slow.* New York, NY: Macmillan.

Lifson, T. (2004). *GWB: HBS MBA, American Thinker.* Retrieved from http://www.americanthinker.com/articles/2004/02/gwb_hbs_mba.html

Locke, E. A. (1996). Motivation through conscious goal setting. *Applied and Preventative Psychology, 5,* 117–124.

Locke, E. A., & Latham, G. P. (2002). Building a practically useful theory of goal setting and task motivation: A 35-year odyssey. *American Psychologist, 57,* 705–717.

Rothkopf, E. Z., & Billington, M. J. (1979). Goal-guided learning from text: Inferring a descriptive processing model from inspection times and eye movements. *Journal of Educational Psychology, 71,* 310–327.

Chapter 6

Understanding Risks and Our Behaviors

Courtesy of Monkey Business/Fotolia.

BIG IDEA:
Our beliefs will drive our financial behaviors.

LEARNING OUTCOMES

- Define *risk* and the four different types of risk outlined in the chapter
- List and describe four basic myths regarding inflation
- Describe how inflation impacts one's retirement planning
- Explain why individuals experience different inflation rates
- Describe ways in which individuals can avoid and/or minimize identity risk
- Understand how to identify and put into perspective your financial fears
- Understand the importance of behavioral finance, and describe the three behavioral biases discussed in the chapter

Introduction

Northpoint Church in Atlanta, Georgia, recently conducted a study of its 300 largest donors in an attempt to understand the relationship between generosity and fear. The results showed that there exists an inverse relationship between generosity and fear. The more fear a person had, the less generous that person tended to be. Fear was a significant driver in reducing generosity.

Because of the end-times mentality of the Christian faith, many Christians are eager to listen to those proclaiming a prophetic message. Hal Lindsey and Larry Burkett, authors of *The Late Great Planet Earth* and *Coming Economic Earthquake*, respectively, and other writers who speculate about the "end times" sell a lot of books, but can also create panic and fear among their readers.

This chapter looks at how we can know and understand risks relating to our finances, which often drive our fear, and helps us gain a perspective of our financial behaviors and how the Bible speaks to those behaviors.

Ron's Corner

With over 35 years in the financial services industry, I have come across countless situations and conversations where people are talking with me about decisions they made in part by fear. One example that comes to mind is that of a friend of mine who publically stated he was worth $6 billion dollars and had no debt; half of his assets were held in publicly traded companies, and when the market crashed in 2008, his net worth went down from $6 billion to $4 billion (still with no debt). However, due to the fear of further losses, he took away his wife's $1 million annual giving fund. On a smaller scale, this would be similar to taking away an expense of $1 for someone with a net worth of $4,000. This is a dramatic example, but not that unusual. Many witnessed a more widespread fear in the late 1990s with the fear of a Y2K computer issue. Stores were consistently out of water and canned goods, and people were preparing as if the end of the world was coming. We know that in the end there was virtually no effect on computers as a result of the turning of the millennium.

RISKS

Risk Hazard, or a potential loss; the idea that some event might occur that does not benefit you.

Risk can generally be defined as "hazard, or a potential loss." In other words, risk is the idea that some event might occur that does not benefit you. Risk, however, does not exist in isolation. There are many different types of risk, and risks are present in every situation, especially those situations that relate to money and possessions. One example is the risks that you have to contend with when you buy a new smartphone. The phone could be dropped and damaged, or it could be stolen or lost. These risks are usually dealt with in one of two ways: minimizing exposure to the risk or assuming the risk. For those people who tend to minimize their risk exposure, we call them risk averse. These people want to reduce their risk as much as possible and normally will not act in ways that they feel are risky. Risk-tolerant people, on the other hand, are those people who will accept a higher degree of risk. Referring back to our purchase of a new smartphone, a risk averse person will likely purchase a hard case (which is a cost of protection) to protect the phone from being dropped as well as purchase an insurance policy (again another cost) that would cover the phone if it is stolen or lost. The hard case and the insurance policy increase the total financial commitment by the consumer in regard to the purchase. This risk-averse consumer is paying to protect the phone and transfer some of the risk to those companies that provided the hard case and the insurance policy.

Investment risk The risk of buying financial investments such as stocks, bonds, art, collectibles, and so forth that have the potential to go down in value and become worth less than what was paid for them.

Diversification Spreading out among various different options.

Let us now look at and review several different types of risks that relate to your money and possessions and then seek what the Bible says about these risks. **Investment risk**, which many can identify with, can be described as the risk associated with buying financial investments. These investments could be classified as all financial investments that have the potential to go down in value and become worth less than what you paid for them and would include stocks, bonds, art, collectibles, and so forth. The idea that what we buy could go down in value holds true for investments we buy, which is why there is risk associated with buying investments. The most prominent way that we can minimize (not eliminate) investment risk is known as diversification. **Diversification** is defined as spreading out investments amongst various different options. When investing, most professionals advise their clients to use portfolio diversification to reduce risk. Portfolio diversification is when various investments are purchased and placed into a *portfolio*, or a group.

So what does the Bible say about this idea of diversification to reduce investment risk? Our Scripture comes from the wisest man who ever lived, Solomon, who in his God-given wisdom provides the following advice:

Ecclesiastes 11:2: Divide your portion to seven, or even to eight, for you do not know what misfortune may occur on the earth.

Robert Katz and Craig Israelsen have both written about and created investment portfolios that represent this notion of diversification into either seven or eight portions. Katz, in his book *Solomon's Portfolio*, outlines the seven portions: (1) large-cap U.S. stocks, (2) small-cap U.S. Stocks, (3) non-U.S. stocks, (4) commodities (i.e., natural resources such as oil and corn), (5) real estate, (6) bonds (specifically intermediate bonds, which will pose less interest rate risk), and (7) cash. We will cover more about these specific types of investments in Chapter 14. Craig Israelsen, a visiting professor at Utah Valley University, has developed a more detailed portfolio he calls, "The 7Twelve® Portfolio." Israelsen uses seven asset classes (U.S. stocks, non-U.S. stocks, real estate, resources, U.S. bonds, non-U.S. bonds, and cash) and then breaks each of those asset categories into subcomponents. For example, U.S. stocks would be partitioned into large U.S. stocks, midcap U.S. stocks, and small U.S. stocks. See Figure 6.1 for the complete breakdown.

Another risk people deal with relating to money and possessions is the risk of inflation. **Inflation** is the overall increase in the cost of goods and services over time. I am sure that many of you have heard from your grandparents about how little things used to cost when they were growing up. In the case of inflation, most will accept the idea that the prices of goods and services will naturally increase over time. The risk, however, comes from the accumulation of these increases over time and how we can

Inflation The overall increase in the cost of goods and services over time.

Figure 6.1

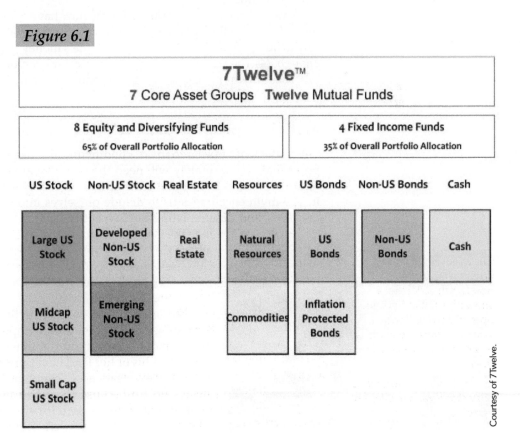

Courtesy of 7Twelve.

prepare to pay for the same items we pay for today in the future. The costs of goods and services is reported by the Bureau of Labor Statistics in its Consumer Price Index. The **Consumer Price Index (CPI)** is a measure of how the costs of goods and services change over a period of time, typically one year. There are certain myths about inflation that should be addressed before concluding our discussion on inflation risk.

Inflated Myths about Inflation

Inflation has been very tame throughout most of the 1990s and 2000s. Many of us, however, who lived through the high inflationary periods of the 1970s and 1980s still have concerns about inflation. I am not a prophet or an economic forecaster. Nevertheless, I believe that the very basic greedy nature of man will force inflation on our society.

> The effects of inflation can be found in Haggai 1:6: "You have planted much, but have harvested little. You eat, but never have enough. You drink, but never have your fill. You put on clothes, but are not warm. You earn wages, only to put them in a purse with holes in it."

The problem with inflation is twofold, and both problems cause fear. First of all, inflation destroys the purchasing power of the money already accumulated, and second, it requires that you continually earn more just to stay even with the increasing costs for the goods and services you need to live on. This is true because inflation has a compounding effect that makes the magic of compounding work against us.

The problem is not so much inflation as it is the fear of inflation. A leftover effect of prior periods of inflation is that we have become a "now" society. Too many of us adopt the philosophy that it will never be any cheaper than it is now, and besides, we only go around once.

Out of this fear and emphasis on the now have evolved four basic myths regarding inflation: (1) Buy it now, because it will cost more later. (2) You should always borrow to buy (the use of OPM—"other people's money"). (3) You can never accumulate enough. (4) The rate of inflation is standard for everyone.

These myths have just enough truth in them to make them believable, and many people govern their economic lives by them.

Myth 1: Buy Now Because It Will Cost More Later

This statement appears to make good financial sense at first reading, but it presupposes that you absolutely will need the item you are buying in the future. The real question, then, is not what it costs or what it will cost, but rather whether you need it. The myth encourages us to delude ourselves into funding our *wants* rather than our *needs*, and differentiating the two is fundamental when it comes to the way we manage God's resources. Advertisers really play on this myth by advertising that next year the cost is going to go up. So what? God has obligated Himself to meet my needs always (see Philippians 4:19), and He didn't qualify that by saying "except for times of inflation."

The second thing that this myth presupposes, of course, is an increasing price; but there is example after example of the fallacy of sure increases, even during times of inflation. Ask any farmer how much his or her land has appreciated over the last few years. Yet just a few years ago, "everyone" knew that farmland would always go up because there is a limited supply of it. Another more recent example is the rise and fall of oil. See Chart 6.1, which shows the price of crude oil from July 2010 to July 2015.

Courtesy of paul prescott/Fotolia.

Chart 6.1 Crude Oil over the Past 5 Years

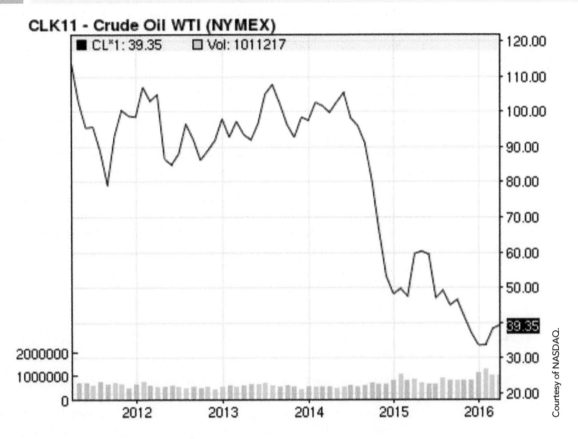

CLK11 - Crude Oil WTI (NYMEX)

CL*1: 39.35   Vol: 1011217

Source: http://www.nasdaq.com/markets/crude-oil.aspx?timeframe=5y

"Everyone" knew that the price of oil would always go up because of the shortage of oil. As shown in the chart, this so-called truth has become a fallacy. Or what about the price of computers and electronic equipment? Or how about the price of milk? Or what about mortgage rates? Those who purchased and mortgaged homes in 1983 at a 14% or 15% fixed rate because they thought the rates would never go down have probably refinanced at least once or twice in recent years.

Be wary of the trap of buying anything because the price is going up in the future. Ask yourself, first of all, "Do I really need this?" Then, the second question is, "If I do, but can't afford it, has God promised to meet my needs?" Of course He has, but not necessarily until you *really have a need* and not for the finest, most costly merchandise when something more affordable will do. He never seems to meet my needs in advance, but always right on time. Larry Burkett often said, "God is seldom early, but never late."

If you decide to fund your *desires/wants* now because of the possibility of future price increases, do so with cash and not with borrowed money. Paying cash will cause you to make a better decision, and at least you will not have compounding working against you.

Myth 2: Always Borrow to Buy

Two elements of truth support this myth. First of all, in times of inflation, the loan is paid back in cheaper dollars than those borrowed (because of the decline in purchasing power); second, the tax deduction for interest expense reduces the cost of interest.

However, the myth has two presuppositions:

1. It presupposes a rate of interest that is less than the inflation rate, and a purchase that appreciates or earns more than the after-tax cost. In other words, it makes economic sense.

2. The cash or investment that could be used for the purchase is earning more than the cost of borrowing. Again, borrowing in that case makes economic sense.

These presuppositions are generally either ignored or not known. The guiding principle now seems to be: Always borrow because you need the interest expense for a tax deduction, and you will always be paying back with cheaper dollars. Tax deductibility is a feature on only a certain number of loan types. These include home mortgages and student loans. Most all other types of consumer debt (car loans, credit cards, department store cards, payday loans, etc.) do not offer any deductibility of interest. Please seek advice from a Certified Public Accountant for more information regarding the deductibility of interest for both personal and business loans.

However, to borrow money for the tax deduction is unwise. If you are in the 25% tax bracket, for every $100 spent on interest, you reduce your taxes by $25, *but* it cost you $100 to do so; therefore, you are out of pocket $75 ($100–$25). Spending more than what you save is hardly the way to achieve financial success, and yet this advice is given regularly, even by professionals who should know better. It is true that in times of inflation you will be paying back borrowed dollars that are worth less than when you borrowed them. However, if you used the borrowed dollars to buy anything that depreciates in value, you have gained nothing financially by doing so and may have even lost in the whole transaction.

In recent years with lower inflation, fewer of these arguments for debt financing during inflationary times seem to arise. But these myths die hard. The point is that always borrowing to buy just because of inflation ignores the presuppositions mentioned previously. Using debt during times of inflation for leverage purposes can make sense, *but* only if these presuppositions are not ignored.

Myth 3: You Can Never Accumulate Enough

Real interest rate The stated interest rate adjusted for inflation.

Understanding the **real interest rate**, which can be defined as the stated interest rate adjusted for inflation, and the magic of compounding are the keys to destroying the myth that you can never accumulate enough to be protected from a continual rise in inflation. Incidentally, this myth is not a myth during times of hyperinflation if *all* of your assets are invested in money market instruments.

Enough An inflow of money (either from wages or accumulated assets/investments) that will support four main objectives: (1) live, (2) give, (3) owe, and (4) grow.

First of all, this myth raises the question of what is "enough." **Enough** can be described as an in flow of money (either from wages or accumulated assets/investments) that will support four main objectives: to (1) live (fund an appropriate lifestyle), (2) give, (3) owe (debt and taxes), and (4) grow. In other words, that investment fund must have sufficient "earning power" to provide for your lifetime.

In times of inflation, the earning power of investment funds will, over time, likely be greater than the inflation rate. When an investor has invested money into a company (usually in the form of stock ownership, covered later in Chapter 14), the investor may be entitled to a portion of that company's profits paid as dividends. Companies, at least in part, can control their prices and costs in order to combat the rise in inflation by increasing the prices of their goods and services. The rise in prices should continue to drive profits to companies (at least by an increase equal to the inflation rate) and thus provide an inflation-neutral return to shareholders. On the other hand, when an investor ties his or her money up at a fixed rate of interest in long-term investments, the interest received from these investments does not change, but will lose its purchasing power over time. For example, if you owned a bond that paid 5% annually, then a $1,000 bond would provide you with $50 annually (or $25 biannually) in interest. The longer you hold that bond, the less your $50 will be able to buy due to the continual rise in prices of goods and services (inflation).

A wise and knowledgeable person can beat inflation by adhering to the first transcendent principle, "spending less than you earn" (covered in detail in Chapter 8). When doing so, the power of compounding is unleashed. If the excess money is put to use in investments such as mutual funds, the earning power of the excess money will, over time, likely be greater than the inflation rate. That earning power will even offset the required increase in income needed just to maintain a standard of living.

We find many variables that are involved when dealing with the specific impact of inflation on your financial plan and accumulating "enough" to meet your retirement goals and objections. A few of these variables are as follows:

1. Time, or the number of years until retirement
2. Short-term goals, excluding children, accumulation needs, and mortgage payments (In other words, what could you live on if you did not have children to support, a mortgage payment, or the need to save?)
3. Additional income from other sources at retirement
4. The inflation rate, CPI changes
5. The after-tax yield now and in the future
6. Your current cash flow margin
7. Your current amount of investment funds
8. Your personal inflation rate (discussed next)

Several factors are assumed when looking at inflation and one's future retirement goals. The retirement income received from other sources will grow at least at the inflation rate, the ability to invest at after-tax yields will be considerably greater than the inflation rate, and the rate of inflation will not reach the level of hyperinflation. The illustration also ignores the impact of inflation on the investment fund at retirement when the entire yield, which had been compounding, is being used to live on. Therefore, the "investment fund needed" is a minimum amount. The point is that if you are spending less than you earn, inflation can work for you rather than against you, and you can fund enough to have in retirement. Even if you do not see how, God is still responsible to meet your needs and only requires that you take the first step of faith and obedience. In this case, that step is to generate a positive cash flow **margin**, which can be defined as the amount of excess over expenditures. Cash inflow minus cash outflow equals margin.

Myth 4: The Rate of Inflation Is Standard for Everyone

In personal financial planning, we figure for the impact of inflation by using the reported inflation rate. Unfortunately, everyone's circumstances are different, and the rates of change of goods and services do not change uniformly. For example, the following chart shows the rate of change in price for the listed goods and services.

When couples plan to have a cash flow margin, they do so by living on some type of workable and simple budget and have some sense of their relative inflation rate. As the previous chart shows, different goods and services differ in their price changes over time. If a couple has three young children, as well as the responsibility for caring for their elderly parents, one might conclude that their personal rate of inflation will be much higher than that of a middle-aged couple with no kids who are not responsible for the welfare of their parents. Using a budget and planning your expenses helps you begin to see what changes are needed in order to continue to generate a cash flow margin out of your earnings.

Margin The amount of excess from our required expenditures (cash inflow minus cash outflow = margin).

			Rates of change			
Good	1913–1929	1929–1941	1941–1951	1951–1968	1968–1983	1983–2013
Food*	3.2%	–1.9%	8.0%	1.3%	7.1%	2.90%
Energy*	3.8%	–0.9%	2.6%	1.9%	9.9%	3.0%
Education**					–3.0%	32.0%
Health Care*			4.3%	38.0%	8.4%	4.9%

			If we start with $1.00 in 1912,				
Good	1913–1929	1929–1941	1941–1951	1951–1968	1968–1983	1983–2013	Total Change from 1912 to 2013
Food*	$1.03	$2.01	$3.09	$4.11	$5.18	$6.21	501%
Energy*	$1.04	$2.03	$3.06	$4.07	$5.17	$6.20	498%
Education**	$1.00	$2.00	$3.00	$4.00	$4.97	$6.29	529%
Health Care*			$1.04	$2.42	$3.51	$4.56	337%

*Source: http://www.bls.gov/opub/mlr/2014/article/one-hundred-years-of-price-change-the-consumer-price-index-and-the-american-inflation-experience.htm

**Source: http://trends.collegeboard.org/college-pricing/figures-tables/tuition-and-fees-and-room-and-board-over-time-1975-76-2015-16-selected-years

DISCIPLESHIP MOMENT AND REFLECTION

Take a few minutes and pray for wisdom (James 1:5) as it relates to knowing and understanding how you personally will be affected by changes in inflation rates. To see the tremendous impact of a personal inflation rate that is less than the reported average annual inflation rate, review the chart above that reflects differences in the cost of goods over time. How do you see these differences impacting you personally? Talk to your accountability and prayer partner and see which ones impact them the most. What do you find the same? Different?

As you review the illustrations in the Appendix, you will notice that the current investment fund provides adequate income to meet the future income needs, with *no* cash flow margin needed for the next 25 years to meet regular living expenses. Of course, if this family lives in such a disciplined way that they have a cash flow margin, they can save for long-term goals, such as major giving or starting a business.

Inflation does not necessarily need to be feared. For those who are wise, knowledgeable, patient, self-disciplined, and mature, it can work to their advantage. The overall global economy is nothing to be feared either. God is ultimately in control of governments and economies.

The concept of inflation, the continual rise of costs over time, leads us to our next risk, longevity in our lives. This may seem unusual, but the reality is that we are generally living longer due to a reversion back to healthy eating habits and medical advances. The risk that we may outlive our financial resources is **longevity risk**. Social resources such as Social Security and other governmental resources might not be sufficient to support our society over longer life spans. As Christians, we must remember the promises provided to us in God's word regarding His provision (see the end-of-chapter Scripture verses). The most effective way to prepare for our longevity is to follow the principles outlined throughout this text, specifically, the five transcendent money management principles: (1) Spend less than you earn. (2) Avoid the use of debt. (3) Maintain liquidity (margin). (4) Save for the long-term. (5) Give generously.

Longevity risk The risk that you may outlive your financial resources.

Political risk The risk associated with changes in the political arena, including changes in power or laws, that could negatively impact our daily lives.

Globalization The interconnectedness of companies across the globe that are involved in supply and demand of their products and services.

Currency risk The risk involved in the fluctuations of the global currencies as they relate to one another.

Political risk is the risk associated with changes in the political arena, including changes in power (people) or laws (regulations) that could negatively impact our daily lives. As we see regularly (every 4 years with our presidential elections), the government is constantly changing the laws and the things it is spending money on and not spending money on. These political decisions are future risks we must assume. Although we have limited ability to minimize political risk, our individual vote for elected officials who match our Christian faith and values should not be undervalued.

With the continued rise of **globalization**, the interconnectedness of companies across the globe that are involved in supply and demand of their products and services, **currency risk** may not be as relevant as it once was. Currency risk is the risk involved in the fluctuations of the global currencies as they relate to one another. Simply, when one currency (the U.S. dollar, for example) rises in value over another (for example, the Japanese yen), then products that are set in U.S. dollars become more expensive than those products priced in Japanese yen. In this example, exports to Japan will decrease because people in Japan will spend less on goods valued by the U.S. dollar (i.e., U.S. goods). In addition, the U.S. dollar will be able to buy more Japanese products, and thus Japanese imports to the United States will likely increase. Over the past several decades, we have seen the U.S. dollar becoming a global currency (Conerly, 2013), which has minimized the risk associated with currency exchanges.

THE IMPACT OF A GLOBAL ECONOMY

In the movie *It's a Wonderful Life*, the main character, George Bailey, is about to realize his dream of travel and adventure and leave Bedford Falls by taking a trip on his honeymoon. During his previous opportunities to leave the town for college or travel, some event or dutiful obligation prevented him from doing so. Leaving the wedding, he and his bride ride away in the taxi, giddy with excitement. Their excitement fades as they see the beginning of the "run" on the town's banks and their Building and Loan. George and his bride, Mary, spend their honeymoon savings to keep the Building and Loan's doors open and depositors happy. The Great Depression had begun—and had ruined their honeymoon plans.

In the real world, the Great Depression, as well as the housing debacle of 2008–2009 in the United States, ruined many people's plans and savings. Even though very little may have changed in their local town or economy from one day to the next, the national changes had a drastic effect on many individuals. It was a classic case of how the overall national economy affects the local economy, or micro-economy, of regions and individuals. Today, the situation has gotten even more complex because countries coexist in a global economy (called the "macro-economy").

HOW THE MACRO ECONOMY AFFECTS YOU

You've seen headlines in the newspapers or heard the lead-in to the economic news stories on TV or radio:

- The Fed Raises Interest Rates
- OPEC Lowers Production, Oil Prices Likely to Increase
- The Dollar Hits Record Low Against the Yen and Euro
- Technology Changes Harm Workers, Help Corporate Earnings
- The Dow Hits Record High, NASDAQ Closes Higher Too
- Internet Increasing Productivity Statistics
- Government Deficit Is Higher, but a Smaller Portion of GNP

- Trade Imbalance Increases
- Lower Unemployment Rattles Bond Market

After perusing these types of headlines, it's easy to want to skip to the comics quickly. Are any of these matters vital to your everyday financial concerns? Well, the answer is both yes and no. These can drastically affect your personal financial situation, yet you could also do well financially without even paying attention to them. In the following sections, I'll explain how this is true.

HAVING SERENITY ABOUT THE MACRO ECONOMY

God grant us the serenity
to accept the things we cannot change,
courage to change the things we can,
and wisdom to know the difference.

When considering the overall economy and how it affects you, it's important to consider what you can control and what you can't. No one individual can affect the long-term stock market changes, the unemployment rate, or inflation. We're not saying those items are unimportant or useless to track. But you can't do much to influence them. Some argue that the global economy is too big and powerful for even the presidents of nations to impact.

The idea of the previously stated Serenity Prayer can apply to the economy. We have to accept the overall economic conditions in which we find ourselves. But we must have the courage to change what we can about our personal financial situation. To better prepare for uncertain changes in the economy, you should spend less than you earn, maintain liquidity, avoid debt, set goals, and continue to give back to God, our Creator.

DOOMSAYERS: "IT'S DÉJÀ VU ALL OVER AGAIN!"

The 1980s witnessed some very interesting economic conditions: (1) interest rates were nearing 20%, (2) inflation was raging, and (3) the stock market had been flat for several years. Those predicting gloom and doom were everywhere. *Ruff Times* was one of the most popular financial newsletters telling people inflation would always be high.

After Black Monday, October 19, 1987, when stock markets across the globe witnessed 30% to 60% declines, various doomsayers were in vogue and in demand. They urged people to take action and take cover.

More recently, many predicted the world would almost stop on 1/1/2000 due to the Y2K issue of how computers would transition from 1999 to 2000. Some people stored up years of food and bought land in rural areas to prepare for the worst.

After the terrorist attacks on the United States. in 2001 and the 3-year downturn in the stock market, some doomsayers were predicting the global economy would be in shambles. The doomsayers were back again in 2008–2009 during the housing crash and the subsequent global recession.

It was challenging to not get depressed during these times because all one would hear was about everything supposedly going wrong. Perhaps the fundamental problem with doomsayers is that although they have a depression mentality, they are unwilling to take "depression actions." If individuals really believed that a depression was coming, they would get out of debt, convert all

Courtesy of O.Farion/Fotolia.

their investments to government securities, buy a one-year supply of food, and otherwise prepare for the worst. The problem is, although people like to talk about and believe that an extreme situation will happen, very few are willing to take extreme steps to plan for it.

Ron's Corner

During my years as a financial planner, I did not believe in emphasizing planning for extremes. Planning for extremes usually dictates radical action. Radical actions can have radical consequences. Radical steps, whatever they may be, usually put one in a high-risk position. One example of planning for extremes is to avoid diversifying and instead put all your investment dollars (or even your margin) into precious metals, based on the theory that the metals market will continue to outperform all other investments. If the extreme happens and you are right, you have won a great reward. But if you are wrong, you have been damaged severely. Not only would you lose the money you put in gold or silver, but you are left without an investment base to cushion the loss. Well, if I don't plan for doomsday or extremes, what should I think? I tend to like balanced practicality.

Identity Theft

Identity theft, or **identity risk**, is the risk associated with having one's identity compromised. This relatively new risk can be experienced by having one's Social Security number or credit card information stolen and used by a person who is not authorized to use the them. Many best practices have been identified by experts to help minimize the risk of identity theft. Some of those practices include the following: cross-shred all of your personal documents, including bank statements, bills, and other documents that have personal and identifying information on them; do not provide any personal or identifiable information through an e-mail request; and use and securely store passwords to access any online sites that provide personal and identifiable information.

Identity theft See *identity risk*.

Identity risk (also known as identity theft) The risk associated with having one's identity compromised, such as having one's Social Security number stolen.

DEALING WITH THE FEAR OF UNCERTAINTY

Ron's Corner

Sherry is a friend of one of my daughters. She had been a missionary, and just before she was to be married, she lived with our family for a few weeks. I'll never forget her.

On December 22, Sherry's wedding was only a few months away. As she dashed out to do some last-minute Christmas shopping, she was bursting with joy amid the sparkling holiday season.

All that changed, though, in a matter of minutes. When Sherry returned to the parking lot where she had left her car, it was gone. Like many young people, she kept virtually everything she owned in there. Her car had been stolen. Frantic, she telephoned her fiancé.

"I've got some bad news of my own," came his reply. "I just lost my job."

As we look at Sherry's story, it is safe to assume that on that frosty December evening, Sherry and her fiancé did not spend their time agonizing over the federal budget deficit or inflation. At that point, they could not have cared less about the tax code changes or oil prices. There's something about genuine, personal fear and anxiety that casts a whole new light on the far-off problems that make for national news.

We have all wrestled with our own private worries. We have examined the impact of large-scale economic concerns. Now, we want to shift the focus to our individual lives, where our personal fears, desires, and long-range dreams often create an anxiety and fear that far outweigh anything we have ever felt over an increase in inflation or a drop in the stock market.

Fears, Desires, and Long-Range Dreams

We live in an imperfect world full of imperfect people. Think, for a brief and somewhat unpleasant moment, of how much and how quickly life can go awry: bankruptcy of a business, divorce, layoffs, a nursing home stay for you or your loved ones, stock market downturn, lawsuits, damage to reputation, disability. How do you respond to the unexpected events of life that directly and indirectly affect your personal finances? Our fears, desires, and dreams are often entirely valid; yet the emotional punch they pack need not be a knockout blow. In this section, you will learn to admit and identify the specific concerns that threaten your personal financial security. Moreover, you will gain a perspective on your financial future that will become the foundation for your ultimate money-management program.

Fears: Examples of the Unknown, the Unexpected, and the Uncertain

Example 1: Unknown Reason

Many years ago, I knew a family who seemed to have everything. They lived in a nice section of Atlanta and had been blessed with five healthy and active children. The father, a man in his early forties, loved spending time with his kids, and he often took them on special outings.

One weekend he took the older children hiking in the mountains of North Carolina. While climbing up to a seemingly safe path beside a waterfall, he grabbed a tree branch. The branch broke, the father lost his balance, and he fell down the mountain. Unfortunately, he did not survive the fall.

How was his wife to cope with rearing five children on her own? In addition to the emotional loss, her financial concerns must have seemed staggering. Could she count on her family and friends? Perhaps. But her former husband's business partner was another matter. He sued to get a bigger share of the business. How do you prepare for something like that?

Example 2: Unexpected Departure

A prominent businessman from a well-known Boston family took his wife and their two children on an annual vacation. Upon arriving home from the airport, he asked the taxi driver to wait a moment after the family unloaded their belongings. "I'm not staying here," the businessman announced. "I'm filing for divorce. I'm just going inside to get my clothes."

Imagine the family's mental and emotional devastation! And then the fear set in: What would this mean financially? Could the wife rely on her ex-husband's support? Would she and the kids have to move? Would she need to find a job to keep the household going?

Example 3: Uncertain Future

A friend of our family recently learned that he has an inoperable brain tumor. He's in his fifties. How will all of his family members respond? Is there ever a way to really be ready to handle the pain and uncertainty of a major illness?

Death, divorce, and unexpected illness all evoke very real and legitimate fears—especially in that they involve factors we typically have little or no control over. Other anxieties include the loss of a job, sudden financial needs (for car repairs or medical expenses, for example), taxes, college costs, and the prospect of living on a fixed income in retirement. Even the impending arrival of a new baby—normally viewed through a window of joyful anticipation—can cause tremendous worry and stress.

Desires: The Goals We Yearn to Achieve

Our desires may not pack the unplanned-for punch of many of our fears; yet, as causes for anxiety, they are every bit as real. Desires include getting out of debt, taking a vacation, buying a home, purchasing new clothes, getting a new car, or providing for a child's higher education bills. The fear that we may fail to realize these goals can exact a devastating emotional toll.

Many of our dreams—in fact, the American dream itself—seem to be vanishing into an early-morning fog. So many of the things we once took for granted seem suddenly out of reach. Is it still reasonable to hope, as our parents did, that at some point we may no longer have a home mortgage? Owning your own home used to be considered almost a right; now it seems more like a privilege.

The same may be said of a college education. According to the College Board, the average annual cost for a private college is $30,367 for tuition, room, and board. That's right—per year. The 4-year total is $121,468. That's today, not years from now. The average annual cost at a 4-year public university is $12,796. And the skyrocketing costs show no sign of slowing. Suddenly, putting your children—or yourself—through college is no longer something to be taken for granted.

According to the National Center for Educational Statistics, the annual cost has climbed from $4,406/year in 1982 to $17,474/year in 2013 for public institutions. Table 6.1 shows the annual costs per year from 1982 to 2013 for public, private, and for-profit universities.

Long-Range Dreams: More Distant Now than Ever Before?

Further off, but no less vivid, are the hopes and dreams that make for long-term planning. This category may include a desire to launch your own business, increase your charitable giving, or gain the financial independence necessary for retirement.

Factors such as changes in the tax code and interest rate can make long-term planning especially difficult. Investment counselors urge their clients to get serious about planning—yet they freely admit the challenge this admonition presents. As a slogan for a mutual fund company once warned: "Planning for retirement is like trying to hit a moving target while blindfolded."

So what are we to do? Throw in the investment towel and simply cross our fingers? Start buying lottery tickets in bulk? Hope that rich Uncle Frank will go before we do and pray that we will get at least some of the inheritance?

One might classify our retirement ideology as to: "Put away as much as I can and hope for the best." That may be a strategy but unfortunately it's no plan.

Table 6.1   Annual Cost of College per Year, 1982–2013

Average total tuition, fees, and room and board rates charged for full-time undergraduate students in degree-granting institutions, by type and control of institution: Selected years, 1982–83 to 2012–13

Year and Control of Institution	Constant 2012–13 dollars[1]			Current Dollars		
	All Institutions	4-year Institutions	2-year Institutions	All Institutions	4-year Institutions	2-year Institutions
All Institutions						
1982–83	$9,138	$10,385	$6,396	$3,877	$4,406	$2,713
1992–93	12,097	14,216	6,830	7,452	8,758	4,207
2001–02	14,775	17,708	7,424	11,380	13,639	5,718
2002–03	15,262	18,344	7,943	12,014	14,439	6,252
2003–04	16,104	19,276	8,336	12,953	15,505	6,705
2004–05	16,647	19,925	8,563	13,793	16,510	7,095
2005–06	17,014	20,289	8,412	14,634	17,451	7,236
2006–07	17,547	20,934	8,461	15,483	18,471	7,466
2007–08	17,737	21,160	8,346	16,231	19,363	7,637
2008–09	18,421	21,996	8,879	17,092	20,409	8,238
2009–10	18,839	22,515	9,109	17,649	21,093	8,533
2010–11	19,355	23,118	9,323	18,497	22,092	8,909
2011–12	19,741	23,409	9,461	19,418	23,025	9,306
2012–13	20,234	23,872	9,574	20,234	23,872	9,574
Public Institutions						
1982–83	$6,941	$7,534	$5,632	$2,945	$3,196	$2,390
1992–93	8,731	9,772	6,166	5,379	6,020	3,799
2001–02	10,415	11,940	6,670	8,022	9,196	5,137
2002–03	10,800	12,434	7,116	8,502	9,787	5,601
2003–04	11,496	13,270	7,474	9,247	10,674	6,012
2004–05	11,905	13,790	7,694	9,864	11,426	6,375
2005–06	12,154	14,077	7,547	10,454	12,108	6,492
2006–07	12,522	14,503	7,723	11,049	12,797	6,815
2007–08	12,647	14,675	7,623	11,573	13,429	6,975
2008–09	13,209	15,371	8,156	12,256	14,262	7,568
2009–10	13,667	16,027	8,223	12,804	15,014	7,703
2010–11	14,194	16,657	8,460	13,564	15,918	8,085
2011–12	14,616	17,084	8,715	14,377	16,805	8,572
2012–13	15,022	17,474	8,928	15,022	17,474	8,928

Private Nonprofit and For-Profit Institutions

1982–83	$16,311	$16,797	$12,644	$6,920	$7,126	$5,364
1992–93	23,754	24,364	16,076	14,634	15,009	9,903
2001–02	29,100	29,727	20,547	22,413	22,896	15,825
2002–03	29,652	30,220	22,554	23,340	23,787	17,753
2003–04	30,613	31,167	24,315	24,624	25,070	19,558
2004–05	31,158	31,693	24,497	25,817	26,260	20,297
2005–06	31,284	31,778	24,885	26,908	27,333	21,404
2006–07	32,231	32,774	22,988	28,439	28,919	20,284
2007–08	32,530	33,032	23,698	29,767	30,226	21,685
2008–09	33,199	33,706	24,494	30,804	31,273	22,726
2009–10	33,116	33,612	26,134	31,023	31,488	24,483
2010–11	33,513	34,131	24,979	32,026	32,617	23,871
2011–12	33,608	34,234	24,049	33,058	33,674	23,655
2012–13	34,483	35,074	23,328	34,483	35,074	23,328

Source: U.S. Department of Education, National Center for Education Statistics. (2015). *Digest of Education Statistics, 2013* (NCES 2015-011), Chapter 3.

[1] Constant dollars based on the Consumer Price Index, prepared by the Bureau of Labor Statistics, U.S. Department of Labor, adjusted to a school-year basis.

There is no getting around the fact that we desperately need an effective plan for retirement. Relying on Social Security alone is not enough. In 2006, the average monthly benefit received by American workers was a meager $1,008[1]—an income scarcely above the poverty level for people older than 65. And that figure is likely to drop as the Social Security system adds more and more retirees to its roster, many of whom will live at least 10 to 20 years longer than their counterparts of the 1930s and 1940s. Average Social Security payments have increased each year, but have risen more slowly than medical costs have increased.

The challenge we face in planning for retirement (or for other long-term dreams) can generate a great deal of tension and anxiety. The fear that we might not realize our hopes and desires may prove just as unsettling as the threat of an unexpected loss or crisis. Yet none of these fears should compromise our security. We must confront our fears head-on, wrestling them into submission before they gain a stronghold in our lives.

Pinpointing Your Fears

So what are you to do with all of these fears and risks? The first step in overcoming financial fear is to face it. It's not sinful or wrong to experience fear, doubt, or uncertainty. Neither is at all uncommon. Moreover, being a Christian does not make you immune to fear.

---

[1] U.S. Social Security Administration, Office of Policy, Monthly Statistical Snapshot, September 2006. Retrieved from http://www.ssa.gov/policy/docs/quickfacts/stat_snapshot/index.html.

As previously mentioned, Larry Burkett's book *The Coming Economic Earthquake*, which was written primarily for the Christian community, sold about a million copies in the 1990s. Our office received hundreds of phone calls in response to the book—almost all from Christians who were frightened about the economic outlook. Larry never intended his message to be received prophetically; rather, he merely pointed out what would happen if things did not change. He simply made a calculated prediction, and yet it was enough to unsettle countless readers!

Fear is a universal emotion. If you doubt me on this, simply open any newspaper and glance through the headlines. The world is glutted with fearful analysts, worried politicians, anxious officials, and countless individuals who are scared about all sorts of things—especially about the future!

We cannot hide our heads in the sand. Refusing to see or acknowledge our fear will not make it go away; in fact, left to fester on its own, it will probably grow to new and more frightening proportions. We must admit that we are afraid, and then move on to tackle our fear.

Identify Your Fear

The second vital step in conquering fear is to identify it. Once you come to grips with the fact that you are experiencing fear (once you admit it, that is), you must label your specific concerns. A correct diagnosis of the problem is essential to discovering the proper cure.

People wrestle with two primary fears: the fear of failure and the fear of the future. I think psychologists would equate the fear of failure with our search for *significance*, whereas the fear of the future represents our search for *security*. In terms of financial planning, our thinking often runs along these lines "If I have enough wealth, I will be secure [or significant, or both]."

The Fear of Failure

Ron's Corner

I grew up in a modest home with parents who never went to college. After becoming a teenager, I stepped from an eighth-grade class of only 12 students into a high school where there were 600 students in my class alone. I desperately wanted to be "someone," and by the time I graduated, I had lettered in two sports, served as senior-class president, and achieved the distinction I craved. I continued to make a name for myself in college and then went on to pass the CPA exam on my first try. Later I acquired my MBA degree and got a job with the world's largest accounting firm. To an outside observer, my life appeared to be woven with the threads of success. I typically worked 70- to 80-hour weeks, relying on my accumulating wealth to give me a feeling of significance and success. What I did not realize, however, was that a fear of failure dictated my every move. Once I committed my life to Christ, nothing changed in terms of my controlling fears. I still worked more than 70 hours a week, this time for the "cause of Christ." I thrived on the recognition I received from the Christian community, and my reputation as a hardworking, dedicated Christian brought me immense satisfaction. It reached the point where, in my mind, it seemed that the church—if not the Lord Himself—was somehow dependent on my outstanding efforts. Finally, a friend pointed out that, as a Christian, I was allowing myself to be driven by the very same force that influenced my lifestyle in the secular world. The fear of failure was just as wrong in the one arena as in the other, with consequences equally as adverse.

Fear of failure A constant search for significance.

1. **The Fear of Failure.** The **fear of failure**, which could also be referred to as the fear of being insignificant, is typically more of a male issue than a female one. Men, more often than women, tend to be driven by the fear that if they don't push hard enough or work long enough, they will fail and as a result be insignificant. Often, this drive can have positive results in terms of increased productivity and greater financial reward. Many successful entrepreneurs and hard-driving business executives are propelled—sometimes unknowingly—by the fear of failure.

   The danger, however, is when money and possessions become the primary measures of success and significance. When this happens, anything that threatens one's ability to accumulate wealth becomes a driving force in one's decision-making process. Ultimately, this mind-set leads to unwise decisions and overly risky financial moves.

   Once we recognized how common—and powerful—the fear of failure is, we begin to recognize its presence in decision making. An example may be when people start a business; there is a very high likelihood that they have a very real fear of failure. Instead of letting this fear prevent them from starting the business, it is important for them to recognize the fear and move toward prayer and seeking confirmation in the call. Once they have given the decision over to God and feel confirmation, they can move with confidence into the opportunity and trust that God will provide for them in their obedience.

   The fear of failure can often push people to new heights. It might cause someone to work longer hours, stay more focused, or be in consistent prayer. However, having an understanding of motives and the driving force behind any action is vitally important. When the fear of failure is removed from the situation, it enables us to rely on God and be guided and directed according to His schedule rather than our own.

   We must face the fear of failure, not only on the financial level, but also on a spiritual level. If you are a Christian, you have already dealt with this issue. You are already an admitted failure! You have recognized that you can do nothing to save yourself or to earn your own significance.

   Jesus Christ is the only true source of personal worth and fulfillment. As 2 Corinthians 3:5 reminds us, we are not "sufficient," or competent, to claim anything for ourselves, "but our sufficiency is from God." Once we truly believe this promise, the fear of failure—and its accompanying desires for material or worldly significance—will no longer dictate our decisions and behavior.

Fear of the future A state of worry in an attempt to control or identify future events.

2. **The Fear of the Future.** Fear of the future can be described as a state of worry in an attempt to control or identify future events. Much of what we worry about never comes to pass. Worry is a common manifestation of the fear of the future. The things we worry about—such as the death of a spouse, a medical emergency, unrealized dreams, or a financial calamity—are the things that affect our sense of security. Because we can readily point to these concerns, the fear of the future is usually much easier to identify than the fear of failure.

   Again, identifying this fear is half the battle. Once we recognize that we're afraid of the future, we can pinpoint the exact problem and develop an effective solution. We must evaluate the fear of the future on two levels, the spiritual and the financial.

   Scripture is loaded with truth and wisdom about the future and how we are to approach it. In Luke 14:28, Jesus asks, "Which of you, intending to build a tower, does not sit down first and count the cost, whether he has enough to finish it?" Obviously, there is wisdom in accurate financial planning for the future.

   At the same time, though, the Bible warns us that we cannot control the future. James 4:14 reminds us that we "do not know what will happen tomorrow. For what is your life? It is even a vapor that appears for a little time and then vanishes away."

One passage about the future and the time we have is **2 Peter 3:8**: "With the Lord one day is as a thousand years, and a thousand years as one day."

When I spoke with Joni Eareckson Tada, she shared her thoughts on this verse. Paralyzed after a diving accident, Joni is a popular author, speaker, and artist who has a dynamic ministry to the disabled. I had always interpreted **2 Peter 3:8** to mean that because a day was like a thousand years, God was not anxious about schedules or timetables. After all, He has all the time in the world! Although I still believe this assessment to be true, Joni opened my eyes to the other side of this verse. Because a thousand years is like a day, Joni said, each day becomes incredibly important in that it can have the eternal impact of a thousand years!

The spiritual principles outlined in **2 Peter 3:8** are also appropriate on a financial level. The knowledge that time is not as short as it may appear to be will keep us from plunging headlong into an ill-considered plan or investment. On the other hand, the realization of each day's potential can motivate us to action where we might otherwise drag our feet. Either way, the smartest approach to any financial decision begins with confronting your concerns.

Nobody is immune to fear: chances are, your personal concerns and private worries will fit into at least one, if not both, of the two fear categories we have discussed: the fear of failure or the fear of the future.

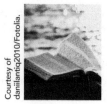

Courtesy of daniilantiq2010/Fotolia.

DISCIPLESHIP MOMENT AND REFLECTION (PART 1)

Have you admitted that there are areas of your financial life that cause you to be afraid? If so, what are they? Take a few moments to mentally catalog your financial fears. Do any of the following items threaten your sense of security? Review the list, marking any areas that reflect your individual concerns. Talk through these with your accountability and prayer partner.

A. Financial mistakes
- Poor investment decisions
- Not saving enough
- Poor buying decisions
- Not being unified with your spouse in terms of financial habits and goals

B. Future dreams, desires, goals, opportunities
- Children's education
- Personal education
- Retirement
- Financial independence
- Starting your own business
- Purchasing first or new home
- Paying off debt
- Other_____

C. Future uncertainties, challenges or fears
- Death of a loved one causing personal financial hardship
- Loss of a job
- Medical-, health-, or accident-related concern
- Business failure
- Investment losses
- Other_____

D. External forces
- The national economy
- Tax-law changes
- Other_____

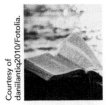

DISCIPLESHIP MOMENT AND REFLECTION (PART 2)

Having pinpointed your specific fears, work through the following steps to deal with your concerns. (Hint: If you can't confidently answer all the questions in this section, come back and complete this page when you finish reading this book.)

A. Of all the fears you identified and checked, cross off those that are out of your control.

B. Of those that are left, identify your top two fears:

C. How likely is it that number 1 will occur? _____percent chance

D. How likely is it that number 2 will occur? _____ percent chance

E. If number 1 does occur, what is the financial cost? $ _____

F. If number 2 does occur, what is the financial cost? $ _____

G. What are the steps you can take to prepare for number 1?

Put Your Fear into Perspective

As we discovered in the lesson from 2 Peter 3:8, understanding and applying God's perspective on time steals much of the thunder from our fears about the future. Likewise, putting our concerns into the proper perspective goes a long way toward rendering our fears powerless to dictate or influence our decision making.

The Bible relates story after story of the fears and concerns that stalked God's people. Joseph, Gideon, and Paul were as flawed and human as any of us—yet in their stories we can find great encouragement and a host of "how-to" guides for putting fear into perspective. See the Appendix for complete readings of these Bible stories.

A. Read Genesis 41. How did Joseph deal with the fear of famine?

B. Read Judges 6 and 7. How did Gideon deal with the fear of a powerful enemy?

C. Read Acts 16:16–40. How did Paul deal with suddenly being thrown into prison?

D. Meditate on Philippians 4:6–7 and Thessalonians 5:18. Have you brought every fear to God, as He commands? Will you resolve to do so?

Admitting and identifying your specific concerns is the first step in dealing with any fear. Even then, though, such fear can worm its way into your financial life and create panic—or, equally devastating, leave you paralyzed and unable to take decisive action. Present your fears to God and allow Him to work in your heart and mind as you learn to experience the peace that comes with trusting God to deliver you through the things that cause you the most fear.

BEHAVIORAL FINANCE

Over the past decade, the idea of behavioral finance has become a significant component of research related to why and how people make decisions in relation to their finances. The amount of research on behavioral finance has become rather robust over this time period. This section provides a brief overview of behavioral finance and identifies several common biases in our decision making that this research has revealed. We also review how the Bible speaks to these biases.

Behavioral finance can be thought of as a blend of three unique fields of study: psychology, economics, and finance. As researchers look at traditional finance theories (modern portfolio theory by Markowitz, as an example) they assume two basic premises: (1) that decisions are made rationally, and (2) that our main goal is to maximize our wealth/resources. Although finance theories have provided people with a foundation from which to create wealth, research has shown that people still make decisions that (1) are not rational and (2) don't always provide us with wealth maximization. **Behavioral finance** attempts to provide a series of explanations as to why people make such decisions. So why do we make irrational decisions and select financial choices that do not maximize our wealth? The best answer can be found in Scripture from the writing of Paul to the Roman church:

> Romans 3:10: As it is written: "There is no one righteous, no not one."

The Bible has provided insight into humankind's behavior for over 3,000 years. No one is righteous and can make righteous decisions. We have all fallen short of the glory of God (Romans 3:23) and thus need a Savior. So, knowing that we are not righteous, what are the biases that influence our decisions when it comes to the way we manage and handle the resources God has bestowed on us? As previously mentioned, we will cover just a few of the most common biases people tend to use in their decision making. Daniel Kahnmann, Richard Thaler, and others have been instrumental in behavioral finance research, particularly with their work on how certain biases determine how people make decisions.

Mental accounting is the tendency to mentally categorize our money into different conscious compartments based on certain criteria, mainly the origin of the funds (salary versus bonus) and purpose of funds (vacation or lunch money). Unfortunately, these mental decisions can subject people to making poor/irrational decisions. Let me give you an example. As you are getting ready to leave work, your boss gives you a check for $500 as a spontaneous bonus. Research suggests (Thaler, 1999) that you are more likely to spend this money than save it. Additionally, if that money was added incrementally over time to a person's regular paycheck, research again suggests that the person would spend that $500 quite differently.

Overconfidence is the incorrect belief that we are above the averages. Let me give you an example by asking this simple question, "Are you a safe driver?" Most people would say that they are! Yet, only half of the population can be above the average. When it comes to managing our resources/investments, do we think we can do better than the average person? The average financial professional? One example that you may be able to relate to personally is that of the amount of time you spent studying for a course and the ultimate final grade you received. If you took a course and didn't study the course material and barely went to class AND received an A, you are probably inclined to repeat that behavior due to an exaggerated self-perception of your own abilities. If you have tendencies to be overconfident in your thinking, seek God's counsel toward humility. The book of Proverbs provides many wise verses relating back to being humble and meek. See the end-of-chapter Scripture verses for reference.

We have already talked about risk and the idea that some people are generally risk averse. Taking this concept further, many people are prone to be influenced by the concept of loss aversion. **Loss aversion** implies that people are more heavily influenced by a loss than by a win. Some research suggests that we feel pain that is 2.5 times stronger when we experience a loss as compared with a gain/win. This "feeling" can thus hinder us from making choices because we "know" that if we suffer a loss, it will be worse than the feeling of being right and experiencing a gain. Think about this scenario: You have a pinwheel that you can spin, with two possible outcomes, a red option where you have to pay and a green option where you get paid. Both outcomes are equally likely; in other words, the odds are 50/50. If the penalty for landing on the red outcome requires that you pay $10, what would you feel you would need for the green outcome to be in dollars for you to play? Most would say they that it would need to be more than $10. This type of situation helps explain the fact that many people experience loss as more painful than winning or gaining.

Another behavioral finance bias is that of anchoring. **Anchoring** is the idea that we get "stuck" on an idea (in finance, it is typically a number) that we use in our decision even though that number may be completely irrelevant. One of the most common anchors in the financial/investment field is that of the average percentage return of the stock market. Some have heard 8%, and some may have heard 12%. Whichever you have heard will typically become the baseline from which you make investment decisions and, more importantly, the way in which you respond to outcomes as they relate to these anchors. According to S&P Dow Jones, the Dow Jones Industrial Average returned 7.26% in 2012 (yearend 2011 value of 12,217.56 and year end 2012 value of 13,104.14). If you had been anchored by the annual rate of return of 12%, you might have walked away very disappointed.

Sunk Cost Dilemma. Most all of us have held onto our pride or felt that more effort or added resources would make an outcome better. In other words, we continue to sink money or time into something that we know is not progressing as we would like and hope that things will change. **Sunk costs** are time, money, or resources that have already been used and cannot be recaptured. Unfortunately, for many people, this idea that time/money/resources have already been spent keeps them from moving away from a project or idea in the hopes that they can ultimately recover the initial investment or at least get back to break even. One example of a sunk cost that may be familiar to many students is the idea of staying with a current major even though you have realized it is not something you want to do or feel called by the Holy Spirit to do any longer. When you take into consideration the time spent on previous coursework or the cost affiliated with courses already taken, you are relying on sunk costs in making the decision.

Confirmation Bias. In the previous chapter, we talked about how to set goals and then make decisions to reach those goals. Careful consideration needs to be evaluated in our research around those decisions. **Confirmation bias** claims that we will not use our research and understanding to make a decision or choice, but rather make a choice and then find the research/data to confirm our decision. I'm sure we have all made a decision to buy a certain item and then used research and evaluations to support our decision, rather than determining all of the factors needed to make the decision prior to making up our minds. For most of us, we confirm our decisions with supporting research.

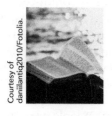

DISCIPLESHIP MOMENT AND REFLECTION

This idea of confirmation bias is one of the main reasons why you should consider seeking professional objective advice from a financial advisor with a biblical worldview. As confirmation bias outlines, we can almost always confirm our decisions with supporting research. Take a moment and think about asking your accountability partner or prayer partner to be a sounding board in addition to your spouse, if married, when making purchasing decisions.

Framing effect or framing bias The influence created based on the way or context in which information was presented.

Framing Effect. The way information is presented usually influences the way we think about certain things. The **framing effect/bias** is the influence created based on the way or context in which information is presented, normally as it relates to decisions or choices. Think of the ways in which many of the disciples viewed Christ in His ministry. The frame in this case is what we think of when we think of a king. Characteristics of great power, influence, prestige, and so forth all frame this idea of what a king looks like. The framing effect/bias is what kept many Jews from believing that Christ was the messiah prophesized by Isaiah and others throughout the Old Testament. Another, more tangible example might be how some people use dollars and percentages based on the manner in which one or the other "looks" better. If you had $5,000 dollars invested in the stock market and 6 months later your portfolio value was $4,500, you would likely receive a call from your financial advisor letting you know that your portfolio was down, and most likely your advisor would frame this information in a way similar to the following:

> John, its Michael, from Biblical Financial Concepts. I was calling to give you an update on your portfolio. Although there have been some struggles in the market lately, you are only down 10% compared to the market averages, which are down about 13%. Looks like we are still beating the market.

This previous conversation sounds better than the following:

> John, its Michael from Biblical Financial Concepts. I was calling to give you an update on your portfolio. Although there have been some struggles in the market lately, you are down $500 from when you first began investing with me.

As one can see, it comes off better to provide a smaller percentage loss than a larger dollar figure loss even though they are the same. It's all in the way it is framed. So much of our financial decisions come from managing our psychological tendencies as opposed to seeing the most efficient or effective, rational choice. By understanding a few of the most common types of behavioral and psychological factors in decision making, we can begin to see when these tendencies are likely to invade our thinking and perhaps we can be mindful to not allow them to cloud our judgements.

SUMMARY

Three main components necessary for us to understand our risks and behaviors were reviewed throughout this chapter. Risk was the first component, and the discussion of risk helped us to see the components that create an opportunity for loss or hazard. An understanding of these risks lead us to an understanding of certain fears, which we described as our fear of failure or a fear of the future. Finally, the risks we perceive and the fears we feel lead us to behave in certain ways as sinful/fallen beings. We can either assume these risks or in some cases we can transfer this risk to others, such as an insurance company. As we evaluate our risks, we then look at how those risks steer us into fears that can influence our decisions. Mark 4:40 provides a snippet of Jesus's response to fear: "He said to his disciples, 'Why are you so afraid? Do you still have no faith?'" Recall that the disciples and Jesus were in the boat when a storm came, and the boat was beginning to take on water from the waves. We are to hold fast to our faith and not be afraid of the things of this world. Because our world involves risk and we all carry with us a certain amount of fear and anxiety, we tend to use risk and fear to make decisions, and ultimately reveal our behaviors and reveal our biases. Many of our behaviors and biases influence our financial decisions, such as how we use mental accounting or confirmation bias to support our actions, and lead us into making decisions based on something other than objective facts and criteria.

SUMMARY REVIEW QUESTIONS

1. Define and describe four different types of risks outlined in the chapter.

2. What are four different myths related to the fear of inflation?

3. How does inflation impact one's retirement planning?

4. Why would individuals experience different inflation rates?

5. What are ways that you can avoid, or at least minimize, identity risk?

6. Explain, through an example in the chapter or a personal example, how fear of the unknown has influenced a decision of yours.

7. What are the two steps in pinpointing your fear?

8. For many people, what are two common types of fear?

9. How do the following Bible verses deal with fear?
    a. Genesis 41
    b. Judges 6 and 7
    c. Acts 16:16–40

10. Why does behavioral finance matter?

11. Explain three of the behavioral biases discussed in the chapter.

Case Study Analysis

After Bob's frustrating set of events, Debbie decided to go ahead and schedule their next meeting with Steve, but she had an agenda of her own. After watching Bob and her struggle with the decision of what to do with the inheritance, she realized how important emotions are in dealing with money. When she set the appointment, she told Steve about the situation that occurred regarding the night of chaos. Steve was all too prepared to help them understand their behaviors toward money because that was his next assignment for them.

Steve provided Debbie a link to a behavioral finance assessment that he wanted both of them to complete, independently. Once they completed the assessment, their results were sent back to them and a copy was sent to Steve to have before their meeting.

Take some time to review Bob and Debbie's financial values questionnaire found in the case study section of this book. Compare Bob and Debbie's assessments and answer the following questions.

Financial Values Questionnaire

NOTE: This questionnaire was designed to help you think about your relationship with money. It asks thought-provoking questions about your financial beliefs, values, and goals. After completing the questionnaire, you will receive a detailed wealth psychology profile. Your customized profile explains your personal \"financial values\", and it is a crucial step towards enhancing your total life (and wealth) satisfaction. Furthermore, a financial advisor can better address your needs and desires after reading your report.

Q1. You shouldn't tell others how much money you have.
- ☐ Strongly Disagree
- ☐ Moderately Disagree
- ☐ Neither Agree Nor Disagree
- ☐ Moderately Agree
- ☐ Strongly Agree

Q2. When it comes to my finances, I don't sweat the small stuff.
- ☐ Strongly Disagree
- ☐ Moderately Disagree
- ☐ Neither Agree Nor Disagree
- ☐ Moderately Agree
- ☐ Strongly Agree

Q3. Poor people are undisciplined.
- ☐ Strongly Disagree
- ☐ Moderately Disagree
- ☐ Neither Agree Nor Disagree
- ☐ Moderately Agree
- ☐ Strongly Agree

Q4. Money provides security.
- ☐ Strongly Disagree
- ☐ Moderately Disagree
- ☐ Neither Agree Nor Disagree
- ☐ Moderately Agree
- ☐ Strongly Agree

Q5. People will want to take advantage of you if they find out you are wealthy.
- ☐ Strongly Disagree
- ☐ Moderately Disagree
- ☐ Neither Agree Nor Disagree
- ☐ Moderately Agree
- ☐ Strongly Agree

Q6. People are essentially honest.
- ☐ Strongly Disagree
- ☐ Moderately Disagree
- ☐ Neither Agree Nor Disagree
- ☐ Moderately Agree
- ☐ Strongly Agree

Q7. The smarter you are, the more money you will make.
- ☐ Strongly Disagree
- ☐ Moderately Disagree
- ☐ Neither Agree Nor Disagree
- ☐ Moderately Agree
- ☐ Strongly Agree

Q8. It's important to diligently keep track of all income and expenditures.
- ☐ Strongly Disagree
- ☐ Moderately Disagree
- ☐ Neither Agree Nor Disagree
- ☐ Moderately Agree
- ☐ Strongly Agree

Q9. If I see a dime on the sidewalk, I'll stop to pick it up.
- ☐ Strongly Disagree
- ☐ Moderately Disagree
- ☐ Neither Agree Nor Disagree
- ☐ Moderately Agree
- ☐ Strongly Agree

Q10. Sometimes I trade stocks for fun.
- ☐ Strongly Disagree
- ☐ Moderately Disagree
- ☐ Neither Agree Nor Disagree
- ☐ Moderately Agree
- ☐ Strongly Agree

Q11. I often worry about how much things cost.
- ☐ Strongly Disagree
- ☐ Moderately Disagree
- ☐ Neither Agree Nor Disagree
- ☐ Moderately Agree
- ☐ Strongly Agree

Q12. I am concerned about others' financial well-being.
- ☐ Strongly Disagree
- ☐ Moderately Disagree
- ☐ Neither Agree Nor Disagree
- ☐ Moderately Agree
- ☐ Strongly Agree

Q13. I am not interested in theoretical discussions about my financial future.
- ☐ Strongly Disagree
- ☐ Moderately Disagree
- ☐ Neither Agree Nor Disagree
- ☐ Moderately Agree
- ☐ Strongly Agree

Q14. I am disciplined with my spending.
- ☐ Strongly Disagree
- ☐ Moderately Disagree
- ☐ Neither Agree Nor Disagree
- ☐ Moderately Agree
- ☐ Strongly Agree

Q15. I like to talk to acquaintances about my investments.
- ☐ Strongly Disagree
- ☐ Moderately Disagree
- ☐ Neither Agree Nor Disagree
- ☐ Moderately Agree
- ☐ Strongly Agree

Q16. I am not bothered by fluctuations in the market values of my assets.
- ☐ Strongly Disagree
- ☐ Moderately Disagree
- ☐ Neither Agree Nor Disagree
- ☐ Moderately Agree
- ☐ Strongly Agree

Q17. I believe people are essentially generous.
- ☐ Strongly Disagree
- ☐ Moderately Disagree
- ☐ Neither Agree Nor Disagree
- ☐ Moderately Agree
- ☐ Strongly Agree

Q18. I enjoy thinking about my investments.
- ☐ Strongly Disagree
- ☐ Moderately Disagree
- ☐ Neither Agree Nor Disagree
- ☐ Moderately Agree
- ☐ Strongly Agree

Q19. I understand just enough about my finances to get by.
- ☐ Strongly Disagree
- ☐ Moderately Disagree
- ☐ Neither Agree Nor Disagree
- ☐ Moderately Agree
- ☐ Strongly Agree

Q20. I enjoy owning big-name stocks.
- ☐ Strongly Disagree
- ☐ Moderately Disagree
- ☐ Neither Agree Nor Disagree
- ☐ Moderately Agree
- ☐ Strongly Agree

Q21. I am relaxed about investing even when the markets are down.
- ☐ Strongly Disagree
- ☐ Moderately Disagree
- ☐ Neither Agree Nor Disagree
- ☐ Moderately Agree
- ☐ Strongly Agree

Q22. I get back at people who rip me off.
☐ Strongly Disagree
☐ Moderately Disagree
☐ Neither Agree Nor Disagree
☐ Moderately Agree
☐ Strongly Agree

Q23. I have difficulty understanding abstract financial concepts.
☐ Strongly Disagree
☐ Moderately Disagree
☐ Neither Agree Nor Disagree
☐ Moderately Agree
☐ Strongly Agree

Q24. I invest my money according to a plan—for example, in fixed percentages of different assets.
☐ Strongly Disagree
☐ Moderately Disagree
☐ Neither Agree Nor Disagree
☐ Moderately Agree
☐ Strongly Agree

Q25. I avoid following the crowd in my investing.
☐ Strongly Disagree
☐ Moderately Disagree
☐ Neither Agree Nor Disagree
☐ Moderately Agree
☐ Strongly Agree

Q26. I never read the business section of the newspaper.
☐ Strongly Disagree
☐ Moderately Disagree
☐ Neither Agree Nor Disagree
☐ Moderately Agree
☐ Strongly Agree

Q27. I try to keep track of economic trends.
☐ Strongly Disagree
☐ Moderately Disagree
☐ Neither Agree Nor Disagree
☐ Moderately Agree
☐ Strongly Agree

Q28. I accurately plan my expenses.
☐ Strongly Disagree
☐ Moderately Disagree
☐ Neither Agree Nor Disagree
☐ Moderately Agree
☐ Strongly Agree

Q29. I like to prepare for the future.
☐ Strongly Disagree
☐ Moderately Disagree

☐ Neither Agree Nor Disagree
☐ Moderately Agree
☐ Strongly Agree

Q30. I feel very excited by the possibility of large investment gains.
☐ Strongly Disagree
☐ Moderately Disagree
☐ Neither Agree Nor Disagree
☐ Moderately Agree
☐ Strongly Agree

Q31. I never feel inclined to follow "hot" stock tips.
☐ Strongly Disagree
☐ Moderately Disagree
☐ Neither Agree Nor Disagree
☐ Moderately Agree
☐ Strongly Agree

Q32. If you had to choose, you would prefer to:
☐ Spend more on lifestyle now and have less savings in retirement.
☐ Spend less on lifestyle now and have more savings in retirement.

Q33. Is your answer to the previous question reflective of how you are actually spending and saving?
☐ Yes
☐ No

Q34. Have financial setbacks from the following events significantly affected you or your parents (please check all that apply)?

Me	Parents	Neither	Both	
☐				Great Depression
☐	☐	☐	☐	Unemployment
☐	☐	☐	☐	Business Failure
☐	☐	☐	☐	Bank Failure
☐	☐	☐	☐	Childhood poverty
☐	☐	☐	☐	Emmigration or refugee status
☐	☐	☐	☐	Bear market
☐	☐	☐	☐	Debt Accumulation
☐	☐	☐	☐	War
☐	☐	☐	☐	Crime or fraud
☐	☐	☐	☐	Divorce
☐	☐	☐	☐	Accident, illness or death
☐	☐	☐	☐	Addictions
☐	☐	☐	☐	Natural disaster

Other Or Explaination:

Q35. If you checked items on 34, please briefly explain how those experiences have changed you. How have your financial values been shaped by these setbacks?

Q36. How concerned are you that you will not have enough money at the end of your life?
- ☐ Extremely
- ☐ Very
- ☐ Moderately
- ☐ Mildly
- ☐ Not at all

Q37. In which of the following domains do you have unmet life goals and dreams?
- ☐ Recreation
- ☐ Travel
- ☐ Education
- ☐ Family
- ☐ Spirituality/Religion
- ☐ Financial

Q38. Do you feel that you have sufficient assets to accomplish your goals and realize your dreams?
- ☐ Need or would like additional income
- ☐ Have sufficient assets

Q39. What are your most valued activities during leisure (or retirement) time? Please select up to four.
- ☐ Recreation (athletics and entertainment)
- ☐ Travel
- ☐ Education
- ☐ Hobbies
- ☐ Community service
- ☐ Continued working
- ☐ Managing my assets
- ☐ Family
- ☐ Religious service
- ☐ To do nothing

Q40. After you retire, what are likely to be your financial priorities? (Please rank from 1 to 3, where 1= most important).
- ☐ Legacy—Charitable giving to foundations, schools, religious bodies, or institutes.
- ☐ Lifestyle—Spending on homes, recreation, travel, education, memberships, healthcare, and luxuries.
- ☐ Thrift—Ensuring I have enough to last until the end of my life.

Q41. What traditions and values in your family or community are important and should be carried on?

Q42. How would you like to be remembered by later generations?

Q43. Do you believe that the amount of money you have impacts your level of happiness? If so, in what ways?

Instructions

Take some time to compare Bob and Debbie's behavioral finance assessments, and answer the following questions:

1. Bob and Debbie differ in many categories of the behavioral assessment. Describe the areas in which they differ.

2. Using information from the chapter, assess how Bob and Debbie differ in their risk tolerance. Provide some examples from what you know of Bob and Debbie to support this assessment.

3. Based on the behavioral finance assessment, what fears do you think Bob deals with? Debbie?

4. Explain how the following behavioral finance biases are at play with Bob and Debbie's dilemma of what to do with the $40,000 inheritance:
   a. Overconfidence
   b. Mental accounting
   c. Anchoring
   d. Loss aversion
   e. Confirmation bias
   f. Framing effect/bias

DEFINITIONS

Anchoring   (p. 133)

Behavioral finance   (p. 132)

Confirmation bias   (p. 133)

Consumer Price Index (CPI)   (p. 116)

Currency risk   (p. 120)

Diversification   (p. 114)

Enough   (p. 118)

Fear of failure   (p. 129)

Fear of the future   (p. 129)

Framing effect or framing bias   (p. 134)

Globalization   (p. 120)

Identity risk (also known as identity theft)   (p. 123)

Identity theft   (p. 123)

Inflation   (p. 115)

Investment risk   (p. 114)

Longevity risk   (p. 120)

Loss aversion   (p. 133)

Margin   (p. 119)

Mental accounting   (p. 132)

Overconfidence   (p. 132)

Political risk   (p. 120)

Real interest rate   (p. 118)

Risk   (p. 114)

Sunk costs   (p. 133)

SCRIPTURE VERSES (ESV)

Ecclesiastes 11:2—Give a portion to seven, or even to eight, for you know not what disaster may happen on earth.

Haggai 1:6—You have sown much, and harvested little. You eat, but you never have enough; you drink, but you never have your fill. You clothe yourselves, but no one is warm. And he who earns wages does so to put them into a bag with holes."

Philippians 4:19—And my God will supply every need of yours according to his riches in glory in Christ Jesus."

Philippians 4:6–7—Do not be anxious about anything, but in everything by prayer and supplication with thanksgiving let your requests be made known to God. And the peace of God, which surpasses all understanding, will guard your hearts and your minds in Christ Jesus."

1 Thessalonians 5:18—Give thanks in all circumstances; for this is God's will for you in Christ Jesus.

2 Corinthians 3:5—Give thanks in all circumstances; for this is the will of God in Christ Jesus for you. Not that we are sufficient in ourselves to claim anything as coming from us, but our sufficiency is from God.

Luke 14:28—For which of you, desiring to build a tower, does not first sit down and count the cost, whether he has enough to complete it?

James 4:14—Yet you do not know what tomorrow will bring. What is your life? For you are a mist that appears for a little time and then vanishes."

2 Peter 3:8—But do not overlook this one fact, beloved, that with the Lord one day is as a thousand years, and a thousand years as one day."

Romans 3:10—As it is written: "None is righteous, no, not one."

Romans 3:23—For all have sinned and fall short of the glory of God.

Acts 16:16-40—As we were going to the place of prayer, we were met by a slave girl who had a spirit of divination and brought her owners much gain by fortune-telling. She followed Paul and us, crying out, "These men are servants of the Most High God, who proclaim to you the way of salvation." And this she kept doing for many days. Paul, having become greatly annoyed, turned and said to the spirit, "I command you in the name of Jesus Christ to come out of her." And it came out that very hour.

But when her owners saw that their hope of gain was gone, they seized Paul and Silas and dragged them into the marketplace before the rulers. And when they had brought them to the magistrates, they said, "These men are Jews, and they are disturbing our city. They advocate customs that are not lawful for us as Romans to accept or practice." The crowd joined in attacking them, and the magistrates tore the garments off them and gave orders to beat them with rods. And when they had inflicted many blows upon them, they threw them into prison, ordering the jailer to keep them safely. Having received this order, he put them into the inner prison and fastened their feet in the stocks.

About midnight Paul and Silas were praying and singing hymns to God, and the prisoners were listening to them, and suddenly there was a great earthquake, so that the foundations of the prison were shaken. And immediately all the doors were opened, and everyone's bonds were unfastened. When the jailer woke and saw that the prison doors were open, he drew his sword and was about to kill himself, supposing that the prisoners had escaped. But Paul cried with a loud voice, "Do not harm yourself, for we are all here." And the jailer called for lights and rushed in, and trembling with fear he fell down before Paul and Silas. Then he brought them out and said, "Sirs, what must I do to be saved?" And they said, "Believe in the Lord Jesus, and you will be saved, you and your household." And they spoke the word of the Lord to him and to all who were in his house. And he took them the same hour of the night and washed their wounds; and he was baptized at once, he and all his family. Then he brought them up into his house and set food before them. And he rejoiced along with his entire household that he had believed in God.

But when it was day, the magistrates sent the police, saying, "Let those men go." And the jailer reported these words to Paul, saying, "The magistrates have sent to let you go. Therefore come out now and go in peace." But Paul said to them, "They have beaten us publicly, uncondemned, men who are Roman citizens, and have thrown us into prison; and do they now throw us out secretly? No! Let them come themselves and take us out." The police reported these words to the magistrates, and they were afraid when they heard that they were Roman citizens. So they came and apologized to them. And they took them out and asked them to leave the city. So they went out of the prison and visited Lydia. And when they had seen the brothers, they encouraged them and departed."

Judges 6—"The people of Israel did what was evil in the sight of the LORD, and the LORD gave them into the hand of Midian seven years. And the hand of Midian overpowered Israel, and because of Midian the people of Israel made for themselves the dens that are in the mountains and the caves and the strongholds. For whenever the Israelites planted crops, the Midianites and the Amalekites and the people of the East would come up against them. They would encamp against them and devour the produce of the land, as far as Gaza, and leave no sustenance in Israel and no sheep or ox or donkey. For they would come up with their livestock and their tents; they would come like locusts in number—both they and their camels could not be counted—so that they laid waste the land as they came in. And Israel was brought very low because of Midian. And the people of Israel cried out for help to the LORD.

When the people of Israel cried out to the LORD on account of the Midianites, the LORD sent a prophet to the people of Israel. And he said to them, "Thus says the LORD, the God of Israel: I led you up from Egypt and brought you out of the house of slavery. And I delivered you from the hand of the Egyptians and from the hand of all who oppressed you, and drove them out before you and gave you their land. And I said to you, 'I am the LORD your God; you shall not fear the gods of the Amorites in whose land you dwell.' But you have not obeyed my voice."

Now the angel of the LORD came and sat under the terebinth at Ophrah, which belonged to Joash the Abiezrite, while his son Gideon was beating out wheat in the winepress to hide it from the Midianites. And the angel of the LORD appeared to him and said to him, "The LORD is with you, O mighty man of valor." And Gideon said to him, "Please, sir, if the LORD is with us, why then has all this happened to us? And where are all his wonderful deeds that our fathers recounted to us, saying, 'Did not the LORD bring us up from Egypt?' But now the LORD has forsaken us and given us into the hand of Midian." And the LORD turned to him and said, "Go in this might of yours and save Israel from the hand of Midian; do not I send you?" And he said to him, "Please, Lord, how can I save Israel? Behold, my clan is the weakest in Manasseh, and I am the least in my father's house." And the LORD said to him, "But I will be with you, and you shall strike the Midianites as one man." And he said to him, "If now I have found favor in your eyes, then show me a sign that it is you who speak with me. Please do not depart from here until I come to you and bring out my present and set it before you." And he said, "I will stay till you return."

So Gideon went into his house and prepared a young goat and unleavened cakes from an ephah of flour. The meat he put in a basket, and the broth he put in a pot, and brought them to him under the terebinth and presented them. And the angel of God said to him, "Take the meat and the unleavened cakes, and put them on this rock, and pour the broth over them." And he did so. Then the angel of the LORD reached out the tip of the staff that was in his hand and touched the meat and the unleavened cakes. And fire sprang up from the rock and consumed the meat and the unleavened cakes. And the angel of the LORD vanished from his sight. Then Gideon perceived that he was the angel of the LORD. And Gideon said, "Alas, O Lord GOD! For now I have seen the angel of the LORD face to face." But the LORD said to him, "Peace be to you. Do not fear; you shall not die." Then Gideon built an altar there to the LORD and called it, The LORD Is Peace. To this day it still stands at Ophrah, which belongs to the Abiezrites.

That night the LORD said to him, "Take your father's bull, and the second bull seven years old, and pull down the altar of Baal that your father has, and cut down the Asherah that is beside it and build an altar to the LORD your God on the top of the stronghold here, with stones laid in due order. Then take the second bull and offer it as a burnt offering with the wood of the Asherah that you shall cut down." So Gideon took ten men of his servants and did as the LORD had told him. But because he was too afraid of his family and the men of the town to do it by day, he did it by night.

When the men of the town rose early in the morning, behold, the altar of Baal was broken down, and the Asherah beside it was cut down, and the second bull was offered on the altar that had been built. And they said to one another, "Who has done this thing?" And after they had searched and inquired, they said, "Gideon the son of Joash has done this thing." Then the men of the town said to Joash, "Bring out your son, that he may die, for he has broken down the altar of Baal and cut down the Asherah beside it." But Joash said to all who stood against him, "Will you contend for Baal? Or will you save him? Whoever contends for him shall be put to death by morning. If he is a god, let him contend for himself, because his altar has been broken down." Therefore on that day Gideon was called Jerubbaal, that is to say, "Let Baal contend against him," because he broke down his altar.

Now all the Midianites and the Amalekites and the people of the East came together, and they crossed the Jordan and encamped in the Valley of Jezreel. But the Spirit of the LORD clothed Gideon, and he sounded the trumpet, and the Abiezrites were called out to follow him. And he sent messengers throughout all Manasseh, and they too were called out to follow him. And he sent messengers to Asher, Zebulun, and Naphtali, and they went up to meet them.

Then Gideon said to God, "If you will save Israel by my hand, as you have said, behold, I am laying a fleece of wool on the threshing floor. If there is dew on the fleece alone, and it is dry on all the ground, then I shall know that you will save Israel by my hand, as you have said." And it was so. When he rose early next morning and squeezed the fleece, he wrung enough dew from the fleece to fill a bowl with water. Then Gideon said to God, "Let not your anger burn against me; let me speak just once more. Please let me test just once more with the fleece. Please let it be dry on the fleece only, and on all the ground let there be dew." And God did so that night; and it was dry on the fleece only, and on all the ground there was dew.

Judges 7—Then Jerubbaal (that is, Gideon) and all the people who were with him rose early and encamped beside the spring of Harod. And the camp of Midian was north of them, by the hill of Moreh, in the valley.

The LORD said to Gideon, "The people with you are too many for me to give the Midianites into their hand,
lest Israel boast over me, saying, 'My own hand has saved me.' Now therefore proclaim in the ears of the people, saying, 'Whoever is fearful and trembling, let him return home and hurry away from Mount Gilead'." Then 22,000 of the people returned, and 10,000 remained.

And the LORD said to Gideon, "The people are still too many. Take them down to the water, and I will test them for you there, and anyone of whom I say to you, 'This one shall go with you,' shall go with you, and anyone of whom I say to you, 'This one shall not go with you', shall not go." So he brought the people down to the water. And the LORD said to Gideon, "Every one who laps the water with his tongue, as a dog laps, you shall set by himself. Likewise, every one who kneels down to drink." And the number of those who lapped, putting their hands to their mouths, was 300 men, but all the rest of the people knelt down to drink water. And the LORD said to Gideon, "With the 300 men who lapped I will save you and give the Midianites into your hand, and let all the others go every man to his home." So the people took provisions in their hands, and their trumpets. And he sent all the rest of Israel every man to his tent, but retained the 300 men. And the camp of Midian was below him in the valley.

That same night the LORD said to him, "Arise, go down against the camp, for I have given it into your hand. But if you are afraid to go down, go down to the camp with Purah your servant. And you shall hear what they say, and afterward your hands shall be strengthened to go down against the camp." Then he went down with Purah his servant to the outposts of the armed men who were in the camp. And the Midianites and the Amalekites and all the people of the East lay along the valley like locusts in abundance, and their camels were without number, as the sand that is on the seashore in abundance. When Gideon came, behold, a man was telling a dream to his comrade. And he said, "Behold, I dreamed a dream, and behold, a cake of barley bread tumbled into the camp of Midian and came to the tent and struck it so that it fell and turned it upside down, so that the tent lay flat." And his comrade answered, "This is no other than the sword of Gideon the son of Joash, a man of Israel; God has given into his hand Midian and all the camp."

As soon as Gideon heard the telling of the dream and its interpretation, he worshiped. And he returned to the camp of Israel and said, "Arise, for the LORD has given the host of Midian into your hand." And he divided the 300 men into three companies and put trumpets into the hands of all of them and empty jars, with torches inside the jars. And he said to them, "Look at me, and do likewise. When I come to the outskirts of the camp, do as I do. When I blow the trumpet, I and all who are with me, then blow the trumpets also on every side of all the camp and shout, 'For the LORD and for Gideon.'"

So Gideon and the hundred men who were with him came to the outskirts of the camp at the beginning of the middle watch, when they had just set the watch. And they blew the trumpets and smashed the jars that were in their hands. Then the three companies blew the trumpets and broke the jars. They held in their left hands the torches, and in their right hands the trumpets to blow. And they cried out, "A sword for the LORD and for Gideon!" Every man stood in his place around the camp, and all the army ran. They cried out and fled. When they blew the 300 trumpets, the LORD set every man's sword against his comrade and against all the army. And the army fled as far as Beth-shittah toward Zererah, as far as the border of Abel-meholah, by Tabbath. And the men of Israel were called out from Naphtali and from Asher and from all Manasseh, and they pursued after Midian.

Gideon sent messengers throughout all the hill country of Ephraim, saying, "Come down against the Midianites and capture the waters against them, as far as Beth-barah, and also the Jordan." So all the men of Ephraim were called out, and they captured the waters as far as Beth-barah, and also the Jordan. And they captured the two princes of Midian, Oreb and Zeeb. They killed Oreb at the rock of Oreb, and Zeeb they killed at the winepress of Zeeb. Then they pursued Midian, and they brought the heads of Oreb and Zeeb to Gideon across the Jordan.

Genesis 41—After two whole years, Pharaoh dreamed that he was standing by the Nile, and behold, there came up out of the Nile seven cows attractive and plump, and they fed in the reed grass. And behold, seven other cows, ugly and thin, came up out of the Nile after them, and stood by the other cows on the bank of the Nile. And the ugly, thin cows ate up the seven attractive, plump cows. And Pharaoh awoke. And he fell asleep and dreamed a second time. And behold, seven ears of grain, plump and good, were growing on one stalk. And behold, after them sprouted seven ears, thin and blighted by the east wind. And the thin ears swallowed up the seven plump, full ears. And Pharaoh awoke, and behold, it was a dream. So in the morning his spirit was troubled, and he sent and called for all the magicians of Egypt and all its wise men. Pharaoh told them his dreams, but there was none who could interpret them to Pharaoh.

Then the chief cupbearer said to Pharaoh, "I remember my offenses today. When Pharaoh was angry with his servants and put me and the chief baker in custody in the house of the captain of the guard, we dreamed on the same night, he and I, each having a dream with its own interpretation. A young Hebrew was there with us, a servant of the captain of the guard. When we told him, he interpreted our dreams to us, giving an interpretation to each man according to his dream. And as he interpreted to us, so it came about. I was restored to my office, and the baker was hanged."

Then Pharaoh sent and called Joseph, and they quickly brought him out of the pit. And when he had shaved himself and changed his clothes, he came in before Pharaoh. And Pharaoh said to Joseph, "I have had a dream, and there is no one who can interpret it. I have heard it said of you that when you hear a dream you can interpret it." Joseph answered Pharaoh, "It is not in me; God will give Pharaoh a favorable answer." Then Pharaoh said to Joseph, "Behold, in my dream I was standing on the banks of the Nile. Seven cows, plump and attractive, came up out of the Nile and fed in the reed grass. Seven other cows came up after them, poor and very ugly and thin, such as I had never seen in all the land of Egypt. And the thin, ugly cows ate up the first seven plump cows, but when they had eaten them no one would have known that they had eaten them, for they were still as ugly as at the beginning. Then I awoke. I also saw in my dream seven ears growing on one stalk, full and good. Seven ears, withered, thin, and blighted by the east wind, sprouted after them, and the thin ears swallowed up the seven good ears. And I told it to the magicians, but there was no one who could explain it to me."

Then Joseph said to Pharaoh, "The dreams of Pharaoh are one; God has revealed to Pharaoh what he is about to do. The seven good cows are seven years, and the seven good ears are seven years; the dreams are one. The seven lean and ugly cows that came up after them are seven years, and the seven empty ears blighted by the east wind are also seven years of famine. It is as I told Pharaoh; God has shown to Pharaoh what he is about to do. There will come seven years of great plenty throughout all the land of Egypt, but after them there will arise seven years of famine, and all the plenty will be forgotten in the land of Egypt. The famine will consume the land, and the plenty will be unknown in the land by reason of the famine that will follow, for it will be very severe. And the doubling of Pharaoh's dream means that the thing is fixed by God, and God will shortly bring it about. Now therefore let Pharaoh select a discerning and wise man, and set him over the land of Egypt. Let Pharaoh proceed to appoint overseers over the land and take one-fifth of the produce of the land of Egypt during the seven plentiful years. And let them gather all the food of these good years that are coming and store up grain under the authority of Pharaoh for food in the cities, and let them keep it. That food shall be a reserve for the land against the seven years of famine that are to occur in the land of Egypt, so that the land may not perish through the famine."

This proposal pleased Pharaoh and all his servants. And Pharaoh said to his servants, "Can we find a man like this, in whom is the Spirit of God?" Then Pharaoh said to Joseph, "Since God has shown you all this, there is none so discerning and wise as you are. You shall be over my house, and all my people shall order themselves as you command. Only as regards the throne will I be greater than you." And Pharaoh said to Joseph, "See, I have set you over all the land of Egypt." Then Pharaoh took his signet ring from his hand and put it on Joseph's hand, and clothed him in garments of fine linen and put a gold chain about his neck. And he made him ride in his second chariot. And they called out before him, "Bow the knee!" Thus he set him over all the land of Egypt. Moreover, Pharaoh said to Joseph, "I am Pharaoh, and without your consent no one shall lift up hand or foot in all the land of Egypt." And Pharaoh called Joseph's name Zaphenath-paneah. And he gave him in marriage Asenath, the daughter of Potiphera priest of On. So Joseph went out over the land of Egypt.

Joseph was thirty years old when he entered the service of Pharaoh king of Egypt. And Joseph went out from the presence of Pharaoh and went through all the land of Egypt. During the seven plentiful years the earth produced abundantly, and he gathered up all the food of these seven years, which occurred in the land of Egypt, and put the food in the cities. He put in every city the food from the fields around it. And Joseph stored up grain in great abundance, like the sand of the sea, until he ceased to measure it, for it could not be measured.

Before the year of famine came, two sons were born to Joseph. Asenath, the daughter of Potiphera priest of On, bore them to him. Joseph called the name of the firstborn Manasseh. "For," he said, "God has made me forget all my hardship and all my father's house." The name of the second he called Ephraim, "For God has made me fruitful in the land of my affliction." The seven years of plenty that occurred in the land of Egypt came to an end, and the seven years of famine began to come, as Joseph had said. There was famine in all lands, but in all the land of Egypt there was bread. When all the land of Egypt was famished, the people cried to Pharaoh for bread. Pharaoh said to all the Egyptians, "Go to Joseph. What he says to you, do."

So when the famine had spread over all the land, Joseph opened all the storehouses and sold to the Egyptians, for the famine was severe in the land of Egypt. Moreover, all the earth came to Egypt to Joseph to buy grain, because the famine was severe over all the earth.

ADDITIONAL READINGS

Malevergne, Y., & Sornette, D. (2006). *Extreme financial risks: From dependence to risk management*. New York, NY: Springer Science & Business Media.

Morley, P. (2009). *How to survive the economic meltdown: Practical and spiritual strategies for you and your friends*. Casselberry, FL: Man in the Mirror Books.

Pompian, M. M. (2006). *Behavioral finance and wealth management: How to build optimal portfolios that account for investor biases*. Hoboken, NJ: Wiley.

Tuma, J. (2011). *From boom to bust and beyond: The hidden forces driving our economy—what you need to know to survive and succeed*. Lake Mary, FL: Charisma Media.

REFERENCES

Burkett, L. (1991). *The coming economic earthquake*. Chicago, IL: Moody Press.

Conerly, B. (2013). Future of the dollar as world reserve currency. *Forbes*. Retrieved from http://www.forbes.com/sites/billconerly/2013/10/25/future-of-the-dollar-as-world-reserve-currency/

Israelsen, C. (2010). *7twelve: A diversified investment portfolio with a plan*. Hoboken, NJ: Wiley.

Katz, R. (2009). *The Solomon portfolio: How to invest like a king*. Sanford, FL: DC Press.

Lindsey, H., & Carlson, C. C. (1972). *The late great planet earth*. Grand Rapids, MI: Zondervan.

Thaler, R. H. (1999). Mental accounting matters. *Journal of Behavioral Decision Making*, 12(3), 183–206.

Courtesy of duncanandison/Fotolia.

Chapter 7

Family Life Stages

BIG IDEA:
Understanding where you are in the financial life cycle may encourage you—you are not alone.

LEARNING OUTCOMES

- Define the family life cycle and describe the six stages within this cycle
- Define the financial life cycle and describe the three phases within this cycle
- Define the income life cycle and describe the three theories

This chapter focuses on learning and understanding the various stages of the family and financial life cycles. Understanding these life cycles can help guide your expectations of goal setting without feeling a sense of having to plan all things at once. We will cover three main types of life cycles: (1) the family life cycle, (2) the financial life cycle, and (3) the income life cycle. All three of these are interconnected; however, because of the uniqueness of every person's life situation, it is important to understand them separately. The second half of this chapter begins to tie all three together.

For everything there is a season, and a time for every matter under heaven: a time to be born, and a time to die; a time to plant, and a time to pluck up what is planted; a time to kill, and a time to heal; a time to break down, and a time to build up; a time to weep, and a time to laugh; a time to mourn, and a time to dance; a time to cast away stones, and a time to gather stones together; a time to embrace, and a time to refrain from embracing; a time to seek, and a time to lose; a time to keep, and a time to cast away; a time to tear, and a time to sew; a time to keep silence, and a time to speak; a time to love, and a time to hate; a time for war, and a time for peace. **(Ecclesiastes 3)**

Ron's Corner

A strange aspect of our inquisitive human nature is that we want to know how we are doing compared to others. Understanding where you are in the typical life cycles may help encourage you—you're not alone. It can also help you to concentrate on the financial planning areas not critical to you now.

First, understanding that family life cycles, financial life cycles, and income cycles exist will help you focus on the important areas of financial planning; second, it should ease your frustration at trying to accomplish goals. The truth is that none of us have unlimited resources. So, we are always faced with financial challenges and decisions, and unless we can realistically look at them, we will certainly experience frustration.

FAMILY LIFE CYCLE

Family life cycle
A concept that attempts to describe the effects of time on a family through marriage and child rearing, specifically in relation to income and expenses.

Much of the development around the **family life cycle**, a concept that attempts to describe the effects of time on a family through marriage, child rearing, retirement, and death, specifically as it relates to income and expenses, was initiated in the early 1900s by researchers seeking to understand how families functioned over time. Several key components have been established in determining where families fall along this cycle.

Several components are used to define the various life-cycle stages. These components are typically age, marital status, and number of children. These characteristics usually move together through time and thus make for an easy way to classify, in general terms, where people can be grouped together.

It is important to note that these stages start as one reaches the age of adulthood, somewhere around the age of 18 years. The various stages of a family life cycle, described next, are identified by utilizing the various components just noted.

Stage 1: Young Adult (Age 18–24)

Individuals in this group have usually just finished high school and may have entered college, the military, or the workforce. This stage consists of beginning training for a first career and beginning to develop **human capital**, or the skills, training, knowledge, and experiences that an individual can bring to his or her role in the labor force. Some may be seeking to start a family in this stage. For many, this stage represents establishing financial independence from parents or guardians through opening checking accounts, budgeting, saving, and seeking basic risk management products such as life insurance or health insurance. This stage may also be where individuals or couples buy their first home.

Human capital The skills, training, knowledge, and experiences that an individual can bring to his or her role in the labor force.

Stage 2: Adult with or without Children (Age 25–34)

When people reach this next stage, many have gotten married and begun to have children, although that is not always the case. Individuals in this group seem to be in the beginning stages of child rearing and will normally begin to shift their energy from themselves to their young children. Future expenditures such as college savings begin to be thought about more, and "what-if" scenarios abound. Risk management products such as car insurance and home ownership/renters' insurance become more

Courtesy of robyelo357/Fotolia.

ubiquitous. During this stage, many couples begin to establish basic estate planning documents such as wills, trusts, and/or guardianship procedures.

Stage 3: Adult with School-Aged Children (Age 35–44)

This stage tends to see upward job mobility and career training and development (which we usually see after 20 years or so in the workforce). During this stage, there is tendency to focus on funding short-term major expenses such as paying for college, cars for the kids, or even weddings. These usually large expenses tend to create a need for larger income, and thus we see either career changes or upward mobility in one's current profession. Financially, people in this stage tend to allocate more of their margin toward future goals, such as retirement, second homes, and so forth.

Stage 4: Midlife (Age 45–54)

This stage tends to see lots of changes, perhaps more than any other stage. For some, kids are graduating high school and leaving the home to go off to college or join the military. Along with the emotional aspect of children leaving the home, there are potentially large expenses still looming, such as helping with college expenses or weddings. Many individuals and couples in this stage will begin to seek professional financial help as they begin to update or solidify retirement plans and update and create more robust estate planning documents.

Stage 5: Preretirement (Age 55–65)

This stage is usually a person's peak earning years. With large expenses usually behind a couple, this stage allows for a substantial peak in asset accumulation for retirement accounts, liquid savings accounts, or even investing in more speculative investments. Continual evaluation of retirement plans takes place, and many in this stage begin to make decisions about how they will spend their time once they leave the workforce, including saving for health-care costs such as long-term care.

Stage 6: Retirement (Age 65+)

During this stage, individuals and couples will begin to monitor their expenditures closely as their ability to generate additional income begins to diminish. More focus is given to social programs such as Social Security and Medicare and Medicaid. Long-term care becomes a concern, and many in this stage complete final updates to their estate planning documents.

FINANCIAL LIFE CYCLE

Financial life cycle The process individuals go through in relation to their asset accumulation and distribution over their lifetime.

It is not completely obvious, but there are patterns that can be drawn out from the family life-cycle stages to the financial life cycle. The **financial life cycle** is described as the process individuals go through in relation to their asset accumulation and distribution over their lifetime. Academic research has not pinpointed exact names for these phases or exactly how each phase is designed. Some use ages, such as the age at which people begin to retire. Some break up the financial life cycle into two phases, and others use three. We will focus on the financial life cycle as three main and distinct phases.

Phase 1: Self-Preservation (Age 18–24)

Self-preservation is the financial phase where your assets (e.g., checking account) are used to cover your basic needs. This will be for items relative to food, shelter, transportation costs, clothing, and so forth. Basic savings should be initiated in this stage to offset any financial hardships such as a car breaking down or having to replace your computer. This phase will tend to be the shortest phase of the three.

Phase 2: Accumulation (Age 25–60)

The accumulation period of life is the longest time period. It typically stretches from ages in the early to mid-20s to as late as age 55 to 60. During this time period, an individual or couple builds a lifestyle and sees their family grow to the point of their children leaving the proverbial nest. Household income tends to go up fairly rapidly, but unfortunately, in many cases not quite as rapidly as the cost of living does. During this phase, individuals and couples are focused on setting aside and delaying the current use of earned income for future uses such as home projects, large expenses, and retirement. The established lifestyle will be influential in determining how much one needs to accumulate, which was reviewed previously in the discussion of "how much is enough?" in Chapter 4.

The biggest tension in this time period of life is the trade-off between the short term and the long term. The short-term needs and desires of providing a house, furniture, cars, or education take away from the long-term goals of financial independence, getting out of debt, providing for retirement, and even major giving. Every dollar spent to fund short-term needs takes away from the amount of available income to meet long-term goals.

One challenge confronting people during this time period (especially during the later part of the phase) is that they have a much shorter time period within which to meet their long-term goals. Now earning more in the prime of their careers, they try to save more to fund their retirement years. Investments become very important to them, and panic can set in when a couple realizes how short a time they have to meet their longer-term goals. They may be tempted to make riskier investments than appropriate for their risk level to try to make up for a late start in their earlier years.

Phase 3: Distribution (Age 65+)

For most folks, the distribution phase is generally after age 65. Distribution has two separate and distinct aspects: indirect drawdown and proactive giving. Indirect drawdown can be defined as the use of accumulated assets for lifestyle expenditures, such as food, travel, housing, hobbies, and so forth. Proactive giving is the intentional giving of assets to others, which can be heirs or organizations such as the church or nonprofit organizations. In many instances, people never reach the proactive distribution of their assets due to fear of outliving what they have. Rather, the distribution phase becomes simply the drawdown of assets to sustain their lifestyle. The distribution phase of life can occur, of course, at any time because we do not know when death will occur. Because of our increased medical care and a trend toward healthier lifestyles, people are living longer, and the idea of distributing wealth can actually be very challenging to deal with. In addition to longevity, another primary challenge in the distribution phase is to make sure that a surviving spouse is taken care of financially.

Determine what financial life-cycle phase you are in (either self-preservation, accumulation, or distribution) and think about the idea that every dollar spent on short-term needs or wants takes away available income to meet long-term goals. If you are in the self-preservation phase, what can you do to move toward the accumulation phase more quickly? If you are already in the accumulation phase, what changes can you make to allocate more toward your accumulation goal? If you are in the distribution phase, reflect on where God wants you to reallocate His resources. Talk through these decisions with your accountability and prayer partner.

Several factors influence the severity and longevity of each of the foregoing financial life-cycle phases. These factors include when you get married, the number of children you have, where you live (cost of living), occupation, and other lifestyle decisions.

When You Start a Family

Deciding to start a family can drastically change when one enters and leaves each financial life-cycle phase. For example, if you decide to get married in your early 30s, there is a chance that you and your spouse had both been employed for nearly a decade and you could have already saved a substantial amount of money in both liquid savings and retirement savings. Debt may have already been eliminated or perhaps paid down to minimize its impact on a newly married couple's financial plan. There are downsides to a late start, which usually come from establishing new norms for the way you decide to spend money, which now has to be done in collaboration with someone else. Refer back to the section on goal setting and decision making if you need to review.

On the other hand, if you get married really early, say when you are 18 or 19, then it may increase your time in the self-preservation phase. The amount of income earned by the couple may not be adequate to support a family or cover the costs associated with starting a family, such as insurance, medical bills, furniture, increases in food, and so forth.

The Number of Children

The number of children you have will impact your financial life cycle and how long you remain in a particular phase. An article posted by CNN in (Hicken, 2014) suggests that it costs parents roughly $245,000 per child from when they are born to the age of 18. This figure is based on national averages and will only be used as a guide. Using this number, a family with four children will spend roughly $1,000,000 on raising their children. The same-aged couple that does not have children could set this income aside for other expenditures such as retirement savings or keep it as liquid savings. Amazingly, these figures do not include the cost of education. The U.S. Department of Education's National Center for Education Statistics (2015) has reported that the cost to attend "all universities" averaged over $34,000 per year. Should the family with four children desire to pay for four years of college, assuming the national average, they will be required to spend an additional $136,000 per child or $544,000 in total for college costs. As one can see, the number of children a person has will have a tremendous impact on the amount of disposable income that is available. Keep in mind that these numbers are not adjusted for inflation and would probably be higher for private schools. Reprinted from www.money.cnn.com, August 18, 2014, by permission of CNNMoney.

Location (Cost of Living)

Where you live can play a significant role in determining how long you remain in the different phases of your financial life cycle. According to the website Expatistan, (www.expatistan.com), which offers a compilation of data collected by individuals from around the globe to provide insights into the costs of living in certain areas, can help individuals compare various locations on a number of different expense categories. For example, in running a comparison between living in Kansas City, Missouri, and in Orlando Florida, the following information was provided:

- Food costs 5% more in Orlando, Florida.
- Housing costs 8% more in Orlando, Florida.
- Clothing costs 8% more in Orlando, Florida.
- Transportation costs are 2% more in Orlando, Florida.
- Personal care costs are 4% more in Orlando, Florida.
- Entertainment costs are 22% more in Orlando, Florida.

The overall comparison established that Orlando, Florida, cost about 8% more to live in than Kansas City, Missouri. The information used in the comparison consisted of a collection of 4,277 prices entered by 408 different people.

Occupation

Another important factor in determining financial life-cycle phases is your occupation. One's occupation can be influenced by many different factors, including education, life experience, parents' occupations, and other influential factors. But to understand the differences in occupation as it relates to your financial life cycle, let's compare the weekly salary rates of several different positions. Keep in mind that the location (as mentioned previously) will also influence the annual compensation and benefits of these positions, so remember that the following numbers are national averages.

Type of Position*	Weekly Earnings	Annual Earnings (weekly × 52)
Clergy	$958	$49,816
Lawyer	$1,807	$93,964
Kindergarten teacher	$634	$32,968
Media editor	$1,018	$52,936

As a Christian, however, our occupations should not be decided on earning potential. Our faith, led by the Holy Spirit, will guide our career choices. Earning potential can be a part of our decision, but it should not be the driving factor of our choice.

Differentiate God's Calling from Our Occupation

As Christians review occupational salaries and job descriptions, many seek to find "God's calling" in what they do. There exists, however, a difference between the two. Bence (2003) identified three components of God's call:

---

* Data collected from the Bureau of Labor Statistics, "Household Data, Annual Averages—Median Weekly Earnings of Full-Time Wage and Salary Workers by Detailed Occupation and Sex." Retrieved from http://www.bls.gov/cps/cpsaat39.pdf.

1. God calls us to salvation: This call comes from hearing the gospel and responding to the good news of Christ's redeeming work that reconciles us back to the Father.

2. God calls us to holiness: Upon our faith in Christ, we become a new creature, "pressing on toward the mark of the high calling of God in Christ Jesus" (Philippians 4:13).

3. God calls us to service: Most notably, this is evident in the Great Commission found in Matthew 28:16–20, which says we are to go and make disciples by baptizing and teaching new believers. All believers, then, are called to serve one another (1 Peter 4:10; Galatians 5:13).

> Now the eleven disciples went to Galilee, to the mountain to which Jesus had directed them. And when they saw him they worshiped him, but some doubted. And Jesus came and said to them, "All authority in heaven and on earth has been given to me. Go therefore and make disciples of all nations, baptizing them in the name of the Father and of the Son and of the Holy Spirit, teaching them to observe all that I have commanded you. And behold, I am with you always, to the end of the age." (Matthew 28:16–20)

> As each has received a gift, use it to serve one another, as good stewards of God's varied grace. (1 Peter 4:10)

> For you were called to freedom, brothers. Only do not use your freedom as an opportunity for the flesh, but through love serve one another. (Galatians 5:13)

As Bence (2003) also writes:

> Unable to find clear Biblical justification for equating one's occupation with divine calling, I would like to abandon two thousand years of linguistic tradition and suggest that a Christian's vocation has more to do with a discerning and responding to God's *leading* than hearing and obeying God's call. God's call is to trust in his saving work, to pursue Christ-likeness and to reach out in service to others. This call to the Christian life cannot be isolated from one's life work, but ought not to be equated with it. (p. 42)

This quote really helps to separate the two notions of "God's call" and that of our occupation. God has called all believers to these three things, and He leads many to a vocation through reading His word, prayer, and the counsel of other believers.

Courtesy of
daniilantiq2010/Fotolia.

DISCIPLESHIP MOMENT AND REFLECTION

Think through this idea of God's calling versus our vocation. How have you understood the two? Do you need to pray for guidance and counsel regarding your vocation? What do you feel the Holy Spirit is leading you to pursue as a vocation? How does this differ from your call? Pray through these decisions with your accountability and prayer partner.

Other Lifestyle Choices

Your choices about house size, cars, boats, entertainment, vacations, and clothes all affect your lifestyle expenses. Just as a business has "overhead costs," these expenses are your household "overhead" costs. These overhead costs dramatically impact your planning during the financial life-cycle phases. Keep in mind that there are costs not only with the original purchase of these types of items (cars, boats, vacation homes, etc.), but in most cases there are upkeep and maintenance costs that are affiliated with each of these, which will increase the overall costs of ownership.

INCOME LIFE CYCLE—A THEORETICAL PERSPECTIVE

Theory   A system of ideas that, taken together, help explain something.

It is important to have a broad understanding of some theoretical research relating to income and expenditures/consumption over one's life. To start, a **theory** can be defined as a system of ideas that, taken together, help explain something. Hence, theoretical research is that research conducted to explain what, why, or how something occurs. There are three general theories introduced here that offer an explanation as to income and consumption patterns of individuals. The information presented here will be a short synopsis; however, you can refer to the works in the Additional Reading section to explore these theories in more detail.

General Theory of Consumption

J. M. Keynes wrote the book *General Theory of Employment, Interest, and Money* in 1936 (2006 reprint). In this book, Keynes discusses a wide variety of economics (keep in mind that this was written just a few years after the Great Depression) with one of the more relevant topics being the formulation of consumption theory. Keynes suggested that consumption increases as income increases, but only by a fraction of that increase. One of the biggest flaws others found in Keynes's theory of consumption was that it

Figure 7.1

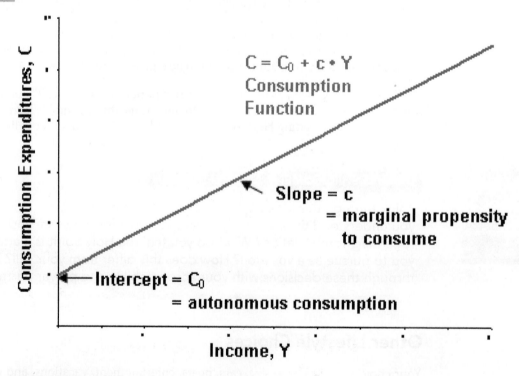

$$C = C_0 + c \cdot Y$$
Consumption Function

Slope = c
= marginal propensity to consume

Intercept = C_0
= autonomous consumption

Consumption Expenditures, C

Income, Y

Retrieved from http://www.lidderdale.com/econ/311/ch5Lect.html

Courtesy of hikrcn/Fotolia.

was only concerned with current income and did not take future income into consideration. In response to this flaw, two additional theories were presented: (1) the permanent income hypothesis by Professor Milton Friedman (1957), and (2) the life-cycle hypothesis by Professors Franco Modigliani and Albert Ando (Ando & Modigliani, 1963).

This graph provides some insight into the general theory of consumption offered by Keynes. The Consumption function line (blue line) intersects with the Y intercept (Income axis) at C_0, which indicates that a certain level of consumption is always required (shelter, food, clothing, etc.). As income increases along the Income axis, you see the level of consumption increasing, but not as fast. The slope of the consumption line is called the *marginal propensity to consume*. In other words, how much of the "extra" income over and above the necessities do you spend? This range will be from zero to one, with zero meaning that none of the extra income is consumed and one meaning that all of the extra income is consumed.

Permanent Income Hypothesis

Milton Friedman took Keynes' general theory of consumption and expanded its reach by taking into consideration the prospect of future income. Friedman's theory posits that people will consume based on their expected long-term average income; in other words, people's current consumption will depend on not only their current income but also their future income, which we refer to as *permanent income*, or what Friedman might refer to as normal income. He noted a secondary type of income as *transitory income*, which would include bonuses received from your employer, birthday gifts, and so forth. Friedman suggested that only increases in permanent income would produce changes in consumption.

The accompanying graph provides a visual to the work of Friedman and the permanent income hypothesis. As people start out, they spend more than their actual income because they know that their future income will increase, but as their income increases, it begins to outpace their consumption.

Figure 7.2

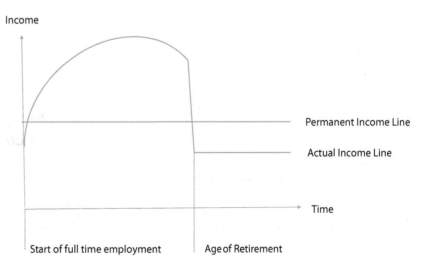

Figure 7.3   Christian Perspective of Permanent Income Hypothesis

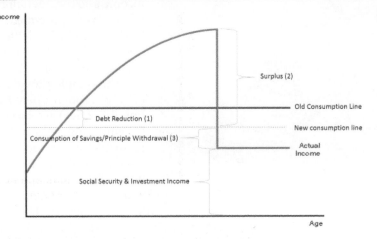

But what would the effect be if there was a slight mind-set change regarding permanent income? When we consider that permanent income is someone's consumption level, not the current income he or she is bringing in, we realize that each individual has the ability to change that line. If an individual were to lower permanent income, the entirety of Friedman's chart would be altered. Lowering the permanent income would allow for an individual to potentially achieve the following benefits:

1. Lowering the consumption line will reduce if not eliminate the initial need to borrow. This can be done by establishing your max consumption level now rather than allowing your emotions to drive how much you spend.

2. By lowering your consumption line, you will achieve more in surplus/savings because you will be spending less. This surplus (compounded over time) will and can create significant benefits in the future.

3. Upon leaving the full-time workplace and lowering your consumption line, you will require less of your savings (i.e., principal withdraws from your savings) to support your lifestyle.

By lowering this consumption line, one could also potentially retire from full-time employment sooner, giving more opportunity for missional or nonpaid work to be completed. Figure 7.3 provides a visual representation of how lowering the consumption line affects the three areas just described.

Life-Cycle Hypothesis

Professors Modigliani and Ando developed another version of Keynes' general theory of consumption in their life-cycle hypothesis (LCH). Very close in nature to the permanent income hypothesis, the LCH seeks to explain that individuals will smooth out their consumption over the course of their lifetime. This "smoothing" process is what we see at early stages in life. For example, people ages 18 to 24 may go into more debt to purchase homes, cars, or even their education because they know that their income will rise over time, allowing them to pay off that debt and begin saving with their surplus income. Modigliani and Ando sought to evaluate the ability to earn future income in terms of human capital, which we previously identified as the skills, training, knowledge, and experiences that an individual can bring to his or her role in the labor force, along with **financial capital,** ownership in assets that produce income.

Financial capital   Owning assets that produce income.

Figure 7.4

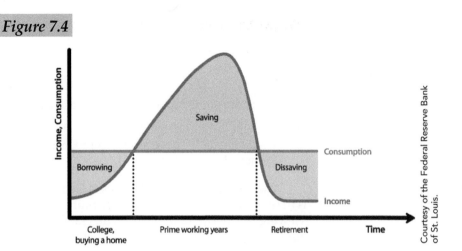

Retrieved from https://research.stlouisfed.org/pageone-economics/uploads/Graphs/POE1114ChartNEW.png

The accompanying graph demonstrates Ando and Modigliani's LCH. You see that this graph is nearly identical to the graph for the permanent income hypothesis presented earlier. The life-cycle hypothesis takes the permanent income hypothesis and adds to it the savings component. You can see that the consumption level is flat over one's lifetime; however, due to the rise and fall of income, it allows for saving and dissaving, which we referred to earlier as the accumulation and distribution phases, respectively.

CHALLENGES UNIQUE FOR EACH TIME PERIOD

There are challenges that exist in every phase of the financial life cycle. In the self-preservation phase, you may find it challenging not to go into debt, such as student loans, car loans, or even credit card debt, because of a lower income or the need to repay student loans. Additionally, based on your life choices, such as marriage and/or having children, and vocation choices, this phase may be prolonged.

During the accumulation time period of life, which is typically from the mid-20s to the mid-60s, a couple is focusing on building their savings and paying for large life-stage-driven expenses such as college tuition or weddings. They are trying to preserve and build upon their savings to achieve their financial and personal goals. Trying to save is more of a challenge while being "sandwiched" between family responsibilities of looking after the older generation and helping the younger generation get established.

The last phase, distribution, could lead to family problems when it comes to outlining how legacy assets (i.e., inheritances) will be distributed. There is often a great deal of conflict that arises when assets are being distributed, and without good clear communication this conflict can escalate into future resentment. Estate distribution is discussed in Chapter 00.

WHY DOES THIS ALL MATTER?

So why is knowing and understanding the different family and financial life-cycle phases important? There are similarities between how families and finances are viewed from a large overall picture similar to what we see in the biblical meta-narrative. When one thinks of God's story from a view at "30,000 feet," one sees four main themes:

1. Creation: God created the world and all that is in it.
2. Fall: Man sinned and separated himself from God.
3. Redemption: Jesus came to earth in human form to be our propitiation.
4. Reconciliation: Those who accept Christ in faith can be reconciled to God the Father.

When one understands that this is God's worldview, it becomes evident that this is the overarching theme of all of Scripture, because this theme is the gospel message. Viewing family and finances from this same viewpoint enables us to see the stages of our lives through the lens of the gospel.

1. For early adults in self-preservation mode, this view is seen in the effort to expand their human capital in order to increase their future income. These individuals are seeking to get married and have children.
2. For midlife adults in an accumulation phase who have peaked their human capital, this view is seen in the effort of transferring the acquired human capital to financial capital—assets that will later provide an income stream to support their lifestyle. This group is in the process of raising children and sending them off once they reach the age of maturity.
3. For senior adults in the distribution phase of life using their financial capital to support their lifestyle, this gospel view is seen in the effort of establishing plans to redistribute their accumulated assets to others. This group is enjoying the benefits of being grandparents!

Although this may oversimplify family and financial life cycles, one can see that it is a process over one's lifetime, and this simplification helps to provide the big picture.

SUMMARY

This chapter focuses on giving a basic understanding of three key life cycles related to family, finances, and income. Six family life stages were described along with several key characteristics of each stage. The first stage is the young adult, followed by the adult with or without children and the adult with school-age children. The fourth stage is the midlife stage, followed by the preretirement stage and, finally, the retirement stage. As individuals progress through these stages, they will also enter and exit three main financial phases: self-preservation, accumulation, and distribution. Next, we looked at three theories that discuss income and consumption and how those can be viewed over the course of the family and financial life cycles. We concluded with an overview of how these life cycles come together and compared these stages to God's overall meta-narrative in order to show how important it is to see the big picture.

SUMMARY REVIEW QUESTIONS

1. What are the characteristics of those in the young adult family life stage?

2. What are the characteristics of those in the stage of adult, with or without children?

3. What are the characteristics of those in the stage of adult with school-aged children?

4. What are the characteristics of those in the midlife stage?

5. What are the characteristics of those in the preretirement stage?

6. What are the characteristics of those in the retirement stage?

7. Name and describe the three phases of the financial life cycle.

8. Explain what factors influence the phases of the financial life cycle.

9. Discuss the difference in God's call versus an occupation.

10. Outline several lifestyle choices that will influence your financial life-cycle phase.

11. Briefly explain each of the three consumption theories presented in the chapter.

12. What are the differences between permanent income hypothesis and the life-cycle hypothesis?

13. What are some of the challenges individuals may face in each phase of the financial life cycle?

Case Study Analysis

Bob and Debbie sat almost completely still as they listened to Pastor Steve go through their behavioral assessments. Although Bob and Debbie differed in the way they viewed money, they never really saw it in this way. As Steve was wrapping up his dialogue, he intended to bring Bob and Debbie out of the "past" and turn to the future.

Steve began with, "As you now have a clearer picture of how you 'behave' around money, it is vital that we use this information as we begin to define our lifestyle going forward, especially as you seek to retire in the next 5 to 10 years. Unfortunately, this can be one of the most challenging times in parents' lives when it comes to thinking through trade-offs, putting money into retirement, or using that money to pay for college expenses—for Chloe, for example. We need to begin to think about when the time frame will be that you and Debbie move from the accumulation phase to the distribution phase. We have already looked at answering the question, "How much is enough?" so now it's time to put in place thoughts about the next 5 to 10 years in relation to your consumption in order to transition smoothly to the distribution phase, when you can begin to withdraw comfortably from your savings to support your lifestyle. In order to get a better grasp of what we are talking about, I would like you and Debbie to complete this diagram. It is really important that the two of you agree and commit to this exercise so that you can commit to making this a reality."

Use the information in their financial statements to review their monthly expenses, and fill in the missing information in the following chart:

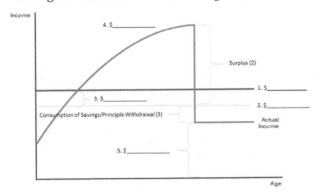

Questions

1. For the first empty space, determine the current consumption line using the expense statement provided in their financial statements.

2. Determine how much Bob and Debbie can reduce their expenses by. Support this by providing specific items that can be minimized.

3. What is the difference that can be used for debt reduction?

4. What is the maximum amount of income that they will commit to? Why is this important from a biblical perspective? (Hint: What can earning too much money lead too?)

5. This number represents how much Bob and Debbie will draw from Social Security and other retirement sources. Not counting Social Security, using all their retirement accounts, determine what 4% annual distribution toward their annual consumption would be. Provide this number here.

How does their financial picture look overall? What observations can you make from the information in this chart?

DEFINITIONS

Family life cycle   (p. 148)   **Financial life cycle**   (p. 149)   **Theory**   (p. 154)

Financial capital   (p. 156)   **Human capital**   (p. 148)

SCRIPTURE VERSES (ESV)

Ecclesiastes 3—For everything there is a season, and a time for every matter under heaven: a time to be born, and a time to die; a time to plant, and a time to pluck up what is planted; a time to kill, and a time to heal; a time to break down, and a time to build up; a time to weep, and a time to laugh; a time to mourn, and a time to dance; a time to cast away stones, and a time to gather stones together; a time to embrace, and a time to refrain from embracing; a time to seek, and a time to lose; a time to keep, and a time to cast away; a time to tear, and a time to sew; a time to keep silence, and a time to speak; a time to love, and a time to hate; a time for war, and a time for peace.

1 Peter 4:10—As each has received a gift, use it to serve one another, as good stewards of God's varied grace:

Galatians 5:13—For you were called to freedom, brothers. Only do not use your freedom as an opportunity for the flesh, but through love serve one another.

Matthew 29:16–20—Now the eleven disciples went to Galilee, to the mountain to which Jesus had directed them. And when they saw him they worshiped him, but some doubted. And Jesus came and said to them, "All authority in heaven and on earth has been given to me. Go therefore and make disciples of all nations, baptizing them in the name of the Father and of the Son and of the Holy Spirit, teaching them to observe all that I have commanded you. And behold, I am with you always, to the end of the age."

ADDITIONAL READINGS

Andresen, T. (1999). The dynamics of long-range financial accumulation and crisis. *Nonlinear Dynamics, Psychology, and Life Sciences, 3*(2), 161–196.

Bewley, T. (1977). The permanent income hypothesis: A theoretical formulation. *Journal of Economic Theory, 16*(2), 252–292.

Campbell, J. Y., & Mankiw, N. G. (1991). The response of consumption to income: a cross-country investigation. *European Economic Review, 35*(4), 723–756.

Carroll, C. D. (1996). *Buffer-stock saving and the life cycle/permanent income hypothesis* (No. w5788). Washington, DC: National Bureau of Economic Research.

Carter, B. L., McGoldrick, M., & Whitbourne, S. K. (2008). The expanded family life cycle: *Individual, family, and social perspective.* Paramus, NJ: Prentice Hall.

Evans, D., McMeekin, A., & Southerton, D. (2012). Sustainable consumption, behavior change policies and theories of practice.

Gandolfo, G., & Padoan, P. C. (2012). *A disequilibrium model of real and financial accumulation in an open economy: theory, evidence, and policy simulations* (Vol. 236). [City, State]: Springer Science & Business Media.

Hall, R. E. (1979). *Stochastic implications of the life cycle-permanent income hypothesis: Theory and evidence* (NBER Working Paper R0015). Washington, DC: National Bureau of Economic Research.

Jappelli, T., & Modigliani, F. (1998). The age-saving profile and the life-cycle hypothesis.

MacDonald, M., & Douthitt, R. A. (1992). Consumption theories and consumers' assessments of subjective well-being. *Journal of Consumer Affairs, 26*(2), 243–261.

Mankiw, N. G., & Shapiro, M. D. (1985). Trends, random walks, and tests of the permanent income hypothesis. *Journal of Monetary Economics, 16*(2), 165–174.

Modigliani, F. (1966). The life cycle hypothesis of saving, the demand for wealth and the supply of capital. *Social Research,* 160–217.

Modigliani, F. (1975). The life cycle hypothesis of saving twenty years later. In M. Parkin & A. R. Nobay (Eds.), *Contemporary issues in economics* (pp.1–35). Manchester.

Modigliani, F. (1986). Life cycle, individual thrift, and the wealth of nations. *The American Economic Review*, 297–313.

Modigliani, F., & Ando, A. K. (1957). Tests of the life cycle hypothesis of savings: Comments and suggestions. *Bulletin of the Oxford University Institute of Economics & Statistics*, *19*(2), 99–124.

Rollins, B. C., & Feldman, H. (1970). Marital satisfaction over the family life cycle. *Journal of Marriage and the Family*, 20–28.

Warde, A. (2005). Consumption and theories of practice. *Journal of Consumer Culture*, *5*(2), 131–153.

Young, C. M. (1977). *Family life cycle*.

REFERENCES

Ando, A., & Modigliani, F. (1963). The" life cycle" hypothesis of saving: Aggregate implications and tests. *American Economic Review*, 55–84.

Bence, C. (2003). *Life calling and God's leading: A Wesleyan perspective on the theology of vocation* (pp. 37–44). Summer Faculty Workshop, a program of the Theological Exploration of

Friedman, M. (1957). The permanent income hypothesis. In *A theory of the consumption function* (pp. 20–37). Princeton, NJ: Princeton University Press.

Hicken, M. (2014). Average cost of raising a child hits $245,000. *CNN Money*. Retrieved from http://money.cnn.com/2014/08/18/pf/child-cost/index.html

Keynes, J. M. (2006). *General theory of employment, interest and money*. [City, State]: Atlantic Publishers & Dist. [Originally published in 1936].

U.S. Department of Education, National Center for Education Statistics. (2015). *Digest of Education Statistics, 2013* (NCES 2015-011), Chapter 3.

Chapter 8

Transcendent Principle 1: Spend Less than You Earn

Courtesy of Monkey Business/Fotolia.

BIG IDEA:
Spending less than you earn is the foundation to wise financial decisions.

LEARNING OUTCOMES

- Explain the benefits of following the principle "spend less than you earn"
- Determine how to calculate your spendable income
- Set categories and dollar figures for those categories in your spending plan
- Identify the four broad categories in which money can be allocated
- Use a cash flow worksheet to monitor your plan for adjustments over time
- Understand the components of and function of a check register
- Identify different types of transactions in a checking account
- Identify various computer software programs and smartphone/tablet apps available for monitoring a spending plan

Prepare a Spending Plan

This chapter will help you become proactive in the daily organization and management of your finances. We seek to provide you information and tools you can use to evaluate your income, develop a spending plan, and come up with a plan to help you reach your financial goals. Unfortunately, this process is not easy and can easily create frustration. As you begin to establish this spending plan, we urge you to continually pray through the material and seek God's power of diligence and perseverance. It is also suggested that you work through the Discipleship Moments and Reflections with your accountability partner and prayer partner. This process will help guide your decisions and help be a sounding board for setting a spending plan that is realistic and achievable.

Ron's Corner

I was a junior at Indiana University when several buddies and I decided to spend the coming summer on Waikiki Beach. As none of us came from wealthy families, we had to scrounge our way to Hawaii. I hitchhiked to California, and then found a "nonscheduled" (read: cheap) flight to the islands.

I'll never forget our first moments near the ocean. How many surfboards should we buy? Would we need two motor scooters or four? As my friends and I stood in the warm island sunshine, the possibilities seemed unlimited.

It took only one week before we were forced to rethink our perspective. We couldn't find any jobs. With no work and no money, we resorted to combing the beach for spare change dropped by sunbathers. Our sand-sifting netted enough nickels and dimes to buy groceries. We survived, but there were no surfboards or motor scooters.

Poking around in the sand to find extra money is one way to survive financially. A much quicker way, however, is to simply reduce living expenses. It may take less mental effort or discipline to sift along a beach, but as one who has tried both methods, I can safely say that curtailing your spending is a far more effective means of retaining the cash you need.

People talk about cutting back, but the truth is that most of us spend as much money as we earn or even more. The key to a smart and successful spending plan, however, is to spend less than you earn. This provides more financial freedom and flexibility. It doesn't matter whether you make $40,000 a year or $140,000. A disciplined spending strategy is critical to achieving and maintaining fiscal fitness.

THE REWARDS OF SMART SPENDING

Spending less than you earn is the commonsense, or even obvious, key to living within your income. Nobody intentionally plans to overspend. On the contrary, many aim to make room in the budget for the things they know are important, such as saving and giving. What happens, though, is that due to not having a budget or plan, many people come up short when it's time to pay the bills.

When people do not have a plan, it is common to see certain negative effects. The first two categories that people tend to give up to meet unplanned obligations are those of saving money and giving money away. These two categories are fundamental, however, to minimizing the impact of not having enough. **Savings**, or resources, usually money, designated for a later use provides people with the ability to pay for unexpected events. Giving is another area that stops when finances come up short of meeting obligations. **Giving** can be defined as freely transferring ownership or possession of something to another individual, group, or business. As Christians, we usually think of giving as it relates to our tithe, or giving to the church, but it should be understood as encompassing significantly more than that. Giving is discussed in more detail in another chapter.

If even after stopping regular saving and giving there is still a deficit, most people's tendency is to rely on credit cards to make up the deficit. **Deficit** is simply defined as the amount by which resources are not sufficient to meet a need. For example, if you have $300 per month in earnings from your job and your monthly obligations together are $350, you have a deficit of $50. If, in this instance, you continue to

Savings Resources, usually money, designated for a later use.

Giving Freely transferring ownership or possession of something to another, such as individuals, groups, or businesses.

Deficit The amount by which our resources are not sufficient to meet a need.

use a credit card to fund the deficit, the balance on the credit card will get larger and thus the payment to the credit card company will get larger. As this tendency continues unchecked, many people fall into the trap of paying the minimum required payment for the credit card.

In this situation, these people are in a vulnerable position. What happens if a financial emergency arises? And it will. A major car repair, a medical emergency, a leaking roof, a broken water pipe—any one of a hundred sudden needs can catapult somebody into additional debt with astonishing force. When peering into a $10,000 or $15,000 hole of debt, a person will teeter on the edge of disaster and wonder, "How in the world did I get here?"

As common as they are, the financial problems associated with unforeseen or unbudgeted expenses are actually fairly simple to prevent. The strategy is to make sure that your inflow (income) exceeds your outflow (expenses)—even in the face of unexpected expenses. Following this rule opens the door to three significant benefits: (1) It eliminates the likelihood of debt, (2) it makes saving money possible, and (3) it eliminates the severity of future financial problems.

1. **Spending less than you earn eliminates the likelihood of debt.** A person who spends less than he or she earns creates **margin**, defined as the amount of excess cash over required expenditures; if cash inflow minus cash outflow is positive, then you have margin. Job losses, investment downturns, and even relatively minor mishaps such as broken appliances or car repairs can drive even the best-intentioned money manager into debt if no savings margin exists.

2. **Spending less than you earn makes saving money possible.** If you think about where your money goes, it might look something like the standard pecking order most people have for their budgets.

   Our first allocation of money is usually for lifestyle, referred to as lifestyle spending. These expenditures include our food, clothing, shelter, hobbies, and so forth. Everyone pays taxes, yet many of us don't actually have to write a check for this expenditure. We will cover taxes in more detail later, but in most cases your employer withholds money from your **gross earnings**, your total annual earnings. Your total tax owed is then calculated when you complete your tax return in April of the following year. Next, we have our debts to repay, such as credit card payments, car loans, student loans, and so forth. After these three critical categories are covered, we then put aside money for savings, and then, finally, we give (usually a very small amount) away. To put it in order using our live, give, owe, grow terminology, most people allocate their money as follows:

   Live
   Owe—taxes
   Owe—debt
   Grow
   Give

   By flipping this order upside down, however, we achieve a biblical—and successful—spending plan:

   Give
   Grow
   Owe—debt
   Owe—taxes
   Live

Margin The amount of excess cash over required expenditures.

Gross earnings Total earnings, usually your annual salary amount or a calculation by which you take your hourly wage and multiply it by the number of hours you worked in a given pay period.

Setting the right priorities is an integral part of controlling your spending. If you set your giving, saving, and debt repayment goals and consider your tax obligation before you allocate your remaining resources, then you will have taken a huge step toward spending less than you earn. By following this giving-and-saving-first spending plan, chances are much better that you will avoid financial trouble. In addition, you will be able to rack up significant savings to help you meet an unpredictable future. As you might suspect, this idea guides God's command for us to give the first fruits of our labor:

> Proverbs 3:9–10: Honor the Lord with your wealth, with the first fruits of all your produce; then your barns will be filled with plenty, and your vats will be bursting with wine.

3. **Spending less than you earn minimizes the possibility of future financial problems.** Because smart spending eliminates the debt option and creates a legitimate savings plan, the longer you follow this practice, the less likely it is that you will encounter severe financial hardship in the future.

Ron's Corner

I know of a man named Jim who was laid off from his six-figure management position and remained jobless for more than a year. With two children to put through college, the family's future might have been grim. But Jim had long practiced frugality in everything from clipping coupons to buying a modest home to setting aside money in an education fund. With little or no debt and a carefully tended nest egg, Jim countered the blow of unemployment and survived far better than most.

Reducing debt, saving money, and establishing a secure financial position for the future may sound like an ideal but impractical or impossible objective. Yet it's actually a relatively straightforward task, provided you follow a sound financial plan. Spending money is easy; knowing how to spend wisely takes common sense, discipline, and occasionally a few tricks from the files of folks who have taken control of their finances and learned how to stretch a dollar in both good times and bad. The following sections describe some of those tricks.

THREE STEPS TO DEVELOPING A SPENDING PLAN

Anyone who has ever tried to live on a budget knows that the process requires both dedication and discipline. There are three basic steps that will guide your spending plan creation. The first step is for you to recognize exactly how much money you have available; you must accurately evaluate your spendable income. Then you will need to determine the categories that money will be allocated to and the amounts for each category. Finally, those categories and allocations need to be evaluated.

Step 1: Evaluating Your Spendable Income

Before we can allocate money toward any categories, there needs to be an assessment of how much money is available to allocate. Money sources can come from the following areas:

> Employment wages/salaries
>
> Bonuses/commissions
>
> Real estate income
>
> Interest income from savings
>
> Investment income from investments (dividends and interest)
>
> Royalties

Caution needs to be taken as these sources are evaluated for two specific components, consistency of payments and amounts of payments. As you begin to evaluate all sources of income, it is important to determine which sources are consistent and can be counted on and which sources are inconsistent. Also, it is important to know which sources provide a reliable amount of income and which sources consist of amounts that can change. In most cases, your employee salary (or hourly wage) will be consistent, and bonuses usually fluctuate.

Table 8.1

Type of Income	Frequency	Consistency	Amount per Payment
Ex. Salary (Gross)	Bi-monthly	Yes	$1,500
Ex. Bonus	Yearly	No	$3,000
Ex. Investment Income	Monthly	Yes	$ 50

As you complete Table 8.1, a decision will need to be made as to whether you want to use all of your inflow sources in your analysis. Remember, we are looking to evaluate our spendable income, which does not require you to use all your income if you choose otherwise.

Once a decision has been made regarding which sources of income will be used, it is important to note that this dollar figure is not what we have to work with for lifestyle spending. For example, let's say a family makes $50,000 per year, and let's assume they have tax withholdings of about 20%; the family is left with no more than $40,000 to cover everything from housing, food, and clothing to entertainment, car repairs, medical expenses, giving, and more. And that does not include any savings! Add outstanding debt to the list, and the belt gets even tighter. The fact is that only about 50% or 60% of your total paycheck can be considered discretionary income. Review the Appendix to complete the Projected Income Worksheet.

Step 2: Establishing Goals for Giving, Saving, and Paying Off Debt

Once your spendable income has been determined (income minus taxes) and before creating a spending plan, it is important to pray and think through what amount or percentage of your income you want to allocate to giving, saving, and paying off debt. These goals will help as you develop your spending plan by creating a sort of check and balance against out of control spending without any attention to long-term or spiritual commitments. When people sit down and think about how much they want to save or give away, they are putting into practice one of the key principles we discussed in an earlier chapter: the longer term your perspective, the better your decisions tend to be. This practice of establishing goals for giving, saving, and repayment of debt prior to considering any other spending will force you to keep the end in mind and to remember the reasons that you are trying to control your spending. If spending is out of control, most people end up without significant savings, without consistently giving, and with making no progress toward the repayment of debt. Therefore, step 2 in creating any spending plan is to establish goals for giving, saving, and paying off debt. After completing steps 1 and 2, you have determined what your live, give, owe, grow pie (see Figure 8.1 later in the chapter for an example) should look like. You should now know how much you plan to allocate to give, to owing taxes, to owing debt, and to growing; the next step is to make allocations within the Live wedge of the pie.

Step 3: Establishing the Categories and Amounts of Where Money Will Be Allocated

Having evaluated your spendable income and established your goals for giving, saving, and repayment of debt, the next step in developing a successful spending plan is to determine where you spend the rest of the money God has given you to steward and how much you spend on each item. By looking at your previous spending habits, you will be able to get a picture as to where your money goes. This step in the process will help you guide where you want to allocate money in the future. For example, let's say after a monthly review of your current expenses, you realize that you spend $150 per month at the local coffee shop ($5 per coffee drink for 30 days). If, when conducting your analysis, you feel this is excessive, then that amount should be lowered, perhaps to $75 (a coffee drink every other day). If, after reviewing your spending habits, you find that the amount spent on coffee drinks is acceptable, then you would allocate $150 per month toward this coffee expenditure. Keep in mind that this process, known as living on a budget, takes self-discipline, realism, and a long-term commitment.

Courtesy of beerphotographer/Fotolia.

Ron's Corner

George is a fellow who once worked in my financial planning firm. He used to play professional football, and although he would never have been considered obese, he did have some leftover weightlifter's bulk he wanted to shed. He changed his eating habits, and at 6 foot 4, he ultimately cut a rather dashing figure.

Meanwhile, I continued to struggle to deflate the spare tire that circled my waistline. "Why don't you look like George?" Judy teased me one day.

"I would," I hastily assured her, "if I were only 7 inches taller!"

Like many people, I have no problem dropping 5 pounds in just a couple of days—only to gain it back again the moment I let down my guard. But I realized I didn't need to lose just 5 pounds; I needed to take off about 15 pounds. Recognizing the importance of setting a "big" goal and allowing ample time to achieve it, I decided to lose 25 pounds and gave myself 6 months to get the job done. I'm happy to report that I accomplished my goal. To do it, I had to change my eating habits and adopt a long-term attitude about the task.

As in the example in Ron's Corner, these same principles hold true in establishing and maintaining a budget. You need to set a worthy faith goal (that is, a big goal). Then you must be realistic about what you are trying to do and give yourself enough time to finish the job. Like the weight loss that results from a change in eating habits, the only permanent solution to spending woes must be fueled by a long-term shift in spending patterns.

Look carefully then how you walk, not as unwise but as wise. (Ephesians 5:15)

This verse should be a focal point as you assign dollar amounts to categories. Food, clothing, shelter, entertainment, utilities, and so forth are all categories that need consideration. Paul writes to the Ephesians that we need to be careful in how we walk, which might be classified as how we spend money. We are not to be like the unwise, but the wise. So what, then, makes us wise? James provides a great perspective on making wise decisions:

Who is wise and understanding among you? By his good conduct let him show his works in the meekness of wisdom. But if you have bitter jealousy and selfish ambition in your hearts, do not boast and be false to the truth. This is not the wisdom that comes down from above, but is earthly, unspiritual, and demonic. For where jealousy and selfish ambition exist, there will be disorder and every vile practice. But the wisdom from above is first pure, then peaceable, gentle, open to reason, full of mercy and good fruits, impartial and sincere. And a harvest of righteousness is sown in peace by those who make peace. What causes quarrels and what causes fights among you? Is it not this, that your passions are at war within you? You desire and do not have, so you murder. You covet and cannot obtain, so you fight and quarrel. You do not have, because you do not ask. You ask and do not receive, because you ask wrongly, to spend it on your passions. You adulterous people! Do you not know that friendship with the world is enmity with God? Therefore whoever wishes to be a friend of the world makes himself an enemy of God. Or do you suppose it is to no purpose that the Scripture says, "He yearns jealously over the spirit that he has made to dwell in us"? But he gives more grace. Therefore it says, "God opposes the proud, but gives grace to the humble." Submit yourselves therefore to God. Resist the devil, and he will flee from you. Draw near to God, and he will draw near to you. Cleanse your hands, you sinners, and purify your hearts, you double-minded. Be wretched and mourn and weep. Let your laughter be turned to mourning and your joy to gloom. Humble yourselves before the Lord, and he will exalt you. (James 3:13–4:10)

In the Appendix, you will find a blank worksheet with a typical list of spending categories that may be helpful in helping you determine where your money is spent. If this granular approach feels overwhelming, it can be helpful to look at spending allocations from a broader perspective. As has been described earlier in this book, there are only four main categories to which money can be allocated: (1) our lifestyle, which is referred to as *live*; (2) our giving, which is referred to as *give*; (3) our debts and taxes, which are referred to as *owe*; and (4) our savings and investing, which are referred to as *grow*. Figure 8.1 is a pie chart that gives a visual of these broad categories.

Once you complete the first three steps in the process of creating a spending plan, you will be able to determine what your pie looks like. This diagram will be explored in more detail throughout the different chapters of this text.

To create a realistic spending plan, begin by answering two questions: (1) What are you spending money on now? (2) What would you like to spend money on in the future? Getting the correct information can take as long as 1 to 2 years, but if you discipline yourself to stick with the process, your eventual budget will be better

Figure 8.1 Category Pie Chart

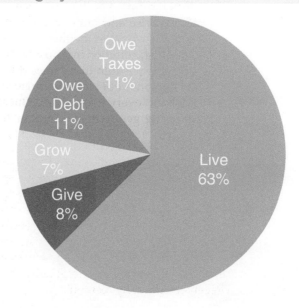

equipped to withstand the ups and downs of family life and uncertain economic conditions.

1. **What are you spending?** To answer this question, go back over the last 12 to 24 months and gather data from bank statements, credit card statements, and other records. Remember to include automatic teller machine (ATM) withdrawals and checks written for cash. If you can't remember what the money was used for, record the amounts in the miscellaneous category. If you don't have this information, take time to keep receipts and track your expenses for a period of at least 6 months. This should give you a good picture of where you currently spend your money.

Courtesy of daniilantiq2010/Fotolia.

DISCIPLESHIP MOMENT AND REFLECTION

Talk to your accountability partner and prayer partner, letting your partner know that you would like to track your expenses over the course of time (you decide—1 month, 3 months, 6 months, etc.). Have your partner encourage you and pray for you during this data-collection period. This can be a challenging task to complete, especially if you are married and both you and your spouse are seeking to track where your money goes. You might set up a reward for yourselves at the end of the time period. Once you are done, consider how the experience changed your perspective on spending money. Talk over the results with your accountability partner.

Proverbs 27:23: Know well the condition of your flocks, and give attention to your herds.

This verse provides us insight that we ought to know the condition of our money—specifically, where it is and where it has gone. We are to pay attention to our flock. In other words, if we think of this verse in the context of our assets and income, we are to make sure we know where our income is and pay attention to where our income is going.

2. **What would you like to spend?** This question reflects your first attempt to develop a budget or a lifestyle spending plan. Ask yourself, "Given my spending history, what would I like the future to look like?" Keep in mind that we need to look at money differently. We act as stewards of God's resources, not owners of our resources. All of us would like to spend more on entertainment, clothes, and so forth, but we need to live within the boundaries of our income. (Note: Most people underestimate how much they spend by at least 5%. After you determine how much you want to spend, add 5% to each budget category to give yourself a more realistic picture.)

Once you have answered these two questions, you will have a baseline for putting together the first draft of your spending plan. You should now have the categories where you currently spend money and categories where you want/need to spend money in the future. You should also know how much you have spent in each of the categories. In the Appendix, you will find the Paid Monthly worksheet, which you can use to identify which expenses you will have and how much will be allocated to each expense. The worksheet records monthly expenses, so if you have expenses that occur less frequently than monthly, you can put those in the Amount Received Annually column.

Table 8.1　Your Living Expenses

HOUSING	MONTHLY PAYMENTS	NON-MONTHLY PAYMENTS	TOTAL ANNUAL AMOUNT
Mortgage/Rent			$ –
Insurance			$ –
Property Taxes			$ –
Electricity			$ –
Heating			$ –
Water			$ –
Sanitation			$ –
Telephone			$ –
Cleaning			$ –
Repairs/Maintenance			$ –
Supplies			$ –
Improvements			$ –
Furnishings			$ –
Total Housing	$ –	$ –	$ –
FOOD			$ –
CLOTHING			$ –
TRANSPORTATION			
Insurance			$ –
Gas and oil			$ –
Cleaning			$ –
Maintenance/Repairs			$ –
Parking			$ –
Other			$ –
Total Transportation	$ –	$ –	$ –
ENTERTAINMENT/RECREATION			
Eating Out			$ –
Babysitters			$ –
Magazines/Newspapers			$ –
Vacation			$ –
Clubs and Activities			$ –
Total Entertainment/Rec.	$ –	$ –	$ –

Table 8.1 Continued

MEDICAL EXPENSES	MONTHLY PAYMENTS	NON-MONTHLY PAYMENTS	TOTAL ANNUAL AMOUNT
Insurance			$ –
Doctors			$ –
Dentists			$ –
Drugs			$ –
Others			$ –
Total Medical	$ –	$ –	$ –
INSURANCE			$ –
Life			$ –
Disability			$ –
Total Insurance	$ –	$ –	$ –
CHILDREN			
School Lunches			$ –
Allowances			$ –
Tuition and College			$ –
Recreation/Lessons			$ –
Other			$ –
Total Children	$ –	$ –	$ –
GIFTS			
Christmas			$ –
Birthdays			$ –
Anniversary			$ –
Other			$ –
Other			$ –
Total Gifts	$ –	$ –	$ –
MISCELLANEOUS			
Toiletries			$ –
Husband			$ –
Wife			$ –
Dry Cleaning			$ –
Animals			$ –
Beauty			$ –
Other			$ –
Other			$ –
Other			$ –
Total Miscellaneous	$ –	$ –	$ –

TOTAL LIVING EXPENSE	$ –	$ –	$ –

Step 4: Analyzing and Adjusting Your Plan

The Your Living Expenses worksheet represents your budget. Once you have attempted to live according to this budget for a period of time (at least several months, but preferably an entire year to get an accurate picture of total spending), you will probably need to make some adjustments.

Obviously, your goal is to live within your budget so that more money comes in than goes out. By analyzing your cash flow, you can determine how much margin your budget includes. Table 8.2 is a simple Cash Flow Analysis worksheet that can help determine what margin you may have, both on your initial budget and then on your adjusted plan.

Table 8.2 Cash Flow Analysis Worksheet

	Initial Plan	Adjusted Plan
1. Total spendable income (from the Annual Spendable Income worksheet total)	$35,000	$35,000
2. Total living expenses (from the Your Living Expenses worksheet total)	$35,578	$33,112
3. Cash flow margin (Line 1 minus line 2)	–$578	$1,888

If you overspend your budget, you will reduce your margin. The only way to live on a negative margin is to borrow money—which only increases your debt commitments, further reducing your future margin.

Again, your goal is to live within your budget. As your income increases through salary raises or other means, your margin will increase, provided your living expenses do not change. Your margin—your extra cash—is the very thing that will enable you to accomplish your goals for giving, saving, and repayment of debt that you set in step 2, as well as enable you to take advantage of the investment strategies and options outlined in a later chapter.

CHECKBOOK BASICS

Ron's Corner

While visiting with a couple regarding their financial situation, the wife explained that keeping a checking account was very simple. She faithfully recorded her checks as she wrote them, and whenever she ran out of money, she used a "neat" column she had discovered in her check register called "deposit." If she ran low on money, she merely added another $1,000 to the deposit column. However, that didn't mean she actually deposited anything in the account. Upon hearing this, her husband was shocked, to say the least. But at least he learned why they were continually overdrawn at the bank when both of them had positive balances on their check registers.

Checking account An account housed at a bank where a depositor can access his or her funds through the use of various negotiable instruments, such as checks, debit cards, cashier's checks, or money orders.

Check register A pamphlet where the depositor can write down all transactions, both deposits and withdrawals, related to the specific account.

Bank statement A collection of all transactions the bank has documented within the specific account, usually categorized by transaction type, first by deposits, then withdrawals.

Federal Reserve Fedwire system A system that allows banks to transfer money from one Federal Reserve Bank to another, which can offer real-time settlement.

The previous sections outlined the basics to creating a spending plan. Unfortunately, creating the spending plan and then analyzing that spending plan requires a method of managing the inflows of income and outflows of expenses. The majority of people use a **checking account**, an account housed at a bank where a depositor can access his or her funds through the use of various negotiable instruments, such as checks, debit cards, cashier's checks, or money orders. In order to track expenses, checking account holders are provided with a **check register**, a pamphlet where the depositor can write down all transactions, both deposits and withdrawals, related to the specific account (Figure 8.2). The register is intended to provide the account of all transactions so that the account holder can verify transactions he or she has recorded with those transactions the bank has reflected on the account holder's **bank statement**. Each account held by an account holder is provided either a monthly or quarterly statement, which is a collection of all transactions the bank has documented within the specific account, usually categorized by transaction type, first by deposits, then withdrawals.

There are seven columns in the register in Figure 8.2, each with a specific purpose. The first column, titled "Check/Code," is where you write in the type of transaction. Examples may include the following: (1) check, (2) ATM withdrawal, (3) debit card (DC) purchase, (4) money order (MO), (5) cashier's check (CC), (6) wire transfer (WT), or (7) electronic transfer (Automatic Clearing House or ACH). ACH is a method in which money is transferred from one entity to another entity through a clearing firm that validates the transaction; using an online bill payment (OBP) system is another way of identifying that transaction as an ACH, so these codes may be interchangeable. This differs from a federal funds wire (or wire transfer) because a wire transfer is money that transfers from one bank to another bank through the **Federal Reserve Fedwire system**. The process of using a fed wire usually provides faster posting times to the receiving bank than having to go through a clearing firm.

The second column is where you provide the date the transaction occurs. It is important to note that the date on which the transaction occurs will be different from the date on which the transaction is posted to your account. For example, if you were to write a check to a friend for a concert ticket, you would write down the date you wrote the check in your register. Your friend may wait for all his friends to pay

Figure 8.2 Check Register

Exhibit C　　Page 4 of 4

Codes DC - Debit Card Transaction　BP - Online Bill Payment
ATM - ATM Withdrawal　EFT - Electronic or Phone Transfer
AD - Automatic Deposit　MD - Manual Deposit

Check /Code	Date	Transaction Description	Payment	Clr'd	Deposit	Balance
		Balance Fwd				1,153.96
BP	2/6/10	Payroll Tax Payment	70.85			1,083.11
BP	2/7/10	BigCo Electric Company	175.25			907.86
BP	2/7/10	Insurance	28.75			879.11

Courtesy of MP Star Financial.

*Retrieved from http://www.mpstarfinancial.com/wp-content/uploads/2012/06/exhibit-c-4.png

him back before he makes the deposit (let's say that it is 3 days). Then he deposits those checks in his account. The money will not be removed from your account for a few days after you have written the check. Hence, there is a time difference between when you write the check and when the money is removed from your account.

The third column is where you write down details regarding the transaction, typically to name the person or entity to which the money is going. As you can see in Figure 8.2, there are three online bill payments (ACHs), one for a payroll tax payment, one to Bigco Electric Company, and one for an insurance bill. These descriptions should be clear enough so that you can quickly see where and what the money was used for.

The next column is the amount that was paid. It is important to keep detailed records of the amounts so that you can accurately track how much money is remaining in your account. This column is followed by a column titled "Clr'd," which stands for "cleared." Cleared indicates that money has actually left your account for this item. Recall in the previous example that your friend waited several days before he deposited your check in his account. Once the total of the check you wrote to your friend for the concert ticket has been withdrawn from your account, the item has "**cleared**" your account.

The next column is where you write any deposit amounts. This column is separated from the payment column to help keep money coming into the account separate from the transactions indicating money leaving the account.

The final column is titled "balance." This column denotes how much should be remaining in your checking account after all items have been accounted for. An important note is to keep track of those expenses that you do not write down in your check register. **Automatic drafts**, defined as money taken out of your account on regular intervals through an automatic process, subscriptions, or bank service fees still need to be accounted for even though they are not items you have recorded. If you are not careful, such automatic payments can create overdrafts in your accounts. **Overdrafts** are items presented for payment on your account for which there are insufficient funds in your account to clear those items.

Finally, at the end of each month, you should reconcile your check register with your bank statement. This is a process in which you check off each item in your check register that has a matching entry on your bank statement. After you have reconciled any discrepancies between your check register and your bank statement, the balance in your check register should match the balance shown on your bank statement. If you find any discrepancies when you are reconciling all the transactions in your check register to your bank statement, call your bank and talk to a customer service representative who can help you determine where the discrepancy may have occurred.

Cleared A term used in describing when the value of a negotiable item has been withdrawn from your account. An example is when a check you write to someone has been withdrawn from your account, which is then said to have cleared.

Automatic drafts Money taken out of your account on regular intervals through an automatic process.

Overdrafts Items presented for payment on your account for which there are insufficient funds in your account to clear the items.

Ron's Corner

Many adults simply don't know how to maintain a checking account. I'm always surprised to discover how many people never reconcile their checkbooks with their bank statements; some don't know that it is even possible to balance with the bank statement.

COMPUTER SOFTWARE AND APPS

Computer software and smartphone and tablet apps can help guide not only your spending plan but also your overall personal financial management. They also take the tediousness out of manually tracking, recording, adding, and subtracting.

Generally, the software/apps track income received and expenses, and then bring the two together to let you know where you stand. This basic process of budgeting and expense tracking allocates resources to various categories and then monitors how your income and spending match up with your predetermined spending plan.

Several good software packages available today are designed specifically for home money management. These range in price from about $30 to $70 for most software packages.

The following are different software and app programs that can help you manage your income and expenses electronically:

Software
- Microsoft Money
- Intuit Quicken
- Mint.com
- DOXO
- Crown Financial Ministry Money Map

Apps
- You Need a Budget (YNAB)
- MoneyWell Express
- BudgetPulse
- PocketSmith
- CalendarBudget
- Mvelopes
- NeoBudget Online
- PearBudget
- Budget by Snowmint Creative solutions
- Inzolo

Additionally, if you don't want to pay for software or an app or don't want to give your personal information to a third party, you can always use a spreadsheet program such as Microsoft Excel to develop your own uniquely personalized budgeting system using various templates found on the Internet.

Several considerations need to be evaluated when seeking to utilize a money management system:

Budgeting: A personal management system must be able to create budget categories and assign income and expenses to them. If this system does not provide for allocation of income to expenses, then you will not be able to make any adjustments.

Check writing: You want to be able to enter your expenses as if you're working directly from your checkbook. Include the date of the expense (or income), the payee (or received from), the amount of the expense or deposit, and the budget allocation. The software or app should have the functionality of a check register.

Reporting: Once your categories and income and expenses are allocated, you want to see how your actual numbers compare to your budget. These reports should clearly tell you whether you are under or over budget by category. They should have enough customizing potential to meet your needs. As previously covered, part of the budgeting process is analyzing your budget and making adjustments as need be, and looking at your reporting will help guide that process.

Standard monthly entries: For most of us who pay bills at home, many checks are written to the same payee, often for the same amount each month. Our paychecks are usually the same each pay period. A good system should have the ability to memorize a standard entry rather than having to reenter every item from scratch. Being able to enter automatic drafts and subscription fees that come out regularly is extremely beneficial.

Bank reconciliation: You will want to balance your checkbook with your bank statement regularly. Personal finance software can help you reconcile your statements easily.

Stability and enhancements: If you're buying commercial software, look for a company with a proven track record of commitment to its customers and to upgrading its product regularly. These updates will help you stay current with any changes that impact your finances, specifically in relation to tax calculations and accounting.

Flexibility: You need the ability to tailor budget categories and reports to meet your personal needs. The software or app you choose should be able to handle multiple banking and credit card accounts as well as investment accounts that you have.

Easy to learn and use: The ideal is to sit down the first time, enter your income and expenses, and produce a set of reports. Some systems are easy to pick up; others are more difficult. Reading reviews on the Internet or talking to others who use the products will help you assess how difficult the software will be to learn.

Affordability: Having a personal budgeting software system can be extremely helpful in saving time and effort in managing God's resources. Keep in mind that most of these software programs and apps do cost money; typically, the more sophisticated they are, the more expensive they can be.

Based on your needs, some budget software offers other unique features, such as the following:

- Address books/contact information
- Income tax estimates
- Investment portfolio tracking/review
- Home inventory management—typically used to track "personal items" such as jewelry, collectibles, furniture, and so forth
- Life insurance needs calculators
- To-do lists

Courtesy of daniilantiq2010/Fotolia.

DISCIPLESHIP MOMENT AND REFLECTION

Take a few moments and pray. Recall that God has given you His provision (income/wealth) to manage on His behalf for the ultimate purpose of giving God the glory. As you pray and seek the Holy Spirit's leading on this process, keep in mind that God owns it all, and we are merely His managers. Pray through each category that you think is important to God and those that are not. The frame of reference is very important when setting up this budget. Talk to your accountability partner and prayer partner about the categories that the Spirit may be leading to you change or adjust.

FOR AN EMERGENCY ONLY

Although budgeting is a process that guides where money will be spent, there will be times that unexpected events require funds to be used, which can alter the most robust budget. Examples include car repairs or unexpected medical bills. These types of expenses are why emergency funds are established. Should emergency funds be used to offset an unexpected financial expense, it will be prudent to replenish those emergency savings as soon as you can.

Unfortunately, some people think this extra savings can be available for other needs that are not really emergencies. After not using the emergency savings for 6 months or a year, it may be tempting to tap into it to fund other wants. The most common reasons for such "unauthorized tapping" are gifts, impulse purchases, and vacations. These are items that should be planned for in your family's budget. Make sure that you and your spouse, if married, are in agreement as to the conditions for which the emergency savings should be used.

SUMMARY

In this chapter, we covered the first transcendent principle of money management: spending less than you earn. In order to accomplish this, a spending plan needs to be established. There are three benefits that this principle will help accomplish: (1) eliminates/minimizes the use of debt, (2) allows for savings, and (3) minimizes the possibility of future financial problems. Four steps were identified in creating a spending plan. First, we need to evaluate our spendable income. Second, we need to establish goals for giving, saving, and repayment of debt. Third, we need to identify the categories and amounts that will be allocated to each category. In order to provide a baseline in this process, two basic questions need to be answered: (1) What are you spending money on? (2) What would you like to spend money on? The former can be answered by tracking your expenses over a period of time, typically a few months, to see what your current spending habits are. Then this information can be used to determine what you will spend money on in the future. Fourth, once we get the allocations assigned to the different categories, the spending plan needs to be monitored and evaluated regularly to make any adjustments as income and expenses change. Finally, we discussed briefly the components of tracking expenses by using a checking account and documenting expenditures in the check register and/or using computer or smartphone/tablet apps to provide an easy method to monitor your spending plan.

SUMMARY REVIEW QUESTIONS

1. Identify the two categories that usually are significantly altered when experiencing financial burdens.

2. Describe the three benefits of following the principle "spend less than you earn."

3. Define the term margin. Why is margin in your finances important?

4. In what order does the world put the five uses of money? How does that differ from a biblical worldview?

5. What are the categories that we should use in determining our spendable income?

6. Explain why our salary does not correspond to our spendable income.

7. Describe the primary method of tracking daily expenditures.

8. Explain three ways money can be withdrawn from a checking account.

9. Describe the ways that computer software or smartphone/tablet apps can help manage and monitor a spending plan.

10. List and describe the critical components required in software to guide a spending plan.

Case Study

Bob and Debbie knew that they had to get their budget in order before they could actually reduce their permanent income line or, as Pastor Steve called it, their consumption line. As they gathered around the table one evening after dinner, Bob and Debbie pulled out all of their bank account statements and credit card statements from the past few months and began to see where all their money was going.

Using the attached Excel sheet, create a spending plan for Bob and Debbie that will provide clear direction as to where their money is actually going from a biblical perspective. Then you can answer the questions that follow.

Use Bob and Debbie's Income and Expenses spreadsheet to answer the following questions:

Questions

1. How much of their income are they giving away?

2. How much of their income are they spending on lifestyle?

3. What areas could be minimized or reduced to provide more margin/liquidity for savings?

4. What would Bob and Debbie's spendable income be?

5. Write down 5 to 10 questions that you would ask Bob and Debbie to learn more about their expenses.

DEFINITIONS

Automatic drafts (p. 177)

Bank statement (p. 176)

Checking account (p. 176)

Check register (p. 176)

Cleared (p. 177)

Deficit (p. 166)

Federal Reserve Fedwire system (p. 176)

Overdrafts (p. 177)

Giving (p. 166)

Gross earnings (p. 167)

Margin (p. 167)

Savings (p. 166)

SCRIPTURE VERSES (ESV)

Proverbs 3:9–10—Honor the Lord with your wealth, with the first fruits of all your produce; then your barns will be filled with plenty, and your vats will be bursting with wine.

Proverbs 27:23—Know well the condition of your flocks, and give attention to your herds.

Ephesians 5:15—Look carefully then how you walk, not as unwise but as wise.

James 3:13–4:10—Who is wise and understanding among you? By his good conduct let him show his works in the meekness of wisdom. But if you have bitter jealousy and selfish ambition in your hearts, do not boast and be false to the truth. This is not the wisdom that comes down from above, but is earthly, unspiritual, and demonic. For where jealousy and selfish ambition exist, there will be disorder and every vile practice. But the wisdom from above is first pure, then peaceable, gentle, open to reason, full of mercy and good fruits, impartial and sincere. And a harvest of righteousness is sown in peace by those who make peace. What causes quarrels and what causes fights among you? Is it not this, that your passions are at war within you? You desire and do not have, so you murder. You covet and cannot obtain, so you fight and quarrel. You do not have, because you do not ask. You ask and do not receive, because you ask wrongly, to spend it on your passions. You adulterous people! Do you not know that friendship with the world is enmity with God? Therefore whoever wishes to be a friend of the world makes himself an enemy of God. Or do you suppose it is to no purpose that the Scripture says, "He yearns jealously over the spirit that he has made to dwell in us"? But he gives more grace. Therefore it says, "God opposes the proud, but gives grace to the humble." Submit yourselves therefore to God. Resist the devil, and he will flee from you. Draw near to God, and he will draw near to you. Cleanse your hands, you sinners, and purify your hearts, you double-minded. Be wretched and mourn and weep. Let your laughter be turned to mourning and your joy to gloom. Humble yourselves before the Lord, and he will exalt you.

ADDITIONAL READINGS

Burkett, L. (1993). *The family budget workbook: Gaining control of your personal finances*. Chicago, IL: Northfield Press.

Burkett, L. (2000). *The family financial workbook: A practical guide to budgeting*. Chicago, IL: Moody Press.

DeVaney, S. A., Gorham, E. E., Bechman, J. C., & Haldeman, V. A. (1996). Cash flow management and credit use: Effect of a financial information program. *Journal of Financial Counseling and Planning, 7,* 71.

Fox, L., Hoffmann, J., & Welch, C. (2004). Federal Reserve personal financial education initiatives. *Federal Reserve Bulletin, 90,* 447.

Gardner, D., & Gardner, T. (2003). *The Motley Fool personal finance workbook: A foolproof guide to organizing your cash and building wealth*. New York, NY: Simon and Schuster.

Godwin, D. D. (1990). Family financial management. *Family Relations, 39*(2), 221–228.

Gorham, E. E., DeVaney, S. A., & Bechman, J. C. (1998). Adoption of financial management practices: A program assessment. *Journal of Extension, 36*(2), 1–9.

Kolb, R. W. (1988). *Principles of finance*. Miami, FL: Scott Foresman.

Lawrence, J. (2008). *The budget kit: The common cents money management workbook*. New York, NY: Kaplan Publishing.

Muske, G. A. (1996). *Family financial management: A real world perspective*. Ames, IA: Digital Repository @ Iowa State University.

Shim, J. K., & Siegel, J. G. (1993). *Complete budgeting workbook and guide*. New York, NY: New York Institute of Finance.

Chapter 9

Transcendent Principle 2: Avoid the Use of Debt

Courtesy of duncanandison/Fotolia.

BIG IDEA:
Borrowing money (debt) always presumes upon the future.

LEARNING OUTCOMES

- Understand the difference between credit and debt
- Explain what the 6 C's of credit are in the credit decision
- Provide an overview to the seven most basic types of loans
- Explain what the Bible *doesn't* say about borrowing
- Explain the three direct points of what the Bible does say about borrowing
- Describe the four main reasons people get into debt problems
- Explain the four considerations for taking on debt
- Explain the four misconceptions about credit card debt
- Describe the three recommendations for battling debt
- Explain the three main ways to reduce and eliminate debt
- Describe four financial deceptions

There is considerable misunderstanding of the biblical perspective on borrowing and related issues. The focus of this chapter is to discuss two components of borrowing: (1) an overview of credit and debt and how they work, followed by (2) a biblical perspective on debt. This text offers a consistent way for Christians, specifically students who are in the infancy of developing personal convictions, to think about the use of credit.

Ron's Corner

When I was practicing as a CPA in Indiana, my firm did a lot of bank auditing and consulting work. As a result, I got to know many small-town bankers. One banker I remember meeting was a young man who had worked in all the departments and through the years assumed increasing responsibilities. Recently his bank was sold to a much larger bank. The new bank wants to build the retail side of its business—that is, consumer lending. Over the next several years, it has plans to greatly increase its credit card and installment loan portfolios. But that raises a serious question for my friend, who's a committed Christian. On the one hand, he's an excellent banker with a chance to become a top executive of his company in the near future. On the other hand, he wonders if encouraging individuals to take on personal debt is consistent with biblical principles. He wrote me a letter and asked, "Can a Christian be a banker?" Trying to discern if he can be true to his spiritual convictions and still promote a business he has serious questions about, my friend has asked many respected Christians for their counsel. He's discovered to his frustration that there's not much clear understanding of or consensus on the biblical teaching about debt.

PART 1: FUNDAMENTALS

Credit An amount of money that a lender is willing to allow to be borrowed and then repaid.

Debt The amount of funds of a credit line that has been used and thus is owed back to the lender.

Throughout this chapter you will see two different terms used in relation to the topic of borrowing: **credit** and **debt**. They seem similar and are often used interchangeably; however, there is a difference. In many cases, when you initiate the process of borrowing, you will likely see terms such as "Credit Application," and everyone is familiar with the fact that the word *credit* is used to name the biggest culprit in most people's debt crisis: credit cards. Credit is simply defined as a person's ability (or worthiness) to borrow. Credit deals with the potential borrower's integrity—his or her faithfulness and timeliness in paying bills. Based on that integrity, a potential lender extends a stated amount of credit. That credit may require either the personal guarantee of the potential borrower, as with a signature loan, or some type of collateral, such as in the form of a security interest in something of value, usually the item purchased.

Credit is not the same thing as debt, but it can be used to go into debt. Debt results when the credit extended is utilized for the purchase of some product or service. A person who believes that having credit cards is wrong should understand that having credit cards does not cause one to go into debt. It only means that credit has been made available to him or her. An individual's use, or misuse, of those credit cards causes him or her to go into debt. It used to be that "being able to afford it" meant you could pay cash for whatever you were purchasing. If you didn't have the cash on hand, by definition, you couldn't afford it. What a difference time makes! Today, "being able to afford it" has nothing to do with whether you have the resources to pay for it. It means strictly "being able to afford the monthly payments." As such, every borrowing decision can be manipulated simply by extending the length of time of repayment in order to make it "affordable." Prior to World War II, home mortgages rarely went beyond 10 years. Today, 30 years is the standard, and in some cases it's possible to get a 40-year or 50-year mortgage. Fifty years is probably longer than the buyer will live. But by extending the terms over half a century, the payments come down to the "affordable level."

For an illustration of the difference, see Figure 9.1.

Figure 9.1 Credit Versus Debt

Card Type	Credit Limit	Card Balance	Available Credit
Visa	$5,000	$1,825	$3,175
MasterCard	$1,500	$ 0	$1,500

In Figure 9.1, the credit limit is the credit available to the creditor, whereas the debt is in the third column, "Card Balance." So, credit is what amount of money has been made available to you to use, whereas debt is the total amount used of that money.

Understanding this difference is critical. Someone may obtain a credit card with a $50,000 limit on it and carry no balance and thus does not have any debt—more on this later in the chapter.

Courtesy of daniilantiq2010/Fotolia.

DISCIPLESHIP MOMENT AND REFLECTION

As you think about credit, do you use credit in the form of credit cards or other forms of lending? Why or why not? What personal convictions do you have about your use of credit? Talk to your prayer and accountability partner about your thoughts and discuss your partner's convictions about credit.

Why Credit Is Used

There are typically four reasons why people use credit. First, they use it to purchase something that they can't pay cash for. Large purchases such as homes, cars, and furnishings are often purchased using some form of credit; however, smaller purchases can be purchased by using credit as well. The second reason people use credit is in an emergency when other payment options may not be available. Loss of a job or a major home repair caused by water damage are examples of emergencies that could require the use of credit. Next, and probably most notably, people use credit strictly for convenience. With the availability of mobile device payment options, using credit has become even easier. Finally, people use credit as a means to fund investments. Investors may borrow to buy investments (margin), or individuals may use credit to start a business.

Establishing Credit

When you begin to think about establishing credit, there are six main factors that influence a lender's decision to extend credit to you: (1) character, (2) capacity, (3) collateral, (4) capital, (5) condition, and (6) co-signer. These factors are usually evaluated in all credit decisions, regardless of the use for the credit (e.g., credit card, home purchase, school loans, car loans, etc.). These factors are usually examined after a potential borrower completes a credit application, which gives the lender an opportunity to gather relevant information about you. During this investigation period, lenders will pull your credit report, which will help the lender evaluate the six factors just mentioned.

Character

When lenders evaluate one's character, they are trying to determine that person's integrity and willingness to repay them. A lender will not want to lend to individuals who will not pay back what they borrow (Psalm 37:21). Lenders will usually conduct this "character" evaluation by looking at the potential borrower's repayment history. This repayment history comes from credit reporting agencies (Transunion, Equifax, and Experian) that provide the lender with basic information on previous credit accounts the borrower has already established. These credit reports show the lender the following information:

- Lenders and type of credit (e.g., mortgages, auto loans, credit cards, etc.)
- Credit limit
- Amount owed
- Monthly payment, if any
- Number of payments on time

Capacity

The term *capacity* refers to the borrower's ability to pay the loan back under the terms set between the borrower and the lender. This decision is usually evaluated based on the borrower's total income less any existing outstanding debt payments. For example, if a borrower has a monthly gross salary of $3,500 and has two credit cards with minimum payments of $120 and $80, then the lender will consider only $3,300 ($3,500 – $120 – $80) when determining that borrower's ability to repay.

Once a borrower's income and other outstanding debt payments are known, the lender will usually determine the borrower's debt-to-income ratio, which will include the potential new debt payment. For example, let's say a borrower is looking to finance a new car and the loan payment would be $400 per month. Using the borrower's financial information, the borrower's debt-to-income ratio is:

Debt-to-income ratio = (Sum of all monthly debt payments)/Monthly gross income

Debt-to-income ratio = ($400 + $120 + $80)/$3500 = $600/$3500 = .1714

In this scenario, the borrower's debt to income ratio is 17%, which means that 17% of the borrower's gross monthly income needs to be used to pay his or her debts. Although there are subjective opinions about how much of gross monthly income should be tied to debt payments, we need to continually and prayerfully seek the Holy Spirit's leading on all credit decisions and seek to maintain a low debt-to-income ratio.

Collateral

In order to protect lenders from the possibility of a borrower not paying back a loan in accordance with the terms of the loan contract, a lender may require the borrower put up **collateral**. Collateral is a pledge or assignment to the lender of something of value that the lender can take if borrower does not repay the loan. In many cases, the collateral item is the actual item being purchased, such as a car, home, or equipment for a business. Should the borrower not repay the loan, the lender can take ownership of the asset that was pledged and sell it to pay off the outstanding loan balance owed by the borrower. Credit cards do not have any collateral securing the amounts borrowed and as a result have a much higher interest rate—this is what is referred to as an unsecured loan.

Collateral Something of value that is pledged or assigned to a lender to hold in case the borrower is unable to repay the loan.

Capital

When lenders are looking at the overall financial health of a borrower, they will look at the borrower's balance sheet to evaluate the types of assets and liabilities the borrower has in general. This evaluation of the borrower's net worth (assets minus liabilities) can give the lender a general overview as to the borrower's financial condition. A positive net worth means that the borrower has extra capital available to repay a loan, and a negative net worth means that the borrower owes more than he or she owns and has no extra funds available to repay a loan.

Condition

Finally, lenders will usually evaluate the existing conditions that could impact the loan. These conditions may include overall economic uncertainty, length of the loans, borrower's job longevity, or perhaps the borrower's future career prospects. There are many other conditions that influence the relative stability of a loan, but it is clear that lenders take into consideration many conditions when making a lending decision.

Co-Signer

After an initial review of the foregoing factors, if a lender does not feel confident in the borrower's ability to repay the loan, it may require an additional person to be responsible for the loan, known as a co-signer. A **co-signer** is someone other than the borrower who agrees to be liable to repay a loan for another person, thus taking full responsibility for the borrower making the loan payments in accordance with the contract between the borrower and the lender. The Bible expressly warns against being a co-signer in **Proverbs 6:1–5**:

> My son, if you have put up security for your neighbor, if you have struck hands in pledge for another, if you have been trapped by what you said, ensnared by the words of your mouth, then do this, my son, to free yourself, since you have fallen into your neighbor's hands: Go and humble yourself; press your plea with your neighbor! Allow no sleep to your eyes, no slumber to your eyelids. Free yourself, like a gazelle from the hand of the hunter, like a bird from the snare of the fowler.

Proverbs 11:15 provides us a glimpse of the effects of becoming a co-signer:

> He who puts up security for another will surely suffer, but whoever refuses to strike hands in pledge is safe.

Credit Report and Credit Score

Understanding the difference between credit and debt leads to the need to understand how your credit and debt are used to develop a credit report and a credit score. A **credit report** is a collection of information from lenders and other credit agencies that provides updates on existing credit accounts as well as a listing of recent inquiries by other potential lenders. A **credit score** is a numerical score based on a mathematical model that each credit reporting agency uses based on a wide variety of risk factors, such as length of credit history, amount of credit available, and number of **credit lines**, defined as the number of credit accounts established, opened.

Co-signer Someone other than the borrower required to sign a promissory note, thus taking equal liability that the loan payments are made in agreement with the contract between the borrower and the lender.

Credit report A collection of information from lenders and other credit agencies that provides updates on existing credit accounts as well as a listing of recent inquiries by other potential lenders.

Credit score A numerical score derived from a mathematical model that each credit reporting agency uses based on a wide variety of risk factors, such as length of credit history, amount of credit available, and number of credit lines opened.

Credit lines The number of credit accounts established/opened on a credit report.

Managing Credit

As Christians, it is highly important to manage credit appropriately. In order to manage credit appropriately and honorably, it is important to understand some key components of credit that occur in all different types of loans:

- Annual percentage rates
- Payments
- Fees and penalties
- Security

Types and Purpose of Loans

Several different types of loans are explored in this section, which we will evaluate and compare based on the previous list of components.

Credit Cards

Revolving line of credit
A type of credit account that does not have a fixed number of payments.

- *Overview*: A credit card account is usually a revolving line of credit. A **revolving line of credit** is a type of credit account that does not have a fixed number of payments and permits money to be borrowed, repaid, and then borrowed again. Each line of credit typically has a maximum amount that can be borrowed or used, known as a credit limit.
- *Annual Percentage Rates*: The rates for credit card accounts will vary based on a wide variety of factors, but will usually fall between 9% and 25%. It is important to note that the interest charged on credit cards is usually compounded interest. This is one of the biggest obstacles to overcome when trapped by credit card debt. Compound interest is the interest that accumulates on both the principal balance plus any unpaid interest. Therefore, the interest that is charged to your account, if not paid in full, will be added to the principal balance on which interest will be charged.
- *Payments*: Payments for credit cards can vary based on the outstanding balance, known as the amount owed; however, a credit card will always have a minimum payment required in order to avoid fees. Additionally, with the passing of the Credit Card Act of 2009, credit card companies are required to show borrowers the cost of repayment should they only make the minimum payment each month. Due to the fact that these accounts are revolving and do not have an end date, payments will occur for as long as an outstanding balance exists.
- *Fees and Penalties*: Fees charged by credit cards vary based on the particular card and lending institution. The most common types of fees associated with credit cards are as follows: (1) late-payment fee, which occurs if the borrower's payment is not received by the due date set on the credit card statement; (2) over-the-limit fee, which can be incurred if you exceed your maximum credit limit; (3) annual fee, which is usually a fee associated with credit cards that offer rewards or other incentives; (4) balance-transfer fee, which is a fee charged to move a balance from one credit card to another; and (5) cash-advance fee, which is a fee charged to the borrower who uses available credit in the form of a cash withdrawal.
- *Security*: Most credit cards do not require any type of collateral or security in order to establish a credit card account.

Installment Loans

- *Overview*: Installment loans are usually **fixed loans**, meaning they have a fixed number of payments. Installment loans can cover a wide array of loans, but the most common types are auto loans and furniture loans.
- *Annual Percentage Rates*: The interest rates charged on installment loans are usually lower than those on credit card accounts, and generally fall in the range of 3% to 12%. With installment loans the interest charged is usually simple interest rather than compound interest. Simple interest is only calculated on the original principal balance and does not consider unpaid interest as a part of the principal balance, as is done with compound interest.
- *Payments*: With installment loans, the interest rate and the number of payments are set from the start. Due to simple-interest calculations, each payment is a combination of interest and principal. As you progress through the **amortization schedule** (a payment table that will reflect the amount of principal and interest paid with each payment until all payments have been made), you will notice that the initial set of payments allocates more of the payment toward interest and less toward reducing the principal amount borrowed. As the borrower continues to make payments, more of each payment is put toward reducing the principal and less toward the interest.

- *Fees and Penalties*: As with credit card accounts, fees and penalties can occur. The most common fees are late fees or returned-payment fees, which are assessed if the borrower's payment does not clear the bank. Another fee, which is becoming less common, is a prepayment fee, which is assessed if the borrower would like to pay the principal balance off sooner than the original due date of the loan.
- *Security*: For most installment loans, the item being purchased can be and usually is used for security/collateral. The collateral, secured by the lender, thus reduces the lender's risk, and as a result the lender can offer lower interest rates to the borrower.

Mortgage Loans

- *Overview*: Home loans will usually fall under two different types of loans, both of which use a home as collateral. The first is a traditional mortgage loan that someone will use to buy a house. This could be either a primary residence, one you will live in regularly, or a second home that will be used sporadically. The most common mortgage terms are 15 and 30 years; however, other lengths are available. The other type of loan is referred to as a **home equity line of credit**, or HELOC. A HELOC is a revolving line of credit, similar in concept to those outlined in the section on credit cards, where the main difference is that the house is used to secure the debt, like a mortgage loan. HELOCs have become an attractive borrowing vehicle over the past decade because of the dual benefits of a revolving line of credit with no fixed payments and the lower interest rate due to the lender having a secure position in your home.

- *Annual Percentage Rates*: Due to a lender having a secure position in your home, the annual interest rates on mortgage loans tend to be lower than those of revolving lines of credit and may even be lower than those of installment loans. The latest interest rates for home mortgage loans range between 2.5% and 8%. Mortgage loans usually charge interest using simple interest and do not add unpaid interest to your principal balance.
- *Payments*: Mortgage loans come in many different structures, which can create different types of repayment options. These will be covered in more detail in

a later chapter on home purchasing. In many cases however, a standard fixed-rate home mortgage will have an amortization schedule with fixed monthly payments. Variable-rate mortgages and HELOCs can have adjusting monthly payments based on the rate or the amount borrowed.

- *Fees and Penalties*: Similar to most all credit lines, mortgage loans can and usually do assess fees for late payments, and returned check fees. In most cases, mortgage lenders usually will not assess any type of prepayment fee, or fee to the borrower for paying off the loan early.

- *Security*: The collateral or security used for home mortgages will almost always be the house that was purchased, although it does not always have to be.

Investment Loans

- *Overview*: Investment loans are usually loans that allow an investor to borrow money to purchase something designed to generate a profit, usually in the context of investable securities such as stocks and bonds. Although loans can be used to fund investments in real estate, land, and businesses, which can then be utilized for their ability to generate a profit, usually the underlying collateral is how loans are defined. Therefore, when we use investments, such as a stock portfolio, as collateral to buy more stocks and bonds, that is referred to as an **investment loan**. In the financial services industry, two terms are usually affiliated with investment loans: (1) security-based lending, and (2) margin. The most significant difference between the two is that security-based lending programs usually allow the borrower to pledge his or her securities and borrow up to 80% of the value of the assets, whereas margin loans will only allow up to 50% borrowing capacity on securities pledged. Another difference is that, in many cases, security-based loans offer lower borrowing costs than do margin loans.

- *Annual Percentage Rates*: The interest rates charged for margin accounts (which will be discussed later in the investment section) will average between 6% and 10%, whereas those for security-based loans will be slightly lower, ranging from 3% to 6%. Investment loans can have both fixed-rate and variable-rate loan options.

- *Payments*: With most investment loans, the payments are usually variable and in most cases require only interest to be paid on a monthly basis.

- *Fees and Penalties*: There are minimal fees in establishing investment loans, but standard fees may apply, such as late-payment fees or returned-check fees.

- *Security*: For investment loans, the borrower's portfolio is used as collateral to fund the loan. It is important to note that some securities are not "marginable," meaning that the security cannot be pledged or used in providing credit to the borrower. Additionally, based on how much an investor may need to borrow, the investor will only have to collateralize a portion of his or her portfolio; in other words, the borrower will not need to pledge his or her entire portfolio if the expected borrowing amount does not warrant the entire portfolio to be pledged.

Business Loans

- Overview: Business loans are loans that are established by a business rather than an individual. For example, a landscape company may decide to upgrade its fleet of lawn mowers and seek a loan to pay for a new fleet of mowers. There are a wide variety of business loans available to meet different requirements. A few examples are (1) start-up loans, (2) equipment loans, (3) construction loans, and (4) real estate loans. Depending on the structure of the business, a business may be able to establish credit and get a loan on its own merit, whereas some businesses may require personal guarantees of the business owners and managers in order to get any form of loan.

- *Annual Percentage Rates*: Business loans, as with many other types of loans, come with a wide variety of structures, terms, and conditions. Keep in mind that a lender is taking a risk when lending money out and thus requires an adequate return in order to accept that risk. As lenders work with businesses, they must determine the amount of risk involved in extending credit to that particular business and charge an interest rate that compensates the lender for the commensurate level of risk. Rates for businesses are very diverse, ranging from 3% to as high as 20%.

- *Payments*: Due to business loans having what seems to be an unlimited number of structures and arrangements, it is difficult to pinpoint a systematic and structured payment schedule that could be called considered normal.

- *Fees and Penalties*: As with most types of credit, the fees associated with personal loans usually also apply to business loans. For example, credit report fees, application fees, and appraisal fees could all be assessed. The **Small Business Association**, commonly known as the SBA, helps small businesses and entrepreneurs by guaranteeing business loans offered by local banks. This guarantee comes at a cost to the bank through a fee paid by the bank, which may be passed down to the borrower.

- *Security*: As previously discussed, business loans can take many different forms. Usually the type of loan will determine what the expected collateral will be. For example, a business equipment loan will require certain equipment to be used as collateral, or if a business was going to get an accounts receivable loan, the accounts receivables would be pledged as collateral to the lender.

Student Loans

- *Overview*: Student loans are loans that both students and parents can obtain in order to pay for secondary education expenses. These expenses can include tuition costs, room and board, and other fees associated with attending a secondary school. There are many different types of student loans, including government-backed loans (subsidized and unsubsidized, Direct PLUS loans, Perkins loans) and private loans from nongovernment lenders.

- *Annual Percentage Rates*: Interest rates on student loans will generally range from 4% to 8%.

- *Payments*: Payment terms for student loans will vary. Private loans act like typical installment loans that require payments to begin, usually a month after the dispersal of the loan proceeds. Government loans have more flexibility. Both subsidized loans and unsubsidized loans allow the borrower to defer payments until after graduation. The one significant difference between subsidized loans and unsubsidized loans is that with subsidized loans, the interest that accrues from the dispersal is paid by the government, whereas with an unsubsidized loan, interest that begins to accrue is the responsibility of the borrower. If a borrower chooses not to make any payments, then the interest **capitalizes** (or adds to the principal balance) until payments begin. Currently, there are eight different repayment plans available. See the Appendix, which provides an overview of each different type of student loan repayment plan.

- *Fees and Penalties*: In establishing or obtaining student loans, there is usually a fee associated with each loan taken out. In a recent review published by the Department of Education, the loan fee ranged from 1% for subsidized and unsubsidized loans to roughly 4% for Direct PLUS loans.

- *Security*: In most cases, there is no security or collateral pledged for student loans. However, some private lenders may require a parent or other co-signer to be on the loan to reduce the risk of nonpayment. Government loans do not require co-signers.

Payday Loans

- *Overview*: A payday loan, sometimes referred to as a cash-advance loan, is usually a very short term, unsecured loan. The name "payday" loan was established due to borrowers taking short-term loans to cover their current expenses until they received their next payroll or salary check from the employer. Banks do not usually enter into such short credit contracts, and thus payday lenders are usually standalone companies.

- *Annual percentage rates*: Rates for payday loans are high, and many accuse them of being in the category of predatory lending due to the substantially high interest rates that are associated with them. The rates will range from 30% to 45%. Until the Uniform Small Loan Laws (USLL) were implemented by legislators, rates were as high as 3,000%.

- *Payments*: Payday loans usually are repaid in one lump sum on a specified date. In a typical example, if you were looking to take out a $300 loan for 8 days, until your next payday, then you might write a postdated check to a payday lender for $300 and receive only $255 of your check in return. The remaining $45 is the fee assessed by the lender for the loan. On the eighth day, the lender will deposit the check for $300.

- *Fees and Penalties*: Usually there are no other fees associated with payday loans because many payday lenders do not pull your credit report or charge for establishing the loan. There may be fees assessed with returned-check fees, however.

- *Security*: Payday loans do not require any type of security. Payday lenders do have certain stipulations before they will make a loan to you, such as that you must: (1) make at least $1,000 per month, (2) have a valid driver's license, (3) have a Social Security number, and (4) provide several pay stubs to prove employment and income.

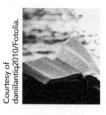

Courtesy of daniilantiq2010/Fotolia.

DISCIPLESHIP MOMENT AND REFLECTION

Review all the different types of loans. Which ones do you have or have you had in the past? Which types do you foresee using in the future? How do you think the use of credit will impact your life, either positively or negatively? Talk to your prayer and accountability partner about your thoughts.

THE BIBLICAL PERSPECTIVE

There are many things the Bible does not say about the subject of debt. The following list is not all-inclusive, but it's a good starting point, because this is where most misunderstandings occur.

It Doesn't Say That It's a Sin to Borrow

The Bible does not say it's a sin to borrow money. Before you react to that statement one way or the other, let me assure you that the Bible does give many warnings about being in debt. However, it doesn't say you are out of God's will or have violated a commandment when you borrow. You may have violated a biblical principle and therefore must bear the consequences, but there's no indication that you need forgiveness for having violated one of God's commandments. That's the difference between an unwise decision and a deliberate decision to disobey God's orders. And in some cases, debt may simply be unavoidable—such as medical emergencies, job layoffs, and business bankruptcy resulting from a lawsuit.

It Doesn't Say That It's Wise to Borrow

A second thing the Bible does not say about borrowing money is that it's wise. Leverage is not biblically condoned as "the way" to prosperity. Many Christians have fallen prey to the misuse of leverage. They believe it's the wise way to conduct business and personal affairs. But absolutely nowhere in the Scriptures are we advised or commanded to use debt to accomplish God-given economic goals. On the contrary, there are many warnings against the use of debt.

Ron's Corner

Early in my practice as a financial planner, I met with a young real estate developer who was getting ready to declare bankruptcy. He had earned a significant income every year, yet he was planning to declare bankruptcy the next week. When I asked how that could be, he made a comment I'll never forget: "Anyone can make money during times of inflation if he's willing to take the risk of high leverage." Unfortunately for him, the economy in his area had become very weak when he was the most highly leveraged, and he was unable to sell the properties he had developed. His cash flow dried up, he couldn't continue making the payments on his properties, and the lenders began calling his loans. Despite a college education and access to the best financial advisors money could buy, his only alternative at that point was to declare bankruptcy. After 15 years of business, he had nothing. The obvious question is, How can such a thing happen to an intelligent businessman with a lot of good financial advisors?

It Doesn't Say That God Will Bail You Out of Debt

Nowhere in the Bible does it say that God is obligated to bail us out of debt. Many Christians who are heavily indebted have the impression that God has promised to get them out of their problems. The verse quoted most often is Philippians 4:19: "And my God shall supply all your need according to His riches in glory by Christ Jesus." That promise is true, of course, and God will meet our needs. But He doesn't promise to overcome the consequences of our unwise behavior.

It Doesn't Say That Debt Is an Exercise in Faith

The Bible talks a lot about faith, but it doesn't say that the use of debt is an exercise of faith. The underlying assumption here is that because you will have to pay debt back in the future from resources you don't already possess, you have to trust God to provide them. This rationale is most often presented by pastors who are getting ready to go into a bond program to raise money for a new church building. They will say that they are taking a tremendous step of faith by obligating themselves to pay back the debt. There is no scriptural basis for this belief, however. In fact, it is most likely a direct contradiction of Scripture. Rather than being a mark of faith, it's testing God, which we are warned not to do.

It Doesn't Say That It's a Sin to Loan Money

Just as the Bible doesn't say that it's a sin to borrow money, it also doesn't say that it's a sin to loan money. Without question, a debtor–creditor agreement changes the relationship between two parties. Anyone who has borrowed money knows the feelings of dread that surround being in debt. It's no fun. Thus, when you loan someone money, you inevitably change your relationship with that person.

So what does the Bible say about debt? The Bible provides wisdom related to debt outlined in three points that have a direct bearing on borrowing decisions:

1. It's wrong not to repay debts.
2. It's foolish to be in a surety situation.
3. Debt may violate two biblical principles that are paramount in our relationship with our Lord: (a) Debt always presumes upon the future, and (b) borrowing may deny God an opportunity to provide.

All Borrowing Must Be Repaid

Psalm 37:21 states, "The wicked borrows and does not repay." The conclusion from this verse is obvious: If you borrow money, you have no alternative but to repay all amounts borrowed. If you don't, by definition, you're what the Bible calls "wicked."

Surety Is Foolish

In reading the book of Proverbs, specifically verse 11:15, you should not go so far as to call surety (guaranteeing another's loan) a sin, but it is explicitly warned against. Look at these strong, vivid words in Proverbs 6:1–5:

> My son, if you have put up security for your neighbor, if you have struck hands in pledge for another, if you have been trapped by what you said, ensnared by the words of your mouth, then do this, my son, to free yourself, since you have fallen into your neighbor's hands: Go and humble yourself; press your plea with your neighbor! Allow no sleep to your eyes, no slumber to your eyelids. Free yourself, like a gazelle from the hand of the hunter, like a bird from the snare of the fowler.

Proverbs 11:15 gives a prediction that I've found usually happens: "He who puts up security for another will surely suffer, but whoever refuses to strike hands in pledge is safe."

The Bible advises that if you find yourself in a surety situation, waste no time getting yourself out of it.

Debt Always Presumes upon the Future

If you borrow money and you believe borrowed money should always be repaid, then you are implicitly presuming upon the future unless you have a guaranteed way to repay the loan. If you think you may have the ability to repay, but, in fact, you don't because your circumstances change, you will have presumed incorrectly upon the future.

Courtesy of renaschild/Fotolia.

The scriptural admonition is found in James 4:13–15:

Now listen, you who say, "Today or tomorrow we will go to this or that city, spend a year there, carry on business and make money." Why, you do not even know what will happen tomorrow. What is your life? You are a mist that appears for a little while and then vanishes. Instead, you ought to say, "If it is the Lord's will, we will live and do this or that."

When borrowing, you need to ask yourself what assumptions and presumptions you are making about the future. If you assume, for example, that your health will remain good, that your job will continue to provide income, that the asset borrowed against will continue to go up in value, or that the business you own will continue to generate profit, you may very well find yourself in bondage if these assumptions do not work out. Again, a distinction needs to be made: The Bible does not say that it's wrong to borrow money, but it does say that it's wrong to presume upon the future. Thus, presuming upon the future to borrow money violates not only a caution, but also a command.

Borrowing May Deny God an Opportunity to Provide

God is interested in increasing our faith. Also, God will meet the needs we have. Therefore, in many cases, borrowing money denies God the opportunity either to meet our needs or to show Himself faithful, thereby increasing our faith.

It's easy, however, to get confused about the difference between a need and a desire. Desires involve the emotions and are very, very strong. Because they are so strong, they are easily misinterpreted as needs. So, if we have a lack of money to meet what we have misinterpreted as a need (e.g., the "need" for a large-screen TV), it is not hard to justify borrowing.

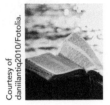

Courtesy of daniilantiq2010/Fotolia.

DISCIPLESHIP MOMENT AND REFLECTION

The two biblical principles just listed show the significant effect that debt can have on our lives. Have you ever felt that God was leading you to do something but felt that your debt had created a barrier to allowing God to move in your life? Pray about this situation and seek God's grace and mercy. May the Spirit be your guiding light in eliminating the bondage debt can create!

THE REASONS FOR DEBT

There are four common causes that tend to create problems with debt. They are somewhat overlapping, and they are shared by all kinds of people—of various cultures, various socioeconomic levels, various races, and various economies. In other words, you may see yourself in more than one category of causes:

1. A lack of discipline
2. A lack of contentment
3. A search for security
4. A search for significance

A Lack of Discipline

Discipline A practice of training someone, to include yourself, to obey rules, or a code of conduct.

As discussed in Chapter 8, creating a spending plan can help eliminate the free flow of money out of our checking accounts. Creating a spending plan, and ultimately sticking to that plan, comes from being disciplined. **Discipline** can be defined as a practice of training someone (yourself included) to obey rules or a code of conduct. This code of conduct is established when you create a spending plan. Discipline requires that you train yourself to follow the guidelines outlined within each category of your spending plan.

If you do not follow those guidelines, you create a free-for-all for spending money wherever and whenever you feel it is okay. For many of us, these free-for-all moments come when we give into our desires and spend money to fulfill a specific want that would normally require debt to be acquired unless money had been specifically allocated for it in our spending plan. If the behavior of free-for-all spending continues, then our level of debt will continue to rise.

The following verses shed some light on God's word relating to discipline and self-control:

> **1 Timothy 4:7:** Have nothing to do with irreverent, silly myths. Rather train yourself for godliness.
>
> **Proverbs 25:28:** A man without self-control is like a city broken into and left without walls.
>
> **Hebrews 12:** Therefore, since we are surrounded by so great a cloud of witnesses, let us also lay aside every weight, and sin which clings so closely, and let us run with endurance the race that is set before us, looking to Jesus, the founder and perfecter of our faith, who for the joy that was set before him endured the cross, despising the shame, and is seated at the right hand of the throne of God. Consider him who endured from sinners such hostility against himself, so that you may not grow weary or fainthearted. In your struggle against sin you have not yet resisted to the point of shedding your blood. And have you forgotten the exhortation that addresses you as sons?

"My son, do not regard lightly the discipline of the Lord,
  nor be weary when reproved by him.
For the Lord disciplines the one he loves,
  and chastises every son whom he receives."

It is for discipline that you have to endure. God is treating you as sons. For what son is there whom his father does not discipline? If you are left without discipline, in which all have participated, then you are illegitimate children and not sons. Besides this, we have had earthly fathers who disciplined us and we respected them. Shall we not much more be subject to the Father of spirits and live? For they disciplined us for a short time as it seemed best to them, but he disciplines us for our good, that we may share his holiness. For the moment all discipline seems painful rather than pleasant, but later it yields the peaceful fruit of righteousness to those who have been trained by it. Therefore lift your drooping hands and strengthen your weak knees, and make straight paths for your feet, so that what is lame may not be put out of joint but rather be healed. Strive for peace with everyone, and for the holiness without which no one will see the Lord. See to it that no one fails to obtain the grace of God; that no "root of bitterness" springs up and causes trouble, and by it many become defiled; that no one is sexually immoral or unholy like Esau, who sold his birthright for a single meal. For you know that afterward, when he desired to inherit the blessing, he was rejected, for he found no chance to repent, though he sought it with tears. For you have not come to what may be touched, a blazing fire and darkness and gloom and a tempest and the sound of a trumpet and a voice whose words made the hearers beg that no further messages be spoken to them. For they could not endure the order that was given, "If even a beast touches the mountain, it shall be stoned." Indeed, so terrifying was the sight that Moses said, "I tremble with fear." But you have come to Mount Zion and to the city of the living God, the heavenly Jerusalem, and to innumerable angels in festal gathering, and to the assembly of the firstborn who are enrolled in heaven, and to God, the judge of all, and to the spirits of the righteous made perfect, and to Jesus, the mediator of a new covenant, and to the sprinkled blood that speaks a better word than the blood of Abel. See that you do not refuse him who is speaking. For if they did not escape when they refused him who warned them on earth, much less will we escape if we reject him who warns from heaven. At that time his voice shook the earth, but now he has promised, "Yet once more I will shake not only the earth but also the heavens." This phrase, "Yet once more," indicates the removal of things that are shaken—that is, things that have been made—in order that the things that cannot be shaken may remain. Therefore let us be grateful for receiving a kingdom that cannot be shaken, and thus let us offer to God acceptable worship, with reverence and awe, for our God is a consuming fire.

A Lack of Contentment

Many things may cause discontentment. Seeing and believing advertisements is a common cause. Another is browsing in shopping malls, which can raise your level of discontentment to the point that it becomes almost impossible not to yield to the temptation to buy. It's the same as putting a drink in front of an alcoholic. It's no coincidence that the level of personal debt and the amount of time people spend in front of television and in shopping malls have both increased dramatically in the last 30 years.

Contentment is found by understanding and accepting a few important truths. First, there is much more lasting joy to be had by nurturing relationships with friends and loved ones than by buying things. Second, it's much healthier to focus on what we have than on what we don't have. Contentment is also a spiritual issue. Replacing an attitude of "I want" with an attitude of "I'm grateful for what I have" begins in the heart.

The following verses provide God's perspective for contentment:

> Hebrews 13:5: Keep your life free from love of money, and be content with what you have, for he has said, "I will never leave you nor forsake you."

> 1 Timothy 6:6–11: Now there is great gain in godliness with contentment, for we brought nothing into the world, and we cannot take anything out of the world. But if we have food and clothing, with these we will be content. But those who desire to be rich fall into temptation, into a snare, into many senseless and harmful desires that plunge people into ruin and destruction. For the love of money is a root of all kinds of evils. It is through this craving that some have wandered away from the faith and pierced themselves with many pangs.

> Matthew 6:30–33: But if God so clothes the grass of the field, which today is alive and tomorrow is thrown into the oven, will he not much more clothe you, O you of little faith? Therefore do not be anxious, saying, "What shall we eat?" or "What shall we drink?" or "What shall we wear?" For the Gentiles seek after all these things, and your heavenly

Father knows that you need them all. But seek first the kingdom of God and his righteousness, and all these things will be added to you.

Philippians 4:19: And my God will supply every need of yours according to his riches in glory in Christ Jesus.

A Search for Security

For many of us, we seek to feel safe and secure. Unfortunately, our security, which can be defined as a state of being free from danger or threat, has more than just physical concerns but emotional and psychological aspects as well. Various aspects help to create a sense of security in our lives, including our income, the stability of our jobs, and our circle of friends, just to name a few. If there are changes to any of these security factors—for example, a loss of a job—most people tend to try to keep as much as possible unchanged and comfortable, such as by staying in the same house or associating with the same social groups even when they cannot afford to do so. These security factors have a tendency to lead people into the belief that they are secure, and when one of them changes, people tend to go into debt in order to regain a sense of security.

God's word says a lot about where our security should be:

Psalm 16:8: I have set the Lord always before me; because he is at my right hand, I shall not be shaken.

Psalm 40:2: He drew me up from the pit of destruction, out of the miry bog, and set my feet upon a rock, making my steps secure.

Psalm 91:1–12: He who dwells in the shelter of the Most High will abide in the shadow of the Almighty. I will say to the Lord, "My refuge and my fortress, my God, in whom I trust." For he will deliver you from the snare of the fowler and from the deadly pestilence. He will cover you with his pinions, and under his wings you will find refuge; his faithfulness is a shield and buckler. You will not fear the terror of the night, nor the arrow that flies by day, nor the pestilence that stalks in darkness, nor the destruction that wastes at noonday. A thousand may fall at your side, ten thousand at your right hand, but it will not come near you. You will only look with your eyes and see the recompense of the wicked. Because you have made the Lord your dwelling place the Most High, who is my refuge no evil shall be allowed to befall you, no plague come near your tent. For he will command his angels concerning you to guard you in all your ways. On their hands they will bear you up, lest you strike your foot against a stone.

A Search for Significance

The drive for significance is another reason people make foolish financial decisions. People often view significance as the quality of being worthy of attention or having a sense of importance. We all strive to be significant in certain areas of our lives. When we search for significance from our culture or society, we often try to achieve it through our possessions. Searching for significance in this way will almost always lead to **materialism**, a tendency to consider material possessions as highly important, such as the cars we drive, the homes we live in, the schools our children attend, and so forth. When we put more weight on our culture's definition of significance, rather

Materialism A tendency to consider material possessions as highly important.

than what God's word says, then our tendency is to buy things we cannot afford by using debt in an attempt to feel significant.

Scripture gives us some great insight into true significance:

> 1 Corinthians 6:19–20: Or do you not know that your body is a temple of the Holy Spirit within you, whom you have from God? You are not your own, for you were bought with a price. So glorify God in your body.

> Galatians 5:22–26: But the fruit of the Spirit is love, joy, peace, patience, kindness, goodness, faithfulness, gentleness, self-control; against such things there is no law. And those who belong to Christ Jesus have crucified the flesh with its passions and desires. If we live by the Spirit, let us also walk by the Spirit. Let us not become conceited, provoking one another, envying one another.

> 2 Corinthians 12:9: But he said to me, "My grace is sufficient for you, for my power is made perfect in weakness." Therefore I will boast all the more gladly of my weaknesses, so that the power of Christ may rest upon me.

Courtesy of daniilantiq2010/Fotolia.

DISCIPLESHIP MOMENT AND REFLECTION

Think back on two or three scenarios where you were affected by one of the common reasons for debt just presented. Describe the process that you used to take on debt and the outcome of that scenario. Spend time thinking about how this may have denied God an opportunity to work in your life.

FOUR CONSIDERATIONS FOR BORROWING

Now that we have considered the reasons that many people assume debt, let's move on to four considerations that should be reviewed before any debt is undertaken:

1. Common sense
2. A guaranteed way to repay
3. Peace of heart and mind
4. Unity

These rules don't necessarily make it easy to decide about taking on debt. The reason we even consider going into debt is to meet a need or desire that has become a high priority to us. In many cases, however, the temptation to use debt to meet the perceived need overwhelms both common sense and spiritual convictions. That's why there are objective considerations to follow. Weighing today's desires against future benefits is a classic psychological definition of maturity. These considerations, then, will help you to act maturely.

Consideration 1: Common Sense

This rule can be stated as follows: For borrowing to make sense, the economic return must be greater than the economic cost. To state it another way, when money is borrowed, the thing it was borrowed to purchase should either grow in value or pay an economic return greater than the cost of borrowing.

Looking at this rule in reverse, it makes no sense at all to borrow money if it's going to cost you more to borrow than what you are going to get in the way of an economic return. That return can be twofold. The thing purchased can grow in value, such as a home, or it can pay a return, such as a stock that pays dividends.

To ignore this rule is to say, in effect, that you are willing to borrow money and pay 12% interest in order to deposit it in a savings account earning 5% interest. I call this a commonsense rule because it makes no sense whatsoever to break it. Yet every day many people agree to "rent" money at a much higher cost than they can ever expect to receive in the way of an economic return. (Things like clothes and restaurant meals, of course, provide no financial return at all.) You may not have thought about paying interest as the privilege of "renting" money, but that is what it is.

Consideration 2: A Guaranteed Way to Repay

If you borrow money to buy a home and the lender is willing to take back the home as full payment of the debt in the event you're unable to pay, you have a guaranteed way to repay the debt. You are not presuming the continuation of favorable economic conditions.

Another example of consistency with this rule is the use of a credit card for the sake of convenience. Suppose you use your credit card to pay for dry cleaning, but you knew that the money was already in the bank to pay for that service. Using a card this way, strictly for convenience with the money in the bank, does not presume upon the future.

There are only three sources from which to repay borrowed money:

1. Income earned from sources other than that for which the money was borrowed
2. The sale of whatever the money was borrowed for
3. The sale or liquidation of some other asset, such as a certificate of deposit or savings account

The reliability of that source of repayment depends on many factors. Only you, as the potential borrower, can make that evaluation.

Consideration 3: Peace of Heart and Mind

To determine whether you satisfy consideration 3, you must ask yourself:

1. Why am I doing what I'm doing?
2. Does what I'm doing violate any ethical or spiritual principle?
3. Do I have peace in my heart, or spirit?
4. Do I have peace of mind when envisioning doing what I'm doing?

The first question gets at motives. Is the reason for borrowing to get rich quick, to avoid working, to satisfy a want, to give an appearance other than the truth, to meet a need, or to attain some other desire?

This is a penetrating question to have to ask yourself. If you can become disciplined enough to ask it and answer honestly before every borrowing decision, at the very least it will cause you to delay making impulsive decisions. In most cases, it will keep you from borrowing for the wrong reasons. If you're unwilling even to ask yourself the question, the chances are pretty good that your motives aren't right.

Another way to check your motives is to explain to your spouse or a good friend why you're doing what you're doing. Most of us are masters at deceiving ourselves so we can justify what we want to do. But when we have to explain our motives to someone else and it's unpleasant or uncomfortable, or if the borrowing "just doesn't sound right" to that person, our motives are most likely wrong.

After answering the first question, you almost always know the answer to the second. If the motive is wrong—greed, lack of discipline, lack of contentment—you know you're violating a spiritual principle.

To illustrate the application of this rule, suppose a man could afford to pay $25,000 cash for a car, enough to buy a moderately priced new car or a nice used one. On the other hand, if he adds $15,000 of debt to this amount, he could drive a new luxury car. He may even be able to "afford" the payments on this luxury car. By asking himself, "Why am I considering going into debt to buy the luxury car?" he's challenging himself to examine his motives.

Closely related to peace of heart is peace of mind. I would separate the two this way: The mind is the intellectual evaluation, whereas the heart is the spiritual and emotional evaluation. Applying this to a borrowing decision, you should ask yourself, "Am I free from confusion about this? Do I have clear thinking and a solid conviction that this is the right decision?"

The questions related to this rule are not all-inclusive. They're meant to get you to examine your motives.

Consideration 4: Unity

A commitment to unity between marriage partners (or, in the case of a single person, with an accountability partner) will help avoid most debt problems. But because accountability and unity go against our nature, this is the rule most often violated. Many husbands don't even consider it unreasonable to make a borrowing decision without consulting their wives.

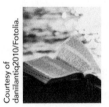

Courtesy of daniilantiq2010/Fotolia.

DISCIPLESHIP MOMENT AND REFLECTION

Reflect on a decision you have made or are planning on making. How did or would you evaluate each of the considerations in that case? Talk through this with your accountability and prayer partner. What insights have you learned through this reflection?

Misconceptions about Credit Card Debt

In this section, we want to review three popular misconceptions about credit card debt. As you will quickly see, these misconceptions appeal to our natural desires or fears.

Misconception 1: You Can't Live Without It

Most advertising is designed to get you to think that you "need" something or, ideally, that you "can't live without it." If a person has succumbed to the latest advertising and has access to a form of credit, specifically a credit card, it will be very easy for that person to make a sudden purchase. One way to avoid the unnecessary use of credit cards is to acknowledge when you are susceptible to making an impulse purchase. A good rule of thumb is to always wait at least 24 hours to buy something you want after you first see it. That means you never buy anything the first time you go to a store unless it is already on your shopping list.

Following this procedure helps you think through what you want to buy and why. It allows the emotion of the impulse to fade and gives you a chance to consider how much you need the item and whether you really want to spend your limited dollars that way. Additionally, if it is a big purchase, run the purchase by your accountability and prayer partner to solicit feedback on the purchase. If, after 24 hours and careful reflection, you still want the item enough to make a second trip back for it, you're more likely to be making a good decision.

Misconception 2: Having a Credit Card Means You're Creditworthy

If you are over the age of 18, you have probably been solicited for a credit card either at your school, in the mail, or via an advertisement on TV. In the advertisement, you were "prequalified" and eligible for up to some dollar amount of a credit line. Interestingly, these credit companies would not be able to determine your creditworthiness without some past credit history. In reality, credit companies do not check your credit history before extending an offer of a credit card to you. Here are a few questions you should answer that can help you determine your ability to handle the credit being offered:

Credit Card Usage Questionnaire

Use the following true/false questions to help determine your credit card behavior:

_____ 1. I have used my credit card to obtain a cash advance.

_____ 2. Credit card companies sometime send customers checks to use to pay bills and other expenses. I have used these checks to pay my bills.

_____ 3. I can only make the minimum payment on my credit card each month.

_____ 4. I have to use credit cards for things that I should be able to pay for with cash.

_____ 5. I am out of money several days before payday.

_____ 6. I am not regularly saving a part of my paycheck.

_____ 7. I could not live off of my savings for at least 2 months if I lost my job.

_____ 8. I have been late paying one or more of my bills in the past 3 months.

_____ 9. My bank has had to charge me for an overdraft or insufficient funds in the past 6 months.

_____ 10. I have borrowed money to consolidate my debts.

Now score your responses. How many times did you answer true?

1–3 True. *You can probably keep going. You don't splurge uncontrollably.*

4–7 True. *Slow down—you have entered the caution zone. It's time to draw up a budget, pay off your bills, and reevaluate your spending habits.*

7–10 True. *You have to stop. You might be wise to consult a credit counselor or financial planner for help in changing your spending habits.*

Adapted from Lawrence, F. C., Christofferson, R. C., Nester, S. E., Moser, E. B., Tucker, J. A., & Lyons, A. C. (2003). *Credit card usage of college students*. Retrieved from http://text.lsuagcenter.com/NR/rdonlyres/4D79415B-DA3E-43B4-9FF6-634F27D0D00C/4106/RIS107CreditCard4.pdf.

Reprinted from *Credit Card Usage of College Students: Evidence from Louisiana State University*, October 6, 2015, Louisiana State University Agricultural Center.

Misconception 3: All Interest Concepts Are Equal

Another misconception is that there's no difference between the stated interest rate and the effective interest rate, when in fact there's a big difference. The stated interest rate is the rate that is used to calculate your interest charge. The effective interest rate, however, is the actual interest charged when there are periods of compounding included over the time a debt is repaid. Here is a simple example: suppose you borrow $10,000 for 1 year at a stated interest rate of 8%.

Scenario 1: You decide to pay off the loan in one payment at the end of the year. When the loan is due, you will owe the principal ($10,000) and the interest (8%, $800), for a total of $10,800. In this situation, your stated rate is equivalent to your effective interest rate.

Scenario 2: You decide that instead of making a one-time payment when the loan matures, you are going to divide up what you will owe ($10,800, which is your principal and interest) over 12 equal payments. See Table 9.1 to see how the monthly payments would change the situation.

Table 9.1

Month	Beginning Balance	Month-End Balance	Payment	Balance
1	10000	10066.66667	900	9166.667
2	9166.667	9289.296296	900	8389.296
3	8389.296	8558.203281	900	7658.203
4	7658.203	7864.473314	900	6964.473
5	6964.473	7199.73845	900	6299.738
6	6299.738	6555.965333	900	5655.965
7	5655.965	5925.24833	900	5025.248
8	5025.248	5299.599297	900	4399.599
9	4399.599	4670.725217	900	3770.725
10	3770.725	4029.783996	900	3129.784
11	3129.784	3367.107143	900	2467.107
12	2467.107	2671.875819	900	1771.876
13	1771.876	1931.733575	900	1031.734
14	1031.734	1132.31484	900	232.3148
15	232.3148	256.6624152	256.66	0.00

As you can see, it would take almost 15 months in order to pay off this loan using 8% as the actual or effective interest rate. If we wanted to keep the payments to 12 months, our effective interest rate would actually be higher than 8%, and we would use the following formula to calculate that interest rate:

Effective annual interest rate (EAR) = $(1 + i/n)^n - 1$, where

i = annual stated interest rate

n = number of periods of compounding (in other words, how frequently the compounding occurs)

If we use this formula to solve for our EAR, we would arrive at:

Step 1: EAR = $(1 + .08/12)^{12} - 1$;

Step 2: EAR = $(1 + .00667)^{12} - 1$; *where we solved for (.08/12)*

Step 3: EAR = $(1.00667)^{12} - 1$; *where we solved for (1 + .00667)*

Step 4: EAR = $(1.0830) - 1$; *where we solved for (1.0667) to the 12th power*

Step 5: EAR = <u>.0830 or 8.30%;</u> *where we subtracted 1 from step 4.*

This effective annual interest rate tells us that we are actually paying more than the stated interest rate by 0.3% by making monthly payments. So why is this the case?

Keep in mind that you owe $800 on $10,000 borrowed. This in essence equates to $66.67 per month in interest ($800/12). So the monthly percentage of interest is .00667 for the first month. If we take our monthly payment amount of $900 (see Table 9.2), then our principal amount will be reduced to $9166. Our second monthly percentage rate is .0133 or ($9289 – $9166)/$9289. As you can see in Table 9.2, each month the rate changes as the amount of principal changes, yet the interest ($66.67) remains the same.

Table 9.2

Month	Beginning Balance	Month-End Balance	Payment	Balance	Monthly EAR
1	10000	10066.66667	900	9166.667	0.006666667
2	9166.667	9289.296296	900	8389.296	0.013377778
3	8389.296	8558.203281	900	7658.203	0.02013363
4	7658.203	7864.473314	900	6964.473	0.02693452
5	6964.473	7199.73845	900	6299.738	0.033780751
6	6299.738	6555.965333	900	5655.965	0.040672622
7	5655.965	5925.24833	900	5025.248	0.04761044
8	5025.248	5299.599297	900	4399.599	0.054594509
9	4399.599	4670.725217	900	3770.725	0.061625139
10	3770.725	4029.783996	900	3129.784	0.06870264
11	3129.784	3367.107143	900	2467.107	0.075827325
12	2467.107	2671.875819	900	1771.876	**0.082999507**

At month 12, our monthly interest rate has risen to 8.3%, which is what we found using our EAR formula. Additionally, at month 12, you still have a balance on the credit card and have to continue paying on it. As you can see, the effective interest rate is actually what you will be paying for the credit over the course of the year when the compounding frequency is greater than 1.

Recommendations for Battling Credit Card Debt

Most of us are going to have to use credit cards at least occasionally to function within our digital society. However, we *don't* have to use them to go into debt. There are three ways to get the benefits of using credit cards without going into debt:

1. Begin with a spending plan.
2. Use a debit card rather than a charge card.
3. Always pay the full balance at the end of the month.

Begin with a Spending Plan

The first recommendation for battling credit card debt is to begin with a spending plan. A spending plan helps give you real control over your spending. To use credit cards to fund your living expenses is to invite temptation in spending decisions.

The way to use credit cards responsibly is for convenience only, staying within your spending plan and paying the balance in full when the bill comes. If you haven't already done so, set up an annual spending plan.

Use a Debit Card

The second recommendation is to use a debit card rather than a normal credit card. An amount charged to a debit card is immediately deducted from your bank or brokerage account balance. It's really no different from writing a check. When using a debit card, the item should be entered in your checkbook just as if you had written a check. Then you deduct it from your available balance. In place of the check number in the check register, you put "Credit Card," or "CC," "VISA," or some other designation to indicate that it was a credit card transaction.

Using a debit card allows you all the convenience of a credit card, but you never have a credit card bill to pay because, in effect, it's paid the moment you use it. The only economic cost is the opportunity cost of not being able to "float" your purchases (i.e., earn interest on your money) for 30 days until the statement is received.

Always Pay the Full Balance

The final recommendation for battling credit card debt is that you should never allow a month to go by without paying off the full balance. If you are tempted not to pay the full amount because it will make a big dent in your available cash, then you are not using the credit card properly. A credit card can be a great convenience, but it should never be used to go into debt. Credit card debt violates the first rule in borrowing presented earlier in this chapter: The economic return should be greater than the economic cost. The cost of credit card debt—12% to 21% interest—is always greater than the economic return of whatever the card was used to buy.

Eliminate Your Credit Cards

If you feel that you cannot control your credit card spending, you should prayerfully consider cutting up your credit cards and throwing them away. In addition, stay away from the numerous unsolicited offers from credit card companies sent to you in the mail.

Debt Reduction and Elimination

To put it simply, you get out of debt little by little over time, and the major requirement is discipline. The challenging part of eliminating debt is that it usually requires a change in lifestyle and a reordering of priorities. That's painful. Our natural human tendency is to avoid such pain or change. You may wish there were some easy, painless way to get out of debt. But no such magic pill exists. If you want to be free of debt problems, you have got to make up your mind, with your family's cooperation, that you will pay the price now to enjoy financial freedom later.

There are only three main ways to gradually repay debt: (1) selling assets, (2) increasing your income, and (3) reducing spending. Selling assets may mean selling a car, a boat, a house, an investment, or something else that's part of your lifestyle now. Generating more income may mean working longer, having both parents work outside the home, obtaining a second job for the breadwinner, or asking adolescent children to work part-time. Each of these alternatives requires a change in lifestyle because something must be given up—namely, time or possessions. The third alternative, reducing spending and applying the new cash flow to debt repayment, is very helpful, but may not go far enough.

Keeping these three general alternatives in mind, there are five specific steps to take in getting out of debt. They are easy to list, but hard to do. But there really is no other moral way.

1. Determine where you are.
2. Stop going into debt.
3. Develop a repayment plan.
4. Establish accountability.
5. Reward yourself.

Step 1: Determine Where You Are

The first step to getting out of debt is knowing your total amount of debt. You can use any type of listing. You will find a Debt Schedule Worksheet in the Appendix that can be helpful. In addition to your credit card balances, include your installment loan balances, student loan balances, mortgage balances, and any other term note balances you owe. Then, you will have a realistic and honest appraisal of your total debt. In listing the amounts owed, do not include such regular monthly expenses as utilities, school tuition, food, and clothing, as those are normal monthly bills and not debts.

Step 2: Stop Going into Debt

This second step is extraordinarily difficult to take. It requires a decision that there will be no additional borrowing for any purpose. Before you even consider taking on more debt, you should go through the process described for evaluating the borrowing decision.

If you are an overspender and in debt, however, then even the latter sections will not be justification for avoiding this step. You absolutely must decide to use debt no longer. If that requires destroying your credit cards, get rid of them completely.

Take some time to read through the following verses, and talk them through with your accountability partner. The commitment to stop using debt in any form needs to be made to another person or couple who will hold you accountable.

> James 1:13–18: Let no one say when he is tempted, "I am being tempted by God," for God cannot be tempted with evil, and he himself tempts no one. But each person is tempted when he is lured and enticed by his own desire. Then desire when it has conceived gives birth to sin, and sin when it is fully grown brings forth death. Do not be deceived, my beloved brothers. Every good gift and every perfect gift is from above, coming down from the Father of lights with whom there is no variation or shadow due to change. Of his own will he brought us forth by the word of truth, that we should be a kind of first fruits of his creatures.

Luke 22:40: And when he came to the place, he said to them, "Pray that you may not enter into temptation."

Luke 11:4: [A]nd forgive us our sins, for we ourselves forgive everyone who is indebted to us. And lead us not into temptation.

Luke 4:13: And when the devil had ended every temptation, he departed from him until an opportune time.

1 Corinthians 10:13: No temptation has overtaken you that is not common to man. God is faithful, and he will not let you be tempted beyond your ability, but with the temptation he will also provide the way of escape, that you may be able to endure it.

1 Peter 4:12: Beloved, do not be surprised at the fiery trial when it comes upon you to test you, as though something strange were happening to you.

2 Peter 2:9: [T]hen the Lord knows how to rescue the godly from trials, and to keep the unrighteous under punishment until the day of judgment.

I Timothy 6:9: But those who desire to be rich fall into temptation, into a snare, into many senseless and harmful desires that plunge people into ruin and destruction.

Step 3: Develop a Repayment Plan

In addition to knowing your current debt level, you need to learn what your cash flow and your living expenses are per year. As you may remember from our financial planning diagram in Chapter 8, you must increase your margin in order to contribute more toward debt repayment. To repay, you must spend less than you make.

After tracking your expenses and developing a spending plan, you should now know how much debt you have, your projected cash flow inflows, and your typical outflows for living expenses. Having also made the commitment to stop going into debt, you can develop a strategy for repaying your current debts. There is no one "right way" of repaying your obligations. Following are several suggestions of sources for repayment. Using a combination of them will provide you with even more momentum in repaying debt.

- *Sell Assets*

The first idea for repaying your debts is to determine if there are any assets that can be sold. Even small things that could be sold through a garage sale or on eBay—clothes that aren't worn anymore, sports equipment that's no longer used, books already read—can help you rid of smaller debts.

The sale of bigger items, such as cars, investments, and perhaps even homes, should also be considered—but only after you have sold the more accessible, less drastic items lying around. Selling the big items may require a change in lifestyle. When considering selling large assets, it is important to remember your commitment to eliminate debt from your life.

- *Use Savings Accounts*

You should consider using "excess" savings in passbook accounts or surplus cash balances in checking accounts to pay off debts. Using a low-yielding savings account to pay off high-cost debt is a guaranteed high-yield investment. If you have a savings account and are still carrying credit card or installment debt, consider using those funds from your savings account to reduce debt. As we discussed previously, it is important and necessary to have emergency savings, but can you temporarily pare down your emergency savings?

If you take this approach, replenish your savings accounts as soon as you can after the debt is paid off. Just keep paying the same amount you had been putting toward credit cards and installment debt—only now it goes into your savings.

- *Double Payments*

A third strategy for getting out of debt is to double up on your payments. By doubling up on the payments and cutting expenses in another area of the budget, it is possible to pay off debt much more quickly. One extra payment—all going toward principal—can make a huge difference. In this situation, you may only be able to double up on one payment, and that is okay. Decide which debt is the most important for you to eliminate and start with that payment first. Many times it makes the most sense to try to eliminate your debts with the highest interest rates first; however, the next strategy may point you toward a different methodology for determining which debt to repay first. Whichever strategy you decide on (and you may decide on a completely different strategy), keep in mind that as you pay off one debt, then the payments that you were making toward that debt should now be used to increase your payment toward the next debt on your list to pay off.

- *Pay Off Smaller Debts First*

A fourth strategy is relatively painless, but can be very effective. Maintain your current debt payments per month, but shift any amount you are paying above the minimum payment on all your debts toward the repayment of your debt with the smallest balance. By paying off the smallest debt first, you can see quickly the progress you are making in eliminating your overall debt, and this may motivate you to keep focused on your debt repayment plan. Once you have paid off this smallest debt, apply all the payments you were making on the smallest debt to your next smallest debt until it is paid off as well. Keep up this process until all of your debts have been repaid. In this strategy, the amount you pay against your debt never changes until all of your debts have been repaid, but you gain momentum over time as you begin repaying some balances in full.

- *Reduce Living Expenses*

A fifth strategy is to review your living expense summary and, as a family, decide where you can cut expenses. Apply the amount cut to specific debts. You might decide to cut down on your entertainment, clothing, food, or home maintenance budgets—whatever fits your family situation. The fact is that in almost every family budget, as much as 10% to 20% could be used to repay debt. Again, it will require a change in lifestyle, but that cost will be more than offset by the sense of satisfaction in seeing yourself gradually get free of payments.

- *Reduce Tax Withholdings*

A sixth strategy is available if you are now receiving a federal income tax refund each year: Reduce your tax withholdings, and apply the increase in take-home pay to your debt repayment. The Internal Revenue Service (IRS) does not require you to pay in withholdings (or estimated payments) any more than what you will actually owe. It is a simple matter to decrease your withholding to the amount of the actual projected liability. This will be covered in greater detail when taxes are discussed.

- *Do Not Decrease Giving*

If you are actively giving to a place of worship or ministry, you should not decrease your giving. For people of faith, giving should be the first-priority use of money. Giving recognizes God's ownership of everything one has.

The only time when a reduction in giving to repay debt might be acceptable is if the debt situation is extremely severe, you have prepared a budget that cuts out all surplus uses of money, and you were already giving a relatively high percentage of income (say, more than 10%).

Strategies to Avoid in Debt Reduction Plans

- *Do Not Use Tax Money*

Do not reduce your tax payments below your projected liability. If you do, you are just borrowing from the government to pay someone else. You are not really reducing your debt at all. The day of reckoning is merely postponed to the following April 15. The IRS is not a pleasant creditor, and you could be subject to underpayment penalties if you withhold too little of your total tax liability.

- *Do Not Use a Debt Consolidation Loan*

In most cases you should not take out a debt consolidation loan. The typical reason for such a loan is that it "feels good," but it does not solve the basic problem. Many people who go for debt consolidation find that they later need another consolidation loan because the first loan did not really solve their spending problems.

If you are seeing a debt counselor, however, and the counselor recommends a debt consolidation loan as your only alternative—and if the counselor will work with you to set up a realistic budget—then it may be appropriate. But it should be a one-time step to relieve symptoms; it never cures the problem.

- *Do Not Seek a Second Full-Time Income*

Most debt problems are spending problems, not income problems. If a homemaker, for example, goes to work to fund a consumptive lifestyle, the root problems have not been identified and dealt with. Keep in mind the difference noted between getting a part-time second job as a means to pay off debt and getting a full-time second job to maintain a lifestyle.

I realize there are exceptions to this general rule: A family may face unexpected medical bills or desire to send their children to a private school for good reasons. But given human nature, extra income tends only to raise the level of discontentment, increasing the desire for more and more "things" that will not meet real needs.

- *Consider Counseling*

In severe debt situations, the repayment plan may require professional assistance. There is nothing disgraceful about asking for help. You might be a single mother with several children to support, for example, and increasing your income, selling assets, or decreasing expenses are not viable alternatives.

Step 4: Establish Accountability

If you report to someone you respect on a commitment you have made voluntarily, such as getting out of debt, you are more likely to follow through. If you are unwilling, however, to verbalize to another person your commitment to get out of debt, the likelihood of your sticking to your payoff plan is reduced dramatically.

Ask someone to hold you accountable, not in a general sense, but specifically to make certain payments on designated dates. Set up a schedule of reporting times. Establish the length of the accountability period. In other words, neither the commitment nor the time is open-ended. When you ask that person or couple to hold you accountable, be honest about why you are doing it. Most people who care about you would be honored to help.

Step 5: Reward Yourself

When we have something positive to look forward to, we are encouraged to maintain the discipline required to get there. Many people who have trouble losing weight, for example, develop a reward system that motivates them to maintain a diet. In the same manner, it is a good idea to reward yourself as you pay off debt.

When you pay off your first debt, for instance, you might treat yourself to a special lunch. When the second debt is paid off, you could enjoy a nice dinner. When the third debt is paid off, it might be time for a more expensive treat, such as a weekend away. Paying off the fourth or final debt could result in a reward such as clothes or furniture.

Be mindful that you don't get yourself into more debt through your reward system. The idea is to find ways to motivate yourself to maintain the discipline required to get out of debt. Rewards don't have to cost much money—or any at all. You might look forward, for example, to a coupon-book-burning ceremony or to hanging a homemade "Graduation from Debt" certificate on the family-room wall. Whatever the rewards you choose, they need to be personally motivational. The most significant reward will be the financial freedom that comes from getting out of debt.

GETTING STARTED AND GETTING OUT

The steps just outlined are designed to eliminate debt. The key is to take the first step. Getting out of debt is done one step at a time. It may appear to be an impossible task at this point, but you can do it, just as many have before you.

How to Keep from Going Back into Debt

If you could continue to be out of debt, would you not want to do so? You might think that's an obvious question. Then why do so many go back into debt? Why would wealthy people still incur debt? The answer is simple but not simplistic: They need to understand and avoid the common deceptions that often lead people into debt.

Ron's Corner

More deception (most of it unintended) is perpetrated by accountants, bankers, business schools, and businesspeople regarding the use of debt than most of us realize. We tend to respect these professional people. Yet they only pass on what they've been taught, and in many cases they've been taught half-truths. Being a CPA, former banker, alumnus of a graduate business school, and businessman myself, I remember what I was taught and have in turn taught others. And there are four major financial deceptions conveyed implicitly or explicitly by my professional peer group. They are as follows:

1. Borrowed money is always paid back with cheaper dollars in the future.

2. The tax deductibility of interest makes using debt a wise thing to do.

3. Inflation is inevitable; therefore, it is always wise to buy now at a lower cost than in the future at a higher price.

4. Leverage (debt) is financial magic.

The assumptions underlying the four statements outlined in Ron's Corner are typically not adequately explained. So to better understand the whole issue of using debt wisely (if, in fact, you should use it at all), you must recognize these deceptions and be able to evaluate them relative to your own circumstances. Otherwise, even after climbing out of your hole of debt, you are likely to find yourself falling right back in.

COMMON FINANCIAL DECEPTIONS

Deception 1: Paying Back with Cheaper Dollars

In times of severe inflation, you will hear lots of people—including experts—saying that prices are going to keep climbing indefinitely. The "wisdom" that goes along with this perspective is that you will always be able to pay back borrowed money with dollars that are worth less in the future, because inflation eats away at the purchasing power of money. This wisdom is true as long as two basic assumptions are met. The first is that you are able to borrow at a fixed interest rate so your rate does not increase with inflation. The second is that inflation will, in fact, continue.

The example used most frequently to sell this deception is the purchase of a home using a fixed-rate, long-term mortgage. This does in fact make sense in a time of inflation, because the dollars used to pay back the principal amount borrowed are worth less and less. In addition, when the interest rate is fixed for the life of the loan, you can't be hurt by the increasing interest rates that go hand in hand with inflation. That approach continues to make sense if the two assumptions continue to be valid.

History proves, however, that there are economic cycles. We can see oil prices boom and bust. High-tech stocks are high flyers; real estate prices soar in certain parts of the country, and then flatten out. Inflation was the threat in the 1970s and early 1980s, but dwindled to very low levels in the early 2000s.

The point is that even if inflation were a valid assumption overall, it may not be valid for the region in which you live. When industries leave an area, deflation, not inflation, occurs. There are not as many people demanding the same goods and services, so prices tend to fall. Thus, what is true today regarding inflation may not be true tomorrow.

Deception 2: The Tax Deductibility of Interest

This deception says that because certain interest is tax deductible, it's a good idea to have interest expense in order to reduce income taxes. There is a certain amount of truth to that, but it does not present the whole picture. First, not all interest is 100% tax deductible. Consumer interest (credit cards, car loans, installment loans) isn't tax deductible. Investment interest has limitations. The primary deductible interest is home mortgage interest, and that has limits too when the taxpayer's mortgage and/ or income goes above a certain amount.

Second, to say that an amount is deductible means only that it's deducted from income before computing the taxes owed. It does not mean that taxes are offset dollar for dollar by the amount of interest.

For example, if you pay a total of 30% in state and federal income taxes, then for every dollar of fully deductible interest you pay, you reduce your taxes by $.30, not $1.00. Thus, the net cost of paying interest is $.70 rather than $1.00. It's still a net cost, and it's never a benefit. To say that interest is tax deductible and therefore a good idea actually means it may offer a partial benefit.

Deception 3: It Will Cost More Later

As mentioned earlier, whenever inflation rates are relatively high, a common advertising theme is "Buy now, because it will cost more later." Many things may cost more later. However, that ploy begs the true question, which is not, "What will it cost later?" but, "Do I really need it?"

The second aspect of this deception is the underlying assumption that everything will continue to go up in price. That's not always the case. Personal computer prices, for example, are lower now than 5 years ago, with far more features available. And almost everything goes on sale periodically.

The way to understand the real question when tempted by this deception is to ask, "So what?" In most cases, the answer to that question is, "I may not need it later" or "The future price makes no difference to me because I have to have it." But making a purchase on the basis of the item costing more later is a very short-term perspective and may well be a financial mistake.

Deception 4: The Magic of Leverage

In graduate school, I was taught the so-called value of OPM—the use of other people's money. The idea is that if you use debt to purchase something, you get a far greater return on your portion of the investment than you would if you paid all cash for it.

The classic example has again been the purchase of a home. If you were to purchase a $160,000 home and put 10% down, you would have a net investment of your own money of $16,000. If that home then appreciated 10% in 1 year (meaning you could sell the house for $176,000), you would have a 100% return on the money you invested (a $16,000 gain on a $16,000 investment).

If, on the other hand, you paid cash for the home, you would have achieved only a 10% return (a $16,000 gain on a $160,000 investment). The difference between a 100% return and a 10% return is the magic of leverage.

During inflationary times, "sophisticated" people expanded the concept to say that it was always unwise to use your own money and always wise to borrow as much as you possibly could for whatever purpose. Those who did not understand the risks and assumptions bought into the idea.

This concept will work as illustrated if the underlying assumptions hold true. The basic assumption is that there will be appreciation rather than depreciation on whatever is purchased—an idea that is clearly false. The second assumption is that if you borrow money instead of paying cash, you have an alternative use for the money that will yield a return greater than your cost of money. Borrowing to buy a car at 6% interest, for instance, assumes that you can earn more than 6% by investing your money. But the only way you can earn that kind of return is to put your money at risk.

Many people have gone bankrupt trying to take advantage of leverage. They did not understand the real assumptions they were making. Even huge lending institutions all over this country have gone bankrupt because they lacked this understanding. Leverage can work for you, but it's like riding a bucking bronco in a rodeo: It's a lot easier to get on than it is to get off safely.

SUMMARY

Throughout this chapter, we covered a wide variety of topics on both credit and debt. First, we distinguished between the two: Credit is an amount of money extended to you that is available for use, and debt is the amount of the credit that has been used for a purpose and must be repaid. We evaluated the 6 "C's" of credit: (1) character, (2) capacity, (3) collateral, (4) capital, (5) conditions, and (6) co-signer. In addition, the most basic types of loans were reviewed. In this chapter, we evaluated misconceptions of debt in relation to the Bible by observing what the Bible does not say about debt while focusing on what the Bible does specifically say about debt. Four main reasons were discussed regarding why people take on debt, and four considerations were given that you should review when seeking to assume debt.

Sometimes it's difficult to make the hard decisions, especially when our desires or the demands of the family are so strong. But choosing to trust God is always the best decision. Hebrews 11:6 is clear in stating, "But without faith it is impossible to please Him for he who comes to God must believe that He is, and that He is a rewarder of those who diligently seek Him." Many times, the borrowing decision precludes the opportunity to see how God might provide, how He might take away the desire, or even how He may come up with a creative alternative to what we think we need.

The bottom line is this: (1) Don't ever put a lender in the place of God by depending on a lender to meet your needs. (2) Don't ever play God by determining that the only way to meet your needs is to borrow. That denies God the opportunity to be who He is. The One who created the universe by a spoken word can certainly meet all our financial needs.

From a biblical perspective, we are free to borrow money, but there are consequences we must bear when we do. In other words, God isn't obligated to bail us out of difficulties resulting from foolish decisions. The nonrepayment of money borrowed is not an option for a Christian. Personal bankruptcy may be warranted in some cases, but never to avoid repayment.

Debt may violate two biblical principles: It almost always presumes upon the future, and it may deny God an opportunity to do what He really wants to do in our lives. All other principles and commandments of Scripture that aren't specifically related to money may have financial consequences as they are lived out in your life.

Should you commit to eliminating your debt, the final sections of this chapter offered some suggestions to accomplish the task and some safeguards to help keep you from getting back into debt.

SUMMARY REVIEW QUESTIONS

1. Explain the difference between credit and debt.

2. List and describe the four reasons people use credit.

3. When establishing a credit account, what six characteristics do lenders usually consider?

4. What are the main components found on a credit report?

5. How can you determine your debt-to-income ratio?

6. What is collateral?

7. How can capital help in determining credit?

8. What are examples of conditions lenders use in evaluating credit?

9. Provide several Scripture verses that deal with co-signing.

10. What can a lender learn from pulling your credit report?

11. What is the difference between a revolving line of credit and a fixed loan?

12. What are the seven most basic types of loans?

13. What is an amortization schedule used for?

14. How do a mortgage and a home equity line of credit differ?

15. What are the two types of investment loans? How do they differ?

16. Which governmental entity helps guarantee loans for businesses?

17. Explain the concept of capitalization.

18. What does the Bible *not* say about borrowing?

19. What are three things the Bible specifically says about borrowing?

20. Explain the four reasons that people usually take on debt.

21. Describe the four considerations used in assuming debt.

Case Study Analysis

Bob and Debbie felt really good going into their next meeting with Pastor Steve. They spent over 3 hours reviewing their bank accounts and really began to get a clear understanding as to where their money was actually going. When they arrived, Bob and Debbie sat around Steve's table and began to show him all that they found by evaluating where all their money was going on a monthly basis.

After about 15 minutes of pleasantries, Steve began, "Bob, Debbie, all this work you accomplished looks great. I am glad that you took time to really see where your money was going. This is the first step to getting your finances in order. I have talked to so many clients over the years who think that because they make such-and-such income, they can exclude this process from meetings. My opinion, however, is that this is the most important part, self-discovery. The two of you together needed to see where your money was going, and, most importantly, you two needed to decide that a change was needed. I can't make that decision for clients. In today's meeting, we are going to discuss a similar task, which is to look at your overall debt and establish a plan to minimize and eliminate your debt. Let me say, debt in and of itself is not always bad, but as an advisor, I have seen time and time again that debt usually holds people back from following the Spirit's leading in their lives, whether that be moving to a certain area, taking a specific job, or going into the mission field. As we begin to unleash this burden from you, I pray that this brings about great joy and freedom in using your financial resources to continue to serve the Great Commission. So, here is the plan. I would like you to complete the following components."

Steve then instructed Bob and Debbie to complete the items in the following list, which you will now complete as if you were Bob and Debbie.

Instructions

Complete the following components for Bob and Debbie using their case file.

- The Debt Schedule
- Develop a repayment plan, using the Debt Repayment Worksheet as it relates to each debt on the Debt Schedule
- Write out a statement (that you both agree to) that holds you accountable to stop going into debt and describes what your accountability measures will be. Additionally, include how you will reward yourself for each debt paid in full.

Debt Repayment Worksheet

STEP 1: List your debts.

Debt	Balance Due	Interest Rate	Minimum Payment
Credit Card #1			
Credit Card #2			
Credit Card #3			
Credit Card #4			
Credit Card #5			
Car Loan #1			
Car Loan #2			
Other Debt			
Other Debt			
Other Debt			
Other Debt			
Other Debt			
Other Debt			
Other Debt			
Other Debt			
Other Debt			
Other Debt			

STEP 2: Decide how much extra you are able to pay each month to reduce your debts.

Debt Repayment Worksheet

STEP 3: Place your debts in the order in which you want to pay them off. You can do this three different ways:

1. You could pay them off from the smallest debt to the largest debt. This will give you the fastest sense of accomplishment.

2. You could pay them off starting with the debt with highest interest rate. This method will save you some money in interest.

3. Or, you can choose which debt to pay off first and just pick your own order. You could do this by deciding to pay off the debt first that is causing you the most stress, or the one that has the biggest minimum monthly payment, or use whatever reason you want.

The most important thing is that you are getting out of debt. The order in which you do that is probably not going to make a huge amount of difference.

	Debt	Balance Due	Minimum Payment	Extra Payment	Months until Payoff
1					
2					
3					
4					
5					
6					
7					
8					
9					
10					
11					
12					
13					
14					
15					

DEFINITIONS

Amortization schedule   (p. 191)

Capitalizes   (p. 193)

Collateral   (p. 188)

Co-signer   (p. 189)

Credit   (p. 186)

Credit lines   (p. 189)

Credit report   (p. 189)

Credit score   (p. 189)

Debt   (p. 186)

Discipline   (p. 198)

Fixed loans   (p. 191)

Home equity line of credit

(HELOC)   (p. 191)

Investment loan   (p. 192)

Materialism   (p. 200)

Revolving line of credit   (p. 190)

Small Business Association
(SBA)   (p. 193)

SCRIPTURE VERSES (ESV)

Proverbs 11:15—He who puts up security for another will surely suffer, but whoever refuses to strike hands in pledge is safe.

Philippians 4:19—And my God shall supply all your need according to His riches in glory by Christ Jesus.

Psalm 37:21—The wicked borrows and does not repay.

Proverbs 6:1–5—My son, if you have put up security for your neighbor, if you have struck hands in pledge for another, if you have been trapped by what you said, ensnared by the words of your mouth, then do this, my son, to free yourself, since you have fallen into your neighbor's hands: Go and humble yourself; press your plea with your neighbor! Allow no sleep to your eyes, no slumber to your eyelids. Free yourself, like a gazelle from the hand of the hunter, like a bird from the snare of the fowler.

James 4:13-15—Now listen, you who say, "Today or tomorrow we will go to this or that city, spend a year there, carry on business and make money." Why, you do not even know what will happen tomorrow. What is your life? You are a mist that appears for a little while and then vanishes. Instead, you ought to say, "If it is the Lord's will, we will live and do this or that."

Titus 1:8—But hospitable, a lover of good, self-controlled, upright, holy, and disciplined.

1 Timothy 4:7—Have nothing to do with irreverent, silly myths. Rather train yourself for godliness.

Proverbs 25:28—A man without self-control is like a city broken into and left without walls.

Hebrews 12—Therefore, since we are surrounded by so great a cloud of witnesses, let us also lay aside every weight, and sin which clings so closely, and let us run with endurance the race that is set before us, looking to Jesus, the founder and perfecter of our faith, who for the joy that was set before him endured the cross, despising the shame, and is seated at the right hand of the throne of God. Consider him who endured from sinners such hostility against himself, so that you may not grow weary or fainthearted. In your struggle against sin you have not yet resisted to the point of shedding your blood. And have you forgotten the exhortation that addresses you as sons?

"My son, do not regard lightly the discipline of the Lord,
    nor be weary when reproved by him.
For the Lord disciplines the one he loves,
    and chastises every son whom he receives."

It is for discipline that you have to endure. God is treating you as sons. For what son is there whom his father does not discipline? If you are left without discipline, in which all have participated, then you are illegitimate children and not sons. Besides this, we have had earthly fathers who disciplined us and we respected them. Shall we not much more be subject to the Father of spirits and live? For they disciplined us for a short time as it seemed best to them, but he disciplines us for our good, that we may share his holiness. For the moment all discipline seems painful rather than pleasant, but later it yields the peaceful fruit of righteousness to those who have been trained by it. Therefore lift your drooping hands and strengthen your weak knees, and make straight paths for your feet, so that what is lame may not be put out of joint but rather be healed. Strive for peace with everyone, and for the holiness without which no one will see the Lord. See to it that no one fails to obtain the grace of God; that no "root of bitterness" springs up and causes trouble, and by it many become defiled; that no one is sexually immoral or unholy like Esau, who sold his birthright for a single meal. For you know that afterward, when he desired to inherit the blessing, he was rejected, for he found no chance to repent, though he sought it with tears. For you have not come to what may be touched, a blazing fire and darkness and gloom and a tempest and the sound of a trumpet and a voice whose words made the hearers beg that no further messages be spoken to them. For they could not endure the order that was given, "If even a beast touches the mountain, it shall be stoned." Indeed, so terrifying was the sight that Moses said, "I tremble with fear." But you have come to Mount Zion and to the city of the living God, the heavenly Jerusalem, and to innumerable angels in festal gathering, and to the assembly of the firstborn who are enrolled in heaven, and to God, the judge of all, and to the spirits of the righteous made perfect, and to Jesus, the mediator of a new covenant, and to the sprinkled blood that speaks a better word than the blood of Abel. See that you do not refuse him who is speaking. For if they did not escape when they refused him who warned them on earth, much less will we escape if we reject him who warns from heaven. At that time his voice shook the earth, but now he has promised, "Yet once more I will shake not only the earth but also the heavens." This phrase, "Yet once more," indicates the removal of things that are shaken—that is, things that have been made—in order that the things that cannot be shaken may remain. Therefore let us be grateful for receiving a kingdom that cannot be shaken, and thus let us offer to God acceptable worship, with reverence and awe, for our God is a consuming fire.

Hebrews 13:5—Keep your life free from love of money, and be content with what you have, for he has said, "I will never leave you nor forsake you."

1 Timothy 6:6–11—Now there is great gain in godliness with contentment, for we brought nothing into the world, and we cannot take anything out of the world. But if we have food and clothing, with these we will be content. But those who desire to be rich fall into temptation, into a snare, into many senseless and harmful desires that plunge people into ruin and destruction. For the love of money is a root of all kinds of evils. It is through this craving that some have wandered away from the faith and pierced themselves with many pangs.

Matthew 6:30–33—But if God so clothes the grass of the field, which today is alive and tomorrow is thrown into the oven, will he not much more clothe you, O you of little faith? Therefore do not be anxious, saying, "What shall we eat?" or "What shall we drink?" or "What shall we wear?" For the Gentiles seek after all these things, and your heavenly Father knows that you need them all. But seek first the kingdom of God and his righteousness, and all these things will be added to you.

Philippians 4:19—And my God will supply every need of yours according to his riches in glory in Christ Jesus.

Psalm 16:8—I have set the Lord always before me; because he is at my right hand, I shall not be shaken.

Psalm 40:2—He drew me up from the pit of destruction, out of the miry bog, and set my feet upon a rock, making my steps secure.

Psalm 91:1–12—He who dwells in the shelter of the Most High will abide in the shadow of the Almighty. I will say to the Lord, "My refuge and my fortress, my God, in whom I trust." For he will deliver you from the snare of the fowler and from the deadly pestilence. He will cover you with his pinions, and under his wings you will find refuge; his faithfulness is a shield and buckler. You will not fear the terror of the night, nor the arrow that flies by day, nor the pestilence that stalks in darkness, nor the destruction that wastes at noonday. A thousand may fall at your side, ten thousand at your right hand, but it will not come near you. You will only look with your eyes and see the recompense of the wicked. Because you have made the Lord your dwelling place the Most High, who is my refuge no evil shall be allowed to befall you, no plague come near your tent. For he will command his angels concerning you to guard you in all your ways. On their hands they will bear you up, lest you strike your foot against a stone.

1 Corinthians 6:19–20—Or do you not know that your body is a temple of the Holy Spirit within you, whom you have from God? You are not your own, for you were bought with a price. So glorify God in your body.

Galatians 5:22–26—But the fruit of the Spirit is love, joy, peace, patience, kindness, goodness, faithfulness, gentleness, self-control; against such things there is no law. And those who belong to Christ Jesus have crucified the flesh with its passions and desires. If we live by the Spirit, let us also walk by the Spirit. Let us not become conceited, provoking one another, envying one another.

2 Corinthians 12:9—But he said to me, "My grace is sufficient for you, for my power is made perfect in weakness." Therefore I will boast all the more gladly of my weaknesses, so that the power of Christ may rest upon me.

Hebrews 11:6—And without faith it is impossible to please him, for whoever would draw near to God must believe that he exists and that he rewards those who seek him.

James 1:13–18—Let no one say when he is tempted, "I am being tempted by God," for God cannot be tempted with evil, and he himself tempts no one. But each person is tempted when he is lured and enticed by his own desire. Then desire when it has conceived gives birth to sin, and sin when it is fully grown brings forth death. Do not be deceived, my beloved brothers. Every good gift and every perfect gift is from above, coming down from the Father of lights with whom there is no variation or shadow due to change. Of his own will he brought us forth by the word of truth, that we should be a kind of first fruits of his creatures.

Luke 22:40—And when he came to the place, he said to them, "Pray that you may not enter into temptation."

Luke 11:4—[A]nd forgive us our sins, for we ourselves forgive everyone who is indebted to us. And lead us not into temptation.

Luke 4:13—And when the devil had ended every temptation, he departed from him until an opportune time.

1 Corinthians 10:13—No temptation has overtaken you that is not common to man. God is faithful, and he will not let you be tempted beyond your ability, but with the temptation he will also provide the way of escape, that you may be able to endure it.

1 Peter 4:12—Beloved, do not be surprised at the fiery trial when it comes upon you to test you, as though something strange were happening to you.

2 Peter 2:9—[T]hen the Lord knows how to rescue the godly from trials, and to keep the unrighteous under punishment until the day of judgment.

1 Timothy 6:9—But those who desire to be rich fall into temptation, into a snare, into many senseless and harmful desires that plunge people into ruin and destruction.

ADDITIONAL READINGS

Cameron, S., & Golby, D. (1990). An economic analysis of personal debt. *Bulletin of Economic Research*, 42(3), 241–247.

Davies, E., & Lea, S. E. (1995). Student attitudes to student debt. *Journal of Economic Psychology*, 16(4), 663–679.

Dayton Jr., H. L. (2011). *Your money counts: The biblical guide to earning, spending, saving, investing, giving, and getting out of debt*. Carol Stream, IL: Tyndale House Publishers, Inc.

Finn, M. C. (2003). *The character of credit: Personal debt in English culture, 1740–1914* (Vol. 1). Cambridge, UK: Cambridge University Press.

Lea, S. E., Webley, P., & Walker, C. M. (1995). Psychological factors in consumer debt: Money management, economic socialization, and credit use. *Journal of Economic Psychology*, 16(4), 681–701.

Livingstone, S. M., & Lunt, P. K. (1992). Predicting personal debt and debt repayment: Psychological, social and economic determinants. *Journal of Economic Psychology*, 13(1), 111–134.

Lunt, P. K., & Livingstone, S. M. (1991). Everyday explanations for personal debt: A network approach. *British Journal of Social Psychology*, 30(4), 309–323.

Papadimitriou, D. B., Shaikh, A. M., Dos Santos, C. H., & Zezza, G. (2002, November). Is personal debt sustainable? *Levy Economics Institute Strategic Analysis Series*.

Stone, B., & Maury, R. V. (2006). Indicators of personal financial debt using a multi-disciplinary behavioral model. *Journal of Economic Psychology*, 27(4), 543–556.

Sutherland, J. R. (1988). The ethics of bankruptcy: A biblical perspective. *Journal of Business Ethics*, 917–927.

Walker, C. M. (1996). Financial management, coping and debt in households under financial strain. *Journal of Economic Psychology*, 17(6), 789–807.

Watson, J. J. (1998). Materialism and debt: A study of current attitudes and behaviors. *Advances in Consumer Research*, 25(1).

Chapter 10

Transcendent Principle 3: Maintain Liquidity

Courtesy of Monkey Business/Fotolia.

BIG IDEA:
Build short-term savings as the only way to meet long-term goals.

LEARNING OUTCOMES

- Understand the importance of maintaining liquidity
- Define and articulate what entails cash management
- Explain the importance of the FDIC and NCUA
- Describe the types of accounts most common in cash management
- Identify other short-term products related to cash management
- Identify common cash management mistakes
- Explain the importance of insurance in a financial plan
- Describe the characteristics of the different types of life insurance: term, whole life, universal life, and variable life insurance
- Provide an overview of health insurance
- Describe the features of different types of health insurance plans
- Identify ways to control health-care costs
- Explain the use of disability insurance
- Explain the use of long-term care insurance
- List some other forms of insurance in the marketplace

This chapter seeks to provide you with concepts that relate to maintaining liquidity. In order to do this, we look at an overview of different ways to build liquidity as well as manage your liquidity. We also cover multiple types of insurance coverage in this chapter. Although it may seem that these two don't fit together, we need to keep in mind that insurance coverage is a risk-protection product that helps us to keep more liquidity than if we did not have appropriate and/or adequate coverage.

So what does the average American family look like from a financial standpoint? Table 10.1 provides a snapshot of the American family, according to 2015 data from the Statistic Brain Research Institute.

Table 10.1	Snapshot of the American Family	
American Family Financial Statistics		**Data**
Average American family savings account balance		$3,950
Percentage of working Americans who are not saving for retirement		40%
Percentage of American families who have no savings at all		25%
Average amount saved for retirement		$35,000
Average American household debt		$117,951
Average American family home value		$160,000
Average amount owed on home mortgage		$95,000
Average American household annual income		$43,000
Average credit card debt		$2,200
Percentage of American workers who postponed their retirement age this year		24%
Percentage surveyed who are very confident about having enough money for retirement		18%
Percentage of American adults who do not have a bank account		7.70%
Percentage of American adults who have an emergency fund to fall back on		38%

Source: http://www.statisticbrain.com/american-family-financial-statistics/

According to the Table 10.1, we see that the average American family has roughly $2,200 in credit card debt and only $3,950 in savings. A more staggering statistic is that roughly 25% of American families do not have any savings at all. So why is this idea of liquidity so important? Because the future is so uncertain—companies downsize, cars break down, medical emergencies occur, and so on. If there was a downsizing and the primary wage earner was released from his or her job, that $3,950 in savings would probably not last very long.

One reason that families have limited liquid assets (cash) is due to the higher costs associated with borrowing money. If, for example, you have money to buy normal consumer items (such as clothes, furniture, etc.), you do not need to use a credit card, which could charge up to 8% to 15% interest—not to mention other fees, such as late fees or annual fees just to carry the card. If you need to borrow money for items such as cars or furniture and use an installment loan, you not only pay the debt service the interest, but you have points, other bank fees, loan insurance, and late-payment penalties. The same applies for purchasing a home, where, in addition to the debt cost, you have credit report fees, settlement charges, and so forth, which can amount to thousands of dollars. When you pay with cash, you create the ability to negotiate and potentially lower the cost of a good or service you are wanting to purchase.

As you can see, cash is important because our culture seems to require that people have an expected amount of money in order to function (to pay for utilities, clothes, mortgage, etc.). If you do not have the money to meet those needs, you are likely to pay a premium for those same services, through borrowing costs or service fees and late penalties.

Think about that as you decide how much money to keep on hand. Cash can work wonders; however, it takes a proactive decision to use cash. So what's the big difference between using cash and using a credit card? Although there are probably many differences, one difference that is significant is the emotional implications of having to give up something (in this case cash) when making a purchase. The tangible act of giving something to someone else can create a hesitation that may prompt us to think again about the financial transaction we are getting ready to enter into.

Courtesy of danillantiq2010/Fotolia.

INVESTING FOR THE SHORT TERM

Cash management The process of handling your cash and cash equivalents in order to meet your immediate obligations.

It is important to know that all money should be given a purpose, especially short-term money. When a purpose is defined for short-term money, the likelihood that you will use the money for another purpose will decrease. There are many different ways in which to allocate short-term money, commonly referred to as cash management. **Cash management** is the process of handling your cash and cash equivalents in order to meet your immediate obligations. In most cases, cash management usually involves money that will be used to fund a purchase in less than 1 year. Examples of short-term uses could be annual property taxes on your home, yearly premiums for your life insurance contracts, or even paying for your car registration fees. These short-term examples are known expenses that have not come due, but will be required to be paid for in usually less than 1 year. The only caveat to this definition of short-term money would be that of an emergency savings fund simply because we anticipate not having to use this money. The money in this emergency account needs to be readily available, so we identify emergency savings as a short-term use of money. The main purpose of short-term money is that the money can be accessed easily and quickly converted into cash at its fair market value. Due to the fact that we typically know which expenses will be due, our willingness to take risk with this allotment of money should be extremely low. We will want to protect these funds so that we are certain enough money will be available for each item we designate to be paid from this allocation of money.

There are a variety of products that you can utilize to manage cash and cash reserves. In this chapter, we identify two of the most common types of accounts to use: checking accounts and passbook savings accounts. We also look at some interest-bearing accounts that can be utilized, such as money market accounts, certificate of deposits, credit union accounts, and brokerage accounts.

Remember that "liquid" means the funds are either in cash or can be readily converted to cash at its fair market value, so each of the options described will provide the account holder with liquidity.

Because most of the accounts discussed here are held by federally insured financial institutions, it is important to note what this "insurance" means and how it applies. The Federal Depository Insurance Corporation, known as the FDIC, is a government bureaucracy that insures financial institutions' depositors from the insolvency of the financial institutions. Credit unions, which are discussed later in the chapter, are insured in the same manner by the National Credit Union Administration (NCUA). Banks and other financial institutions pay a fee to the FDIC/NCUA and in return receive up to $250,000 of insurance for each depositor, not each account. It is important to note that each entity (i.e., depositor) is allowed full insurance coverage. The reason the term *entity* is utilized is that for a married couple, there could be three separate entities that could be entitled to full insurance coverage, as shown in Table 10.2.

Table 10.2

Entity	Account Ownership	Coverage Amount
Husband	Single-name account	$250,000
Wife	Single-name account	$250,000
Husband/wife	Joint account	$500,000/per owner
Husband's trust	Trust	$250,000/per beneficiary
Wife's trust	Trust	$250,000/ per beneficiary
Total insurance for husband and wife		**$1,500,000**

As you can see, federal insurance on your deposits can cover a substantial amount of money held in a variety of accounts at your bank. However, should these limits be insufficient, some banks are members of the Certificate of Deposit Account Registry Service (CDARS), which allows member banks to create certificates of deposit (CDs) in your name at other banks to take full advantage of the FDIC limits imposed on each bank. Based on the number of member financial institutions, a customer could potentially have up to $50 million dollars on deposit in one bank and be fully FDIC insured.

The following list describes several options for parking your margin or savings until the money is needed, while at the same time maintaining a high degree of liquidity and safety and maximizing your investment returns:

1. *Checking Accounts:* Probably the most common type of account used for cash management is a checking account. For most, checking accounts are opened up as soon as they begin to earn income. Checking accounts are standard in their operations. Once an account is opened, the checking account holders, those authorized to transact on the account, can make deposits into the account either through going to the bank, through an automated teller machine (ATM), or by mailing a check to the bank; additionally, some financial institutions will allow customers with camera-enabled mobile devices to take a picture of the front and back of the checks and deposit those funds into their accounts via the camera snapshot. Only checks can be deposited via camera-enabled devices; cash must be brought to the bank for deposit. Upon the deposit of funds into the checking account, those authorized on the account can now begin to transact using

Figure 10.1   Bank Routing Number and Bank Account Number

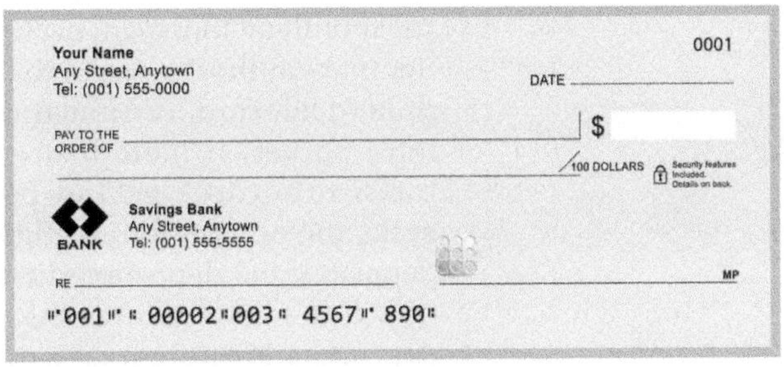

Courtesy of Jamey Ekins/Fotolia.

Check   A written item that gives the payee the ability to have funds withdrawn from the account.

Debit card   A plastic card with a magnetized strip on the back and a series of numbers on the front that provides any merchant electronic approval to remove the authorized amount from the account.

Automated clearing house (ACH)   An electronic network that allows an account holder to electronically approve a withdrawal of money from the account by providing the payee with the banking account number and routing number.

three main methods of payments: checks, debit cards, and automatic clearing house transfers. A **check** is a written item that gives the payee the ability to have funds withdrawn from the account. Another option is the use of a debit card. A **debit card** is a plastic card with a magnetized strip on the back and a series of numbers on the front that provides any merchant electronic approval to remove the authorized amount from the account. This is why you need to sign the receipt; your signature provides written authorization to withdraw the specified amount from your account. Finally, the account holder may authorize money to be withdrawn from the account through an automated clearing house, or ACH. An **automated clearing house** is an electronic network that allows an account holder to electronically approve a withdrawal of money from the account by providing the payee with the banking account number and routing number. The bank account number is the number assigned to the account by the financial institution, and is a way that the bank or credit union can identify different accounts. The routing number is a number that is assigned to each bank by the Federal Reserve system. Some banks may have multiple routing numbers; however, at the bottom of your checks you will have both your bank account number and routing number, as shown in Figure 10.1.

2. *Negotiable Order of Withdrawal (NOW) Accounts*: NOW accounts are checking accounts for which the financial institution will pay the account holder interest. In most cases, the amount of interest is tiered to the amount of money the account holder has on deposit within that account. These accounts usually require a minimum deposit and a minimum amount to keep in the account. The interest rates will usually range from .05% to up to 1%.

3. *Savings Accounts*: Savings accounts, like checking accounts, are accounts that are opened at financial institutions; they are designed for the account holder to put money aside for a later use. Most savings accounts allow for deposits and withdrawals with the same methods as used for a checking account. Savings accounts, in most cases, will pay the account holder interest on the money deposited and maintained in the savings account. For this reason, many people establish savings accounts early in life, some as early as when their parents first receive their Social Security number. Unfortunately, there are limits to how many transactions you can have on your savings account. Federal Reserve Regulation "D" limits the number of withdrawals. The following is an excerpt from the U.S. Government Publishing Office that outlines the rules related to these limitations:

> Under Regulation D, the term "savings deposit" includes a deposit or an account that meets the requirements of and from which, under the terms of

the deposit contract or by practice of the depository institution, the depositor is permitted or authorized to make up to six transfers or withdrawals per month or statement cycle of at least four weeks. The depository institution may authorize up to three of these six transfers to be made by check, draft, debit card, or similar order drawn by the depositor and payable to third parties. If more than six transfers (or more than three third party transfers by check, etc.) are permitted or authorized per month or statement cycle, the depository institution may not classify the account as a savings deposit. If the depositor, during the period, makes more than six transfers or withdrawals (or more than three third party transfers by check, etc.), the depository institution may, depending upon the facts and circumstances, be required by Regulation D to reclassify or close the account.

Source: Retrieved from http://www.ecfr.gov/cgi-bin/retrieveECFR?gp=&SID= 5a348b8e70dec42f8a2caced5c36ed61&mc=true&r=SECTION&n=se12.2.204_1133

The interest earned on savings accounts will range from 1% to as high as 4%, and some financial institutions will base the account holder's interest on the average amount of money kept in the account.

4. *Money Market Accounts*. In an effort to complete with money market mutual funds, banks and other financial institutions have developed money market demand accounts (MMDAs). These demand accounts at local banks pay interest rates that compete with those offered by money market mutual funds. The significant difference is that these accounts are insured by the FDIC. These accounts may require a minimum balance (e.g., $1,000) and will usually only allow a certain number of free transactions each month, normally six. MMDAs usually pay the highest rate of all transaction accounts offered by banks.

5. *Money Market Funds*: Money market funds (MMFs) are usually offered by mutual fund companies rather than banks. MMFs pay higher rates of interest than the bank. The rates vary daily according to the prevailing market interest rates. If prevailing rates increase, the MMF will track this rise. If rates fall, the fund will track downward. The funds are as liquid as accounts with banks or credit unions, and many offer check-writing privileges. Because they are not insured by the government through the FDIC like bank deposits, they have historically had defaults or losses. MMFs are usually used as the cash component of an investment portfolio to pay for new purchases or to park the proceeds from the sale of other securities. These accounts offer liquidity, flexibility, and the ability to write checks, all rolled into one package.

6. *Certificates of Deposit*: Certificates of deposit (CDs) are deposit accounts offered by financial institutions that act like a contract between the depositor and the financial institution, in which the financial institution pays a specified interest rate and the depositor agrees to keep money in the account for a specified time period. For example, you might put money into a 3-year CD at your local bank that earns an interest rate of 2.6%. Usually, the longer the time you commit to the bank, the higher the interest rate. CDs do not offer any deposits or withdrawals once the account is opened until the maturity date of the CD. The maturity date of the CD is the date when you can either add to the CD account or withdraw from the account. Some banks will automatically renew the CD account if no action is taken within a specified time period after the maturity date, usually 7 days. Should the CD holder take out funds from the CD, the financial institution will assess penalties, usually 6 months of interest for premature withdrawal. One common benefit of a CD is that the CD holder can

purchase a CD in varying terms and thus put aside money for a future use and set the terms of the CD so that it will mature when the funds are needed.

OTHER CASH MANAGEMENT AND SAVING OPTIONS

There are several other options you may consider as you seek to be proactive in your cash management responsibilities: treasury bills, Series I savings bonds, and Series EE savings bonds.

Treasury Securities

There are two main methods by which the U.S. government collects money to keep itself in operation: taxes and borrowing. Here we will discuss the borrowing component. There are three main types of borrowing the U.S. government conducts, which are classified by the time in which the borrowed funds need to be paid back. Treasury bonds are U.S. government bonds that range from 10 to 30 years and pay semiannual interest, whereas U.S. Treasury notes have shorter maturities, ranging from 1 year to 10 years. U.S. Treasury notes also pay semiannual interest. The final type of borrowing the U.S. government conducts is in the form of U.S. Treasury bills, also known as T-bills, which are discounted bonds ranging in maturity from 13 weeks to 26 weeks. Treasury bills are short-term government-issued debt and can be attractive because of the inherent safety provided by the full faith and credit of the U.S. government and because they are exempt from both state and local taxes. One of the reasons T-bills are utilized for short-term liquid investments is based on the highly active and stable secondary market. You can purchase T-bills directly over the Internet at www.treasurydirect.gov.

Series I Savings Bonds

Another way the government can borrow money is through the issuance of savings bonds. There are two basic types of bonds that we will discuss: Series I savings bonds and Series EE savings bonds. Series I savings bonds are issued by the U.S. Treasury Department in denominations between $25 and $10,000 and provide an "inflation-adjusted" return to their holders. Series I savings bonds are comprised of two rates: a fixed rate that is constant over the life of the bond and an inflation rate that is adjusted semiannually based on the Consumer Price Index (CPI). Interest earned from Series I savings bonds is free from state and local taxes, although some exclusions apply for financing education. Finally, Series I savings bonds do not exist in a secondary market, meaning you can only buy them through the U.S. Treasury; in many cases, local banks can help facilitate the purchase.

Series EE Bonds

Series EE bonds accrue interest, meaning the interest is not paid until the bond is redeemed, or cashed in. Series EE bonds can be bought in denominations of $25 through $10,000. However, Series EE bonds are bought at half of the face value. For example, should you want to purchase a $1,000 Series EE bond, you would only pay $500 for the bond. When the bond matures, which will vary based on the prevailing interest rates, you will receive the full bond amount. Series EE bonds will continue to earn interest for 30 years and then will stop earning any interest at all. These bonds can be redeemed after the first 12 months; however, some interest may be forfeited in doing so. Both Series I savings bonds and Series EE bonds can be purchased directly from (www.treasurydirect.gov).

Common Cash Management Mistakes

Despite the importance of emergency savings, few people keep savings on hand. It's startling how easily so many would become bankrupt from missing just a few paychecks. When it comes to mismanagement of cash reserves, most turn to debt to fill in the gaps. Unfortunately, this leads to several common mistakes. The first mistake is having a nonworking spouse enter the workforce to provide the necessary means to continue the family's current lifestyle. Two main issues arise in this scenario: (1) There would be additional costs incurred when both spouses work, which need to be carefully considered, and (2) increasing one's consumptive income does not usually solve the cash management problems. The second mistake people make is that after realizing they have used debt to fill their cash management shortfall, many will fall into a debt mentality. This mentality speaks to the idea that having debt is a "way of life" and that it's just too hard to fight it. Once a debt mentality has developed, it can be extremely challenging to overcome these thoughts and behavior changes. Next, and probably the most significant, is the mistake people make if they jump into buying a home prematurely, prior to having their cash management system in a position to afford the costs of home ownership. Finally, should you be disciplined and diligent enough to put aside money for later use, it is extremely important that you are not quick to use that money for nonemergencies. Emergencies do happen, such as car repairs, medical expenses, job layoffs, and so forth, and we need to be thankful that we have savings set aside to meet those contingencies. Unfortunately, some people think this extra savings can be available for other needs that are not really emergencies. After not using the emergency savings for 6 months or a year, it may be tempting to tap into it to fund other wants. The most common reasons for such "unauthorized tapping" are gifts, impulse purchases, and vacations.

DISCIPLESHIP MOMENT AND REFLECTION

Review all of the short-term savings options. Are any of these viable options for you? Speak to your prayer and accountability partner for guidance or additional thoughts.

Ron's Corner

Here are some questions and answers I have put together over my 40 years in practice.

Q: Why is liquidity important?

A: Liquidity, or having readily available cash (such as an emergency fund), is a key aspect of financial flexibility. In many cases it makes the difference between going into debt and remaining debt-free when you encounter unexpected expenses or major purchases. It gives you the choice of how you will pay and where you will buy, and allows you to pay without incurring interest costs.

Q: Where should I invest my emergency fund?

A: The purpose of an investment is to enhance one's income and/or growth. However, this is not the purpose of an emergency fund. It is used to provide liquidity. Your emergency fund should be kept in a place that offers a market rate return (interest) but without any risk, such as a bank money market savings account or a money market fund. The intention is to have these funds readily available as cash without the risk of losing principal. Availability, not return, is the chief criterion.

Q: Isn't having the amount of savings you suggest an evidence of lack of faith?

A: The Bible contains many references of being prudent and prepared. For example, Proverbs 6:6–8 uses a nature example:

> Go to the ant, you sluggard;
> consider its ways and be wise!

> It has no commander,
> no overseer or ruler,

> yet it stores its provisions in summer
> and gathers its food at harvest.

Matthew 25:3–4 says, "The foolish ones took their lamps but did not take any oil with them. The wise, however, took oil in jars along with their lamps."

Finally, Proverbs 21:20 states: "In the house of the wise are stores of choice food and oil, but a foolish man devours all he has."

The key to prudent savings is following a plan. Ask yourself, for example, what you are saving for and how much is needed. If cash is being accumulated simply because it gives you a good feeling or a sense of security, then you're probably following a hoarding plan rather than a savings plan. If your faith increases only as your bank account increases (or vice versa), then you don't have a money problem, you have a spiritual problem.

Q: I have just enough savings to pay off my credit card debt. Should I do this?

A: If you are being charged 18% to 21% in credit card interest and have the savings to pay it off, do so. But this advice is contingent on two factors. First, if an emergency arises you can borrow at an interest rate equal to or less than the current debt you have. Second, you will determine how to replenish your savings with the monthly payments you would have made toward credit card debt.

Q: What amount of liquidity do you recommend?

A: Once again, there are no absolutes. It depends on your job security, level of living expenses, debt situation, plans for major purchases, and your own "comfort level."

For example, for someone with good job stability, 2 months' living expenses would be adequate. If your job is susceptible to strikes and layoffs, it may take 3 or 4 months of living expenses. A person working on a 100% commission basis may need 6 months' expenses (especially if the commissions come in random intervals).

MAINTAINING MARGIN: INSURANCE BASICS

Insurance An agreement between two parties in which one party transfers a risk to another party for a fee.

Situations arise every day that will alter even the most efficient cash management plans. Therefore, it is important to understand how insurance is a complement to meeting and maintaining what God has given to us to manage. **Insurance** is an agreement between two parties in which one party transfers a risk to another party, usually for a fee.

Why Insurance?

The basic purpose of insurance is to transfer the risk that one is not willing to take (or is unable to take) to another party, usually an insurance company, willing to take the risk in return for compensation. We will cover several common types of insurance: (1) life insurance; (2) health insurance, to include vision and dental insurance; (3) property and casualty insurance; and (4) long-term care insurance. So what exactly do we mean by "risk" that the insurance company takes on? In most cases, the risk that is transferred is the "cost" associated with an adverse event. For example, car insurance transfers the risk of repairs or liability damages to those injured from a car accident. If we were to get into an accident and cause damage to our car, the insurance company will take the brunt of the repair costs to get the car fixed. If we didn't have insurance, then our ability to keep liquid funds may be impossible!

One of the key phrases used in insurance sales literature is "protection." Although this is certainly the purpose of insurance, emphasizing it can also induce an attitude of fear. This fear can lead to purchasing insurance on emotions rather than a factual basis. This fear could also be the foundation of overprotection, covering for any and all risks. For the Christian, this may lead to a shifting of trust from God to insurance and to an imbalance between amounts being provided and amounts one can afford.

Provision An amount to be provided.

Protection The act of keeping safe from an adverse event.

The perspective on insurance changes somewhat if the word *provision* is used instead of *protection*. **Provision** is an amount to be provided. When we seek to understand God's provision, our quest comes to understanding why God has provided the amount for our stewardship. Moving from **protection**, which is the act of keeping safe from an adverse event, to provision, which is what needs to be provided, will drastically shift our understanding of insurance. Only God can provide true protection; however, He gives us the ability to determine what provision should be appropriate.

God's purpose for the head of the household, according to the Bible, is to provide for the family:

"If anyone does not provide for his relatives, and especially for his immediate family, he has denied the faith and is worse than an unbeliever" (1 Timothy 5:8).

Under the biblical system, when the father died, the oldest son took the breadwinner's responsibility. If a man had no son, then his brother undertook the care of the family through the laws God had established for widows and orphans (Deuteronomy 14:28, 29; James 1:27). Ideally, these caring functions today would be provided by the body of Christ, the church. Unfortunately, they usually are not. So, a vital part of family financial planning today is for continued provision through the use of life insurance.

You may say that purchasing insurance shows a lack of trust in God to provide. Rather, this is the sound-mind principle being put to use. Insurance is a means that allows a head of household to provide for his or her family (1 Timothy 5:8). Only God knows the future, and insurance is nothing more than transferring the risk to someone else, but does not demonstrate a lack of trust in God.

Life insurance, on the other hand, could give your family the opportunity to continue to live in an environment to which they're accustomed. Insurance may be a form of God's provision when wisely secured. Insurance is acknowledgement of the certainty of death. It's consistent with the whole counsel of Scripture.

Life Insurance

We already mentioned that insurance is a contract between two parties in which one party transfers a risk to another party for a fee. The risk in life insurance is the death of a contributing member of a family. We all know that we are going to die; unfortunately, we don't know when. Life insurance sales literature might use the phrase "premature" death. The message that such terminology is trying to get across is that you might die prior to being financially able to continue supporting your family adequately. For example, suppose you are 28 years old, married, and have two kids. You work full-time and your spouse works part time, with the other time spent at home with the kids. In most cases, a 28-year-old would not be able to provide for a spouse and kids for another 60 to 70 years should that individual go to be with the Lord. Therefore, the 28-year-old would need life insurance, which transfers the risk of supporting the family should something happen to the head of household.

Types of Life Insurance

There are four basic types of life insurance: (1) term, (2) whole life, (3) universal life, and (4) variable life. Each has its unique characteristics and serves a purpose.

Term Life Insurance

Term insurance, as the name implies, is life insurance coverage contracted for a specific time period. Terms vary widely, from as short as 1 year to as long as 30 years, and usually will correspond with a specific event. One example of a short-term life insurance contract, say 5 years, may be to pay off a 5-year installment loan in the event of the borrower's death, which would make the borrower unable to pay. A longer term of use, such as 25 or 30 years, would provide coverage to support a nonworking spouse while raising children. Once the children leave the home and become independent, the need for insurance may change. Term premiums are usually the lowest of all the different types of life insurance contracts. **Premiums** are the amount paid annually to the insurance company for the transfer of risk. Premiums, although calculated annually, can often be broken up into monthly payments. Insurance carriers use **actuaries**, mathematicians and statisticians who deal with risk and risk measurements, to determine the level of risk that the insurance company is taking on and will set their premiums accordingly. In other words, those who are likely to require the insurance coverage (i.e., have more risk of dying) will likely pay more than someone who has a lower risk of using the coverage. The premium of term insurance makes up the mortality and expense fee. The **mortality and expense (M&E) fee** is a fee charged by the insurance company that is intended to cover the cost of death benefits to the beneficiary (mortality) and the expenses of the insurance carrier, such as administration and operations expenses. The following is a list of higher-risk behaviors that may increase one's life insurance premiums:

- Age—as you age, you are getting closer to having to use your insurance coverage.
- Smoking—research suggests that smoking will reduce one's life expectancy.
- Hobbies—some hobbies are more risky (such as skydiving) and may increase premiums.
- Health history—those with poor health may be more likely to have higher premiums.
- Your weight—being overweight, like smoking, leads to health problems and thus higher premiums.
- Your occupation—working in an office is likely to be less risky than, for example, being a commercial pilot.
- Family history—hereditary diseases or other family health issues can increase premiums.
- Gender—due to research suggesting that women live longer than men, in many cases, men will have higher premiums.

Premium The amount paid annually to the insurance carrier for the transfer of risk.

Actuaries Mathematicians and statisticians who deal with risk and risk measurement.

Mortality and expense (M&E) fee A fee charged by the insurance company intended to cover the cost of death benefits to beneficiaries (mortality) and the expenses of the insurance carrier, such as administration and operation expenses.

In addition to these factors (which considered in all life insurance contracts), the longer the term of an insurance contract, usually, the higher the premium. For example, if you took out a 5-year term policy, the premium would be drastically lower than that of a 20-year term policy. The longer the period covered, the more likely something could occur that would require the insurance company to pay the policy holder.

One of the significant drawbacks to term life insurance is that should the contract need to be renewed (there still may be a need for the insurance) at maturity of the contract, then the term policy will likely have much higher premiums due to the age of the insured. If you buy a 20-year term policy at the age of 25, the policy will lapse when you are 45. If you still need insurance coverage and decide to buy another term policy, the premiums are now based on your age of 45, which will make the annual premium much higher than when you originally purchased the insurance at age 25.

Traditional Whole-Life Insurance

As the name implies, whole-life insurance is designed to cover the entire life of the insured. Whole-life insurance is sometimes referred to as *straight-life* or *ordinary life* insurance and usually requires the insured to pay premiums for his or her entire life. The advantage to this scenario is that your premiums are fixed, or remain the same, for the entire duration of the insurance coverage. When a whole-life policy is established, the premiums will be higher than that of term policies due to the longevity of the contract (see reasons for higher premiums in the previous list) as well as the savings portion for account holders. This "saved" portion of your premium is put into a reserve account and is in addition to the M&E fee charged by the insurance company. In addition to the "saved" amount in the premium, whole-life insurance policies can pay policy holders a dividend, which will be added to the cash reserve amount. With this accumulation of the "saved" amount, account holders usually have an option that allows the insured to "pay up" the policy. This means that the account holder can use this reserve cash to pay for the remaining years of the policy so that the policy holder is no longer required to make premium payments. Should the cash reserve not be sufficient to pay up the policy in full, the account holder can choose to reduce the amount of insurance coverage in order to have the policy paid up in full. If the cash reserve amount is not used to pay up the policy, the policy holder can take this amount out of the policy and use it at his or her discretion. This "forced savings" aspect of a whole-life policy has been a controversial subject for many years. Although many people indicate that they do not need this savings option, few have shown an adequate amount of saving for the future, so this aspect of a whole-life policy may be helpful.

The primary disadvantage of a whole-life policy is the higher premiums required in the early years. Although term life insurance provides a cheaper insurance policy, it may be appropriate that some of your insurance protection may be met through whole-life insurance.

Universal Life

Universal life insurance has some similarities to whole-life insurance in that both types of insurance are considered to be permanent; in other words, the policies will not lapse as long as the premiums are paid. Also, both whole-life insurance and universal life policies have an insurance component and a savings component (with a stated rate of interest earned on the savings portion), which can allow the policy owner to make withdrawals from the policy. A universal life insurance contract is a combination of features from term insurance and features from permanent insurance. The most significant difference comes in the flexibility that a universal life offers to the policy holder. The policy holder can adjust the **death benefit**, which is

Death benefit The amount of money the insurance company will pay the beneficiary of the policy.

the amount of money the insurance company will pay the beneficiary of the policy. The **beneficiary** is the person or entity designated by the policy owner to receive the proceeds from the policy. In addition to adjusting the death benefit, the policy owner can also adjust how much in premiums he or she pays into the policy on an annual basis. As long as the premiums and any accumulated cash value (the savings component of the policy) are enough to cover the M&E fee, then the policy will remain in force.

A word of caution about universal life insurance: The same feature that could be an advantage of this contract may become a disadvantage. The ability to vary the premium payments may put the insured in a position of having underfunded the contract in later years and seeing the coverage expire. This is particularly true when an agent or company has projected a high rate of return throughout the life of the policy, when in fact the economic environment dictates that a lower interest rate was actually credited to the account during many of policy's coverage years.

Variable Life

Variable life insurance, like universal life insurance, offers flexible premium payments, and there is generally a minimum guaranteed death benefit. Unlike whole-life and universal life policies, variable life policies permit the policy holder to allocate a portion of each premium payment to one or more investment options after the M&E fees have been deducted. The investment options are typically mutual funds inside the variable life product. Traditional whole-life and universal life policies typically have a fixed dividend or interest rate credited to the accounts on an annual basis. In the last decade, as interest rates have declined, the interest rates credited to these products have also decreased. This has resulted in the current cash values of such policies being significantly less than the projections that were made 5 or 10 years ago. At the same time that interest rates have been declining, the stock market has been achieving double-digit returns. Variable life appears attractive because the cash value builds up inside these policies; if projected at the historical earning rates of the stock market, they can outperform other insurance products.

Although variable life insurance products appear to be superior life insurance products, there is a potential downside. The downside risk of the stock market in the short term may reduce or eliminate the cash value in the policy, and if the policy holder is unaware, the drop in cash value could cause the policy to lapse due to insufficient cash value to cover the M&E fees. Should the cash value drop and the policy holder is aware, the other downfall could be an unanticipated premium to be paid that was not expected and may cause a short-term budget imbalance. Be sure that you fully understand the risks and rewards of purchasing a variable life insurance product.

In order for you to determine what kind of insurance you need, it's important for you to step back and look at these insurance products from an overall perspective. This will mean asking the following questions:

1. How much do I need? (Use the Insurance Needs Analysis worksheet at the end of this chapter.)
2. How long do I need it for?
3. How much can I afford?

Once you answer these questions, the appropriate product should become obvious. Once you feel confident in your life insurance needs, then you will want to spend some time researching which insurance company you feel comfortable with. There are two ways that you can buy life insurance, either directly through the life insurance company or through a broker. A broker is usually a commissioned agent who will search the wide array of insurance products and help you find the right company. However you decide to purchase insurance, a good place to start would be your state's insurance department. The National Association of Insurance Commissioners

(NAIC) has information and links to each state's insurance department. Several questions you will want to ask yourself are as follows:

1. How long has the company been in business?
2. What is the industry rating?

A.M. Best is a third-party company that has analyzed the financial strength of insurance companies for over a century and publishes its findings and profiles on many insurance companies.

Insurance is a wise cornerstone of a complete financial plan, and it's necessary for peace of mind in the family unit. Although the marketplace can be confusing, thinking through the issues raised in this section should help you arrive at a sound decision.

Ron's Corner

Having three daughters is a joyful privilege—and an accompanying challenge. An example of that dual nature of privilege and challenge is the event that causes grown men to shudder: the wedding. To help me cope, I didn't have available to me another of the insurance industry's creative products: wedding insurance policies. No kidding, you can insure against "cold feet."

Imagine what an evacuation of a coastal town from a threatening hurricane or a flu outbreak among the bride and her family could do to the big matrimonial day. A postponement may cause the bride's parents to lose some of those nonrefundable cash deposits to halls, caterers, bands, and the whole range of wedding vendors. Holders of wedding insurance policies may recoup those costs.

As noted in Ron's Corner, there are what seems to be an unlimited number of insurance contracts available. Keep in mind that insurance is nothing more than transferring a risk to someone else for a fee. For example, Lloyd's of London is essentially a market for trading insurance risks of all kinds. Investors and companies can insure a football player's knee, a pop singer's voice, or a special event. Of course, they will do it for a price, called a premium. However, we focus here on the main types of insurance: health insurance, including dental insurance and vision insurance; disability insurance; and long-term care insurance. Property and casualty insurance (insurance that covers your home and car) are covered in the chapter on home and automobile insurance.

Health Insurance

In the United States, we enjoy relatively high-quality, accessible health care. But we certainly pay for it. Health-care costs have increased dramatically in the last generation. Even "minor" outpatient surgery can result in expensive bills from many different sources—some you didn't even know were involved in caring for you. A routine bone break of an active child may easily incur $5,000 in costs throughout the whole process.

Health insurance is probably the most important insurance policy to purchase. The likelihood of you or a family member needing care is almost certain, and the cost of that care is very high. Is it worth transferring that risk to an insurance company? For many, the answer is an astounding yes! Another unique aspect of making health insurance almost a necessity is that insurers have arranged for discounts from health-care providers. So, the actual cost of a procedure, after applying the contractual adjustment with the insurance carrier, is less than the cost to someone without insurance.

There are two main ways in which to obtain health insurance: through your employer or through your state's health-care exchange or the federal health-care exchange. These state and federal exchanges were implemented due to the passing of the Affordable Care Act of 2010 and are designed to provide health-care options to those who are not covered under an existing health-care plan, such as an employer health-care plan, Medicare, Medicaid, or the Children's Health Insurance Program (CHIP).

Costs of Health Care

Whichever method you use to obtain health care, there are some common terms that you should be aware of. First, as with life insurance, there is a premium that is paid on a regular basis to the insurance company. In most instances, the premium is paid monthly; for employees with employer-provided insurance, the premium is usually deducted from the employee's gross wages so that the employee does not have to write a check for the premium. Premiums are determined by the deductible you select and the type of coverage, such as family or individual, and can vary based on the level of benefits the policy holder is entitled to. In addition to the monthly premium, there are two additional costs that you may incur. The first is a **deductible**, which is the total amount of claims that the policy holder is responsible for paying for prior to the insurance company making any payments on behalf of the policy holder. The range of deductibles can be from zero, where the policy holder is not required to pay anything before the insurance company begins to pay, to $5,000. Policies that require a high deductible (and usually a lower premium) are called **high-deductible health plans** and usually require a minimum deductible of $2,500 per person or $3,500 per family. Once a deductible is met by the policy owner, then the second set of costs to the policy owner is referred to as co-insurance. **Co-insurance** is the percentage of all claims, after the deductible has been met, that the policy holder is responsible for. The co-insurance will usually vary depending on the service that is being provided, such as getting an x-ray or having a cast molded for a broken bone. Co-insurance will usually range from 80/20 to 90/10 to 100/0. The first number is the amount the insurance company will pay for each claim, and the second number is the percentage of the claim that is the responsibility of the policy holder.

As an employee, you probably consider health insurance a standard benefit of working for your company. It is important to note that many companies actually pay a portion, if not a significant portion, of each employee's annual premiums. Usually the cost shown to the employee during the **annual enrollment period**, the time that companies will allow employees to adjust their benefits, is only the portion paid by the employee. The total annual premium cost is usually much higher than what is shown. If you're self-employed, unemployed, or retired, the costs for health care can become expensive and in some cases burdensome for small businesses. In fact, one of the highest operating expenses for most businesses over the last several years has been providing health insurance for employees. Cost increases of 25% to 40% per year or more have not been unusual. Therefore, many businesses have been forced to alter benefits to employees related to health care.

Types of Health-Care Plans

There are three main types of health-care plans, each with its own costs, benefits, and exemptions: (1) PPO health insurance plans, (2) HMO health insurance plans, and (3) indemnity plans.

Deductible The total amount of claims that the policy holder is responsible for paying for prior to the insurance company making any payments on behalf of the policy holder.

High-deductible health plan (HDHP) An alternative to a traditional health insurance cost structure that enlists higher deductibles with lower premiums for the policy holder.

Co-insurance The percentage of all claims, after the deductible has been met, that the policy holder is responsible for.

Annual enrollment period A period of time during which companies will allow employees to adjust their benefits.

Courtesy of varenyk/Fotolia.

PPO Health Insurance Plans

PPO stands for preferred provider organization, and PPO plans are one of the most common types of health insurance plans. In a PPO plan, the policy holder must get medical care from a health-care provider that is contracted with the PPO. These medical professionals are on the "list" of preferred providers, and the insurance company will pay the highest percentage of the costs when policy holders see these providers. In a PPO, a policy holder may see someone outside the network of preferred providers, but the insurance company may reduce its coverage amount, in many cases to 50% of the cost. For example, consider a case of a foot injury in which the injured party received quotes from two health-care service providers, both of which indicated $1,800 in cost. The preferred provider would receive 80% of the $1,800 cost from the insurance company, or $1,440. If the other service provider was "out of network," then the insurance company might only pay 50% of the cost, or $900. The difference would thus be the responsibility of the policy holder.

HMO Health Insurance Plans

The second most common type of insurance plan is an HMO, which stands for health maintenance organization. Like the PPO, the HMO offers its health-care services through a network of service providers that contract with the HMO. The most significant difference in the two plans is that a primary care provider is selected from among the network providers and is the first point of contact for most health-care needs. Whereas in a PPO the policy holder can seek any health-care provider in the network of service providers, the HMO typically requires that the policy holder meet with the primary care provider (PCP) first, and if the PCP believes that additional services are required, the PCP will refer the patient to a specialist within the HMO network.

Indemnity Plans

Although they are no longer as common, there are still some indemnity health insurance plans in existence. Indemnity plans allow members to direct their own health care by seeing any doctor or visiting any hospital. Such plans will pay a portion of the health-care costs. In some instances, the employee may be responsible for paying for certain services upfront and then getting reimbursed by the plan provider.

Most people are still covered through the typical health insurance plan in which they choose their own doctor and hospital and pay a deductible on a calendar-year basis. The co-insurance amounts and the out-of-pocket maximum depend on what has been negotiated by the employer with the health insurance provider.

Controlling Costs of Health Care

As mentioned at the beginning of this chapter, insurance can help to keep adequate liquidity on hand; however, costs associated with health care can easily begin to add up. Here are eight ways in which you can help reduce your overall costs:

Claim A request for something to be considered.

1. *Accumulate claims for each family member until each satisfies the deductible.* A **claim** can be described as a request for something to be considered. This is more efficient because it provides more accurate processing on the part of the insurance company. It also benefits the employer because each time the insurance company has to process a claim—even though no claim is paid if the deductible has not yet been met—it goes on record as a claim against that company, and the company's rating has the potential to go up.

Outpatient treatment
Medical services that are not conducted inside a hospital but in many cases a private doctor's office.

2. *Become a careful consumer of health insurance.* Don't go to an emergency room unless it's absolutely necessary. Use **outpatient treatment**, medical services that are not conducted inside a hospital but in many cases in a private doctor's office, rather than inpatient treatment or treatment within a hospital, if at all possible. Do preadmission testing as an outpatient. Be mindful that medical services provided in an emergency setting are more costly services, so try to schedule a visit with your medical professional rather than seeking services in a medical clinic.

3. *Take steps for preventive medical maintenance.* Do things to stay healthy. Get proper exercise, follow a sensible diet, and get an annual physical. Even though the annual physical may not be covered unless some ailment is found, it will help troubleshoot for potential problems. Many employers offer incentives to employees involved in preventive health activities, such as stop-smoking classes.

4. *Keep accurate records of your medical expenses and double-check them when they come back from the insurance processor.* Nobody is infallible, and it's possible the company may have made a mistake in your favor.

5. *Opt for a higher deductible on your health insurance package if your family has been generally healthy.* The cost of your premiums will be less for the higher-deductible insurance.

6. *Use insurance wisely.* Health insurance costs increase partly because of overuse on the part of the insured. Certainly malpractice rates have had an impact on health insurance costs as well, but overuse has also contributed to the increase in expense.

7. *Understand the coordination of benefits if both you and your spouse are covered by separate insurance policies.* The employee's primary coverage is with his or her insurance carrier, and the employee's secondary coverage is with his or her spouse's carrier. Therefore, if you have to pay the deductible and co-insurance through your primary carrier, you may reimburse that amount through your spouse's carrier. Potentially, you could have 100% of your cost covered. However, analyze what it costs to carry insurance separately if you have to pay the premiums. The cost of the premiums may be higher than the benefit.

8. *Become familiar with the details of your company's health insurance package.* Your company's personnel officer should understand fully the benefits and costs, as well as other ways to maximize the benefits to both you and your employer. No one wants you to pay for expenses that you shouldn't. Therefore, be well informed so that you and your employer benefit from wise insurance usage.

Disability Insurance

Disability insurance
Insurance coverage that is designed to provide a percentage of the policy holder's income should the policy holder become unable to work.

Another typical type of insurance provided by employers is **disability insurance**, which is insurance coverage that is designed to provide a percentage of your income should you become unable to work. How dependent is your family on earned income? If you're like most people, you're very dependent! Most people would indeed encounter serious financial difficulties if their regular stream of earned income were to cease. The fact is, you have one chance in three that you'll suffer a long-term disability sometime between the ages of 35 and 65. This is a higher likelihood than that of dying within that time frame. Even so, disability income protection is often overlooked in financial planning.

Several Key Components of Disability Insurance

There are some basics of disability insurance that are paramount in understanding and determining the appropriate policy for you. First, you will need to know the disability benefit level. The **disability benefit level** is the percentage of income that the policy holder is entitled to in the event he or she is unable to work. It is extremely rare to find a disability insurance policy that will cover 100% of your income. Most disability insurance policies will range from 60% to 80% of your income. The second most important factor is the definition of "work" outlined in the policy. There are really two types of coverages for this:

- Your occupation: A *your occupation* policy is a policy that defines work as not being able to conduct the job that the policy holder held prior to the disability.
- Any occupation: An *any occupation* policy is a policy that defines work as not being able to obtain any form of employment due to the disability.

For example, if a professional artist was in an accident and had unrepairable damage to his or her hands, a your occupation disability policy would likely be invoked and pay the policy holder according to the terms of the contract. If that same artist had an any occupation policy, and the insurance company felt that the policy holder could still gain employment, the company might be inclined to not pay the claim.

The final component that needs to be considered is the time length of benefits outlined in the policy. In other words, should a policy be required to pay the policy holder, how long is the policy going to provide benefits? Each policy is different, but short-term policies will usually pay if the disability will last less than 1 year. An example of this may be recovering from a car accident in which the policy holder incurred several broken bones and needed routine physical therapy for a year, but was able to return to work after that. Long-term benefits usually only come into play if the disability will be long term in nature, and such benefits usually cease at age 65. If in the aforementioned example the policy holder was in a car accident that caused the loss of a limb, then the long-term disability policy might be required to pay the policy holder.

The main drivers in the cost of the disability premium are your occupation and your health. The premium for a construction worker is much higher than that for a banker, for example. If you have experienced previous back problems or arthritis, then your premium will be much higher than that of someone without these medical issues. If a person's occupation is very dangerous or his or her health is very poor, then the insurance company may not insure that person at all.

Disability Insurance Coverage

The following terms are associated with disability insurance coverage:

- *Renewal Protection:* An individual policy should be noncancelable and guaranteed renewable. This means the insurer can never cancel the policy as long as you continue to make the premium payments. Your future health will not be a factor in your ability to continue the coverage or the amount of premiums you pay.
- *Waiting Period:* The elimination or waiting period is the length of time after you become disabled before benefits begin. Coverage with a very short elimination period is available, but it's expensive and unnecessary. Waiting periods of 30, 60, 90, and 180 days are common.
- *Cost-of-Living Adjustments:* Some policies allow you to purchase an additional rider that increases your monthly benefit over a period of time tied to an inflation index. Although this may be desirable, the cost for this rider is fairly expensive.

- *Partial Disability*: Under this provision, benefits can continue even after you resume work part-time. Most policies do require that you first be totally disabled for a period of time, usually at least the length of your chosen elimination period. These are called *income replacement policies*, and the benefit paid is strictly a function of lost earnings.

Long-Term Care Insurance

Long-term care (LTC) is an insurance contract that is designed to cover expenses related to extended health-care services, such as living in a nursing home or the care required after being diagnosed with Alzheimer's disease. LTC insurance policies usually take effect when a policy holder meets certain requirements, oftentimes referred to as triggers. One trigger, for example, may be that you are unable to perform two of the following basic personal care activities: bathing, eating on your own, dressing, using the bathroom, or being able to transfer from one location to another. As one ages and draws closer to potentially needing assistance, usually the focus on LTC insurance becomes greater. So what's the big deal? Unfortunately, the cost for long-term care is not cheap. In fact, a Genworth (2007) study found that the average annual cost of 1 year in a nursing home is $74,806, or $204.95/day. Stay a few years, and your individual retirement account (IRA) will take quite a dent. Assisted living facilities have an annual cost of $32,572 for a one-bedroom unit.

Paying for Long-Term Care

The following four basic methods outline how long-term care costs may be covered:

- *Self-insure.* You could pay for the care with your current income (pensions, Social Security) and saved assets. The drawback to this approach is that the significant cost of care could wipe out a lifetime of saving.
- *Rely on the government.* You may use Medicaid if you're poor enough. If you spend all you have, then Medicaid will pay for your nursing home coverage. Few, if any, middle-class Americans will qualify for Medicaid initially. Contrary to the perception of many, Medicare does not cover long-term care costs.
- *Rely upon family members.* Are they nearby? Do they have the time and expertise to care for you? Is there enough room to live together? Can you (or them) stand it?
- *Obtain long-term care insurance.* This option will provide coverage for nursing home stays, home health care, assisted living, and/or other types of care. It will preserve your assets by paying the costs of your care. Of course, this insurance is not free.

The cost for obtaining a long-term care insurance contract will vary based on a wide variety of factors, such as your age, your health, and components of the contract such as daily benefit levels and the length of time that benefits will be paid. There are a variety of options in obtaining LTC coverage, and in some cases, LTC coverage can be wrapped around a life insurance contract so that if the benefit of an LTC policy is not used, the face amount of the policy will be distributed to a named beneficiary.

At times, companies within the insurance industry have used fear and emotional appeals to induce people into buying their product. Some have done this with long-term care insurance. The NAIC, an organization of all the state insurance commissioners, as noted earlier, tried to clarify who should consider long-term care insurance with the following consumer information:

So far in this chapter, we've explored insurance that you likely need. However, it is important to remember that there are lots of different types of insurance on the market. In the following list, we outline several policies for which a thorough analysis of the cost-to-risk tradeoff must be examined. One might suggest, like the title of a popular book, that the attitude of "don't sweat the small stuff" is appropriate regarding the following insurance policies. You can save thousands of dollars over several years when you use this buying principle: Buy insurance for the big risks; ignore the small risks. Here are some examples of insurance for small risks that you probably don't need:

1. *Home warranty/appliance plans*: Although these are fine if a seller of a house buys them for you, you should not buy them yourself. Appliances are generally fairly reliable, the costs of repairs are usually minor, and these plans often limit the coverage on major problems.

2. *Flight insurance*: The selling of flight insurance capitalizes on people's fears at the airport. Flying is statistically safer than driving. If you need life insurance, buy adequate life insurance. It will pay if death occurs by an airline accident. Flight insurance is relatively expensive.

3. *Cancer insurance*: This is another minor insurance policy often bought out of fear instead of need. Cancer insurance pays a fixed dollar amount to someone diagnosed with cancer. It does not pay for the many other diseases or sicknesses possible. If you have good health insurance, then it will pay for your medical bills related to cancer.

4. *Extended warranty and repair plans*: Did you ever notice that right after a salesperson convinces you of the reliability and quality of a new stereo, TV, or computer, the salesperson then tries to sell you insurance in case it fails? The stores get a large commission for selling these policies and aggressively push them. Your new item is usually already covered by an original manufacturer's warranty, and often the replacement cost is manageable by you. Again, self-insure when possible.

5. *Credit life policies*: Direct mail companies, banks, and credit card companies push life insurance, or credit life, that pays off your loan in case of your death. The premium may appear low because the insurance is low and decreases over time as you pay off the loan. These are very expensive for the amount of life insurance dollars they provide. Get enough life insurance coverage elsewhere to pay off any debts and avoid these policies (unless you have poor health and can buy these without a medical evaluation).

6. *Auto comprehensive and collision insurance on older vehicles*: Let's say that your 10-year-old vehicle has a book value of $1,500. If it is stolen or totaled from hitting a deer, the insurance company will only pay the book value. If you can

afford to replace the car, why pay the extra premium for a small possible pay-out? If your net worth is very high, you may be able to self-insure newer cars for collision and comprehensive. If you have $500,000 in the bank, do you need to pay premiums for insuring a $20,000 car? You could afford to replace it.

7. *Dental appliances, contact lenses, and eyeglass insurance*: These are more examples of the endless insurance items that businesses promote. These plans pay if you lose a retainer, tear your contact lenses, or break your glasses. Because these items are relatively inexpensive, just save your money and take the chance.

8. *Pet health care*: Pets can be enjoyable and important parts of your household, but do you really need to insure their health treatment?

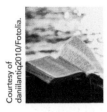

DISCIPLESHIP MOMENT AND REFLECTION

Consider the types of insurance you have and reflect on the following questions. If you don't pay your own insurance, ask those who are responsible for any insurance that you have the following questions.

- Why was the current insurance selected?
- Is there a type of insurance that you should have but do not?
- Is there a type of insurance that you have but perhaps may not need?

Use this time to review the information in this chapter to help determine the answers to these questions. Talk to your prayer and accountability partner about the answers.

SUMMARY

This chapter covered some very important aspects of a financial plan—namely, maintaining liquidity and understanding and using insurance. As we reviewed cash management, we described some of the most common types of accounts that are used when implementing cash management strategies. We also looked at some obstacles that you should be aware of to minimize cash management mistakes. We then turned our attention to insurance and how insurance is vital in being able to maintain financial liquidity. Life insurance policies were reviewed, including term, whole-life, universal life, and variable life insurance, with the characteristics of each explained. An overview of health insurance was provided, with the costs and types of plans that are most common, specifically, PPOs, HMOs, and indemnity plans. Next, both disability and long-term insurance policies were explored. Finally, we listed several other types of noncore insurance that are available in the marketplace.

SUMMARY REVIEW QUESTIONS

1. According to Statistic Brain Research Institute, how much does the average American have in the following areas?
   a. Savings accounts
   b. Retirement balance
   c. Household debt
   d. Home value
   e. Mortgage
   f. Annual income

2. Why is liquidity in a financial plan so important?

3. Define cash management. What type of risk should we take with our cash reserves? Why?

4. How much can a husband and wife potentially have in FDIC insurance? Explain how you arrived at your number.

5. List at least three types of accounts that short-term money might be deposited into and the characteristics of those accounts.

6. Differentiate between money market accounts and money market funds.

7. Differentiate between Series I savings bonds and Series EE savings bonds.

8. Define provision. Define protection. What is the difference between the two?

9. List the characteristics of these types of life insurance:
   a. Term insurance
   b. Whole life
   c. Universal life
   d. Variable life

10. Explain why health insurance is so important in a financial plan.

11. What is the difference between a deductible and co-insurance?

12. What is a PPO health insurance plan?

13. What is a primary care provider, and when is one needed?

14. List and explain the eight ways to help control health-care costs.

15. Define disability benefit level. How do you determine this?

16. What are the two definitions of "work" in a disability policy? Which is preferable?

17. What are the four coverage components of disability insurance contracts?

18. What are the four ways to pay for long-term care?

Case Study Analysis

The meeting between Bob, Debbie, and Steve began to move the conversation toward safety and security, which is exactly where Steve wanted them to be.

Steve began, "Bob and Debbie, we have made some great headway into understanding your finances and hopefully moving you from an owner to a steward mindset. However, as managers or stewards of God's resources, we need not be foolish. So I want to talk about two critical components, your financial asset safety, and (we're not talking about the investments yet) and your personal safety. You see should there be an issue with your financial institution, we want to make sure that you are protected under the FDIC limits. Since what we keep in the bank is usually our most liquid assets, it is so important to know how much we can keep insured under the FDIC guidelines. The second component is to make sure that your insurance coverages are adequate. You see you could have the most sound financial plan, but that plan is usually contingent on everything working perfectly. Most of us forget that we are not immortal, that only Christ is everlasting. As I point out regularly, Timothy in his first letter claims, "If anyone does not provide for his relatives, and especially for his immediate family, he has denied the faith and is worse than an unbeliever" (1 Timothy 5:8). It is important to note also that we as Christians are not using insurance as a replacement of our faith, but rather as a tool to provide for our relatives and families should the Lord call us to his Glory before we have accumulated sufficient financial resources to continually provide for our families. In order for you to complete this task, I want

you to take this life insurance needs worksheet. You will need this to complete part of your assignment from me. So I want you to do a few things before our next meeting:"

Assignment

1. Consider Bob and Debbie's liquid savings (refer to their balance sheet) and evaluate their FDIC coverage limits. Are Bob and Debbie fully insured? If not, what can they do to fully insure their liquid savings?

2. In addition, review Bob and Debbie's life insurance contracts and determine if they are under, over, or adequately covered to meet and provide for their family should either (or both) of them pass away prior to not having any financial dependents. Use the Life Insurance Needs worksheet as a guide.

DEFINITIONS

Actuaries (p. 235)

Annual enrollment period (p. 239)

Automated clearing house (ACH) (p. 229)

Beneficiary (p. 237)

Cash management (p. 227)

Check (p. 228)

Claim (p. 240)

Co-insurance (p. 239)

Death benefit (p. 236)

Debit card (p. 228)

Deductible (p. 239)

Disability benefit level (p. 242)

Disability insurance (p. 241)

High-deductible health plan (HDHP) (p. 239)

Insurance (p. 233)

Long-term care insurance (LTC) (p. 243)

Mortality and expense (M&E) fee (p. 235)

Outpatient treatment (p. 241)

Premium (p. 235)

Protection (p. 234)

Provision (p. 234)

SCRIPTURE VERSES (ESV)

Proverbs 6:6–8—Go to the ant, you sluggard; consider its ways and be wise! It has no commander, no overseer or ruler, yet it stores its provisions in summer and gathers its food at harvest.

Matthew 25:3–4—The foolish ones took their lamps but did not take any oil with them. The wise, however, took oil in jars along with their lamps.

Proverbs 21:20—In the house of the wise are stores of choice food and oil, but a foolish man devours all he has.

1 Timothy 5:8—If anyone does not provide for his relatives, and especially for his immediate family, he has denied the faith and is worse than an unbeliever.

Deuteronomy 14:28–29—At the end of every three years you shall bring out all the tithe of your produce in the same year and lay it up within your towns. And the Levite, because he has no portion or inheritance with you, and the sojourner, the fatherless, and the widow, who are within your towns, shall come and eat and be filled, that the LORD your God may bless you in all the work of your hands that you do.

James 1:27—Religion that is pure and undefiled before God, the Father, is this: to visit orphans and widows in their affliction, and to keep oneself unstained from the world.

ADDITIONAL READINGS

Beutler, I. F., & Mason, J. W. (1987). Family cash-flow budgeting. *Home Economics Research Journal*, 16(1), 3–12.

Chen, H., & Volpe, R. P. (1998). An analysis of personal financial literacy among college students. *Financial Services Review*, 7(2), 107–128.

Danes, S. M., & Hira, T. K. (1987). Money management knowledge of college students. *Journal of Student Financial Aid*, 17(1), 4–16.

Elizabeth, V. (2001). Managing money, managing coupledom: A critical examination of cohabitants' money management practices. *The Sociological Review*, 49(3), 389–411.

Golub, B., Holmer, M., McKendall, R., Pohlman, L., & Zenios, S. A. (1995). A stochastic programming model for money management. *European Journal of Operational Research*, 85(2), 282–296.

Henry, R. A., Weber, J. G., & Yarbrough, D. (2001). Money management practices of college students. *College Student Journal*, 35(2).

Lea, S. E., Webley, P., & Walker, C. M. (1995). Psychological factors in consumer debt: Money management, economic socialization, and credit use. *Journal of Economic Psychology*, 16(4), 681–701.

MacGregor, M., & Baldwin, S. C. (1988). *Your money matters: A CPA's sometimes humorous, consistently practical guide to personal money management, based on Scripture and with an emphasis on family living*. Ada, MI: Bethany House Publishers.

Mitchell, T. R., & Mickel, A. E. (1999). The meaning of money: An individual-difference perspective. *Academy of Management Review*, 24(3), 568–578.

Nürnberger, K. (2008). *Making ends meet: Personal money management in a Christian perspective*. Pietermaritzburg, South Africa: Cluster Publications.

Pahl, J. (1980). Patterns of money management within marriage. *Journal of Social Policy, 9*(03), 313–335.

Pahl, J. (1995). His money, her money: Recent research on financial organisation in marriage. *Journal of Economic Psychology, 16*(3), 361–376.

Ranyard, R., & Craig, G. (1995). Evaluating and budgeting with instalment credit: An interview study. *Journal of Economic Psychology, 16*(3), 449–467.

Scott, D. L. (1995). *The guide to personal budgeting: How to stretch your dollars through wise money management*. Guilford, CT: Globe Pequot Press.

Taylor-Hough, D. (2011). *Frugal living for dummies*. New York, NY: John Wiley & Sons.

REFERENCES

Genworth. (2007*). Genworth Financial 2007 cost of care survey*. Retrieved from https://www.longtermcare.genworth.com/comweb/consumer/pdfs/long_term_care/Cost_Of_Care_Survey.pdf

INSURANCE NEEDS ANALYSIS

Needs Analysis Chart

Income goals for your family (monthly):

Living Expenses	$_____
Taxes	_____
Giving	_____
Miscellaneous	_____
Education Expenses	_____
Debt Repayment	_____
Total Uses	$_____

Income sources (monthly):

Social Security	$_____
Retirement Assets	_____
Interest and Dividends	_____
Earned Income	_____
Unearned Income	_____
Disability	_____
Total Sources	$_____

Courtesy of duncanandison/Fotolia.

Chapter 11

Home Buying Decisions

BIG IDEA:
Purchasing a home is a privilege, not a right.

LEARNING OUTCOMES

- Know the common misconceptions regarding home ownership
- Explain the components of financing a home
- Know how to qualify for a home mortgage
- Explain the costs associated with buying a home
- Describe the methods used for selecting the best home
- Know how to make an offer on a home
- Understand how to choose between renting and buying
- Know the components of homeowners' insurance

Introduction

One of the largest purchases most individuals make is that of a home. This chapter seeks to provide a biblical lens through which to make this purchase.

Ron's Corner

Perhaps I'm showing my age, but I remember when the sound of a "home worth a quarter of a million dollars" sounded like a mansion. In today's real estate market, that's a bit below average! The average price for a new home in the United States, according to the Bureau of Labor Statistics, is $346,500, and the average price of an existing home is $224,100, according to an online site (www.ycharts.com) that tracks U.S. existing home sales. Some readers, particularly on either coast of the United States, would say those prices sound like a bargain compared to the real estate market they face.

Because these prices are far higher than average family incomes, the purchase of a home is a major financial commitment. You'll probably never make a single purchase of any item as expensive as a house. Housing prices have historically increased. But that doesn't mean a home purchase is a no-brainer. Thousands and thousands of houses are foreclosed upon every year. These foreclosures indicate that many house-purchase decisions were bad decisions.

Judy and I used to teach a Sunday school class for young married couples at our church. During one of the first Sundays we taught, we asked the group to name some of their personal goals and objectives. We had a spirited conversation that was finally summarized by one young man who said that most of them expected to start financially where their parents had left off after 25 to 40 years of hard work. They wanted to have two cars and a three- to four-bedroom home in a nice area that was close to work. They also wanted the home to be fully furnished when they moved in.

Judy and I had to laugh in private afterward. We had been married 28 years at the time of our hearing the comments of these young married couples, and our home still wasn't fully furnished as we would like. It had taken us a long time to get where we were. (I expect that about the time we finally finish decorating, we'll want to move into another home.)

In this chapter, we first look at some of the common misconceptions concerning buying and owning a house. Next we examine how to select an affordable house and how to select a real estate agent. Then we review the different types of mortgages, discuss refinancing, and offer thoughts regarding paying off a mortgage early. Finally, we go over some helpful hints that appear to provide a "free lunch."

COMMON MISCONCEPTIONS

As we have already been pointing out, owning a home is not a right. The idea that it is a right is one of the most common misconceptions about home ownership. No one has a right to a house. Home ownership is part of the American dream, but it certainly is not a right. When and if God chooses to provide a house should be considered a privilege.

> Proverbs 3:5–6: Trust in the LORD with all your heart, and do not lean on your own understanding. In all your ways acknowledge him, and he will make straight your paths.

A second misconception is that conventional wisdom is always right and never changes. The conventional wisdom has always been that home ownership is better financially than renting, and renting is simply "throwing money down the drain." That's generally been true since World War II because of three things:

- fixed-rate, long-term mortgages;
- appreciation (inflation); and
- the tax deductibility of mortgage interest.

Notwithstanding this general truth through the years, we will look more closely at the numbers later in this chapter. Renting generally provides more flexibility, and may sometimes make more financial sense.

One final common misconception is the belief that a home is a good investment. However, to understand this misconception, one must consider the idea of what an investment is supposed to do: generate income, which a home does not do, or appreciate enough in value that at some determined point you can sell it for a profit. A home is rarely purchased with the idea of selling it when the value reaches a particular point. Even if it increases in value, you are no better off selling it if you must buy another house to replace it in the same area that has also realized appreciation.

Ron's Corner

A better way to state what most people mean by a home being a good investment is that a home may be a good purchase, but it's seldom bought with true investment intent. I can assure you that most wives would be pretty upset if their husbands advised them that as soon as their home had appreciated 20% in value, it was going to be sold. This would be especially true if the wife had expended any time or emotional energy in redecorating and refurnishing the home. A house may be an investment, but a home is not. At best, it's a good purchase.

Courtesy of daniilantiq2010/Fotolia.

DISCIPLESHIP MOMENT AND REFLECTION

What are your initial thoughts as you think about home ownership and the "American dream"? When you purchased your home (if you own a home), can you recall your reasons for buying the house you chose? Did you feel you had the right, perhaps even an obligation, to buy? What would you tell members of the next generation if they were asking you about a decision to buy a home?

BUYING A HOUSE

Buying a home can be an intimidating and exhilarating experience, especially the first time. It involves so many decisions! In this section we provide some guidelines that will help you avoid most of the pitfalls of finding and purchasing a home.

Once you have made the decision to buy, your first consideration is money: How much do you have, and how much can you borrow? The answers to these two questions will control the location and price range of your home. The best way to buy a home is to pay cash, but most homebuyers must arrange financing for a portion of their purchase. Although borrowing money is not prohibited in Scripture, Proverbs 22:7 tells us that the borrower becomes "the servant of the lender." So use restraint and proceed cautiously when borrowing money. Remember, just because a bank is willing to lend you a certain amount of money does not mean you can actually afford to repay that amount in accordance with the bank's terms.

Many types of loans are available. Most are arranged through banks and lending institutions, but it is possible to finance a home through its owner or other private individuals. In either case, the terms of the loan will specify the minimum down payment, interest rate, the length of the loan, repayment terms, and qualifying criteria.

Down Payments. A **down payment** is the difference between the purchase price of the home and the loan amount. It is an upfront payment toward the purchase price of the house. Historically, lenders have required a down payment of at least 20% of the purchase price. In recent years, as home prices increased and lenders became more aggressive, many lenders began accepting a down payment of as little as 3% or 5%. Mortgages with down payments under 20% will usually require the purchase of private mortgage insurance, known as PMI, to protect the lender against default.

Private mortgage insurance (PMI) is an insurance policy that many lenders will require borrowers to purchase in order to protect the lender from the borrower not making payments, known as a default. **Default** means that a borrower has not met his or her obligations under the loan documents, including the failure to make payments as outlined by the lender. When a borrower pays a down payment that is lower than the standard 20%, lenders believe that borrowers are more likely to default on their loans and thus require borrowers to purchase PMI. PMI premiums can be removed from the borrower's requirements once the loan on the property is less than 80% of the value. For example, suppose you find a condo for sale listed at $100,000 and decide to buy it by getting a mortgage. You decide to put down 5% ($5,000) and thus borrow $95,000. The loan-to-value ratio on the home would be $95,000/$100,000, or 95%. In this instance, you would almost certainly be required to have PMI when borrowing the $95,000. After some time, you review your monthly mortgage statement and realize that you only owe $78,000 on the same $100,000 home. In this case, your loan-to-value ratio is $78,000/$100,000, or 78%, and you may be able to contact your lender and get the PMI premiums removed from your monthly payment.

Interest Rates. The **interest rate** is the percentage rate charged for the use of the money.

There are two standard types of interest structures in lending. The first is referred to as a fixed rate. **Fixed-rate mortgages** are mortgages with the same interest rate throughout the duration of the loan period.

Several characteristics of fixed-rate loans are as follows:

- Rates are usually higher than those of adjustable-rate options at the original time of the loan.
- Rates stay the same during the duration of the loan.
- Payments stay the same during the duration of the loan.
- Such loans are advantageous in periods of rising interest rates.

The other common interest rate type is an adjustable rate, commonly referred to as an **adjustable-rate mortgage** (ARM). Adjustable-rate mortgages, as the name implies, allow for changes in the interest rate to occur during the loan period. So what makes the rates go up and down? ARMs are generally tied to some standard interest rate index, usually the current rate on U.S. Treasury bills, and can adjust up or down. Several characteristics of ARMs are worth noting:

- Rates are usually lower than those of fixed-rate mortgage rates at the original time of the loan.
- They usually have a fixed period during which the rate does not change.

Down payment The upfront payment toward a purchase, usually for a home.

Private mortgage insurance An insurance policy that many lenders will require borrowers to purchase in order to protect the lender from the borrower not making payments or defaulting on the loan.

Default When a borrower does not meet his or her obligations in making payments on a loan.

Interest rate The percentage rate charged for the use of money.

Fixed-rate mortgage A mortgage loan type in which the interest remains the same during the duration of the loan period.

Adjustable-rate mortgage A mortgage loan type that includes an interest rate that can fluctuate or change during the loan period.

- The interest rate can go up and down based on the tracking index used to set the rate.
- Payments can change based on changes in the interest rate.

Loan Term. The length, repayment terms, and qualifying criteria of a loan can vary. Most home mortgage loans are set up for 15 or 30 years with monthly payments. The length and repayment terms affect the repayment amounts and the total amount paid for interest over the term of the loan. Most loans have monthly payments; however, some loans have a payment due only upon maturity. Some common loan payment terms are as follows:

- Interest-only loan: This loan structure only requires the borrower to pay interest during the term of the loan.
- Balloon loan: A balloon loan is a loan type that will usually have minimal or no payments during the term of the loan, with the balance of the loan (plus interest) being due at the end of the term. These are usually short-term loans. One example of a balloon loan, as it relates to mortgages, comes in the form of a construction loan in which the borrower is borrowing funds to build a home. The balance of the loan in a construction loan will be due upon the completion of the home being built. When the balloon loan is paid off, the borrower will roll into longer-term financing, such as a 15-year mortgage.

QUALIFYING FOR THE LOAN

There are multiple factors that influence a lender's decision to extend a loan to an individual. Several factors are discussed in this section (recalling the 6 C's of credit outlined in Chapter 9), including credit scores, income, and outstanding debts.

Credit Scores

One of the most reviewed components for determining your creditworthiness as a borrower is your personalized credit score, often referred to as your FICO score. Bill Fair and Earl Isaac established a company, Fair, Isaac, and Company (which is where we get the term *FICO* from), in order to create a scoring system to quantify consumer risk. The scores range from 300 to 850, where higher scores indicate lower risk to the lender. According to myFICO, the consumer division of FICO, the FICO score is derived by the following categories and is determined only from what is on your credit report:

- Payment history: Thirty-five percent (35%) of your FICO score is based on your past payment history because this is one of the primary concerns lenders have regarding extending credit. Considerations for this category include the following:
  - Credit payment history on many types of accounts
  - Public record and collection items
  - Details on late or missed payments (delinquencies)
  - How many accounts show no late payments
- Amounts owed: Thirty percent (30%) of your FICO score is based on how much credit you already have outstanding. Considerations for this category include the following:
  - The amount owed on all accounts
  - The amount owed on different types of accounts (credit cards, installment loans, student loans, etc.)

- How many accounts have balances, with a higher number of accounts with balances indicating higher risk
- How much of the total credit line is being used and other "revolving" credit accounts, or how close one is to using the total amount of credit available
- How much of an installment loan is still owed compared with the original loan amount

- Length of credit history: Fifteen percent (15%) of your FICO score is determined by how long your credit history is. Generally, the longer your credit history is, the higher your score will be. Considerations for this category include the following:
  - How long your credit accounts have been established
  - How long it has been since you used various accounts

- Credit mix in use: Ten percent (10%) of your FICO score is based on the mix of credit products used, such as credit cards, retail accounts, installment loans, mortgages, and so forth.

- New credit: Ten percent (10%) of your FICO score is based on the amount of new credit you have sought to establish. Attempts to open multiple credit accounts in a short time period generally are viewed as a higher credit risk. Considerations for this category include the following:
  - How many new accounts you have
  - How many recent inquiries into your credit report you have
  - Length of time since your credit report inquiries were made
  - How long it has been since you opened a new account

Figure 11.1 summarizes these FICO score factors.

Figure 11.1 FICO Score Breakdown

Source: http://www.myfico.com/CreditEducation/WhatsInYourScore.aspx

Ratios

Once the credit report has been pulled and the credit score is provided, lenders begin to use various ratios to determine how much a borrower is qualified to borrow. The two main ratios used by lenders are the housing expense ratio and the debt-to-income ratio.

The first ratio, the **housing expense ratio**, is determined by comparing the amount of the anticipated house payment (including principal, interest, taxes, and insurance) and the borrower's gross monthly income. It is recommended that this ratio determination be less than 25% of gross monthly income. For example, suppose your lender informs you that your monthly payment is expected to be $1,000 and your monthly gross income is $5,000. Then your housing expense ratio would be 20% or $1,000/$5,000.

The second ratio, the debt-to-income ratio, is determined by comparing all *monthly* debt payments (including the loan payment on the loan being sought) with gross income. This ratio is important to understand because it informs the lender how much of your gross income is needed to make all of your debt payments. Ideally, you want to keep this debt-to-income number low, and in no event should you permit this ratio to exceed 40%. For example, suppose you have the following monthly debt payments:

- Student loan: $200
- Credit card: $100
- Car loan: $250
- Mortgage: $1,000

In this scenario, the total debt payments would be $1,550 ($200 + $100 + $250 + $1,000). If this person's gross monthly income was $5,000, then the individual's debt-to-income ratio would be 31%, or $1,550/$5,000.

It is important to keep in mind that these ratio limits are not formalized but rather guidelines that bankers and real estate agents ordinarily use. These examples have been used for illustration purposes, so do not think that you need to get as close to these ratio maximums as possible. You are better off if you can find a home meeting your needs—but maybe not all your wants—at a lower price so that your ratios are in the lower range. This will reduce your financial pressures and debt load. In the booming U.S. real estate market of the 2000s, some bankers and real estate agents advocated even higher ratios (meaning higher debt loads compared to income) based on the assumption that real estate prices were rapidly moving higher each year. This is a dangerous assumption and one that has been proven false in recent history. There was a drastic spike downward in real estate prices during the recession of 2008–2009.

Housing expense ratio
A financial ratio that compares the amount of an anticipated house payment to include principle, interest, taxes, and insurance to that of the borrower's gross monthly income.

DISCIPLESHIP MOMENT AND REFLECTION

As you look on your financial and living situation, how much could you put toward a mortgage considering your debts? Would you be under the recommended 40% debt-to-income ratio?

With these ratios in mind, how do you determine what the price range for your home should be? There are several ways to help determine where to start. First, you can use what Freddie Mac, the common name for the Federal Home Loan Mortgage Corporation, a private corporation chartered by Congress to increase the supply of mortgage funds available to homebuyers, suggests about affordability in its blog post titled "Mansion or Yurt: What Can You Afford?" (Freddie Mac, 2014):

You can get a very rough estimate of your affordable home price range by multiplying your annual gross income by 2.5 (this, of course, varies depending on current interest rates, your debt and credit history).

Using this 2.5 number as a guideline, if you had an annual salary of $60,000, then it is likely you could afford a home that is selling for $150,000 ($60,000 × 2.5). Keep in mind that this is just a generalization and will change based on other factors, such as credit score, debt ratios, and so forth.

Another method could be to use an online calculator or tablet app that provides deeper analysis for determining how much you can afford to pay for a home. Many of these tools will ask you to provide the following:

- Expected interest rate
- Initial down payment
- Term of loan (years expected to pay, such as 15 or 30)
- Other debt payments you are currently making

These factors can usually give you a good idea as to the cost of a home you can reasonably afford considering the inputs you enter.

A mortgage lender, a housing counselor, or consumer credit counselor can also help you better understand these guidelines. Don't forget that you also have to save for the down payment, closing costs, inspections costs, moving expenses, and other related expenses.

Finally, you may decide to talk directly with a loan officer or a mortgage lender. Most lenders offer a "prequalifying" interview at no charge, which is an excellent way to learn about loans, closing costs, and prepaid items involved in purchasing a home and receive a personalized evaluation of how much the lender may be willing to loan. It is important, however, that you understand that the lender will most likely be willing to loan you more than you should borrow. Prayerfully consider the information provided to you by the lender and evaluate it with your spouse.

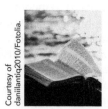

Courtesy of daniilantiq2010/Fotolia.

DISCIPLESHIP MOMENT AND REFLECTION

Take a few minutes to read through some of these passages as you think about your home-buying experience. What prompting do you feel the Holy Spirit leading you to do? If you were to implement the 2.5 multiplier of income guideline, how much could you afford to pay for a home?

Proverbs 23:3–4: By wisdom a house is built, and by understanding it is established; by knowledge the rooms are filled with all precious and pleasant riches.

Proverbs 24:27: Prepare your work outside; get everything ready for yourself in the field, and after that build your house.

Psalm 1:1–2: Blessed is the man who walks not in the counsel of the wicked, nor stands in the way of sinners, nor sits in the seat of scoffers, but his delight is in the law of the Lord, and on his law he meditates day and night.

Philippians 4:19: And my God will supply every need of yours according to his riches in glory in Christ Jesus.

CLOSING COSTS AND PREPAID ITEMS

Closing costs Costs that are associated with servicing a home purchase, such as attorney's fees, loan processing fees, and appraisal fees.

Escrow account A designed account where a third party holds funds to be later used for specific purposes, mainly paying property taxes and annual homeowner's insurance.

In addition to the down payment, there are other costs associated with purchasing a home. These costs are usually separated into two different categories; closing costs and prepaid items. **Closing costs** are costs for services in the home buying process such as attorney's fees, loan processing fees, and a property appraisal. Prepaid items are not really closing costs, but are payments you may be required to make in advance for various items, such as prorated property tax and homeowner's insurance premiums. These prepaid items (taxes and insurance) are usually put into an account called an escrow account to be distributed when the payments come due. An **escrow account** is a designated account where a third party holds funds to be later used for specific purposes. The mortgage lender will usually set up an escrow account for insurance and property taxes and will pay the borrower's homeowners' insurance and property tax bills from this account on an annual basis.

The costs associated with buying a home can be estimated as a percentage of the loan amount, with closing costs generally running about 3% to 4% and prepaid items about 1%. Keep in mind that on any loans in which the purchaser pays less than 20% down, lenders also usually require the purchaser to pay for PMI which will be added to the house payments.

There are many costs associated with borrowing money and purchasing a home. Obviously, the less money you borrow, the more you save on financing costs. Because first-time homebuyers' down-payment money and monthly income are usually limited, some homebuilders and sellers offer to pay some of the closing costs. Depending on the loan, lenders place some restrictions on the percentages a seller can pay. Check with a loan officer or real estate agent about these restrictions.

SHOPPING FOR A HOUSE

Now that you have a general understanding of financing and how to determine how expensive of a house you can afford, you can realistically begin listing and prioritizing your housing needs and wants. The wants and needs of people in different stages of life will differ greatly. However, whether you are interested in single-family housing or a condominium, you can venture out on your own or contact a real estate agent. The Internet is a useful tool to reduce time spent in home shopping because it helps you determine whether or not you want to visit a home without having to go inside of it. When getting ready to go through the process of purchasing a home, you will find the following steps beneficial as you begin.

List Your Needs

Before you start house-hunting, you should make a list of all of the features that you really need. Then list the features that would be nice to have. Once you have a clear idea of what you need as well as what you would like to have in a house, finding a house will be much easier. Be realistic. Looking for a home takes time, so focus on what's important to you. After looking at lots of homes, the line between "I need a garage" and "I want a garage" can get very blurry. Many people focus more on what they would like to have instead of focusing on what they actually need—that can mean they pass up a home that meets their needs in hopes of finding one that meets their wants. Ultimately, you should be able to find a home that is a blend of your needs and wants.

Find a Real Estate Agent

One common way people find homes in their price range is by using a real estate agent. The agents can look for homes that meet their clients' needs and financial circumstances and can help them narrow their choices. Usually the seller pays the agent's fee, so there's no direct cost for you to hire an agent. One of the best ways to find an agent is to ask your family and friends for referrals. You can also look at newspaper ads for "open house" listings and talk with the professionals showing houses. You will want to choose an agent who makes you feel comfortable and can provide the knowledge and services you need.

Real estate agents can help you find the kind of home you want, examine comparable homes, and compare different neighborhoods. Agents will usually rely on an Internet tool known as the Multiple Listings Service, or MLS, to conduct their searches for homes. The **Multiple Listing Service** (MLS) is a comprehensive listing of properties within a given geographic area updated continuously and is only accessible through real estate agents that subscribe to or are members of the MLS. The MLS provides the agent with a significant amount of information, including property descriptions, photos, previous sales, and so forth. Additionally, agents are able to establish a buyer's profile by including the specific requirements of the type of home a buyer is searching for, including the number of bedrooms and bathrooms (see previous "List Your Needs" section), and have listings automatically sent to the buyer that meet those requirements.

When you are ready to make an offer on a home, an agent will usually handle the negotiations with the seller, including presenting your bid. Your agent can also refer you to a mortgage broker for getting proposals for a mortgage, although you should still shop around. The mortgage broker will provide you with a preapproval letter, handle prequalification, and help you secure mortgage financing.

As you seek to find a real estate agent, the following are some questions you should ask to help determine which agent may be right for you:

- How long has the real estate agent been in the real estate business?
- Is this person a full-time agent?
- Is the real estate agent familiar with your preferred community?
- How many homes has the real estate agent sold in the past year?
- What's the average sale price of those homes?
- Does the real estate agent usually work with sellers or buyers?
- How many buyers is the real estate agent presently working with?
- Is the real estate agent acting as an exclusive "buyer's agent," meaning that the agent work exclusively with people like you who are interested in purchasing a home, as opposed to property owners who are selling a home?
- How many sellers is the real estate agent presently working with?
- What are the real estate agent's strengths?

Multiple Listing Service (MLS) A database of property listings usually providing access to available homes within a geographical area and is continuously updated. The MLS is accessed through real estate agents that subscribe to the MLS service.

- Will the real estate agent offer you three homebuyer references?
- For how long will the agent's contract with you be valid?

Choosing a Neighborhood

When you can tell the difference between your housing wants and needs, you will probably have an easier time deciding what you want and need from a neighborhood. Where you live can be as important as the house you live in. You may already have a good idea about the neighborhood you would like to live in. Don't let that keep you from looking at other neighborhoods with similar qualities based on recommendations from your agent.

The following are some questions you should ask about any home you are considering buying (your realtor will be a great resource in helping you answer many of these questions):

PERSONAL QUESTIONS

- How long will it take to get to work, and what will it cost?
- Is this country, suburban, or urban living?
- How far will you be from family members?
- How far will you be from religious activities, night school, or other regular activities?
- Are there any homeowners' association fees?
- Are there any homeowners' association rules or restrictions?
- Can you afford the county and/or city taxes?

NEIGHBORHOOD-SPECIFIC QUESTIONS

- What are the schools, hospitals, and other public services like? How close are they?
- Is it an older, established neighborhood or a younger, still-growing community?
- Are there signs of new construction in the area?
- What will this neighborhood look like in 10 years?
- What are the values of other homes in the neighborhood?
- If there are nearby restaurants and other businesses, do they bring people out during the day or at night?
- What's the traffic like during the week? In the evenings? On weekends?
- Is the empty lot behind the house going to be developed?
- Are there plans for a mega-mall or sports facility nearby?
- Are there mass-transit options within walking distance?

If you like a neighborhood, you should talk to people who live there. As you are driving through a neighborhood and see people outside, you can ask them about the neighborhood. They will be the most knowledgeable about the area and may be your future neighbors.

Even if you know exactly what you are looking for, the house-hunting process can be overwhelming. It takes time.

Compare Homes

Before you make a decision about a home, you should compare your wants and needs against that home. Also look at the short-term and long-term costs associated with each house you are considering. Are the appliances in good condition? What about the backyard? Will there be commuting costs?

Should you decide to use a real estate agent, you can begin to make notes in the MLS listings that your agent sends you, and you can use those notes when you begin to narrow down your search. As you go through each listing, make specific notes about your likes, dislikes, concerns, and questions. These notes will be helpful later as you begin to cross off homes and pray through the remaining homes on your list.

Use written descriptions of each home—from your worksheets or your real estate agent—to help you compare. Don't feel rushed to make a decision. Remember that God will provide the right home at the right time.

> Matthew 6:26: Look at the birds of the air: they neither sow nor reap nor gather into barns, and yet your heavenly Father feeds them. Are you not of more value then they?

MAKING AN OFFER

Once you have found the home you want to buy, you will need to make an educated and reasonable offer. Knowing a home's real value can help you make a fair offer. In determining what a fair offer is, you should consider each of the following:

- **Sales price history**
  You may be able to get the home's past sale prices through county courthouses and recorder's offices, many of which have this public information also available online. You can also check with your real estate agent because the MLS will usually contain this information. See if the value has risen or fallen over time.
- **Home characteristics**
  The number of bedrooms and bathrooms, square footage, and other characteristics greatly affect the value. In many cases, the seller and the seller's agent provide this information to all prospective buyers. You can also get this information from the tax assessor's office.
- **Similar home prices**
  Ask your real estate agent for sale prices of comparable homes in the same neighborhood.

Once an offer is made and accepted, the buyer(s) and seller(s) will enter into a written purchase and sale agreement that will include the buyers' and sellers' information, a description of the property being sold, the agreed-upon purchase price, any conditions to the sale of the home, and signatures from both buyer(s) and seller(s). The process of buying a home can extend from weeks up to months as you work through obtaining necessary financing, getting home appraisals completed, having title work completed, and then scheduling the date of the sale, known as closing.

RENTING OR BUYING: WHICH IS SMARTER?

Most Americans want to experience the pride of ownership. And the personal residence is probably the most sought-after asset. Although owning a home means mowing the grass, fixing leaky roofs, and replacing worn-out furnaces, it's still something nearly every American desires. Rising prices have sometimes pushed the price of a home out of the range that many beginning homebuyers can afford; even so, creative financing, longer terms, equity sharing arrangements, and the like have made it possible for many Americans to own a home. No matter the cost, most attempt to buy a home as soon as they can.

But there are several issues to consider before rushing into the purchase of a home. Many have heard the myth that renting is simply throwing money down a hole, and that purchasing a home is the only smart way to go. But, depending on your particular economic condition and vocational situation, that is not always the case.

Table 11.1 provides a brief overview of the benefits of home ownership and the benefits of renting.

Table 11.1   Home Ownership versus Renting

Benefits of Home Ownership	Benefits of Renting
A portion of mortgage payments will go toward building equity	Flexibility in moving later—no waiting on a house to sell
Owner keeps any price appreciation	No maintenance worries
Pride of ownership—it belongs to you	Low amount of initial savings needed to begin renting
May make home improvements and keep the benefit of those	Rent payments may be lower than mortgage payments with interest, taxes, and home insurance

When individuals graduate from college, start in the workforce, and begin to accumulate cash, they should resist the urge to jump immediately into buying a house without having *an emergency fund and a significant down payment*. Otherwise, they may end up needing to use credit cards to buy the many things needed to operate the house and keep it going. This can start an unending cycle of credit. A good goal is to pay at least 20% of the purchase price as a down payment on a house because that will eliminate additional costs such as mortgage insurance. From a practical standpoint, this means one should save a little longer to buy that first house than expected, or longer than is considered "normal" among most Americans. Remember, God desires that His children be different.

> **Proverbs 1:15**: My son, do not walk in the way with them; hold back your foot from their paths.

Even if you have an emergency fund and a significant down payment, it may still not be economically wise to buy a home. In the following chart, note that the total outflow on rent at $400 is practically the same as the outflow on a $50,000 home with a $10,000 down payment. As a matter of fact, the outflow is greater for owning than renting. In most cases the appreciation of the house is what the purchaser is counting on to make it a "good purchase." Therefore, the key is the inflation rate. With 5% appreciation at the end of 1 year, the $50,000 house had a net cost of $3,327, whereas renting had a cost of $5,375. If that house were to be sold at the end of the year and the 7% real estate commission paid, the cost of that house would be $6,827 or $1,500 more than renting. This is because of a $3,500 reduction from the sales commission. (Over 90% of all houses are sold through a realtor; therefore, it's realistic to assume your home would be.) Of course, if you get a great deal in selling your house, your home purchase would be a better deal. But that does not usually happen.

Assume that you hold on to the $50,000 house for 2 years and have appreciation of approximately $5,000 ($2,500/year). Without considering appreciation, you have about $500 a year more in expense ($5,827 − $5,375) than renting, so the appreciation is offset by $1,000. If we remove the real estate commission of $3,500, you may just about break even ($5,000 − $1,000 − $3,500). Therefore, *in most cases you are better off to buy only if you can live in a house for at least 2 years.* This assumes a sale through a realtor and no special appreciation factors such as buying below market (a foreclosure) or selling above inflation appreciation. *As the price of a house goes up, the longer you must live in it to make it cost-effective over renting.*

In considering whether or not to buy or rent, you should take into account the nature of your occupation, the location, and your needs and goals. It may be that your vocation requires you to move every 2 to 5 years. If so, renting would probably be just as wise as purchasing. However, because of your family's desires and ministry opportunities, owning a house may be more appropriate than renting.

Purchase Price		$50,000	$70,000	$80,000
Expenses	Rent	Buy #1	Buy #2	Buy #3
Mortgage or rent	$4,000	$3,972	$5,856	$6,684
Utilities	600	1,200	1,500	1,800
Taxes	0	800	900	1,000
Insurance	350	400	425	450
Repairs/maintenance	0	250	300	350
Tax savings	0	−1,000	−1,500	−2,000
Total outflow	$4,950	$5,622	$7,481	$8,284
Gain				
Appreciation (5%)	0	2500	3500	4500
Interest income (net of tax)	375	0	0	0
Effect on net worth	($4,575)	($3,122)	($3,981)	($3,784)
Commission on sale (6%)	$0	$3,000	$4,200	$4,800
Effect on net worth after sale w/6% commission	($4,575)	($6,122)	($8,181)	($8,584)

*Scenario is based on $10,000 down, 5% interest on mortgage, 25% tax bracket. Appreciation is assumed at 5% annually of sales price, and interest income assumes renter invests $10,000 at 5% (less taxes).

Remember, these calculations do not take into consideration buying costs such as loan origination fees, appraisal fees, tax service fees, attorney fees, points, and selling costs such as title insurance, which can amount to 2% to 3% of the original loan balance and must also be recovered in the appreciation of the residence. (In our previous illustration, these costs would range from $1,000 to $2,400.) This is another reason why you need to live in the house for more than 2 years to make it pay compared to renting.

In this illustration, you can see that a home is not always a good investment in the short term. In summary, evaluate the purchase of a house with a long-range perspective and also in light of your vocation and lifestyle desires. Buying a home may be the American dream, but use wisdom in deciding whether it's best for you.

A Note to Young Couples

Living the "American dream" and buying a first home seems to be a common desire for many young couples after they get married. We want to note a few suggestions to reflect on as you think through the idea of buying a home.

First, unless you have financial help from relatives, a new house, or a house purchase, right after marriage may very well be out of reach. With the run-up in real estate prices, the average price of a house is so high that it's difficult for any couple, especially a young couple, to afford one unless they both work or are willing to overextend themselves financially.

Second, owning a house is not a right, but a privilege. When it's viewed as a privilege, the appreciation of ownership is much greater when it's finally achieved. When something is perceived as a right, however, there is a high level of frustration if that "right" seems impossible to achieve.

Third, purchasing a home will require financial sacrifices in some other part of the budget. Many ancillary costs of home ownership aren't usually taken into account because they're unknown or not anticipated. The following is a listing of common costs of home ownership that should be considered:

- Initial home changes/repairs (blinds, carpet cleaning, adding fixtures or ceiling fans)
- Pest inspections
- Furniture
- Decorations
- Moving costs
- Trash removal (if items were left by previous homeowner)

Fourth, God can be trusted to meet our needs. He won't necessarily meet our wants, but without question He will meet our every legitimate need. And although everyone has a need for shelter, that doesn't necessarily mean a house, and certainly not a dream house. Many times God will withhold a blessing until it can be provided in such a way as to demonstrate His faithfulness, goodness, and trustworthiness.

SOLVING THE MORTGAGE MYSTERY

For most families, the single biggest loan decision of their lives will be how to finance their home purchase. Ten years ago that was a "plain vanilla" decision: everyone got a 30-year fixed-rate mortgage and made this payment faithfully each month. Times have changed, however, and people are looking at a variety of options for paying off mortgages early.

The next section looks to help you as you filter through many of the concepts previously covered and will help you to figure out which type of mortgage is best for your situation. We present this section in a question-and-answer format.

What Type of Mortgage Should You Get, and What Term, or Length-of-Repayment Terms, Should You Agree To?

In trying to evaluate what type of mortgage to get, you will have to learn many terms: ARMs, PLAMs, Fannie Mae, Freddie Mac, VA loans, buydowns, and so on (the variety in terminology is limited only by lenders' creativity). Mortgage loans can be entered into for almost any number of years, up to at least 30 years, and in some cases up to 50.

We suggest that anything other than a fixed-rate, fixed-term loan is an attempt to make it "easy" on the buyer and to protect the lender in the event of changed circumstances (i.e., rising interest rates). Therefore, ARMs (adjustable-rate mortgages) and PLAMs (price-level-adjusted mortgages) are not wrong, just much riskier. The lender in each case is protected, and you, the buyer, are the one taking all the chances. You are implicitly assuming either deflation (which is a rare economic occurrence) or an income rising faster than interest rate and payment increases.

If you are considering taking any type of adjustable mortgage, make sure it includes two things. First, there should be absolutely no possibility of **negative amortization**, where the amount you owe actually goes up rather than down, on the loan. Second, there should be caps on possible increases in the interest rate charged. For ARMs, that cap has typically been 5% or 6% over the life of the loan (1%–2% per year), and there is no reason to ever agree to a higher total cap. The notion of "being able to afford it" by accepting a smaller payment at the beginning but taking the risk of a larger payment or negative amortization later in the loan life is an unnecessary risk and should not be taken.

In evaluating mortgages other than the fixed-rate, fixed-term type, you should assume the payments are going to go up by the maximum amount each year and do your planning accordingly. Don't assume your income will go up proportionately. The safest way to plan for that type of mortgage is to assume that your income is constant and your mortgage payments will go up as much as possible each period. Then ask yourself, "Can I afford it?"

Recommendations on Mortgage Terms

You are better off in the long run to use a fixed-rate mortgage rather than any type of adjustable loan. The latter almost always forces you to assume favorable economic circumstances in the future, and they may not in fact occur. You should *put down at least 20%* when buying a house, even though it's possible to put down as little as 5%. Once again, the reason is to reduce the danger of presuming upon the future. If at all possible, *choose a 15-year loan* instead of a 30-year loan. The payments are typically only 20% to 25% more per month, but the total amount paid over the life of the mortgage is significantly less.

As you seek to determine your mortgage, consider ways to get out of the mortgage faster, specifically, paying more than the monthly payment. There are several other ways to make early payments or additional payments. You can pay one-half your usual monthly payment twice a month and reduce your interest costs. You can add one-twelfth of a payment to each payment and thereby end up with one extra payment per year. You can also make periodic lump-sum payments of principal.

Negative amortization
The process by which the amount you owe actually goes up rather than down due to adding interest to the balance of the loan.

However, before doing any of these things, you need to check with the lender to determine that prepayments will be accepted without penalty. Ask also about rules regarding those prepayments. Some mortgage companies, for example, will use them to reduce the principal amount owed but not to reduce the payments; and if you are in default one payment in the future, you are in default on the mortgage. This is true even if you have prepaid a significant part of the principal amount borrowed.

All of us are stewards or managers of our spending decisions. Even the traditionally mundane mortgage payment should be proactively managed from a stewardship perspective. After all, it's probably the one area that takes most of your cash flow.

Are Home Equity Loans Wise?

Forget the fancy label—home equity loans are simply second mortgages. They may be useful in certain circumstances when you are in need of cash or if they can convert what would typically be a nondeductible interest expense into a deductible mortgage interest expense. They can also be useful in meeting short-term needs, such as for a college education. However, like any other form of debt, they are easy to enter into but deceptively difficult to pay off. The greatest danger with a home equity loan is that it risks a valuable asset, your home equity, for something less secure, such as an automobile, a vacation, or a boat.

In addition, home equity loans typically have variable rates of interest, with no cap on how high the interest rate can go. Thus, when interest rates rise, these loans can be tremendously expensive to repay. Be extremely careful about entering into a home equity form of debt, as it may become a real burden and put your house in jeopardy.

Is It Advisable to Pay Off a Mortgage Early?

When contemplating the idea of paying off your mortgage early, there are four considerations you should think about. First, consider your *marriage relationship*. The wife's security orientation generally causes her to be more averse to risk; as a result, she typically wants to avoid debt—particularly when it involves the home. Therefore, for marital harmony, it may be a good idea to pay off a mortgage to remove the house from any economic risk.

Second, consider your *investment return*. If individuals maintain a home mortgage and yet have available cash to make other investments, they are implying that they can earn "risk-free" with their other investments more than they are paying on their home mortgage. The idea of "risk-free" is used because paying off the home mortgage is not a risky investment. For example: If you owe $100,000 on a 5% mortgage, then you will pay $5,000 a year in interest and thus $5,000 out-of-pocket. If you pay off your mortgage, then you don't have the outflow of $5,000 and so in essence have earned $5,000 on your $100,000 investment without any risk; you simply paid off your mortgage. If you elect not to pay off your home mortgage and invest $100,000, you must more than 10% with your investment of $100,000 to have the same net worth at the end of the year. However, if you keep debt (even home mortgage debt), then you are implying that you can earn "risk-free" on your investments *more* than you are paying on the debt. However, experience suggests that it is very difficult to consistently earn more each year than the interest rate you would pay on your home mortgage on a risk-free basis. Therefore, the repayment of the home mortgage as the first use of excess funds is a good investment move.

Third, consider your need for *liquidity*. If you have $20,000 in savings, it probably is not a good idea to use that entire amount to pay down the mortgage. If you did that and then had an emergency, you would have to borrow at a higher interest rate than your home mortgage rate to fund the emergency. You should maintain an ample level of liquidity (usually 3–6 months' living expenses) to meet emergencies, and only then should you consider using excess funds to pay off the home mortgage.

Fourth, consider *why you would not want to pay off your home mortgage.* The answer is typically a feeling that you can earn a higher investment return with the money somewhere else. You need to weigh your motives and make sure greed is not driving you. Paying off your home mortgage not only gives you a decent investment return, but peace of mind, a strengthened marriage relationship, and other benefits.

Ron's Corner

I typically ask couples to close their eyes and think about not having a home mortgage. Do they feel better about that alternative or about having the money in the bank? Almost always the answer is, "We have a greater sense of security when the mortgage is paid off." If so, I always recommend that they go ahead and pay the mortgage off. My answer is that it may not be as much of an economic question as it is a peace-of-mind question.

Some people believe that it is better to have a mortgage so that they can take advantage of the mortgage interest deduction on their individual tax return. In fact, there really is no true benefit from a tax standpoint of not paying off a mortgage. If you have a $100,000 mortgage costing 10% and a $100,000 investment earning 10%, you're earning and paying taxes on $10,000 and paying $10,000 of interest with the same tax impact. Therefore, it's a "wash" situation. The best alternative is to pay off the mortgage and then go on paying yourself (saving) an amount equal to the mortgage payments.

What about Refinancing a Mortgage during Times of Falling Interest Rates?

Over the past few years, mortgage rates have come to near all-time lows due to a push to stimulate the economy after the 2008–2009 recession. With the resulting decline in mortgage interest rates, there has been a virtual stampede to refinance. For many people, refinancing their mortgage was an easy decision. As rates have stabilized and moved up in recent years, refinancing a mortgage requires a little bit more analysis.

Remember that refinancing involves some costs. What are the costs? To the lender, refinancing a mortgage is just like starting all over again. So, the lender charges the borrower for a credit report, origination fees, closing costs, legal fees, fees for title search, a new survey, an appraisal, deed recording expenses, discount points, and possibly private mortgage insurance.

A widely quoted rule of thumb for refinancing is that the new interest rate should be at least 2 percentage points below your present rate for it to make sense. The question is, does this rule fit your situation? The real issues are, how long does it take to recover the costs of refinancing, and how much can you save? The answer may depend on the financing fees, the time you intend to remain in your house, and your tax bracket. The less difference between the existing and new mortgage rates, the more time will be required to recover the refinancing costs. Additionally, because the closing costs can be a total of 3% to 5% of the loan amount, it will usually take about 2 years to recoup those expenses at the "2%-rule-of-thumb" differential in rates. Therefore, one other consideration is that you should be planning on staying in the home for at least 2 more years.

Another consideration in refinancing is whether you have the freedom to do so without paying a prepayment penalty. By checking your current loan documents or calling your current lender, you can determine whether or not you are subject to a prepayment penalty and your cost to refinance. It may very well be that you can negotiate those costs with the lender, even though the lender will be taking a lower interest rate (better that than have you borrow from someone else).

WHAT YOU NEED TO KNOW ABOUT HOMEOWNERS' INSURANCE

We will finish up this section on the home-buying decision by reviewing the topic of insuring your residence, whether you own it or are renting it. For many, a home represents one of the most expensive purchases they will make during their lifetime. You likely paid dearly for your home and the belongings that fill it. Therefore, you will probably want to ensure that all of it is properly insured. If you rent rather than own a home, the issues regarding insurance still apply equally to you. The only difference is that you are insuring your belongings only, not the physical building in which you live.

Homeowners' insurance protects against the risk of loss from certain obvious perils, such as damage from fire, storm, and loss through theft or lawsuit. Some perils you wish would be covered often are not, such as flood and earthquake damage. If you live in an area that is often affected by those problems, it is possible to purchase separate coverage.

As with any insurance, the primary consideration is whether or not you are adequately insured. That way, in the event of a partial or complete loss, your insurance will provide adequate money to allow you to replace what you lost in the calamity. For instance, if your home was totally destroyed by fire and you were insured with full replacement costs, it would be the responsibility of the insurance carrier to rebuild the house, furnish it to the same standards you had before the loss, replace lost clothing items, and even stock your refrigerator and cupboards.

Homeowners' policies include five basic coverages:

1. Dwelling (referred to as Coverage A)
2. Other structures (referred to as Coverage B)
3. Personal property (referred to as Coverage C)
4. Additional living expenses (referred to as Coverage D)
5. Liability

The first part of a homeowner's policy covers the dwelling or structure of the home. This part of the policy covers walls, foundations, and other structural components damaged by perils not otherwise excluded, such as flood.

The second part of a homeowner's policy covers other structures on the property. Common examples are detached garages, storage sheds, and barns.

The third part is one of the most important because it covers *personal property*, items that are by their nature movable and not attached to the dwelling. This reimburses you for loss or damage to contents inside the home.

The amount of coverage is usually determined as a percentage of replacement cost of the home. However, there are two different ways insurance companies will value these belongings. First is through an actual cash value of the items. Actual cash value refers to the value of an item being equal to the replacement cost of that item minus depreciation of that item. One easy way to think about this is to think of the value of an item if you were to sell it at a garage sale, usually not the best way to value your prized belongings. The other way insurance companies can value your belongings is on replacement value. This is the most advantageous way to protect your belongings because you will receive the value to replace each item that is damaged. There are, however, monetary limits for specific types of possessions within the home, such as currency, jewelry, furs, and electronic equipment. You want to be sure you understand these limits. If you believe you have certain high-value items in your house, such as a piano, special artwork, or any expensive jewelry, you can talk to your insurance agent to purchase a separate policy for these items. This separate policy would be coverage that is over and above the coverage amounts in your homeowner's policy.

The fourth part of a homeowner's policy covers your out-of-pocket expenses associated with being impacted by the covered peril. For example, if during a hail storm several windows in your home were damaged and needed to be replaced, and as a result you could not stay in your home, then your stay in a hotel during the time it takes to repair the windows would be covered or reimbursed through this section of your policy.

Finally, the last part of a homeowner's policy is the coverage referred to as *liability protection.* This section covers injury or damage to others on your property or caused by you or your family members. It includes accidents that happen around your home. For instance, if a neighborhood kid was playing in your yard and tripped over a rake you left on the ground and suffered a broken bone, your property insurance would more than likely pay for his medical expenses. In the event that his parents filed a lawsuit, your insurance would more than likely pay any settlement costs and legal costs.

Some of the factors that influence home insurance premiums are the cost of your home and furnishings, the availability of fire protection, the liability coverage limits, and the proximity to special risk areas, such as living on a waterfront lot. The key factor in determining how much insurance you need is the value of your house. If you are unsure of the value of your home, you can consult your county tax assessor and find out the value the county uses to assess your property taxes. Keep in mind that the price you paid for your home is not necessarily a good guide, particularly if you bought the house some time ago.

You would be most protected by an insurance policy that covers 100% of repair and replacement costs. This shifts the risk to the insurance company. Therefore, even if your home were valued at $100,000 but it cost $115,000 to rebuild, then the burden for the extra cost is on the insurance company.

In the event of a major claim, the insurance carrier will require you to document all your possessions. It is virtually impossible for you to remember the contents of one room of your house, much less the entire house. For most of us, the challenge of keeping a detailed inventory is one we do not do thoroughly. However, a very easy and cost-effective way of inventorying your house is to record a video of the contents of your house. With most smartphones having video capabilities, it is simple to walk through your home and film the major contents of each room. You can quickly film closets and drawers as well. Once you have this video, you may consider uploading it to a secure server or cloud-based platform so that you can access it even if your home computer is damaged.

You should evaluate your insurance regularly, particularly if you make any major changes to your home (remodeling, relocation, new furniture, etc.). In addition to a video inventory, you should record serial numbers, model numbers, and purchase dates, and retain sales receipts for significant items for proof in the event of a major claim. One recommendation is to meet with your insurance agent at least annually to go over any significant changes required in your coverage.

As with all insurance, it pays to shop the market. Insurance is very competitive. Deal with a reputable agent and a quality insurance carrier. Be careful not to be underinsured; in the event you have a claim, you will go through enough trauma to deal with without having to come up with out-of-pocket money to replace items that were not covered by insurance just because you didn't pay the additional small premium dollars to properly insure them up front.

Courtesy of daniilantiq2010/Fotolia.

DISCIPLESHIP MOMENT AND REFLECTION

Reflecting back on the information presented in this chapter, what were your original goals regarding housing? How has your perspective changed since reading the chapter? Talk to your accountability and prayer partner about what you have learned thus far, and talk through any potential decisions you may need to make.

SUMMARY

We have covered a lot of information in this chapter related to home buying. We started by looking at several common misconceptions in relation to homeownership. We then looked at the different components of financing a home, such as interest rates and terms. We transitioned into how lenders will review borrowers in getting qualified for a home mortgage and what these homebuyers need to bring to the table in terms of costs. We discussed methods you can use to select the most appropriate home as well how to make an offer on a home. We spent some time reviewing renting versus buying and completed the home-buying section with a review of homeowners' insurance policies.

SUMMARY REVIEW QUESTIONS

1. What are two common misconceptions concerning homeownership?

2. Describe the following components in relation to buying a home:
   a. Down payment
   b. Private mortgage insurance
   c. Interest rate
   d. Loan term
   e. Balloon loans

3. What are the five components that influence your FICO credit score?

4. Explain how to calculate the two fundamental ratios used in determining the home price you may be able to afford.

5. Describe the difference between closing costs and prepaid items when buying a house.

6. What are some benefits to using a real estate agent in the home-buying process?

7. Provide at least three critical questions to ask when selecting the area or location you want to live in.

8. List four benefits of homeownership and four benefits of renting.

9. List five of the six common costs usually incurred once a home is purchased.

10. What are the recommended loan structures mentioned in the chapter for buying a home?

11. Explain the four considerations that a homeowner must ponder prior to paying off a mortgage early.

12. Give a brief description of each of the five components of a homeowner's policy.

13. What is the difference between replacement cost and actual cash value cost in a homeowner's policy?

Case Study Analysis

Bob immediately picked up the phone and called Steve. It's not that often that your only son calls and says he is thinking of getting engaged and that he wants to buy a house. Was Sean rushing this? Bob thought, "I can't even recall how long Christine and Sean have been dating." Other thoughts crossed Bob's mind as the phone rang. He knows that he bought a few homes in his day, but probably couldn't articulate the home-buying process, especially because so much has changed since Debbie and he bought their home roughly 8 years ago.

"Hello, this is Steve. How can I help you?"

"Steve, this is Bob Smith, and I was hoping you had a few minutes."

"Sure, Bob, what's going on?" Steve could feel the panic in Bob's voice.

"Our son Sean, who is only a year or so from finishing medical school, just called and said that he is considering proposing to Christine, his girlfriend, and potentially wanting to buy a house. He said that he talked to a buddy of his who is a mortgage lender at a local bank and could get him into the 'home of his dreams,' as Sean put it. I think Sean mentioned that he could get a 2.5% rate with little to no down payment. Steve, I am not equipped well enough to have an intelligent conversation with Sean about the home-buying process. Would you have some time to sit down with the two of us and go through this? Sean will be coming home next weekend, and I thought we could visit then."

Steve sat quietly on the other end of the line until Bob finished, almost out of breath.

"Bob, absolutely. Let's plan for next Saturday morning to go over a simple worksheet that usually helps these 'dreamers' come down to reality." I will send over that form so you have it to review before our meeting. Oh, have Sean bring some basic information regarding the homes he was looking at—we both know as soon as the lender told him about the 'great deal' he started looking up homes in the area!"

Assignment

Look up three homes in the area on a local real estate site and complete the Rent versus Buy: Effect on Net Worth worksheet. Answer the following questions:

- How much should Sean bring to the closing on the three different homes?
- What are the annual costs associated with buying the three properties?
- How does renting an apartment for $800/month impact Sean's net worth compared to buying any of the three home options?
- What are some considerations for Sean as he thinks through this decision?

DEFINITIONS

Adjustable-rate mortgage (p. 254)

Closing costs (p. 259)

Default (p. 254)

Down payment (p. 254)

Escrow account (p. 259)

Fixed-rate mortgage (p. 254)

Housing expense ratio (p. 257)

Interest rate (p. 254)

Multiple Listing Service (p. 260)

Negative amortization (p. 266)

Private mortgage insurance (p. 254)

SCRIPTURE VERSES (ESV)

Proverbs 3:5-6—Trust in the LORD with all your heart, and do not lean on your own understanding. In all your ways acknowledge him, and he will make straight your paths.

Proverbs 22:7—The rich rules over the poor, and the borrower is the slave of the lender.

Proverbs 23:3-4—By wisdom a house is built, and by understanding it is established; by knowledge the rooms are filled with all precious and pleasant riches.

Proverbs 24:2—Prepare your work outside; get everything ready for yourself in the field, and after that build your house.

Psalm 1:1–2—Blessed is the man who walks not in the counsel of the wicked, nor stands in the way of sinners, nor sits in the seat of scoffers, but his delight is in the law of the Lord, and on his law he meditates day and night.

Philippians 4:19—And my God will supply every need of yours according to his riches in glory in Christ Jesus.

Matthew 6:26—Look at the birds of the air: they neither sow nor reap nor gather into barns, and yet your heavenly Father feeds them. Are you not of more value then they?

Proverbs 1:15—My son, do not walk in the way with them; hold back your foot from their paths.

Proverbs 21:25–26—The desire of the sluggard kills him, for his hands refuse to labor. All day long he craves and craves, but the righteous gives and does not hold back.

ADDITIONAL READINGS

Brueggeman, W. B., & Fisher, J. D. (2008). *Real estate finance & investments*. New York, NY: McGraw-Hill/Irwin.

Case, K. E., & Shiller, R. J. (1988). *The behavior of home buyers in boom and post-boom markets*. New England Economic Review, pp. 29–46.

Forrest, R., & Kemeny, J. (1982). Middle-class housing careers: The relationship between furnished renting and home ownership. *The Sociological Review*, 30(2), 208–222.

Franke, D. S., Schulenburg, N. W., & Remer, D. S. (1990). Buying a home versus renting an apartment: A case study. *The Engineering Economist*, 35(3), 191–214.

Friedman, M. R. (1961). Buying a home: Representing the purchaser. *American Bar Association Journal*, 596–604.

Gilbert, A. (2014). Renting a home. In J. Bredenoord (Ed.), *Affordable housing in the urban global south: seeking sustainable solutions* (p. 87). London, England, Routledge.

Hempel, D. J. (1969). *Search behavior and information utilization in the home buying process*. Mansfield, CT: Center for Real Estate and Urban Economic Studies, The University of Connecticut.

Hempel, D. J. (1977). Consumer satisfaction with the home buying process: Conceptualization and measurement. *Marketing Science Institute*, 6, 7–21.

Irwin, R., & foreword by Galen, D. (1998). *Buying a home on the Internet*. New York, NY: McGraw-Hill School Education Group.

Morrow-Jones, H. A. (1988). The housing life-cycle and the transition from renting to owning a home in the United States: a multistate analysis. *Environment and Planning A*, 20(9), 1165–1184.

Razzi, E., & Parmelee, J. (1995). Buying a home before it's built. *Kiplinger's Personal Finance Magazine*, 49(8), 77–79.

Schoeni, R. F., & Ross, K. E. (2005). *Material assistance from families during the transition to adulthood*. Chicago, IL: University of Chicago Press.

Shelton, J. P. (1968). The cost of renting versus owning a home. *Land Economics*, 44(1), 59–72.

Shiller, R. J. (1990). Speculative prices and popular models. *Journal of Economic Perspectives*, 4(2), 55–65.

Sindell, K. (2000). *The unofficial guide to buying a home online*. Hoboken, NJ: Hungry Minds, Incorporated.

REFERENCES

Freddie Mac (2014). Mansion or yurt: What can you afford? Retrieved from http://www.freddiemac.com/blog/homeownership/20140515_home_affordability.html

Chapter 12

Auto Decisions

Courtesy of Monkey Business/Fotolia.

BIG IDEA:
A car will not make you, but it may break you.

LEARNING OUTCOMES

- Understand why people buy cars
- Provide a process for buying a car
- Explain available options for paying for your next vehicle
- Understand the opportunity cost of consumption
- List the methods available for buying a used car
- Know the components of car insurance

Introduction

Having evaluated what is for most people the largest purchase decision they will make, a home, in the last chapter, we now turn our attention to the second most significant purchase decision most people make: vehicles.

As a society, Americans are notorious for their love affair with the automobile. Will Rogers once said, in the days when having an automobile was more of a luxury, "We're the only nation in the world to go to the poorhouse in an automobile." That wisecrack still has some truth to it. Many people barely have a positive net worth, yet they drive cars with every known option. We use our cars for far more than basic transportation. We eat and get dressed in them—just watch what happens on the highways of major cities during the morning commute. They are mobile entertainment compartments—observe the DVD players and TV screens, satellite radio, stereos, and the current ability for our vehicles to be turned into mobile command centers with Wi-Fi capability. From heated car seats to mapping screens to cars that automatically parallel park, they do it—*for a price.*

In this chapter, we review the financial principles for purchasing vehicles. We examine the ways to finance their purchase, from leasing to borrowing to using cash. We cover the common deceptions found in financing cars. We also go over where you can find the cheapest car you will ever own.

TRANSPORTATION OR SIGNIFICANCE?

Have you ever asked yourself, "Should I buy a new car or not?" Many of us have, of course. Unfortunately, this is usually the wrong question to ask.

In many instances, people regard cars as a purchase that provides ego satisfaction, which implies that driving a new car outweighs the economic criteria. It is amazing how egos can justify a new car when in fact it never makes economic sense to purchase one! A quality foreign or American car may have a better resale value than another car, but rarely does a car (other than a rare antique model) appreciate in value. Therefore, due to cars being depreciating assets, it is probably best to not think of a car as a good "investment." At best, it may be a wise purchase. (And when you pay cash, you typically make a better purchase then when you finance—but more on that later in this section.)

The real question should be "How can I best provide transportation?" The answer depends on your objectives and the priority of those objectives. For example, some of your objectives may be to (1) minimize the annual cost, (2) provide comfort, (3) provide safety, (4) minimize the down payment, (5) minimize the annual financing cost, or (6) achieve a dream car (a Jaguar or BMW).

Believe it or not, the cheapest car you will ever own is almost always the one you are presently driving. The reason is that the cost of financing a new car plus the depreciation of a new car minus the lost opportunities for the use of your down payment will always more than offset the annual maintenance and upkeep of an older car, even though the newer car may have some advantages, such as better gas mileage. The higher the price of the car, the higher the actual cost to drive that car, and therefore the more desirable it becomes to drive the older car. A new car will also require more expensive maintenance, insurance, and license fees than an older car.

Ron's Corner

I received this question years ago, and I still believe that my response holds true today. The question was, "What's a financial decision that you have made in the past and are still benefiting from today?" My response was and still is to pay cash for cars. Finishing a close second would be our decision to pay off our mortgage. That was, and is, such a sense of freedom.

After I decided to pay cash for all cars, several related decisions followed to help my financial position. We kept cars longer. We bought less expensive cars because we didn't have enough saved for the luxury cars. So, we lost less to depreciation. Avoiding debt to buy an item that rapidly depreciates in value is one of the best decisions I made.

Although economically it never makes sense to get a new car, obviously there comes a time when one must get a *different* car. There are three legitimate reasons to consider getting a different car:

1. The cost of repairs become greater than the value of the car
2. Safety reasons require a different vehicle
3. Time of upkeep outweighs the economic cost of a different car

Let's look at each of these reasons in a little bit more detail:

- *When the cost of repairs becomes greater than the value of the car.* Suppose you have a car that is to the point of needing a new transmission or, worse, a complete engine overhaul. Such repairs may make it too costly to repair the car rather than replace it.
- *When a different car is needed for safety reasons.* If you drive a two-seat pickup truck and you learn that your family is getting ready to expand (having a baby!), a car seat would not be safe (perhaps even legal) if strapped in the front seat of a pickup truck. For this safety reason, you would need to purchase a different car.
- *When the cost of your time to continually take a car in for repairs outweighs the economic cost of a different car.* For example, if you need your car for your business or occupation, time spent in a repair shop prevents you from realizing your full income potential. This is a high "opportunity cost." If your cars are unavailable 1 or 2 days a week because of repairs or maintenance, it makes sense to replace them and get back that 1 or 2 days of productive time. Only you can put a value on your time and determine if keeping your old car is costing too much. Obviously, time spent in the repair shop is time you can't spend on other activities, including those that generate income. But valuing your time can be a highly subjective exercise.

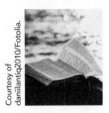

Courtesy of daniilantiq2010/Fotolia.

DISCIPLESHIP MOMENT AND REFLECTION

As you think about a time when you replaced a car, what was your motivation to do so? Talk with your accountability and prayer partner and talk about how you can hold each other to staying with your current vehicle until one of the three reasons for replacing your car occurs.

Be careful in using any of these three reasons for making the decision to replace your car. They are legitimate reasons, but don't use them to kid yourself. Is your plan to replace a car really rooted in discontentment, or do you have a valid reason?

HOW TO BUY YOUR NEXT CAR

Without question, the best way to purchase a different car is to pay cash for it. Unfortunately, many people do not have adequate liquidity to be able to keep adequate reserves in their emergency savings accounts and purchase a car with cash. Therefore, we want to demonstrate the best to way to "pay" for your next car. The process can be outlined in several steps.

Step 1: Keep Your Current Vehicle

This first step requires you to keep your current vehicle. Two items must be addressed: (1) pay off your first vehicle as soon as you can, and (2) be prepared to keep your car a few years longer than you anticipate.

Step 2: Make Continued Payments

Once you pay off your vehicle, you can move to the next step by continuing to make car payments but to your own savings account. Let's say that you originally were making a $400 car payment each month for 48 months. Because the car is paid off, you can take that $400 per month and put it into a savings account. Let's assume you can keep your current vehicle for another 4 years with no payments and have been able to put aside that same $400 into a savings account earning 3%; in that case, you would have accumulated roughly $21,000 over that period of time. Now you can take that $21,000 and pay cash for your replacement vehicle. As an added bonus, you can probably get a car valued in the $25,000 to $30,000 range if you are able to pay cash for it.

Step 3: Continue the Process Over and Over

Let's say that the replacement vehicle you are able to purchase will last you 8 years and you continue to save the $400 per month. Over the 8 years, you will accumulate just under $47,000, assuming a 3% interest rate, which can be used to replace your then current car. If you had financed the purchase of a car with a $400-per-month payment, assuming an interest rate of 4% and a loan term of 8 years, you could only afford a car costing $33,000. This means that you have saved an additional $14,000 toward a new car.

As you can see, you will have saved money by paying for the car in advance and delaying your gratification of your car purchase until you have the cash to pay for it. Also, keep in mind the additional bonus of not having any obligation to the car (debt). Because you own the car outright, you can keep your insurance premiums lower and potentially have lower overall costs.

We have just reviewed some overall recommendations with respect to cars; let's now dig a little deeper. Three topics need to be addressed regarding the buying and selling of cars. (1) Why buy a particular car? (2) When should you replace your car? (3) How should you pay for the replacement car?

WHY BUY A PARTICULAR CAR?

It is rare to find a family that does not have at least one car. And some families have three, four, or even five vehicles. The need for cars is obvious, and that's to provide transportation.

Cars these days have all kinds of "bells and whistles" that can make them attractive even though they are not necessary. They are luxuries. Whether you are willing to pay for them comes back to what you are really trying to do in buying a particular car. If you are searching for significance or you lack contentment, then you may make foolish economic decisions.

WHEN SHOULD YOU REPLACE YOUR CAR?

Your current car is almost always the cheapest car you will own because even though some costs go up the longer you own a car, many other costs go down. Even though it is cheaper to keep a car rather than replace it, there does come a time when it becomes necessary to replace your car. A few base guidelines are provided in the accompanying box.

An article in *Money* (1989) magazine titled "The Case for Hanging on to Your Aging Family Car for 100,000 Miles" said the following: "The considerable financial advantage of hanging on to a car for at least eight years has been demonstrated by Runzheimer International of Rochester, Wis., a worldwide transportation consultant to corporations. Runzheimer's analysts posed two choices last year for the owner of a mid-size, six-cylinder car, then four years old and free of debt: drive it another four years or trade it in on a new model and drive that car for the next four years."

The main finding, outlined in Table 12.1, was that by sticking with his older car, the owner would stand to save $5,036 despite the analysts' estimate that in 4 years of steady driving (60,000 miles), repair costs for the older car would exceed those of the new car by $1,179 and that the old model would consume $428 more in gas and oil.

"There are, however, offsetting economies. One is modestly lower insurance premiums on an older car. As an auto loses trade-in value, you pay less to insure it for theft and collision damage. But the lost value, together with financing costs, is what knocks the new car out of contention. Those two items would be expected to account for nearly 55% of the total costs of keeping a new model on the road during its first four years of life. On the debt-free older model, depreciation would total just 35% of expenses. And in this regard, a Chevy is no different from a Ford, Cadillac or Mercedes."

The analysis in this article, done by an independent, worldwide transportation consultant, bears out what we have discussed in this chapter.

Table 12.1 Four-Year Cost of Ownership

FOUR-YEAR COST OF OWNERSHIP

	Old Car	New Car
Loan Payments (Interest and Principal)	$0	$10,166
Gas and Oil	3,428	3,000
Insurance	2,213	2,403
Repairs Maintenance, and Tires	2,582	1,383
Total Expenses	8,203	16,952
Trade-in-Value	924	4,637
Net Cost of Ownership	7,279	12,315
Saved by Not Trading In	5,036	

Source: Runzheimer International

HOW SHOULD YOU PAY FOR THE REPLACEMENT CAR?

Once you feel that one of the three legitimate reasons to get a different vehicle has occurred, you need to understand the various ways that a different vehicle can be paid for. It would be naïve to believe we are not tempted to go overboard when we get into car-buying mode. There are times when it's okay to buy a car that's more than you need in terms of basic transportation. And there are three issues to consider when it comes to funding the replacement:

1. New versus used
2. Lease versus buy
3. Cash versus borrow

New versus used. In almost every case, it will be less expensive to buy a used car rather than a new one, providing you do a good job of evaluating the alternatives. Frequently the reason given for purchasing a new car is that you won't be buying someone else's problems. But new cars break down, too. What you are really looking for is a reliable car that will get you to the areas you need to get to, such as school or work.

Proper shopping can help you fund a good used car. Never buy one without first taking it to a mechanic to have it checked. There will be a cost associated with this but it is well worth the cost to have a certified mechanic inspect the vehicle. We would also recommend examining the service records of the previous owner to determine the kind of care the car received. Questions you may consider:

- How often was the oil changed?
- Did the owner have regularly scheduled maintenance performed (e.g., service at 30,000 miles and 60,000 miles)?
- Were any recall issues resolved?
- How many owners owned the car before you?
- Was the car in any accidents?
- What did the CARFAX report indicate?

Assuming you can satisfy yourself that the car you are buying is in good shape, a used car will always be the wisest economic choice.

Buying a new car can be a legitimate decision, however, if you follow two rules. The first is that you plan to drive the new car for at least 8 to 10 years. That way the heavy early depreciation of the car is irrelevant, because you will have spread out the total depreciation over that lengthy time period. The second rule is that you pay cash for the new car. As has been proven already, it is always more advantageous economically to pay cash rather than borrow. This is never truer than when buying a new car.

Paying cash generally causes you to make a better decision than you would if you borrowed. It's much easier to borrow $20,000 to $25,000 because you have "easy payments" of $350 per month than to write a check for $20,000. Somehow it is difficult to part with money that has been hard earned and hard saved in one lump sum. And that is exactly why it is recommend that you always pay cash for a car, especially a new one.

Every major purchase, in fact, should be made with cash. It could even be a radical idea to go the bank and withdraw the amount needed for a purchase in large bills. Conducting such a transaction will help you focus on the reality that you are trading part of your hard-earned money to acquire something you desire so strongly.

Lease versus buy. As will be discussed later in the chapter, it is better to buy a car with cash than with financing. Leasing, however, should be viewed differently. Leasing is defined as a contract in which one party (lessor) allows another party (lessee) to use a product or service for a specified time and agreed-upon payment. In other words, a lease is nothing more than a rental agreement between two parties. Leases are attractive for a wide variety of reasons, but the most prominent advantage of a lease seems to be the lower monthly payment. Due to the fact that leases offer lower monthly payments, many people fall into the trap of getting a more expensive vehicle with what amounts to "reasonable" monthly payments. The deception of "easy payments" is always appealing to consumers. The lease-versus-buy decision, which is becoming more and more common, preys on this deception.

The leasing decision, however, will never be more advantageous than financing, let alone paying cash. A lease is set up strictly for convenience. The lessor (car dealer) allows the lessee (customer), within limits, to set up his or her own convenient lease plan. All the lessor does to make it work for the lessee is to adjust the time period of the lease and/or the back-end replacement cost the lessee must guarantee (more on this later in the chapter).

In calculating how much to charge on a lease, the lessor does the same calculations you should do when buying a car. The lessor determines what the actual cost is going to be depending on the terms the lessee desires; the lessor adds to it the financing cost the lessor will have to bear (dealers buy their inventory on credit); and then the lessor adds on a profit margin. All the lessor is really doing is giving you the ease of renting rather than taking the multiple responsibilities of ownership. You can put the license plates and insurance in the lessor's name. Repairs and maintenance can be handled by the lessor. But for that convenience, the lessor charges you all those costs plus a profit margin. It is never economically advantageous to lease. At best it can only be more convenient.

Two arguments are given for leasing even when it's clear you pay a premium to do so. One is that it's easier to take a tax deduction for a business car by leasing rather than buying. The other is that it's more convenient to replace the car because you do not have to sell it at the end of the lease.

However, if you can meet the requirements of the Internal Revenue Service (IRS) for deducting a lease payment, you can certainly qualify to deduct the costs of owning a car. Those costs are depreciation, repairs and maintenance, parking, tolls, and so on. The determining factor for the deductibility of a car is not whether it's leased or purchased, but whether it's used for business purposes. Leasing has nothing to do with tax deductibility.

It's true that with a lease you can replace your car at the end of 3, 4, or 5 years merely by turning it in for another leased car. However, there is a cost associated with doing so. The lessor will require you to guarantee the lessor's back-end value on that car. When you turn it in, if the actual value is less than the originally estimated value (because of depreciation, high mileage, or the condition of the car), you may be responsible for the difference.

Additionally, you are paying the lessor a premium to do something you can do yourself: sell the car or trade it in. If you are following the rules regarding "new versus used" given previously, you will be driving it for at least 8 to 10 years anyway. And to say that it's more convenient to lease because of the trade-in or replacement aspect is to say that you prefer to be what the Bible calls "slothful." It is also short-sighted and foolish.

> Proverbs 21:25–26: The desire of the sluggard kills him, for his hands refuse to labor. All day long he craves and craves, but the righteous gives and does not hold back.

Cash versus borrow. Cars are commonly financed with installment debt. So, we are going to look briefly at the deceptions related to this type of borrowing and discuss an important principle called the *opportunity cost of consumption*. Then, we will discuss tips on purchasing used cars and auto insurance.

Deception 1: It Makes More Sense to Borrow than to Pay Cash for a Car

Let us suppose you go to a car dealer and get this comment from the salesperson:

> I can get you in this car and you will come out ahead financially if you put your money in a certificate of deposit paying 5 percent and finance the car with us at 9 percent. I can prove it!

What would you say?

The logic inside you says, "There is no way—show me!"

The salesperson then proceeds to draw you a chart, shown here as Table 12.2.

Table 12.2 Pay Cash or Finance?

Cost of Car	$15,000
Cash in Bank	$15,000
Payments on Car Loan	$311.38 per month for 60 months
Interest Rate	9.0%
CD Saving Rate	5.0%
Dealer's Analysis	
$15,000 Invested at 5% for 60 Months Grows to	$19,144
Original Investment	$15,000
Interest Income	$ 4,144
Total Payments on Car Loan	
($311.38/Month × 60 Months)	$18,683
Original Amount Borrowed	($15,000)
Interest Expense	$3,683
Advantage of Financing	**$461**

As you work out the numbers on different options, you may conclude that if you took the 14.2% loan, you could break even with just a 7% return on your investment. If you could earn 10%, you would make almost $1,500 more than you paid out over the 4 years of the loan.

By calculating both the cost of the loan and the investment earnings month by month, you can see that the deal works so well because the 14% is charged against a declining balance, whereas the 9% is paid on a growing balance. As a general rule of thumb, if you can earn an interest rate equivalent to half the interest rate of your loan, you will come out ahead.

There is one alternative, however, that has not been considered yet, and that is to use the cash to pay for the car and then make the monthly payment to yourself and deposit it in an interest-bearing account. Table 12.3 shows this in application.

The gain would be $2,310 if cash was paid for the car and a monthly payment of $311.38 was made to yourself and invested at 9%, as opposed to keeping the cash and financing the car. The idea that financing may put you in a better position really is only a half truth. It's always financially advantageous to pay cash for a car and save the monthly payment, literally as well as figuratively.

Table 12.3 Advantage of Paying Cash

Investment Value of a Monthly Savings of $311.38	
Earns 5% for 60 Months	$21,176
Taxes Paid on Interest Earned (15%)	($ 396)
Net Investment	$20,780
True Investment Value from Table 12.2	
Future Value of CD	$19,144
Taxes Paid on Interest Earned*	($ 674)
Net Investment	$18,470
Advantage of Paying Cash	$ 2,310

*The difference in taxes is due to the difference in interest income from the average principal actually invested. One begins with a large principal—producing more interest income—whereas the other amount grows over time.

Courtesy of mizuno555/Fotolia.

The only time this would not be true is if the interest rate charged by the lender dropped to about half the rate that could be earned through investment. If the lending rate ever drops that low, however, the dealer is assuredly making up the lost interest by charging a higher price for the car. In that case, you would still be better off paying cash for the car and negotiating the price down accordingly.

Finding an alternative better than paying cash for a car just does not seem possible. A vehicle is a depreciating item; borrowing to buy it does not make sense. Many times someone will say, "Well, I can't afford to pay cash." In that event, the answer is simple: "You can't afford that car."

A money maxim summarizes the situation well: "If you can't afford to save in order to pay cash, you can't afford to buy it on credit." For example, if you can find room in your budget for $400 truck payment, then you should be able to save $400 per month. Don't kid yourself.

Deception 2: Easy Payments

The second common deception with using installment debt to purchase a car is the idea of "easy payments." There is no such thing. Again, if you cannot afford to save, you cannot afford to make payments. Payments appear to be easy only when you extend the term of repayment. Car loans used to be made for 24 months. Now they are commonly extended to 60, or even 72 months. As prices go up, the length of repayment becomes longer. Notice, too, that interest rates do not drop with longer-term loans; they usually rise. This is demonstrated by the standard yield curve. The **yield curve** is a graphical representation in which interest rates are plotted against time, usually designed by a determined maturity. Figure 12.1 is a normal yield curve. As you can see from Figure 12.1, the longer the time to maturity of a loan, the higher the interest rate.

Yield curve The graphical representation in which interest rates are plotted against time, usually designed by a determined maturity.

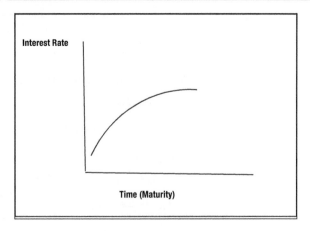

Figure 12.1 Yield Curve

THE OPPORTUNITY COST OF CONSUMPTION

Opportunity cost The value associated with any potential gain foregone by any other possible alternatives.

Consumption The use or using up of a resource.

Opportunity cost of consumption The foregone future value of money due to the use or using up of that money now.

In order to help explain the concept of opportunity cost of consumption we will go over an example. First, let's define several of these terms. **Opportunity cost** is defined as the loss of potential gain from other alternatives when one alternative is chosen. In other words, any gain you could have received by choosing a different option is referred to as an opportunity cost. The other important term is **consumption**, which is simply the use or using up of a resource. Therefore, when the terms are combined, the **opportunity cost of consumption,** in relation to finances, is the foregone future value of money due to the use or using up of that money now.

On to the example. Assume that you borrow $10,000 to buy a used car and pay off the loan over 4 years. In this situation, you would average having about $5000 per year outstanding in borrowed dollars. The reason it is not $2,500 ($10,000/4 years) is that the principal balance decreases slowly at first due to the majority of the first few years' payments being devoted toward interest payments. See the Appendix for a complete amortization schedule for $10,000 borrowed at 6% for 4 years. Think of this as an inverse yield curve, as shown in Figure 12.2.

Further assume that you continue to borrow $10,000 every 4 years in order to replace your car throughout a working life of 40 years. You have thus borrowed an average of $5,000 for 40 years. Assuming a 6% annual interest rate at which to borrow, you will have paid $12,720 in interest over the course of 40 years and paid back the principal balance of $100,000 totaling $112,720 dollars in total.

On the other hand, suppose you were to invest $5,000 at 8% and leave it untouched for 40 years. Your account balance would be roughly $108,500.

Thus, when you choose to borrow rather than save, you are giving up the opportunity to earn. That opportunity given up is what is referred to as the opportunity cost of consumption. You can do your own calculations to see what you are likely to give up (or maybe have already given up) when you borrow.

If you are feeling a need to replace a car now and you do not think you can afford to pay cash, let me show you a way to be able to pay cash for your cars.

Let's assume you have a $1,000 repair bill facing you on your car, which is why you think you should trade it in and get a newer model. If you spend that $1,000 now and then save $100, $200, or $300 per month in a savings account earning 6%, you

Figure 12.2 Amortization Curve

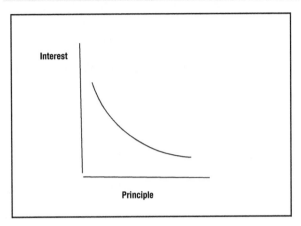

will have one of the amounts shown in Table 12.3 at the end of whatever time period you choose.

If, instead of spending $300 per month on car payments, you put that amount in savings and wait 1 year, you can have a $3,700 car (less taxes) for which you could pay cash. It's true you won't be driving the same luxury car that $300 per month could buy. But it's also true that you won't have the installment debt. If you continue to save the $300 per month, 3 more years later you'll have another $11,121 (less taxes on the interest), and then you can upgrade to a car costing that amount. If you keep that car for just 4 years, you'll have saved $14,831 (less tax) more to buy the next new car.

Table 12.3 Saving to Buy Later

	Save to Buy		
Amount in fund at the end of year (before taxes) with 6% interest compounded monthly			
Year	$100/Mo	$200/Mo	$300/Mo
1	$ 1,233	$ 2,467	$ 3,700
2	2,470	4,940	7,410
3	3,707	7,417	11,121
4	4,943	9,887	14,831

You can see from this chart that the longer you save to buy the car, or the longer you drive the car you now have and make the payments to yourself, the more you will be able to pay for a car later. This again illustrates the value of delaying gratification of your desires, as well as the truth of our maxim "If you can't afford to save for it, you can't afford to borrow for it." If the money is available to make payments, the money is also available to be saved. All you have to do is delay making the decision to buy until later.

It's easy to find some justification for any decision we make, called confirmation bias, even if it's a bad decision. There will always be an advertiser, a salesperson, or a friend to point out some great-sounding deal.

You may be thinking that this type of lifestyle amounts to living like your parents or grandparents. Absolutely! We would benefit greatly from getting back to their definition of "being able to afford it," which is that you can afford to pay cash. Old-fashioned? Yes. Revolutionary? We hope so!

BUYING A USED CAR

As we have already discussed, when buying a car, a used car is in many cases the most economical choice. And although it may seem obvious, the primary motivation for purchasing a used car is affordability. With new car and truck prices easily approaching $40,000, a used car looks more attractive in terms of price. When you buy a used car, even if it is only several months old, you avoid paying for the privilege of driving it off the showroom floor. Because most new cars have lengthy warranties, from 36 to 60 months, that are transferable, buying a used car does not necessarily lose the benefits of the warranty from the manufacturer. However, if the warranty is still in effect, you may pay more for the car.

It is important to understand the psychology that is involved in buying a car. For some reason many people believe that if they buy a used car from a dealer, it will run better than if they buy it from someone off the street. There seems to be a degree of comfort in seeing a dealer's nameplate on the back of the car, perhaps because the dealer will "back up" the deal with appropriate service and repairs. However, there is a price for that degree of comfort. There is another side to the same coin. There are people who will trade in their problem cars to dealers because they do not want to be individually hassled by an unhappy buyer. So the problem cars can end up on the dealer's lot, which is where most people buy.

Another fallacy that leads a person to the dealer's showroom is that the dealer is the only place to get financing. As previously mentioned, you are encouraged to purchase your vehicles with cash if at all possible. If this is not possible, however, realize that there are multiple different places to secure financing. You should call local banks in your area as well as check with various online lenders that offer competitive rates for vehicles. Take the time to do your homework. Incidentally, you can finance a used car bought from an individual.

There are three basic steps to buying a used car. The first step is to *determine in advance how much you can pay for a car*. This will require a great deal of discipline to not go after a more expensive car or a newer model that still has that "new car smell." This is another reason to avoid a dealer's lot: you are always tempted to buy up. In America, cars are a status symbol—the more status, the higher the cost. By following this step, you won't get caught in the trap of paying more than you can afford.

Second, *do your homework by researching what is on the market*. Give yourself 4 to 6 weeks to do this. Keep your eyes open for "For Sale" signs, particularly around your neighborhood. Check the newspapers or used car guidebooks available at convenience stores. The Internet offers a productive way to compare prices and availability, from eBay to superstore dealers. Select several potential vehicles and then begin the interviewing process. Contact the sellers and ask about these items:

1. Correct mileage (Generally, you can assume about 15,000 miles per year times the age of the car.)
2. Number of owners

3. Whether the car has been wrecked
4. Whether the car has been used to tow a boat or a trailer
5. The reason the car is for sale
6. Availability of the car's service records
7. The asking price, and what the seller is willing to accept for the car

In addition to these questions, you can also pull a car's CARFAX vehicle history report. According to the CARFAX website, the vehicle reports may include the following:

- Title information, including salvaged or junked titles
- Flood damage history
- Total loss accident history
- Odometer readings
- Lemon history
- Number of owners
- Accident indicators, such as airbag deployments
- State emissions inspections results
- Service records
- Vehicle use (taxi, rental, lease, etc.)

Source: http://www.carfax.com/company/about

From your interview list, select the cars you want to see and test drive. Then allow yourself plenty of time. Consider taking a friend with you who can objectively look at the car and not fall prey to "new-car fever."

Finally, if you feel this is the car for you, you should arrange to have the car checked at a reputable mechanic. Plan to pay up to $100 to $200 for this inspection, which should include a complete check of the car from top to bottom, especially the engine, including compression, transmission, electrical system, and fuel and brake systems. Do not buy the car without this examination. If the seller hesitates to let you get the car checked, that is the key sign that the car is not for you. Once the mechanic provides you with a "clean bill of health on the car," you can then make the purchase.

Once you have decided to purchase the car, there are two items that you need to make sure that you have upon completing the transaction: (1) the title and (2) a bill of sale. The title is the documentation that proves ownership. Both the previous owner and the new owner should sign the title. In many cases, the signatures need to be notarized by a Notary Public, which can be completed at your local bank. The second item, a bill of sale, is a record of the sale/transfer and will include:

- Date of the purchase or transfer
- Price that was paid for the vehicle
- Identifying information of the vehicle, to include year, model, and vehicle identification number (VIN)
- Names and address of both the buyer and seller

To the extent you follow these steps, you will end up with a better car for your money. Remember: There is no such thing as a perfect car; whether it's a BMW or a Geo Metro, it will give you problems. The goal is to minimize your problems in advance by not buying the wrong car.

DISCIPLESHIP MOMENT AND REFLECTION

Reflect back on any car-buying decisions you have made in the past. What would you do differently? If you have not bought a car, ask your accountability and prayer partner about his or her experiences. What would he or she have done differently? Talk about what you have learned thus far.

SHOPPING FOR AUTO INSURANCE

Nobody enjoys paying for automobile insurance. Rates seem to rise continually. As a matter of fact, in the past 10 years they have risen at twice the rate of inflation—but not without cause. New car prices, repairs, personal injury lawsuits, and health-care costs have all jumped dramatically. The auto insurers have passed these costs on to the buyer.

In light of this, here are some tips to consider when choosing automobile insurance to keep your rates as low as possible:

1. *Choose the right car.* Make insurance costs a part of your criteria in selecting a car. You may be able to afford the car, but can you afford to insure it? The cost of insurance is influenced by the driver of the car and the make, model, and year of the car. High-performance cars cost the most to purchase, replace, and repair, and they are stolen more often than "family cars." They also tend to be driven by people who are higher insurance risks. Take time to shop different insurance costs for different types of cars.

2. *Youthful drivers.* The industry recognizes that accidents happen more with 16- to 25-year-olds. Therefore, they are charged higher rates. Here are several options to reduce them:

   i. Higher student grades can be helpful in keeping car insurance premiums lower. GPAs with at least a B average may provide a 5% to 25% discount.

   ii. Taking driver's training may bring another 5% to 10% discount. Both of these must be documented for your insurance carrier. There are many online options for driver safety courses that can be completed in the comfort of your own home.

   iii. Make the youthful driver an "occasional driver" on a family car rather than a "principal driver" on his or her own car. If the insurance company sees more drivers than cars, they may allow the young driver to qualify as an occasional driver. However, if the number of cars and drivers is equal, it would be hard to avoid the principal driver classification and higher rate. You may also consider raising the deductible on insurance for the car driven by the younger person if he or she is the principal driver.

   iv. Youthful drivers are those under 25 (sometimes 30). But females who marry by age 25 are rated as adults.

3. *Maintain a safe driving record.* Most insurance companies have discounts after 3 to 6 years of driving without a chargeable accident or a moving violation. If either is on your driving record, you may pay additional premiums for 3 years. In some cases, taking a driving safety course may keep your premiums from going up if you are involved in an accident or receive a violation.

4. *Consider your location.* Where you live definitely affects your insurance rates, although it hardly makes sense to move into rural areas from the city to reduce your insurance rates! However, it is important to know that where you work and live can both make a difference in your insurance premiums.

Umbrella policy An insurance policy that provides liability coverage over and above the coverage listed on one's auto and homeowner's insurance policies.

5. *Understand liability insurance.* Liability insurance is a very critical part of an insurance policy. This section in an insurance policy provides the amount of coverage paid to other individuals who are injured during an accident. It is never good to be underinsured. Each state has minimum requirements for liability insurance. These amounts, however, may be very impractical. Remember, you can't choose what kind of car you may hit or driver you may injure. If you hit a Ferrari and have only $100,000 in property damage insurance, you may be personally responsible for an additional $150,000 of repair costs! If you injure or kill a professional such as a medical doctor, the courts may assess a large "loss of earnings" claim against you. Your $50,000 of minimum liability won't go very far. You should spend more of your insurance dollars on liability coverage instead of comprehensive and collision coverages. One way to help ensure you are adequately covered from liability is to purchase what is referred to as an umbrella policy. An **umbrella policy** is an insurance policy that provides liability coverage over and above the coverages listed on your auto and home policies. Most agents would recommend at least $100,000 per person and $300,000 per accident for personal liability coverage and $300,000 for property damage.

6. *Raise the deductible on your auto policy.* When thinking about insurance, understand that insurance is nothing more than a transfer of risk. The more of the risk we transfer, the more expensive or costly the policy will be. The deductible on an insurance policy is what a policyholder must pay out-of-pocket for damages covered by the policy prior to the insurance company paying anything. Therefore, when you increase your deductible, you are taking more ownership in paying for the damages associated with an accident and thus will reduce what an insurance company will be required to pay out. This in turn will reduce your monthly premiums. The same holds true if you decrease your deductible; you are moving more responsibility of paying a claim to the insurance company, and will thus increase your monthly premium.

7. *Shop the market.* Rates are competitive, but make certain you compare "apples to apples." Great differences exist between companies in their service, products, ability to do on-site claims, and so forth. You may save money dealing with a less expensive company, but be sure you know what you are giving up. It often pays to develop a long-term relationship with an insurance agent and a company. In the event you get into a bad situation, they can help work you through all your options.

8. *Check with the state insurance commission on questions involving carriers.* Your state insurance commission can be useful in helping to review and evaluate insurance companies as well as insurance agents. Also, ask friends for references on companies you are considering.

Some of these options may not apply to your situation; others may require some thought or research. A little of your time could save you a lot of money.

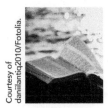

Courtesy of daniilantiq2010/Fotolia.

DISCIPLESHIP MOMENT AND REFLECTION

We hope that you have limited experience in filing auto insurance claims. Ask some of your mentors about their experiences, including your accountability and prayer partner. What types of claims did they file, what were the outcomes, and what advice could they give to you prior to filing an auto claim?

SUMMARY

This chapter looked at how we make vehicle purchasing decisions, starting with why we buy cars and how to most appropriately answer the question as to a vehicle's purpose. We then provided a process that you can follow to buy a car. Next we looked at ways to pay for a car and considered the differences between buying and leasing. We spent some time looking at the opportunity cost of consumption as it relates to car buying and offered some strategies for buying a used vehicle. We finished up the chapter by looking at the components of an auto insurance policy.

SUMMARY REVIEW QUESTIONS

1. Explain the real question that needs to be answered when deciding to get a vehicle.

2. Describe the three legitimate reasons to get a different car.

3. Explain the three steps recommended in the car-buying process.

4. Determine the 4-year cost of ownership between a new car and a used car you like. Include the following:
   a. Get an auto insurance quote for both vehicles.
   b. Assuming that you drive 12,000 miles per year, determine your gas consumption based on the tank size of each vehicle.
   c. Assume that it will cost $550/year for the used vehicle and $250/year for the new vehicle for maintenance, repairs, and tires.

5. Compare and contrast the three ways to replace a vehicle:
   a. New versus used
   b. Lease verse buy
   c. Cash versus borrow

6. What does "opportunity cost of consumption" mean in the case of car buying?

7. Explain the three steps to buying a used car.

8. What two fallacies exist in buying a car from a dealer? How can you overcome these tendencies?

9. What information can you obtain from a CARFAX report?

10. Give an explanation of to five to eight factors that will influence your auto insurance premiums.

Case Study Analysis

"Mom? Dad?" Chloe asked as she entered the family room. Bob and Debbie were both sitting down watching the nightly news and discussing the fact that news stories are always so depressing.

"Yes, Chloe?" Bob responded.

Chloe responded, "I was thinking that I think I am ready to get a car of my own. I don't really like having to always wait on when either of the cars are free from being used by you and mom. I know this probably isn't the best time to ask, but I'm not sure there will ever be a good time to ask. I know that you bought Sean his Ford Escape when he was 16."

Debbie interrupted, "Chloe, we bought Sean that car so that he could help transport you and Clara to some of your activities that your father and I couldn't always get to."

Chloe, in a soft voice, said, "I know—but it doesn't seem fair that he was able to drive whenever he wanted and I have to wait and ask to use the cars when you or dad are home or aren't using them. Plus, and I know this seems petty, but all my friends are starting to get their own cars, and I always feel that even though I have my license, I am always having to hitch rides with everyone. It just is really getting it to me."

Bob just sat there listening, although he hadn't fully turned his attention to Chloe from the news.

Chloe continued, "I know that dad doesn't ride his motorcycle very much, and I thought that if money was tight, we could use that to get me a car."

Bob's attention quickly turned to Chloe, "Chloe, I work extremely hard so that we can have the things we have, and therefore I get to buy things that I want. If you want to go buy a car, then go get a job—"

Bob paused, realizing that his harshness was out of line, and quickly apologized.

"Chloe, I'm sorry to snap at you. Let your mom and me talk about this and we will let you know in a few days what we decide."

A few days later, Bob and Debbie sat down with Chloe in her room and talked to her about their decision.

Bob started off, "Chloe, your mother and I have decided that we are going to help you get a car of your own; however, you need to complete an assignment first. This assignment is hopefully going to help you understand the process and details required to think about in relation to buying and owning a car. So, are you willing to do this assignment?"

Without hesitation, Chloe screamed, "Yes, anything! What is it?"

Bob and Debbie handed Chloe an envelope and left her room. Chloe quickly tore open the envelope and read the instructions.

Dear Chloe,

We are excited to see you go through this assignment. This is not just about busy work, but is intended to provide you the opportunity to go through the car-buying process and learn the true costs of ownership of a car. Once you complete this assignment, you should be ready to make a wise decision. Provide us a written response to each of the following steps.

Step 1: Before starting this process, we want you to pray about this decision. Pray that the Holy Spirit will guide you through this process and that you will remain focused on Him and not on your desires. Make sure that you are focused on answering the right questions.

Step 2: Find three cars that you might consider buying and complete the list below of the characteristics of each car in an Excel spreadsheet.

Car Characteristics	Option 1	Option 2	Option 3
Year			
Make			
Model			
Body style (two-door, etc.)			
Color			
Mileage			
Transmission type			
Engine size			
Is a CARFAX report available?			
Is the car under warranty?			

Price _____

Step 3: Do some research on the maintenance costs for a car, in general, by completing the following chart and determining which services are annual or monthly. (If something is less frequent than annual, put the charge in annual costs because it's better to overestimate costs than to underestimate them). Convert all your costs to monthly costs (divide annual total costs by 12).

Item	Frequency	Cost	Where You Found This Information
Oil change			
30k mileage service			
60k mileage service			
90k mileage service			
120k mileage service			
150k mileage service			
New tires			
New battery			
Insurance			
Option 1: full coverage			
Option 2: collision only			
Annual registration fee			
Annual state inspection (if any)			
Toll payments (if any)			
Gas consumption			
Option 1: 14-gallon tank (2 fill-ups per month)			
Option 2: Hybrid option (1 fill-up per month)			
OnStar service (optional)			
Sirius satellite radio (optional)			
Total annual cost			
Total monthly cost			
Total average per-month cost of ownership			

Step 4: Using the information from steps 1, 2, and 3, determine which of the three cars you would potentially buy. Assuming you are able to put 5% down based on the price of the car, do some research with three different lenders and compute the following.

	Bank 1	Bank 2	Bank 3
Price of car			
Down payment			
Interest rate			
Total monthly payment			

Step 5: Determine your total monthly costs for owning the car by adding the results from step 3 and step 4.

Step 6: Assume that you can get hired at the YMCA this summer as a summer camp counselor, working 35 hours per week earning $10/hour.

Step 7: Knowing your total wages from step 6, would you be able to put any additional money toward the payment of the car? Why or why not?

Step 8: Provide an explanation as to how you will continue to make car payments when the summer is over and you are back in school, when you may be unable to work with volleyball and softball activities.

Step 9: Summarize your findings and present this information to your parents. The outcome will be determined based on your findings.

We are praying for you during this exercise that the Lord will lead you through this process with wisdom and understanding.

Mom and Dad

DEFINITIONS

Consumption   (p. 286)

Opportunity cost   (p. 286)

Opportunity cost of consumption   (p. 286)

Umbrella policy   (p. 291)

Yield curve   (p. 285)

SCRIPTURE VERSES (ESV)

Proverbs 21:25–26—The desire of the sluggard kills him, for his hands refuse to labor. All day long he craves and craves, but the righteous gives and does not hold back.

ADDITIONAL READINGS

Advani, R. (2013). Buying a car. In *Financial Freedom: A Guide to Achieving Lifelong Wealth and Secuirty* (pp. 85–90). New York, NY: Apress.

Bell, G. D. (1967). Self-confidence and persuasion in car buying. *Journal of Marketing Research*, 46–52.

Dasgupta, S., Siddarth, S., & Silva-Risso, J. (2007). To lease or to buy? A structural model of a consumer's vehicle and contract choice decisions. *Journal of Marketing Research, 44*(3), 490–502.

Dijksterhuis, A., Bos, M. W., Nordgren, L. F., & Van Baaren, R. B. (2006). On making the right choice: The deliberation-without-attention effect. *Science, 311*(5763), 1005–1007.

Goldberg, P. K. (1996). Dealer price discrimination in new car purchases: Evidence from the consumer expenditure survey. *Journal of Political Economy*, 622–654.

Greene, D. L. (2010). *How consumers value fuel economy: A literature review* (No. EPA-420-R-10-008). Washington, DC: Environmental Protection Agency.

Hendel, I., & Lizzeri, A. (1998). *The role of leasing under adverse selection* (No. w6577). Washington, DC: National Bureau of Economic Research.

Johnson, J. P., & Waldman, M. (2003). Leasing, lemons, and buybacks. *RAND Journal of Economics*, 247–265.

Miller, M. H., & Upton, C. W. (1976). Leasing, buying, and the cost of capital services. *Journal of Finance, 31*(3), 761–786.

Miller, S. E. (1995). Economics of automobile leasing: The call option value. *Journal of Consumer Affairs, 29*(1), 199–218.

Oppenheimer, P. (2002). Including real options in evaluating terminal cash flows in consumer auto leases. *Financial Services Review, 11*(2), 135.

Pirotte, H., Schmit, M., & Vaessen, C. (2004). *Credit risk mitigation evidence in auto leases and residual value risk*. Working Paper 04/008, Centre Emile Bernheim, Solvay Business School, Université Libre de Bruxelles.

Pykhtin, M., & Dev, A. (2003). Residual risk in auto leases. *Risk, 16*(10), 10.

Rachlin, H., Logue, A. W., Gibbon, J., & Frankel, M. (1986). Cognition and behavior in studies of choice. *Psychological review, 93*(1), 33.

Tollefson, J. (2008). Car industry: Charging up the future. *Nature News, 456*(7221), 436–440.

REFERENCES

The case for hanging on to your aging family car for 100,000 miles. (1989, March). *Money*, pp. 165–166.

Chapter 13

Personal Income Taxes

Courtesy of duncanandison/Fotolia.

BIG IDEA:
We should pay taxes with gratitude because they are a result of God's provision (income).

LEARNING OUTCOMES

- Understand the three components relevant to having a proper perspective on taxes
- Provide Scripture verses that support a positive view of taxes
- List and explain the various types of taxes we pay
- Understand the difference between marginal and effective tax rates
- Know when to use different tax-filing statuses
- Explain the four steps for determining taxable income from gross income
- Explain how to best prepare for your annual tax filings
- Understand the tax-withholding process and how to match withholdings to expected tax liability
- Explain the difference between tax deductions and tax credits
- Know the different forms used in a tax return
- Explain how three strategies can reduce taxes legitimately: timing, shifting, and investments

Introduction

If there's one cash outflow that everyone is eager to reduce, it's taxes. From ancient Rome to modern civilizations, people grouse about taxes.

When reflecting on this attitude toward taxes, the question arises, "Why is it that many Americans detest paying taxes?" The answer is multifaceted, but the primary reason is that there is no visual perceived benefit from paying taxes. Only in this area of our finances do we feel that once the money is gone, it seems to be gone forever.

Ron's Corner

When I was a practicing CPA, I prepared hundreds of tax returns each year and was asked hundreds of times over the course of several years, "How can I reduce my taxes?" I had a facetious answer for that question: "It's easy to reduce your taxes—just reduce your income." It's a guaranteed way to reduce taxes, and there is no audit risk to it. The point is that if your taxes are going up, your income is also going up.

PROPER PERSPECTIVE ON TAXES

In this chapter we cover three main topics that seem to greatly influence our general perceptions of taxes. First is the idea that we must do everything in our power to reduce or eliminate our taxes. There are two ways to view this strategy, and one is right and the other is wrong. Next, we highlight some general cultural thoughts that reflect our (society's) view of taxes. Finally, we look at two potential detrimental behaviors that are typical in relation to taxes: acting as if free tax deductions exist and receiving a large tax refund.

Legitimate Tax Reduction

Tax avoidance (*see also* Tax minimization) The use of legitimate processes offered through the tax code that can reduce the amount of tax owed.

Tax minimization (*see also* Tax avoidance) The use of legitimate processes offered through the tax code that can reduce the amount of tax owed.

Tax evasion The intentional act of preparing misleading tax documents and/or avoiding paying what is legitimately required.

Having the right attitude about taxes does not imply that you need to pay more than you rightfully owe in taxes. There is a big difference, however, between tax avoidance and tax evasion. **Tax avoidance**, or **tax minimization**, is the use of legitimate processes offered through the tax code to reduce the amount of tax owed. **Tax evasion** is the intentional act of preparing misleading tax documents and/or avoiding paying what is legitimately required. Tax avoidance is planning wisely and prudently to pay a fair share of taxes, but not more than what is legally owed.

Attitudes Toward Taxes

Taxes need to be put into proper perspective, and the proper perspective is that income taxes are levied only when there is income earned. Also, although tax dollars may not always be used in the most effective way possible, tax dollars go toward paying for services that are used by everybody. We are not "entitled" to those services for free. If we benefit from them, we must pay for them. Entitlement is definitely an attitude bred by our have-it-all culture, not by God. Check your perspective and thank God for your government.

There seems to be a cultural perspective toward taxes that says the following:

- Paying taxes is bad.
- Cheating by the other guy is normal, so a little "fudging" by me is acceptable.
- I shouldn't have to support an irresponsible government.
- I'm paying more than my fair share, but the rich aren't.

Although these perspectives on taxes may not have crossed your mind, you probably do not approach the topic of taxes with delight. Here are several suggestions of ways that you can view taxes with a more positive perspective:

- Paying income taxes is not a "bad" thing.
- Integrated tax planning is critical to long-term financial success.

- A direct correlation exists between income and income taxes due.
- Tax reduction is a legitimate goal.
- Income taxes may be an indicator of God's blessings.
- Income tax planning requires highly specialized expertise.
- Inability to pay taxes due is symptomatic of poor planning.
- Taxes should never be a source of cash flow problems.
- Tax reduction and debt reduction are in direct conflict with one another.
- Getting a large refund check may be a sign of poor stewardship.

TAX BEHAVIORS

In the Ron's Corner section earlier in this chapter, Ron Blue offers some amusing advice for lowering your taxes—lower your income. There is another surefire way to lower your tax liability, and that is to spend all your money on items that can be deducted from your income, such as charitable contributions, medical bills, mortgage interest, and retirement account/401(k) contributions. It is important to highlight that there is no such thing as a free tax deduction. If you are in the 15% tax bracket, then a dollar spent on a deductible item costs you 85 cents cash out-of-pocket. True, it reduces your taxes, but there is a cost to it.

There is no free tax deduction anywhere, at any time, for anything!

It's easy for an accountant to make the client happy by having the client overpay on withholdings and quarterly tax estimates during the year so that he or she always gets a refund. Unfortunately, this practice, if done intentionally by the accountant, borders on being unethical, and it certainly does not make good economic sense. When we view our resources from the perspective of a steward, receiving a large refund check is a sign of improper management of resources. There are several reasons why this is the case:

1. Going back and forth: When you receive a refund, you are merely receiving money that you have already paid in to the government. It is as if you sent a check to the government, and the government sent the check back to you.

2. No compensation: Our withholding, from earnings, is sent to the government to cover our expected tax liability. If we withhold too much or pay too much in estimated payments, we miss out on any earning potential from this money. The government does not pay interest on this money that is being held. Therefore, when you get a refund check back, the entire amount has been earning 0% for the duration of time the government had access to it.

    a. Suppose you paid $1,000 per month ($12,000 per year) in withholdings and had a total tax liability at the end of the year of $6,000. We could say that your tax liability was covered through the first six payments, and the last six payments of $1,000 each could have earned 6% if that money had been invested instead. By sending the government too much money (six payments of $1,000) you lost the opportunity to earn $75.50 over that 6-month period. To highlight the extreme, suppose you had this same scenario for your entire working life of 40 years. You would have lost the ability to have $11,607 at 6% annual interest rate.

3. Regular pay versus bonus pay: It is interesting how we view expected income, our regular wages and earnings, versus unexpected income from bonuses or, in this case, tax return checks. Mental accounting, the notion that we put

money into mental accounts and use each account for specific purposes, helps explain this phenomenon. Our regular wages are put to use to cover our daily living expenses and thus are usually spent less frivolously. When we receive a sum of money from a different source that has not been allocated toward our daily living expenses, we feel that the sum of money may be used in other (less rigid) ways.

Understand that these behaviors may be difficult to deal with because they go against the grain of everything we see in our culture. For example, many people plan to have that refund check in order to make major purchases each year, such as vacations or home remodels. Unfortunately, what they are really doing is admitting that they do not have the discipline to save for that major purchase. You will gain more in interest if you learn to save that money little by little each month through more accurate withholding. Please remember that tax planning does not have to be a mystery or even very difficult, especially if you understand the two pieces of advice just given.

BIBLICAL INSIGHTS ON TAXES

Although the Bible does not provide us specifics as to how much tax we should pay and the Bible does not say that we should not pay taxes, it does give us many principles that directly apply to income taxes, such as the following:

- **Proverbs 13:11**: Dishonest money dwindles away, but he who gathers money little by little makes it grow.
- **Luke 16:10**: Whoever can be trusted with very little can also be trusted with much, and whoever is dishonest with very little will also be dishonest with much.
- **2 Corinthians 4:2**: Rather, we have renounced secret and shameful ways; we do not use deception, nor do we distort the word of God. On the contrary, by setting forth the truth plainly we commend ourselves to every man's conscience in the sight of God.
- **Romans 13:7**: Give everyone what you owe him: If you owe taxes, pay taxes: if revenue, then revenue; if respect, then respect; if honor, then honor.
- **Luke 20:22, 24, 25**: Is it lawful for us to pay taxes to Caesar, or not? "Show Me a denarius. Whose portrait and inscription are on it?" "Caesar's," they replied. He said to them, "Then give to Caesar what is Caesar's, and to God what is God's."
- **Matthew 5:16**: In the same way, let your light shine before men, that they may see your good deeds and praise your Father in heaven.
- **Proverbs 15:22**: Plans fail for lack of counsel, but with many advisors they succeed.

So how do these verses really apply to our understanding of taxes? Here are some insights applying these verses to how we view and understand taxes:

- You are called to be a light to a dark and dying world. One of the ways that you reflect light is by your good stewardship, which requires paying taxes.
- Your choice is fraud or faithfulness. You may reduce taxes by illegal or questionable means, but faithfulness requires you to use good planning and

honesty to reduce taxes or to pay the full amount without begrudging where no deductions can be taken. Your objective is faithfulness—not tax reduction. It is God's money. Remember that he owns it all. If He does not resent that you have to use it for that purpose, then why should you?

- Some taxes are certainly due because our government has supplied services. Quite frankly, the freedoms and protection we enjoy in the United States are unparalleled anywhere in the world, and thus we all have a part in paying for these privileges.
- Be a planner, not a responder. It's especially important to plan in the tax area because of the many types of taxes that we must pay.

"Render *cheerfully* unto Caesar what is Caesar's, but no more than he requires."

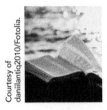

Courtesy of daniilantiq2010/Fotolia.

DISCIPLESHIP MOMENT AND REFLECTION

Reflect back on your attitude toward paying taxes. Pray that God gives you the right attitude. Discuss your thoughts with your prayer and accountability partner.

With this theological background in mind, we now turn our attention toward how taxes work and offer strategies to legitimately minimize tax liability.

TYPES OF TAXES

You are taxed when you earn, when you spend, when you use your phone, when your investments do well, and when you die. As a matter of fact, you are taxed almost any time there is a money transaction.

The following list is a summary of some of the many types of taxes:

- *Income taxes*—This tax is levied on all earned income during each calendar year. Income taxes can be assessed at various levels, including federal, state, city, and county. At the federal level, the majority of income tax is used to pay for the following programs and services:

  - Health care   27.49%
  - National defense   23.91%
  - Job and family security   18.17%
  - Net interest   9.07%
  - Veterans benefits   5.93%
  - Education and job training   3.59%

  Source from: https://www.whitehouse.gov/2014-taxreceipt

- *Sales taxes*—States can impose sales taxes on retail purchases, leases, rentals, and the exchange of goods and services in that state. These taxes are used to support the operations of state, city, and local governments.
- *Intangible taxes*—Taxes on various intangible properties owned, usually including stocks, bonds, and other investments. State governments generally impose this tax.

- *Use taxes*—Taxes for the use of goods and services provided by taxing authorities, such as gasoline taxes for the use of roads and airport taxes for the use of airports. These taxes are usually imposed at the state level.
- *Estate taxes*—Taxes imposed by the federal and state governments on the accumulation of material wealth when a person dies. The estate tax is a tax on the value of property left by the decedent.
- *Inheritance taxes*—Taxes imposed by state and local governments, again, on estates accumulated. Inheritance tax is a tax imposed on the beneficiary of assets from a decedent.
- *Gift taxes*—Taxes imposed on the transfer of various kinds of property to another person. Gift taxes and estate taxes are typically referred to as transfer taxes. In other words, the transferring of property from one person to another may result in a tax. Gift taxes can be imposed by both federal and state governments.
- *Property taxes*—Taxes imposed by local authorities on property owned. The tax is usually assessed by the jurisdiction where the property is located and is used to fund local schools and governmental services, such as police and fire departments.
- *Social Security and Medicare taxes*—Taxes imposed by the federal government on wages, earnings, and self-employment income to pay for Social Security and Medicare benefits.

This list is not meant to be all-inclusive, but merely to illustrate that you do pay taxes at almost every turn of your financial life. Due to the complexity of our income tax code and the variety of taxes we just identified, we will focus our discussion on tax planning in the area of income taxes at the state and federal levels only.

Albert Einstein once said, "The hardest thing in the world to understand is the income tax."

INCOME TAX RATES

There are two different "tax rates" that will be explained in the upcoming section: marginal tax rates and effective tax rates. It is important to understand the difference and when each of these terms is used in relation to taxes.

Marginal, by definition in finances, means the impact of the next unit. Applying this to taxes, the **marginal tax rate,** or **marginal tax bracket**, is the tax rate at which the next dollar of income will be taxed. What does this mean? The federal income tax system is set up as a progressive scale. In other words, as you earn more money, the amount of your income that is subject to taxes increases. Table 13.1 provides the 2015 Internal Revenue Service (IRS) tax table.

Marginal tax rate, also marginal tax bracket   The tax rate at which the next dollar of income will be taxed.

Table 13.1 2015 IRS Tax Table

Tax Bracket (Single)	Tax Bracket (Married)	Tax Bracket (Head of Household)	Marginal Tax Rate
$0–$9,074	$0–$18,149	$0–$12,949	10%
$9,075–$36,899	$18,150–$73,799	$12,950–$49,399	15%
$36,900–$89,349	$73,800–$148,849	$49,400–$127,549	25%
$89,350–$186,349	$148,850–$226,849	$127,550–$206,599	28%
$186,350–$405,099	$226,850–$405,099	$206,600–$405,099	33%
$405,100–$406,749	$405,100–$456,999	$405,100–$432,199	35%
$406,750+	$457,000+	$432,200+	39.6%

Source: http://www.tax-brackets.org/federaltaxtable

As you can see from Table 13.1, as your income goes up and reaches the next income bracket, each additional dollar of earned income is then taxed at a higher marginal tax rate.

For example, a husband and wife filing taxes jointly who earn $80,000 might say that they are in the "25% tax bracket" because their next dollar of income would be taxed at 25%.

As the income reaches a higher level, the rate goes up, but—and this is important to remember—*the rate does not go up on all of the previously earned and taxed income.* It only applies to that next dollar of income. So what would the tax liability be for this couple earning $80,000? Let's work out how to calculate the tax liability on $80,000. (It's important to note that this is for illustrative purposes only; we will discuss later in this chapter how to calculate taxable income from gross income.)

Because this couple is married, we will use the second column titled "Tax Bracket (Married)" in conducting this calculation.

- Between $0 and $18,149, 10% of this amount of income (10% of $18,149) = $1,850
- Between $18,150 and $73,799, 15% of this amount of income (15% of $55,649) = $8,347.35
- Between $73,800 and $80,000, 25% of this amount (25% of $6,200) = $1,612

So we add up these numbers to determine the couple's total tax ($1,850 + $8,347.35 + $1,612) = $11,809.35

In order for this example to be clear, we need to clarify one thing. Keep in mind that the $80,000 in the example is taxable income. **Taxable income** is the portion of your earned income that is ultimately taxed after taking into account all deductions, exemptions, and other reductions. We will discuss how to derive taxable income later in this chapter.

The following bar chart illustrates how the maximum marginal tax rate has changed over time. Note how low the marginal rate was during the 2000s relative to other time periods. The first thing to realize is that the lower the marginal rate, the less tax-motivated any financial decision should be. Second, be on guard, because marginal tax rates can be (and will be) changed at the whim of Congress. What's true today regarding wise tax planning may not be true next year.

Taxable income The portion of your earned income that is ultimately taxed after taking into account all deductions, exemptions, and other reductions of income.

Figure 13.1 Marginal Tax Rates

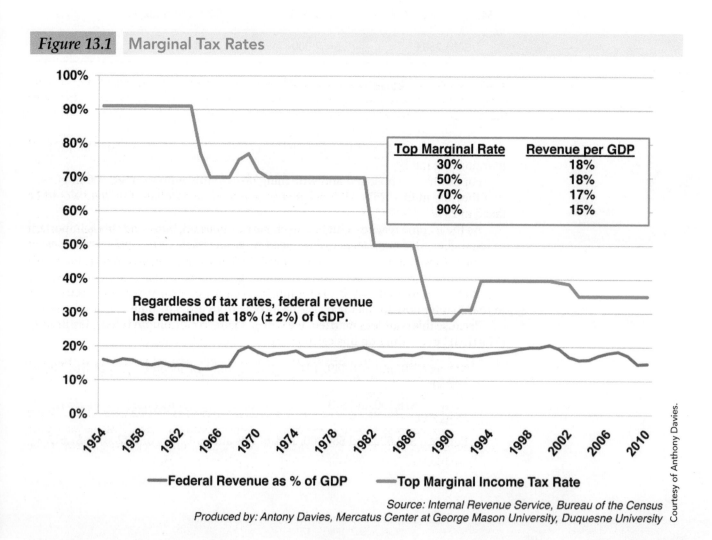

Top Marginal Rate	Revenue per GDP
30%	18%
50%	18%
70%	17%
90%	15%

Regardless of tax rates, federal revenue has remained at 18% (± 2%) of GDP.

Federal Revenue as % of GDP   Top Marginal Income Tax Rate

Source: Internal Revenue Service, Bureau of the Census
Produced by: Antony Davies, Mercatus Center at George Mason University, Duquesne University

Courtesy of Anthony Davies.

Source: https://thescoietypages.org/socimages/files/2012/12/1.png

Effective Rate

The other rate that deserves attention is the effective tax rate. The **effective tax rate** is found as the ratio of the total amount of taxes paid to the total earned income. Let's assume that our married couple earned $110,000 in gross wages (giving us a taxable income of $80,000) and paid their tax due of $11,809.35; they would have the following tax identifiers:

- They are in the 25% marginal tax bracket.
- The have an effective tax rate of 10.75% ($11,809.35/$110,000).

The effective rate is the key number. It is much more important than the marginal tax rate because it tells you what percentage of your gross income was paid in taxes. The simple objective in tax planning is to reduce the effective tax rate in order to generate after-tax dollars for any goals that you have.

TAX-FILING STATUS

Your tax calculations can be influenced by your tax-filing status, which is primarily based on your marital status and your family structure. The U.S. tax code provides filers with five different status options when they file:

1. *Single*: This status is for those who are not married. You can be legally separated from a spouse through either a separation or divorce decree and file as a single taxpayer.

2. *Married filing jointly*: This status allows married couples to combine their earnings into one joint tax return

3. *Married filing separately*: This status allows a married couple to file their own tax returns using their income and respective deductions only. Although there may be personal reasons to file separately, the most common reason to explore this option is that two spouses have either large discrepancies in income between the two or spouses have brought complicated separate property producing income into the marriage and it makes economic sense to calculate the income toward each spouse separately. If you think you fall into this category, we would recommend discussing your filing status with a tax professional.

4. *Head of household*: Any taxpayer who is not legally considered married and pays more than half the cost to support him- or herself AND a qualifying dependent can file as this type of a filer.

5. *Qualifying widow or widower with a dependent child*: This benefit is good for 2 years after a spouse dies; however, you must remain unmarried and have a qualifying dependent. The main benefit of this status is that allows you to continue to be classified in the favorable married-filing-jointly tax brackets.

TAX CALCULATIONS: FROM GROSS EARNINGS TO TAXABLE INCOME

Regardless of the tax-filing status that you use, the transition from gross earnings to taxable income is the same, with the only difference being the specific qualifiers for each step. We will go through this process in steps. Each of these steps is somewhat technical and fills thousands of pages of the Internal Revenue Code (IRC), so only the major categories will be explained, and we will only list some of the provisions within each step. Review this information and seek advice from a professional if you think it is applicable.

Step 1: Determine Your Gross Earnings

According to tax law, you will normally receive documentation of your earnings through W-2s (if you are employed), 1099s (if you are a subcontractor or self-employed), or K-1s (if you have partnerships) prior to the end of February of each year. These are added together to generate your total gross annual income.

Step 2: Determine Your Deductions from Income

This step allows you to reduce your gross income (found in step 1) by subtracting certain expenses allowed by the IRS. Although this is not an all-inclusive list, the most prominent adjustments to gross income are listed below (found on Form 1040 as items 23–37):

Alimony   Payments to or for a spouse or former spouse under a separation or divorce decree.

- Unreimbursed educator expenses
- Certain business expenses
- Health savings account contributions
- Unreimbursed moving expenses
- Part of self-employment tax (if self-employed)
- Self-employed health insurance premiums
- **Alimony**—payment to or for a spouse or former spouse under a separation or divorce decree
- Individual retirement account (IRA) contributions
- Student loan interest
- Tuition and school fees

Adjusted gross income (AGI)   The amount used to compute various limitations imposed by the tax code.

Once these adjustments have been determined and added together, the summed total is subtracted from gross income (step 1). The new figure is referred to as **adjusted gross income (AGI)** and will be used to compute various limitations on deductions to which you may be entitled.

Step 3: Determine Between a Standard Deduction or the Use of Itemized Deductions

Once you have determined your AGI, you now need to refer back to your records and do some calculations to determine between the *greater amount* of allowed deductions from the following two options:

1. Option 1: The standard deduction is a flat amount that you can reduce your AGI by. The amount of the deduction for each type of filer is as follows:
    a. Single: $6,300
    b. Married Filing Jointly: $12,600
    c. Married Filing Separately: $6,300
    d. Head of Household: $9,250
    e. Surviving Spouse: $12,600

2. Option 2: The itemized deduction is the sum of certain expenses paid throughout the year (certain restrictions apply):
   a. Medical and dental expenses (only expenses over 10% of AGI)
   b. Deductible taxes (state and local taxes: income, property and sales tax)
   c. Home mortgage points (prepaid interest may be deductible)
   d. Interest expense (limitations apply usually to investment interest and qualified home mortgage interest)
   e. Charitable contributions
   f. Business use of home
   g. Business use of car
   h. Educational expenses (such as tuition, books, supplies, research costs)
   i. Employee business expenses (unreimbursed work-related expenses)
   j. Casualty, disaster and theft losses

PREPARING AND PLANNING FOR TAX TIME

As you can see from the itemized deduction section, there are many different numbers that you as a taxpayer will need to collect and calculate in order to determine which deduction method is most advantageous. In order to make this process as efficient as possible, several suggestions are offered:

1. Get an accordion file or a multiple-pocket expandable file folder and label the following:
   a. Income
      i. Wages (W-2)
      ii. Dividends and interest (1099s)
      iii. Capital gain/loss
      iv. Other
   b. Expenses
      i. Medical and dental
      ii. Taxes (property, sales tax on large items)
      iii. Interest on qualified debt (home mortgage/investments)
      iv. Charitable contributions
      v. IRA contributions
      vi. Child-care expenses
      vii. Miscellaneous
   c. Special Items
      i. Closing statements
      ii. Moving expenses
      iii. Prior year's tax return
      iv. K-1 (for partnership ownership)
      v. Rental property statements
   d. Self-Employed
      i. 1099—miscellaneous
      ii. Accounting documentation
      iii. Payroll

Throughout the year, you can use the folder to hold relevant tax information. During January and February, you will be receiving a number of statements from your employer and other financial companies that should be filed in this folder under the appropriate headings. In mid-February, you should be in a position where most, if not all, of your information is in hand.

File the documentation in the folder and you will be ready to total the numbers for your return. In addition to filing your receipts, you should also spend some time going through all your canceled checks and credit card statements (if any) for the year. Pull out or highlight those items that are tax deductible and file them in the appropriate folder.

By spending the time pulling your data together in an organized fashion, you will actually save yourself time in preparing your returns. Furthermore, if you are using a professional tax preparer, you will save yourself money because it should significantly aid the tax preparer in completing your return.

After going through the previous itemized deduction list (remember, the list is not all-inclusive) and your file folder of accumulated yearly receipts, you can make the determination of which option (the standard deduction or the itemized deduction) provides the greater reduction to your AGI.

One question that is often asked is whether contributions of time are deductible as charitable contributions, and the answer is no. If you do not receive income for the time spent, you already have received, in effect, a deduction by not having the income to report as taxable income.

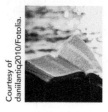

DISCIPLESHIP MOMENT AND REFLECTION

Review your tax paperwork organization. Do you feel you need to make any changes to how you organize your tax documents to make your tax filing easier? Talk to your prayer and accountability partner how he or she organizes tax documents throughout the year.

Step 4: Determine Personal Exemptions

Personal exemptions are the final deduction from AGI based on the number of people supported by the taxpayer.

- Taxpayer: $4,000
- Taxpayer's spouse: $4,000
- Each dependent child under 24 years of age: $4,000 (each)*
- Any relative for which the taxpayer provides more than half of the individual's financial support: $4,000*

*Both children and dependent relatives must not earn a certain level of income.

These personal exemptions, however, do have what the IRS labels as *phase-out levels*. In other words, if you make over a certain amount of income, you will no longer be eligible to take this deduction from AGI. These levels are as follows:

- Single: Phase-out begins at AGI of $258,250; no deduction allowable over $380,750.
- Married filing jointly: Phase-out begins at AGI of $309,900; no deduction allowable over $432,400.

Step 5: Determine Taxable Income

After you have determined how many personal exemptions you are eligible to include, you are now ready to determine your taxable income:

> **Gross Income**
> (−) Minus Adjustments to Income
> (=) **Adjusted Gross Income**
> (−) Greater of **Standard Deduction** or **Itemized Deduction** Amount
> (−) **Personal Exemption** Amount
> (=) Taxable Income

Now that you have your taxable income subject to tax, you can go the tax table (Table 13.1) and determine your tax liability. Once you understand the general process of tax calculations, you can begin to appropriately adjust your withholding from your employer to match what you will owe in taxes.

TAX WITHHOLDING

You may recall that on your first day of employment, you completed a wide variety of forms, one of which determines the amount of tax withheld from your gross income each pay period. That form is called a W-4 and allows you to choose how many allowances you want to take against your withholdings. Each allowance reduces the amount of tax withheld from your pay, thus increasing your take-home pay. The most common allowances you are eligible to take as an employee are for:

- Yourself
- Your spouse
- Each dependent child claimed on your tax return
- Another allowance if you are single with only one job
- Another allowance if you are married with one job and a nonworking spouse
- Another allowance if you have income from a second job less than $1,500

It is important to note that you are not required to take these allowances and can indicate "0" allowances on the W-4 form. By doing this, the maximum allowable tax will be withheld from your pay, which may result in you overwithholding. The IRS offers a tool that can help you calculate the number of allowances you may need to take through the IRS Withholding Calculator (https://www.irs.gov/Individuals/IRS-Withholding-Calculator).

At the end of the year, you will receive a W-2 indicating how much in taxes were withheld and sent to the IRS during the year. The W-2 will provide you with your overall earnings and the tax withheld from such earnings. The three tax withholding components found on a W-2 are for federal income tax (box 2 on a W-2), Social Security tax (box 4 on a W-2), and Medicare tax (box 6 on the W-2). The W-2 will also tell you the amount of any state withholding as well. Figure 13.2 gives a sample of a W-2.

Tax Credits

Even after your taxable income is determined and you have calculated your tax liability, you still may not owe that amount in taxes. In addition to deductions and adjustments to income, the tax law provides for tax credits against your tax liability

Figure 13.2 Sample W-2

22222	**a** Employee's social security number	OMB No. 1545-0008		
b Employer identification number (EIN)			**1** Wages, tips, other compensation	**2** Federal income tax withheld
c Employer's name, address, and ZIP code			**3** Social security wages	**4** Social security tax withheld
			5 Medicare wages and tips	**6** Medicare tax withheld
			7 Social security tips	**8** Allocated tips
d Control number			**9**	**10** Dependent care benefits
e Employee's first name and initial Last name Suff.			**11** Nonqualified plans	**12a**
			13 Statutory employee Retirement plan Third-party sick pay	**12b**
			14 Other	**12c**
				12d
f Employee's address and ZIP code				

15 State	Employer's state ID number	**16** State wages, tips, etc.	**17** State income tax	**18** Local wages, tips, etc.	**19** Local income tax	**20** Locality name

Form **W-2** Wage and Tax Statement   **2015**   Department of the Treasury—Internal Revenue Service

Copy 1—For State, City, or Local Tax Department

amount, thus reducing how much you owe in taxes on a dollar-for-dollar basis. This means that for every $1 in tax credit you have, you can reduce your tax liability by $1. Adjustments and deductions are designed to offset income, whereas tax credits are designed to offset taxes owed. The most common types of tax credits are child tax credits, child- and dependent-care credit for expenses paid by a working couple, adoption credit, college credit, and credit for a contribution to a retirement plan. Only once you have reduced you tax liability by any tax credits that you are entitled to will you know how much you owe in taxes for that year.

Completing the Tax Return

All of the information covered in the previous sections is included on tax forms that are ultimately submitted (in many cases electronically) to the IRS. The most common forms are as follows:

Tax return forms:

- 1040—Standard tax form used when itemizing deductions.
- 1040A—This is a short form of the 1040.
- 1040EZ—This is a short form usually used for single tax filers with no dependents.
- 1040X—This form is used when a previous tax return needs to be amended.

Schedules:

- Schedule A—This schedule lists all itemized deductions.
- Schedule B—This schedule provides interest and ordinary dividends received.
- Schedule C—This schedule is used to show any profit or loss from a business.
- Schedule D—This schedule is used to show capital gains and losses.

- Schedule E—This schedule is used to identify any supplemental income or loss.
- Schedule EIC—This is the schedule that determines eligibility to receive the Earned Income Credit.
- Schedule F—This schedule is used for any farming profit or loss.
- Schedule F—This schedule determines elderly or disabled credits.
- Schedule SE—This schedule determines any self-employment tax.

Forms
- 2106—This form is used when you have unreimbursed business expenses.
- 2119—This form is used when you have sold a home.
- 2441—This form is used when you have child- and dependent-care expenses.
- 3903—This form is used when you have moving-related expenses.
- 4868—This form is used when you need to file for an extension of time to submit your return.
- 8839—This form is used when you have qualified adoption expenses.

TAX-PLANNING STRATEGIES

Now that we have a firm grasp on how taxes are calculated, let's turn our attention to some tax-planning strategies that can be legitimate ways to reduce your tax liability. The most popular time for tax planning by taxpayers is December, with the second most popular month being April. However, both months are too late to do any serious tax planning. Once December 31 has passed, little can be done, except perhaps an IRA contribution, to reduce taxes for the previous year. Most people know this and become rather panicked in the month of December, wondering how they are going to reduce their taxes. Most income tax planning should be done at least 1 year in advance, with monitoring and the necessary adjustments made in the plan at least quarterly during the year. This means that the tax planning you do on December 31 would *not* be for the current year, but for the next year, so that you are always 1 year ahead.

Tax planning can be divided into three general tax-planning strategies: timing, shifting, and investing. You don't need to be an expert to understand these three general strategies; you need merely to ask yourself three questions:

1. *Timing.* Can I reduce my taxes by changing the year in which I am to receive income or to claim deductible expenses?
2. *Shifting.* Can I reduce my taxes by shifting my income to someone in my family who is in a lower tax bracket?
3. *Investing.* Can I reduce my taxes through the use of investments?

TIMING STRATEGIES

Delaying Income

Timing strategies involve deciding when to recognize income and deduct expenses. The general rule is that you should always push income into a future year and pull expenses into the current year. Why? Because even if these actions do not change the tax bracket one way or the other, they do delay the payment of taxes.

For example, if a taxpayer is in the 15% tax bracket and has the opportunity to delay $1,000 of income, it will reduce the current taxes by $150. But, because that income went into the next year, it increases the taxes paid next year by $150. That may not seem to make any difference; however, the taxpayer, not the government, has had the use of $150 for 1 year and the time to earn interest on that $150. Previously, we saw how a little bit over a long time period can add up to a great deal through the magic of compounding.

As noted, this strategy enables the taxpayer to control the $150 for a longer time. In considering this strategy, the doctrine in tax law called "constructive receipt" must be understood. The **doctrine of constructive receipt** simply says that if you earn the income and have a right to receive it, you cannot postpone the taxes incurred on that amount by merely choosing not to receive it.

For example, a contractor offering his services receives checks near the end of the year, but in an effort to avoid taxable income, he merely sticks them in a bottom drawer and does not deposit them until after December 31. This violates the doctrine of constructive receipt. He is attempting to use a timing strategy to reduce his income, but as a matter of fact, this is tax evasion, not tax avoidance. He must receive and report the income.

There are many legal ways to defer income, such as postponing the work that would generate the income so that the payment received for it is not due until the following year. Also, money invested in a savings type of account, such as a money market fund, is taxed because the interest is earned on a daily basis. Instead of leaving the money in such an account, invest it in a U.S. savings bond that is a zero-coupon bond and does not require interest to be paid until it is redeemed.

A self-employed person can choose to pay bonuses after the end of the calendar year, thereby postponing the tax on that income until the next year. There are other ways to defer income, but the objective here is to challenge your thinking and your own creativity rather than to provide a tax manual.

Paying Expenses

Accelerating or pulling deductions into the current year has the same effect. For example, if a taxpayer is in the 15% tax bracket and pulls $1,000 of deductions from next year into this year, the tax liability goes down $150 for the current year and up $150 for the next year.

One of the obvious ways to pull deductions into the current year is to make a charitable contribution in the current year rather than waiting until January. One of the principal advantages that our government allows in this area is the deduction of the full fair-market value of a gift of property. For example, let's say you purchased a stock for $10,000 and it had appreciated in value to $20,000. If you sold that stock and paid the tax on it of, say, $1,500, you would have $18,500 left to give to a charitable organization. The $18,500 contribution would further reduce your taxes by (for illustration purposes) 25% or $4,625. The net cost to making the charitable contribution would be the $20,000 property less the $4,625 tax savings, or $15,375. If, on the other hand, you contributed the appreciated stock directly to the charitable organization, you would receive a $20,000 contribution deduction with a tax savings of $5,000, for a lower net cost to you of $15,000. The charity, in turn, could sell the property for $20,000 and have $20,000 rather than $18,500, and it would have cost the taxpayer $375 less ($5,000 − $4,625) to give a charity $1,500 more ($20,000 − $18,500). Obviously, this is a "win-win" situation.

Courtesy of christianchan/Fotolia.

Doctrine of constructive receipt A tax concept that if one earns income and has the right to receive that income, he or she is in constructive receipt and must therefore pay tax on that amount of money.

Other strategies to do this are to pay for all expenses incurred, but not yet due, prior to the end of the year—for example, interest on debt that has been incurred, medical expenses that have been incurred but not yet paid, property taxes, legal fees, state income taxes, and so on. You cannot, according to the law, prepay interest and medical expenses, but you can bring the payments up to date, thereby deducting them in the current year as opposed to the following year. You will need to be alert for these deductions because delayed billing in December is increasingly common by professionals (they are trying to work their own timing strategy for income).

One recommendation is that you review last year's tax return and ask yourself the following question for each item of income: "Could it have been deferred into the subsequent year?" And for each deduction you took, ask yourself the question: "Could I have pulled more deductions in this area from the subsequent year?" Because of their nature, timing strategies are just about the only strategies that work near the end of the year. Almost all of the other strategies must be implemented earlier in the year.

SHIFTING STRATEGIES

Although not as common as it has been in the past, the second tax-planning strategy is referred to as shifting. Shifting occurs when income-producing assets are moved to someone in a lower tax bracket, usually your children. Understanding tax brackets is essential for understanding shifting strategies. The shifting strategies ask the question, "Can I shift what would be taxable income to me to a taxpayer in a lower tax bracket?" For example, "Can I shift income from my wife and me, who are in a high tax bracket, to our children, who are in a very low tax bracket, and perhaps pay no taxes at all?" The assumption in using this type of strategy is that you can shift the income and either still retain control of that income or use it for an item that you would have paid for anyway.

Probably the classic example of shifting income is in the area of college education for children. Many times parents will have the opportunity to give their children income-producing assets so that the child can pay the income taxes earned on that income rather than the parent. One of the most common ways to establish this shifting strategy is through the use of a state-sponsored education savings account, known as a 529 college saving plan. Named after the Section 529 of the tax code, a 529 plan allows for tax-free growth and can be income-tax-free if the money held by the plan is used to pay for eligible college expenses such as tuition, books, supplies, and equipment. One added benefit is that with a 529 account, a single person can contribute up to 5 years' worth of contributions of $14,000, or $70,000 (for 2015) without triggering any gift tax. Using this option does eliminate the ability to make any further gifts for 5 years, but with the magic of compounding, it is worth the tradeoff. The 529 legal landscape continually changes, so it is recommended that you work with a financial advisor who can guide you as to the best choice.

Another college saving vehicle is the Coverdell Education Saving Account (ESA). An ESA provides tax-free growth if the withdrawals are used to pay education expenses. Parents may contribute up to $2,000 each year for each child/student. The ESA may be invested in various mutual funds. Let's say that a parent contributes $2,000 for 1 year only. Over time, the investments in this ESA increase to $5,000. When the parents withdraw the $5,000 to help pay for education costs, there is no tax due! The growth is not simply tax deferred, but tax-free.

Unfortunately, there are few other ways to shift income-producing assets to children due to the IRS implementing limits on these strategies. What is known as the Kiddie Tax substantially limits these strategies. The Kiddie Tax says that if a child's interest, dividends, and other unearned income exceed a certain limit ($2,000 for 2015), then part of that income will be subject to tax at the parent's marginal tax rate.

The shifting strategy includes *gifting* to another family member income-producing assets, such as cash, real estate, stocks, bonds, closely held stock and notes, or mortgages receivable. Frequently these items are gifted in the form of a trust, which is explained in greater detail in another chapter.

INVESTMENT STRATEGIES

The basis of every investment you make is to produce more value (referred to as capital gain) or more income over time. Income from investments is taxed in various ways and can therefore have a great impact on total taxes paid. Income investments are taxed in four ways.

Tax-Exempt/Tax-Free

The income from some investments, such as many municipal bonds, is tax-exempt by law, and as a result, this income is substantially lower than the fully taxable income earned on similar types of investments.

Roth IRAs, named after Senator William Roth, who initially proposed the legislation authorizing them, provide tax-free returns. Any contribution to a Roth IRA is an after-tax deduction, but any appreciation, interest, or dividends are tax-free. Inside of your Roth IRA you can invest in mutual funds, individual stocks, or certificates of deposit. Roth IRAs are excellent vehicles for retirement and long-term savings. To be eligible, you must have earned income and total AGI less than $183,000 (2015 limit) for a married couple filing jointly.

Tax-Deferred

Some investments require that no tax be paid on the income earned until some time in the future. Almost all retirement plans fall into this category, whether it is an employer-sponsored plan such as a 401(k) or 403(b), or one of your own retirement plans such as a traditional IRA, SEP, or another qualified retirement plan. In addition, tax-deferred annuities from insurance companies allow you to earn a return on a tax-deferred basis.

The value of a tax-deferred investment is that compounding works for you not only on your portion of the income earned on the investment but also on the portion that would have gone to pay taxes if they not been deferred. Additionally, when it is time to pay taxes on the investment income that has been generated, presumably the investor is retired and in a lower tax bracket, so, therefore, in real dollar terms, the investor would pay less in income taxes. These instruments are excellent ways to avoid taxes now and save for future long-term goals.

Tax-Favored

Tax-favored investments are investments having special income tax allowances and provisions, again merely as a matter of law and not because of the nature of the investment. For example, dividends from stocks or from stock mutual funds enjoy a favored status. Dividend income is taxed at a maximum of 15%—even if your marginal income tax bracket is 35% or 39.6%.

Fully Taxable

The fourth type of investment is one that is fully taxable and includes almost all interest-bearing types of investments other than those described in the previous sections.

Remember that any time there is a favorable tax consequence to an investment, there is a corresponding cost somewhere. For example, in the tax-exempt investments, the cost is that the yield is not as high as in fully taxable investments. In the case of tax-deferred investments, the cost is that the investment is not accessible—unless you pay the penalties for early withdrawals.

To give you an idea of the consequences of the taxability of income and what that means in terms of your ability to accumulate, Table 13.2 assumes a $1,000 investment per year. It shows a Roth IRA (tax-free), a traditional IRA (tax-deferred), and a joint account (taxed ongoing). While saving during 40 years, it's assumed the taxpayer is in the 25% tax bracket. Upon withdrawals, it's assumed the tax bracket drops to 15%.

Table 13.2 Fully Taxable, Tax-Deferred, and Tax-Free Growth Results

Summary	Fully-Taxable	Tax-Deferred	Tax-Free
Current investment balance	$0	$0	$0
Annual contributions	$1,000	$1,000	$1,000
Number of years to invest	40	40	40
Before-tax return	8%	8%	8%
Marginal tax bracket	25%	25%	25%
After-tax return	6%	8%	8%
Future account value*	$154,762	$259,057	$259,057
Future account value (after-tax)	$154,762	$204,292	$259,057

Source: https://www.calcxml.com/calculators/inc07?skn=#results
*The lump sum shown after taxes is based on the marginal tax rate that you selected. This lump sum after tax figure does not take into account the possible change in tax bracket that might occur due to a lump sum distribution of the taxable amount, nor does it take into effect any applicable tax penalties.

In reviewing the chart, note how the type of account (or tax vehicle) you are using and your tax bracket make a big difference. It proves that tax-deferred investments can accumulate more than after-tax joint accounts. But a Roth is superior to all three. At the end of 40 years, in the tax-deferred investment, you have an ending balance of $204,292, far above the $154,762 balance in a fully taxable account. Due to the tax implications of withdrawals from a tax-deferred account, the tax-free account (Roth IRA) could have an ending balance of $259,057, almost $35,000 more.

As you get older, the tax-free nature of certain income may appear desirable. However, the illustration shows the value of compounding on a tax-deferred basis as compared to any other alternative. Tax-free investments do not yield enough to offset the compounding impact on a tax-deferred basis, nor do they offset the compounding associated with fully taxable amounts for the taxpayer in the 25% bracket in this illustration.

The primary point is that there are different types of tax-favored investments. When making an investment decision, base your decision, first of all, on investment considerations, and then on tax considerations.

SUMMARY

The topic of taxes can be a difficult and frustrating topic due to the typical negative emotions it creates when we approach the subject. Hopefully, we have come to realize that taxes are nothing more than an implication of God's provision for our lives. In this chapter, we discussed how to view taxes with a proper perspective by looking at the ideas of tax reduction, our attitude toward taxes, and how we make decisions based on how the decisions will impact our taxes. We reviewed some foundational Scripture verses that help us to view taxes in a biblical context. Once the theological perspective of taxes was covered, we moved into looking at the different types of taxes we pay, such as income tax and property taxes. We spent some time on the progressive nature of our income tax structure and explained the difference between marginal rates and effective tax rates. We reviewed the different tax-filing statuses and walked through the four steps in determining your taxable income from your gross income. We reviewed how taxes are withheld and ways to match your withholding to your expected tax liability. In the last half of the chapter, we looked at ways to legitimately reduce your tax liability through timing strategies, shifting strategies, and investment strategies.

SUMMARY REVIEW QUESTIONS

1. Differentiate between tax minimization and tax evasion.

2. What are the differences in the cultural perspectives on paying taxes versus the perspective we as Christians should have toward taxes?

3. What does the phrase "There is no free tax deduction anywhere, at any time, for anything!" mean?

4. Give and explain three reasons why a large refund check demonstrates a lack of good stewardship.

5. Provide insight into the following Scripture verses as in relation to taxes:
   a. Proverbs 13:11
   b. Luke 16:10
   c. 2 Corinthians 4:2
   d. Romans 13:7
   e. Luke 20:22, 24–25
   f. Matthew 5:16
   g. Proverbs 15:22

6. Give a description of these types of taxes:
   a. Income taxes
   b. Sales taxes
   c. Intangible taxes
   d. Use taxes
   e. Estate taxes
   f. Inheritance taxes
   g. Gift taxes
   h. Property taxes
   i. Social Security and Medicare taxes

7. Differentiate between your marginal tax rate and your effective tax rate.

8. What are the various tax-filing statuses and their significance?

9. What is step 2 in determining your tax liability, and why is that step so important?

10. How do you determine which deduction is best, itemized or standard?

11. What are ways that you can keep your tax information organized throughout the year?

12. How can you determine how much money should be withheld from your paycheck?

13. What is the difference between tax credits and tax deductions?

14. What is an IRS 1040 form? 1040EZ?

15. What information do the following tax schedules provide the IRS?
    a. Schedule A
    b. Schedule C
    c. Schedule D
    d. Form 2119
    e. Form 2441

16. What are three ways that you can implement appropriate tax minimization strategies?

17. Define constructive receipt.

18. What are the differences among tax-deferred, tax-favored, and fully taxable?

Case Study Analysis

Taxes

Sean paced the shiny wooden floors of his new home with mixed emotions and thoughts firing. "What's this property tax statement? I thought I already paid my taxes at closing. I remember signing about a thousand pages of documents and contracts. Buying a new house seemed exciting at first, but there are so many expenses besides just the price of the house that I did not put much thought into." At that moment, he paused and lifted the property tax bill that he had been holding tightly in his fist to eye level. With reality starting to sink in, Sean said aloud and in a panic, "I don't know what I am doing with this property tax statement, let alone any other taxes that I might owe! I have to call my dad!" Sean quickly pulled his new phone out of his pocket and called his dad.

"Hey, Sean, what's going on?" Bob answered.

"Dad! I need your help!" Sean quickly exclaimed.

"Well, certainly! It's not every day that your oldest son admits he needs his father's help. What do you need?" Bob replied.

Sean went on to unload the stress he was under with the sudden burden of taxes on his mind. Along with the property tax statement, Sean explained that he was realizing how little he knew about taxes and wanted to see if he would run into any other tax issues when dealing with the house.

When Sean completed his rant, Bob felt confident that he could help his son.

"Sean, I am meeting Karl Thompson, my tax accountant, this week. Why don't you come along? You can observe the process I go through with my taxes and ask as many questions as you wish, specifically in relation to the ongoing tax adjustments that result from being a homeowner. I may even be able

to set up an appointment specifically for your taxes if you don't feel comfortable doing them on your own."

Later, when Bob and Sean showed up at Karl's office, Karl, a no-nonsense man with a type A personality, cut the pleasantries short and decided it was best to review last year's tax return to ensure that Bob knew exactly where he stood before they began to plan for the upcoming year.

Assignment

Refer to the tax return documents found in the Case Study section, and, in written form, answer the following questions:

1. Where did the number in line item 7 on the 1040 come from?

2. How was the $395 determined on line item 9a and 9b on the 1040?

3. What is line 13 on the 1040? Why is there a number there? Why is there not a number in box 14?

4. What is line 22 on the 1040 commonly called?

5. What would Bob and Debbie's itemized deductions be? What would their standard deduction be? Which option was selected for Bob and Debbie? (Use the IRS Deduction for Exemptions Worksheet and the IRS Standard Deduction Worksheet for Dependents.)

6. What is the difference between "above-the-line" adjustments to income and deductions from income?

7. Using the 2014 Tax Computation Worksheet, explain how the total tax (line item 44) was figured.

8. Where does the number on line 74 come from?

9. What are the following forms, and why would you receive them?
    a. 1099-SA
    b. 1098-T
    c. 1098—Mortgage Interest Statement
    d. 1099-Div (Dividends and Distributions)
    e. 1099-B (Capital Gains Transactions)

DEFINITIONS

Adjusted gross income (AGI) (p. 308)

Alimony (p. 308)

Doctrine of constructive receipt (p. 314)

Effective tax rate (p. 307)

Itemized deduction (p. 311)

Marginal tax rate, also marginal tax bracket (p. 304)

Standard deduction (p. 311)

Tax avoidance (*see also* **Tax minimization)** (p. 300)

Tax evasion (p. 300)

Tax minimization (*see also* **Tax avoidance)** (p. 300)

Taxable income (p. 306)

SCRIPTURE VERSES (ESV)

Proverbs 13:11—Dishonest money dwindles away, but he who gathers money little by little makes it grow.

Luke 16:10—Whoever can be trusted with very little can also be trusted with much, and whoever is dishonest with very little will also be dishonest with much.

2 Corinthians 4:2—Rather, we have renounced secret and shameful ways; we do not use deception, nor do we distort the word of God. On the contrary, by setting forth the truth plainly we commend ourselves to every man's conscience in the sight of God

Romans 13:7—Give everyone what you owe him: If you owe taxes, pay taxes: if revenue, then revenue; if respect, then respect; if honor, then honor.

Luke 20:22, 24, 25—Is it lawful for us to pay taxes to Caesar, or not? 'Show Me a denarius. Whose portrait and inscription are on it?' 'Caesar's,' they replied. He said to them, 'Then give to Caesar what is Caesar's, and to God what is God's.'

Matthew 5:16—In the same way, let your light shine before men, that they may see your good deeds and praise your Father in heaven.

Proverbs 15:22—Plans fail for lack of counsel, but with many advisors they succeed.

ADDITIONAL READINGS

Aidt, T. S., & Jensen, P. S. (2009). The taxman tools up: An event history study of the introduction of the personal income tax. *Journal of Public Economics*, *93*(1), 160–175.

Andrews, W. D. (1974). A consumption-type or cash flow personal income tax. *Harvard Law Review*, 1113–1188.

Bakija, J., & Slemrod, J. (2004). *Do the rich flee from high state taxes? Evidence from federal estate tax returns* (No. w10645). Washington, DC: National Bureau of Economic Research.

Bergstresser, D., & Poterba, J. (2002). Do after-tax returns affect mutual fund inflows? *Journal of Financial Economics*, *63*(3), 381–414.

Bryan, J. (2012). Individual income tax returns, 2010. *Statistics of Income Bulletin*, *32*, 5–78.

Heim, B. T. (2009). The effect of recent tax changes on taxable income: Evidence from a new panel of tax returns. *Journal of Policy Analysis and Management*, *28*(1), 147–163.

Kopczuk, W. (2006). *Bequest and tax planning: Evidence from estate tax returns* (No. w12701). Washington, DC: National Bureau of Economic Research.

Kopczuk, W., & Saez, E. (2004). *Top wealth shares in the United States: 1916–2000: Evidence from estate tax returns* (No. w10399). Washington, DC: National Bureau of Economic Research.

Manzi, N. (2004). *Use tax collection on income tax returns in other states*. St. Paul, MN: Research Department, Minnesota House of Representatives.

Miller, M. H. (1977). Debt and taxes. *Journal of Finance*, *32*(2), 261–275.

Miller, M. H., & Scholes, M. S. (1978). Dividends and taxes. *Journal of Financial Economics*, *6*(4), 333–364.

Saez, E. (2009). *Striking it richer: The evolution of top incomes in the United States (update with 2007 estimates)*. Berkeley, CA: retrieved on April 12, 2016 from: http://eml.berkeley.edu/~saez/saez-UStopincomes-2012.pdf.

Tanzi, V. (2008). *Inflation and the personal income tax*. New York, NY: Cambridge Books.

Taussig, M. K. (1967). Economic aspects of the personal income tax treatment of charitable contributions. *National Tax Journal, 20*(1), 1–19.

Wallace, S., & Edwards, B. M. (1999). Personal income tax. *Public Administration and Public Policy, 72*, 149–190.

Chapter 14

Employee Benefits

Courtesy of Monkey Business/Fotolia.

BIG IDEA:
Employee benefits create a foundation on which to build your financial plan.

- Review the two main types of retirement plans offered to employees

- Be able to describe and explain two other types of investment accounts that employees may have access to through their employers

- Explain the Affordable Care Act, and provide ways in which the ACA has impacted health-care benefits

- Explain the three main types of group health plans offered by employers

- Explain the benefits of both dental and vision insurance

- List the various life changes that can allow for changes in benefits

- Explain the benefits of health savings accounts

- Identify how life insurance and disability insurance play a role in employee benefits

- Describe ADD insurance and when it is appropriate

- Explain how tuition reimbursements and adoption assistance programs work

- List several of the main types of discounts provided by employers

- Explain some common mistakes employees make in utilizing their employee benefits

Introduction

For many of us, benefits provided by our employers are the foundation on which we build our financial plans. For example, health insurance, basic life insurance, and retirement benefits are common in today's employee benefits packages offered by employees, in most cases to full-time employees and in some cases even part-time employees. This chapter reviews some of these many benefits, although some of the information may be an overview of other sections already covered. We review many benefits that may be available to you through your employer; however, you will want to check with your human resources department to see which specific benefits your company offers.

RETIREMENT PLANS AND OTHER SAVINGS BENEFITS

Probably the most discussed benefit offered by employers is the retirement plans offered to their employees. Each retirement plan can be customized to the company and its needs; however, we review and highlight the most common types, such as the defined benefit plan, the defined contribution plan, stock options, and employee stock purchase plans. A more thorough description can be found in the long-term savings section.

DEFINED BENEFIT PLANS

Defined benefit plans were at one point the most prominent retirement plan offered by employers. Defined benefit plans are plans in which the employee, based on his or her length of service with the company, would receive a specific annual retirement income (also known as a pension) from the employer. The amount the employee would receive would typically be based on the employee's last annual salary amount and the years of service with the company. Unfortunately, these plans are becoming rare in the workforce due to the future liability the pension payouts cost the employers. There are, however, still a few companies that offer a defined benefit plan to their employees, for example:

- ExxonMobil
- Lockheed Martin
- United Parcel Service (UPS)
- Johnson and Johnson
- 3M (MMM)
- Bank of America
- Wachovia
- Coca Cola
- Accenture
- Liden Nestle Soled & Associates (Nestle)

Based on actuarial calculations, defined benefit plans usually take into consideration several factors, including the average of the final 3 years of salary, a pension factor usually arrived at by statisticians and actuaries, and the total number of years employed. The following is an example of how a defined benefit may be calculated:

Year 1 salary: $108,000

Year 2 salary: $112,000

Year 3 salary: $118,000

Years worked: 30 years

Actuary factor for pension = .02

The average 3-year salary was $112,666.

Once we know the last 3 years' average salary, we multiple that figure ($112,666) by the pension factor (.02), which is $2,253. Because you worked for 30 years for the company in this example, you multiply the result ($2,253) by 30 to get the annual payout of $67,600, or $5,633 per month. This amount would represent a payment made for your entire life, commonly known as a **single life annuity**. A single life annuity is a series of equal payments made to someone over their lifetime. This is just one example, so if your company has a defined benefit amount, you should check with your human resource department and see what calculations are used to determine your benefit.

Single life annuity
A series of equal payments made to someone over their lifetime.

DEFINED CONTRIBUTION PLANS

With the limited number of defined benefit plans still in existence today, most employers now offer defined contribution plans (although some employers, such as those listed earlier, offer both to their employees). Defined contribution plans are retirement plans in which employers have defined how much they will contribute to their employees' retirement accounts. Most defined contributions plans will specify a percentage of an employee's salary to the employee's account. Some companies will only match what an employee contributes to the retirement account as a motivation tool to entice employees to make contributions. The matching amount of many companies falls within 50% to 100% of employee contributions up to a certain maximum. There are, however, maximum allowable limits to contribution amounts in defined contributions accounts such as 401(k), 403(b), or 457 plans. These amounts are adjusted frequently by Congress, but for 2016 the annual amount was set at $18,000. If you are over the age of 50, you can contribute a catch-up amount of $6,000 allowing for a combined contribution up to $24,000. An employee can contribute up to a 100% of his or salary but, with employer contributions, not in excess of $49,000.

Defined contribution plans can also attach a profit-sharing component to the retirement account, in which a company may contribute a portion of excess profits to employees through their retirement accounts. Although employees were limited to $18,000 in contribution amounts in 2016, employers through their contributions and profit sharing can add up to an additional $31,000, for a total combined contribution of $49,000. Profit-sharing plans can contribute up to 25% of employee salary to the maximum of $49,000 total contribution (to include employee contributions).

Ron's Corner

When people ask my advice on personal investments, I automatically ask them if their employer offers a pension, profit sharing plan, or 401(k) plan into which they can make voluntary contributions. I am amazed by how many people don't know. So I give them a homework assignment: to bring their employee manual or a description of their company retirement plan to our next meeting. They usually discover that the first place they should invest is through their own company.

OTHER SAVINGS PLANS

Besides retirement specific plans as previously mentioned, companies usually offer other types of savings that employees can benefit from. Two of the most common are stock options and employee stock purchase plans. These plans should be considered in conjunction with an employee's overall financial assets and be discussed in greater detail with a Christian financial planner.

Stock Option Plans

A more complex plan, which can be part of or separate from the retirement plans themselves, is the stock option plan. Used by many companies for mid-level and above managers to establish company loyalty and to align company performance with employee benefits, stock option plans can be attractive to company employees.

An option, specifically a stock option, is nothing more than an agreement to buy a stock in specific quantities, at a specific price referred to as the exercise price, during a specific time frame. In order to entice managers to stay "motivated," they may receive an option to buy 1,000 shares of the company's stock at an exercise price of $30 with an option expiration date of 2 years from now. The goal of stock options is to reward employees when the market price of the stock exceeds or is greater than the exercise price ($30 in this case). If in a year and half, the stock is trading at $60, then the employee will buy the stock for $30,000 ($30/share × 1,000 shares) and can then sell those shares in the open market for $60,000 ($60/share × 1,000), creating a $30,000 gain.

Due to the complexity of stock options, we cover the basics of what a stock option is and discuss how stock options can be beneficial to employees. There are many different aspects to stock options that, should you be in a position of receiving stock options, you will want to discuss with your Christian financial planner.

Employee Stock Purchase Plans

Although not a retirement plan specifically, an employee stock purchase plan (ESPP) can be a great benefit for companies to offer. Most common in publicly traded companies, an ESPP is a plan designed to offer employees a discount, usually 5% to 10%, on the quoted market price of the company's stock. For example, if an ESPP plan offers a 5% discount and the stock is trading at $50, then the employee would be able to buy the stock at $47.50. Also, in many cases, no transaction costs occur to the employee when enrolling in this service.

An employee who is interested in buying company stock using this plan will usually need to complete paperwork (an enrollment form) with the human resources department that will allow the employee to select either a percentage of income or a flat dollar amount to be invested at specific intervals (usually each pay period). The company, however, will usually make these "purchases" on behalf of the employee more sporadically, usually quarterly. Therefore, the employee will have money set aside from each paycheck, and then the company will allocate the stock on a quarterly basis to the employee's account. The discount is then applied to the market price on the day the stock is allocated. Although many companies do not have the capacity to manage these types of accounts themselves, companies will usually outsource this service to a third party, such as Computershare (www.computershare.com). Because these purchases are not part of a retirement plan, sales and withdrawals can be taken without penalty to the employee, although capital gains or losses will be imposed based on the selling price.

HEALTH INSURANCE

Our health is such a significant and often underappreciated component of our lives. We rarely stop to think about staying healthy unless we are ill or are overcoming ailments. For many of us, the feeling of invincibility can become too strong until the moment when our health fades. As quoted so eloquently in Proverbs 31: 17, "She sets about her work vigorously; her arms are strong for her tasks." Our health is what gives us the ability to work unto the Lord (Colossians 3:23). For these reasons, health insurance through employers is one of the most critical benefits that companies offer their employees. There are several different types of plans offered by companies: (1) health maintenance organizations (HMOs), (2) paid provider organizations

(PPOs), and (3) indemnity (pay-for-service) plans. These health insurance plans are usually classified as **group health plans** or health plans that cover a group of individuals based on some common affiliation in which all individuals help share in the cost of coverage. In this case, the common affiliation would be the employer for which the employees work. There are other common types of affiliations, such as civic organizations (Lions Club) or even ministries. Some organizations, such as Samaritan's Purse and Christian Care Ministries, are **health-care share ministries** in which members share in one another's health-care costs rather relying on an insurance company. Table 14.1 lists the top 10 group health insurance companies.

Table 14.1 Top 10 Group Health Insurance Companies

Rank	Insurer
#1	UnitedHealth Group
#2	Kaiser Foundation Group
#3	Wellpoint Inc. Group
#4	Aetna Group
#5	Humana Group
#6	HCSC Group
#7	Cigna Health Group
#8	Highmark Group
#9	Blue Shield of California Group
#10	Independence Blue Cross Group

Courtesy of US News & World Report.

Source: http://health.usnews.com/health-news/health-insurance/articles/2013/12/16/top-health-insurance-companies

Companies will usually seek bids for coverage from several health insurance providers and then select the proposal from the health-care company that best fits their employees' needs. Many companies will offer, through the same health insurance company, several different health insurance options to their employees with different types of coverage (e.g., individual, family, individual with children) and different deductibles (high-deductible plan or traditional major medical plan). Some plans may even customize co-pays, co-insurance, and in-network or out-of-network benefit amounts; however, most companies usually follow industry standards. The array of options provided by employers will impact the cost of the plans. Unfortunately, over the past decade, health-care costs have continually increased, and much of these increases are being passed on to the employees. A study by Claxton et al. (2015) of employee benefits reported the following:

Average annual premiums in 1999
Single: $2,196
Family: $5,791

Average annual premiums in 2015
Single: $6,521
Family: $17,545

The differences over the last 16 years suggest an annual increase of over 196% for single coverage and 203% for family coverage.

AFFORDABLE CARE ACT

With the passing of the Affordable Care Act (ACA) in 2010 (known as Obamacare), the anticipation that health-care costs will continue to increase has yet to be determined. According to the Health and Human Services government website (www .hhs.gov), the Affordable Care Act:

> Put in place comprehensive health insurance reforms that have improved access, affordability, and quality in health care for Americans. (p. 1)

Several key features of the ACA are as follows:

- Denial of coverage for children with preexisting conditions is abolished. The age of coverage for children is extended to age 26 under their parents' health plan.
- Coverage cannot be terminated due to "honest mistakes."
- The insured is guaranteed the right to appeal any denial of payments.
- Lifetime limits for coverage were removed from all health insurance plans.
- Rate increases in health plans must be made public and justifiable.
- Premiums must be primarily allocated toward health-care costs, not administrative costs.
- Preventative care costs are covered, with no co-payments.
- Emergency coverage is provided for out-of-network providers.

REVIEW OF PLAN TYPES

Indemnity plans A type of health insurance plan that allows the insured to pay for services as those services occur, usually requiring an annual deductible to be met.

If you have been through the insurance section, then this may be somewhat of a review. There are two main types of health insurance plans, indemnity plans and managed care plans. **Indemnity plans** are health insurance plans that are straightforward "pay-as-you-require-service" plans. Many indemnity plans have an annual deductible that must be met, which can range from $0 to several thousand dollars. As with most insurance plans, the lower the deductible, the higher the premiums for the insured. Along with the deductible, the insured also pays a percentage of co-insurance, which is usually 20%. With indemnity plans there are three main parties involved, the insured (you), the plan provider (the company you pay your premiums to), and the health-care professionals you see. With an indemnity plan, you pay your annual premiums and the insurer then pays the health-care providers (the insurer's portion usually is 80%) once your deductible is met. Indemnity plans do not require the insured to see any specific health-care professional. Many companies are moving away from indemnity plans, and very few remain in the United States.

Many companies have transitioned to a managed care plans, which are typically one of the either health maintenance organizations or preferred provider organizations.

HEALTH MAINTENANCE ORGANIZATIONS

A health maintenance organization (HMO) is group of health service providers that have formed an alliance or group in order to provide health-care services to those subscribing to this organization. HMOs will have a monthly fee (similar to that of a monthly premium) based on the number of people covered in your family in addition to an office visit fee for seeing one of the health-care providers. These office fees

Courtesy of Halfpoint/Fotolia.

will vary and will usually be no more than $50. Because of the structure of this organization, the biggest benefit is that members do not pay deductibles for the services used, and because of the size of these organizations, members can usually receive nearly all major medical services from the organization's health-care providers. One of the biggest disadvantages in HMOs is that the subscriber usually must see a doctor who is part of the alliance, thus limiting the choice of providers the insured can select from. In addition, HMOs have the insured select a primary care physician who acts like the "quarterback" for the insured and will help determine if other health-care providers may be needed for more specialized services; if so, the primary care provider will provide the insured a referral, for example, to a cardiologist.

PREFERRED PROVIDER ORGANIZATION

A preferred provider organization (PPO) offers similar characteristics to traditional indemnity plans. Unlike HMOs, where doctors join together and offer subscribers (i.e., members) health-care services, PPOs formulate around the health insurance company. Health-care providers agree to certain fees that will be charged for services provided to those who use the PPO for their insurance. One of the biggest benefits with PPOs is the selection of doctors from which to choose because PPOs offer coverage for both in-network doctors (those who have agreed to the fees with the PPO) and out-of-network doctors (those health-care providers that are not contracted with the PPO). The biggest difference lies in the amount the insurance will cover of the health-care professionals' fees. In most cases, when you see an in-network provider, the PPO will usually pay 80% to 90% of the fees, whereas out-of-network care typically receives 50% coverage.

CONSUMER DIRECTED HEALTH PLANS

In order to help control rising health care costs, a new structure of health care has emerged called Consumer Directed Health Plans, otherwise High Deductible Health Plans. These plans are designed to put more control in the hands of the consumer by allowing consumers flexibility by pairing these high deductible plans with a health savings account which will be discussed in more detail later. These high deductible plans are designed to help consumers control their own health care costs and thus are paired with a company's HMO or PPO plan which determines a consumer's health care providers.

DENTAL PLANS

Although a subcategory of health insurance, dental insurance usually is provided under a different policy of your employer than health insurance (although this is not always the case). Dental insurance covers dental care, preventative dental procedures, and other dental work needed due to an incident. Major dental surgery or reconstructive procedures may fall under the coverage of major medical or health-care insurance depending on the type of specialist that is required to be seen. In many cases, dental insurance will cover (many times without a co-payment) preventative services such as biannual teeth cleaning, fluoride treatments, and annual x-rays. Other procedures covered include fillings and root canals, and there is usually a maximum amount allowable for orthodontia work; usually the maximum allowable is per plan participant. Dental plans usually carry a small maximum coverage amount, less than $2,000 in most cases, so extensive dental work may require out-of-pocket payment.

VISION PLANS

Vision plans are another component of the health insurance benefit offered by many employers with minimal cost. Most vision plans, like dental plans, offer preventative care such as annual eye exams, without any co-pay or office visit fee. Vision plans will usually cover a certain maximum for glasses, frames, and contacts and some have a built-in maximum allowable amount for eye surgery, such as Lasik eye surgery.

SELECTING THE RIGHT PLAN

Now that we have reviewed the top health-care plans offered by most companies, it is imperative that you understand what your company offers specifically and then decide which plan is right for you. Most companies offer a benefit window in which all existing employees have a specific time frame in which to make changes to their existing benefits, which include health, dental, and vision insurance. In addition to these open-enrollment periods, you can make changes when you are first employed and eligible for benefits or when a life event occurs. Life events usually consist of:

- Moving
- Having a baby
- Getting married
- Getting divorced
- Taking or returning from a leave of absence
- Work schedule changes that change eligibility of benefits
- Having a child "age out" and no longer eligible under your benefits

During one of these times in which you are eligible to make changes, take time to review the worksheet in Figure 14.1 found on pp. 341–345, which can help you determine the services most likely to be used, the cost of each of those services within each plan, and your total out-of-pocket cost for each insurance plan. We also suggest that you seek wise counsel from colleagues and co-workers as to their experience with the plans they use, how they use the plan, and what they like and dislike about their plan coverage.

HEALTH SAVINGS ACCOUNTS

Depending on the type of plan you enroll in, specifically in relation to the deductible amount, you may be eligible to enroll in either a health reimbursement account (HRA) or a health savings account (HSA). These accounts are very similar, but there are a few main differences. An HRA is an account that is funded by employer dollars only and used to help employees cover medical expenses (typically the deductible) if they are in a high-deductible health plan. Contributions to these accounts by the employer are tax deductible to the employer and do not count as wages for the employees. Any unused contributions to the HRA can be rolled over year to year in order to continue to accumulate funds to help cover medical expenses. As for the company, it does not need to fund the account until reimbursement claims are filed. In other words, an HRA is a "promise to pay" by employers without having to actually allocate funds to specific accounts. The drawback to an HRA is that if you leave the company, you will forfeit any accumulated balance in the HRA.

HSAs have a few differences compared with HRAs. First, employers, employees, or both can contribute to HSAs. Like HRAs, HSAs allow for rollover of unused funds from year to year in order to accumulate funds for future health-care expenses. The notable difference between the two accounts is that HSA accounts are owned by the employee and the employee can move the account should the employee leave the current employer. From the perspective of the employer, funds must be deposited (allocated to employee accounts), which creates an opportunity cost of using those funds for other expenses.

DISCIPLESHIP MOMENT AND REFLECTION

Take a moment to review your health insurance plan(s). Ask your prayer and accountability partner about his or her plan. Compare and contrast the differences and consider any changes you may want to make.

LIFE AND DISABILITY INSURANCE

Besides health insurance, probably the second most beneficial benefit offered by most insurance companies comes from life and disability insurance. We will review how each of these policies is structured.

Life Insurance

It may be suggested that life insurance is the foundation for every financial plan. Many of us can save and invest with great returns, but unless we live long enough to save or invest enough, both saving and investing will not allow us to support our families should we die before we can "self-insure." Recall what Paul penned to Timothy:

> Anyone who does not provide for their relatives, and especially for their own household, has denied the faith and is worse than an unbeliever. (1 Timothy 5:8)

Companies offer two different types of life insurance for employees, one of which usually does not cost employees any out-of-pocket costs and another that is optional for the employee and does have a cost associated with it. The first, often called *group term life insurance*, is a basic term life insurance policy that is in force as long as the employee is employed by the company and usually is set to the maximum of $50,000. This group term life insurance policy does not usually require the employee to pay any premiums. Companies are eligible to deduct the premiums of this group term life policy if they choose to offer it as a benefit to their employees. Once employees are benefit eligible (based on each company's guidelines), the employees automatically qualify for this coverage.

The second option is not required and needs to be enrolled in along with other benefits during the enrollment period. Although referred to as supplemental life insurance because this insurance would be in addition to the $50,000 group term life insurance, this insurance exhibits one significant advantage, which is the lack of medical exam required to receive coverage—traditional life insurance coverage usually will require the insured to receive a medical exam by a health-care professional prior to issuance of a life insurance policy. With supplemental life insurance through your employer, you can usually forgo a medical exam, although you may need to have your doctor complete a form to attest to your general state of health. These types of life insurance will give employees an option to select from 1 to up to 8 times their annual base salary. Bonuses do not count in this calculation. Each company will have its own limits to the multiple of annual base salary, so make sure you check with your employer for what is offered. Two important considerations are as follows: (1) the employee (you) is responsible for the premiums, which are usually deducted from gross earnings, and (2) the premiums for supplemental life insurance are typically paid with pre-tax dollars. In other words, the premiums you pay will reduce your taxable wage amount (just like health insurance and other benefits are withdrawn from your gross earnings).

In addition to you as an employee, many companies will provide you the option to buy supplemental insurance for your spouse (if married) and dependents (if any). For spousal supplemental life insurance, there is normally a maximum dollar amount that you can buy, and each company's plan will be different. Depending on the amount of spousal supplemental life insurance coverage, your spouse may need to provide proof of insurability, referred to as **evidence of insurability** or EOI, from a health-care professional. In addition to your spouse, you can choose to purchase supplemental life insurance for your qualified dependents. Although every company differs, the standard amounts of life insurance available to employees range from $10,000 to $15,000 per dependent. This cost is typically set by the average cost of funeral expenses for a child because this insurance is not set to replace any income or other financial support.

Disability

As previously mentioned, life insurance may be the foundation of every financial plan; however, disability insurance is just as, if not more important. According to a Cornell University study on disability statistics, an estimated 12.5% of non-institutionalized males and females of all ages have a disability. In other words, over 10% of the population (roughly 1 out of every 10 people) have a disability (https://www.disabilitystatistics.org/glossary.cfm?g_id=286&view=true). Disability, according to the American Community Survey (ACS), is based on affirming or positively identifying with any of these six categories:

- Hearing Disability—Are you deaf or have a serious difficulty hearing?
- Visual Disability—Are you blind or have serious difficulty seeing even when wearing glasses?
- Cognitive Disability—Due to a physical, mental, or emotional condition, do you have serious difficulty concentrating, remembering, or making decisions?
- Ambulatory Disability—Do you have series difficulty walking or climbing stairs?
- Self-Care Disability—Do you have difficulty dressing or bathing?
- Independent Living Disability—Due to a physical, mental, or emotional condition, do you have difficulty doing errands alone such as visiting a doctor's office or shopping?

Source: https://www.disabilitystatistics.org/glossary.cfm.
Courtesy of Cornell University.

Due to the varying types of disabilities with which one could be diagnosed employers usually offer a form of disability insurance. **Disability insurance** is a type of insurance that offers the insured income protection in the event that he or she

Evidence of insurability
Proof of insurability or general health provided by a health-care professional.

Disability insurance
A type of insurance that offers the insured income protection in the event that he or she becomes unable to work due to a qualified disability.

becomes unable to work due to a qualified disability. Unfortunately, disability insurance can be somewhat complex, so we want to provide you some basic terminology that you will encounter in dealing with most disability policies. It is important to understand that disability insurance is an income replacement policy, which requires the insured to have working income. In other words, someone who is unemployed or someone who receives passive income (passive income being investment income) would not be eligible to get a disability insurance policy. Due to the wide flexibility of disability insurance policies, it will be important to go over these terms with your human resource staff to ensure you have a complete understanding of the policies specific to your company.

Important terms to understand include the following:

Benefit Amount—As you look at a disability insurance (DI) policy, it is important to know and understand what the benefit of the policy will be should you need to file a claim. The **disability benefit amount** is usually set as a percentage of your gross annual salary. DI typically covers 50% to 70% of your annual income. It is vital to understand that DI polices do not provide the insured a 100% income replacement benefit.

Benefit Period—The **disability benefit period** is the period of time that a disability insurance policy will provide your replacement income. Some policies may only pay for several years (e.g., 5 years), whereas other policies may pay out until the insured reaches the age of 65. Keep in mind that the longer the payout period is set for, usually the more expensive the policy will be.

Elimination Period (Waiting Period)—Unfortunately, disability insurance policies do not go into effect on day 1 of a disability. There is a time period that must lapse prior to any benefits being paid out in a disability policy, known as the **elimination period** or **waiting period**. DI policies will establish, in many cases, a period of 90 days from the onset of a disability prior to the insurance company paying benefits. This time period accomplishes two main purposes. First, it allows an insured to seek medical treatment and get a sound diagnosis regarding the disability. In other words, having a 2-week flu that prevents you from working would not classify as a "independent living disability." Second, this elimination period minimizes nonlegitimate claims so that disability premiums do not become so expensive as to make them cost prohibitive.

Disability Classification—Based on the disability policy, there are two types of disability classifications used, and it is very important that you know which classification is used in your company's policy. The two classifications are (1) own occupation and (2) any occupation. Own occupation disability means that if you are unable to perform the functions of your current occupation, then you will be eligible for benefits. For example, suppose you are a trainer for your company and your function is to travel around the country and give presentations to your employees on different initiatives your company establishes. If you were to come down with chronic laryngitis, for example, you may not be able to perform your function as a presenter. This would be an example of an "own occupation" disability. On the other hand, if the policy classified a disability as "any occupation," then in our example you would not be classified as disabled if you were able to write training guides that other presenters can use in training sessions. You could also become a medical transcriptionist, which would not require talking. Although it may seem obvious, the most attractive classification for employees is the "own occupation" classification.

Inflation protection provisions—As you are probably aware, prices of everyday goods and services usually always go up over time, which is in part due to inflation, or the general increase of prices over time. Therefore, some policies offer inflation provisions in the policy that will increase the benefit amount received by the insured, usually annually. The increase amount will be determined by some index;

Disability benefit amount
The amount, usually established as a percentage, of replacement income a disability policy will pay out. The amount is often between 50% and 70% of the employee's salary.

Disability benefit period
The amount of time that a disability policy will provide benefits to the insured.

Elimination period (waiting period) A time period that must lapse prior to any benefits being paid out in a disability policy.

in many cases it is the change in the Consumer Price Index (CPI). Again, if a policy has inflation provisions, the premiums will be higher than if the policy did not.

ACCIDENTAL DEATH OR DISMEMBERMENT INSURANCE

Accidental death or dismemberment (ADD) insurance policies can act as a stand-alone policy or can be added as a supplemental insurance to an existing life or health insurance policy. Most employers will offer this policy to employees on a voluntary basis; in other words, it is an option in which the employee will pay the premiums. If an insured dies accidentally (e.g., not by natural causes related to the body), then the beneficiary of the policy may receive double indemnity, or two insurance settlements: (1) from the ADD policy and (2) from a traditional life insurance policy. Due to the rarity of deaths by accident, the costs of ADD policies, in the context of a group life or group health add-on, can be minimal to the employee. Even though the cost of coverage may be minimal, it is important to understand what defines an accidental death or dismemberment within the policy. It is important to know and understand how the terms are defined to ensure you are comfortable with when a policy will pay out any benefits and when it will not.

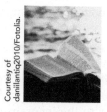

Courtesy of daniilantiq2010/Fotolia.

DISCIPLESHIP MOMENT AND REFLECTION

Take a moment to review your own life and disability insurance contracts or those of your parents. What type of insurance do they have, and what types of coverage do they have? Consider what you may need to change, and talk through these thoughts with your prayer and accountability partner.

TUITION ASSISTANCE

One benefit that can be highly attractive to potential employees is the idea of free or reduced education through tuition assistance programs. The rationale behind such a benefit may seem obvious, that the more education employees receive the better employees they will be. Jones (1999) found that, in general, two main points were upheld in relation to such programs: (1) educated workers were more productive than noneducated workers, and (2) those who earned more did so due to the fact that they were more productive. The study also reported, specifically in relation to high-tech firms, that an additional year of education led to a roughly 12.5% increase in productivity.

Courtesy of krasnevsky/Fotolia.

Companies have a wide variety of options when it comes to building a tuition reimbursement plan, ranging from the company receiving and paying your tuition bill to a traditional reimbursement plan in which the employee pays the cost and then submits receipts showing proof of payment and a grade report for reimbursement. In addition to the way a company can reimburse the employee, companies can also have different reimbursement rates at which employees can receive benefits. Some companies will offer reimbursement if the employee receives a C grade or higher, whereas other companies offer a sliding scale in which the employee may get the highest reimbursement amount for an A, a smaller percentage reimbursed for a B, and further reduction in reimbursement for a C. Finally, some companies will reimburse up to 100% of the tuition expenses, whereas some companies will only cover a portion (e.g., 80%) as a means of sharing the cost with the employee.

Due to the fact that companies are putting their resources toward benefiting their employees, there is a risk that employees will work for an employer only through their schooling and then leave to find a better-paying job. One way that employers have helped to reduce employee turnover is to attach time frames during which an employee must work for the company after a reimbursement has been awarded. For example, a company may require an employee to sign a 2-year working commitment to the company so that if an employee leaves within the 2 years, the employee will be responsible for paying the employer back for the costs of education. These payback policies are usually structured in a gradually decreasing scale so that if an employee leaves after 1 year, the employee only is responsible for, say, 50% of the reimbursement amount, and so forth. Be mindful of any payback provisions as you seek to apply for tuition assistance.

ADOPTION ASSISTANCE

Adoption assistance benefits are not a typical benefit that all employers offer; however, such assistance has continued to become a more prevalent benefit to employees over time. Hewitt and Associates studied adoption assistance programs in the United States and found that in 1999, roughly 12% of employers offered adoption assistance, whereas in 2004 that figure rose to roughly 39%. The latest Aon Hewitt study (2012) found that over 52% of surveyed companies reported having an adoption assistance program. The financial reimbursements were found to range from $500 to $25,000, averaging about $7,000 in benefits to employees. You can find the Dave Thomas Foundation's Top 100 List of companies that offer adoption assistance for 2015 in the References section of this chapter.

In addition to the benefit itself, the Internal Revenue Service (IRS) has allowed any adoption assistance or subsidy to generally not be included in income in the year the subsidy is awarded. The one precaution is that if any assistance or subsidy exceeds the cost of the adoption, then that amount may be included in taxable earnings. Please be mindful of adoption costs and any employer assistance should you use this benefit to ensure accurate reporting on your yearly tax return.

PAID LEAVE

Paid leave is an obvious benefit to employees, and most companies offer some form of paid time off or paid leave to their benefit-eligible employees. However, keep in mind that each day of paid leave is a cost to your employer. Considering that the average number of days of paid vacation per year for employees is 10 days, you can quickly calculate what the cost to your company will be by multiplying your hourly wage by the number of hours you work by the number of days you are eligible to take off. For example, if you make $15.75 per hour, work on average 8 hours per day, and are eligible for 10 days of paid leave, then the financial benefit to you as the employee is $1,260 ($15.75 × 8 hours × 10 days). In order to provide incentives for employee loyalty, many companies will offer a progressive time-off policy that increases the amount of paid time off based on the years of service with the organization. For example, if you start with a company you may be entitled to 10 days of paid time off, which may increase to 15 days after 5 years of continual employment.

In addition to the vacation days for which you are eligible, most companies will accompany paid leave with time off for illnesses, often referred to as sick leave. Every company offers sick time differently, so it is important to understand your employer's specific policies. In some cases, sick leave can be used in the event that dependents (children or dependent parents) need support in the event that they are unable to take care of themselves.

In addition to paid time off, the Family and Medical Leave Act (FMLA) allows eligible employees to take unpaid time off for certain specified medical and/or family reasons while protecting the jobs of those employees and their continuation of group health insurance coverage. According to the U.S. Department of Labor (2015), the following are the conditions in which unpaid leave can be taken:

12 weeks of leave in a 12-month period:

- The birth of a child or care for a newborn within the first year of the child's life
- Receiving an adopted child and being able to care for that child during the first year of placement (includes foster children as well)
- To care for a spouse, child, or dependent parent who has a serious health condition
- A serious medical condition that makes the employee unable to perform the essential functions of the job
- Any qualifying urgent demand arising out of the fact that the employee's spouse, child, or parent is a covered military member on "covered active duty"

26 weeks of leave during a 12-month period:

- To care for a covered service member with a serious injury or illness if the eligible employee is the service member's spouse, child, parent, or next of kin

Source: http://www.dol.gov/whd/fmla/

DISCOUNT PROGRAMS

Discount programs
Voluntary benefits offered by employers that are established to offer reduced costs or discounts on products and services offered by other third parties.

In an effort to continually provide employee benefits, special discount programs have been implemented in many large companies, although you do not necessarily have to work for a large company in order to have these benefits. **Discount programs** are voluntary benefits offered by employers that are established to provide reduced costs for or discounts on products and services offered by other third parties. Employers will establish an agreement with other vendors that offer a discount to employees, which can range anywhere from 10% to 50% off retail prices. These agreements can be established with little, if any, cost to the company but with great benefits to employees. Common discounts are in the following areas:

- Fitness or gym memberships
- Cellular service discounts
- Discounts on loan fees or account fees at financial institutions
- Discounts on spa or health-related services (spa treatments, acupuncture)
- Computer (hardware and software) discounts
- Child-care discounts
- Travel discounts (rental cars, hotels, travel planning fees)
- Restaurants
- Legal services (wills, trusts, estate documents)
- Other retail products (clothes, accessories, camping gear, etc.)

More important than just third-party discounts, employers will usually offer reduced or in some cases free products and services that the employer provides. For example, if you were to work for a food service company, you may be entitled to one free meal per your working shift. If you work for a computer technology company, you may be eligible to receive free software from the company. Make sure that you inquire into these types of programs offered by your company.

COMMON MISTAKES WHEN USING EMPLOYEE BENEFITS

Many of the previously mentioned benefits can be extremely important to us as we make decisions about where we work. However, it is important to understand several key mistakes that seem common among employees, especially for couples who both work and have different options with each employer.

Here is a quick list of the most common mistakes people make when working with and implementing fringe benefits in their financial planning:

- *Failing to review beneficiary choices.* It is important to review your beneficiary designations (those who will receive the benefit should something happen to you) at least annually. This allows you to ensure that each beneficiary is up-to-date because the human resources department or the insurance company will not make these changes automatically. You do not want to put your family members in a bad situation when they realize that the beneficiaries are not who you said they were.

- *Assuming that the human resources department will be your reminder.* As companies grow, employee turnover grows, and it can be an impossible task for human resources personnel to make sure that each employee has been reminded of all the different options and benefits offered by the company. We urge you to be proactive in making sure that you know and understand all the benefits that your company offers.

- *Failing to take advantage of available employee fringe benefits.* As just mentioned, it is imperative that you keep aware of all the benefits that your employer offers. Remember, these are for your benefit, so you are encouraged to see how they best fit your situation.

- *Failing to fully consider stock option plans.* Some more robust benefit plans offer employees the option to purchase company stock. These can be extremely lucrative benefits, but can also lead to an overconcentration of owning your own company's stock, which could be risky. It is recommended that you talk to a Christian financial advisor to help you appropriately manage any company stock that you own to balance the reward with the risk you are comfortable taking.

- *Failing to review your fringe benefit choices annually.* Remember that your circumstances change all the time, and it is your responsibility to make changes to your benefits. You should review all benefits at least annually. We recommend going through the benefits package during your company's annual open-enrollment period.

- *Contributing too much to flexible spending plans.* Although the tax benefits can be nice, and the rollover feature is attractive to many employees, you don't want to contribute so much that you begin to create a need to use debt to sustain your lifestyle due to a shortfall in take-home pay. It is prudent to try to match your health-care expenses to that of your health-care flexible spending plans.

- *Failing to obtain professional consultation outside the company.* We are told repeatedly in Proverbs to seek wise counsel. It is strongly encouraged that you meet with a Christian financial professional in order to wade through the many options and pray for guidance as you begin to make benefit choices.

- *Failing to fully consider options when both spouses have benefits.* Make sure that you review the benefits offered to both you and your spouse if you are both eligible employees at different companies. Couples have the tendency to review only the cost of health insurance from both plans, but rarely focus on the other benefits offered, such as supplemental life insurance, travel discounts, and so forth. This area of coordination may be best determined with a Christian financial professional who has some experience in employee benefits.

Keep in mind that most of your decisions regarding fringe benefits fall under the category of being a wise and good steward as you live in this fallen world.

SUMMARY

This chapter focused on the varying options companies offer to their employees as benefits. The chapter started off by reviewing the two main types of employee retirement accounts: defined benefit and defined contribution plans. We also provided an overview of stock option accounts and employee stock purchase plans. These non-retirement accounts are benefits that help employees manage employee stock purchases. We then reviewed health-care benefits and the impact of the 2010 Affordable Care Act on these benefits. In addition to the various health-care plans, we highlighted dental insurance, vision insurance, and accidental death and dismemberment insurance. Many of these insurance policies require the employee to pay out-of-pocket expenses, and thus we reviewed the importance and significance of health savings accounts.

Besides retirement and health benefits, the last most significant benefit is that of life insurance, and we discussed the ways in which employees can maximize their coverage. We also reviewed some other common benefits, such as tuition reimbursement programs, adoption assistance programs, and the various discount programs offered by many companies. Finally, we wrapped up the chapter by reviewing several common mistakes that employees make when utilizing employee benefits.

Figure 14.1 Health Insurance Worksheet

Deductible	$500.00		
Max out-of-pocket	$5,000.00		
Coinsurance %	20%		
Office Visit Cost	$25.00		
Monthly premium	$200.00		
Annual premium	$2,400.00		
Number of office visits/year	8		
Total Office Visit Costs	$200.00		
If hospital expenses are...	$0.00	$2,500.00	$20,000.00
Deductible cost	$0.00	$500.00	$500.00
Covered amount	$0.00	$2,000.00	$19,500.00
Coinsurance cost	$0.00	$400.00	$3,900.00
Total Hospital Costs	$0.00	$900.00	$4,400.00
	Generic	Generic Specialty	Specialty
If prescriptions cost...	$5.00	$85.00	$250.00
Number of perscriptions...	2	3	0
Times per year refilled...	4	1	0
Total Presription Costs	$40.00	$255.00	$0.00
Out-of-pocket costs	$40.00	$900.00	$4,400.00
TOTAL COST	$2,640.00	$3,755.00	$7,000.00
Compared to...			
First Health Insurance Plan A			
First Health Insurance Plan B	($380.08)	($1,495.08)	($4,740.08)
First Health Insurance Plan C	($40.00)	($1,075.00)	($4,320.00)
First Health Insurance Plan D	($0.00)	($1,115.00)	($4,360.00)

		First Health Insurance Plan B
Deductible		$1,000.00
Max out-of-pocket		$5,000.00
Coinsurance %		25%
Office Visit Cost		$0.00
Monthly premium		$185.00
Annual premium		$2,220.00
Number of office visits/year	8	
Total Office Visit Costs	$0.00	
If hospital expenses are...	$0.00	$20,000.00
Deductible cost	$0.00	$1,000.00
Covered amount	$0.00	$19,000.00
Coinsurance cost	$0.00	$4,000.00
Total Hospital Costs	$0.00	$1,375.00 / $5,000.00
	Generic	Generic Specialty
If prescriptions cost...	$4.99	$75.00 $200.00
Number of perscriptions...	2	3 / 0
Times per year refilled...	4	1 / 0
Total Presription Costs	$39.92	$225.00
Out-of-pocket costs	$39.92	$5,000.00
TOTAL COST	$2,259.92	$3,820.00 / $7,220.00
Compared to...		
First Health Insurance Plan A	$380.08	($1,180.00)
First Health Insurance Plan B		($4,580.00)
First Health Insurance Plan C	($420.08)	($1,140.00) ($4,540.00)
First Health Insurance Plan D	($380.08)	($1,180.00) ($4,580.00)

First Health Insurance Plan C

Deductible		$250.00
Max out-of-pocket		$5,000.00
Coinsurance %		30%
Office Visit Cost		$50.00
Monthly premium		$245.00
Annual premium		**$2,940.00**
Number of office visits/year	8	
Total Office Visit Costs		**$400.00**
If hospital expenses are...	$0.00	**$2,500.00**
Deductible cost	$0.00	$250.00
Covered amount	$0.00	$2,250.00
Coinsurance cost	$0.00	$675.00
Total Hospital Costs	**$0.00**	**$925.00**
	Generic	Generic Specialty	Specialty

	Generic		Specialty
If prescriptions cost...	$10.00	$105.00	$280.00
Number of perscriptions...	2	3	0
Times per year refilled...	4	1	0
Total Presription Costs	$80.00	$315.00	$0.00

Out-of-pocket costs	**$80.00**	**$925.00**	**$5,000.00**
TOTAL COST	**$2,680.00**	**$3,840.00**	**$7,600.00**
Compared to...		
First Health Insurance Plan A	($40.00)	($1,200.00)	($4,960.00)
First Health Insurance Plan B	($420.08)	($1,580.08)	($5,340.08)
First Health Insurance Plan C			
First Health Insurance Plan D	($40.00)	($1,200.00)	($4,960.00)

			First Health Insurance Plan D
Deductible			$2,500.00
Max out-of-pocket			$7,500.00
Coinsurance %			25%
Office Visit Cost			$10.00
Monthly premium			$145.00
Annual premium	$1,740.00		
Number of office visits/year			8
Total Office Visit Costs			$80.00
If hospital expenses are...	$0.00		$20,000.00
Deductible cost	$0.00		$2,500.00
Covered amount	$0.00		$17,500.00
Coinsurance cost	$0.00		$4,375.00
Total Hospital Costs	$0.00		$6,875.00
	Generic	Specialty	Generic Specialty
If prescriptions cost...	$5.00	$85.00	$250.00
Number of perscriptions...	2	3	0
Times per year refilled...	4	1	0
Total Presription Costs	$40.00	$255.00	$0.00
Out-of-pocket costs	$40.00	$2,500.00	$6,875.00
TOTAL COST	$2,640.00	$5,355.00	$9,475.00
Compared to...			
First Health Insurance Plan A	$0.00	($2,715.00)	($6,835.00)
First Health Insurance Plan B	($380.08)	($3,095.08)	($7,215.08)
First Health Insurance Plan C	($40.00)	($2,675.00)	($6,795.00)
First Health Insurance Plan D			

SUMMARY REVIEW QUESTIONS

1. What is a defined benefit plan? What is a defined contribution plan? What are the differences between the two?

2. Why have defined benefit plans become obsolete in today's workforce?

3. In what ways can an employer contribute to a defined contribution plan?

4. For 2016, what are the IRS contribution limits established for defined contribution plans?

5. Explain briefly what a stock option plan is and how these types of plans can benefit employees.

6. What are the usual characteristics of an employee stock purchase plan?

7. For group health coverage, what are the two most prevalent options listed in the chapter?

8. List and explain the three main types of group health insurance plans.

9. How do HMO plans differ from PPO plans?

10. What is one significant flaw or downfall in most dental plans?

11. List approved events that allow employees an opportunity to change their health benefits.

12. What are the advantages associated with using a health savings account?

13. What is the amount that is not taxable to employees in group life insurance?

14. How can an employee exceed the typical standard coverage of life insurance?

15. What is evidence of insurability, and how do you get it?

16. List reasons why disability insurance is so important.

17. What are the six different types of disability?

18. Define the benefit amount, the benefit period, and the elimination period for a disability insurance policy.

19. Why is it so important to know the difference in occupation classification when choosing a disability policy?

20. What does double indemnity mean in an accidental death and dismemberment policy?

21. How can companies help employees succeed in their education through their tuition reimbursement policies?

22. What are the three ways that employers offer paid leave for time away from work?

23. What are some common discounts offered by employers to employees in a discount benefit program?

24. List and explain the eight common mistakes employees can make in dealing with their employee benefits.

Case Study Analysis

Bob always seemed to get agitated around this time of year when he had to "waste time" in selecting the same old insurances policies each year during open enrollment. Debbie decided that because they have been working with Steve, she would give him a call to make sure that what benefits they signed up for at Lextin Oil Supply would not be counter to all the work they have been doing with their new financial plan.

"Steve, this is Debbie Smith, and I wanted to ask your advice. Do you have a few minutes?"

"Sure, Debbie, what's up?" replied Steve.

"It's that time of year," Debbie responded, "where we need to select our benefits at Bob's work, and I just wanted to see if there is anything we need to be aware of because we have been working with you and didn't want to do anything that would be counter to your advice. Should we come in and meet?"

"Debbie, thanks for calling. Employee benefits can be daunting and overwhelming for people because there always seems to be an overwhelming number of choices that can create a lot of anxiety among employees. Let's do this: why don't you and Bob bring in your employee benefits package, and we can review each option and make sure that everything lines up. We can also review any benefits that you may not be taking advantage of that might be incorporated in our planning, such as travel discounts or even tuition assistance. What

does next Thursday afternoon look like? Will that give you time to complete your enrollment prior to the deadline set by Bob's employer?"

"I think next Thursday would work. I will make sure Bob and I meet you at your office then—say, four o'clock?"

"Four o'clock it is. I am looking forward to it, Debbie. See you then."

"Thanks, Steve. Bye."

As Debbie hung up the phone, she felt an immediate sense of relief. Perhaps Bob will feel relieved too as we go through all these options with Steve, she thought.

Assignment

Take time to review the employee benefits package provided. Go through each section and select which options would be best for Bob and Debbie to consider. Make sure you justify why you selected each type of plan. Also, provide any benefits that Bob and Debbie need to consider taking advantage of that they may not already be using.

DEFINITIONS

Disability benefit amount   (p. 335)

Disability benefit period   (p. 335)

Disability insurance   (p. 334)

Discount programs   (p. 338)

Elimination period (waiting period)   (p. 335)

Evidence of insurability   (p. 334)

Group health plans   (p. 329)

Health-care share ministries   (p. 329)

Indemnity plans   (p. 330)

Single life annuity   (p. 326)

SCRIPTURE VERSES (ESV)

1 Timothy 5:8—Anyone who does not provide for their relatives, and especially for their own household, has denied the faith and is worse than an unbeliever.

ADDITIONAL READINGS

Beam, B., & Mcfadden, J. J. (2007). *Employee benefits*. Fort Lauderdale: Kaplan Publishing.

Bergmann, T. J., Bergmann, M. A., & Grahn, J. L. (1994). How important are employee benefits to public sector employees? *Public Personnel Management, 23*(3), 397–406.

Cole, N. D., & Flint, D. H. (2004). Perceptions of distributive and procedural justice in employee benefits: flexible versus traditional benefit plans. *Journal of Managerial Psychology, 19*(1), 19–40.

Dencker, J. C., Joshi, A., & Martocchio, J. J. (2007). Employee benefits as context for intergenerational conflict. *Human Resource Management Review, 17*(2), 208–220.

Dulebohn, J. H., Molloy, J. C., Pichler, S. M., & Murray, B. (2009). Employee benefits: Literature review and emerging issues. *Human Resource Management Review, 19*(2), 86–103.

Estreicher, S., & Reilly, D. J. (2010). *Employee benefits and executive compensation: Proceedings of the New York University 59th Annual Conference on Labor*. New York: NY: Kluwer Law International.

Fronstin, P. (1999). Retirement patterns and employee benefits: Do benefits matter? *The Gerontologist, 39*(1), 37–48.

Gerber, P. D., Nel, P. S., & Van Dyk, P. S. (1987). *Human resources management*. Birmingham, AL: Southern Book Publishers.

Hong, J. C., Yang, S. D., Wang, L. J., Chiou, E. F., Su, F. Y., & Huang, S. L. (1995). Impact of employee benefits on work motivation and productivity. *International Journal of Career Management, 7*(6), 10–14.

Kennedy, K. J., & Shultz, P. T. (2012). *Employee Benefits Law: Qualification and ERISA requirements*. Durham, NC: Carolina Academic Press.

Martocchio, J. J. (2011). *Employee benefits: A primer for human resource professionals*. New York: NY: McGraw-Hill Irwin.

McCaffery, R. M. (1988). *Employee benefit programs: A total compensation perspective*. Independence KY: Brooks/Cole.

Milkovich, G. T., Newman, J. M., & Milkovich, C. (1999). *Compensation*. Burr Ridge, IL: Irwin/McGraw-Hill.

Rosenbloom, J. S., & Hallman, G. V. (1991). *Employee benefit planning*. Upper Saddle, River, NJ: Prentice Hall.

States, U. (2004). *Pension and employee benefits: Preambles to final and temporary regulations*. New York, NY: Commerce Clearing House.

REFERENCES

American Consumer Survey, (2015). *Disability statistics.* Retrieved from https://www.disabilitystatistics.org/glossary.cfm

Claxton, G., Rae, M., Panchal, N., Whitmore, H., Damico, A., Kenward, K., & Long, M. (2015). Health benefits in 2015: Stable trends in the employer market. *Health Affairs*, 10, 1779–1788.

Dave Thomas Foundation for Adoption. (2015). *100 overall best companies for adoption.* Retrieved from https://dciw4f53l7k9i.cloudfront.net/wp-contentuploads/2014/11/100-Best-01.jpg

Jones, P. (1999). *Are educated workers really more productive?* Retrieved from http://www.cid.harvard.edu/archive/events/cidneudc/papers/jones.pdf

U.S. Department of Labor. (2015). *Family Medical Leave Act.* Retrieved from http://www.dol.gov/whd/fmla/

Chapter 15

Transcendent Principle 4: Set Long-Term Goals

Courtesy of duncanandison/Fotolia.

BIG IDEA:
Set long-term goals because there is always a trade-off between the short term and the long term.

LEARNING OUTCOMES

- Understand and apply the six time-value-of-money calculations
- Be able to explain the five steps in the sequential investing diagram
- Describe the purpose of stocks as investments
- Explain how mutual funds work and how they can be a vital part of an investment portfolio
- Articulate the eight basic rules of investing in stocks
- Describe and characterize different types of fixed-income securities
- Understand the differences in government, municipal, and corporate bonds
- Know how other assets, such as real estate and commodities, can be used in an investment portfolio
- Differentiate between the types of accounts used for investing
- Explain the biblical and practical purposes of investing

Time Value of Money

Before we get into looking at setting long-term goals, it is important to have a grasp on six fundamental finance concepts. Known as time-value-of-money (TVM) calculations, these six concepts allow us to track the value of a dollar over time and determine what its worth will be. The six concepts are future value, future value of an annuity, future value of a series of unequal cash flows, present value, present value of an annuity, and present value of unequal cash flows. As we unpack each of these TVM calculations, it is important to understand the several key factors that we will use to conduct these calculations. These functions will be used in almost all of the TVM formulas, so it is important to know what they are and how they are used. Table 15.1 gives an overview of the different functions and their abbreviations.

Table 15.1

Name	Abbreviation	Description
Present value	PV	The value today of a future value
Present value of an annuity	PVA	The value today of a series of payments
Future value	FV	The value in the future of a present value
Future value of an annuity	FVA	The value in the future of a series of payments
Payment	PMT	The amount of each payment
Time periods	N (or sometimes t)	The number of periods during which the calculation will be conducted
Interest rate	I (or sometimes r)	The interest rate that will be used to calculate the problem
Cash flow	CF_t	The cash flow at a specific time (t)

TIME VALUE OF MONEY: FUTURE VALUE

Future Value of a Single Cash Input

Probably the most common TVM calculation is to determine a future value. In other words, what will a dollar today be worth in the future? For this calculation, we need to know several key components from Table 15.1, the initial starting value (PV), the interest rate at which we will "invest" the money for future use (I), and the number of times we will apply our interest rate to our number (N).

We can enter those numbers in the following formula:

$$FV = PV(1 + i)^n$$

Using this equation in an example, suppose we want to know what the future value will be of $100 if we were to save our money in a savings account paying 3% for 2 years. We would simply plug the numbers into our equation using the following inputs:

PV = $100

I = 3%

N = 2

Therefore, FV = $100 $(1 + .03)^2$ = $106.09. After 2 years with a 3% annual interest rate, we would have earned $6.09 in interest.

Future Value of an Annuity (or Equal Cash Flows)

The second future value TVM calculation consists of determining the future value of a series of payments, or equal cash flows. We may or may not have an initial starting value, but for this example, we will assume our starting value (PV) is zero. To solve this problem, we will need to know the payment amount (PMT), the rate at which interest will be compounded (I), and the number of periods in the calculation (N).

Suppose that at your birth, your grandfather decided to put $100 each year (on your birthday) for 18 years into a savings account that earned an annual rate of interest of 4%. What would the value be in the savings account at the end of year 18? To solve this problem, we will use the following formula with the appropriate inputs:

$$FVA = PMT[(1 + i)^n - 1)/i)]$$

PMT = $100
N = 18
I = 4%
Therefore, FV = $100[(1 + .04)^{18} - 1)/.04) = $2,564.54.

What makes this so interesting? If you think about how much the grandfather actually put away, $100 times 18 years, that's $1,800. Over the course of 18 years, the account with a 4% annual interest rate earned $764.54.

Future Value of Unequal Cash Flows

The final future value calculation in TVM problems consists of unequal cash flows. Understanding the concept is fairly easy, but the calculation can be a bit time consuming. Using Excel or your financial calculator can be really helpful in these more complicated TVM problems. In order to solve this TVM problem, we will need to know the different cash flows (CF_t), the interest rate at which our value will compound (I), and the number of periods in the calculation (N).

For example, suppose that your grandfather decided that instead of $100 per year, he would give you $100 for each year you were alive, up to the age of 18. In other words, $100 on your first birthday, $200 on your second birthday, and so on. What would the value of the account be in 18 years if you were to earn a 2.5% annual interest rate? To solve this problem, we will use the following inputs and the following formula:

$$FVn = {}^n_{t=0}\Sigma CF_t(1 + I)^{n-t}$$

where Σ is the sum of each year's future cash flow value.

CF1 = $100	CF8 = $800	CF15 = $1,500
CF2 = $200	CF9 = $900	CF16 = $1,600
CF3 = $300	CF10 = $1,000	CF17 = $1,700
CF4 = $400	CF11 = $1,100	CF18 = $1,800
CF5 = $500	CF12 = $1,200	N = 18
CF6 = $600	CF13 = $1,300	I = 2.5%
CF7 = $700	CF14 = $1,400	

You may notice that the exponent in this equation is n−t, where N is the number of periods we have in our calculation and t starts at a value of 0 and increases by 1 for each subsequent year. For example, in year 1, we have n−t = 18 − 0 = 18. Year 2 is thus 18 − 1 = 17, all the way to year 18, which is 18 − 17 = 1.

So, to solve this problem, our first few years would look like the following:

$$FV_{18} = $100(1.025)^{18} + $200(1.025)^{17} + \ldots + $1800(1.025)^1 = $20,278.63.$$

When we calculate what the grandfather put into the account, we see that he deposited only $17,100 over the 18 years, and the account grew to $20,278.63, a difference of $3,178.63.

DISCIPLESHIP MOMENT AND REFLECTION

Suppose you were to save $10,000 and knew that you could invest that money and earn 8% annually. What would the value be in 20 years if you did not add any more money to it? What other goals should you jot down for which it would be helpful to know the future value, such as an education or home value? Talk this through with your prayer and accountability partner.

TIME VALUE OF MONEY: PRESENT VALUE

Similar to the way future value calculations work, we can also look to find what we need today if we know a future amount. These calculations can be extremely helpful when we know our desired retirement account balance and wish to determine how much we need to put aside on a regular basis to achieve a known future account balance. Just as with future value, there are three different calculations for present value: present value of a single future cash outcome, present value of an annuity (or equal cash flows), and present value of unequal cash flows.

Present Value of a Future Output

If we desire to know the present value of a given future value, we can use the following equation as long as we know three main components, the interest rate we are discounting, the time by which the amount will be discounted, and the ultimate future value.

$PV = (FV/(1 + i)^n)$

Where,

FV = the amount to be received in the future,

I = interest rate by which we are discounting to the present, and

N = the number of periods we will be discounting.

Let's go to our grandfather example and look at it with a present value perspective. Suppose that at your birth, your grandfather decides that he wants you to have $20,000 to pay for your first year of college 18 years later, and he knows that he can earn 5% annually in a conservative mutual fund. He wants to know how much to put aside today to be able to give you this gift on your 18th birthday. We would use the previous equation and the following inputs:

FV = $20,000

I = 5%

N = 18

PV = $20,000/(1 + .05)18 = $20,000/2.41 = $8,298.75

Your grandfather would only have to deposit $8,298.75 today and earn 5% annually to have $20,000 18 years later. In other words, your grandfather would earn $11,701.25 over the course of those 18 years.

Present Value of an Annuity (or Equal Cash Flows)

The second present value TVM calculation consists of determining the present value of a series of payments, or equal cash flows. To solve this problem, we need to know the payment amount (PMT), the rate at which interest will be discounted (I), and the number of periods in the calculation (N).

Let's go through an example. Let's suppose your grandfather is looking at pre-payment options for your first year of college. The choices are to pay $1,000 a year to the university or to give a check today for $12,000. He knows that the current interest rate is 5%. What would be the best option for him?

To solve this problem, we use the following formula with the appropriate inputs:

$$PVA = PMT[1 - (1/(1 + i)^n)/i)]$$

Where,

PMT = $1,000,

I = 5%, and

N = 18.

$$PVA = \$1,000[(1 - (1/1+.05)18)/.05)] = \$1,000[(1 - /1/2.41)/.05)] = \$1,000[(1 - .415)/.05] = \$1,000[(.585)/.05] = \$1,000[11.7] = \$11,700.$$

So, what should he choose? It seems logical to select the option where he pays $1,000 to the university because the present value of that cash flow is $11,700, which is less than the other option, which is to pay the school $12,000 today.

Present Value of Unequal Cash Flows

This last section looks at determining the present value of a series of unequal cash flows.

Let's revisit the future value of unequal cash flows example and see what the present value of those cash flows would be using the same figures. The equation that we use is as follows:

$$PVn = {}^n_{t=0} \Sigma CF_t/(1 + i)^n$$

Where,

Σ is the sum of each year's cash flow value,

$CF_{(t)}$ = the cash flow at each time period (t),

I = discounting interest rate, and

N = number of time period the cash flow occurs.

Going back to the previous example, we want to determine what your grandfather would need to have today to pay you an increasing amount on your birthday. In other words, what does he need to have today to accomplish this if he could earn a 2.5% annual interest rate? To solve this problem, we will use the following inputs in the formula:

CF1 = $100	CF9 = $900	CF17 = $1,700
CF2 = $200	CF10 = $1,000	CF18 = $1,800
CF3 = $300	CF11 = $1,100	N = 18
CF4 = $400	CF12 = $1,200	I = 2.5%
CF5 = $500	CF13 = $1,300	$PV_{18} = \$100/(1.025)^{18}$
CF6 = $600	CF14 = $1,400	$+ \$200/(1.025)^{17} + \dots$
CF7 = $700	CF15 = $1,500	$+ \$1800/(1.025)^{1}$
CF8 = $800	CF16 = $1,600	$= \$16{,}682.93.$

This means that your grandfather would need $16,682.93 today in order to provide your birthday gifts at a $100 increasing level for the next 18 years. Recall that the total amount given is $17,100. By having $16,682.93, he was able to save over $400.

LONG-TERM INVESTING

Now that we have a foundation as to the use and calculations of TVM problems, we can begin to look at components of our long-term investing. Before we get too deep into investments and the types of investments, it is important to provide a bit of a recap as to the sequential order of our margin, or extra monthly spendable income, so we stay on the same page.

Figure 15.1   Sequential Investing

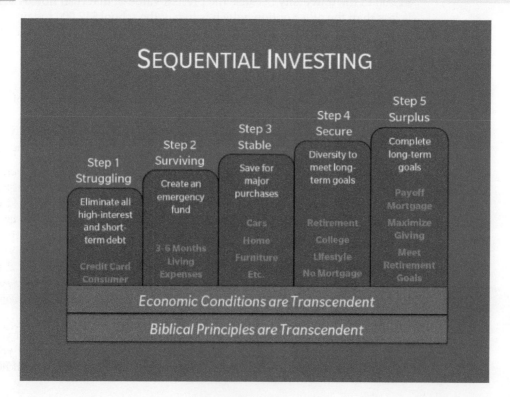

In looking at this diagram, we see that our investment decisions are on top of the foundation of biblical principles and the current economic conditions. These two components are imperative as you understand when to begin investing. First, we must always remember that biblical principles transcend time, meaning they are always right and always relevant. Additionally, it is important to remember that markets, industries, and companies all experience cycles, which include peaks, troughs, expansionary periods, and contractionary periods. More specifically, a **business cycle** is defined as a repeatable pattern of growth (expansion) and decline (contraction) related to economic activity. It is important to have a general idea as to where the general economy is positioned prior to making any investment decisions.

Ron's Corner

The Bible has much to say about the principle of sowing and reaping. In 2 Corinthians 9:6 Paul said, "Whoever sows sparingly will also reap sparingly, and whoever sows generously will also reap generously." There is a lot to be learned from sowing and reaping, and I want to pull out one small part of that principle in talking about delayed gratification.

Delayed gratification means that I give up today's desire in order to save for a future benefit. This principle is critical to financial success because unless you receive an inheritance, strike it rich with an investment, or otherwise receive a windfall, you will not be able to have everything immediately. This can cause frustration if you have a totally short-term perspective. Delayed gratification requires a long-term perspective and is key to financial maturity.

Proverbs 24:27: Put your outdoor work in order and get your fields ready; after that, build your house.

The sequential investing diagram helps to explain that there is a proper order related to investing, and if the sequence gets out of order, we can fall prey to disaster. We will review each step in order.

Step 1: Eliminate all high-interest and short-term debt.

High-interest and short-term debt usually consists of credit cards, store charge accounts, payday loans, and perhaps even automobile loans. When you rid ourselves of these debts, you have already made an "investment return" because when you pay off high-interest debt you are "earning" the interest rate that you were previously paying. For example, suppose you had a $5,000 credit card balance for which you were charged 10% annually. Your annual interest payment would be $500. If the debt were eliminated, you would have earned 10% just as a result of not having to pay that amount of money again. Putting it another way, instead of spending $500 in interest, you now can save that money; you are no longer obligated to make that payment, and thus you are earning a return of 10%.

Step 2: Create an emergency fund of 3 to 6 months of living expenses.

Once you have all your high-interest debt paid off, you can now move into step 2, which is to start building up your emergency fund. The money placed in this fund should be in a liquid account that, if possible, should be an interest-bearing account. It is important to note that these funds are used for emergency purposes that should be discussed and outlined in advance. In other words, you (and your spouse if you are married) need to identify what an emergency is, such as a loss of a job or a car repair costing over $500. If you do not do this, then it will be much easier to tap into this fund even if there is no emergency. Each person's living expenses will vary, and each person's risk level will vary, so here are a few items to consider:

- Calculate your monthly expenditures over 2 or 3 months and average those expenditures to get what you "usually" spend in a month. This is the monthly amount you will need to save for.
- The less risk you are comfortable taking, the more months of expenses you should put aside. If you feel extremely uncomfortable with the idea of a possible job loss, then you will want to be conservative and put aside 6 months of living expenses. If you feel you are adequately protected against most emergencies, then you may only want to keep 3 months of living expenses in a liquid savings account.

Should you need to use these funds in an emergency, it is imperative that you replace the used funds as soon as possible. Keep in mind that these funds are your safety net and help create a sense of peace as you manage your finances.

Step 3: Save for major purchases.

Once you have money set aside in an emergency fund, you next need to evaluate any major purchases you will make over the next few years (yes, this takes some planning!). Items you may want to consider are furniture replacements, car replacements, or even down payments for your next house. Think about how much time you think you have, and then, using TVM calculations, determine what you should start putting away for those items. This should be feasible if you have no debt and feel comfortable with your emergency savings.

Step 4: Diversify and save for long-term goals.

At this step, you are now free to begin to put aside money for long-term goals such as college education, giving generously, paying off your home mortgage, and so forth. These investments usually carry higher risks yet yield higher rewards. Without any debt obligations and with your emergency savings set aside, you may feel better about accepting these more risky investment options.

Step 5: Complete long-term goals.

This step finalizes progress toward financial independence. This step allows you the flexibility to maximize your giving, start a business, or fund other lifelong passions.

The information presented in this chapter ideally comes into play during and after step 3.

Investing, or an investment, is an activity undertaken with the hope of making a profit. In other words, an investment is something that is purchased with one or two expectations: **capital gains**, which is a gain from selling something at a price higher than what it was purchased for, or for income. Before we get into the discussion on

Capital gains   A gain from selling something at a higher price than what it was purchased for.

investments, we need to identify what is *not* an investment. The following do not qualify as investments:

- Home
- Car
- Diamond ring
- Jewelry
- Furnishings
- Second homes

Depending on conversations you have been involved in, you may have heard at least some, if not all, of the listed items mentioned as investments. It's important to keep in mind that investments are a tool one uses to accomplish financial objectives. Investments are not an end in themselves. Many things, like the items in the list, may have "value," but they are not considered investments. Jewelry has value, but it isn't purchased with the purpose of creating capital gains or income. It may grow in value, but just try selling your wife's wedding ring. It's not going to happen.

There are biblical examples of investing, such as the wise woman investing in land and selling it for a higher price (Proverbs 31:16), to farmers planting seeds (2 Timothy 2:6), to the parable of wise servants increasing the master's allotment (Matthew 25:14–30). These are more primitive types of investments compared to the more sophisticated financial instruments we have available today in our economy, but they still apply.

Before we delve into the more detailed explanations of investments, it's important to ask the following questions:

- What are my reasons for making this investment?
  - Becoming debt free: Proverbs 22:26–27
  - Providing for my family, meeting future needs, and establishing an inheritance: Proverbs 30:25
  - Allowing increased giving: Proverbs 22:9
- Could I be investing unwisely due to an attitude of:
  - Greed? 1 Timothy 6:9; Proverbs 22:9
  - Pride? Proverbs 16:5
  - Fear? Proverbs 18:11
- Am I presuming on the future and creating anxiety for myself or my family? Matthew 6:25; Philippians 4:6–7

STOCKS OVERVIEW: WHAT ARE THEY?

At the top of the annual riches list are business owners—Bill Gates (Microsoft), the Sam Walton family (Wal-Mart), or Warren Buffet (Berkshire Hathaway), for example. In countries where capitalism is the economic system, owning a successful business is one way of greatly increasing wealth. Owning a business is a challenge. Unfortunately, having an idea, meeting a need, executing a plan to deliver a product or service, making a profit, and staying ahead of competition are very difficult tasks fraught with much uncertainty. In the financial world, we refer to uncertainty as risk. Owning a business involves a high potential for reward—and much risk, or uncertainty.

Not everyone has the opportunity or the willingness to own their own business on a full-time basis. Many, however, do own small percentages of companies by owning stock, or equity, in those companies. When referring to *stock*, we simply mean a certificate showing a percentage of ownership of a company. These certificates, or stocks, are traded between people at a stock market. The value of a stock goes up or down depending on the general demand of others wanting to own that stock.

When you own stock of a company, for example General Electric (GE), you own a small, tiny piece of the company. So how does an investor in stocks make money? Typical investors seek to buy a stock at a certain price and then sell the stock at a later date for more than what they paid for it. What, then, makes a stock go up? The basic answer is the law of supply and demand.

Because businesses are designed to make a profit, investors invest in companies because they want to share in the profits (also known as earnings) of that company. If people begin to think that a company will make a lot of money (high earning potential), then more investors will want to own that stock. If more people demand a certain stock (which is limited in nature due to only having one initial public offering), then the value of that stock will rise due to there being more buyers than sellers. On the contrary, if a company is not making enough earnings to satisfy investors, they will sell their stakes in the company and go invest in another company. When more sellers of the stock appear than buyers, the value of the stock will go down.

Because the value of a stock usually depends, in large part, on the company's future earning potential, stock prices can and do move up and down rather quickly. This up-and-down movement, referred to as **volatility**, or the rate at which a stock price will go up and down, is why stocks are more risky or uncertain than other types of investments.

Some companies have reached certain points along the business cycle (part of the economic conditions noted in the sequential investing chart) and may decide to start giving their owners cash payments from their excess revenue as opposed to using that money to grow the company. These cash payments from the company's excess earnings to its shareholders are referred to as **dividends**. In many cases, once a company starts paying shareholders a dividend, the company will usually continue to do so. Why? By not paying the dividend, investors may look upon the company as not being able to pay and thus lose confidence in the company's earning ability and may decide to sell their shares.

One of the many advantages offered by owning stocks is the ability to receive both price appreciation and dividend payments. In order to determine your rate of return, which is the desire of all investors, you can use the following formula:

Rate of return = ((Sales price of the stock − Purchase price of the stock) + Dividends received)/Original investment

For example, suppose you received $1,000 from your grandfather to invest, and you bought shares of Apple when the stock was $100 a share. When you check the stock 1 year later, the stock is now trading at $118 per share, and you decide to sell it. You also received a $2/share dividend ($2 × 10 shares = $20.00) while you owned the stock. In order to determine your rate of return, you would use the previous equation with the following numbers:

Rate of return = ((118 − 100) + 20)/$1,000 = .038 or 3.8%.

Volatility The rate at which a stock will go up and down.

Dividends Cash payments from the excess earnings of a company to its shareholders.

Unfortunately, we don't always sell stocks at a higher price than the price for which we bought them. Suppose in our previous example that the price of Apple stock had declined to $75 per share when we sold it. We still received the $2-per-share dividend. Our return would be as follows:

Rate of return = (($75 − $100) + $20)/$1,000 = −.005 or −.5%.

As you can see, the dividend payment can help to offset any negative price changes in the stock, which can help reduce the risk in owning dividend-paying stocks. However, a dividend alone may not be sufficient to minimize the risk in owning one stock by itself. Thus, many investors will buy more than one stock and create a portfolio of stocks. An **investment portfolio** is a collection of different stocks (or other investments) that make up one's overall investment holdings.

When you invest in multiple different stocks, there are several different risks that you can help to minimize (although you can't avoid all risk):

- Business Risk: **Business risk** is the inherent risk that a company has by being in business. These risks include poor operations, bad management, fraud, unsuccessful products, and competition, to name a few. There is not a company that is perfect, and all companies have risk associated with being in business.

- Market Risk: **Market risk** is the risk one takes by investing in the stock market as a whole. Certain factors can influence how investors feel the economy is headed, which can lead to a pessimistic view that companies overall will have reduced earning potential. Market risk is also referred to as **systematic risk**, which is the risk of the overall market and economy. Examples of systematic risk include wars, terrorist attacks, rising interest rates, and economic crises like those experienced between 2008 and 2009. Another type of risk is **unsystematic risk**, which is the risk that is associated with investing in a specific company or industry. The most common way to reduce unsystematic risk is through **diversification**, or diversifying your portfolio by owning a variety of shares in different companies in different industries.

Ecclesiastes 11:2: Divide your portion to seven, or even to eight, for you do not know what misfortune may occur on the earth.

Solomon, the wisest man who walked the earth, penned these words. The idea of diversification is nothing new. Unfortunately, many investors may find it hard to know which stocks to buy in order to diversify or don't have the time required to do so. Due to these issues (and others), the emergence of mutual funds have become one of the most popular investment tools in our day.

Investment portfolio A collection of different stocks (or other investments) that make up one's overall investment holdings.

Business risk The inherent risk that a company faces by being in business. Examples include poor management and unsuccessful products.

Market risk The risk one takes by investing in the stock market as a whole.

Systematic risk The risk of the overall market and economy.

Unsystematic risk The risk associated with investing in a specific company or industry.

Diversification Owning a variety of different companies in different industries in your portfolio.

MUTUAL FUNDS: A MEANS OF DIVERSIFICATION

A mutual fund is an investment tool that allows people to pool their money into a single investment company that in turn invests in stocks or bonds to meet an investment objective. This type of arrangement offers several advantages to the average investor, including access to professional investment managers, the ability to diversify investments, accessibility through liquidity, and recordkeeping.

The first significant advantage of this type of investing is professional management. Fund managers have access to research sources and work full-time at selecting and analyzing the investments for the fund. Although professional management is never a guarantee for success, many mutual funds have shown consistent performance above market averages for many years. With a mutual fund, you are really buying the professional management expertise.

Another major advantage of mutual funds is diversification. Typically, the small investor may own two to three stocks. The mutual fund may own anywhere from 100 to 500 stocks in many different industry categories. Diversification gives a measure of safety by reducing your risk of loss. Losses on a few stocks are not likely to have a serious impact on the fund's performance.

Mutual funds also provide liquidity. This means shares in the fund can be sold easily, allowing ready access to your money. In addition, many funds offer different options on the use of dividends they earn. You can reinvest them automatically or take them in cash, which gives you greater control of cash flow.

Finally, mutual funds provide the investor with recordkeeping services. When the stocks held by the mutual fund merge, split, or pay dividends, the mutual fund keeps track of these transactions for you. Mutual funds provide simplicity, summarized statements periodically, and regular reports of what is happening in the fund. And, as with the stock market, you can track the fund's performance on a daily basis in the newspaper.

So how does a mutual fund help to diversify your investments? Mutual funds are a tool to help put your investment dollars in different companies and different industries. Mutual funds each have an investment purpose, and investors should select the fund that matches their investment objectives. For example, American Funds offers a mutual fund titled Growth Fund of America (AGTHX), and the summary of this fund is as follows:

> Paints with a broad brush. Takes a flexible approach to seeking growth opportunities, seeking out classic growth stocks, cyclical stocks and turnaround situations.

Source: https://www.americanfunds.com/individual/investments/fund/agthx

In this example, the mutual fund seeks to invest in growth stocks that appear to be overcoming adversity and have an optimistic future. Because each company and industry has varying characteristics, such as large companies, small companies, international (global) companies, and so forth, mutual funds can help provide a form of *asset allocation*, which, by definition, is spreading your investments over varying asset classes. The following list provides the most common types of asset classes:

- Large U.S. stocks
- Mid-sized U.S. stocks
- Small U.S. stocks
- Large international stocks
- Emerging market stocks
- Real estate
- Resources
- Commodities
- U.S. bonds

Value investment
Investments sought after due to trading below their intrinsic value.

Intrinsic value The difference between the market price of a company and the per-share value of its book value, or company assets less company liabilities.

Growth investment
Investments that are expected to grow quickly over a short period of time.

- TIPS
- International bonds
- Cash

In addition to these asset classes, there are two other classifications that many investors will add to investments: value investments and growth investments. **Value investments** are classified as investments that trade below their **intrinsic value**, meaning the price of the company is valued at less than its book value (or the value of all its assets less its liabilities). The other classification is referred to as **growth investments**, which are investments that are expected to grow quickly over a short time period. In many cases, start-up companies fall within this category due to new products or technology being offered in the marketplace.

INVESTING IN STOCKS: SOME BASIC RULES

When asked to summarize their key investment philosophies, most investors—including professional money managers—would have a difficult time giving an answer. Why? Because the most used investment approach is the "seat-of-the-pants" method. Investment results from this approach are usually mediocre, at best.

Over the long-term periods of time, the overall U.S. stock market has increased significantly, a shown in Figure 15.2. Various studies have shown, however, that the average individual investor has not realized returns as high as the average of the overall market. The bar graph in Figure 15.2 shows that overall market returns are three times greater than the return actually received by individual investors.

Not many investors have consistently produced returns close to, much less exceeding, market investment returns. With that in mind, here are eight common-sense suggestions relating to investing in stocks:

1. *Set realistic, achievable investment goals.* Based on the stock market's past performance and returns achieved by successful money managers, a goal of an 8% to 12% annual total return, on *average,* is considered reasonable. Keep in mind that this is an average annual return; actual returns can and will vary greatly from this average.

2. *Value wins out.* The most successful investors develop a method of measuring value. A stock is bought only when its price is significantly undervalued in relation to the company's earnings and assets. When a stock is overvalued, it is sold, without exception.

3. *Know the financial stability of the companies you buy.* Don't buy stocks of companies with poor financial quality. These companies have a much higher probability of cutting dividends, declaring bankruptcy, or announcing some other negative surprise.

4. *Diversify.* To minimize risk, hold at least 10 stocks in your portfolio and have representation in at least five different industries. Figure 15.3 shows the various different sectors from which you can select investments.

5. *Don't listen to rumors.* When someone tells you about a "hot tip," there's probably a 95% chance or more that it's false and that you will lose money. The few times a rumor turns out to be true, you may actually be relying on "inside information," which is illegal.

Figure 15.2 Stock Market Growth, 1871—2010

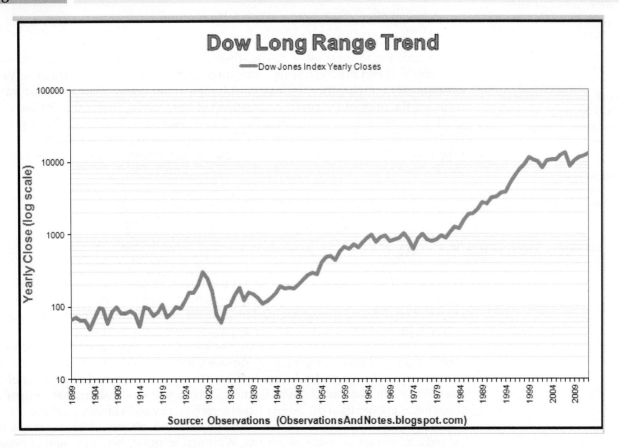

Source: http://observationsandnotes.blogspot.com/2008/10/100-years-of-stock-market-histsory.html

6. *Be patient.* Understand that you are buying an ownership interest when you buy a stock. It takes time for owners to reap the rewards on their investments. Only buy a stock that you are willing to hold for at least 3 years. Studies have shown that investors who buy and hold stocks realize better returns than those who trade often. Long-term investing is the right frame of mind. (Of course, the cynic wisecracks that a long-term investment is a short-term investment that failed.)

7. *Exercise discipline.* Develop a set of investment rules, and *never* stray from them. By sticking to the investment rules you establish, you help to minimize—if not eliminate—the opportunity to begin to make emotional investment decisions. These decisions are usually sparked by greed or fear, both of which are wrong motivators when making investment decisions.

8. *Use common sense.* We have all been blessed with a measure of common sense. In evaluating an investment, consider whether it makes sense. If a stock sounds too good to be true, it probably is! In addition, talk to your spouse, if you are married, or your accountability partner. We also recommend that you seek professional counsel that aligns to your biblical worldview.

Applying all of these rules will not guarantee investment success, but the chances of achieving attractive returns will be much higher.

Figure 15.3 U.S. Stock Market Sectors

Courtesy of John Takai/Dreamstime.

FIXED-INCOME SECURITIES

Fixed-income investments are different from equity investments and serve a different purpose. Some investors are not interested in seeking to grow their assets as much as they are hoping to protect their assets and to use their assets to generate a stream of income. Fixed-income securities are investments that usually offer a steady stream of income to the investor. Fixed-income securities can vary in maturity, ranging from a few weeks to as long as 30 years. You may recall that, usually, the further out in time is the maturity of the investment, the higher is the yield (or rate of return) on that investment. Some of the most common types of fixed-income securities are the following:

- Certificates of deposit
- U.S. savings bonds
- U.S. Treasuries (bills, notes, and bonds)
- Municipal bonds
- Corporate bonds

These vehicles, which offer relatively little risk, can be purchased at a bank or brokerage firm. When making an investment selection, people often wrongly let current market conditions change their decision parameters. Some individuals who want complete safety and cannot live with market fluctuations generally buy CDs. We will briefly review each of these different types of fixed-income securities.

Certificates of Deposit

Certificate of deposit (CDs) are investments offered by banks in which money is placed in an account for a specific period of time, ranging from 7 days to 7 years, that will earn a specific interest rate. Interest accumulation for a CD will usually depend on the length to maturity. For example, a CD with a maturity of 1 month (30 days) will usually credit the account with interest at maturity. If, for example, you had a 5-year CD, your interest may be credited annually, in some cases monthly. CDs are great investments when you are trying to match the need for specific funds with a specific date in the future. Let's say you have saved funds for your family vacation but will not take the vacation for another 6 months. You may decide to put that money in a 6-month CD to earn interest prior to your trip. CDs will usually have a penalty if the money is taken out prior to the selected maturity date; in most cases the penalty is equal to 2 months of interest. This penalty is what can make using a CD for your vacation money attractive in order to help you avoid using the money for another purpose.

Investors seeking income and protection of principal may decide to use what is known as a *CD ladder*. This process is established by setting up CDs with different maturity dates in order to maintain a certain level of liquidity while still providing a return on the invested money. Let's suppose that your grandfather has $500,000 in investable assets and wants to have access to some of the money but wants to put some of it in investments that are insured by the Federal Deposit Insurance Corporation (FDIC). He could set up five CDs as follows:

> CD 1: $100,000, which matures in year 1
>
> CD 2: $100,000, which matures in year 2
>
> CD 3: $100,000, which matures in year 3
>
> CD 4: $100,000, which matures in year 4
>
> CD 5: $100,000, which matures in year 5

In this situation, each year your grandfather will be able to have access to $100,000 plus the interest he earned on that specific CD. If he realizes that he doesn't need the money, he can buy another 5-year CD, knowing that in 1 year, he will have another CD come due, and the cycle can repeat.

U.S. Savings Bonds

U.S. savings bonds are structured like CDs in that you buy a savings bond (or loan the U.S. government money) and hold the savings bonds until you are ready to redeem the bond. At redemption, you will receive your original investment back plus accrued interest. **Accrued interest** is all interest that has accumulated from an investment that has not been paid to the investor. The most significant difference between U.S. savings bonds and CDs is that savings bonds do not have a specific maturity. There is, however, a point in the future when interest will stop accruing on a savings bond, although that does not require you to redeem the bond.

There are two main types of saving bonds: Series EE/E bonds and Series I bonds.

Accrued interest All interest that has accumulated from an investment that has not been paid to the investor.

Series EE/E Bonds

Series EE/E bonds usually will earn a stated rate of interest, which can be found on the U.S. Treasury's website (www.treasurydirect.gov). U.S. savings bonds require a minimum purchase of $25 and a maximum of $10,000 for each Social Security number per calendar year. This means that each person can only buy up to $10,000 per year in these savings bonds. The interest accrual period for these bonds is 30 years. These bonds require at least a 1-year holding period, the time period that must lapse prior to redeeming the bond. If the bonds are redeemed prior to the 5th anniversary year, then a penalty of 3 months of interest will be forfeited. Although the interest on these bonds is subject to federal tax, if the money from the bonds is used for a qualified taxpayer's higher education expenses, the interest may be excluded from the taxpayer's gross income.

Series I Bonds

The other form of U.S. savings bonds is referred to as a Series I bond, which implies that the interest is indexed or adjusted for inflation. There are two components to the interest rate, a fixed rate and an inflation rate, which, when combined, give the bondholder the total interest rate. The rate is usually adjusted twice a year based on the changes in the Consumer Price Index (CPI). Like their counterpart EE/E bonds, the minimum purchase is $25, with an annual maximum of $10,000. Interest continues to accrue for 30 years, and I bonds have the same redemption requirements as EE/E bonds.

Bond Price to Yield

Before we dive further into other types of bonds, it is important to note the way in which a price of a bond (what you pay for it) relates to its yield (or your overall return), specifically as it relates to its coupon rate. A bond's coupon rate is the stated rate of interest that the bond will be paying the bondholders, usually with semi-annual payments. For example, if you bought a $1,000 bond with a 5% coupon rate, your annual interest would be $50, and you would receive $25.00 twice a year. However, the coupon rate is not typically what you earn on your investment in a bond. Because bonds can be traded in security markets, their price will fluctuate, as often as every second.

Let's go through an example. Suppose you bought a bond from a local restaurant that is looking to expand. In order to entice you to give the restaurant your $1,000, which is the **par value**, or initial value associated with each bond, its owners tell you that they will pay you 10% interest annually (payments twice per year), and then in the 10th year, they will repay your $1,000 plus the last interest payment. In this situation, you will receive $50 twice a year ($100 total). Several months later you are at a coffee shop with your friends when the topic of local expansion comes up, and you hear that the restaurant has issued another round of bonds, only this time those bonds are paying 12% interest. Now you begin to wonder, "What happens now to my 10% bond?"

Unfortunately, you come to realize that your bond, which is receiving 10% interest, is of lower value than the new bonds paying 12%, thus making your bond less desirable. You know that due to the desirability of your bond going down, if you wanted to sell the bond to someone else, you would have to lower the price, because no one would pay full price ($1,000) for a 10% bond when they could pay $1,000 and get a 12% bond. After some contemplation, you recall that at the end of the 10 years, the owner of this bond will receive $1,000 back plus the last interest payment. You begin to think that if you lower the price of the bond, knowing someone is going to get the $1,000 back, then you could create a bond that is equivalent to earning 12% on

Par value The initial value associated with each bond when issued.

the bond. You recall your present value calculation equations and believe you can use that as a way to calculate and determine the new price of your bond:

Bond price at a discount = Coupon value $((1 - 1/(1 + I)^n)/I + M/(1 + I)^n$

Where,

Coupon value = Semiannual payments,
I = Current interest rate in the market,
M = Maturity value (or par value), and
N = Number of payments we expect to receive (years left × 2 payments per year)

When we replace our equation with actual numbers, we get the following equation:

Bond price at a discount = $50[1 - (1/(1.06)^{20})]/.06 + $1000/(1.06)^{20}$
Coupon value = $50 ($50 per year divided by 2 payments per year)
I = 6% (our annual rate expectation is 12%, but we receive semiannual payments, so we divide the annual rate by the number of payments we receive per year, 2 in our example)
M = $1,000
N = 20 (10 years × 2 payments per year

Thus, the bond price would be $885.15 if you wanted to sell it to someone and provide a current rate of return of 12%. This same philosophy would hold true if the current interest rates declined and were only 8%. In this case, your bond would be more valuable and would increase in price over and above the par value of $1,000.

U.S. Treasuries (Bills, Notes, and Bonds)

In addition to savings bonds, the U.S. government also issues three main securities, which are defined by their maturity, as follows:

Treasury Bills: Commonly referred to as "T-bills," Treasury bills are short-term government fixed-income securities that range in maturity from several days to up to 52 weeks (1 year). These securities are usually sold at a discount and redeemed at par value. The minimum purchase amount is $100, and purchases by institutions can range up to millions of dollars.

Treasury Notes: These fixed-income securities are intermediary in length, with 2-, 3-, 5-, 7-, and 10-year maturities. Treasury notes pay interest semiannually. As with T-bills, you can purchase Treasury notes with as little as $100.

The 10-year treasury note, however, holds some significance worthy of note (no pun intended!). The 10-year Treasury rate (yield) is oftentimes used as an index on which other rates are based, such as the mortgage rate. So if the 10-year Treasury rate drops, you will likely see a drop in the current mortgage rates. Additionally, the 10-year Treasury note has been used by some economists to evaluate investor confidence. As investors feel a sense of confidence or the desire to take on more risk, these investors will be less likely to buy safe government-backed securities, and thus the price of Treasury notes will fall. This implies that investors are not "playing it safe" and are seeking riskier investments, thus showing confidence in the ability to earn higher rates elsewhere. Conversely, when the demand for the 10-year Treasury note goes up and there are more investors in these bonds than usual, economists suggest that investors are fearful and are wanting to put their money in safer government-backed securities. This, in turn, indicates low confidence in the ability to earn a return in riskier assets.

Treasury Bonds: The final subset of bonds offered by the U.S. government is Treasury bonds, which are only issued in maturities of 30 years. Interest is paid semi-annually, and they can be purchased with a minimum investment of $100. Most Treasury bonds are purchased by corporate entities through an auction bid.

Municipal Bonds

Municipal bonds are bonds that are issued by municipalities (cities and counties), usually for capital to fund building or improvement projects in their districts. For example, suppose a city feels it needs to update its local hospital. The city may issue a bond that will raise money in order to pay for the hospital renovation. Municipal bonds are usually offered in two forms, revenue bonds or general obligation bonds. **Revenue bonds** are bonds issued by cities in which the funds are used to improve or create a structure that will generate revenue. The revenue generated will then be used to repay the bond. **General obligations bonds** (GO bonds) are bonds that do not have a revenue source and thus must be repaid by the ability of the municipality to tax its constituents (residents). In most cases, the residents must vote on whether to accept the raise of taxes and thus allow the issuance of the bonds by the municipality.

Municipal bonds carry a very special incentive for investors: In many cases, these bonds are tax-exempt from federal tax. In other words, the interest that is received from many municipal bonds will not be subject to being included in your income when determining your tax liability. In some cases, municipal bond interest may be exempt from state and local taxes as well.

The structure of municipal bonds is very broad in that cities and counties can issue bonds from only several years to up to 30 years in maturity. They also have flexibility in what rates they offer to attract investors to buy their bonds. Because each municipality is run differently, third-party rating agencies, such as Fitch, Standard and Poor's (S&P), and Moody's, offer an evaluation of a municipality's creditworthiness by analyzing its ability to make the debt obligation payments. An overview of these three rating agencies and their rating systems is provided in Table 15.2. When bonds are rated as investment grade, they are usually lower-risk bonds; bonds classified as speculative are bonds that are more risky, in other words, are more likely to default on their payments. In order to reduce any potential anxiety an investor may have regarding the financial stability of a municipality, many municipalities will buy insurance on their bonds in order to pay investors should they be unable to make their future payments.

Corporate Bonds

Companies can also issue bonds in order to help raise capital to finance expansion, to increase working capital, or to refinance existing debt. Corporate bonds work just as previously discussed for U.S. Treasury bonds and municipal bonds. Because the federal government and municipalities have the power to tax and pay off debt, Treasury securities and municipal bonds are lower-risk bonds and thus carry lower prevailing interest rates. Companies, on the other hand, are considered more risky than the government and municipalities. In order to help reduce the interest rate, corporations have the ability to entice potential investors to buy their bonds by offering incentives such as the option to convert their bonds to equity shares, called **convertible corporate bonds**, or attach warrants to the bonds. **Warrants**, in finance, are securities that allow the owner to buy the underlying stock at a specific price (known as the exercise price) for a certain period of time.

Revenue bond Bonds issued by cities in which the funds are used to improve or create a structure that will generate revenue.

General obligation bonds (GO bonds) Bonds that do not have a revenue source and thus must be repaid through the ability of the municipality to tax its constituents (residents).

Convertible corporate bonds Corporate bonds that have the ability to be converted into a specific number of equity shares by the issuer of the bond.

Warrants Securities that allow the owner to buy the underlying stock at a specific price (known as the exercise price) for a certain period of time.

Table 15.2 Rating Agency Chart

Fitch	S&P	Moody's	Rating grade description (Moody's)	
AAA	AAA	Aaa	Investment grade	Minimal credit risk
AA+	AA+	Aa1		Very low credit risk
AA	AA	Aa2		
AA-	AA-	Aa3		
A+	A+	A1		Low credit risk
A	A	A2		
A-	A-	A3		
BBB+	BBB+	Baa1		Moderate credit risk
BBB	BBB	Baa2		
BBB-	BBB-	Baa3		
BB+	BB+	Ba1	Speculative grade	Substantial credit risk
BB	BB	Ba2		
BB-	BB-	Ba3		
B+	B+	B1		High credit risk
B	B	B2		
B-	B-	B3		
CCC+	CCC+	Caa1		Very high credit risk
CCC	CCC	Caa2		
CCC-	CCC-	Caa3		
CC	CC	Ca		In or near default, with possibility of recovery
C	C			
DDD	SD	C		In default, with little chance of recovery
DD	D			
D				

Courtesy of VerticalScope Inc.

Source: http://www.thetruthaboutcars.com/wp-content/uploads/2013/09/zoi_2011_IV_box_2_tab_1_en.gif

Courtesy of daniilantiq2010/Fotolia.

DISCIPLESHIP MOMENT AND REFLECTION

If you had your choice, what types of investments would you feel comfortable investing in—stocks? bonds? CDs? What other types of investments make you uncomfortable? Talk to your prayer and accountability partner about each of these types of assets and get his or her opinion.

HARD ASSETS, HARD CHOICES

> Take my instruction, and not silver, and knowledge rather than choicest gold. (Proverbs 8:10)

Gold and silver are mentioned frequently in the Bible. As precious and valuable as they are, they are nothing when compared to the attributes of God. Even so, history has shown that God knew what He was talking about when He placed a special significance on gold and silver. Over the centuries, they have always signified wealth.

When you listen to the business news, two indicators of our economy are frequently mentioned: the changes in the Dow Jones Industrial Average (DJIA) and the

Courtesy of marilyn barbone/Fotolia.

current price of gold. One reason gold is so important is that it is used as a barometer to indicate the direction people think our economy is going; second, it gives a tangible measure of wealth.

There are typically two strategies when purchasing gold and silver, as an investment opportunity and/or as a wealth preservation tactic. The first strategy is buying and trading it for investment purposes. Precious metals are traded in the commodity markets, which are markets focused on trading primary products, such as gas, coal, gold, silver, and sugar, to name a few, and can be very speculative (risky) investments due to the fact that should an investment not be watched carefully, you could end up with tons of sugar, for example, on your doorstep.

The second strategy of buying gold as a "wealth preserver" is a valid one. Gold will protect your purchasing power in times of runaway inflation or help to protect your assets in times of market fear. As people become fearful, they will begin to buy hard assets such as gold and silver, which in turn will increase in value during times of unease.

One of the challenging questions for someone seeking to buy gold or silver is, "Where do I store these metals?" There are three main options. First, when you buy gold you have the option to take possession of your metal and store it where you feel comfortable. Many investors may decide to store it in a bank safety deposit box or in a home safe, or bury it in the backyard (although we don't recommend that!). The second option is to have your broker store the metals on your behalf. You will receive a "receipt" that shows your ownership; the receipt will usually have some identification numbers that match those of the physical gold or silver stored on your behalf. Finally, if you are unsure of whether you want to buy the actual hard assets of gold and silver, you may decide to invest in a mutual fund or other investment vehicle that tracks the price of gold, such as the Gold Index Exchange Traded Fund (ETF) with the ticker GLD.

Real Estate

Investing in real estate can be another option for investors. Specifically, real estate investing offers the potential for both income from rents and capital gains from the sale of the property at a future date. Unfortunately, real estate investing has demonstrated that, although contrary to what many property owners and investors want, real estate is just as susceptible to wide swings in valuations, as seen in the housing bubble crisis of 2007 through 2009, when people were thinking that real estate would never go down in value.

The asset class of real estate can include many different types of property, such as the following:

- Homes
- Multifamily units
- Apartment buildings
- Undeveloped land
- Commercial property
- Shopping centers
- Warehouses
- Office buildings

In many cases the motivation to invest in real estate is primarily for the rent income that is generated from the contract between the renter and owner of the property. These agreements can be short in nature, month to month, for example, for an apartment complex, to 10- or 15-year contracts for office space. Although real estate can offer the investor both an income stream and price appreciation, the most significant disadvantage is the substantial amount of capital it takes in order to participate in these types of investments.

In the mid-1960s, legislative changes allowed for average investors to participate in real estate investments through the development of a product called a real estate investment trust, or REIT. REITs, similar to mutual funds, pool capital from many different investors and acquire real estate for a portfolio. The income generated by this portfolio of real estate investments is then distributed to those owning shares in the REIT. There are lots of different types of REITs, some that invest exclusively in office buildings and others that invest in shopping malls, for example, so some research is required as to what type of real estate an investor is interested in prior to investing.

There are three basic types of REITs in which you can invest:

- Equity REITs
  - Equity REITs invest in income-producing real estate, as mentioned earlier.
- Mortgage REITs
  - Mortgage REITs focus on the loans or debts that are attributed to real estate, such as construction loans and mortgage loans.
- Hybrid REITs
  - Hybrid REITs are a combination of equity and mortgage REITs.

REITs are required by the tax code to distribute 90% of the income to their shareholders, which is part of the reason that REITs offer higher yields or returns for the investors who seek to generate income. Furthermore, REITs can help create a more diversified portfolio for investors than that attainable just through stocks and bonds. Real estate has a completely different set of reasons for the rise and fall in prices as compared with stocks and bonds, thus minimizing how much these stocks will go up or down in price at the same time, which is what is referred to as correlation.

Correlation is the relationship (and the strength of that relationship) between two investments. In a portfolio of investments, assets that are not highly correlated (do not move together) are preferable to a portfolio comprised of assets that all move in the same direction at the same time. An example of a correlated portfolio would be owning both Apple stock and Microsoft stock. Both will decline if computer or technology changes, and both will go up with technology advancement (although not at the same rate). Therefore, a better option might be to own Apple stock and Bank of America stock. One company is focused on technology and the other on financial services. If the technology industry changes, either positively or negatively, the impact on Bank of America mostly likely will not be correlated. Real estate holdings can help create this type of diversification.

Correlation The relationship (and strength of that relationship) between two investments.

INVESTMENT ACCOUNTS

In the previous section we looked at various types of investments, such as stocks, mutual funds, and various fixed-income investments, and reviewed a few types of nontraditional investments, such as gold and silver and real estate. But it is important to also have an understanding as to the types of accounts that are used to not only hold these types of investments but also to allow investors to buy and sell these securities. We will focus our attention on two main types of accounts: nonqualified (taxable accounts) and qualified accounts (tax-deferred accounts). We will also discuss annuities and their characteristics.

It's important to understand that the investments (as reviewed up to this point) are distinct from the accounts in which those investments are transacted. Many people, in their dialog regarding finances, can easily get these two components confused. For example, we would not say, "I'm selling my IRA to pay for my school tuition," but rather, "I'm selling the investments inside my IRA and will be closing my IRA to pay my tuition bill." The IRA is an account, not something that is sold or bought. Hopefully, this will become clearer as we go over the types of accounts.

Nonqualified Accounts

Most all people have nonqualified accounts. Accounts such as checking accounts and savings accounts are nonqualified. What does that mean? **Nonqualified accounts** are accounts that are not qualified, or eligible, to receive special tax considerations under the tax code of the Internal Revenue Service (IRS). In relation to investments, these accounts can usually buy and sell all types of investments; however, the income and capital gains received from the investments inside a taxable account will be subject to the marginal tax rate of the account holder, or holders if the account is jointly owned.

In the mid-1970s, individual retirement accounts (IRAs) were established within the legislative act of the Employee Retirement Income and Security Act (ERISA) due to several large companies mismanaging their employee pension funds. These accounts were established in order to transition from a **defined benefit plan**, a retirement plan that provides a set benefit to employees upon retirement for the rest of their lives, to that of a **defined contribution plan**, where employees are allowed to control or direct their own contributions and fund selections. These defined contribution plans, however, do not provide a specific level of benefit to the employee. The benefits are contingent upon the performance of the funds selected and the total amount contributed by the employee.

Qualified Accounts

Qualified accounts, commonly referred to as tax-deferred accounts, do have special tax considerations attached to them. There are several categories of qualified accounts, as follows:

- Traditional IRA: A traditional IRA, normally just called an IRA, is a type of retirement account that is funded with pre-tax dollars (dollars that have not be taxed) and used for withdrawals during retirement. The IRS allows a taxpayer to deduct contributions to retirement accounts in order to help incentivize people to save for their retirements. In 2016, individuals with earned income could deduct contributions of up to $5,500 toward an IRA. Several exceptions must be noted:
  - A spouse of a working employee may also contribute to an IRA even if the spouse is not employed. A joint tax return must be filed in order to do this.
  - If you are over the age of 50, you may deduct contributions up to $6,500. You are ineligible to contribute to an IRA after the age of 70½.
  - You have up to April 15 of the following year to contribute to an IRA and deduct the contribution on your current year's tax return.

Table 15.3   2015 IRA Deduction Phase-Out Schedule

If Your Filing Status Is . . .	And Your Modified AGI Is . . .	Then You Can Take . . .
Single or head of household	$61,000 or less	a full deduction up to the amount of your contribution limit
	more than $61,000 but less than $71,000	a partial deduction
	$71,000 or more	no deduction
Married filing jointly or qualifying widow(er)	$98,000 or less	a full deduction up to the amount of your contribution limit
	more than $98,000 but less than $118,000	a partial deduction
	$118,000 or more	no deduction
Married filing separately	less than $10,000	a partial deduction
	$10,000 or more	no deduction

If you file separately and did not live with your spouse at any time during the year, your IRA deduction is determined under the "Single" filing status.

Source: https://www.irs.gov/Retirement-Plans/2015-IRA-Deduction-Limits-Effect-of-Modified-AGI-on-Deduction-if-You-Are-Covered-by-a-Retirement-Plan-at-Work

The deductibility of IRA contributions, unfortunately, is phased out when someone makes over a specified amount of money. See Table 15.3 for 2015 phase-out limits.

- Roth Individual Retirement Account (Roth IRA): In the late 1990s, Senator William Roth Jr. from Delaware introduced the Roth IRA. Characteristics of Roth IRAs are as follows:
  - A Roth IRA allows taxpayers to contribute to their retirement accounts with after-tax dollars with the ability to withdraw or make qualified distributions tax-free.
  - If distributions from the Roth IRA are taken before 59½ years of age, the distribution may receive a 10% early withdrawal penalty on the gains.
  - You must have earned income, but only up to certain limits.
  - Contribution amounts match those for a traditional IRA.
  - Contribution deadlines match those for a traditional IRA.
  - The original owner is not required to take out distributions.
- Rollover Individual Retirement Account (RIRA): When an employee leaves a company and has a balance in his or her retirement plan at the former place of employment, the employee can roll the funds into a RIRA. The characteristics of rollovers match those of traditional IRAs or Roth IRAs for whichever type of rollover it is. The reason it is important to keep these funds separated is that these funds will be eligible to be put back into a new company retirement plan at a future date. The funds, however, cannot be intermingled with traditional IRA funds or Roth IRA funds in order to complete the transfer to a new company retirement plan such as a 401(k).
- 401(k)/403(b) Retirement Accounts: Created under section 401(k) of the IRS tax code, 401(k) accounts are employer-sponsored retirement plans in which

employees are permitted, up to certain limits, to contribute pre-tax or post-tax earnings designed specifically for retirement. In many cases, employers will also contribute to these employee accounts, either as a flat percentage of their income or by matching specific amounts of employee contributions, or some combination of the two. The maximum allowable contribution to 401(k) accounts in 2015 was $18,000 ($23,000 for those over the age of 50).

Many public schools, nonprofit organizations, and certain tax-exempt organizations, such as churches, offer 403(b) plans, which are also known as tax-sheltered annuities (TSAs). These plans will usually consist of one of three different formats:

- An annuity contract provided by an insurance company
- A custodial account in which the employee can buy certain mutual funds
- A retirement account that allows for a combination of annuities and mutual funds

These accounts usually will follow the same contribution and distribution limits as those of a traditional IRA. At this point, there does not exist a Roth version of a 403(b) account.

- 529 College Savings Accounts: The 529 college savings accounts is another form of qualified account that receives special tax incentives. 529 plans are established individually by each state, but 529 plans usually have the following characteristics:
  - Proceeds are tax-free if they are used for qualified higher education expenses, such as room and board and tuition.
  - Many states will also provide a state tax deduction for contributions made to a 529 plan.
  - One special component of 529 plans is that a husband and wife can use 5 years' worth of the annual gift tax exclusion ($170,000 for 2015) to fund a 529 plan. In other words, a husband can give to his son $85,000 into a 529 plan for his education. If he does this, though, he cannot make any gifts to his son for the next 5 years. Each spouse has the ability to do this, which could allow for up to $170,000 of contributions for a husband and wife to a 529 account per beneficiary (or each child).

SOCIALLY RESPONSIBLE INVESTING, OR VALUES-BASED INVESTING

In recent decades, more investors are concerned about investing surplus dollars in a way that reflects their values. Their main concern is to avoid "ill-gotten gains," or profits from companies engaged in immoral activities.

Ethical or socially conscious investing can mean different things to different people. Generally it involves following one's moral principles in choosing specific investments. For example, in the 1980s some sincere groups refused to invest in companies with ties to South Africa during the tenure of the government that enforced apartheid policies. Another equally sincere group didn't find South African investments objectionable. Some people want to invest only in companies that are environmentally responsible. Most mutual funds available today for those concerned with "socially responsible investing" tend to be focused on the more liberal political spectrum.

More recently, Christians have expressed interest in investing according to their values. Rather than socially responsible investing, a more reasonable term is to call this *values-based investing*. **Values-based investing** is the idea that investors can incorporate their values and personal convictions by aligning those values with

Values-based investing
The idea that investors can incorporate their values and personal convictions by aligning those values with the companies they invest in.

Courtesy of Ian Law/Fotolia.

the companies they invest in. Traditionally, most Christians do not want any of their money invested directly in companies with operations in alcohol, tobacco, gambling, or pornography. Some have opposed investments in China, Sudan, or Iran.

Is there a pure values-based biblical investment? No, because we live in a fallen, imperfect world. When the prospect arises that we have found the perfectly pure Christian investment, somebody usually will remind us of its flaws. Thus, we find that we must put a degree to the value in which we invest, because no company will be perfect.

Although no investment will be perfect, we can utilize certain screeners that can help guide and direct our investment decisions. One resource that you should consider as a Christian is the Biblically Responsible Investing Institute (BRII), which is an organization that helps guide investors so that they can stay away from companies that might be directly against the values of a Christian worldview. Specifically, the BRII describes itself as follows:

> An investment research firm that examines publically-traded companies for involvement in ten areas: abortion, alcohol, anti-family activity, bioethics, gambling, human rights, low-income financial services, pornography, tobacco, and the homosexual agenda. Although other business activities could be included, BRII has identified these areas as clearly conflicting with biblical values. The alcohol, gaming, and tobacco industries profit from man's addictions and weaknesses. Abortion, bioethics, and human rights relate to the sanctity of life. Pornography, anti-family activity and homosexuality undermine marriage and the family, while advancing destructive and impure lifestyles. (BRII, p. 1, http://www.briinstitute.com/about.htm)

Although the goal is the same—investing according to one's principles—the implementation varies greatly. Many may find owning stock in a distillery objectionable. But many would not be uncomfortable investing in a company that makes and sells bottles to various customers, one of which is a whiskey maker. The problem is that when one attempts to invest responsibly, it can drift toward legalism. The danger of legalism is that we begin to substitute outward behavior for inward faith and obedience.

THE BIBLICAL APPROACH

What does the Bible say about ethical investing? First, we need to consider two types of investments: active and passive. Active investments are those in which we are actively owning or participating in the management of a business. If the purpose of that business is clearly not honoring God, then we have a real problem. A second problem to consider is to be in partnership with an immoral non-Christian, and therefore be unequally yoked (2 Corinthians 6:14). Someone who is yoked can be controlled, and no one should be controlled by an investment or business partner who would force compromise.

God gives us obvious guidelines on how to allocate our resources in activities in which we are actively involved to make a profit. But what about passive investing—those investments you have no control over? Passive investments—such as a mutual fund, real estate property, or bank—with a stated purpose that does not disagree with any of God's principles and whose only "violations" are solely incidental to the operation of the investment should be prayerfully considered. Remember, we have been given the Spirit of Truth (John 16:13), so we need to seek the Lord in prayer and know that the Spirit will guide our thoughts and actions toward what is in the will of the Lord.

A PRACTICAL APPROACH

Unfortunately, all Christians may not see the same way on this issue, and that is okay. As we just said, the Spirit should be our guiding light, and He will direct us (Proverbs 3:5–6). Recall, also, Paul's words in Romans 14 that address this idea of believers not agreeing in areas that do not conflict with scriptural doctrine. Romans 14:5 says, "One man considers one day more sacred than another; another man considers every day alike. Each one should be fully convinced in his own mind."

How can we approach this subject practically? First, we should realize that we are *in the* world but not of it. God has given Christians a soul mind in which to deal with the world (2 Timothy 1:7). For instance, we should actively avoid business partnerships and investments in which the stated purposes are not acceptable to God. In passive investments, however, use common sense. Find a bank with a good reputation in the community. Ask a bank officer about the types of loans the bank makes. Find out if the bank has ever been involved in a scandal. When investing in a mutual fund, realize that you are insulated from the management decisions of that fund. Look for funds with a widely diversified portfolio that have dealt honestly and ethically with their shareholders over a long time. If you are investing in real estate, ask the general partner or manager what types of tenants have rented the office building, apartment complex, or shopping center. Perhaps the manager's standards are the same as yours. Consider undeveloped land as an investment because it has no tenants.

Above all, make a positive investment of your time. People often worry about what not to do so much that they don't actively invest even an hour a week in an activity that can have a significant impact in their sphere of influence.

Finally, avoid legalism and tunnel vision. Recognize that we do live in an imperfect world. Your passive investments are merely a tool to provide you returns that will ultimately go to fulfill the Great Commission.

SUMMARY

This chapter seeks to provide an understanding of the "grow" section of our pie chart. The first part of the chapter reviewed and explained the six fundamental time-value-of-money problems: future value calculations and present value calculations, and equal and unequal cash flows. Next, we transitioned into the sequential investing diagram in order to show the appropriate use of margin funds prior to investing. We then looked at an overview of stocks, or equity, and highlighted the two fundamental investing rationales, income and capital gains. We then explored risk and how some risk can be minimized through mutual funds and diversification. Eight basic rules were given to help in making appropriate investment choices. We then transitioned into various types of fixed-income securities, where we focused mainly on government, municipal, and corporate bonds. We provided an overview of other asset classes, such as real estate and commodities, and how those investments can be used in an investment portfolio. This chapter also provided an overview of the different types of accounts in which investments can be held and traded. Finally, we ended by looking at the biblical and practical applications of investing.

SUMMARY REVIEW QUESTIONS

1. What is the purpose of the time-value-of-money formulas?

2. What information do you need to compute a FV calculation of a single PV sum?

3. How can knowing the TVM formulas help in setting long-term financial goals?

4. What are the five steps in the sequential investing chart? Explain each step.

5. How does Proverbs 24:27 shed light on the sequential investing process?

6. What are the two reasons investments should be made?

7. Why would a diamond ring and a car not be considered investments?

8. Provide a brief overview of what stocks represent to an investor.

9. In what ways do stocks provide an investor a return?

10. How do you calculate the return on an investment?

11. List different types of risk that investors may face by investing in stocks.

12. How can risk be minimized while investing?

13. What is the difference between value and growth investing?

14. What are the eight investment guidelines mentioned in the chapter?

15. List the 12 different sectors within the U.S. stock market.

16. List several of the fixed-income securities mentioned in the chapter and provide an overview of those securities.

17. Explain the relationship between bond prices and interest rates (yields).

18. What is significant about the 10-year U.S. Treasury note?

19. What are the two types of municipal bonds? What is the difference between the two?

20. What do rating agencies provide to investors in fixed-income securities?

21. List at least five types of real estate property that an investor can invest in.

22. What are the three basic types of REITs? What differentiates them?

23. Provide an overview of the three account types that allow an investor to hold and trade securities.

24. Describe the differences between socially responsible investing and values-based investing.

Case Study Analysis

As they drove home from church, Bob begin to reflect on Pastor Steve's message in relation to following Christ.

"Honey," Bob said as he turned to Debbie, "do you think we can take what Steve said today literally? I know that he was talking about how we must count the cost to us as we seek to follow Christ, but as he was talking about it, and with us going through building a solid financial plan with Steve, it really got me thinking about all the things we want to do—for our retirement, the kids, and so forth."

He paused.

"I don't see why not," Debbie replied. "So much of the Bible can be applied to our lives because it is a living document."

"After dinner tonight, let's sit down and go over some of our main goals, and let's 'count the cost,'" Bob said.

"Okay. While you are getting everything ready, I need to start baking a pie for Clara's 4H event on Monday night."

Later, as they sat down at the table after dinner, Bob began to jot down all of their goals.

Assignment

Determine the outcome using time-value-of-money calculations to see if Bob and Debbie can complete their financial goals, which they stated as follows:

- Be able to generate $36,000/year from my retirement accounts for 30 years, ending with a $0 balance.
  - Use the balance sheet to determine the starting value of Bob and Debbie's total retirement funds.
  - Anticipate an annual rate of return of 8%.
  - Bob is putting aside $11,000 annually ($917/month), and his employer is matching his contributions dollar for dollar of up to 4% of his annual salary of $167,480.
  - Hint: Determine future value and then use that as present value to determine payment amount.

- Provide 5 years of undergraduate school for Chloe and Clara at $18,000 per year.
  - Chloe has 2 years until college.
  - Clara has 4 years until college (she also has a $10,000 scholarship, which should reduce the amount she requires for school).
  - No college fund was established, but you can use Bob and Debbie's taxable account statement from the Case Study as the present value.
  - The interest rate that those funds will earn is 8%.
  - Assume no educational inflation because the need to fund college is only a few years away.
  - Bob and Debbie put away $500 per month in this account to save for their children's college.
  - Hint: Determine future value when Chloe starts school and then use this as present value to determine 2 years of payments. Then use the new value (after 2 years of payments) as the new present value to include the 2 years both girls are in school. Then do present value calculations one more time to finish Clara's school costs. Also, Clara will use the $10,000 scholarship for books and supplies, so you do not need to include that in your calculation.

DEFINITIONS

Accrued interest (p. 365)

Business cycle (p. 355)

Business risk (p. 359)

Capital gains (p. 357)

Convertible corporate bonds (p. 368)

Correlation (p. 371)

Defined benefit plan (p. 371)

Defined contribution plan (p. 371)

Diversification (p. 359)

Dividends (p. 358)

General obligation bonds (GO bonds) (p. 367)

Growth investment (p. 361)

Intrinsic value (p. 361)

Investment portfolio (p. 359)

Market risk (p. 359)

Nonqualified account (p. 371)

Par value (p. 365)

Revenue bond (p. 367)

Systematic risk (p. 359)

Unsystematic risk (p. 359)

Value investment (p. 361)

Values-based investing (p. 374)

Volatility (p. 358)

Warrants (p. 368)

SCRIPTURE VERSES (ESV)

Proverbs 24:27—Put your outdoor work in order and get your fields ready; after that, build your house.

Proverbs 31:16—She considers a field and buys it; with the fruit of her hands she plants a vineyard.

2 Timothy 2:6—It is the hard-working farmer who ought to have the first share of the crops.

Matthew 25:14–30—For it will be like a man going on a journey, who called his servants and entrusted to them his property. To one he gave five talents, to another two, to another one, to each according to his ability. Then he went away. He who had received the five talents went at once and traded with them, and he made five talents more. So also he who had the two talents made two talents more. But he who had received the one talent went and dug in the ground and hid his master's money. Now after a long time the master of those servants came and settled accounts with them. And he who had received the five talents came forward, bringing five talents more, saying, "Master, you delivered to me five talents; here I have made five talents more." His master said to him, "Well done, good and faithful servant. You have been faithful over a little; I will set you over much. Enter into the joy of your master." And he also who had the two talents came forward, saying, "Master, you delivered to me two talents; here I have made two talents more." His master said to him, "Well done, good and faithful servant. You have been faithful over a little; I will set you over much. Enter into the joy of your master." He also who had received the one talent came forward, saying, "Master, I knew you to be a hard man, reaping where you did not sow, and gathering where you scattered no seed, so I was afraid, and I went and hid your talent in the ground. Here you have what is yours." But his master answered him, "You wicked and slothful servant! You knew that I reap where I have not sown and gather where I scattered no seed? Then you ought to have invested my money with the bankers, and at my coming I should have received what was my own with interest. So take the talent from him and give it to him who has the ten talents. For to everyone who has will more be given, and he will have an abundance. But from the one who has not, even what he has will be taken away. And cast the worthless servant into the outer darkness. In that place there will be weeping and gnashing of teeth."

Proverbs 22:26–27—Be not one of those who give pledges, who put up security for debts. If you have nothing with which to pay, why should your bed be taken from under you?

Proverbs 30:25—[T]he ants are a people not strong, yet they provide their food in the summer.

Proverbs 22:9—Whoever has a bountiful eye will be blessed, for he shares his bread with the poor.

1 Timothy 6:9—But those who desire to be rich fall into temptation, into a snare, into many senseless and harmful desires that plunge people into ruin and destruction.

Proverbs 16:5—Everyone who is arrogant in heart is an abomination to the LORD; be assured, he will not go unpunished.

Proverbs 18:11—A rich man's wealth is his strong city, and like a high wall in his imagination.

Matthew 6:25—Therefore I tell you, do not be anxious about your life, what you will eat or what you will drink, nor about your body, what you will put on. Is not life more than food, and the body more than clothing?

Philippians 4:6–7—Do not be anxious about anything, but in everything by prayer and supplication with thanksgiving let your requests be made known to God. And the peace of God, which surpasses all understanding, will guard your hearts and your minds in Christ Jesus.

Proverbs 8:10—Take my instruction instead of silver, and knowledge rather than choice gold

ADDITIONAL READINGS

Adams, G. A., & Rau, B. L. (2011). Putting off tomorrow to do what you want today: Planning for retirement. *American Psychologist, 66*(3), 180.

Bodie, Z., Detemple, J. B., Otruba, S., & Walter, S. (2004). Optimal consumption—portfolio choices and retirement planning. *Journal of Economic Dynamics and Control, 28*(6), 1115–1148.

Brown, J. R. (2007). *Rational and behavioral perspectives on the role of annuities in retirement planning* (No. w13537). Washington, DC: National Bureau of Economic Research.

Elder, H. W., & Rudolph, P. M. (1999). Does retirement planning affect the level of retirement satisfaction? *Financial Services Review, 8*(2), 117–127.

Gleeson, T., Alley, W. M., Allen, D. M., Sophocleous, M. A., Zhou, Y., Taniguchi, M., & VanderSteen, J. (2012). Towards sustainable groundwater use: Setting long-term goals, backcasting, and managing adaptively. *Ground Water, 50*(1), 19–26.

Harackiewicz, J. M., Barron, K. E., Tauer, J. M., Carter, S. M., & Elliot, A. J. (2000). Short-term and long-term consequences of achievement goals: Predicting interest and performance over time. *Journal of Educational Psychology, 92*(2), 316.

Kosloski, K., Ekerdt, D., & DeViney, S. (2001). The role of job-related rewards in retirement planning. *The Journals of Gerontology Series B: Psychological Sciences and Social Sciences, 56*(3), P160–P169.

Lusardi, A., & Mitchell, O. S. (2007). Financial literacy and retirement planning: New evidence from the Rand American Life Panel. *Michigan Retirement Research Center Research Paper No. WP, 157.*

Taylor-Carter, M. A., Cook, K., & Weinberg, C. (1997). Planning and expectations of the retirement experience. *Educational Gerontology: An International Quarterly, 23*(3), 273–288.

Topa, G., Moriano, J. A., Depolo, M., Alcover, C. M., & Morales, J. F. (2009). Antecedents and consequences of retirement planning and decision-making: A meta-analysis and model. *Journal of Vocational Behavior, 75*(1), 38–55.

Van Rooij, M. C., Lusardi, A., & Alessie, R. J. (2012). Financial literacy, retirement planning and household wealth. *The Economic Journal, 122*(560), 449–478.

Chapter 16

Transcendent Principle 5: Give Generously

Courtesy of Monkey Business/Fotolia.

BIG IDEA:
Giving generously breaks the power of money.

LEARNING OUTCOMES

- Understand why, as Christians, we should give

- List and describe five good reasons to give

- Learn a five-step process that can guide you in establishing a giving plan

- Describe how giving was crucial in a biblical context (Widow's mite) and a current example (Jack and Lisa)

- Explain the ladder of giving

Introduction

Giving is the second piece of the pie in the live, give, owe, grow construct for allocating resources. Even though *give* is listed second in this construct, it is the most important piece of the pie for Christians. It is the piece that should be determined first before any of the other pieces are considered. God commanded the Israelites to give their first fruits to the Lord (**Leviticus 23:9–14**) as an act of recognition of God's provision and sovereignty. Paul also instructed the Corinthian church to set aside something at the beginning of each week so that there would be money available (**1 Corinthians 16:2**). Similar to the understanding of the Israelites and Paul, it is important for Christians to give to God their offerings (giving) first before committing other money to other purposes. This habit and practice has a way of recognizing God's ownership and our thanksgiving.

The secret to financial contentment is not couched in wise investments, meticulous budgets, or debt-free living. All these things are valuable—yet even the highest investment return or the most carefully constructed budget affords very little in the way of real confidence and joy if one key ingredient is neglected. That one ingredient—and the ingredient that makes true freedom possible—is generosity: the willingness to give your time, talents, and material wealth to benefit others and impact eternity.

Understanding what giving is and what the Bible tells us about giving is important to being able to prayerfully allocate resources to the "give" piece of the pie. This chapter discusses the biblical basis for giving and helps you understand what the Bible actually teaches on the topic of giving.

THE TREASURE PRINCIPLE

In order to understand nearly everything that the Bible teaches about giving, one must understand one of the most significant verses in the Bible: Matthew 6:21. It says, "For where your treasure is, there your heart will be also." Your treasure in this verse refers to the thing or things that are most important to you. Maybe it's a job promotion, a new house, or a new car. Maybe you want to get married or have a child. Maybe you just need a vacation, and you dream about soft white beaches and vibrant sunsets. Regardless of your particular passion, your treasure is what you think about, what you go after, what you want to attain. It's what your heart longs for.

Two stories from the Bible shed tremendous light on how you can identify where your heart is. The first story is from Matthew 19:16–22. In this story, a rich young man came up to Jesus to discern what he needed to do to inherit eternal life. After asking the man about keeping the commandments from the Old Testament and determining that he is a follower of the law, Jesus tells him that if he wants to inherit eternal life and have treasure in heaven, he must sell all he possesses and give it to the poor. The man goes away sad and presumably does not follow Jesus's instructions. The second story is from Mark 12:41–44. In this story, Jesus was watching people give money to the temple, and He saw a poor widow give a few pennies, which was all that she had. After seeing this, Jesus remarked that the widow gave more than anyone else because she gave out of her poverty.

From these two stories, it is plain to see where the treasures are for the main characters. The rich young man treasures his earthly riches more than inheriting eternal life, and the poor widow treasures eternity more than she does her daily comfort. Further, it is easy to conclude that the heart of the widow was fully devoted to God and that the heart of the rich man was devoted to his earthly possessions. These two stories offer great illustrations as to what it looks like to place our treasure in God and how when that is true, our money practically follows our hearts.

Why should you store up treasures in heaven instead of on earth? Is it because things on earth are bad? No, it is because the things in heaven are so much better and the things on earth will not last. Everything on earth is going to end up at the dump. No matter what it is, how shiny it is, how innovative it is, over time, everything ends up in the garbage and wastes away. There is only one place where moth and rust do not destroy: heaven. Isn't it much better to store up treasures in a place where they will last and have eternal consequence rather than investing in things that are just pre-trash?

Why was Christ so eager to separate the rich young man from his money? Was He holding out the promise of heaven like a carrot, as the ultimate fundraising gimmick? The Bible never applauds an accumulator. Over and over again, God's praise is reserved for the giver. With the rich young man, Jesus knew he was wealthy and that he had placed his trust in his own wallet. Until he could bring himself to part with that financial security blanket, the rich young man would never be free to place his trust in Christ. He would never know the true riches and security of eternal life.

Like the rich young man, you have a choice to make. Will you control your money, or will it control you? Our tendency, particularly during financially trying times, is to want to hang on to what we have. As we do that, though, we transfer our trust further and further away from God and deeper and deeper into our own inadequate resources.

How should you store up treasures in heaven? 1 Timothy 6:18–19 (NIV), in speaking of those who are rich, tells us: "Command them to do good, to be rich in good deeds, and to be generous and willing to share. In this way they will lay up treasure for themselves as a firm foundation for the coming age, so that they may take hold of the life that is truly life." We are all rich and should take to heart these words from Paul to Timothy regarding how we can store up treasures in heaven.

Ron's Corner

Looking back, I can honestly say that there was a time when my treasure was couched in the recognition and success I achieved in business. When I became a Christian, though, those priorities began to change. My heart turned toward my family, and I began to think more about their eternal destiny than about our material needs and desires. My heart—and my treasure—was no longer bound up in money and worldly ambition.

What about you? God knows your heart can't be devoted both to him and to wealth or material pursuits. You cannot, as Matthew 6:24 puts it, serve both God and money. God does not say it's difficult to serve both. He does not say we should try really hard to serve both. He says it's impossible to serve both. You must make a choice.

God asks you to give because he wants your heart. Your behavior says a lot about what you truly believe. How do you feel about giving? Do you really believe God loves a cheerful giver and that He will reward your generosity? Can you hold your treasure—your money, your possession, your time, your talents—with an open hand? Are you willing to give Him your heart?

If your answers to questions like these point to a need for a change, you need to know that the transformation will come as a process. Generosity doesn't happen overnight. But God does promise us this: If we seek Him first, and keep on seeking Him first, everything else—food, clothing, and all of our needs—will be taken care of (see Mathew 6:33).

All God asks is that we be good stewards of the resources He gives us. Understanding our role as a steward is a very practical manifestation of living out the treasure principle. It is saying that our treasure is in God and we are willing to do whatever He asks of us. Good stewardship means making wise decisions regarding how you use your money—from how much you spend on your children to how you maximize the effectiveness of your contributions to church and God's work.

The idea of stewardship and the treasure principle is not to get you to simply empty your pockets. Nor is it to hand you some kind of magic number of formula to allow you to figure your "tithe." Instead, this chapter seeks to teach you to give generously and wisely. God asks us to give. Our job is to step out in obedience and faith.

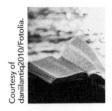

Courtesy of daniilantiq2010/Fotolia.

DISCIPLESHIP MOMENT AND REFLECTION

Take a few minutes to think about the things you treasure most in the world. Write down where you think your treasure is currently and write down where you believe God wants it to be. Share these reflections with your prayer and accountability partner.

Why Should You Give?

From a purely financial perspective, giving never really "makes sense," because we always have less money after we've given than before we've given. Nevertheless, there are many studies and spiritual philosophies (beyond just the Christian one) that encourage giving as a means to satisfaction or fulfillment for the giver. The Bible encourages us to give as a way to break the power of money, as a means of laying up treasure in heaven, as a way to gain an eternal perspective, as a way to recognize God's ownership, and as a means of obedience.

Financial contentment and freedom begins with a willingness to give. The poor widow recognized this principle, and in making her resources available to God, she received a liberating and eternal reward. Giving should be an integral part of every maturing believer's life. Giving is commanded in Scripture, for the benefit of both the giver and the recipient. This advantage is readily available to each one of us once we discover exactly why, and how, we should give.

The money-management objectives we have considered so far in this textbook are logical supports in a well-built financial plan. Giving, however, is often relegated to a discretionary category. It becomes no more than a noble pursuit that can be postponed until later when funds "become available." Yet financial contentment and freedom begin with giving. Giving should not be merely a pillar in your financial plan; it should be the cornerstone.

Ron's Corner

I've learned and clearly observed that generosity and financial freedom are inextricably linked. The Bible supports this principle. "Give, and it will be given to you," promises Luke 6:38. "He who gives to the poor will lack nothing," says Proverbs 28:27. And, according to 2 Corinthians 9:6–7, "Whoever sows generously will also reap generously . . . for God loves a cheerful giver."

The folks who enjoy genuine contentment and freedom are those who give the most, relative to their incomes. Giving is more than just a way to use your money. It is a lifestyle, a way of living that allows you to hold all that you own—including your time and your talents—with an open, generous hand.

This chapter about giving is designed to get you to that place. I want to challenge you, philosophically, to evaluate your willingness and ability to give. I want to teach you how to make sense out of all the requests for your money, your time, and your talents so you can maximize the effectiveness of your giving. I want to help you ungrasp your hand.

Five Good Reasons to Give

The ultimate goal of this textbook is to enable others, through wise financial planning, to free up more of their resources for giving. Hopefully, readers will be encouraged to give generously—regardless of their income level.

In an effort to encourage people to give, it is important to understand what does and does not motivate giving. Is it the strength of some heart-wrenching financial appeal? Is it genuine altruism—the desire to help someone or something? Is it the perceived need for a tax write-off? Guilt?

People give for all sorts of reasons. For some, giving meets an ego need because their names appear on a plaque or an impressive list of friends or benefactors. For others, giving—usually some token amount—is merely a way to avoid or lessen the nuisance of fundraising appeals.

Whatever the motivation, though, one fact is clear: Financially speaking, giving doesn't make sense. When you give your money away, you always have less of it for yourself. Even the much-ballyhooed tax breaks for charitable contributions do not keep pace with the size of the gifts themselves. If you give $1,000, then your tax bill is reduced by $250 if you're in the 25% federal income tax bracket. Any donation—no matter how large or how small—reduces your total net worth.

So why should you make giving part of your financial plan? There are at least five good reasons, every one of which will contribute to your financial contentment.

Giving Breaks the Power of Money

Let's say that you're in a time period of global uncertainty and fear. In times of economic uncertainty, the only people who seem to be free of financial worry are the naïve, the uninformed, and the givers.

The naïve simply do not have a clue as to the severity or urgency of their situation. "Don't confuse me with the facts," they seem to protest. Like Scarlett O'Hara in *Gone with the Wind*, they prefer not to concern themselves with potentially difficult circumstances, reasoning that they can "worry about that tomorrow."

The uninformed may be perceptive people, yet they simply do not have the necessary facts to come to any educated conclusions. Ignorant about matters such as the government debt or global economic effects of terrorism, they fail to grasp the total financial picture and operate from a false sense of security.

The givers, on the other hand, understand the economic causes of fear. Yet, because they have a biblical perspective on money, they experience real security and contentment. They have learned, firsthand, the truth of Matthew 6:8, that "your Father knows the things you have need of before you ask Him." Their trust in God's provision allows them to give with an open hand.

The world's perspective—that accumulation should be our ultimate goal—creates a bondage to money. Under this philosophy, any thought of giving money away comes as a threat to our overall security. So, we simply can't give freely. We become slaves to our finances.

Givers, on the other hand, master their money. In giving their resources away, they relinquish worldly security and significance; they acknowledge their dependence on and service to God. Money no longer has any hold on them. David Robinson, a retired all-star basketball player who has given millions of dollars to the foundation he established to help underprivileged children, wisely said, "If I'm clutching on to my money with both hands, how can I be free to hug my wife and kids?"

Either we control our money, or it controls us. We cannot be accumulators first and still serve God. Luke 16:13 explains why this is so: "No servant can serve two masters; for either he will hate the one and love the other, or else he will be loyal to the one and despise the other. You cannot serve God and mammon." God really wants your heart, not your money.

Giving Is a Way to Lay Up Treasures in Heaven

Again and again throughout Scripture, God's command to give goes hand in hand with a promise:

- Honor the LORD with your possessions . . . so our barns will be filled with plenty (Proverbs 3:9–10).
- Well done good and faithful servant. You have been faithful with a few things, now I will put you in charge of many things. Come and enter the joy of your master (Matthew 25:33).

- Give, and it will be given to you. (Luke 6:38).
- For whoever sows generously will also reap generously . . . (2 Corinthians 9:6b)
- A generous man will himself be blessed, for he shares his food with the poor. (Proverbs 22:9)

God is serious about giving. He knows—and He promises—that we will be better off for it. Many people interpret these promises to mean that the more they give, the more they will get. Were this actually the case, giving would become the hottest investment strategy on Wall Street. It would make unquestionably good economic sense.

The truth is that God's promised rewards are much more significant than financial blessing. If the rewards were simply financial blessing on earth, then that would be a very fleeting reward indeed. Matthew 6:19 tells us that we should not lay up for ourselves treasures on earth, "where moth and rust destroy . . ." In other words, we should not seek treasures of earthly things that will just pass away at some point anyway. We should desire rewards in heaven that will never be destroyed. God may reward givers on earth with more to give, but it is not promised or expected. If we truly understand eternal value, then earthly things will become much less desirable.

Instead of looking for more earthly goods, expect God to bless you in ways you may never have imagined. Perhaps He will give you good health, favor with your boss, or wisdom in your financial decision making. He may use your gift mainly to draw you closer to Himself. He may, in fact, choose to bless you with an eternal reward—one that you will never see on this side of heaven. Whatever the case, give cheerfully. Your promised reward will surely come, and it will be better than whatever you could conjure up.

Giving Provides an Eternal Perspective

When we give, we are reminded of our true home as well as of God's greater purposes. Luke 16:11–13 and 1 Timothy 6:18–19 both reveal the fact that giving allows us to attain allegiance to God and His kingdom in ways that other habits simply cannot. In Philippians 4:17, Paul commends the church members for their generosity toward him—not because of his needs, but because of the gifts that would be credited to their account. Paul was talking about the Philippians' eternal account, the place where, as Christ put it, "neither moth nor rust destroys and where thieves do not break in and steal" (Matthew 6:20).

Few people have articulated the importance of maintaining an eternal perspective better than the missionary Jim Elliot. Jim and his wife Elisabeth went to South America during the 1950s to work with the Auca Indians. Jim and four other men took a small airplane into the jungle to meet the tribe. They landed and were immediately murdered by headhunters.

When Elisabeth received the word that her husband had been murdered, she resolved to stay in South America and live among the Indians, sharing with them the message of Jesus Christ. Today, many years after Jim's death, many in the Auca tribe have become Christians. How did Elisabeth find the strength to see their mission through? How was she able to respond to the uncertain future with such courage and faith? A key to her resolve may be found in her husband's letters and journals: "He is no fool," Jim wrote, "who gives up what he cannot keep to gain what he cannot lose."

Applying Jim's message to giving and reaping eternal rewards, why would you not want to give up something you cannot keep to get something you cannot lose? Why would you hang on to your money when you could have an eternal reward instead? If you are truly concerned about planning for the future and withstanding economic uncertainty, it only makes sense to pursue that which is both certain and secure. It only makes sense to give. As Randy Alcorn says in his book *The Treasure Principle*, "You can't take it with you—but you can send it on ahead."

Giving Demonstrates God's Ownership

When we give to the church or to the poor or to other needs, we are doing so out of an understanding that what we have is not really ours, and that God's resources are sometimes best deployed by being spent on behalf of others. Giving is a very tangible way of living out the principle that God owns it all. If it is all God's, shouldn't He help you determine where you should give it?

The Bible says, "The earth is the Lord's and everything in it. The world and all its people belong to Him" (Psalms 24:1, NLT). When we give, all we are really doing is demonstrating this fact. King David declares,

> "Yours, O Lord, is the greatness, the power, the glory, the victory, and the majesty. Everything in the heavens and on earth is yours, O LORD, and this is your kingdom. We adore you as the one who is over all things. Riches and honor come from you alone, for you rule over everything. Power and might are in your hand, and it is at your discretion that people are made great and given strength." (1 Chronicles 29:11–12, NLT)

Recognizing God's ownership in our resources—actually of all resources—is probably the biggest key to financial freedom.

Ron's Corner

Kathy is a young mother I know. Not long ago she lost 20 dollars—a bill she had hurriedly thrust into her pocketbook as she dashed out the door for a quick trip to the grocery store before she was due to pick up a carpool of five preschoolers. She discovered the loss when she started to pay for her groceries and realized the money was gone.

Looking for a sympathetic ear, Kathy later confided her trouble in the carpool. "Children," she sighed, "I just lost 20 dollars, and I'm feeling sad."

The questions and advice came with rapid fire:

"What did you need the money for?"

"Can't you just go to the bank and get some more?"

"Maybe, if you ask her, my mommy will give you some of her money."

Kathy could not help but smile at the youngsters' eagerness to help—and suddenly her spirits lifted.

"You know what?" she said to herself as much as to the children, "God owns everything. He can help me find that money, or He can provide for us in some other way. We don't need to even worry about it!"

Thus liberated, Kathy cheerfully finished her carpool rounds and drove home with a newfound peace and sense of security. She knew God would take care of her, and as she pulled into her driveway, she saw it. Tucked among the blanket of fall leaves that covered her drive was a 20-dollar bill.

In acknowledging God's ownership of her resources, Kathy was able to mentally release the 20 dollars and experience a true freedom from worry. She learned a valuable lesson about financial security: Financial freedom does not come with having money in your wallet when you go through the grocery store checkout line. Financial freedom comes when you turn your resources fully over to God.

When you manage your money with the conviction that it is actually God's money, giving becomes a logical, natural part of your total financial plan. It confirms God's ownership of your resources, demonstrating, again, that He really does "own it all."

Giving Demonstrates Obedience to God's Commands

Obedience to God's commands really comes as the first reason why you give. It is the over-arching reason to give, inclusive of many other reasons. God tells us to give. Therefore giving is an act of obedience. How do you show your love for God? There are many ways to answer this question, but Jesus summed it up for us in John 14:15. "If you love Me," He said, "keep My commandments."

The secret to giving generously is deciding, in advance, how much money you really need to live on. Plan to give. One of the biggest barriers to giving is that people wait until needs are presented to them and then they react to them. At that point, the money is rarely available—and no matter how much individuals may want to help, they are simply unable to do so.

There are many more reasons that people give, but these five reasons are the primary reasons that most Christians give. Understanding what may (or should) motivate you to give is a very important step in determining how and where you actually give. Before talking about where to give and how to give, let us look at a few reasons why people do not give more.

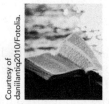

Courtesy of daniilantiq2010/Fotolia.

DISCIPLESHIP MOMENT AND REFLECTION

Take a few moments to reflect on the reasons we should give. Ask God to help turn your heart to becoming more generous, and ask Him to give you a bigger picture of heaven and eternity. Discuss with your accountability partner the challenges you face in giving and the barriers that you face when trying to be more generous.

Why We Don't Give More

As important as it is to understand the motivation behind giving, it is just as important to understand the reasons keeping people from giving more. There are many reasons that people do not give, but the seven primary reasons behind an attitude of not giving are as follows:

1. Spiritual problems
2. Financial problems
3. Limited vision
4. Limited relationships
5. Don't know they can
6. Don't know how to
7. Don't plan to

The underlying root cause keeping most people from giving is ultimately a spiritual problem. Financial problems, such as carrying too much credit card debt, are probably the next biggest reason people do not give. Even if a person is spiritually mature and doesn't have financial problems, he or she may not give because of a multitude of other reasons, such as limited vision, limited relationships, not knowing his or her ability to give, not knowing how to give, or not planning to give. It is interesting that people are very willing to talk about financial planning, but most are not willing to talk about giving planning. Planning giving is probably the most important spiritual and financial decision you can make. Do not neglect planning giving.

Getting Started: A Five-Step Plan

How do you develop a giving plan? When you think about giving, don't just think of writing a check. Start there—and put your money where your mouth is. But you can give so much more than money. Just as having a financial plan can help you free up more money for giving, so having a lifestyle strategy can help make generosity a reality in your life. Here are five action steps to help you identify and take advantage of the opportunities God gives you in the area of giving:

1. Examine your priorities. Do you live with an eternal mind-set? Where is your treasure? Take some time to examine your priorities, remembering the words from Philippians 2:3, "Do nothing out of selfish ambition or vain conceit, but in humility consider others better than yourselves." Determine what things are most important to you and what you want to care about the most, and then direct some of your giving to those arenas.

2. Inventory your assets. Literally make a list of all of the things you have been given: time, influence, treasure, talents, relationships, and so forth. This list should not be limited to your money because you have so much more to give than just money. According to Romans 12:6, all of us have different gifts or talents. Whatever your gifts are, those were meant to be shared with others. Don't waste your resources; instead, be prepared to use them when the opportunity arises.

3. Ask the right questions. When presented with an opportunity to give of time or gifts, instead of asking "Can I do it?" or "Do I have time to do it?" ask God "How would you have me use these resources and gifts?" You have limited resources, but God has unlimited resources. Prayerfully consider where and how God may be leading you.

4. Eliminate expectations. When you decide to give of your possessions or gifts, approach the gift without any expectation of a return. Do not think about what you may get out of it. Don't do your good works as the Pharisees did, in order to "walk around in flowing robes and be greeted in the marketplaces, and have the most important seats in the synagogues and the places of honor at banquets" (Mark 12:38–39). Instead, remember that sacrificial giving involves a cost to yourself, not a reward for your generosity.

5. Give your schedule to God. Begin every day by committing your steps to God. This means that you are open to being interrupted by something that He is moving you into. He may have very different plans for how to use your time and resources during the day than you did. Be open to His voice and ask Him to lead you throughout the day.

All that we have learned in this chapter will help point you toward living a lifestyle of generosity. This will not happen overnight. This is a growth process in which you move into a more generous lifestyle marked by joy and contentment. The next part of this chapter deals with the questions of how to give and where to give. You must understand the why first, and then you will be ready to think about the how and where. As you work through generosity in your own life, you will discover how generosity—in your finances and in your lifestyle—really is the key to freedom, satisfaction, and contentment.

Determining Where to Give

Once one accepts the proposition that we are told by God to give and understands the joys that come from giving, then the question of where to give must be examined.

This section examines giving to the local church, to fulfillment of the Great Commission, and to the needy.

The Old Testament required the Israelites to give to three specific places. First, the Israelites were to give to support full-time religious workers who were not given land of their own (Numbers 18:8–32). Second, the Israelites were instructed to give to provide a meal for community celebration and religious fellowship (Deuteronomy 14:22–29). Third, the Israelites were told to give to provide for the needs of the poor (Deuteronomy 14:28–29). Each of these offerings was supposed to be a tithe, which literally means "a tenth." The first two offerings were yearly offerings, and the third offering was to take place once every third year. A more complete discussion of the tithe concept can be found in the following section.

Similar to the Old Testament, the New Testament tells Christians to give to three specific places. First, Christians are to give to the local church (Galatians 6:6). Second, Christians are told to give to help support the Great Commission (Matthew 28:18–20). Third, Christians are instructed to give to help the needy (1 John 3:17). The New Testament is generally not specific as to the amount required to give.

Looking at these lists from the New and Old Testaments, it seems that they are largely the same, or they at least go toward nearly identical purposes. The first place we are to give in both the Old Testament and the New Testament is to the church and its workers. The second place we are to give in the Old Testament is to celebrate the good things that God has done and in the New Testament is to preach God's word—both of these places will go toward spreading the goodness of God and who He is. The third place we are to give in both the Old and New Testaments is to the poor and needy. When we break down these requirements, it becomes clear to whom we are commanded to give: the local church, to spread the good news about Jesus, and to the needy.

Giving to the local church and to missions is pretty straightforward. (In the next section, we discuss how much we should give as we break down what the Bible teaches us about tithing and giving.) Giving should always begin with the local church. The local church is the primary tool that God has chosen to spread the message of the good news of Jesus Christ. Additionally, the New and Old Testaments are full of instructions and examples of supporting the local church and other believers inside the church. Once somebody is giving at a foundational level to the church, only then should he or she begin to look outside of the church for additional places to give. Remember that when you give to the church, you are (or should be) also indirectly giving to missions and to the poor. One of the functions of the local church is to spread the gospel to the world and to minister to the poor, sick, and the imprisoned. However, just because you give to the church does not mean that giving to the poor and sick is no longer needed.

The much more challenging place to give is to the needy. Matthew 25:31–46 makes it very clear that we are to give the hungry, naked, sick, and imprisoned help, but the challenge comes in giving that help in a way that does not ultimately make the problem worse. There is a well-known book that does a great job of discussing this tension: *When Helping Hurts*. This book helps point out that a continual stream of handouts can rob recipients of their dignity and create a culture of entitlement. However, on the other side of the struggle, if those with abundant or excess resources do not think to use those resources to help the needy, then that creates a problem for both the potential giver and the potential recipient. This is a very real struggle that must be thought through in giving.

There are no easy answers to the challenge of giving to the needy. The most important thing is that we do not ignore the needy because we cannot figure out the best way to help. God gave us the needy to give us opportunities to give and to teach us to rely on

Courtesy of Mele Avery/Fotolia.

His provision. Additionally, the Gospel of Matthew records Jesus's teachings about what will happen to those who ignore the hungry, the stranger, the sick, the naked, or the prisoner: They will be sent to eternal punishment (Matthew 25:31–46). If this is Jesus's warning, then the needy must be helped and cared for. Giving to them is certainly a big part of this assistance, but simply giving a handout without determining what the root of the issue is can often do more harm than good. These are important issues to pray about and struggle with, but the main point is to determine how you can help the needy with your money and with your time and other resources.

Figuring out where to give can be one of the most rewarding and most difficult things that any giver has to determine. The Bible has much to say about giving and to whom we should give, but it does not give us easy or pat answers. It is very important to seek God's wisdom in this process, and it is very important to be giving to all three areas identified. As the treasure principle taught us, where our money is, there our heart is also. When we give to all three of these areas, our hearts follow. If you want a heart for your church, missions, and the needy, then give to those entities and people.

Now that we have figured out why people do and don't give and where the Bible instructs us to give, we next explore the topic of how much to give. These are very personal subjects, but there are truths that apply to each person.

How Much to Give?

How is one supposed to determine how much to give? What does the Bible even say? Is the Old Testament tithe still required? There is much debate over this last question, but one thing is certain: The Bible is very clear that we are to give generously and with a joyful heart. Starting with the basic understanding that the Bible does not leave an option open for us to give nothing, we will discuss in this section what the Bible has to say about how much we are to give. There may be no more controversial issue in the Christian life—and I would venture to say, no greater issue of disobedience—than tithing and giving. How much to give can be one of the most difficult questions for the Christian to answer.

Ron's Corner

I love the story about three men who were discussing the proper way to determine how much money to give to the Lord. The first man said that they should draw a circle on the ground, take all the money out of their pockets and throw it into the air; whatever landed inside the circle is the Lord's, and the rest is theirs to spend. The second man disagreed; he said the proper way to determine how much was the Lord's was how much fell outside the circle. They could then spend the money that fell inside the circle. The third man, being more "spiritually mature," said they should throw their money into the air; whatever God wanted He could keep, and whatever fell to the ground was theirs to spend! This clearly is not a good way to determine how much money to give, so let's look at Scripture to see what it says.

The Internal Revenue Service (IRS) reports that Americans, on average, give approximately 1.8% of their adjusted gross income for charitable contributions. If this percentage were based off of reported gross income, then this percentage would be even lower. Over the years, studies have shown that people who identify themselves as evangelical Christians tend to give more than this 1.8%, but not significantly more. Evangelical Christians do not come anywhere close to approaching giving to

Tithe A tenth; a portion of your income set aside for giving.

the level of a **tithe**, which simply means "a tenth." A lot of people think that the more money people make, the less trouble they have tithing—but these statistics prove otherwise. As salaries grow, giving percentage does not keep pace. In fact, as America has prospered, it has become increasingly stingy. The organization called Empty Tomb, Inc. provides a very interesting analysis of giving and lifestyle research. The organization found the following:

> In 1916, Protestants were giving 2.9% of their incomes to their churches. In 1933, the depth of the Great Depression, it was 3.2%. In 1955, just after affluence began spreading through our culture, it was still 3.2%. By 2004, when Americans were over 555% richer, after taxes and inflation, than in the Great Depression, Protestants were giving 2.6% of their incomes to their churches."

These statistics alone should be convincing enough, but if one looks at giving in America versus other spending, the conviction leads to despair. A study in 2006 showed that Americans donated $93.2 billion to religious organizations (that includes all church types and religions). That same year Americans also spent money as follows:

Entertainment and recreation[1]	$705.0 billion
Fast-food restaurants[2]	$135 billion
Weddings and jewelry[3]	$110.6 billion
Lawn and gardening[4]	$101.6 billion
Soft drinks and salty snacks[5]	$ 86.0 billion
Legal gambling[6]	$ 84.6 billion

So, much of the discretionary lifestyle expenditures by Americans exceed what is given to churches. These numbers and statistics are pretty sobering even without looking at what the Bible teaches. But let's look at giving through the lenses of the Bible and see if this level of giving is in line with Scripture or against Scripture.

Most Christians have heard someone say that every Christian should give a minimum of 10% of their income, or a tithe. Where did this number and idea come from? In the Old Testament, the concept of the tithe is very prevalent. The most widely discussed tithe is an offering of the first 10% of any livestock, produce, or other sources

---

[1] The spending amount for 2004 as cited in an online article dated January 1, 2005, "Self-Actualization Drives Spending on Entertainment and Recreation," http://www.unity marketingonline.com/events/index.php.

[2] As cited in an article by Kirby Pringle, staff writer, "Fast Food: How America (and the World) Traded Genteel Dining for a Good, Fast Meal," *Champaign-Urbana News Gazette*, January 23, 2000, E-1. The 1999 figures reported are adjusted for annual inflation of 3%.

[3] As noted in "Bridal Guide InfoSource USA Today Snapshot," by Darryl Haralson and Keith Simmons, *USA Today*, June 23, 2004, Section B, p. 1. The amount spent on weddings was $57 billion in 2003. Per the Empty Tomb organization, the amount spent on jewelry and watches was $53.6 billion in 2003.

[4] As noted in an Associated Press article, "Accessories Keep Lawn and Garden Industry Growing," *Champaign-Urbana News Gazette*, August 19, 2001, C-5. The amount spent in 2000 was $85 billion, adjusted for 3% annual inflation and growth.

[5] The amount spent on soft drinks was $64 billion in 2003 per an Associated Press article, "Diet Soda Inches Up in Soft Drink Market," *Champaign-Urbana News Gazette*, December 22, 2004, C-9. The amount spent on salty snacks, such as potato chips, pretzels, and so forth, was $22 billion, per an article by Patrick Walters, an Associated Press writer, appearing in the *Champaign-Urbana News Gazette*, March 26, 2004, D-2.

[6] Industry data for 2005 are from the American Gaming Association at http://www.american gaming.org.

of income. In Deuteronomy 26:11–15, Moses provides specific guidelines for the Israelite people. There were actually three different tithes that were required by law! The first tithe was for the yearly first fruits of produce or flocks. This is what we typically think of as the 10%. However, there were two other tithes that were mandated by law!

The second tithe was the yearly first fruits tithe that was to be eaten as a celebration. God had blessed the Israelites quite generously, and this was a way of thanking God for the many blessings.

Finally, every third year, there was a tithe that would go to a local storehouse. This tithe was used to care for and support sojourners, orphans, and the widows of the land. Think how differently our world would be today if everyone continued this tradition.

As a result of all three tithes (remember they were required by law), the Israelites were essentially paying a 23.3% annual tithe.

Now, to further complicate matters, the tithe was to be paid on your increase—hence the reason the first crops were what was "taxed." Not only was a tithe required, but Malachi 3:8–10 tells us that God promised a curse for those who withheld their tithe and great blessings for those who gave wholeheartedly. Likewise, the promise in Proverbs 3:9–10 is that if we honor our Lord with our wealth, with the "first fruits" of all our crops, our "barns will be filled with plenty," and our "vats will overflow with new wine."

Understanding the Old Testament is imperative, but the real debate around how much the Bible tells people to give comes in the New Testament. Did the New Testament completely abolish the law, or has some of it survived? If some or all of it survived, how do we follow it today? These questions are the subject of much debate, and there are many on both sides of the tithing debate with credible arguments. This book does not have the space to try to answer the tithing debate, but the basic premise that all believers should base their giving on is the concept of grace.

1 Corinthians 16:2 provides a glimpse as to what grace means in our giving. In this passage, Paul instructs the church to do weekly collections, but to do so according to the prosperity of each. Not everyone has the same level of income. Hence, giving amounts will be different for different people, and that's okay. The point is that we should be giving according to what God has given us. For those who have been blessed more, more is expected. Additionally, if we have been freed from the law and are living under grace, shouldn't we expect that God would expect more generosity from us than He commanded for the poorest of the Israelites? The New Testament did not lower the standards of holiness; if anything, it raised them. There were no exemptions in the Old Testament for the poor—everyone was expected to contribute. If, then, we have been given such grace, our gratitude should overflow with more giving than that of the poorest of the Israelites.

Too often people want to debate the amount that they should or should not give instead of just giving. People will even argue about whether we are supposed to tithe off of our gross paycheck or wait until the taxes and other withholdings have been taken out and then tithe off of what we actually receive, the net amount. It seems that people want to set an amount so that they can figure out what the minimum they have to give is. We should not be looking for the minimum requirement, and we certainly should not be arguing about it. Giving is not really about the money we give; it is about the attitude of our hearts toward God and His ownership of the money He has entrusted to us. If our treasure is in heaven and we recognize that God owns it all, then our giving should overflow in a spirit of thanksgiving, and our minimums and arguments should wash away.

All of the arguments around giving lose much of their relevance, however, when we consider Paul's admonishment in 1 Corinthians that the Christian should give "as he may prosper." We are to give as God has prospered us.

Also, our gifts should be generous because, as Christ tells us in Luke 6:38, we get what we give: "Give, and it will be given to you: good measure, pressed down, shaken together, and running over will be put into your bosom. For with the measure that you use it, it will be measured back to you." In 2 Corinthians 9:7, we read that our giving should be done "not grudgingly or of necessity; for God loves a cheerful giver." In 2 Corinthians 8:9, Paul gave us the example of Christ to suggest the right attitude toward giving: "For you know the grace of our Lord Jesus Christ, that though He was rich, yet for your sakes He became poor, that you through His poverty might become rich." So, the attitude of giving must be one of cheerfulness and grace. Freely we have received, and freely we must give.

One danger of sticking too closely to the Old Testament specifics is that our perspective may get skewed. If we only give 10% again and again out of every paycheck, we may begin to feel that 10% is God's, and the remaining 90% belongs to us. Remember: God owns it all.

Having determined that how much to give in quantitative terms is not as important as our attitude toward giving, let us now address a good starting place for people to begin thinking about how much to give. Although you may want a legalistic formula, such as give 13.5% of gross income or 8.9% of net take-home pay, the Bible is not that rigid or dogmatic.

> For I testify that they *gave as much as they were able, and even beyond their ability* [emphasis added]. Entirely on their own, they urgently pleaded with us for the privilege of sharing in this service to the saints. And they did not do as we expected but they gave themselves first to the Lord and then to us in keeping with God's will. (2 Corinthians 8:3-5)

Therefore, we are not limited in how much we give either by what we can see or according to our abilities, but what God instructs us each to do. That will vary for each Christian family.

A good framework to think about giving is based on three "Ps": give *proportionately*, give on a *planned* basis, and give on a *pre-committed* basis. This can be further defined as give what you should, give what you could, and give what you would. In other words, you should give an amount that is proportionate to the amount that God has prospered you. You could, by planning, give more than a proportionate amount. You would, if God makes a way, give some of the amount God provides on a totally unexpected basis.

First, the "should give" level includes our proportionate giving. Each Christian should give in proportion to the amount that he or she has received. The best place to start for this type of giving is a basic tithe, 10% of our gross income.

Second, the "could give" level is the amount that one could give if one were willing to give up something else. It may mean giving up a vacation, a savings account, a lifestyle desire, or something else. Giving at this level is probably the closest an American Christian can come to sacrificial giving as described in Luke 21:4: "For all these out of their abundance have put in offerings for God, but she out of her poverty has put in all the livelihood that she had."

Sacrificial giving is giving up something in order to give to the Lord. After putting together a financial plan, it is a great idea to regularly choose to give up something in order to give at the "could give" level. This level requires little faith, so it is not a faith pledge. There is no faith required because you can see the amount, and faith, by definition, requires seeing the unseen. It is simply a sacrificial love gift, an exercise to tangibly show God your love, your willingness to trust Him, and your loose hold on the things and desires of earth.

Figure 16.1 Spending Plan—Giving

GIVING	Goal
Do you plan to give?	Yes
If so, what percentage of your income will you give?	0%

	List the charities that you will give to and then describe why you want to support that charity, how you made your decision and how much you will give:
1	
2	
3	
4	
5	
6	

The third level of giving more clearly approximates faith giving, and is called pre-committed giving (committing in advance), or the "would give" level. We commit ourselves to giving if God provides a certain amount supernaturally. God can do this only if there is a financial plan in place that allows us to see His provision of an additional cash flow margin through either additional income or decreased expenses. Unless a person is pre-committed to give the additional surplus, it will not be given, and that person may miss out on having the incredible blessing of seeing God's hand at work to provide in unique ways.

In summary, how much we can give is dependent upon three levels: You should give an amount proportionate to your income; you could give an additional amount by giving up something; and you would give more if God increased your cash flow margin. The how much is not dependent upon a set formula, and it gives us the opportunity to see God at work in our financial lives.

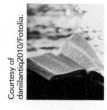

Courtesy of daniilantiq2010/Fotolia.

DISCIPLESHIP MOMENT AND REFLECTION

Write down how much you think God wants you to give. Reflect on why we often look to find minimum requirements in giving. What does this reflect about our hearts?

EXAMPLES IN GIVING

As you reviewed the list of how much we spend relative to giving to mission organizations earlier in the chapter, you may have thought, "But I have to live in the world I'm in and eat!" Certainly, you need to purchase food, clothing, and other things your family needs first. From a strictly economic standpoint and logically speaking, giving never makes sense.

For one thing, we can never meet all the needs. Like a drop in the ocean, our dollar or two (or even thousand dollars or two) will hardly be noticed in the grand scheme of things. Viewed in this light, our giving may seem pointless.

Moreover, we may question where the money will come from. Rarely do we feel financially able to give generously toward a newly recognized need while continuing to fund the people or projects we already support. Like robbing Peter to pay Paul, we would have to shortchange somebody—no matter how valid the need.

Finally, no matter how much money you have or what tax bracket you fall into, you can never gain financial ground by giving. Even when you factor in the deductions for charitable contributions, you would still be better off, financially, if you simply kept all the money for yourself. It always costs money to give.

Giving costs—but therein lies the point. When Jesus talked about giving, He applauded those who gave what they could not logically afford to give. He reserved his praise for those who gave extravagantly—regardless of the amount of the gift. Consider the poor widow whose offering the Lord commended in Mark 12:41–44.

Imagine the scene. Jesus sat across from the temple treasury, watching people make their contributions. Many rich people dressed in fine clothes approached the offering box with a sense of religious pomp and ceremony. The Bible says they "threw" their money in and no doubt heard a satisfying "ch-ching" as the coins fell into the box.

Then a poor widow came along. She probably went almost unnoticed in the hustle and bustle that marked the temple courtyard—and she probably liked it that way. Unlike her wealthy neighbors, she could not afford to make a hefty donation. In fact, she could not really afford to give anything. But still she came, hoping to slip unobtrusively alongside the money box and quietly drop in her offering—two small coins that were all but worthless.

Unwilling to embarrass the woman, Jesus did not make a scene. Yet He called His disciples to His side to let them know what the woman had done. "The truth is that this poor widow gave more to the collection than all the others put together. All the others gave what they'll never miss; she gave extravagantly what she couldn't afford—she gave her all" (**Mark 12**, *The Message*).

For that woman, two cents was everything. The Lord singled her out—both from the temple crowd and from all the other examples in Scripture. The poor widow's story stands as the only direct reference Jesus makes to the manner in which Christians should give. That widow gave God all that she had.

A Modern Example of Giving: The Couple with a Cap on Their Lifestyle

When Jack and Lisa bought their first home, the real estate agent who sold it to them figured it wouldn't be long before the $71,000 house would be on the market again. She knew Jack was a doctor, fresh out of medical school, and she reasoned that he would want to upgrade to a larger home in a fancier neighborhood within 2 or 3 years. She didn't know any young professionals who would live in such a modest little home—but then, she didn't really know Jack and Lisa.

Throughout med school and his subsequent residency, Jack had seen other doctors pursue wealth and prestige, usually at the expense of their families. Many had wrecked their homes as they concentrated on their careers, and Jack wanted no part of that life. Instead, he felt compelled to reach for something more—and, as he read his Bible, he unconsciously found himself at the start of the generosity process, the preparation phase. He could not escape the power of Luke 6:38: "Give, and it will be given to you," the verse promised. "For with the measure you use, it will be measured to you."

As Jack's medical practice grew, that verse replayed itself over and over again in his mind. "Maybe," he confided to Lisa, "the extra money I'm making is not meant for us. Maybe God is increasing my income so we'll have more money to give away."

Jack had an eternal perspective. He understood the basic truth that God owns it all. He asked himself, "How much is enough?" As a result of their convictions, he and Lisa made a remarkable decision. They set a cap on the lifestyle they wanted to attain. They resolved not to move the markers as their income rose; instead, they planned to use the extra—their cash margin—for strategic "investing": giving to God's kingdom.

Right away, the couple recognized the financial implications their decision would have. They knew they could not, for example, always follow their friends as they moved into larger homes. Instead, the couple stayed in their three-bedroom house for 7 years, despite the increasingly crowded conditions as the first four of their five children were born. "It was cramped," Jack admits, "but the kids learned a lot about how to share space."

Likewise, their self-imposed lifestyle cap meant that every spending decision had to be made with the big picture—the eternal perspective—in mind. As Jack continued to drive the Buick sedan he had bought from his mother during medical school, his friends and colleagues must have wondered at his priorities. Why would a doctor drive such an old car? Why didn't Jack and Lisa take many vacations or live in a fancier home? And why, they might have asked (had they known), would anyone walk around with holes in his shoes when he could easily afford to buy a new pair?

The matter of his shoes taught Jack an important lesson. Making his rounds at the hospital, Jack was on his feet almost constantly. He had to wear costly orthopedic shoes—and he knew that to replace them when they began to wear out would leave that much less for him and Lisa to give away. One day, as Jack knelt at the bedside of a young patient, the boy's father noticed the holes in the doctor's shoes. "Please," the man asked, "allow me the privilege of putting new soles on your shoes. It's my business—and I want to thank you for the care you have given my son."

Jack recognized the man's offer for what it was: God's way of providing for his material needs in order to free up more money for giving. He accepted the man's proposition—and from that day on he took his worn-out shoes to his friend whenever they needed repairing.

Over the years, Jack and Lisa's willingness to receive God's provision became a critical factor in their ability to live within the parameters of their chosen lifestyle. Once, when Lisa's parents invited their family to visit them on the West Coast, Jack and Lisa felt they had to decline. They were eager to make the trip, but the only way they could afford to fly all seven family members across the country would be to increase their lifestyle spending and cut into their giving budget. It was a difficult decision, but Jack hoped his in-laws would understand why they couldn't accept the invitation.

Lisa's parents understood perfectly. Even so, they were eager to see their grandchildren, so they sent Jack a check to help cover the cost of the trip. Again, Jack saw God's hand at work, and gladly received his blessing.

Stories like these go on and on as Jack and Lisa recount the times when God met their expenses in ways they had not imagined—from family vacations to the kids' education (which Jack's father unexpectedly offered to help fund). Had they been too proud or unwilling to receive from others, none of these blessings would have come to pass.

Jack and Lisa are real people, and their story is true. By maintaining their lifestyle boundaries, Jack and Lisa were able to steadily increase their giving over the years. Today—even with five children to feed, clothe, and educate—they manage to give away half of everything they earn. But the road has not always been easy. Many times, Jack says, they felt—and still feel—the pinch of sacrifice. Sometimes they battle self-pity or the temptation to increase their living expenses and upgrade their lifestyle. Even so, their commitment to giving has provided them with firsthand exposure to God's promise in Luke 6 (*The Message*): "Give away your life, you'll find life given, back, but not merely given back—given back with bonus and blessing."

In effect, what Jack and Lisa did was to set a "finish line" on their lives. This concept is a biblical one. In Hebrews 12 (*The Message*), for example, Paul admonishes us to do the following:

> Strip down, start running—and never quit! No extra spiritual fat, no parasitic sins. Keep your eyes on Jesus, who both began and finished this race we're in. Study how he did it. Because he never lost sight of where he was headed—that exhilarating finish in and with God—he could put up with anything along the way.

If you choose to run life's race with an eternal perspective, that decision will be evidenced by your lifestyle—specifically, how you choose to use the money you have.

Think about where you are headed. Is your focus on eternity? Are you keeping your eyes on Jesus? Or have you allowed the "fat" and "sin" of things such as materialism, covetousness, and self-centeredness to drag you down? If you choose to run life's race with an eternal perspective, that decision will be evidenced by your lifestyle—specifically, how you choose to use the money you have.

Ron's Corner

R. G. LeTourneau

In my book *Splitting Heirs*, I highlighted modern-day examples of generous givers and those who did it right. One of those was R. G. LeTourneau who, at age 30, dedicated his life to being God's businessman. He ran into early problems in the earthmoving business, but was granted his first U.S. patent at age 35 for a scraper. His last patent was granted in 1965 when he was 77 years old. In the 42 years between these two inventions, he was granted 297 more patents and became one of the top inventors of all time.

LeTourneau is credited with the creation of the modern mechanized earthmoving industry. These 297 inventions included the bulldozer, scrapers of all sorts, dredgers, portable cranes, dump wagons, bridge spans, and logging equipment. He invented mobile sea platforms for oil exploration that now dot the seas throughout the world. He introduced the rubber tire into the earthmoving and material-handling industries.

His company built 70% of the heavy earthmoving equipment used by the Allied forces in World War II. During the height of the war, from 1942 to 1945, his fertile mind pumped out 78 inventions, many of which were instrumental in helping to win the war.

His business efforts—although incredibly successful—never deterred him from what he felt was his reason for existence: to glorify God and spread the gospel message. For over 30 years he traveled across the United States, Canada, and other foreign countries at his own expense, sharing his testimony about the satisfaction and joy of a businessman serving Jesus Christ. Each time he spoke, he began by saying, "Friends, I'm just a sinner saved by grace. Just a mechanic that the Lord has blessed."

LeTourneau felt it was God's business and he was simply a temporary "partner in business." Eventually, he increased his annual giving to 90% and lived off 10%. He later gave 90% of his company to a foundation. He invested millions of dollars in missionary development projects in less-developed countries of Africa and South America. Even in times when his business was in financial jeopardy, he continued giving his sacrificial pledges to Christ's work. "The question," he said, "is not how much of my money I give to God, but rather how much of God's money I keep for myself."

LeTourneau found he couldn't give it away fast enough. In an appropriate earthmoving metaphor, he said, "I shovel it out and God shovels it back—but God has a bigger shovel."[7]

USE A "TARGET" FOR GIVING

George Dayton founded the Dayton's department store in Minneapolis, the beginning of a very successful retail empire. The grandsons of George Dayton grew the retail business and expanded the Dayton Corporation. The company acquired other

[7] Material summarized from LeTourneau's biographical information included in his autobiography, *Mover of Men and Mountains* (Moody's, 1967) and a biographical sketch from the LeTourneau University's site at http://www.letu.edu.

stores, including Hudson's, Mervyn's, and Marshall Field and Co. The Dayton grandsons created a discount store concept in 1962, called Target, which became the company's most profitable store. The company renamed itself in 2000 from Dayton's to the Target Corporation.[8]

The founding Dayton had instructed his children and then grandchildren to be generous givers. In 1946, near the beginning of their management of the company, the George Dayton grandsons instituted a policy of giving 5% of the company's pre-tax profits to charity. At the time, 5% was the maximum amount deductible for corporations under the tax code; the Dayton Corporation was only the second company to institute such a policy.

Kenneth Dayton, one of the grandsons of George Dayton, became a public advocate for giving. He had started as a tither and carefully tracked his giving for over 50 years. In what would make Grandpa George Dayton proud, Kenneth Dayton identified nine stages of giving, and he encourages others to progress through these stages. (He acknowledged he is in the seventh stage and trying for the final stages.)

What is most useful about Mr. Dayton's use of the stages of giving is its planned nature, its challenge beyond taxes, its "finish line" aspect, and its plan of giving after death. As you review these stages, try to see where you are currently and how you can move up his suggested "ladder of giving":

1. *Minimal Response*—Giving because we were asked and only because we were asked.

2. *Involvement and Interest*—As soon as one becomes involved . . . giving becomes more meaningful.

3. *As Much as Possible*—Giving this amount requires a plan and a budget.

4. *Maximum Allowable*—Giving the most that IRS allows as deductible.

5. *Beyond the Max*—No longer would we let the IRS tell us how much (or how little) we could give . . . [however], we no longer had a benchmark . . . we, therefore, needed to invent one.

6. *Percentage of Wealth*—Until we started to measure our giving against our wealth, we did not fully realize how much we could give away and still live very comfortably.

7. *Capping Wealth*—Giving each year a percent of one's wealth forces one to start thinking about the relative importance of increasing giving vs. increasing wealth.

8. *Reducing the Cap*—We can visualize the possibility of doing so . . . we cannot say whether we will ever have the courage.

9. *Bequests*—Having given our heirs enough assets, we are able to leave almost all our remaining assets [to charities].[9]

SUMMARY

Experience shows that cheerful and generous givers exhibit humility, and they are usually joyful. Which comes first, the generosity or joy? Probably joy is the result of their generous lives. Be a cheerful giver. You may want a set of rules, but God doesn't want a set of rules. That's what the Pharisees did. God wants it all—all of our hearts, that is.

---

[8] As noted in *Notable American Philanthropists*, Robert T. Grimm, Jr. editor (Greenwood Press, pp. 73–76).
[9] As noted by Kenneth N. Dayton in *The Stages of Giving* (Washington, DC: Independent Sector, 1999).

SUMMARY REVIEW QUESTIONS

1. What is the true secret to financial freedom and contentment?

2. Briefly describe the treasure principle. Give an example of how this applies to your life.

3. Why is it better to store up treasures in heaven instead of on earth?

4. List the five good reasons to give as described in this chapter.

5. What are some reasons that people don't give more than they do?

6. Describe the five-step plan to getting started with giving as outlined in this chapter.

7. To what causes or people does the Old Testament tell us to give?

8. To what causes or people does the New Testament tell us to give?

9. What does it mean to tithe?

10. Is the tithe still required by the New Testament?

11. How do you determine how much is an appropriate amount for you to give?

12. Where would you place yourself on the ladder of giving? Where do you want to place yourself on the ladder of giving?

Case Study Analysis

Clara burst through the door, eyes bloodshot red and tears streaming down her face. She ran straight to her room and slammed the door. Bob was sitting in his office and quickly got up to find out what the commotion was all about. Debbie was just entering through the garage door, carrying an armful of stuff.

"What's going on?" Bob asked inquisitively.

"The stable is closing down at the end of the month" Debbie replied. "They just had a meeting to tell all the girls that they were not able to raise all the money they needed to keep the horses and maintain the facility."

Debbie lowered her head into Bob's chest, still holding all her stuff, and began to cry. As she gathered herself, she started up again as she began to put everything down.

"The therapeutic stable helped so many kids with disabilities and was such a wonderful thing, especially because the stable was Christ-centered and focused on giving all the glory to God. On top of that, it gave several kids after-school jobs in order to help pay for riding lessons. I just can't imagine that there wasn't enough support from the community to keep it open. They told the girls this afternoon that they are likely going to shut down, although they have one last shot tomorrow night—they have several influential community members who could help support them if they agree. Unfortunately, the staff members at the stable don't think these community leaders are willing to give any money; they told me this is the last group of people to listen and these are all the folks that are super-stingy with their money. Several of them actually go to our church, from what I understand. Bob, what can we do to help?"

Bob stood there in silence, not sure exactly what to say.

That night Bob couldn't sleep as he kept thinking about this situation, and he couldn't help but to ponder why he and Debbie hadn't given any money to the stable, knowing they were a nonprofit organization. He thought about what they could do to help. He decided to take action.

Bob thought to himself, "I know we didn't give, but that can change. I am going to write a letter that will, God willing, convince this group of community members of the power of giving. He began to write.

Assignment

Write a speech/letter to this group of community leaders as if you are Bob, explaining to them the power of giving and why it is so important. In your letter, acknowledge your own lack of giving and how you are going to provide a financial commitment (determine what commitment Bob will make by reviewing where and how much he will give to the stable) while asking the community leaders to understand how giving will Glorify God in this Christ-centered facility. Support your speech/letter with appropriate Scripture references.

DEFINITION

Tithe   (p. 398)

SCRIPTURE VERSES (ESV)

Leviticus 23:9–14—⁹ And the Lord spoke to Moses, saying, ¹⁰ "Speak to the people of Israel and say to them, When you come into the land that I give you and reap its harvest, you shall bring the sheaf of the first fruits of your harvest to the priest, ¹¹ and he shall wave the sheaf before the Lord, so that you may be accepted. On the day after the Sabbath the priest shall wave it. ¹² And on the day when you wave the sheaf, you shall offer a male lamb a year old without blemish as a burnt offering to the Lord. ¹³ And the grain offering with it shall be two tenths of an ephah of fine flour mixed with oil, a food offering to the Lord with a pleasing aroma, and the drink offering with it shall be of wine, a fourth of a hin. ¹⁴ And you shall eat neither bread nor grain parched or fresh until this same day, until you have brought the offering of your God: it is a statute forever throughout your generations in all your dwellings.

Numbers 18:8–32—⁸ Then the Lord spoke to Aaron, "Behold, I have given you charge of the contributions made to me, all the consecrated things of the people of Israel. I have given them to you as a portion and to your sons as a perpetual due. ⁹ This shall be yours of the most holy things, reserved from the fire: every offering of theirs, every grain offering of theirs and every sin offering of theirs and every guilt offering of theirs, which they render to me, shall be most holy to you and to your sons. ¹⁰ In a most holy place shall you eat it. Every male may eat it; it is holy to you. ¹¹ This also is yours: the contribution of their gift, all the wave offerings of the people of Israel. I have given them to you, and to your sons and daughters with you, as a perpetual due. Everyone who is clean in your house may eat it. ¹² All the best of the oil and all the best of the wine and of the grain, the first fruits of what they give to the Lord, I give to you. ¹³ The first ripe fruits of all that is in their land, which they bring to the Lord, shall be yours. Everyone who is clean in your house may eat it. ¹⁴ Every devoted thing in Israel shall be yours. ¹⁵ Everything that opens the womb of all flesh, whether man or beast, which they offer to the Lord, shall be yours. Nevertheless, the firstborn of man you shall redeem, and the firstborn of unclean animals you shall redeem. ¹⁶ And their redemption price (at a month old you shall redeem them) you shall fix at five shekels[b] in silver, according to the shekel of the sanctuary, which is twenty gerahs. ¹⁷ But the firstborn of a cow, or the firstborn of a sheep, or the firstborn of

a goat, you shall not redeem; they are holy. You shall sprinkle their blood on the altar and shall burn their fat as a food offering, with a pleasing aroma to the Lord. ¹⁸ But their flesh shall be yours, as the breast that is waved and as the right thigh are yours. ¹⁹ All the holy contributions that the people of Israel present to the Lord I give to you, and to your sons and daughters with you, as a perpetual due. It is a covenant of salt forever before the Lord for you and for your offspring with you." ²⁰ And the Lord said to Aaron, "You shall have no inheritance in their land, neither shall you have any portion among them. I am your portion and your inheritance among the people of Israel.

²¹ "To the Levites I have given every tithe in Israel for an inheritance, in return for their service that they do, their service in the tent of meeting, ²² so that the people of Israel do not come near the tent of meeting, lest they bear sin and die. ²³ But the Levites shall do the service of the tent of meeting, and they shall bear their iniquity. It shall be a perpetual statute throughout your generations, and among the people of Israel they shall have no inheritance. ²⁴ For the tithe of the people of Israel, which they present as a contribution to the Lord, I have given to the Levites for an inheritance. Therefore I have said of them that they shall have no inheritance among the people of Israel."

²⁵ And the Lord spoke to Moses, saying, ²⁶ "Moreover, you shall speak and say to the Levites, 'When you take from the people of Israel the tithe that I have given you from them for your inheritance, then you shall present a contribution from it to the Lord, a tithe of the tithe. ²⁷ And your contribution shall be counted to you as though it were the grain of the threshing floor, and as the fullness of the winepress. ²⁸ So you shall also present a contribution to the Lord from all your tithes, which you receive from the people of Israel. And from it you shall give the Lord's contribution to Aaron the priest. ²⁹ Out of all the gifts to you, you shall present every contribution due to the Lord; from each its best part is to be dedicated.' ³⁰ Therefore you shall say to them, 'When you have offered from it the best of it, then the rest shall be counted to the Levites as produce of the threshing floor, and as produce of the winepress. ³¹ And you may eat it in any place, you and your households, for it is your reward in return for your service in the tent of meeting. ³² And you shall bear no sin by reason of it,

when you have contributed the best of it. But you shall not profane the holy things of the people of Israel, lest you die.'"

Deuteronomy 14:22–29—22 "You shall tithe all the yield of your seed that comes from the field year by year. 23 And before the Lord your God, in the place that he will choose, to make his name dwell there, you shall eat the tithe of your grain, of your wine, and of your oil, and the firstborn of your herd and flock, that you may learn to fear the Lord your God always. 24 And if the way is too long for you, so that you are not able to carry the tithe, when the Lord your God blesses you, because the place is too far from you, which the Lord your God chooses, to set his name there, 25 then you shall turn it into money and bind up the money in your hand and go to the place that the Lord your God chooses 26 and spend the money for whatever you desire—oxen or sheep or wine or strong drink, whatever your appetite craves. And you shall eat there before the Lord your God and rejoice, you and your household. 27 And you shall not neglect the Levite who is within your towns, for he has no portion or inheritance with you.

28 "At the end of every three years you shall bring out all the tithe of your produce in the same year and lay it up within your towns. 29 And the Levite, because he has no portion or inheritance with you, and the sojourner, the fatherless, and the widow, who are within your towns, shall come and eat and be filled, that the Lord your God may bless you in all the work of your hands that you do.

Deuteronomy 26:11–15—11 And you shall rejoice in all the good that the Lord your God has given to you and to your house, you, and the Levite, and the sojourner who is among you.

12 "When you have finished paying all the tithe of your produce in the third year, which is the year of tithing, giving it to the Levite, the sojourner, the fatherless, and the widow, so that they may eat within your towns and be filled, 13 then you shall say before the Lord your God, 'I have removed the sacred portion out of my house, and moreover, I have given it to the Levite, the sojourner, the fatherless, and the widow, according to all your commandment that you have commanded me. I have not transgressed any of your commandments, nor have I forgotten them. 14 I have not eaten of the tithe while I was mourning, or removed any of it while I was unclean, or offered any of it to the dead. I have obeyed the voice of the Lord my God. I have done according to all that you have commanded me. 15 Look down from your holy habitation, from heaven, and bless your people Israel and the ground that you have given us, as you swore to our fathers, a land flowing with milk and honey.'

1 Chronicles 29:11–12—11 Yours, O Lord, is the greatness and the power and the glory and the victory and the majesty, for all that is in the heavens and in the earth is yours. Yours is the kingdom, O Lord, and you are exalted as head above all. 12 Both riches and honor come from you, and you rule over all. In your hand are power and might, and in your hand it is to make great and to give strength to all.

Psalm 24:1—The earth is the Lord's and the fullness thereof, the world and those who dwell therein,

Proverbs 3:9–10—9 Honor the Lord with your wealth and with the first fruits of all your produce; 10 then your barns will be filled with plenty, and your vats will be bursting with wine.

Proverbs 22:9—Whoever has a bountiful eye will be blessed, for he shares his bread with the poor.

Malachi 3:8–10—8 Will man rob God? Yet you are robbing me. But you say, 'How have we robbed you?' In your tithes and contributions. 9 You are cursed with a curse, for you are robbing me, the whole nation of you. 10 Bring the full tithe into the storehouse, that there may be food in my house. And thereby put me to the test, says the Lord of hosts, if I will not open the windows of heaven for you and pour down for you a blessing until there is no more need.

Matthew 6:19–21—19 "Do not lay up for yourselves treasures on earth, where moth and rust destroy and where thieves break in and steal, 20 but lay up for yourselves treasures in heaven, where neither moth nor rust destroys and where thieves do not break in and steal. 21 For where your treasure is, there your heart will be also.

Matthew 19:16–22—16 And behold, a man came up to him, saying, "Teacher, what good deed must I do to have eternal life?" 17 And he said to him, "Why do you ask me about what is good? There is only one who is good. If you would enter life, keep the commandments." 18 He said to him, "Which ones?" And Jesus said, "You shall not murder, You shall not commit adultery, You shall not steal, You shall not bear false witness, 19 Honor your father and mother, and, You shall love your neighbor as yourself." 20 The young man said to him, "All these I have kept. What do I still lack?" 21 Jesus said to him, "If you would be perfect, go, sell what you possess and give to the poor, and you will have treasure in heaven; and come, follow me." 22 When the young man heard this he went away sorrowful, for he had great possessions.

Matthew 25:31–46—31 "When the Son of Man comes in his glory, and all the angels with him, then he will sit on his glorious throne. 32 Before him will be gathered all the nations, and he will separate people one from another as a shepherd separates the sheep from the goats. ³³ And he will place the sheep on his right, but the goats on the left. ³⁴ Then the King will say to those on his right, 'Come, you who are blessed by my Father, inherit the kingdom prepared for you from the foundation of the world. ³⁵ For I was hungry and you gave me food, I was thirsty and you gave me drink, I was a stranger and you welcomed me, ³⁶ I was naked and you clothed me, I was sick and you visited me, I was in prison and you came to me.' ³⁷ Then the righteous will answer him, saying, 'Lord, when did we see you hungry and feed you, or thirsty and give you drink? ³⁸ And when did we see you a stranger and welcome you, or naked and clothe you? ³⁹ And when did we see you sick or in prison and visit you?'⁴⁰ And the King will answer them, 'Truly, I say to you, as you did it to one of the least of these my brothers, you did it to me.'

⁴¹ "Then he will say to those on his left, 'Depart from me, you cursed, into the eternal fire prepared for the devil and his angels. ⁴² For I was hungry and you gave me no food, I was thirsty and you gave me no drink, ⁴³ I was a stranger and you did not welcome me, naked and you did not clothe me, sick and in prison and you did not visit me.' ⁴⁴ Then they also will answer, saying, 'Lord, when did we see you hungry or thirsty or a stranger or naked or sick or in prison, and did not minister to you?' ⁴⁵ Then he will answer them, saying, 'Truly, I say to you, as you did not do it to one of the least of these, you did not do it to me.' ⁴⁶ And these will go away into eternal punishment, but the righteous into eternal life."

Matthew 28:18–20—¹⁸ And Jesus came and said to them, "All authority in heaven and on earth has been given to me. ¹⁹ Go therefore and make disciples of all nations, baptizing them in[b] the name of the Father and of the Son and of the Holy Spirit, ²⁰ teaching them to observe all that I have commanded you. And behold, I am with you always, to the end of the age."

Mark 12:38–39—³⁸ And in his teaching he said, "Beware of the scribes, who like to walk around in long robes and like greetings in the marketplaces ³⁹ and have the best seats in the synagogues and the places of honor at feasts,

Mark 12:41–44—⁴¹ And he sat down opposite the treasury and watched the people putting money into the offering box. Many rich people put in large sums. ⁴² And a poor widow came and put in two small copper coins, which make a penny. ⁴³ And he called his disciples to him and said to them, "Truly, I say to you, this poor widow has put in more than all those who are contributing to the offering box. ⁴⁴ For they all contributed out of their abundance, but she out of her poverty has put in everything she had, all she had to live on."

Luke 6:38—give, and it will be given to you. Good measure, pressed down, shaken together, running over, will be put into your lap. For with the measure you use it will be measured back to you."

Luke 16:11–13—¹¹ If then you have not been faithful in the unrighteous wealth, who will entrust to you the true riches? ¹² And if you have not been faithful in that which is another's, who will give you that which is your own? ¹³ No servant can serve two masters, for either he will hate the one and love the other, or he will be devoted to the one and despise the other. You cannot serve God and money."

Luke 21:4—For they all contributed out of their abundance, but she out of her poverty put in all she had to live on.

John 14:15—If you love me, you will keep my commandments.

Romans 12:6—Having gifts that differ according to the grace given to us, let us use them: if prophecy, in proportion to our faith.

1 Corinthians 16:2—On the first day of every week, each of you is to put something aside and store it up, as he may prosper, so that there will be no collecting when I come.

2 Corinthians 8:3–5—³ For they gave according to their means, as I can testify, and beyond their means, of their own accord, ⁴ begging us earnestly for the favor of taking part in the relief of the saints— ⁵ and this, not as we expected, but they gave themselves first to the Lord and then by the will of God to us.

2 Corinthians 8:9—For you know the grace of our Lord Jesus Christ, that though he was rich, yet for your sake he became poor, so that you by his poverty might become rich.

2 Corinthians 9:6—The point is this: whoever sows sparingly will also reap sparingly, and whoever sows bountifully will also reap bountifully.

2 Corinthians 9:7—Each one must give as he has decided in his heart, not reluctantly or under compulsion, for God loves a cheerful giver.

Galatians 6:6—Let the one who is taught the word share all good things with the one who teaches.

Philippians 2:3—Do nothing from selfish ambition or conceit, but in humility count others more significant than yourselves.

Philippians 4:17—Not that I seek the gift, but I seek the fruit that increases to your credit.

1 Timothy 6:18–19—[18] They are to do good, to be rich in good works, to be generous and ready to share, [19] thus storing up treasure for themselves as a good foundation for the future, so that they may take hold of that which is truly life.

1 John 3:17—But if anyone has the world's goods and sees his brother in need, yet closes his heart against him, how does God's love abide in him?

ADDITIONAL READINGS

Blanchard, K., & Cathy, S. T. (2009). *The generosity factor: Discover the joy of giving your time, talent, and Treasure*. Grand Rapids, MI: Zondervan.

Blue, R., & Berndt, J. (1997). *Generous living: Finding contentment through giving*. Grand Rapids, MI: Zondervan.

Ewert, M. V. (2014). *The generosity path: Finding the richness in giving*. Boston, MA: Unitarian Universalist Association of Congregations.

Formsma, B. (2014). *I like giving: The transforming power of a generous life*. Colorado Springs, CO: WaterBrook Press.

Hamilton, A. (2012). *Enough, revised and updated: Discovering joy through simplicity and generosity*. Nashville, TN: Abingdon Press.

Hinze, D. W. (1990). *To give and give again: A Christian imperative for generosity*. Boston, MA: Pilgrim Press.

Kapic, K. M., & Borger, J. (2010). *God so loved, He gave: Entering the movement of divine generosity*. Grand Rapids, MI: Zondervan.

Newlands, G. M. (2008). *Generosity and the Christian future*. Eugene, OR: Wipf and Stock Publishers.

Rowell, J. (2007). *To give or not to give? Rethinking dependency, restoring generosity, and redefining sustainability*. Colorado Springs, CO: Biblica.

Schnase, R. (2014). *The grace of giving: The practice of extravagant generosity*. Nashville, TN: Abingdon Press.

Sider, R. (2005). *Rich Christians in an age of hunger: Moving from affluence to generosity*. Nashville, TN: Thomas Nelson Inc.

Smith, C., & Davidson, H. (2014). *The paradox of generosity: Giving we receive, grasping we lose*. New York, NY: Oxford University Press.

Templeton, J. M. (2004). *Thrift and generosity: Joy of giving*. Conshohocken, PA: Templeton Foundation Press.

Willard, C., & Sheppard, J. (2012). *Contagious generosity: Creating a culture of giving in your church*. Grand Rapids, MI: Zondervan.

Willmer, W. K. (2008). *A revolution in generosity: Transforming stewards to be rich toward god*. Chicago, IL: Moody Publishers.

REFERENCES

Accessories keep lawn and garden industry growing. (2001, August 19). *Champaign-Urbana News Gazette*, C-5.

American Gaming Association. 2005. Casino Gaming in America. Retrieved from http://www.americangaming.org

Corbett, S., & Fikkert, B. (2009). *When helping hurts*. Moody Publishers, Chicago, IL. 101, 14.

Dayton, K. N. (1999). *The stages of giving*. Washington, DC: Independent Sector.

Diet soda inches up in soft drink market. (2004, December 22). *Champaign-Urbana News Gazette*, C-9.

Grimm, R. T. Jr. (Ed.). [(date)]. *Notable American philanthropists*. Westport, CT: Greenwood Press.

Haralson, D., & Simmons, K. (2004, June 23). Bridal guide InfoSource USA Today snapshot. *USA Today*, B-1.

LeTourneau, R. G. (1967). *Mover of men and mountains*. Chicago, IL: Moody Publishers.

LeTourneau University. (2016). About LeTourneau. Retrieved from http://www.letu.edu.

Pringle, K. (2000, January 23). Fast food: How America (and the world) traded genteel dining for a good, fast meal. *Champaign-Urbana News Gazette*, E-1.

Self-actualization drives spending on entertainment and recreation. (2005, January 1). *Unity Marketing Online*. Retrieved from http://www.unitymarketingonline.com/events/index.php.

Walters, P. (2004). Snack food makers on defensive. *Champaign-Urbana News, Gazette*, D-2.

Chapter 17

Estate Planning

Courtesy of duncanandison/Fotolia.

BIG IDEA:
Pass wisdom before wealth.

- Know the components that make up an estate plan

- Understand why estate planning is so important

- Explain the three principles in estate planning (treasure principle, wisdom principle, unity principle)

- Know and explain the six decisions to be made prior to transferring wealth

- Understand how an estate is administered and the functions of those who are involved in that administration

- Discuss various tools utilized to most effectively plan for passing of assets to beneficiaries

Introduction

Regardless of one's age, it is never too early to begin to think about the fact that God can call us home on His time, not ours. However, we all have an opportunity to be wise stewards in preparing the next beneficiary of God's resources when God deems it necessary. This chapter focuses on the components of estate planning, how to administer an estate, and the tools used to pass property to the next beneficiary.

THE ESTATE PLANNING PROCESS—WHEN TO BEGIN, WHY IT IS IMPORTANT

No matter who you are, how healthful your lifestyle, or how good your genes are, you will die one day. Although everyone understands and acknowledges this truth, far too few plan for their death appropriately. No matter how much or how little you have, when you die, all of your possessions will be distributed to someone. The

Estate planning The planning of how you want your possessions to be distributed and handled at your death.

planning of how you want your possessions to be distributed and handled at your death is called **estate planning**. Unless you plan the distribution of your possessions prior to your death, the government will determine how and where your assets will be distributed. Your surviving spouse, parents, kids, or other relatives will have no say in how your possessions will be distributed. In limited cases, the government's distribution of your possessions will exactly match what you want to do, but that is the extreme exception to the rule.

Even if your desires to distribute your possessions exactly align with the government's, your relatives and beneficiaries will have to go to court to get your possessions distributed if you do not leave instructions. This process is timely, expensive, and frustrating, and to put others through it because of lack of planning is inconsiderate. These two huge issues can both be largely avoided if a little bit of estate planning is done prior to death.

If all of this is true, why doesn't everyone properly plan their estate? Most people have very good intentions with respect to creating an estate plan, but there are so many relational and spiritual issues involved in the estate planning process that people tend to make excuses for not getting it done. Some of the challenges everyone faces and that cause a lot of people to procrastinate are as follows:

- Helping children and grandchildren without harming them
- Managing expectations of children and spouse
- Dealing with sons-in-law, daughters-in-law, stepchildren, and step-grandchildren
- Providing for a spouse
- Providing for God's kingdom purposes
- Deciding which charities to support
- Avoiding family conflict and sibling rivalry
- Admitting that you are going to die
- Acknowledging that all of your hard earned-wealth will be left to someone else
- Talking about a difficult subject
- Reaching agreement with your spouse
- Desiring to control your possessions after death
- Handling change in personal and family circumstances
- Experiencing significant changes in wealth
- Desiring to leave a legacy
- Learning about complex legal and financial matters

Because of the complexity of developing an estate plan and the many reasons why people procrastinate, it is very helpful to outline a good and orderly process for developing an estate plan. As with any process, the order is very important. You would not start making a pizza by throwing the toppings on a pan. You would make your dough and lay it out first before adding any toppings. Similarly, you should not start to determine tools and techniques in estate planning until you have answered the fundamental questions of who you are giving your estate to, how much you are giving, when you are giving, and so forth. The following process will ensure that all of the right questions are thought through when preparing an estate plan.

	Life Overview	*The Why*
Decision 1:	Transfer	*To Whom?*
Decision 2:	Treatment	*How Much?*
Decision 3:	Timing	*When?*
	Current Deferred	
Decision 4:	Title	*What?*
Decision 5:	Tools & Techniques	*How?*
Decision 6:	Communication	*Communicate the why, who, how much, when, and what, and how*

Decision 1: Transfer—To Whom?

A large part of being a good steward includes choosing and preparing the next best steward for the resources that God has entrusted to us. The first thing to understand in this process is whom can you choose to be the next best steward. Looking at the big picture, there are really only three choices for the next steward:

1. Heirs
2. Charity
3. Government (by taxes)

The transfer decision is the first and most important decision in the wealth transfer process. No other decision should be made before this decision has been fully considered. The transfer decision will drive all the other decisions in the process. To help with your transfer decision, consider the following three principles:

- **The treasure principle—You can't take it with you, but you can send it on ahead.**
- **The wisdom principle—Transfer wisdom before wealth.**
- **The unity principle—Your spouse completes you, not competes with you.**

The Treasure Principle—You Can't Take It with You, But You Can Send It on Ahead

In the book *The Treasure Principle*, Randy Alcorn summarizes this principle: "You can't take it with you—but you can send it on ahead."[1]

Randy says it like this:

Many have stored up their treasures on earth, not in heaven. Each day brings us closer to death. If your treasures are on earth, that means each day brings you closer to losing your treasures. . . . He who lays up treasures in heaven looks forward to eternity; he's moving daily toward his treasures. To him, death is gain. He who spends his life moving away from his treasures has reason to despair. He who spends his life moving toward his treasures has reason to rejoice.[2]

In other words, what you do on earth will be rewarded. Financially speaking, we can give some of our resources to churches, missions, charities, and needy individuals and be rewarded. Of course, you should not give solely in order to get, but it is a valid motivation for giving. Unfortunately, too many people fail to grasp the eternal significance of their actions.

The transfer decision is too often decided by default and without thought, prayer, or much consideration. Too many people simply choose to leave their estate to their relatives in a relatively equal manner. The key in this process is that the transfer decision is thought through, prayed over, and considered carefully. Remember, not deciding is a decision.

Ultimately, many people will conclude that their children should get all of their wealth. That's fine. But this should be a decision and not a default. The next steward

---

[1] Randy Alcorn, *The Treasure Principle: Discovering the Secret of Joyful Giving* (Multnomah Publishers, 2001), p. 17.

[2] Randy Alcorn, *The Treasure Principle: Discovering the Secret of Joyful Giving* (Multnomah Publishers, 2001), pp. 40, 43.

should be chosen and prepared and not simply named because this choice is the default or because everyone else does it this way. To know if the next steward is ready, wisdom should be transferred before wealth. This is the next principle.

The Wisdom Principle—Transfer Wisdom Before Wealth

Wealth never creates wisdom. However, wisdom may create wealth. If you pass wisdom to your children, you probably can pass wealth to them. If they have enough wisdom, then they may not need your wealth.

Too often in our culture, the attitude of the parents is, "I'll take care of the money. You kids just stay in school or play the piano or play soccer." This is a dangerous philosophy. With each passing year, more and more practical experience and needed knowledge about handling money can be passed to kids by teaching them how it should be handled and used. The worst thing a person can do is to pass wealth if they have not passed wisdom.

The Bible says, "An inheritance gained hurriedly at the beginning will not be blessed in the end" (Proverbs 20:21). In biblical times, the sons inherited their fathers' properties and thus provided for the rest of their families. What is not so obvious is that, in most instances, the sons received their inheritances while their fathers were still living, enabling the fathers to oversee their sons' stewardship.

In turn, the sons, particularly the oldest, inherited great responsibility for providing for the parents and extended family. Would you be more interested in training your children to handle money wisely if you knew that one day your estate would be in your children's hands and you would have to depend on them for their support?

Good stewardship includes not only providing for your family, but also being sure that every family member knows how to manage it. It's so easy to procrastinate. It's a "tyranny of the urgent" type of problem that keeps us from doing the important items.

The Unity Principle—Your Spouse Completes You, Not Competes with You

Finally, if you are married, or one day get married, unity with your spouse regarding who the next steward is to be is of utmost importance. King Solomon, who had some experience with money and wives, said the following:

> Two are better than one, because they have a good return for their work: If one falls down, His friend can help him up. But pity the man who falls And has no one to help him up! Also, if two lie down together, they will keep warm. But how can one keep warm alone? Though one may be overpowered, Two can defend themselves. (Ecclesiastes 4:9–12)

Ron's Corner

My friend and mentor, noted teacher and author Dr. Howard Hendricks, first told me the phrase behind the unity principle. In Dr. Hendricks's words, "God did not give you a spouse to frustrate you but to complete you." He helped me see that Judy and I can make better decisions together than either one of us can alone.

Spouses tend to have different strengths and weaknesses. Marriage brings about a challenging but complementary blend of emotions and logic, estrogen and testosterone.

When you are making these decisions related to wealth transfer, unity is necessary between husband and wife. If at first you don't succeed, keep talking, keep listening, keep compromising, and keep praying together.

THREE QUESTIONS TO ASK FOR THE TRANSFER DECISION

Once the transfer decision has been made between your heirs, charity, and the government, you should always consider the following three questions:

1. What is the worst thing that can happen if I transfer wealth to the chosen steward?
2. How serious is it?
3. How likely is it to occur?

You can then repeat these three questions in a more positive frame of mind: "What is the best thing that can happen if I transfer wealth to the chosen steward?" If the answer to these questions scares or worries you, then you probably need to rethink the transfer decision.

Decision 2: Treatment—How Much?

Probably every parent of more than one child feels the same way regarding their children's individuality: How can children coming from the same two parents with the same gene pool living in the same environment with the same stimuli be so different?

If children are so different, is it unfair to treat them differently based on their different needs? For example, if one of your children is a single parent with multiple kids and the other one is single without any kids, would it be unfair to treat them differently? Not necessarily. A unique approach to the second decision, the treatment decision, in the wealth transfer process is based on the following "uniqueness principle": **If you love your children equally, you will treat them uniquely.**

To do otherwise would dishonor them. Sons are different than daughters, sons-in-law are different from daughters-in-law, grandchildren are different from other grandchildren. Some of your children may be much better equipped to handle wealth than others. Some may have more genuine needs than others. Love them unconditionally, but treat them uniquely. They are unique in their character, values, and ability to deal with life; they are unique in their vocation, health, and immediate family situation.

Furthermore, it is a parent and grandparent's responsibility to entrust God's resources to children only if they have demonstrated the ability to handle those resources in a manner that would be pleasing to Him who is the owner of all. If a parent entrusts God's resources to a slothful child, it's no different than giving those resources to any slothful stranger. Just because you have a child does not make the child the automatic beneficiary of your estate.

Much prayer, wisdom, and courage are needed in making the treatment decision. Obviously, great emotion and perhaps tradition are involved. This is why you ultimately must talk with your family about your decisions. It's better to discuss unequal distributions to children while you are alive than to run the risk of bitterness toward you, or among your children, after you are dead.

You are a steward of God's resources on His behalf. You are *not* a steward of your children's resources. You are *not* accountable to your children on how you transfer or spend His money. *You are* accountable to God.

With your will and wealth transfer decisions, it's easy to become legalistic and rigid. Sometimes you can be too close to an issue, emotionally speaking, to think clearly and ask the right questions. When that happens, it's important to pray diligently for God's direction, work through this process of thinking and decision making, and seek professional counsel from a Christian perspective.

The first two decisions of "to whom?" (transfer) and "how much?" (treatment) pave the way for the next decision of "when?" (timing).

Courtesy of daniilantiq2010/Fotolia.

DISCIPLESHIP MOMENT AND REFLECTION

Take a moment to think about the statement that if you love your children equally, you will treat them uniquely. Do you think that this is sound advice for parenting? Did your parents treat you and your siblings this way? Reflect on what this statement means in our relationship with God and how He treats His children differently.

Decision 3: Timing—When?

Once the transfer and treatment decisions have been made, the question arises of whether it is better to give the gift now, at some other time before death, or upon death.

There are two principles that help in balancing the timing decision:

- The kingdom principle: Time your wealth transfer to maximize its use by you, your heirs, and kingdom servants.
- The living principle: Do your giving while you are living, so you know where it is going.

These principles often work together. They apply to timing decisions for wealth transferred to charities or to adult children or grandchildren.

Imagine that you have resources that are sufficient for your retirement, and a ministry you are involved with has a current need to complete an obviously God-directed mission. By waiting to give (through your will) until after you die, you may outlive the usefulness of that ministry, and your gift may not be needed as much later as it is now. By applying the kingdom principle and the living principle, you may choose to make substantial gifts now instead of later.

The same principles may apply to your heirs. They may have more need for your inheritance now—to allow a young mother to stay at home, to pay off student loans, or to replace an aging car—instead of when they are 50 or 60. You can also receive the joy of giving now and seeing them benefit. You could train them further and be around to share wisdom in their management of portions of wealth received now.

Another problem with giving out of your estate—instead of currently—is that you don't know the future. Let's say that Bob made a will in 1985 that says half of his estate goes to free Christian prisoners in the USSR. In 1988, Bob experienced a debilitating stroke causing him to lose mental capacity. When Bob died in 1996, several years after the Iron Curtain fell in the former Soviet empire, the organizations he named no longer existed.

It can be dangerous presuming upon the future. There is no way to know what the most important needs are years from now. If you limit your giving until after you die, then you may be giving to a need that is not nearly as urgent or important as present needs.

Decision 4: Title—What?

After the transfer, treatment, and timing decisions are made, the actual transfers may need to take place. Unfortunately, many people erroneously focus more of their efforts on the technical aspects of the title decision instead of thinking through the other decisions first. Remember that this is a process, and the title decision should only be made after the other decisions have been thought through. A person should only transfer title in order to accomplish the other decisions already made. The title decision is a simple ministerial act of transferring ownership and is really nothing more.

Even though this is the simplest of the decisions so far, it can often be the hardest. Actually writing the check or transferring an asset takes faith that the Lord will provide enough for the rest of your life. The business owner may agree with the idea that he needs to set up succession planning for his business, but actually transferring the stock is difficult. Signing the wills to treat your children uniquely takes courage.

Decision 5: Tools and Techniques—How?

Unfortunately, most people deal with the tools and techniques of wealth transfer too early in the planning process. However, a person's wealth transfer planning is more competent and complete when it addresses the decisions such as *to whom* and *how much* before addressing the *how*.

Only after considering the other decisions in the wealth transfer process should a person begin drafting wills, trusts, or other legal instruments. Unfortunately, the tools and techniques, particularly among lawyers and accountants, become the focus of planning rather than a tool of planning. It is, after all, the most complex area and the primary reason that people engage them for their services. The underlying principles of the tools and techniques decision are the following:

- The tools principle ⇒ Estate planning tools and techniques help you accomplish objectives, but are not *the* objective.
- The trust principle ⇒ Never use a trust because of a lack of trust.
- The KISS principle ⇒ Keep your estate matters as simple as possible.

Much of the remainder of this chapter deals with the tools and techniques of estate planning, and those matters will be addressed in detail there. Even though these tools and techniques take up the bulk of this chapter, do not forget that they are simply the means to the ends you have determined in advance. The tools are necessary, but they are the last thing that should be considered when planning an estate.

Decision 6: Talk—Communicating the Why, Who, How Much, When, What, and How

Is it easier to share wealth transfer plans with your heirs around the coffee table or from a coffin? Who can better share your motivations, hopes, desires, and blessings with your heirs: you or your lawyer reading your will?

If a person fails to complete this last decision after working through the wealth transfer process presented in this chapter, then the impact of his or her plans will be greatly reduced, and it may even cause harm to the heirs. It is hard enough to talk about money, and even harder talking about money and death. Regardless of the difficulties, this last part of the process must be done, so *just do it*.

Here's the underlying principle of the talk decision:

- The expectation principle: Communicate to align expectations with plans.

The aim of the expectation principle is to get everyone on the same page with no surprises. Try to avoid creating a "coping gap" for your heirs. If the expectations are at one level and reality is at a much different level, then the difference between them is a coping gap.

For example, imagine a decedent has an adult child who is expecting an inheritance of about $500,000. The decedent planned on giving substantially to mission work, and that adult child actually receives only a $5,000 inheritance. That is a $495,000 coping gap! An heir may have difficulty coping with a gift that is significantly different than his or her expectations.

Failure to have a talk about the distribution of an estate oftentimes will result in a coping gap. At the very least, having a family conference relating to the distribution of your estate allows for open dialogue and discussion about expectations, both now and after your death.

Every family will ultimately have a family conference, it is just a matter of whether you will be alive to attend. Isn't it far better to have the family conference prior to death? A family conference can be an invaluable time of bringing a family closer together.

The families who have a family conference, meeting, or retreat to discuss their wealth transfer plans rarely regret it. Communication is the final and very important step for implementing your wealth transfer plans.

TOOLS, TECHNIQUES, AND TERMINOLOGY

Now that we have a good understanding of the decisions that need to be made with respect to the transfer of wealth, we will spend the rest of this chapter exploring basic tools, techniques, and terminology encountered in the planning of estates.

Wills

The will is the most basic tool in the estate planning process and should be present in nearly every single estate. A will is the foundational cornerstone of any estate plan. It is a written, witnessed document that defines a person's final wishes and desires regarding many things, including property distribution. A person who dies with a will is called one who dies **testate**. A person who dies without a will dies **intestate**, and the laws of intestacy apply.

Typical wills contain the following elements:

- Recitation of the **testator** (the person whose will it is)
- Declaration of competency and sound mind of the testator
- Statement regarding marital status and children, if any
- Appointment of an executor to administer the testator's estate
- Description of the powers of the named executor
- Instructions as to how the testator's property is to be distributed

Wills can contain many other elements, but those just listed are the ones that will be found in nearly every will. If a person has minor children, his or her will would usually contain a clause that appoints a guardian for the children.

If a person dies intestate (without a will), then the state government of his or her state of residency will have the right to determine:

Testate   A person who dies with a will.

Intestate   A person who dies without a will.

Testator   The person who is the writer of the will.

Estate Planning   **423**

- The control of the individual's financial resources
- The distribution of those resources
- The choice of executor
- The choice of a guardian for minor children
- The ability to waive fiduciary bonds
- The right to authorize a business continuation plan

In some cases the state government's distribution of assets will be exactly the same as the wishes of the person who died, but that is extremely rare to see and would frankly be a lucky coincidence. If individuals do not want the state government to have the authority to determine the beneficiaries of their estate, then they must take the step of creating a will.

Despite these truths, many Americans do not have a will. Survey after survey reveals that the number of Americans without wills ranges from 50% to 60%. That means that more than half of all Americans "trust" their state governments to determine the proper distribution of their estates, the appointment of an executor to administer their assets, and potentially the right to determine the guardian of their minor children.

An important step for all good stewards is to implement the basic tool of a will. A will does not have to be complex and may be only a page or two long. Good intentions or prayerful consideration of the wealth transfer process will not get the job done. In many states, the surviving spouse has no say in the matter if there is no will. Your estate becomes subject to the responsibility and function of the court system. The will is the first step in putting together a plan of distribution of an estate.

ADMINISTRATION OF AN ESTATE

The administration of an estate refers to the management and distribution of the assets and liabilities of a decedent's estate following his or her death. It involves gathering the assets of the decedent, paying the debts of the decedent, and distributing the remaining property to the beneficiaries of the estate. The process can be very daunting and cumbersome and will vary depending on the state of residence of the decedent. If an executor has been named in the will of the deceased person, then that person will be in charge of administering the estate. If no executor has been named in the will or there is no will, then the court will have to appoint a person as the executor of the estate.

Probate The process of proving up a will and transferring assets through the court system.

Generally speaking, an executor is only going to handle and distribute **probate** assets. Probate assets are assets that transfer under the will. Nonprobate assets are assets that transfer outside of the will—for example, life insurance proceeds, retirement assets, community property, rights of survivorship property, and so forth. The next section discusses many of the most common types of nonprobate assets.

In handling the probate assets of an estate, the estate will be administered in one of two ways: formal administration or informal administration. Formal administration is the more complex and drawn-out version of administration. It requires significant court involvement and will usually take much longer than informal administration. Informal administration can be much easier and will oftentimes only require an initial and final filing with the court. All actions taken in between those two filings may be taken without court approval. The state you live in, the maturity of your executor, and the size of your estate will determine which form of administration is most advantageous for your situation.

TITLED ASSETS

Titled assets are a specific form of ownership for assets that are held in common with another person. By nature, many of these assets will pass to another person outside of the probate process and independent of a will.

The most common forms of titled assets are (1) joint tenants with rights of survivorship, (2) tenants in common, and (3) community property.

Joint tenants with rights of survivorship is a type of ownership by two or more persons. As joint tenants, all of the owners share equal ownership of the property, and they all have the equal, undivided right to use and enjoy the property. Upon the death of one of the owners, the deceased person's interest in the property automatically passes to the other owners without any action on the part of the remaining owners. These types of interests can arise by deed or contract and are commonly seen as a way to hold bank accounts and real estate.

Tenants in common is a type of ownership that is similar to a joint tenancy with rights of survivorship, with the biggest differences being that owners do not have to have equal rights in the property and there is no automatic transfer at the death of an owner. Each owner is free to dispose of his or her portion of the property in any way that the owner sees fit, and the interest of each owner will pass upon such owner's death by will or by the laws of intestacy. These interests usually arise by deed, will, or by operation of law.

Community property is another form of joint tenancy, but it can only exist between a married couple. The community property form of ownership will only exist in certain states. In these states, all property accumulated by a spouse during a marriage automatically is owned jointly by both spouses absent an agreement to the contrary. As a result, all property acquired or accumulated during a marriage is owned 50/50 by each spouse. Upon the death of a spouse, the deceased spouse's 50% portion of the property will pass by will or by the laws of intestacy, and the 50% interest of the surviving spouse will remain with the surviving spouse.

There are other ways to title assets, and many will vary based on the state in which you live. The important thing to remember is that owning property with another person carries with it certain rights and responsibilities. You need to know how your joint ownership with another person will affect your estate and the transfer of those assets upon your death.

TRUSTS

Trust A fiduciary relationship that appoints a third party, a trustee, to hold assets for the benefit of a beneficiary.

Trusts are another tool that can be used to hold assets and possibly to transfer them to another party outside of probate. Simply put, a **trust** is a fiduciary relationship that appoints a third party, a trustee, to hold assets for the benefit of a beneficiary. Trusts typically have three parties: the trustee, the trustor, and the beneficiary. These three parties can be three different people, but they do not have to be. The trustor is also called the settlor and is the party who establishes the trust. The trustee is the party who is responsible for managing the trust in accordance with the trustor's stated wishes in a trust agreement. The beneficiary is the party who receives the distributions of the trust and benefits from the assets of the trust.

There are many different types of trusts, and we do not have the time or the space to discuss them all. However, the two main classifications of trusts are irrevocable

Irrevocable trust A trust that cannot be revoked.

Revocable trust A trust that is able to be cancelled.

trusts and revocable trusts. An **irrevocable trust** is a trust that cannot ever be revoked; thus, once an asset is put into an irrevocable trust, it has been given away forever. A **revocable trust**, on the other hand, can be revoked; thus, the trustor can get his or her assets back at some point in the future. Revocable trusts are often set up as a way to avoid probate, and they allow the trustor to maintain control of his or her assets during the trustor's lifetime.

The main types of trusts and their purposes are described in Table 17.1.

Table 17.1 **Types of Trusts**

Marital Trust	A trust that is designed to provide benefits to a surviving spouse.
Bypass Trust	A trust that is designed to provide benefits to a surviving spouse while bypassing the surviving spouse's estate. These are sometimes also called credit shelter trusts.
Testamentary Trust	A trust that is created and described in a will after the death of the trustor.
Irrevocable Life Insurance Trust	A trust that is designed to exclude life insurance proceeds from the taxable estate of the deceased while providing liquidity to the estate or the beneficiaries of the estate.
Charitable Lead Trust	A trust that provides income to a charity for a set amount of time, with the remainder going to the beneficiaries of a trustor.
Charitable Remainder Trust	A trust that provides income to the trustor for a defined period of time, with the remainder going to a charity.
Qualified Terminable Interest Property Trust	A trust that is designed to provide benefits to a surviving spouse, with the remainder of the property passing to additional beneficiaries named by the trustor upon the surviving spouse's death.

Trusts can be used to accomplish many purposes and are a very useful tool in estate planning. Trusts are a good way to protect young adults from inheriting money before they are mature enough to handle it, and they can be used to protect assets from creditors if a beneficiary is prone to poor decisions. Trusts are wonderful tools to be used for planning and prudence, but do not fall into the trap of relying on trusts to control from the grave. Trusts pose a very real temptation to try to control beneficiaries long after the death of the trustor. Although there are very legitimate uses of trusts, simple control from the grave should not be one of them. Train your beneficiaries before you die, and then let them deal with what is left behind.

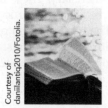

Courtesy of daniilantiq2010/Fotolia.

DISCIPLESHIP MOMENT AND REFLECTION

Think about reasons you may want to use a trust when leaving assets to another person. Think about how a trust works to protect assets, but may not work to protect legacy. Think about the best way to leave a legacy and how these tools and techniques fit into that plan.

TAXABLE ESTATE

Since 1916, the federal government of the United States has levied taxes on estates. The original and continuing official rationale is that the estate tax prevents the concentration of wealth.

In a technical sense, you do not pay the estate tax. You have to die before it applies. Your estate will pay the tax. So, your heirs would receive fewer assets. Here's the equation: Your total assets owned at death minus any estate taxes owed equals the amount available for your heirs. The irritating aspect of the estate tax is that much of your wealth has already been taxed for income taxes when you earned it. Let's say that you worked as an employee for 40 years and diligently saved and invested your earnings. You paid income tax throughout your working life on the wages earned and the interest and dividends earned. If you did a great job of saving and investing to build an account of $6 million, then your estate may have to pay estate taxes too—at very high rates (minimum of 15%, rising very quickly to a top rate of 40%).

Notice in the last sentence that it said your estate "may" have to pay estate taxes. Despite the bad news that wealth may be potentially taxed twice, the good news is that everyone receives a standard credit from estate and gift taxes. (Gift taxes are added here because the estate and gift taxes are related to each other. You can't escape estate taxes by giving away everything—because gift taxes would likely then apply.) This standard credit is technically called the *unified credit*. It is an estate and gift tax credit allowed by law to offset any estate or gift tax due on any transfers of property that are taxed. The amount of the unified credit effective for 2015 was $2,117,800. This credit will offset the tax on an estate totaling $5.43 million. So, you can give away or transfer to individuals up to $5.43 million without triggering estate or gift taxes. Accountants and lawyers refer to this amount as the technical term exemption equivalent, but we will refer to it as the lifetime exemption.

For many years, the lifetime exemption was $600,000. In response to constituents, Congress raised the lifetime exemption effective in 2000. The Tax Act of 2001 implemented a gradual phase-in of increasing it to $3.5 million in the year 2009. Briefly for 2010, the estate tax was entirely repealed. Then, in a strange result of political compromise, the estate tax came back, but only for estates of $5 million or more.

The past chaos in the federal estate tax code is mentioned to point out that these rates and approaches to taxation are in constant change. Congress and the president may radically change the nature and amount of the estate tax rules again, but many of the tools and techniques described in this chapter will remain relevant and important.

1. **How do estate taxes apply if I leave everything to my spouse?**

   You can leave an unlimited amount of property to your spouse and your estate will not have to pay any estate taxes. This sounds too good to be true, right? It is true, but there may be a trap. Let's use the concept of lifetime exemption discussed in the last section to explain.

   A **marital deduction** refers to property that one spouse can transfer to the living spouse at his or her death without paying an estate tax. The amount is unlimited. This can enable a person to avoid all estate tax at the death of the first spouse. The same idea applies to lifetime gifts. The **marital gift exclusion** allows one spouse to transfer an unlimited amount to the other spouse before death without paying a gift transfer tax.

   As an illustration, let's say that Bill dies and leaves his land holdings worth $13 million to his wife, Sally. Because of the unlimited marital deduction, no estate tax is due upon his death. Sounds good so far, but the trap comes at Sally's death without proper planning. Let's further assume that Sally suffered

Marital deduction
Property that one spouse can transfer to the living spouse at his or her death without paying an estate tax.

Marital gift exclusion
Allows one spouse to transfer an unlimited amount to the other spouse before death without paying a gift transfer tax.

from extreme grief from Bill's death and died the following month. Her estate will be taxed. How much of Sally's estate will be taxable? The taxable portion will be $7.57 million ($13 million less her lifetime exemption of $5.43 million).

Remember that the lifetime exemption applies to *each* person. Bill has $5.43 million and Sally has $5.43 million that they can exempt from estate taxes. The lifetime exemption dies with you. So, Bill did not benefit from his $5.43 million lifetime exemption. He transferred everything to his wife, Sally. No estate taxes were owed because of the unlimited marital deduction. He didn't use the lifetime exemption, it died with him, and his family lost the benefit of it. We will look at tools and techniques to preserve the value of the lifetime exemption in a following section.

2. **How do gifts affect estate taxes?**

The estate and gift tax laws state that any gifts made during the last 3 years of a person's life must be counted in the deceased person's estate. Gifts are still considered, on paper at least, as part of a person's estate and are taxed if given within the last 3 years of life. These laws thus effectively limit the "deathbed" gifts or signing over of deeds to reduce estate taxes.

Another important concept with gifts is the **annual gift exclusion**. The annual gift exclusion is simply the dollar amount of an asset that can be transferred every year from any person to any other person or persons free from any gift taxes and without using up any of your unified credit. As of 2015, the annual gift exclusion amount was $14,000. For many years the amount was $10,000 per person, but this amount has been gradually increasing over the past 10 years.

Remember that the estate and gift taxation system works together; it is unified. If John makes a single gift of $500,000 in stock to his son, then gift tax is due (because this is more than the $14,000 annual exclusion amount). John can pay the gift tax in the year the gift was made. Or, John may choose to not pay the gift tax now, but he will use up $468,000 of his lifetime exemption for estate taxes. If John's total estate is expected to be less than $5.43 million, he can safely use up some of his unified credit because his estate will not owe estate taxes.

Annual gift exclusion The dollar amount of an asset that can be transferred every year from any person to any other person or persons free from any gift taxes and without using up any of your unified credit.

Is Life Insurance a Part of a Taxable Estate?

Yes—if you own the policy. Life insurance proceeds made payable to your beneficiaries will be added back to your estate for purposes of the estate taxes.

Many people wisely use life insurance to provide liquidity at the time of death, to provide for survivors, and perhaps to pay estate taxes. However, keep in mind that unless the ownership is properly structured, the life insurance will be added back to your estate's value when computing the estate tax due.

Tools and Techniques for Saving Estate Taxes

Now that you have some facts, let's see how they might apply. Although the estate tax seems onerous, the good news is that it is the easiest tax to legally avoid. Minimizing your tax is a valid goal of a good steward, but it is not the most important aim. Remember the tools principle: Estate planning tools and techniques help you accomplish objectives, but are not the objective. If your objective is to give generously to charity and to your adult children, then minimizing taxes supports your objective. Less to the government means more to charity and to your children.

After you have thought through the wealth transfer decisions presented earlier and if the value of your estimated estate is likely to be more than $5.43 million, then consider the following ideas to save literally hundreds of thousands of dollars in estate taxes. These are simple steps. They are not the most advanced steps, but the KISS principle (of course, the acronym for this principle is from the saying "keep it simple, stupid") reminds us that we do not need to be more complex than necessary to reach our objectives and to minimize taxes.

1. *Maximize the lifetime exemption by retitling property between the spouses and passing some property to eventual heirs upon the death of the first spouse.* Because each person gets a lifetime exemption ($5.43 million in 2015), use that exemption. Instead of transferring all your assets to your spouse, transfer an amount equal to the lifetime exemption to your adult children or some organization upon your death. The benefit: Your eventual heirs will get assets earlier and there is less property in the estate of the second spouse. Less property means less tax.

   Although this idea may work in some cases, there may be practical problems. What if the assets are not easily divisible into a portion equaling the lifetime exemption? What if the surviving spouse needs the income from the assets to live on? These practical challenges lead to the second idea—another way to maximize the lifetime exemption.

2. *Maximize the lifetime exemption by using portability or a marital (or A-B) trust.* In 2010, Congress enacted a new concept into estate tax law called portability. This concept basically says that a surviving spouse is allowed to "inherit" the decedent spouse's unused lifetime exemption. (There are some concrete steps that must be made within a certain period of time in order to benefit from this concept, so if you are in this situation, you should seek professional advice.) This means that even if planning has not been done, the surviving spouse is allowed to take advantage of the spouse's unused lifetime exemption. That could mean that the surviving spouse has $10.86 million of lifetime exemption to use during his or her lifetime or at his or her death.

   The old way that estate attorneys used to take advantage of both spouses' lifetime exemption while still allowing the surviving spouse to have access to the funds is what is known as an A-B trust. The objective is to keep a portion of the assets in the estate of the first spouse to die to utilize the lifetime exemption. (Sometimes the resulting trust is called a bypass trust because the principal bypasses the surviving spouse.) These trusts would allow the use of all of the decedent spouse's lifetime exemption while still providing for the surviving spouse. These trusts are fairly technical, so we will not get deep into the details, but be aware that they may be of use to limit or eliminate estate taxes.

3. *Begin giving gifts now to individual heirs to take advantage of the annual gift exclusion.* If your estate may be subject to taxes, an added reason to give now is the reduction in your estate and, consequently, the reduction in taxes. Every $14,000 gift can save up to $5,600 in taxes. Everyone wins—except the Internal Revenue Service (IRS).

   The exclusion provides for an attractive way to remove assets from one's estate with no legal fees or complications—a great example of the KISS principle. For an illustration of how this can work in fairly large numbers, let's assume that Jay and Carol have plenty of income to live on through pensions and rental income and plan on transferring their wealth to their children and grandchildren. They have three children, all of whom are married with two children. The 3 children plus 3 spouses plus 6 grandchildren make a total of 12 family members. Because both the husband and wife can each give $14,000 to each family member, potentially they can give $168,000 ($14,000 × 12 each). Combined, they can give $336,000 every year to their family—$14,000 from each parent to each child, spouse, and grandchild.

Remember that the 3-year time limit must be satisfied for gifts to be excluded from your estate, so this is not a deathbed planning option. This technique can save a very significant amount of estate taxes. The amount saved depends on how large your estate is, how long you live, how long you give, and the number of people you give to. But it could be significant.

4. *Give away assets that will likely appreciate rapidly in value to reduce the future potential value of your estate.* This idea is essentially a turbo-charged version of item 3. Instead of giving cash each year, you could give shares of stock or land that may increase in value in the future. By doing so, you eliminate future growth of your estate and limit estate taxes.

   Let's say that in 2010 you bought 600 shares of a growing software company for $30,000. The stock began to increase, and you believed that one day this relatively small software company could dominate the technology world. You gave 150 shares to each of your four children at Christmas 2010. Based on the value of the stock at Christmas, you gave each of them a gift that was valued at $9,000— less than the annual gift exclusion. Therefore, no taxation resulted at the time of the gift, and no usage of your lifetime exemption occurred.

   Your children held on to the shares of that company, which later did dominate the technology world. If you had held on to the stock within your estate, then all of the increase would be subject to estate tax. But giving away the stock before it appreciated allowed you to leverage your tax-free wealth transfer. The potential tax savings could range from a few thousand to theoretically a few million dollars given the right circumstances.

5. *Use an irrevocable life insurance trust (ILIT) to exclude life insurance proceeds from your estate.* With a little bit of legal work, setting up an ILIT can save a very significant amount of estate taxes. In simplified terms, here's how this idea works.

   The ILIT, that is, the trust, owns an insurance policy. You are the insured. When you set up the ILIT, you name the beneficiaries of it. You also name the trustee of the ILIT. You pay the premiums each year; this action is considered a contribution to the trust. The trustee makes sure the premiums are paid, receives notices, notifies the insurance company upon your death, and basically has the power to act on behalf of the trust.

   In essence, you have given up ownership of the policy in exchange for getting proceeds to beneficiaries of your choice. Because life insurance proceeds are not taxable for income taxes, your beneficiaries receive the full value of the insurance death benefit. No estate taxes are subtracted and no income taxes are subtracted.

More Advanced and Creative Tools and Techniques

In addition to the tools and techniques described thus far in the chapter, a whole alphabet soup of creative tools and techniques exists. Acronyms such as CRAT, CRUT, CLAT, GRIT, GRAT, and GRUT all represent types of trusts that can be established to provide significant tax savings to an estate. To help see how some of these trusts are used, we will look at an example of Patrick.

Patrick is the third generation of his family to farm 250 acres located near a major metropolitan area. When Patrick's grandfather originally bought the land, it was way out in the country and was an hour's drive over gravel roads and two-lane highways to reach the major city. As the city grew and its suburbs expanded, Patrick's farm was surrounded by affluent houses and interstate highways.

Patrick resisted the many offers over the years for his land. Farming was all he had known, and he held the hope that his sons might want to join him. Eventually,

Patrick saw that the land was worth far more than he could ever earn farming. His sons graduated from college, obtained advanced degrees, and went off to high-paying jobs in other large cities. A shopping mall developer recently called Patrick with an offer for an eye-popping $25 million for his land.

As he considered whether or not to sell the land, Patrick reviewed his wealth transfer plans with his financial and legal advisors. Patrick and his wife, now in their 70s, needed regular income to support them. They were very interested in funding mission work through their church and other ministries. Their sons were in sound financial condition. Patrick's tax basis for income tax purposes in the land was only $1 million. If he sold the land and received the proceeds, then he would have to pay more than $5 million in income taxes. Then, upon their deaths, their estate would have to pay even more in estate taxes if the remaining proceeds remained in their bank accounts or investment accounts. What could they do?

Their advisors recommended a charitable remainder trust (CRT). The concept of a CRT is that Patrick and his wife donate the property to a trust, the trust sells the property, and the trust invests the proceeds. Patrick and his wife receive an annual income stream from the trust. After their deaths, the remaining principle in the trust is transferred to charity. Hence the name—charitable remainder trust.

What are the benefits of a CRT? First, income tax is avoided. Because Patrick does not sell the property and receive all the proceeds, he does not have to pay income taxes. Not only does Patrick avoid income taxes, he gets a charitable deduction (for a small portion—computed according to IRS formula) for his future gift to charity. Another advantage is that the land and its proceeds are excluded from their estate. The CRT results in millions of dollars of tax savings for Patrick. Patrick and his wife can name one or more charitable beneficiaries and have the power to change beneficiaries if desired.

While living, Patrick and his wife will continue to receive a regular income stream. They may choose the method of receiving that income. If they chose to receive a fixed dollar amount, then it is called a charitable remainder annuity trust (CRAT). If they chose to receive 5% (the required minimum), then they would receive $1,250,000 per year—far more than they earned farming! The other choice is to receive a fixed percentage. The fixed percentage, called a unitrust (CRUT), is applied against the trust assets. If the investments in the trust increased in value, then the annual payout would increase in value. If the investments decreased, then the annual payout would decrease.

We used Patrick's situation as an example of using a more advanced technique to achieve his objectives. Using a CRAT or CRUT is not always the perfect solution. Remember the tools principle—it depends on your objectives. The CRAT or CRUT costs additional legal fees, trust administration fees, investment fees, and tax preparation fees. Another potential concern is that the charities do not benefit until later. If you consider the timing decision and prayerfully conclude that the Lord is leading you to give now, then a "remainder" trust would not be the appropriate tool to reach your objectives.

Another tool to benefit a charity now and your family later is a charitable lead trust (CLT). This flip-flops the CRT. With a CLT, you transfer assets to a trust and the charity receives the income now. Your heirs will receive the remaining principal later upon your death. The CLT works well if you have other sources of income now, the charity needs the income now, and you desire the asset to revert back to your heirs.

Many other advanced tools and techniques exist that are beyond the scope—and perhaps beyond the attention span of readers—of this book. The important takeaway is that there are multiple tools and techniques for reducing and avoiding estate taxes, but do not let the tax tail wag the dog and control all of your planning. Walk through the process described at the beginning of this chapter, and then decide if any of these advanced tools and techniques are necessary or make sense.

POAS

Power of attorney
A written authorization appointing a person to act on your behalf in your personal or business matters.

POA is an abbreviation for *power of attorney*. A **power of attorney** is a written authorization appointing a person to act on your behalf in your personal or business matters. The person appointing another person is referred to as the principal or grantor of the power. The person being appointed is referred to as the agent or the attorney in fact. There are different types of POAs with specific purposes.

A durable power of attorney is a power of attorney that appoints a person to act in specified personal or business matters even after you become incapacitated and unable to act on your own behalf. It is referred to as a durable power of attorney because its duration continues beyond a disability. A durable power of attorney is a necessary consideration in every estate plan, and it avoids the need for loved ones to go to court to obtain permission to manage your assets if you ever become unable to handle your own affairs due to a disability or illness.

A health-care power of attorney is another type of power of attorney that is prudent to include in every estate plan. A health-care power of attorney gives the attorney in fact the authority to make health-care-related decisions for the principal, including so-called end-of-life determinations. The principal can restrict the power of the attorney in fact and can give instructions as to how he or she wants to see decisions made. These powers of attorney generally need to be current and should be refreshed every few years.

SUMMARY

The focus of this chapter was to help identify the various components that make up an estate plan as well as focus on why estate planning is vital. We reviewed three main principles—the treasure principle, the wisdom principle, and the unity principle—and how these principles apply to establishing a biblically framed estate plan. Next we looked at the six decisions that need to be made in developing how an estate plan should be established. We looked at what to transfer, how to transfer, when to make these transfers, how to title the transfers, and the tools and techniques used in establishing the transfers. The final decision or process is to communicate the decisions to those who will be impacted. We then looked at the process of administering an estate and the roles and responsibilities of those involved in an estate distribution.

SUMMARY REVIEW QUESTIONS

1. What are some reasons that people put off planning for their death?

2. Describe the treasure principle, wisdom principle, and unity principle as they relate to your transfer decision in estate planning.

3. What are three important questions to ask regarding the transfer decision in estate planning?

4. What is the uniqueness principle? Do you agree with this principle?

5. What do the kingdom principle and the living principle say about when you should give assets to an heir or a charity?

6. Describe the tools principle, the trust principle, and the KISS principle as they relate to determining the best method to transfer assets.

7. Why is it so important to communicate your estate plans to your beneficiaries prior to death?

8. What are the main components of most wills?

9. What is the job of an administrator of an estate?

10. What is the current amount of assets that can be transferred by a person before those assets are subject to gift and estate taxes?

11. What is the annual exclusion amount?

12. How does the marital deduction work?

Case Study Analysis

Several days had passed after the meeting at which Bob had encouraged leaders to commit to giving generously to keep the stable open. While Bob and Debbie were preparing dinner, Debbie stopped and gave Bob a big hug and said, "I've been thinking a lot about this whole process of finding out about our finances with Steve, and with your wonderful speech the other day, I feel that we have grown so much closer together through this entire process. I have a better feeling about what we have and where we will be in the future, especially during retirement. I know we don't have everything in order like we should, but we are working toward becoming better stewards, as Steve would say. And although we are on track, there is a nagging in me about what will happen when we are gone. I remember Steve saying in one of our first meetings that everything belongs to God and we are just stewards. So when we pass along, what happens to what God has given us to steward?"

"I know," Bob jumped in. "If I think you are saying what I think you are saying, then, yes, we need to evaluate our plan for when we die. We need to evaluate our estate planning documents and probably do some updating. However, I think it even goes beyond just updating the documents—we need to make sure that Sean, Chloe, and Clara are prepared to take responsibility for what they will be entrusted to take care of."

Debbie smiled and let out a sigh of relief as she sat listening to her husband. "That's it, honey. We need to make sure the kids are prepared to be stewards as well."

Bob continued, "I think Sean will be back visiting in a couple of weeks for a break in school. Let's have a family evening where we can talk through our estate planning documents, show the kids where everything is, and identify how we plan on leaving them ready to be the next stewards. This will also give us some time to prepare ourselves for that meeting."

Assignment

Review the estate planning documents in the Case Study and identify what updates/changes need to be made in the following items, along with support for your recommended changes (explain why the changes are suggested):

- Will
- Medical directive

- Bob's durable power of attorney
- Debbie's durable power of attorney
- Guardianship forms
- Living Trust

Respond to the following questions regarding Bob and Debbie's preparation for this meeting:

1. Assuming the final value of all assets to be $3 million, how much should be allocated to each of the following?
   a. Sean
   b. Chloe
   c. Clara
   d. Charity
   e. Government (in taxes)

2. How do the following principles apply as we think about these decisions of wealth transfer?
   a. Treasure principle
   b. Wisdom principle
   c. Unity principle
   d. Kingdom impact principle
   e. Living principle

3. Create an assignment that should be given to Sean, Chloe, and Clara that will allow them to understand that what they are given is a responsibility as a steward and not a right to spend when they inherit money from their parents.

DEFINITIONS

Annual gift exclusion   (p. 428)   **Marital deduction**   (p. 427)   **Revocable trust**   (p. 426)

Estate planning   (p. 416)   **Marital gift exclusion**   (p. 427)   **Testate**   (p. 423)

Intestate   (p. 423)   **Power of attorney**   (p. 432)   **Testator**   (p. 423)

Irrevocable trust   (p. 426)   **Probate**   (p. 424)   **Trust**   (p. 425)

SCRIPTURE VERSES (ESV)

Proverbs 20:21—An inheritance gained hastily in the beginning will not be blessed in the end.

Ecclesiastes 4:9–12—[9] Two are better than one, because they have a good reward for their toil. [10] For if they fall, one will lift up his fellow. But woe to him who is alone when he falls and has not another to lift him up! [11] Again, if two lie together, they keep warm, but how can one keep warm alone? [12] And though a man might prevail against one who is alone, two will withstand him—a threefold cord is not quickly broken.

ADDITIONAL READINGS

Blue, R. (2008). *Splitting heirs: Giving your money and things to your children without ruining their lives.* Chicago, IL: Moody Publishers.

Blue, R., & White, J. L. (2008). *Faith-based family finances: Let go of worry and grow in confidence.* Carol Stream, IL: Tyndale House Publishers.

Celia, D., & Kroll, W. (2009). *Bigger kingdom or bigger barns: Estate planning from a biblical perspective.* Mustang, OK: Tate Pub. & Enterprises LLC.

Dockery, D. S. (2011). *Christian leadership essentials: A handbook for managing Christian organizations.* Nashville, TN: B&H Academic.

Ives, J. P., & Ives, S. C. (2013). *Growing love in Christian marriage. Pastor's manual* (3rd ed., 2012 rev.). Nashville, TN: Abingdon Press.

Joiner, D. W. (1991). *Christians and money: A guide to personal finance.* Nashville, TN: Discipleship Resources.

Pope, E. (2003). *Creating your personal money map.* Carol Stream, IL: Tyndale House Publishers.

Ramsey, D. (2015). *The legacy journey: A radical view of biblical wealth and generosity.* Nashville, TN: Ramsey Press.

Reid, G. E. (1993). *It's your money isn't it?* Hagerstown, MD: Review and Herald Pub. Association.

Samp, R. H. (2005). *The final tithe: A Christian approach to estate planning.* Sioux Falls, SD: Rushmore House Publishing.

Union, C. o. C. i. C. (1991). *Advocate.* St. Stephen, NB: Advocate Publishing House.

Chapter 18

Governmental Support Programs

Courtesy of Monkey Business/Fotolia.

BIG IDEA:
We are to be obedient to those over us as they are ordained by God.

LEARNING OUTCOMES

- Understand the role of the family in relation to supporting your family
- Know and explain the requirements of receiving retirement benefits from Social Security
- Explain the disability component of Social Security
- List the benefits associated with survivor's benefits as part of Social Security
- Understand who is eligible for Supplemental Support Income (SSI) as part of Social Security
- Know and explain the four main parts of Medicare
- Explain how recipients of Medicare can "fill in the gaps" in their coverage
- Describe the advantages and disadvantages of FHA and VA loans
- List the benefits of programs such as unemployment, SNAP, and TANF

This chapter highlights the various governmental programs that can be utilized in conjunction with a solid biblically based financial plan. It provides an overview of programs such as the six types of Social Security benefits, with special attention to retirement benefits and Medicare (the health insurance program for retirees).

SOCIAL PROGRAMS HISTORY

The **Social Security Administration** (SSA) was created in 1935 under the Old-Age and Survivors Insurance program (known as the Social Security Board until 1946) as part of the Social Security Act signed into law by President Roosevelt. It's important to understand, however, that the development of social programs to support those in need reaches back to centuries earlier.

ROLE OF THE FAMILY AND THE CHURCH

Social Security Administration
A governmental organization created in 1935 under the Old-Age and Survivors Insurance program (known as the Social Security Board until 1946) as part of the Social Security Act signed into law by President Roosevelt.

As life unfolds for each of us, we see that there are times of desperation, especially financially. There will be times of unemployment, disability, illnesses, and death, along with the inevitability of old age, all of which may leave us unable to contribute to the economic well-being of our families.

God's word reveals us this very truth:

1 Timothy 5:8: But if anyone does not provide for his relatives, and especially for members of his household, he has denied the faith and is worse than an unbeliever.

Leviticus 19:3: Every one of you shall revere his mother and his father, and you shall keep my Sabbaths: I am the Lord your God.

Taking care of our parents and family is just one aspect of our role in taking care of those who need help.

Exodus 22:22–24: You shall not mistreat any widow or fatherless child. If you do mistreat them, and they cry out to me, I will surely hear their cry, and my wrath will burn, and I will kill you with the sword, and your wives shall become widows and your children fatherless.

1 Timothy 5:3–6: Honor widows who are truly widows. But if a widow has children or grandchildren, let them first learn to show godliness to their own household and to make some return to their parents, for this is pleasing in the sight of God. She who is truly a widow, left all alone, has set her hope on God and continues in supplications and prayers night and day, but she who is self-indulgent is dead even while she lives.

Psalm 68:5: Father of the fatherless and protector of widows is God in his holy habitation.

Zechariah 7:10: Do not oppress the widow, the fatherless, the sojourner, or the poor, and let none of you devise evil against another in your heart.

God's word instructs his body to take care of those who are unable to take care of themselves, specifically widows and children if they do not have any relatives to provide for them. Unfortunately, we find that society has seemed to fall short of fulfilling this command.

STATISTICS ON CHURCH GIVING

From the beginning of the church, we find a call to give to those in need. For example:

Acts 20:35: In all things I have shown you that by working hard in this way we must help the weak and remember the words of the Lord Jesus, how he himself said, "It is more blessed to give than to receive."

Proverbs 19:17: Whoever is generous to the poor lends to the LORD, and he will repay him for his deed.

Matthew 25:35–40: For I was hungry and you gave me food, I was thirsty and you gave me drink, I was a stranger and you welcomed me, I was naked and you clothed me, I was sick and you visited me, I was in prison and you came to me. Then the righteous will answer him, saying, "Lord, when did we see you hungry and feed you, or thirsty and give you drink? And when did we see you a stranger and welcome you, or naked and clothe you? And when did we see you sick or in prison and visit you?"

Galatians 6:2: Bear one another's burdens, and so fulfill the law of Christ.

Matthew 5:42: Give to the one who begs from you, and do not refuse the one who would borrow from you.

Proverbs 14:31: Whoever oppresses a poor man insults his Maker, but he who is generous to the needy honors him.

There are many other Scripture verses that provide us insight into God's heart toward His people, all of His people. As we seek to understand the church's role in providing for the support of others in the body of Christ, we find three main ways in which to provide help. First is through our time in helping those who need help. This may require sacrificing by going to a soup kitchen or other local ministry to volunteer to feed those in need. Second, we can provide help through our talents. Perhaps you have the ability to build homes or other structures that could be useful toward God's kingdom. Finally, we can use our financial resources in support of those who give time or talents in their work.

When you begin to consider how you can support those in need, you may begin to feel overwhelmed. How can the church support everyone? Keep in mind, however, that we have different levels of support. We need to know that we support our families differently than we will financially support the homeless or a local women's shelter. Deciding on the level of support can be and needs to be a prayerful decision; unfortunately, it is not the most pressing. The question is not what to support, but more importantly, how we support. Unfortunately, the answer is not optimistic.

In a research study on church giving, Ronsvalle and Ronsvalle (2015) reported the following statistics on church giving from 1968 through 2013:

- Using a percentage of income, member giving among Protestant-denominated churches dropped from 3.02% to 2.17% of income.
- Using an inflation-adjusted dollar figure (2009), member giving was $470.10 in 1968 and increased to $800.64 in 2013. When considering the inflation adjustment in 2009 of $330.54, we find that the average increase was $7.35 per year in member contributions.
- Cash contributions to charitable giving of income after taxes by age:
  - Under 25 years old   1%
  - 25–34 years old   1.1%
  - 35–44 years old   1.0%
  - 45–54 years old   1.4%
  - 55–64 years old   2.0%
  - 65–74 years old   3.1%
  - Over 75 years old   4.3%
- If church members gave 10% of their income rather than the 2.17%, the church would have an additional $180.9 billion to fund the kingdom of God.

Such statistics are staggering. Paul, in his letter to the Corinthians, helps the church understand the aspect of giving (1 Corinthians 8–9) that is beyond just the

Old Testament structure of 10%. In fact, the Apostle Paul, a Jew of Jews, did not even mention the tithe in his letter. The lack of mention of the tithe helps us see the importance of this new idea of giving, which can be defined as *according to our ability*. However, because the church has not taken this concept to heart, we find that our ability to help those in need, including the elderly, sick, disabled, and children, is severely deficient.

Due to the decline in financial support for the body of Christ, the government thus has created programs designed to help provide support. The primary support components in the United States are from those programs implemented through the Social Security Act, which created both retirement and disability income programs as well as programs offering health-care coverage for eligible individuals. The remaining part of this chapter focuses on describing the components of the various Social Security programs.

RETIREMENT BENEFITS

One of most notable topics in the components of Social Security is the benefits received when reaching what is known as "retirement age." In 2016, the full retirement age was designated as age 67, which has been increasing over the years. Table 18.1 provides an overview as to the retirement age based on when you were born.

Table 18.1 Full Retirement Age by Year of Birth

Year of Birth*	Full Retirement Age
1937 or earlier	65
1938	65 and 2 months
1939	65 and 4 months
1940	65 and 6 months
1941	65 and 8 months
1942	65 and 10 months
1943–1954	66
1955	66 and 2 months
1956	66 and 4 months
1957	66 and 6 months
1958	66 and 8 months
1959	66 and 10 months
1960 and later	67

*If you were born on January 1 of any year, you should refer to the previous year. (If you were born on the 1st of the month, your benefit (and your full retirement age) are figured as if your birthday was in the previous month.)
Source: https://www.ssa.gov/planners/retire/retirechart.html

Your age, however, does not automatically qualify you to receive retirement benefits. Your benefit level is determined by establishing "credits," which are achieved by working. In addition to retirement benefits, Social Security credits are used to determine other benefit types through the Social Security program. **Social Security credits** are calculated using two components: your earnings (wages) and your work history (how long you have worked). The premise behind these two components is that your benefit should be comparable to what you have paid into the Social Security system; the more you earn and the longer you pay into Social Security, the larger your benefit will be at retirement. In 2015, an employed person received 1 credit for $1,220 of income, with a maximum of 4 credits available in a given year. The earnings amount is increased each year as average earnings increase.

The Apostle Paul lays out a similar plan in his second letter to Thessalonians (2 Thessalonians 3:10): "For even when we were with you, we would give you this command: If anyone is not willing to work, let him not eat." Those not willing to contribute should not be willing to receive. It is important to note, however, that the key phrase here is "willing to"—this is different from when someone is unable to work.

In order to receive retirement benefits from Social Security, you need to have worked for at least 10 years, or have 40 credits, to be eligible, which is known as being **fully insured**. However, as part of the Social Security process, you are eligible to determine when you receive the retirement benefits, which was alluded to earlier in this section. As you recall, the full retirement age at which you receive 100% of your eligible benefits is determined by the year in which you were born (see Table 18.1). You can, however, select to either (1) take a percentage less than 100% of your benefit by selecting to take benefits sooner, or (2) defer your eligible benefit and delay taking your benefit, which will give you a higher percentage in the future. The earliest that one can begin to take retirement benefits from Social Security (and assuming the required number of credits is met) is at age 62. The latest you can delay, and thus increase your benefit amount, is up to age 70. At age 70, you can still defer your Social Security retirement benefits; however, the benefit amount will not continue to increase.

Based on the table for full retirement age, should you decide to take Social Security benefits early, say at age 62 when you are eligible, your benefit amount will be reduced roughly by 5/9ths of 1% (.55%) per month prior to full retirement age up to a maximum of 36 months. If your decision to take Social Security benefits exceeds 36 months early, then the benefit is reduced 5/12ths of 1% (.416%) for the remaining 24 months that you would be eligible to take benefits. Taken together, the 60 months in early benefits (taking benefits at age 62 when your full retirement age is 67 equals 60 months) would thus amount to roughly a 30% reduction in the benefit amount. This reduction is sustained for the duration of your lifetime. In other words, your benefit amount will not increase, whether at full retirement age or beyond.

On the other hand, you can elect to defer taking Social Security benefits past your full retirement age, which will provide an increase in your eligible benefit. The current annual increase stands at 8% per year of delayed benefit. One caveat is that you must meet the requirements for benefits at full retirement age. In other words, delaying benefits in order to receive additional "credits" will not increase your benefit. All credits must be established at full retirement age in order to increase your benefit amount.

Ron's Corner

In general, I recommend waiting until full retirement age to begin Social Security because it provides a higher benefit for life and because longevity trends show that most people are living longer.

DISABILITY BENEFITS

Social Security disability benefits Benefits received by those who meet the two criteria for being disabled: (1) being unable to work due to a medical condition lasting or expected to last at least 1 year or (2) having a condition that could lead to death.

Most people don't realize that disabilities are far too common than we would like to accept. According to the Social Security Administration, a 20-year-old worker has a one in four chance of becoming disabled at some point before reaching full retirement age. In order to receive **Social Security disability benefits**, you must be unable to work due to a medical condition that lasts or is expected to last at least 1 year or could lead to death. These conditions must be documented by your medical practitioner and given to the Social Security Administration representative. In order to become eligible for Social Security disability benefits, you must be able to prove two main criteria:

1. You must show, based on your age when a disability occurs, that you have recently worked a minimum number of years out of a set range of years. For example, if your disability happens after you turn 31, you must have worked 5 out of the last 10 years (see Table 18.2).

Table 18.2 Rules for Work Needed Test

If you become disabled . . .	Then, you generally need:
In or before the quarter you turn age 24	1.5 years of work during the 3-year period ending with the quarter in which your disability began.
In the quarter after you turn age 24 but before the quarter you turn age 31	Work during half the time for the period beginning with the quarter after you turned 21 and ending with the quarter in which you became disabled. Example: If you become disabled in the quarter you turned age 27, then you would need 3 years of work out of the 6-year period ending with the quarter in which you became disabled.
In the quarter you turn age 31 or later	Work during 5 years out of the 10-year period ending with the quarter in which your disability began.

Source: https://www.ssa.gov/pubs/EN-05-10029.pdf

2. You must show, based on your age when a disability occurs, that you have collectively worked enough years in order to qualify for benefits. For example, if you were to become disabled at age 50, then you must have a 7-year duration of work history in order to receive benefits (see Table 18.3).

Table 18.3 Rules for Duration Needed Test

If you become disabled . . .	Then, you generally need:
Before age 28	1.5 years of work
Age 30	2 years
Age 34	3 years
Age 38	4 years
Age 42	5 years
Age 44	5.5 years
Age 46	6 years
Age 48	6.5 years
Age 50	7 years
Age 52	7.5 years
Age 54	8 years
Age 56	8.5 years
Age 58	9 years
Age 60	9.5 years

Source: https://www.ssa.gov/pubs/EN-05-10029.pdf

In order to receive benefits, both criteria must be met. Once the Social Security Administration representative determines your eligibility, the representative will conduct a review of your medical records and employment status in order to make a determination of your benefits.

SURVIVOR'S BENEFITS

Another section of Social Security is designed to help those who have experienced the death of a family member who was eligible for benefits. Two main benefits may be received, with the first being a $255 one-time payment to the spouse if they were living together at the time of the decedent's death. The second part of the benefit package to survivors includes potential benefits to certain family members, as follows:

- A widow or widower age 60 or order (age 50 if disabled) may be eligible for survivor benefits.
- A widow or widower of any age who is caring for the decedent's child under the age of 16 or if the child is disabled may be eligible for survivor benefits.

- Unmarried children may be eligible if they are:
  - Younger than 18 (19 if still enrolled in an elementary or secondary school)
  - Age 18 or older and disabled, as long as the disability was established before age 22
  - Stepchildren, step-grandchildren or adopted children (limits are established)
- Dependent parents age 62 or older who are dependent on the decedent for at least 50% of their support may be eligible for survivor benefits.
- A surviving ex-spouse (limits are established) may be eligible for survivor benefits.

Once a family member becomes deceased, it is important to notify the Social Security Administration to determine if any survivors are eligible for benefits. In many cases the funeral home will notify the Social Security Administration of the death.

SUPPLEMENTAL SECURITY INCOME BENEFITS

Supplemental Security Income Governmental financial support for those adults who have a disability and children who have limited income and other resources for their support.

Although less common in the dialogue about Social Security, **Supplemental Security Income** (SSI) helps to support those adults who have a disability and children who have limited income and other resources for their support. Although part of the Social Security benefit ensemble, SSI is not paid from Social Security taxes, but rather through the U.S. Treasury Department's general funds.

The general purpose of the SSI section is to pay monthly benefits to three main groups of low-income people:

- Those age 65 years old or older
- Those who are blind
- Those who are disabled (as outlined earlier in the section on disability benefits)

Children with disabilities or who are blind are also eligible for SSI if their parents have limited income. When determining your eligibility for SSI, two components are evaluated: (1) your income and (2) your resources (material things you possess). There are certain adjustments that can be made to your gross earnings or other income that is not counted toward your eligibility, and so we urge you to contact the Social Security Administration to determine these criteria. The second component, your resources, includes such assets as your checking account balance, your home and land, stock portfolios, cars, and so forth. As a general rule, you must possess less than $2,000 in resources, including your checking and savings account balances.

MEDICARE

Medicare A social health-care program designed to supplement the cost of health care for those over the age of 65.

As our society continues to age and with the continued rise in health-care costs, Medicare and its components have become a major political agenda item. This section provides an overview of **Medicare**, a social health-care program generally for those over the age of 65. It is important to note that Medicare is designed to supplement the cost of health care, but usually will not cover all medical costs for those enrolled. These uncovered costs can usually be covered under a different policy (Medigap), which is covered later in this section.

Courtesy of WavebreakMediaMicro/Fotolia.

There is an enrollment process that must be completed for Medicare. In 2016, eligible recipients needed to enroll up to 3 months before their 65th birthday and had until 3 months after their 65th birthday to enroll to avoid any penalties. Medicare offers various enrollment periods for different parts of its coverage.

Medicare is funded in part by Social Security payroll taxes paid by both employees and employers. Where the funds come from has been up for debate; some speculate that Medicare will be unable to be sustained as more and more aging Americans continue to become eligible combined with the rising costs of health care in our country. Those who are enrolled in Medicare pay a monthly premium, which does help offset the cost of coverage.

Medicare is broken down into four main parts: A, B, C, and D.

Part A—Hospital Coverage

The first section of Medicare is for costs associated with hospital coverage, known commonly as Part A. This coverage helps offset the cost of care while in a hospital, post-hospital care in a nursing facility, or in some cases home health or hospice care. In many cases, Part A is provided to recipients at no cost. You are eligible for Part A if you have earned enough credits for benefits. If, however, you are not eligible, you may be able to obtain Medicare Part A by paying a small monthly premium. There are certain circumstances in which certain individuals may receive Medicare Part A prior to age 65, such as those receiving Social Security disability benefits for the past 24 months.

Part B—Medical Coverage

The next section covers the medical practitioners and other health-care professionals. Medical insurance, known as Part B, also helps cover outpatient care, medical equipment, and some preventative services. Although this is an optional component to Medicare coverage, you may be assessed a penalty if you do not enroll during your first enrollment period. Should you elect to enroll in Part B, you will be assessed a monthly premium that is based on your income.

Part C—Medicare Advantage Plans

Medicare Advantage Plan A third-party plan that offers Social Security Medicare plans to participants. Typically, these plans offer more benefits and generally lower costs to participants.

The benefits of Part A and Part B can be provided in one of two ways: (1) you can enroll directly through the government (Social Security Administration) or (2) you can enroll through private health-care companies that are approved Medicare Advantage organizations. If you have elected to have your Part A and Part B benefits through a third party, you have a **Medicare Advantage Plan,** which in many cases offer more benefits to its insured and the opportunity to have lower out-of-pocket costs. These plans may have a higher monthly premium than that of just Part B due to the other benefits the plan may cover. Enrollment in a Medicare Advantage Plan eliminates your ability to enroll in a Medigap policy due to the Medicare Advantage Plan covering many of the services not covered by government-sponsored Medicare, known as "original Medicare."

Medicare Advantage Plans have open enrollment, usually from October 15 through December 7, in which eligible participants in Medicare Part A and Part B can enroll in a Medicare Advantage Plan that becomes effective on January 1 of the following year.

Part D—Prescription Drug Plans

If you are enrolled in either Part A or Part B, you are eligible for Part D, which covers prescription drugs. These plans are optional as well, and those enrolled will pay a monthly premium. Like Part B, the prescription drug plan premiums are usually determined by one's income, where higher incomes usually have higher premiums. Similar to the other components, if you do not enroll in Part D upon your first eligibility, you may be assessed a penalty for later enrollment. You can enroll in Part D during the open enrollment period of October 15 through December 7 for effective coverage beginning January 1 of the following year.

Medigap Policies

Medigap Policies sold to Social Security beneficiaries that help to cover costs that are not covered by Medicare programs. You must be enrolled in Part A or Part B of Medicare to qualify for a Medigap policy.

Medicare Supplement Insurance plans, known as **Medigap**, are polices that are sold to those who have enrolled in the "original Medicare" program through the government. These policies can help offset the cost of co-payments, co-insurance, deductibles, and other services that are not necessarily covered by Part A or Part B. In order to be eligible for a Medigap policy, you must be aware of the following guidelines:

- You must be currently enrolled in either Part A or Part B.
- You are required to pay the Medigap monthly premium, which is over and above the Part B premium.
- Medigap policies only cover one individual; spouses must each have their own policy.
- Medigap policies are guaranteed renewable, meaning the policy cannot be cancelled as long as the premiums are paid.
- Medigap policies do not include any prescription drug coverage (after 2006).
- If you are enrolled in a Medicare Advantage Plan (MAP), you are not eligible for a Medigap policy.

Although Medigap is designed to cover expenses not covered by Part A and Part B, there are some services that a Medigap policy will usually not cover, such as long-term care, vision services, and dental services. In addition, policies may not cover medical devices such as hearing aids or eyeglasses.

MEDICAID

Medicaid A health-care coverage program designed for low-income adults, children, and pregnant women and eligible people with disabilities.

Medicaid is a health-care coverage program designed for low-income adults, children, pregnant women, and eligible people with disabilities. Designed as a cooperative between states and the federal government, it covers over 60 million people in the United States. Although dually funded by the states and the federal government, Medicaid is a state-run program in which benefits are designed by each state, with federal oversight and guidelines. Each state must provide "mandatory" benefits and have the option to include other benefits at the state's discretion. In order to become eligible for Medicaid, you must meet requirements set forth by the states, which must meet federal minimum standards. The federal minimum income standards have been defined mostly by the Federal Poverty Line (FPL). With the passing of the Affordable Care Act in 2010, the new legislation requires eligibility for Medicaid at 133% of the FPL, which would be $32,252 for a family of four in 2016. The FPL is usually adjusted annually for cost-of-living increases.

GOVERNMENTAL HOUSING PROGRAMS

Federal Housing Administration
A home loan program in partnership with the Department of Housing and Urban Development and local lenders offering governmental guarantees to borrower loans.

Although there are various governmental programs related to housing, this section will cover two of the most prominent: Federal Housing Administration (FHA) loans and Veterans Affairs (VA) loans offered by the Department of Veterans Affairs.

Federal Housing Administration loans, commonly referred to as FHA loans, are home loan programs in partnership with the Department of Housing and Urban Development (HUD) that allow borrowers the following benefits:

- Low down payments (as low as 3.5% of the purchase price)
- Low closing costs
- Lower qualifying standards

Private mortgage insurance An insurance policy that is required by lenders when borrowers put down less than 20% of the purchase price in order to protect the lender from borrower default.

When evaluating housing options, you may select to choose an FHA loan; however, there are limitations to doing so. First, all FHA loans that have a down payment of lower than 20% of the purchase price require the borrower to get FHA mortgage insurance, or **private mortgage insurance** (PMI). As indicated in the chapter on home buying, PMI is a type of insurance that is required by the lender and paid by the borrower that protects the lender from default. FHA loans are also capped to the amount that a borrower may borrow under this governmental program, which varies by state and county. For example, a borrower in Baker County, Georgia, could only borrow $271,050 using an FHA loan, whereas in Butts County, Georgia, the borrower could borrow up to $342,700 (both of these values are for single-family homes). Another component to FHA loans is that although the amounts may vary based on the location of each lender, many of the fees are standardized and are set within reasonable and customary ranges. Other fees are usually not permitted, or the seller pays those fees.

Mortgage-payment-expense-to-income ratio
(also known as mortgage-to-income ratio) A ratio found by taking the total house payment (to include principal, interest, PMI, insurance, and taxes) and dividing that payment by the household's combined gross income.

Debt-to-income ratio This ratio is found by taking the sum of all your monthly debt payments (including your expected house payment) and dividing that by the household's combined gross income.

As you evaluate FHA loans, there are two main ratios that you must be aware of. First is the ratio of **mortgage payment expense to income** (also known as the mortgage-to-income ratio). This ratio is found by taking the total house payment (to include principal, interest, PMI, insurance, and taxes) and dividing that payment by your combined gross income. The mortgage-to-income ratio must fall under 31% in order to qualify.

The next ratio that you must understand is the total **debt-to-income ratio**. This ratio is found by taking the sum of all your monthly debt payments (to include your expected house payment) and dividing that by your combined gross income. This total debt-to-income ratio must fall under 43%. In other words, this number will give you the percentage of your income that is committed to your debt payments.

Finally, FHA loans provide guidelines for approval even when the borrower's credit may be subpar. For example, a borrower paying off a Chapter 13 bankruptcy may still be eligible for an FHA loan as long as the agreed-upon payments are up-to-date and satisfactory. Similarly, two years of a usual 7-year credit evaluation will be reviewed in a Chapter 7 bankruptcy when debts have been forgiven. Although slow or late payments may come up in a credit report, the analysis of an FHA loan will take into consideration the overall pattern of payments versus those that are late in isolation. Finally, collections or other judgments that are minor in nature (subject to the FHA loan reviewer) should not be required to be paid off in order to qualify for an FHA loan.

Men and women of the armed services may be eligible for VA loans based on their length of service, current duty status, and character of service. The Department of Veterans Affairs office insures these loans and offers the following benefits:

- Down payment may be waived.
- Usually PMI is waived.

Courtesy of Ig0rZh/Fotolia.

The process for VA loans is just like that of FHA loans, in that they are handled by mortgage bankers for the loan process but will follow the guidelines set forth by the Department of Veteran Affairs, which guarantees or insures the loan from any default risk by the borrower.

OTHER GOVERNMENTAL PROGRAMS

The government provides support in other ways as well, such as through various welfare programs. Before any debate occurs regarding the efficiency of such programs, we provide an overview of several of the other main social welfare programs: unemployment, the Supplemental Nutrition Assistance Program, and Temporary Assistance for Needy Families.

Unemployment

Unemployment A benefit program that pays money to formerly employed workers who have become unemployed by no fault of their own and meet certain requirements determined by the state in which the worker lives.

Unfortunately, the loss of a job can lead a family into financial disaster, especially without adequate liquid savings to support a time of no employment. In order to help support families through job transitions, there is a governmental benefit known as unemployment. **Unemployment** is a benefit program that pays money to formerly employed workers who have become unemployed by no fault of their own and meet certain requirements determined by the state in which the worker lives. Unemployment benefits must be applied for through the state's unemployment office. Keep in mind that each state has different eligibility requirements.

Supplemental Nutrition Assistance Program

Supplemental Nutrition Assistance Program (SNAP) A federally funded program that helps low-income families buy food. These programs are mainly run through state or county offices.

The **Supplemental Nutrition Assistance Program (SNAP)**, formerly referred to as the food stamp program, is a federally funded program that helps low-income families buy food. SNAP programs are mainly run through state or county offices. SNAP works by allowing low-income individuals and families to apply for aid by supplying an overview of their income and assets in an online eligibility tool (or through a SNAP office) to determine eligibility. This calculation will let individuals know how much they may qualify for in food benefits. This calculation tool is not considered an application, so should you become eligible, you then apply through your state's online application or the closest SNAP office. After your application is approved, your benefit amount is added to an Electronic Benefits Transfer (EBT) card, which is similar in nature to a debit card. The benefit amount is added to the EBT card and can be used at authorized SNAP retailers for certain products.

Temporary Assistance for Needy Families

Temporary Assistance for Needy Families (TANF) A federal program that provides grant money to states in order to provide short-term financial support to low-income families who have dependents under the age of 18.

Formerly known as welfare, **Temporary Assistance for Needy Families (TANF)** is a federal program that provides grant money to states in order to provide short-term financial support to low-income families who have dependents under the age of 18. This program offers support for buying food and paying for housing, utilities, child care, job training, and other necessities. Differentiating it from its predecessor, TANF supports individuals and families by promoting job preparation, work, and marriage. Furthermore, TANF is designed to reduce the number of out-of-wedlock pregnancies while encouraging and promoting the formation and sustainability of two-parent families.

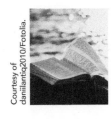

DISCIPLESHIP MOMENT AND REFLECTION

Eligibility for government housing programs, unemployment, SNAP (food stamps), and TANF generally isn't a life state that is dreamed of or sought after. How would you respond and how would you be challenged if you found yourself in need of one of these programs? Talk through this with your prayer and accountability partner.

SUMMARY

Although we may not want to accept social programs or even agree with how social programs function, we can't deny that these programs offer support for many Americans over the course of their lives. In this chapter, we looked at the history of many of our current social programs and why these programs were created. We need to understand that God's word speaks to the idea that the body of Christ should be taking care of the body of Christ; unfortunately, we could be doing a far better job than we are. In this regard, government has taken ownership of our social programs to help our retirees through retirement programs (Social Security) and health-care programs (Medicare). We reviewed the different aspects of Medicare and then reviewed the options for coverage of gaps within those policies (Medigap or Medicare Advantage Plans). We then looked at an overview of Medicaid, which is a state-supported program for low-income individuals to receive medical coverage. We then transitioned into housing programs offered through the government (FHA loans and VA loans). Finally, we provided an overview of some other governmental programs: unemployment, SNAP, and TANF.

SUMMARY REVIEW QUESTIONS

1. What do 1 Timothy 5:8 and Leviticus 19:3 say about providing for our families?

2. What factor determines your full retirement age? What is the current full retirement age?

3. How are Social Security credits earned? How many credits do you need to be eligible for most benefits through Social Security?

4. What are the two main criteria to indicate a disability for Social Security eligibility?

5. How does someone usually get survivor benefits from Social Security?

6. What are the three main categories of people who qualify for Supplemental Security Income benefits of Social Security?

7. Describe the four main parts of Medicare and the benefits of each part.

8. Explain how a Medicare recipient can "fill in the gaps" in Medicare coverage.

9. Explain how Medicaid works.

10. Describe the benefits associated with getting an FHA loan. What are the disadvantages?

11. What are the two ratios that lenders review in relation to the debt and income of borrowers? What are the significant levels of each ratio?

12. How can a U.S. veteran seek information regarding VA benefits in relation to buying a home?

13. What is the primary purpose of unemployment benefits?

14. How can individuals determine whether they qualify for SNAP and the level of benefits they are eligible for?

15. Outside of financial assistance, what other components of support does TANF offer?

Case Study Analysis

Bob walks through the door from a long day of work.

"Hey honey," yells Debbie from the kitchen as she is preparing dinner. "Steve from church called earlier for you. He told me that he was sending you an e-mail and that he is looking forward to our last meeting with him on Friday."

"What a day! We received a notice that the government is seeking to tax oil suppliers and that there may be a significant impact on our revenues. Although they didn't mention this directly, I assume that they may begin to have to lay off workers."

"Oh no! Do you think your job is in jeopardy?" Debbie blurted out in a panic.

"I don't think so, honey! Although this will all be in God's hands. I just get so frustrated that people in the government always feel that they have to keep changing things when, from the outside, it doesn't seem that anything is broken."

"Well don't get too mad, but Steve mentioned something about Social Security benefits and that he would put everything in an e-mail."

"Oh boy," Bob said with a sigh. "What now? I suppose we won't be entitled to Social Security with the way things seem to be going. Let me change clothes and sit down and read Steve's e-mail before dinner. Perhaps a good meal will put me back in a cheerful mood—I am hungry!"

Bob sat down and opened up Steve's e-mail.

Bob,

I hope things are going well. I am looking forward to our last scheduled meeting on Friday. I received a call from a friend of mine who is a financial advisor, and he mentioned that there seemed to be a reported discrepancy on the last batch of Social Security statements sent out. I was reviewing yours and wanted to make you aware of this. I have included a copy of the estimate calculation that you should receive and wanted you to calculate this before we meet. This will allow us to compare what you calculate with the statement sent by the Social Security Administration. As you go through this, note that you have exceeded the maximum earnings each year you have been employed (since 1983 when you started full time—at least that is what you mentioned to me).

I wanted to make you aware of this and hope that when we meet we can plan on using an accurate number as your plan continues to come together.

I look forward to Friday.

God Bless,

Steve

Assignment

1. Use the "Your Retirement Benefit: How It's Figured" document from the Social Security Administration to calculate Bob's estimated benefit from Social Security. Provide an answer to each step if it has a blank next to it.

2. After you have determined the estimated Social Security benefit, answer the following questions:

   - The amount you have determined is Bob's full retirement benefit. When do you believe you will take your benefit? Early at age 62? At full retirement age 67? Or delay to age 72? What factors do you need to consider in making this decision?

   - Based on your personal convictions, what is your overall thought of using Social Security in your retirement plan?

   - How does Bob's Social Security benefit help Bob and Debbie's overall retirement plan?

DEFINITIONS

Debt-to-income ratio   (p. 447)

Federal Housing Administration   (p. 447)

Fully insured   (p. 441)

Medicaid   (p. 446)

Medicare   (p. 444)

Medicare Advantage Plan   (p. 445)

Medigap   (p. 446)

Mortgage-payment-expense-to-income ratio (also known as mortgage-to-income ratio)   (p. 447)

Private mortgage insurance   (p. 447)

Social Security Administration   (p. 438)

Social Security credits   (p. 441)

Social Security disability benefits   (p. 442)

Supplemental Nutrition Assistance Program (SNAP)   (p. 448)

Supplemental Security Income   (p. 444)

Temporary Assistance for Needy Families (TANF)   (p. 449)

Unemployment   (p. 448)

SCRIPTURE VERSES (ESV)

Acts 20:35—In all things I have shown you that by working hard in this way we must help the weak and remember the words of the Lord Jesus, how he himself said, 'It is more blessed to give than to receive.'

Proverbs 19:17—Whoever is generous to the poor lends to the LORD, and he will repay him for his deed.

Matthew 25:35–40—For I was hungry and you gave me food, I was thirsty and you gave me drink, I was a stranger and you welcomed me, I was naked and you clothed me, I was sick and you visited me, I was in prison and you came to me.' Then the righteous will answer him, saying, 'Lord, when did we see you hungry and feed you, or thirsty and give you drink? And when did we see you a stranger and welcome you, or

naked and clothe you? And when did we see you sick or in prison and visit you?

Galatians 6:2—Bear one another's burdens, and so fulfill the law of Christ.

Matthew 5:42—Give to the one who begs from you, and do not refuse the one who would borrow from you.

Proverbs 14:31—Whoever oppresses a poor man insults his Maker, but he who is generous to the needy honors him.

2 Thessalonians 3:10—For even when we were with you, we would give you this command: If anyone is not willing to work, let him not eat.

ADDITIONAL READINGS

Benítez-Silva, H., Buchinsky, M., Chan, H. M., Rust, J., & Sheidvasser, S. (1999). An empirical analysis of the Social Security disability application, appeal, and award process. *Labour Economics*, 6(2), 147–178.

Conesa, J. C., & Krueger, D. (1999). Social Security reform with heterogeneous agents. *Review of Economic Dynamics*, 2(4), 757–795.

Duggan, M. (2006). *The growth in the Social Security disability rolls: A fiscal crisis unfolding* (No. w12436). Washington, DC: National Bureau of Economic Research.

Gillion, C. (Ed.). (2000). *Social Security pensions: Development and reform*. Geneva, Switzerland: International Labour Organization.

Gruber, J., & Wise, D. A. (Eds.). (2009). *Social Security programs and retirement around the world*. Chicago, IL: University of Chicago Press.

Huggett, M., & Ventura, G. (1999). On the distributional effects of Social Security reform. *Review of Economic Dynamics*, 2(3), 498–531.

Kline, A. (n.d.). *Social Security disability*. Retrieved from http://lprb.mncourts.gov/Articles/ArticleImages/A%20Lawyer's%20Role_Image.pdf

Samuelson, P. A. (1975). Optimum Social Security in a life-cycle growth model. *International Economic Review*, 539–544.

Social Security Administration Staff. (2005). *Fast facts and figures about Social Security 2005*. Washington, DC: Government Printing Office.

Von Wachter, T., Song, J., & Manchester, J. (2011). Trends in employment and earnings of allowed and rejected applicants to the Social Security disability insurance program. *The American Economic Review, 101*(7), 3308–3329.

REFERENCE

Ronsvalle J. L., & Ronsvalle, S. (2015). *The state of church giving through 2013*. Champaign, IL: Empty Tomb Publishing.

Chapter 19

Courtesy of duncanandison/Fotolia.

Choosing a Financial Advisor

BIG IDEA:
Listen to and accept godly advice from godly advisors.

- Understand the value that a financial professional can provide
- Describe the role and function of financial counselors
- Describe the role and function of brokers/financial managers
- Describe the role and function of financial planners
- Explain the differences in the business structures/models in which financial professionals are employed
- List the education, experience, and exam requirements for different professional designations
- Understand the value of biblical advice and wisdom regarding financial planning
- Establish guidelines to interview and manage financial advisors

Introduction

With all the material covered in the previous chapters, you might be thinking how overwhelming finances can be in our personal lives. In this section, we want to ensure that you are aware that you don't have to do it on your own. In the previous discussions of various topics, we have encouraged you to talk and pray through topics with your prayer and accountability partner, which we hope was valuable to you and your accountability partner. However, those who help keep us accountable and those we can seek prayer from may not be in a position to offer us advice in relation to making financial decisions, especially when we know that there seem to always be an infinite number of options. This chapter provides information you can use as you think about choosing a financial advisor. First we look at why it is important to have a financial advisor, focusing specifically on why a Christian financial advisor is ideal. We also review professional designations in the financial field and then provide a guide to help you interview various professionals.

Information available via the Internet on financial literacy topics, retirement, savings, and investing, just to name a few topics, continues to grow. Moreover, the number of websites offering financial products and services to individuals also continues to grow, making deciphering truth from fiction almost impossible. Unfortunately, many people argue that due to the amount of information available to individuals, professional financial advisors are no longer needed. Additionally, you may have a stereotype about financial advisors or financial planners that they are just salespeople trying to sell you something that you don't need. Keep in mind that there are always those who are out for their own benefit, seeking their own financial gain. 1 John 4:1: "Beloved, believe not every spirit, but try the spirits whether they are of God: because many false prophets are gone out into the world." That said, there are many financial professionals who are in their profession to help. Financial professionals, however, can be found in a wide variety of firms and business types, and it is important to understand how each business structure is set up in order for you to best evaluate what structure best meets your needs in financial planning.

Without going into the legislation that has been instrumental in creating these differences, we do want to make a few points before we begin. First, depending on the services provided by financial professionals, they might fall into several different roles. It is important to be aware when your financial professional is acting in a different capacity. This section will help you identify in what capacity your financial professional is being engaged depending on the services being supplied. This should make more sense as we progress through the different roles. Another note is that the terms used to describe your financial professional may be interchangeable, so it is critical to understand the different roles and how they apply to your situation.

Financial Counselors

Financial counselors
Those in a position to work with individual clients, usually one on one, to assist clients with establishing personal budgets, evaluating their current debts, helping set financial goals, and working to create an action plan to help reach those goals.

Financial counselors are those in a position to work with individuals, usually one on one, where the counselor can assist clients with establishing personal budgets, evaluating their current debts, setting financial goals, and working to create an action plan to help reach those goals. Financial counselors are usually trained in counseling techniques as well as basic fundamentals of personal financial management. In addition, financial counselors abide by various codes of ethics and consumer protection guidelines. Several training courses are designed to prepare financial counselors, such as the Certified Personal Finance Counselor offered by the Center for Financial Certifications. In December 2015, the National Commission for Certifying Agencies (NCCA) granted the Association for Financial Counseling, Planning, and Education (AFCPE) accreditation for its Accredited Financial Counselor® (AFC®) designation. According to the AFCPE's competencies, an AFC should be able to:

1. Gather pertinent client information
2. Assist clients in creating an action plan
3. Analyze client financial statements, financial ratios, and spending plans
4. Understand clients' spending habits and other money management techniques
5. Guide clients in the area of credit and debt
6. Provide clients information on consumer protection
7. Educate clients on managing property (rent/own)
8. Educate clients on financial risks and risk management
9. Provide an overview of investments to clients
10. Educate clients on retirement and estate planning

Financial counselors usually are compensated in one of two ways. First, financial counselors may charge a session fee to their clients. Each session may be related to a specific topic or topics and may be from an hour to several hours in length. The other compensation structure (although very similar) is to charge an hourly fee, usually ranging anywhere from $50 to $150 per hour. One important note is that financial counselors are not regulated and are not required to obtain any specific training in order to use the title of financial counselor.

Brokers—Financial Managers

Stock brokers Originally, those who would buy and sell financial securities (stocks and bonds) and earn a commission on what they bought or sold for a client; more generally, those who receive compensation, usually in the form of commissions, for each transaction they help a client complete.

Stock brokers, or simply brokers, originally referred to those who would buy and sell financial securities (stocks and bonds) and earn a commission on what they bought or sold for a client. These financial professionals are those who receive compensation, usually in the form of commissions, for each transaction they help a client complete. Unfortunately, for the investing public, the title of these financial professionals is not standard or consistent within the industry. Some firms call these brokers *financial advisors*, some use *financial managers*, and others use *financial consultants*, just to name a few. Due to the number of titles used in the financial industry, it may be best to decipher how an advisor gets paid. Brokers get paid when they conduct a transaction on your behalf. In order for brokers to be eligible to transact sales for a client, they must pass two national exams sponsored by the **Financial Industry Regulatory Authority (FINRA),** which is a regulatory body overseeing those who conduct financial transactions on behalf of clients. The two exams are the FINRA Series 7—General Securities Representative exam and the FINRA Series 63—Uniform Securities Agent State Law exam. The Series 7 exam tests the applicant's knowledge of and technical competence in financial products and services, legislation, and ethics, whereas the Series 63 exam tests the applicant's robust understanding as to the differences in state legislation and registrations. Passing these two exams requires a thorough understanding of and ability to apply a range of financial services, thus ensuring the competency of those who seek to engage in financial transactions on behalf of clients. Unfortunately, there does exist a potential issue for investors.

Financial Industry Regulatory Authority (FINRA) A self-regulatory organization whose role is to oversee those who conduct financial transactions on behalf of clients.

Suitability In regard to financial planning, investments that meet the objectives of an investor and that fall within the client's means.

Risk tolerance The level of risk a client is willing to take.

According to FINRA, a broker must ensure that two main client characteristics are analyzed before a security can be determined suitable. **Suitability** refers to an investment meeting the objectives of an investor and falling within the client's means. Three main characteristics are considered in order to understand or determine whether an investment is suitable for a client: a client's risk tolerance, a client's time horizon, and a client's liquidity. **Risk tolerance** is determined by how much risk a client is willing to take. Risk tolerance is usually determined by a subjective question posed to the investor, such as, "What would classify your risk tolerance?" In this case, answer choices are aggressive, moderate, and conservative. Another option is to have an investor answer a series of questions, and those answers are then given a score. The scores are then summed to determine a client's risk level. Financial professionals need to use this information to make sure that an investment falls within a risk level that is comfortable for the client.

Time horizon The length of time that an investor has before potentially needing to access the capital used to purchase an investment.

The second component is a client's **time horizon,** the time period before they may need access to the money used to purchase the investment. Investments range widely in the duration of their maturity, from several weeks to those that are established in perpetuity—in other words, forever. Some investments require an investor to hold on to the investment for a specific period of time or a penalty can be assessed. Financial professionals are required to document how long an investor has before the invested money must be available. This determination keeps a financial professional from buying an investment that will require a longer holding period than an investor has before needing to access the investment money. This issue of time horizon is especially important to elderly investors who may have needs to pay for and could be placed in an inappropriate investment if the financial professional is unaware of the client's need for money.

Finally, financial professionals need to make sure that they understand a client's **liquidity**, or available cash reserves. Although this is similar in nature to time horizon, a financial professional needs to make sure that the investment does not put a client in an inappropriate position relative to the ability to access other forms of liquid capital. For example, if a client has $5,000 in savings, it would not be prudent to purchase a $5,000 investment for that client if the client knows he or she will need that money for emergencies.

When considering these three characteristics of investors that need to be determined, it is important to note that even though an investment may satisfactorily meet these requirements for the client, it does not mean that the investment is appropriate for the client. Let's give an example of how this may play out.

Suppose Bob, whose net worth is $800,000 has $80,000 (1/10 of his assets) in cash reserves that he wants to invest. He hears from a friend that a new company, Xcaliber Technologies, is coming out with a device that controls your car, allowing you to remotely control your car from anywhere. In this situation, is an investment in this company suitable for the client? If Bob's risk tolerance is classified as aggressive, his time horizon is 10 to 20 years, and he has other liquid investments so that he has liquidity, this investment would satisfy the FINRA criteria. The financial professional could satisfy the regulatory obligation for the purchase of this investment (risk tolerance, time horizon, and liquidity), but would that make it an appropriate investment? The unfortunate answer is *it depends*. We don't know about the other investments Bob holds, what his objectives in investing are, and many other components in Bob's financial picture to make an appropriate determination. The point here is that for financial professionals who act as a broker, the requirements for determining suitability for a client do not always clearly suggest what is appropriate for a particular client.

Registered Investment Advisors (Fee Only)

Registered Investment Advisors are quite a bit different than brokers or those who buy and sell on a commission basis. Registered Investment Advisors, commonly referred to as RIAs, do select from the same pool of investments as brokers do for clients, but their pay structure and regulation vastly differ from that of brokers. Although still regulated by FINRA, RIAs must pass the FINRA 65—Uniform Investment Advisor Law Exam or FINRA 66—Uniform Combined State Law Exam in order to charge a fee for ongoing financial advice. This fee for ongoing advice is usually structured by charging a percentage of the investment dollars that are managed by the RIA, known as assets under management (AUM). The industry has some variation in the percentages charged to clients, but the fee charged by many advisors will fall within 50 basis points (.5%) to 2 percentage points (2%) of the value of a client's account, charged annually. Because these accounts have AUM fees, clients receiving advice from their RIA usually are not charged transactions fees or commissions on the transactions that occur in their accounts.

The advantages of this model are found in the fee structure. A financial professional who charges a commission gets paid once the transaction occurs, regardless of the outcome of that financial transaction. In other words, a financial professional gets paid upon the transaction being completed and is not impacted, either positively or negatively, after the transaction. An RIA, however, is compensated by the amount of assets under management. Therefore, if a client's account values go down, then the amount of fees

Liquidity The amount of cash reserves a client has available.

Registered Investment Advisor (RIA) A financial professional who is able to offer financial advice and charge an ongoing fee for that advice. The ongoing fee is usually established as a percentage of the assets managed or advised on for a client.

Courtesy of Galyna Andrushko/Fotolia.

collected by an RIA will subsequently go down as well. This thus aligns an RIA to the client because both the client and the RIA are positively rewarded with account increases and negatively impacted with account decreases. It is in the best interest of the RIA to continually seek financial investments that are likely to increase over time because that will reward the RIA with an increase in fee income.

There is, unfortunately, a drawback to this model, though. Recall that this model is such that the investor is paying a continual fee for advice from the RIA. What happens if the RIA does not look at your account often enough? In this situation, you are being charged fees when your financial professional may not be providing you adequate service. Thus, it is best to determine and articulate the appropriate amount of engagement prior to establishing a relationship between the RIA and the client.

Financial Planners

The final model we will discuss is that of a financial planner. Financial planners can come in all sorts, so it is important to understand their expertise and experience. There is, unfortunately, no specific requirements that need to be met in order to call oneself a financial planner. That said, you should look for someone who holds the Certified Financial Planner™ (CFP®) designation issued by the Certified Financial Planner (CFP) Board of Standards, Inc. In order to hold the CFP® designation, a financial professional must complete the following requirements:

- Complete a CFP®-registered educational program. which covers topics in:
  - Financial planning
  - Investment planning
  - Income tax planning
  - Estate planning
  - Insurance and risk management planning
  - Retirement planning
  - Comprehensive case study analysis
- Pass the CFP Board of Standards, Inc., national exam given three times annually.
- Complete 3 years (6,000 hours) of experience in any of the following areas:
  - Establishing and defining the client/advisor relationship
  - Gathering client data
  - Analyzing and evaluating the client's financial status
  - Developing and presenting financial planning recommendations
  - Implementing the financial planning recommendations
  - Monitoring the financial planning recommendations

Although there are other designations, which are discussed later in this section, the CFP® designation is probably the most notable in terms of financial planning due to the vast amount of depth that is required in the educational requirements. As far as compensation, financial planners will usually establish one of two different compensation structures; some may use a combination of both depending on the needs of a client. The first compensation structure is that of charging an hourly fee. These planners will sit down with clients (similar to financial counselors) but will be able to bring more depth to the components of a comprehensive plan and guide clients in the implementation of that plan. Some CFPs® will work with other financial professionals, such as estate planners, insurance agents, and certified public accountants (CPAs), to ensure that the client's goal and objectives are being met. Like an attorney or CPA, when a CFP® is working on an hourly basis, the CPA will clock the amount of time devoted to each client and then bill for those hours. The second compensation structure for financial planners is that of charging a flat rate for a financial plan along with an annual fee for reviewing and updating the plan. These fees may vary but will range from as low as $1,500 to as high as $25,000, or more, depending on the financial plan and the complexity of the plan that needs to be created.

Courtesy of daniilantiq2010/Fotolia.

PROFESSIONAL DESIGNATIONS

We have covered several professional designations that you will find in the area of financial planning. To recap, we reviewed the AFC certification for financial counseling and the CFP™ designation for financial planning. There are many designations, each with different educational and experiential requirements. We will review the most common that you will find in the field of financial planning.

Charted Financial Analyst (CFA®)

Charted Financial Analyst (CFA®) is a designation offered by the Charted Financial Analyst (CFA) Institute, and those who have earned the CFA are referred to ask CFA charter holders. The CFA consists of three exams (Level I, Level II, and Level III). Once the applicant has passed these three exams (Level I is offered twice per year, and Level II and Level III are only offered once per year), 3 years of professional experience must be documented. Many CFAs are portfolio managers or conduct security analysis as they receive extensive training in accounting, corporate finance, security analysis, and portfolio management.

Chartered Financial Consultant (ChFC®)

The Chartered Financial Consultant (ChFC®) designation is awarded by the American College, and is known as an advanced financial planning designation. The educational requirements for the ChFC® require the student to take the seven CFP courses (identified in the previous section) coupled with three additional courses (electives) that the student may find interesting. In total, this designation requires completion of 10 courses, with each requiring a passing exam upon the completion of that course. ChFCs® have extensive knowledge in financial planning applications; however, they are not required to obtain any specific experience requirement to be able to use the designation.

Certified Investment Management Analyst (CIMA)

The highly acclaimed Certified Investment Management Analyst designation is offered by the Investment Management Consultants Association (IMCA), which was established to offer "premier investment consulting and wealth management credentials and world-class educational offerings through membership, conferences, research, and publications" (IMCA, 2016). One of the significant educational aspects of the CIMA® is the focus on portfolio construction for clients integrating the following five main areas of financial analysis:

1. Governance of the financial services industry
2. Investment fundamentals
3. Portfolio performance and risk measures
4. Traditional and alternative investments
5. Portfolio theory and behavioral finance
6. Investment consulting process

To qualify to become a CIMA®, the candidate must complete an application and pass a background check. Then the candidate will study (roughly 100 hours of instruction) in order to pass the qualifying exam. Once the candidate has passed the qualification exam, the candidate moves into a week-long intensive program offered by either Wharton School of Business or Booth School of Business. During this week-long intensive program, the candidate completes a rigorous executive education curriculum which prepares them for the final step. Upon the completion of this week-long course, the candidate takes a 4-hour comprehensive exam. Candidates will usually receive their scores several weeks later. Upon passing the comprehensive exam, candidates must satisfy their 3-year experience requirement in order to present themselves as a CIMA® designee.

Certified Public Accountant (CPA)

Although CPAs are not specifically focused on financial planning, they do have an important role in financial planning. That said, some CPAs hold a Personal Financial Specialist (PFS) designation, which signifies completion of a curriculum built for CPAs who desire to engage in financial planning with clients. CPAs are governed by state laws, and each state may be different. The process to become a CPA is somewhat standard across states, though. As with many of the professional designations mentioned thus far, the CPA requires an education component, completion of an examination, and completion of an experience requirement. Although the education requirement is not standardized, many states require 150 hours of instruction. Of these 150 hours, states vary on the number of undergraduate and graduate accounting courses. It is likely that an accounting student will take roughly 24 hours of accounting courses at the undergraduate level and another 12 to 15 hours of graduate courses in accounting. There are four sections in the CPA exam:

- Auditing and Attestation
- Business Environment and Concepts
- Financial Accounting Reporting
- Regulations

As for experience, states will usually require 1 to 2 years of experience in working alongside or under a licensed CPA. The majority of people seek the services of CPAs in preparing and submitting their tax returns. However, those CPAs who also hold the PFS® designation can offer tax planning services and integrate the complexity of financial planning into the client's experience.

Chartered Life Underwriter (CLU)

The Chartered Life Underwriter (CLU®) designation is offered by the American College to those who seek additional training in risk management and insurance for individuals, business owners, and other professionals. CLU candidates must take the following five required courses and take an additional three courses offered by the American College. The five required courses are:

- Fundamentals of Insurance Planning
- Individual Life Insurance
- Life Insurance Law
- Fundamentals of Estate Planning
- Planning for Business Owners and Professionals

CLU® designees can help clients understand and determine the types and amounts of insurance coverage they may need. Additionally, CLU® holders can help clients in estate planning in terms of understanding how insurance can play a significant part in the wealth transfer process.

Courtesy of danilantiq2010/Fotolia.

DISCIPLESHIP MOMENT AND REFLECTION

In the previous Discipleship Moment, you gathered information on five financial advisors. Next, determine what certifications each advisor holds and reflect on which advisor would be most helpful in your circumstances.

WHY BIBLICAL ADVICE

As you can see, there are a vast array of financial designations that offer clients a sense of the education and experience that financial professionals have. However, is that all? Is that the only criteria that you should evaluate in seeking financial advice? These designations can suggest the technical competence of a financial advisor, but may not offer the full picture, especially regarding his or her worldview or Christian perspective.

We believe that your financial advice needs to have technical competence but also must never stray from biblical wisdom. Why? For several main reasons: (1) God's word is always true (Proverbs 30:5, John 17:17), (2) God's word is unchanging (Matthew 5:18, Matthew 24:35), and (3) God's word is our source of life (Deuteronomy 8:3, Romans 10:17, 1 Peter 1:23).

As we look at these biblical truths, we can infer the following:

1. A biblical worldview of finances works across every economic environment and for any economic social class. In other words, God's word on finances relates to all people under all circumstances.

2. God's word on finances is and will always be transferrable through replication and teaching.

Knowing these truths and understanding them may seem somewhat obvious, but applying them in our finances may prove to be challenging. Seeing this dilemma and the lack of biblical wisdom in the professional world, Ron Blue was instrumental in establishing Kingdom Advisors, which is described as:

A professional association that offers in-depth training and a tight-knit community to Christian financial professionals who want to integrate their faith with their practice. (Kingdom Advisors, 2016. Retrieved from Kingdomadvisors.com)

With the establishment of Kingdom Advisors, there is a now a platform through which Christian financial professionals can receive the three E's (education, experience, and examination) through an integration of their faith. In order to qualify to become a Certified Kingdom Advisor (CKA®), an advisor must complete the following components:

- Complete the education training offered by two prestigious Christian Universities, which covers roughly 100 hours of instruction
- Pass the CKA® national exam offered at various proctored testing facilities
- Hold an industry-approved designation or have at least 10 years of financial planning experience
- Complete the CKA® application

Ron's Corner

I often get asked why I started Kingdom Advisors, which was formed originally with 16 members. The answer is that I believe there is a very real difference between a Christian who is a financial advisor and a Christian financial advisor. I wanted to train people to integrate their faith into their jobs so that they could become Christian financial advisors instead of simply financial advisors who also happened to be Christians. Additionally, I had observed over many years in my practice that the financial services world does a very good job of training people to analyze financial situations, but does a very poor job of training people in how to incorporate values and morals into their professional advice. These things should not be kept separate! Starting Kingdom Advisors gave me an avenue to train a new group of Christian financial advisors!

Courtesy of daniilantiq2010/Fotolia.

DISCIPLESHIP MOMENT AND REFLECTION

Finally, take a third step in looking at the advisors you have chosen and examine whether they follow biblical principles.

HOW TO SELECT A FINANCIAL ADVISOR

Many professional organizations that grant financial designations also offer search capabilities to find professionals with those designations based on your specific location. Within the websites of the organizations, you may find information such as the location, contact information, and short biographies of the financial professionals in your area.

Another way to inquire about financial professionals is to sit down with your pastoral staff and see who in your local church provides these services. Talking to a financial professional in your church does not automatically mean that you must hire that individual, but it can be a good starting point for your interview process.

It is vital that as you seek out financial guidance, you learn to ask the right questions. In order to provide you some guidance, Table 19.1 lists several questions that you should be ready to ask a potential financial advisor.

Table 19.1 Questionnaire for Interviewing a Financial Advisor

1. Tell me about how you became a financial advisor/planner.
2. What are some of the reasons you decided on this career path?
3. How long have you been an advisor?
4. What is your educational background?
5. What professional designations do you have, and how long have you had them?
6. What is your role in terms of taking on a fiduciary relationship?
7. Tell me about any legal actions that have taken place against you.
8. Tell me about your average client (age, income, asset level, experience).
9. Could you provide me several clients' contact information so that I may use them as references?
10. Tell me about your firm.
11. What services do you provide on behalf of your clients?
12. Tell me about any other professionals you engage with in order to provide services to your clients (CPAs, attorneys, etc.).
13. Tell me about your fee structure and how you get compensated.
14. Tell me about the cost structures associated with the products and services you utilize for your clients.
15. Tell me about how you help assess my financial situation and risk tolerance.
16. How do you use that information (question 15) to determine the most appropriate mix of investments for me?
17. What type of guidelines do you rely on when making investment decisions?
18. How do you incorporate my future income (such as Social Security) in the analysis of my outcomes?
19. How often do usually meet with clients?
20. When creating a portfolio or adjusting a current plan, what assumptions are usually made (inflation rates, expected returns, market performance, etc.)?
21. How do you incorporate the impact of taxes in clients' portfolios?
22. As a Christian, I like to make sure that my Christian values are incorporated into my finances. What are your spiritual beliefs?
23. How do you incorporate your values into your practice?
24. Based on our conversation today, do you feel that you would be a good advisor for me? Why or why not?

As you think about other questions you may ask a financial advisor/planner, it is probably more important to keep track of the questions that the financial professional asks you. One of the most rewarding aspects of having a Christian financial planner is that he or she (hopefully) is engaged in the faith and will ask you questions that you may not find relevant at first. For example, you will begin to know the heart of the advisor should you be asked questions like the following:

- How do you feel about your investments matching your values?
- How much is enough to you?
- What are your personal convictions as they relate to money?
- Whom do you have to hold you accountable in ensuring your actions align with our role as stewards?

MANAGING MULTIPLE ADVISORS

With the plethora of financial designations, you may find it challenging to choose just one advisor to guide you through your financial affairs. Perhaps you choose to have a CPA do your taxes, have a CFP® help to map out your financial future, have a CLU® buy and manage your insurance and risk management products, and have a CFA put together a portfolio of investments that will guide you in reaching your goals in accordance with your risk profile. As we see in **Proverbs 15:22**:

> Without counsel plans fail, but with many advisors they succeed.

Although each one of these financial professionals will bring a certain level of expertise to your finances, this setup may be problematic if not appropriately handled. Farming out different aspects of your finances to different financial professionals creates a new role for you as their client, an advisor. One of the many reasons to hire financial professionals (outside of their obvious technical competence) is to delegate responsibility. If you have multiple advisors, then the management of this "team" of advisors ultimately falls on you. Your responsibilities now include:

- Manage the responsibilities, strategies and recommendations from each advisor
- Coordinate recommendations to ensure no overlapping or conflicting advice
- Establish guidelines for changes that reflect a combined coordinated effort

These three responsibilities force you to become an active manager of managers and can become very complicated, especially if you don't have the expertise to handle such a task. In order to make having multiple advisors manageable, we suggest following these simple steps to ensure your team is efficient and effective.

Step 1: Make sure that the team members know of one another.

This first step may seem obvious, but can actually be missed if not taken as a proactive step. If you have multiple people helping you, make sure that each financial professional is aware of the other professionals by giving each of your advisors the other advisors' contact information.

Step 2: Provide advisors documented approval to talk to one another on your behalf.

In this era of privacy and protection, it can be cumbersome for financial professionals to talk to other professionals on your behalf. Therefore, you should provide in writing your approval to provide information regarding your accounts and transactions to other members of your team of financial professionals. Although this may seem uncomfortable, we hope that you have diligently vetted each of your financial professionals through an interview of sorts and trust those whom you have hired to provide you advice. If you trust these professionals, then you should trust them enough to allow them to talk to other professionals you trust in order to most appropriately serve your best interest.

Step 3: Establish a "primary" advisor on the team.

You need to select a primary advisor who will support the other professionals who provide you advice; you can think of this individual as the team's quarterback. For many, this is the CFP® because those who hold this designation have a general, broad overview of most aspects of financial planning topics and can ensure a comprehensive evaluation from each of the other professionals. Also, you will want to make sure that your primary advisor aligns with your spiritual values, such as by selecting a Certified Kingdom Advisor.

Step 4: Establish regular team meetings.

Once your team of advisors is established and you have set a primary advisor to lead the team, it is important to establish an effective communication strategy to bring everyone together and discuss your finances as well as address any changes. This can be accomplished by setting up an annual conference call for all your advisors to take part in, or it may be an informal gathering for lunch at a local restaurant. There is no particular venue that is required; what is important is that you, as the client, make sure that all your advisors meet at least annually to discuss your situation. This will help all the advisors stay in agreement regarding how to best manage your financial situation and work toward goal attainment.

SUMMARY

This chapter focused on providing you relevant information regarding identifying and selecting the right financial professionals to help you meet your needs, whether that is in the form of financial counselors or professional money managers. We looked at the structure of each of the different types of positions for financial professionals, focusing on how they are compensated, which is one of the most significant differentiators. Each financial professional can gain educational acumen by obtaining professional designations. The main financial professional designations were described in terms of their educational, experience, and exam requirements. We then turned our attention to establishing a basis for seeking not only technical competence through professional designations, but also why you should seek those who offer advice from a biblical perspective. We know that God's word is always true, unchanging, and transferrable to others. Finally, we sought to provide you a guide to interviewing financial advisors and steps to take to ensure an appropriate management of multiple financial professionals.

SUMMARY REVIEW QUESTIONS

1. What are reasons to work with a financial advisor?

2. In your own words, define the role and functions of a financial counselor.

3. What professional designations would you find appropriate for those practicing as financial counselors?

4. According to the AFCPE, what are the 10 competencies of a financial counselor?

5. What does successful completion of the FINRA Series 7 exam allow a broker to do? FINRA Series 63?

6. What does suitability mean, and how does it relate to investments and investors?

7. What are the components of suitability? How can suitability become problematic?

8. What differentiates a registered investment advisor from a stock broker?

9. What are the topics that CFP candidates must be competent in?

10. How are the different models discussed in this chapter differentiated by their fee structures?

11. Describe the characteristics of the following designations:
    a. CFA®
    b. ChFC®
    c. CIMA
    d. CPA
    e. CLU

12. What are the reasons that we should seek biblical wisdom in relation to our finances?

13. In Ron's Corner, what did Ron explain that he observed in relation to integrating biblical wisdom into a financial advisory practice?

14. Outline reasons why you should interview advisors. (Feel free to use questions in the interview guide for help.)

15. What are the steps you can take to help make working with a team of advisors more effective?

Case Study Analysis

As Bob and Steve finalized their conversation regarding the Social Security discrepancy (Debbie was caught up in a text conversation with Chloe about driving to the high school basketball game with friends), the conversation quickly changed.

Steve paused and then said, "Bob, Debbie, it has been great working with you, but I must make a comment. I am no longer a financial planner. I have a true passion for helping people with their finances, but I can't be your full-time advisor. I hope that our time has helped you and, most importantly, that you have had an opportunity to grow closer to Christ during this time. However, I believe it is now time to have you seek an advisor who is in a position to be in a hands-on, active, ongoing relationship."

Bob and Debbie knew that what Steve was saying was correct, although it did make them feel a bit uneasy because both Bob and Debbie truly felt good about their relationship with Steve during this process.

Steve continued, "I have prepared an assignment for you to complete that will help you seek a financial advisor who aligns with your values and convictions. I have put many of the items in perspective in terms of importance, but keep in mind that each advisor has his or her own set of experiences and ideas as to what is in the client's best interest. I pray that you will be as open-minded with your new advisor as you were with me.

"Before we wrap up, let me pray for us:

Heavenly Father,

I want to thank you for your great mercy and grace that you give to us each and every day. Father, as we think about the way we manage money, I want us to acknowledge that our handling of money is an act of worship to you—that we may honor you with what you have entrusted to us and that the way we handle our finances will bring you glory. Lord, I pray that the Spirit will be with Bob and Debbie as they prepare to seek wise counsel to continue to guide them in being good stewards. I pray that you will encourage and instruct them in their decision-making process as they start to look for a financial advisor. And Father, I pray that whomever you lead them to will be focused on your word and provide Bob and Debbie biblically wise counsel—that the advisor's convictions, attitudes, and focus toward you will align with those of Bob and Debbie. Lord, be with Bob and Debbie and their wonderful family,

so that they may continue to be fruitful stewards of what you have entrusted to them.

Amen."

Assignment

Prepare a list of the characteristics, experience, education, and designations of a financial professional that you feel would be best suited for your financial situation. Then, search the Kingdom Advisors website (www.kingdomadvisors.com) and find an advisor in your immediate area. Contact the advisor to set up an interview appointment, and use the interview guide as a baseline to conduct an interview with this individual. If you do not have an advisor nearby, you can find someone in your state whom you can call and interview. Then answer the following questions:

- What was your impression of this advisor?
- How long has this advisor been in the business?
- What education does the advisor have?
- What firm does the advisor work for?
- Does the firm allow the advisor to identify as a Kingdom Advisor?
- What designations does the advisor have?
- Do the advisor's values align with yours? How did you determine whether your values were in alignment?
- How did this assignment prepare you to talk to an advisor in the future?

DEFINITIONS

Financial counselors (p. 456)

Financial Industry Regulatory Authority (FINRA) (p. 457)

Liquidity (p. 458)

Registered Investment Advisor (RIA) (p. 458)

Risk tolerance (p. 457)

Stock brokers (p. 457)

Suitability (p. 457)

Time horizon (p. 457)

SCRIPTURE VERSES (ESV)

1 John 4:1—Beloved, believe not every spirit, but try the spirits whether they are of God: because many false prophets are gone out into the world.

Proverbs 30:5—Every word of God is flawless; he is a shield to those who take refuge in him.

John 17:17—Sanctify them by the truth; your word is truth.

Matthew 5:18—For truly I tell you, until heaven and earth disappear, not the smallest letter, not the least stroke of a pen, will by any means disappear from the Law until everything is accomplished.

Matthew 24:35—Heaven and earth will pass away, but my words will never pass away.

Deuteronomy 8:3—He humbled you, causing you to hunger and then feeding you with manna, which neither you nor your ancestors had known, to teach you that man does not live on bread alone but on every word that comes from the mouth of the LORD.

Romans 10:17—Consequently, faith comes from hearing the message, and the message is heard through the word about Christ.

1 Peter 1:23—For you have been born again, not of perishable seed, but of imperishable, through the living and enduring word of God.

Proverbs 15:22—Plans fail for lack of counsel, but with many advisers they succeed.

ADDITIONAL READINGS

Bae, S. C., & Sandager, J. P. (1997). What consumers look for in financial planners. *Journal of Financial Counseling and Planning, 8*(2), 9.

Brown, C. E., Nielson, N. I., & Phillips, M. E. (1990). Expert systems for personal financial planning. *Journal of Financial Planning, 3*(3), 137–143.

Callan, V. J., & Johnson, M. (2002). Some guidelines for financial planners in measuring and advising clients about their levels of risk tolerance. *Journal of Personal Finance, 1*(1), 31–44.

Dubofsky, D., & Sussman, L. (2009). The changing role of the financial planner part 1: From financial analytics to coaching and life planning. *Journal of Financial Planning, 22*(8), 48–57.

Hanna, S. D., & Lindamood, S. (2010). Quantifying the economic benefits of personal financial planning. *Financial Services Review, 19*(2).

Hutchison, P. D., & Fleischman, G. M. (2003). Professional certification opportunities for accountants. *The CPA Journal, 73*(3), 48.

Miller, S. A., & Montalto, C. P. (2001). Who uses financial planners? Evidence from the 1998 Survey of Consumer Finances. *Consumer Interests Annual, 47*, 1–9.

Oleson, M., Nielsen, R. B., & Martin, T. (2004). Accredited financial counselor: The state of the designation. *Journal of Financial Counseling and Planning, 15*(2), 23–26.

Rattiner, J. H. (2010). *Getting started as a financial planner* (Vol. 8). New York, NY: John Wiley and Sons.

Thaler, R. H., & Benartzi, S. (2004). Save more tomorrow™: Using behavioral economics to increase employee saving. *Journal of Political Economy, 112*(S1), S164–S187.

REFERENCES

Investment Management Consultant Association. (2016).

Kingdom Advisors. (2016). Retrieved from Kingdomadvisors .com

Case Study

Case Study Disclaimer

The information contained in this Case Study is to be used only as a case study example for teaching purposes. The information in the Case Study is both factual and fictional. This case is designed exclusively for the purposes of this textbook and should not be intended for financial advice. Please consult a financial professional for customized advice for your personal information.

Bob and Debbie Profile

Bob and Debbie Smith Background

Bob and Debbie Smith were married on September 25, 1992 (their 25th wedding anniversary is approaching). Bob was 25 years old and Debbie was 23 when the couple was married. They both attended New Mexico State University, where they met and dated off and on until a mutual friend suggested they "just commit already!" and they finally tied the knot. Upon graduation, Bob began working as a project manager for a small oil and gas exploration company and was making pretty good money ($55,000 per year), and Debbie was working as a receptionist for a local bank in their new hometown of Lovington, New Mexico.

Bob is a very pragmatic thinker. As a project manager, he is constantly looking for the solution that makes the most sense and that can be completed in the most cost-effective manner. He is well respected within his organization; however, in 2012 Bob was involved in a lawsuit filed by a county in which his firm, Lextin Oil Supply, was hired to design and build a new drilling site. A county geologist believed an oil pocket was located near the drilling site, and the lawsuit claims the drilling rigs were not inspected for safety. A leak in the pipes spewed over 50,000 barrels of oil, causing damage to the soil and wildlife in the area. Bob was not specifically named in the lawsuit, but he was the manager over the installation of the rigs for this project. Even though this event took place several years ago, Bob still gets upset when it comes up in conversation because the lawsuit took a big toll on his family.

Debbie grew up in a Christian home. She is quiet and heavily conservative. She would admit that she doesn't speak up during many family decisions, especially in relation to money, which she thinks is appropriate, but rather defers to Bob for most family decisions because she trusts Bob's judgment. As the kids have gotten older, she has more free time and has been comfortable moving away from the paradigm that the husband should be the only decision maker. This transition has been heavily influenced by spending time with her mom, who has been a widow for the past few years. Now that her mom has had to learn how to make decisions and take care of herself, she has really reinforced this idea to Debbie, hoping she doesn't fall into the trap that she becomes incapable of managing the family should something happen to Bob.

Bob and Debbie feel that they are doing okay financially. Through Bob's retirement, he has saved up some money and feels that it might be time to start thinking about retiring and living on what they have. Bob is not sure what the numbers look like over the next 25 to 30 years, but now that he is a millionaire, he feels confident he is ready. Debbie, on the other hand, feels very insecure at the idea of Bob stopping work and only living on what they have. Debbie worries that there are still so many things to pay for: college, retirement, health care, and so forth. These worries have been the main focus of her prayers over the past 6 months, as Bob and Debbie have differing views on the possible outcomes. Due to the known differences of opinion, the topic of retirement hasn't been brought up in conversation lately, but both know a decision needs to be made.

SPIRITUAL BACKGROUND

Bob grew up going to church with his family on occasion when they were in town and not traveling due to sporting events. His parents rarely discussed spiritual matters and rarely prayed or read the Bible in their home. Bob became a Christian several years after being married to Debbie as a result of her influence and witness. Now as a Christian, he is committed to attending church regularly and raising his kids in a more biblically based home.

Debbie is the daughter of a military chaplain and lived at various military bases across the country and overseas where her father was ministering. Her parents prayed with her regularly and often read the Bible with her and her siblings. She enjoyed a close relationship with them, and they often discussed spiritual matters together. She committed her life to Christ at the age of 9 while overseas with her family. From that point forward, she was active in her church and often helped in the nursery.

EXTENDED FAMILY

Bob's parents are frail. They live in Florida in a senior living facility. His father is 74 and his mother is 71. His father is on blood pressure medication, and his mother recently had a hip replacement. Bob's parents are starting to consider their long-term health-care plans as they are aging.

Bob has one older brother who is a doctor in northern California, practicing orthopedic medicine. He is divorced and has two children, ages 24 and 20.

Debbie's father passed away 4 years ago from bone cancer. Her mother sold their house when her husband passed and bought a small condo in a senior living community. She is 78. She is in good health and enjoys her time in the community playing bridge with a small group of widows. She also volunteers in a nearby food pantry.

Debbie has two older brothers and one younger brother. Her oldest brother is now a missionary in the Philippines, where he helps build new church buildings for the growing church there. He is married and has three children who are grown and living in the states. Her second oldest brother is divorced and lives in Texas, where he works as a highway patrolman. He does not have any children. Her younger brother is a worship leader at a local church in Colorado and he just released his first solo album. He is married and has four children who are 13, 15, 18, and 19.

CHILDREN

Sean graduated high school with honors and attends New Mexico State University, where his parents both attended. He is a pre-med major and hopes to attend UCLA medical school upon graduation. His goal is to become a surgeon. He is active in his fraternity and plays drums for the church worship band. He enjoys snow skiing in the nearby mountains. He has a girlfriend who also attends school with him. They've been dating for about 18 months.

Chloe is a high school sophomore and recently got her driver's license. She plays volleyball on her high school team and softball for a club league. She is a B student and wants to attend an out-of-state school. She plans to study communications and hopes to get into the sports commentary world. One year ago she injured her elbow and still works with a physical therapist and sports trainer at school.

Clara is in eighth grade and looks forward to high school next year. She enjoys reading and playing piano. She won the state's creative writing story competition last year, and was awarded a $10,000 scholarship to put toward the college of her choice. She has not yet decided where she wants to attend college but plans to become an author or an English teacher. After school she works with handicapped children at a horseback riding facility. She also rides and shows horses herself and recently won the state equestrian title. Her work at the stable helps pay for some of her riding lessons.

Over the last year and half, the more demanding schedules of both Chloe and Clara have caused the family to miss a lot of church. The girls would both rather spend time with their friends from school and in their extracurricular activities than with the teens in the church youth group. They are both becoming resistant about attending church and rarely participate in the youth activities at church.

Bob recently purchased a custom-ordered Harley Davidson motorcycle for himself. He enjoys riding in the evenings and on weekends. He has also considered buying a time-share for a ski-in ski-out condo in Colorado, rationalizing that this will put Debbie closer to her brother and his family.

Personal Data

Bob T. Smith	**Debbie Smith**
DOB: 5/18/1963	**DOB:** 1/27/1965
SS No.: 123-45-6789	**SS No.:** 987-65-4321
Occupation	**Occupation**
Lextin Oil Supply Project Manager 123 Industrial Blvd. Lovington, NM 11111 (936) 273-0000	Homemaker

Children

Sean Smith
DOB: 8/15/1995 (20 years old)
SS No.: 456-78-1234

Chloe Smith
DOB: 2/20/1999 (16 years old)
SS No.: 123-98-4567

Clara Smith
DOB: 5/02/2001 (14 years old)
SS No.: 98-123-4567

Home

1000 Residential Lane
Lovington, NM 11111
(936) 233-1234
(936) 233-0000 fax
(936) 695-0000 cell
Bsmith@lextinoilsupply.com
Debbiesmith63@gmail.com

CLIENT GOALS AND OBJECTIVES

Bob and Debbie would like to:

A. Complete a comprehensive financial plan.

B. Provide for 5 years of undergraduate college expenses for Chloe and Clara and provide the remaining year of Sean's undergraduate school.

C. Provide for at least $25,000 of graduate work for each of the three kids should they decide to further their education. They desire to provide for Sean to go to medical school and to provide additional assistance up to $50,000 for him to complete medical school.

D. Determine if assets will be sufficient to provide for their goals and objectives.

E. Include the purchase of replacement automobiles for Bob and Debbie.

F. Evaluate their life insurance needs to determine the amount and type of life insurance that is actually needed.

G. Seek to provide financial support for Bob's parents and potentially Debbie's mom.

H. Evaluate the different alternatives available to them in dealing with their stock options.

I. Determine if Bob will be able to retire in one more year.

J. Complete an estate analysis.

IDENTIFICATION OF ISSUES AND PROBLEMS

A. Bob and Debbie want to pursue a financial plan that is in line with their biblical beliefs. It is important to Bob and Debbie that they show and practice good biblical stewardship with the resources they have been given by God. They would like to ensure their investments, insurance, estate plan, and the training of their children are all in line with their spiritual convictions.

B. Based on the amount of life insurance that is needed, what type of coverage should be purchased?

C. Determine how to best handle their current debt obligations and understand their true need for both current debt and any future debt. (They are seeking a car for Chloe now and will for Clara once she turns 16.)

D. Understand the unique financial planning opportunities, challenges, and requirements that Bob and Debbie face related to Bob's stock options.

E. What additional expenses will Bob and Debbie have that are not included in the analysis (such as health-related expenses, additional expenses related to their home, or additional expenses relating to Sean)?

F. What additional strategies can be implemented to reduce the cost of passing their estate from one generation to the next?

G. What are the objectives with regard to the estate?

ASSUMPTIONS

A. Unless otherwise indicated, ages referred to in the analysis apply to Bob's age.

B. An average annual inflation rate of 3.0% is used in the analysis.

C. Personal living expenses and miscellaneous insurance premiums increase at a 3.6% average annual inflation rate.

D. College expenses for Sean, Chloe, and Clara are based on 5 years of undergraduate school, although 4 would be ideal.

E. Report illustrates no reduction in income needs.

F. Retirement at the age of 66 is used in the analysis.

G. Joint filing status is used in the tax analysis.

H. Social Security benefits for Bob begin at age 66.

I. Social Security benefits for Debbie begin at age 66.

J. Retirement account distributions begin at age 70 or when required by income needs.

K. Life expectancy for Bob is age 90.

L. Life expectancy for Debbie is age 95.

M. The tax calculations assume the use of the 2015 tax tables provided by the Internal Revenue Service (IRS).

N. Estate administration rate is 3.25%.

CASH FLOW

Earned Income

This annual breakdown includes a gross salary of $167,480 with quarterly bonus payments of $25,000. Although these quarterly bonuses are not guaranteed, they have been consistently paid out by the company for the past 8 years.

Smith Financial Plan

The following is a breakdown of their annual expenses.

1.	Personal Expenses:	$ 81,200
2.	Life and Misc. Ins. Premiums:	37,729
3.	Debt Payments:	42,144
4.	Retirement Account Deposits:	11,004
5.	Other Expenses:	24,759
6.	Itemized Deductions:	29,677
7.	Income Tax:	74,274
	Total:	$300,787

1. Personal Living Expenses

Personal living expenses do NOT include scheduled outlays for items covered in other areas of the report, such as loan payments, insurance premiums, savings, investment additions, and income taxes. Personal living expenses are an after-tax dollar amount that is available for various living expenses, such as food, gas, entertainment, hobbies, etc.

In each analysis, personal living expenses are based on $6,767 a month or $81,200 a year. Personal living expenses inflate at a 3.6% annual inflation rate. There is no reduction in personal living expenses in either analysis.

2. Life and Misc. Ins. Premiums

In each analysis, the following miscellaneous insurance premiums are included:

Auto Ins.	**$1,838**
Volvo	$821
Ford	$773
Harley	$244
Homeowners Ins.	**3,151**
Medical	**4,153**
Total:	$9,142

Life Insurance

Bob: Mutual Life: $1,500,000 term (10 years left on 30-year term)	$156/month
Debbie: Mutual Life: $250,000 term (10 years left on 20-year term)	$65/month
Bob: Group Term: $50,000 (pre-tax)	$25/month
Debbie: Group Term: $50,000 (pre-tax under Bob's employer)	$20/month
Total:	$266/month

3. Debt Payments

The *Smith Financial Plan* includes several liabilities in the analysis: the mortgage for their residence, two automobile loans, and one credit card. Automobile payments for the Ford Expedition equal $608 a month, the new Harley Davison Motorcycle is $325 a month, and their credit card is $250 a month (outstanding balance is $28,145). Mortgage payments for principal and interest equal $2,329 a month. The mortgage payments are based on a principal balance of $262,481 financed at a 5.0% interest rate.

A. Automobile payments for their Ford Expedition equal $608 a month, the new Harley Davison Motorcycle is $325 a month and their two credit cards are $250 a month and $358 a month for their Bass Pro card and Chase credit card respectively.

4. Retirement Plan Deposits

Contributions to Bob's 401(k) continue for one more year until retirement.

5. Itemized Deductions

- Charitable contributions are based on annual contributions of $12,000 a year.
- Medical expenses are based on $3,832 a year.
- Property taxes in the first year of the analysis equal $13,845.
  - Property tax calculations are based on a tax rate percentage of 2.13% of the county tax value. In each analysis the annual inflation rate for the residence is 3.6% per year. As the residence increases in value, property taxes adjust accordingly.

6. Taxes

Federal income tax liability in the first year of the analysis equal $74,274, which is based on the tax liability from the previous year. Beginning in year 2, the tax liability is recalculated annually based on the individual circumstances of that particular year.

Information that follows is outlined year by year in the Cash Flow section of each analysis under Other Income (Expense), Other Single-Year Income or Expense, and Multiple-Year Income and Expense):

Other Single-Year Income or Expense

1. Automobile

In each analysis, five automobiles are purchased throughout the planning period. The automobiles are purchased at age 56, 60, 64, 68, and 72. The purchase price of the automobiles is based on a current out-of-pocket cost of $30,000 inflated at a 3.6% annual inflation rate. The analysis assumes that cash is paid for each of the automobiles at the time of purchase.

Multiple-Year Income and Expense

1. College Education Expenses

Bob and Debbie would like to help pay for college expenses for Sean, Chloe, and Clara. Annual college expenses are based on $20,000 a year for 5 years, inflated at a 4% annual inflation rate. College expenses increase each year based on a 4% inflation rate.

2. Parents

To assist in the support of Bob's parents, an additional expense of $5,000 a year is included in the analysis for the next 20 years. Support payments increase each year at a 3.6% annual inflation rate. Bob and Debbie would like to allocate an additional $3,600 a year to help Debbie's mom should she need any help.

INVESTMENTS

Asset values are based on their current values. The analysis assumes that investment assets will earn a 9% return in the future, even though the assets may currently be worth less than their original purchase price. Where the cost basis of the assets is higher than their current value, the amount of the loss is reflected in the unrealized appreciation figure. This enables the investment assets to appreciate by that amount without any additional tax consequences.

Assets in checking accounts and the Woodlands Golf Club membership are considered personal assets and are not included in the analysis.

Taxable Money Market Accounts:	$ 87,674
Equity & Other:	370,690
Tax Deferred:	78,541
Qualified Retirement Accounts:	1,194,546
Roth IRA:	8,436
Total:	**$1,739,887**

Variables

1. The returns consist of 20% dividends and 80% appreciation of assets.

2. All equity assets earn a 9% annual rate of return except Roth IRAs and the variable annuity.

3. Roth IRAs earn an 8% annual rate of return.

4. The variable annuity earns a 6% annual rate of return.

5. Corporate bonds earn a 6% annual rate of return.

6. Government bonds and T-bills earn a 4% annual rate of return.

7. Money accounts earn a 2% annual rate of return.

8. Partnership assets appreciate at a 3.6% annual appreciation rate.

9. In the analysis, when there is a cash surplus, it is reinvested, with 10% allocated to a fully taxable account money B and the remaining 90% into an equity account.

10. As income is needed in the future, assets in the taxable account are accessed first, then assets in the equity account, and finally assets in the retirement account.

11. Current management fees of assets are negotiated with their financial advisor at 1.75% for their brokerage accounts.

STOCK OPTIONS

The stock option analysis consists of examining the effect that the stock options would have on the overall financial plan based on two possible scenarios. The annual appreciation rate that stock option proceeds receive after the stock has been sold is 9% a year. Other variables used in the analysis are as follows:

Name	Lextin Oil Supply
Current Date	6/6/2015
Current Price per Share	39.56
Annual Appreciation Rate	5%

RISK MANAGEMENT

Property and Casualty Insurance

- Liability bodily injury is set for $100,000.
- Bodily injury is set for $300,000.
- Property damage is set for $50,000. Property damage limits should be sufficient to replace an automobile if an accident was caused by an uninsured or underinsured motorist.
- Uninsured and underinsured motorist bodily injury and property damage coverage is set at $100,000/$300,000 bodily injury.
- Deductibles are set at $500.

The homeowner insurance policy is set to cover the replacement value of the home. Personal liability coverage is limited to $300,000, and medical coverage is limited to $5,000.

Umbrella Liability Policy

Currently there is no umbrella liability policy coverage.

Disability

Bob and Debbie are currently covered through Bob's employee benefits. The current disability coverage is 70% of income replacement for Bob's base salary. Bonus payments are not included in the coverage.

Health Insurance

Bob and Debbie are covered by Lextin Oil Supply under a PPO plan for which they pay $420 per pay period (paid on the 15th and 30th of each month). Dental and vision are also employee benefit, that they receive, and the premiums for those (for family coverage) are $25/per pay period and $18/per pay period, respectively. Other medical plans are available, and further consideration should be taken to examine the best options.

Life Insurance

According to the information provided, Bob is currently insured by three separate individual life insurance policies, with a total death benefit of $1,550,000. Debbie is currently insured by a group life insurance policy under Lextin Oil Supply, with a total death benefit of $50,000.

TAXES

The Smiths are currently in the 33% tax bracket. They do have a concern as it relates to their tax situation should they exercise their stock options and generate a significant tax liability this coming year.

The following 2015 tax table will be used to calculate taxes due:

2015 Tax Year Brackets (Jan. 1–Dec. 31, 2015); Tax Return Due on April 15, 2016

Tax Rate	Single	Married/Joint	Married/Separate	Head of Household
10%	$1 to $9,225	$1 to $18,450	$1 to $9,225	$1 to $13,150
15%	$9,226 to $37,450	$18,451 to $74,900	$9,226 to $37,450	$13,151 to $50,200
25%	$37,451 to $90,750	$74,901 to $151,200	$37,451 to $75,600	$50,201 to $129,600
28%	$90,751 to $189,300	$151,201 to $230,450	$75,601 to $115,225	$129,601 to $209,850
33%	$189,301 to $411,500	$230,451 to $411,500	$115,226 to $205,750	$209,851 to $411,500
35%	$411,501 to $413,200	$411,501 to $464,850	$205,751 to $232,425	$411,501 to $439,200
39.60%	over $413,200	over $464,850	over $232,425	over $439,200

FINANCIAL INDEPENDENCE AND RETIREMENT

The following factors will be used to determine the likelihood of retirement outcomes.

- Income needed for basic living expenses and the number of years required
- Income available from Social Security, pensions, and other sources
- Extraordinary income or expense items that will affect the retirement capital
- Existing savings, investment, and retirement funds, as well as annual additions to the accounts
- The effect of inflation on income and expenses
- The rate of return earned on the accounts
- The effect of income taxes on income sources and accounts

In disbursing assets to satisfy income needs, assets are disbursed in the following order:

1. Earned income (e.g., part-time consulting, pension income, and Social Security)
2. Taxable assets (nonqualified assets)
3. Tax-deferred accounts (qualified accounts)
4. Tax-free sources (e.g., municipal bonds)

A year-by-year breakdown of income should be calculated to determine total income, which can then be adjusted for factors such as inflation and other expenditures per year, such as car purchases and vacations.

ESTATE

Bob and Debbie need to evaluate their current estate plan. Items that should be considered include determining their estimated estate value, ensuring all wills have been updated within the last few years, determining whether any trusts should be established, and evaluating whether their current giving plan aligns with their estate plan. Tasks involved include the following:

- Determine estate value at end of life.
- Review and update wills for both Bob and Debbie.
- Evaluate any need for trusts (revocable trusts, credit shelter trust, etc.).
- Create a living gift plan that is in conjunction with their legacy estate plan.

GIVING

Bob and Debbie desire to set up a giving plan that aligns with their spiritual convictions. Unfortunately, they have only sporadically given their "tithe" but know that this has been something that needs to be proactively decided on. Their mentality over the past few years has been to put $20 in the offering plate when they do attend church (which is not consistent due to sporting events).

Church Covenants

CHURCH HISTORY

Lovington Community Church began in the hearts of members of the World Evangelism organization as they were targeting strategic areas in the United States in which to establish Bible-believing local churches. On April 25, 1980, the dream became a reality when Lovington Community Church was started in a storefront building in downtown Lovington, New Mexico.

Within a few years, the church bought property and began to build on its present location in Lovington. Now with 20 acres of land and over 80,000 square feet of building space, every week 600 to 700 people from all over Gaines County (and beyond) come together to worship the great God and King, to study His word, to serve and encourage one another, and to intentionally take the saving Gospel of Jesus Christ to the community.

For more than 30 years the goal has been to *"Touch Lives with the Gospel Truth."* And although God has certainly done wonderful things in and through His church, there is still so much more to do. And so, until He comes, members of the church are committed to be the Church in this place, in this day!

CHURCH COVENANTS

We, the members of Lovington Community Church of Gaines County, New Mexico, desiring to faithfully serve the Lord Jesus Christ, to foster the spirit of harmony, to promote good order in the church, and to better set forth our position before the world, do ordain and establish the following articles, to which we voluntarily submit ourselves.

Article I—Name

This assembly is incorporated as Lovington Community Church Inc. We shall be known as Lovington Community Church.

Article II—Statement of Purpose

A. To exalt the Lord Jesus Christ as the Son of God, the Savior of the world, and the Head of His church (Matthew 16:13–18; Romans 10:8–11; Ephesians 5:23; Colossians 1:15–19).

B. To establish a local congregation of believers patterned after the New Testament Church and obedient to the teaching of the Scriptures.

C. To build and advance the true church of which Christ is the Head:

1. By preaching the Gospel of Christ to the lost and leading them to the Savior, beginning in our "Jerusalem" and extending to the "uttermost parts of the earth" (Matthew 28:18–20; Acts 1:8).

2. By providing a place where believers can assemble to worship the Lord (Hebrews 10:25).

3. By teaching believers the doctrines of Scripture and training them for the work of the ministry (2 Timothy 2:15; Ephesians 4:11–12).

D. To administer the ordinances of Baptism and the Lord's Supper as set forth in the New Testament.

Article III—Church Covenant

Having been led by the Holy Spirit to receive the Lord Jesus Christ as our Savior, and on the public confession of our faith, having been immersed in the name of the Father, and of the Son, and of the Holy Spirit, we do now, in the presence of God and His assembly, solemnly and joyfully enter into covenant with one another as one body in Christ.

We purpose, therefore, by the aid of the Holy Spirit, to walk together in Christian love; to strive for the advancement of this church body in knowledge and holiness to promote its prosperity and spirituality; to attend its services regularly; to sustain its worship, ordinances, discipline, and doctrines; to give it a sacred preeminence over all institutions of human origin; to give faithfully of time and talent in its activities; and to contribute cheerfully and regularly, as God has prospered us, to the support of the ministry, the expenses of the church, the relief of the poor, and the spread of the gospel throughout all nations.

We also purpose to maintain family and private devotions; to train our children according to the word of God; to seek the salvation of our kindred and acquaintances; to walk circumspectly in the world; to be just in our dealing, faithful in our engagements, and exemplary in our conduct; to avoid all gossip, backbiting, and unrighteous anger; to abstain from all forms of activity that dishonor our Lord Jesus Christ, cause stumbling to a fellow believer, or hinder the winning of a soul to Christ; to be zealous in our efforts to advance the cause of Christ, our Savior; and to give Him preeminence in all things.

We further purpose to encourage one another in the blessed hope of our Lord's return; to watch over one another in brotherly love; to remember each other in prayer; to aid each other in sickness and distress; to cultivate Christian sympathy in feeling and courtesy in speech; and to be slow to take offense but always ready for reconciliation and mindful of the rules of our Savior, to seek it without delay.

We moreover purpose that when we remove from this place, we will as soon as possible unite with some other church of like faith and practice, where we can carry out the spirit of this covenant and the principles of God's word. In the event there is no such church, we shall seek, with the Lord's help, to establish one.

Article IV—The Statement of Doctrinal Belief

The Statement of Doctrinal Belief is that which was ratified by the church and is on file in the church office. The Statement of Doctrinal Belief is presented to all candidates for membership in the church.

Article V—Association

This church, recognizing Christ as its Head, shall not be subject to any other authority. It may associate in fellowship with those of like faith and practice and may declare itself in agreement with others in a common cause, but under no circumstances shall such association or agreement ever be construed as bringing this church under the authority of any person, group, or body.

Article VI—Membership

SECTION 1. Adult membership in this assembly shall be restricted to regenerated believers, ages 18 and older, who have followed the Lord in baptism by immersion following conversion or who have affirmed their intent for membership having previously held child membership at Lovington Community Church.

SECTION 2. Youth membership in this assembly shall be restricted to regenerated believers, under 18, who have followed the Lord in baptism by immersion following conversion.

SECTION 3. Applicants for membership will be received upon their confession of faith. Applicants shall be interviewed by the Elders, who shall make a recommendation to the church for reception; otherwise the applicant's name shall not come before the church. An attempt shall be made to notify the church where the applicants have been members.

SECTION 4. Applicants for membership shall give their testimony concerning their assurance of salvation and baptism to the Elder Body. They shall declare their substantial agreement with the statement of doctrinal belief of this church and their willingness to be governed by it, the constitution and by-laws. They shall be encouraged to become actively involved in at least one area of ministry within the church.

SECTION 5. Applicants deemed eligible for membership by the Elder Body shall be received into the membership of the church by a majority vote of the Lovington Community Church membership.

SECTION 6. Letters of transfer shall be granted for members in good standing upon request from churches of like faith and practice. Letters of dismissal shall be granted to members in good standing who are uniting with churches other than those of like faith and practice. If a member is not in good standing, churches requesting a letter will be notified as to their standing and status in the church.

SECTION 7. Members demonstrating a pattern of prolonged absenteeism from all services of the church shall be contacted by an Elder regarding their absence to encourage faithfulness in attendance. Members unwilling to resume regular attendance shall be excluded from membership by a majority vote of the Lovington Community Church membership at a duly called business meeting. The delinquent member shall be notified of such action. Exemptions in this matter shall apply in cases of illness, infirmity, missionary/Christian service, school, and so forth.

SECTION 8. Members of this church who shall err in doctrine or conduct shall be subject to dismissal according to Matthew 18:15–18. Before such dismissal, however, it shall be the duty of any member of this church who has knowledge of the erring member's heresy or misconduct to warn and to correct him or her in private. If the member does not heed this warning, then the warning member shall again go to the erring member accompanied by one or two witnesses to warn and correct him or her. If the erring member still refuses to heed this warning, it shall be brought to the attention of the Elder Body. The Elders shall seek to aid the erring member to restoration. They may recommend to the church proper action in relation to the erring member who declines restoration. He or she shall be subject to public dismissal from the church. A majority vote in a regular or duly called business meeting shall be sufficient for dismissal. The erring member shall be notified of such action.

Article VII—Elders

Section 1. Organizational Structure

Although we recognize that Jesus Christ is the head of the church, the Elder Body will organize itself in the following manner:

A. The Senior Pastor/Teacher will serve as the head of the Elder Body. He shall have the main teaching and preaching responsibilities within the church family. Although he functions as the leading Elder, he is to approach his position as a leader among peers.

B. The Elder Body will meet on a monthly basis. Special meetings may be called when deemed necessary. A quorum, which shall consist of at least 51% of the total number of Elders, shall be present to conduct any business.

C. The Elder Body will organize itself in order to provide oversight for all ministries of the church.

D. The Elder Body will annually select from its number both a chairman and secretary. The chairman's responsibility will be to provide oversight for the Elder Body in the absence of the Senior Pastor. The secretary's responsibility will be to record and distribute the minutes of the Elder Body meetings.

E. The Elder Body will be responsible for determining and upholding the doctrinal truths believed and practiced at Lovington Community Church.

F. The Elder Body will provide oversight for accountability and ministry partnership over the Deacon flock ministry and ensure that the spiritual and physical needs of each individual and/or family are being met. The Elder/Deacon relationship shall be viewed as a team ministry, with the Elders primarily responsible for the spiritual needs and the Deacons primarily responsible for the physical needs.

G. The Elder Body will be responsible for developing goals, projects, and ministries for Lovington Community Church. The Elder Body will also develop direction to implement the plans it suggests.

Section 2. The Authority of the Elder Body

A. The Elder Body will have complete authority in any area involving questions relating to scriptural truth.

B. The Elder Body will have oversight over all ministries and committees of the church. The ministries and committees shall not meet without Elder approval.

C. The Elder Body will have authority to initiate the process for disciplining individuals for violating scriptural purity. Dismissal shall only come after all attempts at restoration have failed according to the biblical pattern of Matthew 18. Any matters that cannot be decided upon unanimously by the Elder Body may be brought before the congregation for their input and discussion. This is to be done for the purpose of gathering input. It will remain the responsibility of the Elder Body to come to a unanimous decision before any action is taken.

D. Be it resolved that all decisions relating to doctrinal truth and spiritual direction must be decided by unanimous vote by all Elder Body members.

E. If, after having followed the pattern of Matthew 18, the Elder Body fails to regulate itself biblically, they disqualify themselves from office and may be voted out by the congregation. This vote must be taken by a written, signed ballot and be passed by a vote of 80%.

Article VIII—The Staff Elders of the Church

Staff Elders shall consist of the Senior Staff Elder and Associate Staff Elder(s).

Section 1. Qualifications

A. They must have been called of God to the work of the gospel ministry and be adequately trained for the preaching/teaching of the gospel and the pastoral ministry.

B. They must meet the scriptural qualifications set forth in 1 Timothy 3:1–7, Hebrews 13:7 and 17, Acts 20:28, and 1 Peter 5:1–4.

C. They must be men of unquestionable character as determined by careful search into their past history prior to extending the call to minister at Lovington Community Church.

D. They must be in agreement with the Statement of Doctrinal Belief of this church and be willing to work under its Constitution and By-Laws.

Section 2. Call

A. When the need arises to add or replace a Staff Elder, the members of the congregation shall be encouraged to present their recommendations of persons for the office of Staff Elder to the Elder Body. The Elder Body shall interview qualified men recommended for the office.

B. The Elder Body, after prayerful deliberation, will present to the congregation approved candidates for the position of Staff Elder. The congregation will be given an opportunity to hear them preach and to question them.

C. Following unanimous approval among the Elder Body, a candidate's name will be submitted to the membership of Lovington Community Church for two consecutive Sundays prior to a vote of confirmation by the members. During this 2-week period, any objections to the candidate's appointment should be brought before an Elder privately. If no objections are raised or if the objection(s) is (are) found to be invalid by the Elder Body, the candidate will be submitted to the membership for a public vote of confidence. A candidate must receive 80% approval to be confirmed to the office of Staff Elder.

Section 3. Tenure

A. A Staff Elder is called to serve an indefinite term.

B. He may terminate his ministry by submitting in writing his resignation to the Elder Body, no less than 30 days and no more than 60 days prior to the effective date. The Elder Body will announce the resignation to the congregation. The 30-day notice or the 60-day notice may be waived by mutual consent.

C. A Staff Elder's ministry may be terminated under the following circumstances:

1. Definite and Deliberate Sin

    a. Two or more persons who believe that a Staff Elder is involved in definite and deliberate unscriptural or sinful activity should submit to the Elder Body a written statement regarding the accusation supported by the reasons for such an accusation (Matthew 18:16; 1 Timothy 5:19).

    b. The Elder Body will investigate the accusation by interviewing all parties involved.

    c. If the Staff Elder is proven to be involved in definite and deliberate unscriptural and/or sinful activity, which would disqualify him from serving as an Elder, he will be relieved of his duties, his employment will be immediately terminated, and he will be given 30 days of severance pay. The church will be notified of such action at the earliest possible date.

2. Dereliction of Duties

   a. Two or more persons who believe a Staff Elder is failing to discharge his biblical and/or assigned responsibilities should submit to the Elder Body a written statement regarding the accusation supported by the reasons for such an accusation.

   b. The Elder Body will fully investigate the accusation.

   c. If the Staff Elder is proven to be failing in the discharge of his biblical and/or assigned responsibilities, the Elder Body will counsel with him to attempt to correct the situation. The Staff Elder will then be given specific goals and a timeline to correct the problem. If the problem is not corrected within the established time frame, the Staff Elder will be relieved of his duties, his employment will be immediately terminated, and he will be given 30 days of severance pay. The church will be notified of such action at the earliest possible date.

Section 4. Duties

A. SENIOR STAFF ELDER

1. He shall be responsible for the preaching/teaching ministry of the congregation and the spiritual welfare and general oversight of the church.

2. By virtue of his office, the Senior Staff Elder will serve as the moderator of the Elder Body.

B. ASSOCIATE STAFF ELDER(S)

He or they shall be responsible for duties as agreed upon by himself or themselves, the Senior Staff Elder, and the Elder Body. He or they will also assist the Senior Staff Elder in the oversight and shepherding of the church.

Section 5. Compensation

The Staff Elders of the church shall be financially compensated for their service to the church and receive other benefits as defined by present church policy set by the Non-Staff Elders and approved by the membership.

Article IX—Non-Staff Elders

Section 1. Qualifications

A. Elders must fulfill the scriptural requirements as outlined in 1 Timothy 3:1–7 and Titus 1:5–9.

B. Elders must be men who have been believers for at least 5 years.

C. Non-Staff Elders must have been members of Lovington Community Church for 1 year, which is a sufficient period of time to demonstrate a lifestyle pattern that is in harmony with the biblical qualifications as stated in 1 Timothy 3:1–7 and Titus 1:5–9.

Section 2. Selection

A. The selection of new Elders can occur whenever the Elder Body deems necessary.

B. The Elder Body is responsible for selecting men to serve in available positions. This process involves the following steps:

    1. An interview with the Elder Body.

    2. The sharing of public testimony.

C. After unanimous approval by all Elder Body members, a candidate's name will be submitted to the membership of Lovington Community Church for two consecutive Sundays prior to a vote of confidence by the members. During this 2-week period, any objections to the candidate's appointment should be brought before a member of the Elder Body privately. If no objections are raised, or if the objection(s) is (are) found to be invalid by the Elder Body, the candidate will be submitted to the membership for a public vote of confidence. A candidate must receive 80% approval to be confirmed to the office of Elder.

Section 3. Tenure

A. Non-Staff Elders are called to an indefinite term.

B. If the non-Staff Elder desires to resign from the Elder Body, 30 days' notification prior to the effective date of his resignation is requested.

C. A Non-Staff Elder's ministry may be terminated by the following procedure:

    1. Two or more persons who feel that a Non-Staff Elder is involved in definite and deliberate unscriptural or sinful activity, or is failing to discharge his biblical ministry duties, should submit to the Elder Body a written statement regarding the accusation supported by the reasons for such an accusation (Matthew 18:16; 1 Timothy 5:19).

    2. The Elder Body will investigate the accusation and then proceed to call for a vote of confidence from the congregation, if such action is justified. An 80% affirmative vote will support the Non-Staff Elder's continued ministry. The vote must be by ballot in a business session announced for this purpose on two consecutive Sundays.

    3. Depending upon the severity of the offense, the Non-Staff Elder may be relieved of his duties, pending the vote of confidence.

Section 4. Duties

A. Elders are expected to devote themselves to prayer, reading, and studying the Bible daily.

B. Elders are expected to shepherd the members of Lovington Community Church and manage the church body.

Article X—The Role of a Deacon

Section 1. Qualifications

A. They must meet the spiritual qualifications set forth in 1 Timothy 3:8–13.

B. Deacons must be male members 21 years of age or older who have been members of the church in good standing for a period of 1 year.

C. The Board of Deacons will be determined by the size of the congregation, the demands of the ministry, and the availability of biblically qualified men (1 Timothy 3:1–13). The Elder Body will recommend to the congregation when additional members should be added.

Section 2. Selection

A. The Elder Body shall select those they believe are qualified for the office of Deacon. Each voting member is encouraged to contact an Elder with recommendations for Deacon selection.

B. Those selected will then be personally interviewed by the Elder Body regarding their desire to serve in this capacity and their individual qualifications as determined by Scripture and the Constitution of the Lovington Community Church.

C. The names of those selected shall be posted 2 weeks prior to the election meeting. Public testimony will be given prior to the election.

D. The Elder Body will then submit a ballot of name(s) to the church, giving each voting member of the congregation an opportunity to elect said Deacon(s). Each candidate on the ballot will be presented to the church for an affirmation vote. Each candidate receiving at least 2/3 of the votes cast will serve as Deacon.

E. The Deacons shall serve as the official trustees of the corporation.

Section 3. Tenure

A. Once confirmed by congregational vote, each Deacon will be considered to be called to serve an indefinite term, as long as he continues to meet the scriptural requirements for the position.

B. Recognizing that life events may require such, a Deacon may step out of service at any time and for any period of time by notifying the chairman of the Deacons of his intent.

C. However, for the sake of continuity in ministering to the flock, a minimum term of 3 years is the expectation, unless there are extenuating circumstances as stated in item B.

D. If there has been a period where a Deacon is not actively serving and he is then ready to return to service, he must meet with a member of the Elder Body or their designee to discuss his return. Upon approval by that Elder or designee, he will be considered an active Deacon. An additional public testimony and congregational vote will not be required in that instance.

E. The same procedure will be followed for the dismissal of a Deacon as is outlined for the dismissal of an Elder (Article VIII, Section 3).

Section 4. Organization/Duties

A. The Board of Deacons shall organize itself in such a way so as to effectively pray for and minister to the physical needs of the congregation.

B. In the discharge of their duties, members of the Board of Deacons are under the supervision of the Elder Body.

C. The Deacons shall be organized as a board. The board shall annually select a chairman and a secretary from among their number. They shall meet each month and whenever requested by the Elder Body.

D. The Deacon Board shall keep minutes of its meetings and shall submit these minutes to the Elder Body regularly. The Deacon Board shall meet with the Elder Body in joint session once a quarter to confer on matters of common interest.

Article XI—The Church Moderator

SECTION 1. The Senior Staff Elder, by virtue of his office, will moderate all public meetings and business sessions of the congregation.

SECTION 2. At the request of or in the absence of the Senior Staff Elder, another Elder will moderate.

Article XII—Finances

SECTION 1. The fiscal year shall be from January 1 through December 31.

SECTION 2. The primary means of disbursement of moneys shall be by check. All cash disbursements shall be properly receipted and accounted for.

SECTION 3. All regular moneys for the church shall be raised only by voluntary tithes and offerings from the congregation.

SECTION 4. Special moneys for property or buildings may be financed, by vote of the church, by loans, mortgages, or bonds.

SECTION 5. No individual or committee shall have the authority to obligate the church to any indebtedness without the prior approval of the church congregation.

SECTION 6. The Finance Committee will oversee the receipt and disbursal of all funds of the church and will monitor budgetary spending in cooperation with the Elder assigned to the various budget categories. An Elder selected by the Elder Body will oversee the Finance Committee.

SECTION 7. Designated gifts will be accepted only toward projects approved by the church and are encouraged to be over and above the tithe.

SECTION 8. All church moneys will be distributed in accordance with the annual church budget as approved by the congregation. Any expenditure outside of the church budget must be approved by the Elder Body. Any unfavorable variance of $2,500 or more within the expense categories must be approved by the congregation. These unfavorable variances will be brought to the congregation for approval shortly after the release of each quarterly financial report.

SECTION 9. Financial reporting will take place on a quarterly basis.

Article XIII—Missions

SECTION 1. It will be the policy of this church to promote and support missionaries whose doctrine is in conformity with that of our church as outlined in our Statement of Doctrinal Belief.

SECTION 2. The church will strive to designate not less than 10% of its annual operating budget toward mission work.

SECTION 3. All committed missionary support will be approved by the congregation.

Article XIV—Meetings

SECTION 1. The church body shall meet each Sunday morning for corporate worship and at other designated times as recommended by the church leadership and approved by the congregation.

SECTION 2. The Annual Business Meeting shall be held no later than the last Sunday in January of the following year. Special Business Meetings may be called by the Elder Body.

SECTION 3. The Annual Budget Meeting will be held prior to the start of the next fiscal year.

SECTION 4. Where applicable, Robert's Rules of Order shall govern the conduct of business in all sessions.

Article XV—Amendments

SECTION 1. The Constitution and By-Laws of this church may be amended at any duly announced business meeting by a majority vote of members present.

SECTION 2. The proposed amendments or changes will be available for the membership two consecutive Sundays prior to the next business meeting.

Article XVI—Quorum and Voting Age

SECTION 1. A minimum of 25% of the voting members shall constitute a quorum.
SECTION 2. The voting age shall be 18 years or older.

Article XVII—Dissolution Clause

In the event of the dissolution of this corporation, all of its debts shall be fully satisfied. None of its assets or holdings shall be divided among its members or other individuals, but shall be irrevocably designated by corporate vote prior to dissolution to such other nonprofit religious corporations as are in agreement with the letter and spirit of the articles of doctrinal belief adopted by this church, and in conformity with the requirements of the U.S. Internal Revenue Service's Code of 1954 (Section 501-C-3).

This Constitution and By-Laws were adopted on April 1, 1980, and were last amended on December 19, 2010, and supersede any and all constitutions previously adopted.

Transactions

JULY

Date	Expense	Category	Amount
7/1/15	ATM WITHDRAWAL	ATM/Cash Withdrawals	-$42.00
7/17/15	ATM SURCHARGE REBATE	ATM/Cash Withdrawals	$2.00
7/20/15	ATM WITHDRAWAL	ATM/Cash Withdrawals	-$203.00
7/27/15	ATM WITHDRAWAL	ATM/Cash Withdrawals	-$20.00
Total			**-$263.00**
7/31/15	CABLE, INTERNET, HOME PHONE SERVICE	Cable/Satellite Services	-$106.20
Total			**-$106.20**
7/9/15	CAR REGISTRATION	Car Maintenance	-$204.85
7/9/15	LICENSE RENEWAL	Car Maintenance	-$17.50
Total			**-$222.35**
7/10/15	COMPASSION INTERNATIONAL	Charitable Giving	-$38.00
Total			**-$38.00**
7/13/15	CHECK # 0xxxxx1655	Checks	-$110.00
7/14/15	CHECK # 0xxxxx1653	Checks	-$448.00
7/17/15	CHECK # 0xxxxx1656	Checks	-$240.00
7/23/15	CHECK # 0xxxxx1657	Checks	-$250.00
Total			**-$1,048.00**
7/6/15	EXPRESS MART	Clothing/Shoes	-$43.03
Total			**-$43.03**
7/24/15	CHRISTIAN BOOKSTORE	Educational Supplies	-$81.00
7/24/15	BIBLE STUDY GUIDE FOR ALL AGES	Educational Supplies	$47.60
Total			**-$33.40**
7/6/15	BEST BUY	Electronics	-$85.58
7/9/15	BEST BUY	Electronics	$63.07
7/16/15	BEST BUY	Electronics	-$74.89
Total			**-$97.40**
7/3/15	PARTY CITY	Entertainment	-$11.72
Total			**-$11.72**
7/17/15	KROGER FUEL CTR	Gasoline/Fuel	-$41.00
7/31/15	SPEEDWAY	Gasoline/Fuel	-$39.14
Total			**-$80.14**
7/6/15	TARGET	General Merchandise	-$152.70
7/20/15	TARGET	General Merchandise	-$62.40
Total			**-$215.10**

Date	Expense	Category	Amount
7/6/15	KROGER	Groceries	-$51.21
7/8/15	KROGER	Groceries	-$76.54
7/15/15	COMPANY MEAL PLAN	Groceries	-$91.25
7/16/15	The Harbour Market	Groceries	-$23.23
7/20/15	KROGER	Groceries	-$32.22
7/27/15	KROGER	Groceries	-$339.37
7/31/15	FRESH THYME GROCERY STORE	Groceries	-$113.68
Total			**-$727.50**
7/8/15	Great Clip	Hair Cuts	-$62.00
Total			**-$62.00**
7/13/15	CVS PHARMACY	Healthcare/Medical	-$117.09
7/15/15	CVS PHARMACY	Healthcare/Medical	-$13.25
7/29/15	CVS PHARMACY	Healthcare/Medical	-$47.17
Total			**-$177.51**
7/6/15	GOLF GALAXY	Hobbies	-$181.88
7/20/15	BARNES & NOBLE	Hobbies	-$2.56
Total			**-$184.44**
7/6/15	MENARDS HOME SUPPLY STORE	Home Improvement	-$115.30
7/6/15	THE HOME DEPOT	Home Improvement	-$47.88
7/13/15	MENARDS	Home Improvement	-$180.82
7/27/15	THE HOME DEPOT	Home Improvement	-$32.14
Total			**-$376.14**
7/17/15	INTEREST PAID	Interest	$0.02
Total			**$0.02**
7/13/15	Horse Stables	Memberships	-$150.00
7/27/15	AMERICAN HERITAGE GIRLS	Memberships	-$26.00
Total			**-$176.00**
7/20/15	POST OFFICE	Postage and Shipping	-$11.66
7/14/15	THE UPS STORE	Postage and Shipping	-$16.31
Total			**-$27.97**
7/27/15	PUREFLIX ONLINE SUBSCRIPTION	Online Services	-$7.99
Total			**-$7.99**
7/6/15	PAYPAL PURCHASE	Other Expenses	-$17.21
Total			**-$17.21**

Date	Expense	Category	Amount
7/2/15	CHICK-FIL-A	Restaurants/Dining	-$32.42
7/6/15	CHICK-FIL-A	Restaurants/Dining	-$35.52
7/9/15	CHICK-FIL-A	Restaurants/Dining	-$43.91
7/9/15	MCALISTER'S DELI	Restaurants/Dining	-$4.78
7/10/15	First Watch Res	Restaurants/Dining	-$23.00
7/13/15	PANERA BREAD	Restaurants/Dining	-$7.83
7/13/15	PANERA BREAD	Restaurants/Dining	-$6.31
7/17/15	CHICK-FIL-A	Restaurants/Dining	-$17.96
7/20/15	10 WEST	Restaurants/Dining	-$80.00
7/20/15	ORANGE LEAF YOGURT	Restaurants/Dining	-$12.71
7/24/15	WHICH WICH	Restaurants/Dining	-$7.79
7/24/15	PARADIES	Restaurants/Dining	-$5.33
7/27/15	MIKE'S CAFÉ	Restaurants/Dining	-$37.89
7/27/15	PF CHANGS	Restaurants/Dining	-$18.70
7/27/15	MONTEREYS	Restaurants/Dining	-$14.46
7/27/15	Mama's Café	Restaurants/Dining	-$13.50
7/27/15	CHICK-FIL-A	Restaurants/Dining	-$9.33
7/27/15	PARADIES	Restaurants/Dining	-$2.39
7/28/15	BUFFALO WILD WINGS	Restaurants/Dining	-$11.87
7/30/15	WHICH WICH	Restaurants/Dining	-$26.46
7/31/15	SEASONS RESTAURANT	Restaurants/Dining	-$30.00
Total			**-$442.16**
7/1/15	Duke Energy	Utilities	-$139.62
7/6/15	L2GNOBLESVILLE	Utilities	-$37.69
7/7/15	VECTREN ENERGY	Utilities	-$50.27
7/29/15	WATER BILL	Utilities	-$98.39
Total			**-$325.97**

AUGUST

Date	Expense	Category	Amount
8/4/15	ATM Withdrawal	ATM/Cash Withdrawals	-$20.00
8/12/15	ATM Withdrawal	ATM/Cash Withdrawals	-$25.00
8/17/15	CARDTRONICS - ATM WITHDRAWAL	ATM/Cash Withdrawals	-$103.00
8/18/15	ATM SURCHARGE REBATE	ATM/Cash Withdrawals	$6.00
8/25/15	ATM Withdrawal	ATM/Cash Withdrawals	-$25.00
8/31/15	ATM Withdrawal	ATM/Cash Withdrawals	-$83.00
8/31/15	ATM Withdrawal	ATM/Cash Withdrawals	-$30.00
Total			**-$280.00**
8/4/15	ALUMNI FOUNDATION DONATION	Charitable Giving	-$200.00
8/11/15	COMPASSION INTE	Charitable Giving	-$38.00
Total			**-$238.00**

Date	Expense	Category	Amount
8/4/15	CHECK # 0xxxxx1661	Checks	-$300.00
8/6/15	CHECK # 0xxxxx1660	Checks	-$1,800.42
8/18/15	CHECK # 0xxxxx1662	Checks	-$75.00
8/19/15	CHECK # 0xxxxx1663	Checks	-$90.00
8/20/15	CHECK # 0xxxxx1664	Checks	-$52.00
Total			**-$2,317.42**
8/12/15	EXPRESS MART	Clothing/Shoes	-$38.19
8/12/15	EXPRESS MART	Clothing/Shoes	-$23.53
8/17/15	ALTAR'D STATE 1	Clothing/Shoes	-$219.21
8/31/15	ALTAR'D STATE 1	Clothing/Shoes	-$195.66
8/31/15	DESTINATION CLOTHIER	Clothing/Shoes	-$80.25
Total			**-$556.84**
8/3/15	LANDRY CONSULTING - ONLINE COURSE	Education Supplies	-$573.00
8/12/15	BIBLE STUDY GUIDE FOR ALL AGES	Education Supplies	-$61.03
8/19/15	CHRISTIANBOOK STORE	Education Supplies	-$14.98
8/26/15	RAINBOW RESOURCE CENTER - EDUCATION SUPPLIES	Education Supplies	-$64.45
Total			**-$713.46**
8/3/15	CONNER PRAIRIE-	Entertainment	-$54.00
8/17/15	FANDANGO.COM	Entertainment	-$25.00
8/31/15	FRESH THYME	Entertainment	-$285.51
Total			**-$364.51**
8/11/15	KROGER FUEL CTR	Gasoline/Fuel	-$7.77
8/17/15	SPEEDWAY GAS STATION	Gasoline/Fuel	-$45.08
Total			**-$52.85**
8/3/15	TARGET DEBIT CRD ACH TRAN	General Merchandise	-$87.54
8/10/15	BIG HOFFAS	General Merchandise	-$52.98
8/12/15	TARGET DEBIT CRD ACH TRAN	General Merchandise	-$82.24
8/24/15	WAL-MART	General Merchandise	-$27.01
Total			**-$249.77**
8/3/15	FRESH THYME GROCERY STORE	Groceries	-$399.11
8/3/15	BUILDING CONVENIENCE STORE	Groceries	-$86.00
8/5/15	VINTAGE SPIRITS	Groceries	-$5.34
8/7/15	BUILDING CONVENIENCE STORE	Groceries	-$12.83
8/10/15	MEIJER INC	Groceries	-$47.53
8/11/15	BUILDING CONVENIENCE STORE	Groceries	-$30.56
8/14/15	MEIJER	Groceries	-$34.85
8/18/15	KROGER	Groceries	-$111.53
8/24/15	KROGER	Groceries	-$178.30
8/27/15	MEIJER INC	Groceries	-$43.46
8/28/15	COMPANY MEAL PLAN	Groceries	-$97.50
8/31/15	KROGER	Groceries	-$218.91
Total			**-$1,265.92**

Date	Expense	Category	Amount
8/3/15	Great Clip	Hair Cuts	-$28.76
8/31/15	Great Clip	Hair Cuts	-$44.00
Total			**-$72.76**
8/17/15	CVS PHARMACY	Healthcare/Medical	-$10.57
Total			**-$10.57**
8/3/15	HOBBY-LOBBY	Hobbies	-$26.74
Total			**-$26.74**
8/6/15	GREEN VISTA LANDSCAPING	Lawn Care	-$254.36
8/28/15	GREEN VISTA LANDSCAPING	Lawn Care	-$220.00
Total			**-$474.36**
8/6/15	American Heritage Girls	Membership	-$26.00
Total			**-$26.00**
8/17/15	SEPHORA 268	Personal Care	-$147.66
Total			**-$147.66**
8/5/15	THE MARINA LIMITED - BOAT RENTAL	Recreation/Entertainment	-$125.00
8/5/15	THE MARINA LIMITED - REFUEL FEE	Recreation/Entertainment	-$8.52
Total			**-$133.52**
8/3/15	CHICK-FIL-A	Restaurants/Dining	-$42.37
8/3/15	PANERA BREAD	Restaurants/Dining	-$18.34
8/4/15	WHICH WICH	Restaurants/Dining	-$28.08
8/6/15	STARBUCKS #0988	Restaurants/Dining	-$172.38
8/10/15	CHICK-FIL-A	Restaurants/Dining	-$50.61
8/10/15	CHICK-FIL-A	Restaurants/Dining	-$16.19
8/12/15	CHICK-FIL-A	Restaurants/Dining	-$34.20
8/14/15	CHIPOTLE	Restaurants/Dining	-$28.34
8/17/15	MAGGIANOS	Restaurants/Dining	-$65.00
8/17/15	CHEESECAKE FACTORY	Restaurants/Dining	-$17.33
8/19/15	CHICK-FIL-A	Restaurants/Dining	-$43.50
8/19/15	STARBUCKS	Restaurants/Dining	-$29.85
8/21/15	MCDONALD'S	Restaurants/Dining	-$5.70
8/24/15	THE OLIVE GARDEN	Restaurants/Dining	-$49.66
8/24/15	CHICK-FIL-A	Restaurants/Dining	-$39.89
8/24/15	PAPA JOHN'S	Restaurants/Dining	-$29.59
8/26/15	BUFFALO WILD WINGS	Restaurants/Dining	-$25.36

Date	Expense	Category	Amount
8/28/15	CHICK-FIL-A	Restaurants/Dining	-$41.78
8/28/15	PAPA JOHN'S	Restaurants/Dining	-$29.59
8/28/15	BUFFALO WILD WINGS	Restaurants/Dining	-$15.03
8/31/15	RUTH'S CHRIS ST	Restaurants/Dining	-$168.32
8/31/15	OCHARLEYS RESTAURANT	Restaurants/Dining	-$50.00
8/31/15	CHICK-FIL-A	Restaurants/Dining	-$37.92
8/31/15	ORANGE LEAF YOGURT	Restaurants/Dining	-$11.97
8/31/15	MCDONALD'S	Restaurants/Dining	-$6.57
Total			**-$1,057.57**
8/31/15	PUREFLIX ONLINE SUBSCRIPTION	Subscriptions	-$7.99
Total			**-$7.99**
8/3/15	Duke Energy - ELECTRICITY	Utilities	-$171.46
8/12/15	VECTREN UTILITY - GAS BILL	Utilities	-$80.05
8/12/15	CITY SANITATION/TRASH	Utilities	-$39.03
8/28/15	WATER BILL	Utilities	-$117.25
Total			**-$407.79**

Balance Sheet

Bob and Debbie Smith - Balance Sheet *Updated June 2015

Assets	Location	Ownership Structure	Rate	Balance	
Checking Accounts	Lovington National Bank	Joint with rights of survivorship	0%	$ 7,000.00	
Savings Accounts	Lovington National Bank	Joint with rights of survivorship	0.25%	$ 80,674.00	
Money Market Accounts	Lovington National Bank	Joint with rights of survivorship	1.10%	$ 44,368.00	
Taxable Investments	Camelot Portfolios			$ 23,229.97	*Annual average rate of return has been 9%
IRA Accounts	Camelot Portfolios	Debbie's IRA		$ 92,524.66	*Annual average rate of return has been 7% (net of 1.75 fee)
401K Accounts	Lextin Supply 401K			$ 1,170,036.15	*Annual average rate of return has been 7.5%
Total Current Assets				$ 1,417,832.78	
Real Estate	1000 Residentail Lane	Joint with rights of survivorship		$ 375,000.00	*Appraisal completed on June 2014
Auto		Joint with rights of survivorship			
Volvo		Bob Smith		$ 9,800.00	
Ford Escape		Joint with rights of survivorship		$ 16,000.00	
Harley Davidson		Bob Smith		$ 20,000.00	
Personal Property					
Furniture				$ 20,000.00	
Jewelry				$ 18,000.00	*Rolex Watch, Engagement ring, Wedding band, Pearl neckalce
Art work				$ 20,000.00	*Russian painting given as inheritance from Debbie's father
Life Insurance (Cash Value)				$ -	
Other				$ -	
Total Assets				$ 1,896,632.78	
Liabilities					
Bass Pro Visa		Joint with rights of survivorship	9.99%	$ 13,567.00	
Chase Credit Card		Joint with rights of survivorship	7.75%	$ 18,000.00	
1st Primary Mortgage		Joint with rights of survivorship	5%	$ 262,481.00	
Ford - Lovington State Bank		Joint with rights of survivorship	3.75%	$ 11,723.00	
Harley Davison - HD Financial		Bob Smith	0%	$ 18,000.00	
Total Liabilities				$ 323,771.00	
Net Worth				$ 1,572,861.78	

Financial Values Questionnaire

BOB'S FINAL REPORT

There are no right or wrong scores in your report. This report describes your own beliefs and values compared to the averages of other test-takers. A financial planner who reads this report can gain a deeper psychological understanding of you. Please discuss results of interest with your financial advisor.

Self-Interest

Self-Interest Level: High

Self-interested people are often more financially independent. Additionally, high-scorers are likely to be autonomous decision makers, even to the point where they mistrust outside financial advisors' intentions. Planners may find that high-scorers are more decisive and more concerned about fees, and are less interested in charitable giving. Low-scorers are more financially open and accommodative toward others. Although low-scorers are more likely trusting and generous, they may have difficulty resisting inappropriate requests for money from relatives and friends, are likely to experience more financial guilt about their wealth, and may be indecisive when considering financial plans.

Worry

Worry Level: Below Average

"Worry" refers to financial anxiety. High-scorers experience more financial stress when thinking about their finances. Financial planners can help high-scorers by encouraging them to think long-term and to reduce the frequency of price-checking of their assets (such as stocks). Furthermore, it is often helpful if they are less aware of the details of how their planner is investing their assets, although an emphasis on risk management is often soothing. Conversely, low scorers may be financially reckless, and advisors can often help by helping them implement risk management plans.

Motivation

Motivation Level: High

Motivation refers to one's level of interest in learning about investments, keeping track of economic trends, and managing money. High-scorers are likely to have some enthusiasm for managing their own finances. Planners can assist low-scorers by educating them in simple, accessible terms. Planners should help to stoke low-scorer's engagement in their financial future while emphasizing those aspects of the financial markets that their clients find interesting. High-scorers are likely to be self-starters who will perform requested research and take an interest in co-managing their funds.

Courtesy of MarketPsych LLC

Discipline

Discipline Level: Below Average

Discipline refers to one's ability to organize his or her and prepare for contingencies. Discipline is necessary in order to follow an investment plan. High scorers are more likely to stay consistent with a plan. Low-scorers may not have prioritized financial planning in the past. For low-scorers, it can be helpful to locate one's emotional triggers around financial discipline. By learning how to see opportunity in the organization of their finances, and working to manage emotional blocks, their financial planning can become more effortless and fun.

Excitement

Excitement Level: Very High

Excitement refers to those investors who seek thrills in their investing. Financial excitement-seeking is not necessarily bad—it can motivate investors to find opportunities. Excitement-seeking can be a problem if it leads to excessive risk-taking. Financial planners may find that high-scorers are inclined to chase fast-moving stocks, buy stocks based on tips, request high risk investment strategies, and have high performance expectations. Low-scorers are likely to be more sober and deliberate decision makers.

Text Responses

- **If you had to choose, you would prefer to:**
  Spend less on lifestyle now and have more savings in retirement.
- **Is your answer to the previous question reflective of how you are actually spending and saving?**
  No
- **Have financial setbacks from the following events significantly affected you or your parents? (Please check all that apply.)**

Me	Parents	Both
Debt accumulation	Accident, illness, or death	Bear market, war

- **Other:**
- **If you identified any financial setbacks listed in the previous questions, please briefly explain how those experiences have changed you. How have your financial values been shaped by these setbacks?**
  My parents are aging, and I am concerned with their health and how that impacts me financially. I know I have some debt as well.
- **How concerned are you that you will not have enough money at the end of your life?**
  Not at all
- **In which of the following domains do you have unmet life goals and dreams?**
  - Travel
  - Education
  - Financial

- **Do you feel that you have sufficient assets to accomplish your goals and realize your dreams?**
  Have sufficient assets
- **What are your most valued activities during leisure (or retirement) time? Please select up to four.**
  - Recreation (athletics and entertainment)
  - Travel
  - Hobbies
- **After you retire, what are likely to be your financial priorities? (Please rank from 1 to 3, where 1 = most important.)**
  3: Legacy—Charitable giving to foundations, schools, religious bodies, or institutes.
  1: Lifestyle—Spending on homes, recreation, travel, education, memberships, health care, and luxuries.
  2: Thrift—Ensuring I have enough to last until the end of my life.
- **What traditions and values in your family or community are important and should be carried on?**
  I want my kids to be able to see the world. Debbie and I have never really had the opportunity to travel together, and that is really important.
- **How would you like to be remembered by later generations?**
  I want my kids to know that I was a good dad and that I loved them.
- **Do you believe that the amount of money you have impacts your level of happiness? If so, in what ways?**
  Yes, money is the source by which all things can be accomplished. Money allows us to spend time together on vacations and traveling.

DEBBIE'S FINAL REPORT

There are no right or wrong scores in your report. This report describes your own beliefs and values compared to the averages of other test-takers. A financial planner who reads this report can gain a deeper psychological understanding of you. Please discuss results of interest with your financial advisor.

Self-Interest

Self-Interest Level: Below Average

Self-interested people are often more financially independent. Additionally, high-scorers are likely to be autonomous decision makers, even to the point where they mistrust outside financial advisors' intentions. Planners may find that high-scorers are more decisive and more concerned about fees, and are less interested in charitable giving. Low-scorers are more financially open and accommodative toward others. Although low-scorers are more likely trusting and generous, they may have difficulty resisting inappropriate requests for money from relatives and friends, are likely to experience more financial guilt about their wealth, and may be indecisive when considering financial plans.

Worry

Worry Level: Very High

"Worry" refers to financial anxiety. High scorers experience more financial stress when thinking about their finances. Financial planners can help high-scorers by encouraging them to think long-term and to reduce the frequency of price-checking of their assets (such as stocks). Furthermore, it is often helpful if they are less aware of the details of how their planner is investing their assets, although an emphasis on risk management is often soothing. Conversely, low-scorers may be financially reckless, and advisors can often help by helping them implement risk management plans.

Motivation

Motivation Level: Low

Motivation refers to one's level of interest in learning about investments, keeping track of economic trends, and managing money. High-scorers are likely to have some enthusiasm for managing their own finances. Planners can assist low-scorers by educating them in simple, accessible terms. Planners should help to stoke low-scorer's engagement in their financial future while emphasizing those aspects of the financial markets that their clients find interesting. High-scorers are likely to be self-starters who will perform requested research and take an interest in co-managing their funds.

Discipline

Discipline Level: High

Discipline refers to one´s ability to organize his or her finances and prepare for contingencies. Discipline is necessary in order to follow an investment plan. High scorers are more likely to stay consistent with a plan. Low-scorers may not have prioritized financial planning in the past. For low-scorers, it can be helpful to locate one's emotional triggers around financial discipline. By learning how to see opportunity in the organization of their finances, and working to manage emotional blocks, their financial planning can become more effortless and fun.

Excitement

Excitement Level: Below Average

Excitement refers to those investors who seek thrills in their investing. Financial excitement-seeking is not necessarily bad—it can motivate investors to find opportunities. Excitement-seeking can be a problem if it leads to excessive risk-taking. Financial planners may find that high-scorers are inclined to chase fast-moving stocks, buy stocks based on tips, request high risk investment strategies, and have high performance expectations. Low-scorers are likely to be more sober and deliberate decision makers.

Text Responses

- **If you had to choose, you would prefer to:**
  Spend less on lifestyle now and have more savings in retirement.

- **Is your answer to the previous question reflective of how you are actually spending and saving?**
  No

- **Have financial setbacks from the following events significantly affected you or your parents? (Please check all that apply.)**

Me	Parents	Both
Debt accumulation		War, accident, illness or death

- **Other:**
- **If you identified any financial setbacks listed in the previous questions, please briefly explain how those experiences have changed you. How have your financial values been shaped by these setbacks?**
  My father died of cancer a few years ago, so my mother, my siblings, and I have dealt with that loss.
- **How concerned are you that you will not have enough money at the end of your life?**
  Very
- **In which of the following domains do you have unmet life goals and dreams?**
  - Family
  - Spirituality/Religion
  - Financial
- **Do you feel that you have sufficient assets to accomplish your goals and realize your dreams?**
  Need or would like additional income
- **What are your most valued activities during leisure (or retirement) time? Please select up to four.**
  - Travel
  - Hobbies
  - Community service
  - Religious service
- **After you retire, what are likely to be your financial priorities? (Please rank from 1 to 3, where 1 = most important.)**
  2: Legacy—Charitable giving to foundations, schools, religious bodies, or institutes.
  3: Lifestyle—Spending on homes, recreation, travel, education, memberships, healthcare, and luxuries.
  1: Thrift—Ensuring I have enough to last until the end of my life.
- **What traditions and values in your family or community are important and should be carried on?**
  I want to make sure my kids continue to serve the Lord and raise their kids, my grandkids, up in the name of the Lord.
- **How would you like to be remembered by later generations?**
  I want to be remembered as a mother who stood as a servant wife in the name of the Lord. I also want my kids to know that we gave to others as Christ gave to us.
- **Do you believe that the amount of money you have impacts your level of happiness? If so, in what ways?**
  I believe money can be used to fulfill projects, but most importantly, I believe that our happiness comes from having a deep relationship with Jesus Christ.

Insurance

BOB SMITH LIFE INSURANCE DECLARATION 1

ABC Life Insurance Company
Policy Declarations Page

Insured:	Bob Smith	**Death Benefit:**	$ 1,000,000.00
Policy Date:	10/1/09	**Policy Number:**	ABC12345
Initial Premium:	$ 89.00	**Age/Sex:**	44/Male
Premium Mode:	Monthly	**Premium Class:**	Preferred Non-tobacco
Owner:	Bob Smith	**Policy Type:**	20 Year Level Term
Beneficiary:	As Requested On Application	**Total Annual Premium:**	$ 1,068.00

BOB SMITH LIFE INSURANCE DECLARATION 2

ABC Life Insurance Company
Policy Declarations Page

Insured:	Bob Smith	**Death Benefit:**	$ 300,000.00
Policy Date:	2/1/12	**Policy Number:**	ABC12345
Initial Premium:	$ 53.50	**Age/Sex:**	46/Male
Premium Mode:	Monthly	**Premium Class:**	Preferred Non-tobacco
Owner:	Bob Smith	**Policy Type:**	20 Year Level Term
Beneficiary:	As Requested On Application	**Total Annual Premium:**	$ 642.00

ABC Life Insurance Company
Policy Declarations Page

Insured:	Bob Smith	Death Benefit:	$ 250,000.00
Policy Date:	6/15/14	Policy Number:	ABC12345
Initial Premium:	$ 57.00	Age/Sex:	49/Male
Premium Mode:	Monthly	Premium Class:	Preferred Non-tobacco
Owner:	Bob Smith	Policy Type:	20 Year Level Term
Beneficiary:	As Requested On Application	Total Annual Premium:	$ 684.00

SMITH AUTO DECLARATION

Auto Policy Declarations

Coverage provided by:
Mutual Insurance
100 Mutual Pl., Mutual, NM 11111

Named Insured	Policy Number	Your Insurance Agent	Agent Phone
Bob Smith &	ABC-12345	Jones Insurance Agency	(936)111-1111
Debbie Smith	**Policy Period**	200 Main St	
1000 Residential Lane	12/1/2015 to 12/1/2016	Lovington, NM 11111	
Lovington, NM 11111			

Total Annual Policy Premium: $ 1,838.00

Vehicles Covered:

Vehicle Rating Information:

Vehicles	VIN	State	Use	Annual Miles
1. 2009 Volvo	ABC11111112222222	NM	To work 6-10	12,000 Miles
2. 2013 Ford	EFG33333334444444	NM	Pleasure	8,000 Miles
3. 2014 Harley Davidson	HJK55555556666666	NM	Pleasure	8,000 Miles

Driver Rating Information:

Drivers Included	Age	Status	Gender	Vehicle	FT/PT
Bob Smith	50	Married	Male	1	FT
Debbie Smith	52	Married	Female	2	FT
Sean Smith	20	Single	Male	1	PT
Chloe Smith	16	Single	Female	2	PT

Coverage Information:

	Vehicle (premium in $)		
	1	2	3
Liability Protection			
Bodily Injury $100,000 per person/ $300,000 per accident	178	165	68
Property Damage $50,000 per accident	157	152	46
Medical Payments			
$5,000 per person	30	28	14
Uninsured/Underinsured Motorists			
Bodily Injury $100,000 per person/ $300,000 per accident	60	55	22
Property Damage $50,000 per accident	20	18	9
Physical Damage			
Comprehensive- $500 deductible	115	107	28
Collisioin- $500 deductible	241	228	57
Optional Coverages			
Transportation Expenses- Comprehensive $30/day- $900 maximum	5	5	0
Transportation Expenses- Collision $30/day- $900 maximum	15	15	0
Annual Premium per Vehicle	**821**	**773**	**244**

Discounts That Apply:	Vehicle:
Anti-Lock Brake Discount	1,2
Anti-Theft Discount	1,2
Multi-Car Discount	1,2
Multi-Policy Discount	1,2
Passive Restraint Discount	1,2
Prior Bodily Injury Discount	1,2

SMITH HOMEOWNER DECLARATION

Homeowner Policy Declarations

Coverage provided by:
Mutual Insurance
100 Mutual Pl., Mutual, NM 11111

Named Insured	**Policy Number**	**Your Insurance Agent**	**Agent Phone**
Bob Smith &	Home-12345	Jones Insurance Agency	(936)111-1111
Debbie Smith	**Policy Period**	200 Main St	
1000 Residential Lane	12/1/2015 to 12/1/2016	Lovington, NM 11111	
Lovington, NM 11111			

Location Address:
1000 Residential Lane
Lovington, NM 11111

Total Annual Policy Premium: $ 2,002.00

Policy Form- HO5

Homeowner Coverages:

Policy Deductible: $ 1,000.00

	Coverage Amount	Premium
Section I- Property Protection		
Coverage A (Dwelling)	$ 375,000.00	$ 1,852.00
Coverage B (Other Structures)	$ 37,500.00	$ 193.00
Coverage C (Personal Property)	$ 262,500.00	$ 343.00
Coverage D (Loss of Use)	$ 75,000.00	$ 199.00
Section II- Home and Family Liability Protection		
Personal Liability- Each Occurrence	$ 300,000.00	$ 125.00
Medical Payments to Others- Each Person	$ 5,000.00	$ 24.00
Policy Endorsements		
Coverage A Extension	50%	$ 119.00
Water/ Sewer and Drain Backup	$ 20,000.00	$ 151.00
Scheduled Personal Property	$ 15,000.00	$ 145.00
Personal Property Replacement Cost	Yes	Included
Total Annual Policy Premium		$ 3,151.00

Discounts That Apply:

Alarm Credit		$ (143.00)
Multi- Policy Discount		$ (521.00)
New Home Discount		$ (485.00)
Total Annual Policy Premium (After Discounts)		$ 2,002.00

XYZ Life Insurance Company
Policy Declarations Page

Lextin Oil Supply Group Life Insurance

Employee:	Bob Smith	**Relationship:**	Spouse
Insured:	Debbie Smith	**Death Benefit:**	$ 50,000.00
Policy Date:	1/1/15	**Policy Number:**	JKL12345
Amount Deducted	$ 11.00	**Age/Sex:**	52/Female
Premium Mode:	Per pay	**Premium Class:**	Non-tobacco
Owner:	Debbie Smith	**Policy Type:**	Group Term
Beneficiary:	As Requested On Application	**Total Annual Premium:**	$ 264.00

RST Life Insurance Company

Guaranteed Universal Life Illustration

For:	Bob Smith			Initial Death Benefit:			$	3,000,000.00
Age:	51			Planned Modal Premium (Monthly EFT):			$	2,929.85
Sex:	Male							
Class:	Preferred Non-Tobacco							

Guaranteed 2.00% Interest/Guaranteed Charges

End Of Year	Age	Annual Premium Outlay	Net Policy Value	Surrender Value	Death Benefit
1	52	$ 35,158.00	$ 3,840.00	$ -	$ 3,000,000.00
2	53	$ 35,158.00	$ 6,647.00	$ -	$ 3,000,000.00
3	54	$ 35,158.00	$ 8,307.00	$ -	$ 3,000,000.00
4	55	$ 35,158.00	$ 8,460.00	$ -	$ 3,000,000.00
5	56	$ 35,158.00	$ 6,701.00	$ -	$ 3,000,000.00
6	57	$ 35,158.00	$ 2,948.00	$ -	$ 3,000,000.00
7	58	$ 35,158.00	$ -	$ -	$ 3,000,000.00
8	59	$ 35,158.00	$ -	$ -	$ 3,000,000.00
9	60	$ 35,158.00	$ -	$ -	$ 3,000,000.00
10	61	$ 35,158.00	$ -	$ -	$ 3,000,000.00
		$ 351,580.00			
11	62	$ 35,158.00	$ -	$ -	$ 3,000,000.00
12	63	$ 35,158.00	$ -	$ -	$ 3,000,000.00
13	64	$ 35,158.00	$ -	$ -	$ 3,000,000.00
14	65	$ 35,158.00	$ -	$ -	$ 3,000,000.00
15	66	$ 35,158.00	$ -	$ -	$ 3,000,000.00
16	67	$ 35,158.00	$ -	$ -	$ 3,000,000.00
17	68	$ 35,158.00	$ -	$ -	$ 3,000,000.00
18	69	$ 35,158.00	$ -	$ -	$ 3,000,000.00
19	70	$ 35,158.00	$ -	$ -	$ 3,000,000.00
20	71	$ 35,158.00	$ -	$ -	$ 3,000,000.00
		$ 703,160.00			
21	72	$ 35,158.00	$ -	$ -	$ 3,000,000.00
22	73	$ 35,158.00	$ -	$ -	$ 3,000,000.00
23	74	$ 35,158.00	$ -	$ -	$ 3,000,000.00
24	75	$ 35,158.00	$ -	$ -	$ 3,000,000.00
25	76	$ 35,158.00	$ -	$ -	$ 3,000,000.00
26	77	$ 35,158.00	$ -	$ -	$ 3,000,000.00
27	78	$ 35,158.00	$ -	$ -	$ 3,000,000.00
28	79	$ 35,158.00	$ -	$ -	$ 3,000,000.00
29	80	$ 35,158.00	$ -	$ -	$ 3,000,000.00
30	81	$ 35,158.00	$ -	$ -	$ 3,000,000.00
		$ 1,054,740.00			

31	82	$	35,158.00	$	-	$	-	$	3,000,000.00
32	83	$	35,158.00	$	-	$	-	$	3,000,000.00
33	84	$	35,158.00	$	-	$	-	$	3,000,000.00
34	85	$	35,158.00	$	-	$	-	$	3,000,000.00
35	86	$	35,158.00	$	-	$	-	$	3,000,000.00
36	87	$	35,158.00	$	-	$	-	$	3,000,000.00
37	88	$	35,158.00	$	-	$	-	$	3,000,000.00
38	89	$	35,158.00	$	-	$	-	$	3,000,000.00
39	90	$	35,158.00	$	-	$	-	$	3,000,000.00
40	91	$	35,158.00	$	-	$	-	$	3,000,000.00
		$	1,406,320.00						
41	92	$	35,158.00	$	-	$	-	$	3,000,000.00
42	93	$	35,158.00	$	-	$	-	$	3,000,000.00
43	94	$	35,158.00	$	-	$	-	$	3,000,000.00
44	95	$	35,158.00	$	-	$	-	$	3,000,000.00
45	96	$	35,158.00	$	-	$	-	$	3,000,000.00
46	97	$	35,158.00	$	-	$	-	$	3,000,000.00
47	98	$	35,158.00	$	-	$	-	$	3,000,000.00
48	99	$	35,158.00	$	-	$	-	$	3,000,000.00
49	100	$	35,158.00	$	-	$	-	$	3,000,000.00
50	101	$	35,158.00	$	-	$	-	$	3,000,000.00
		$	1,757,900.00						
51	102	$	35,158.00	$	-	$	-	$	3,000,000.00
52	103	$	35,158.00	$	-	$	-	$	3,000,000.00
53	104	$	35,158.00	$	-	$	-	$	3,000,000.00
54	105	$	35,158.00	$	-	$	-	$	3,000,000.00
55	106	$	35,158.00	$	-	$	-	$	3,000,000.00
56	107	$	35,158.00	$	-	$	-	$	3,000,000.00
57	108	$	35,158.00	$	-	$	-	$	3,000,000.00
58	109	$	35,158.00	$	-	$	-	$	3,000,000.00
59	110	$	35,158.00	$	-	$	-	$	3,000,000.00
60	111	$	35,158.00	$	-	$	-	$	3,000,000.00
		$	2,109,480.00						
61	112	$	35,158.00	$	-	$	-	$	3,000,000.00
62	113	$	35,158.00	$	-	$	-	$	3,000,000.00
63	114	$	35,158.00	$	-	$	-	$	3,000,000.00
64	115	$	35,158.00	$	-	$	-	$	3,000,000.00
65	116	$	35,158.00	$	-	$	-	$	3,000,000.00
66	117	$	35,158.00	$	-	$	-	$	3,000,000.00
67	118	$	35,158.00	$	-	$	-	$	3,000,000.00
68	119	$	35,158.00	$	-	$	-	$	3,000,000.00
69	120	$	35,158.00	$	-	$	-	$	3,000,000.00
70	121	$	35,158.00	$	-	$	-	$	3,000,000.00
		$	2,461,060.00						
71	122	$	-	$	-	$	-	$	3,000,000.00
72	123	$	-	$	-	$	-	$	3,000,000.00
73	124	$	-	$	-	$	-	$	3,000,000.00
74	125	$	-	$	-	$	-	$	3,000,000.00
75	126	$	-	$	-	$	-	$	3,000,000.00
		$	2,461,060.00						

Taxes

Taxes

| Form **1040** | Department of the Treasury - Internal Revenue Service (99) | **2014** | OMB No. 1545-0074 | IRS Use Only - Do not write or staple in this space. |

U.S. Individual Income Tax Return

For the year Jan. 1-Dec. 31, 2014, or other tax year beginning _____ , ending _____ | See separate instructions.

Your first name and initial	Last name	Your social security number
Bob T	Smith	123-45-6789

If a joint return, spouse's first name and initial	Last name	Spouse's social security number
Debbie	Smith	987-65-4321

Home address (number and street). If you have a P.O. box, see instructions. | Apt. no.
1000 Residential Lane

Make sure the SSN(s) above and on line 6c are correct.

City, town or post office, state, and ZIP code. If you have a foreign address, also complete spaces below (see instructions).
Lovington, NM 11111

Foreign country name | Foreign province/state/county | Foreign postal code

Presidential Election Campaign
Check here if you, or your spouse if filing jointly, want $3 to go to this fund. Checking a box below will not change your tax or refund. ☐ You ☐ Spouse

Filing Status
Check only one box.
1. ☐ Single
2. ☒ Married filing jointly (even if only one had income)
3. ☐ Married filing separately. Enter spouse's SSN above and full name here. ▶
4. ☐ Head of household (with qualifying person). (See instructions.) If the qualifying person is a child but not your dependent, enter this child's name here. ▶
5. ☐ Qualifying widow(er) with dependent child

Exemptions

6a ☒ Yourself. If someone can claim you as a dependent, **do not** check box 6a
b ☒ Spouse

Boxes checked on 6a and 6b **2**

c Dependents:

(1) First name Last name	(2) Dependent's social security number	(3) Dependent's relationship to you	(4) ✗ if child under age 17 qualifying for child tax credit (see instr.)
Sean Smith	456-78-1234	Son	☐
Chole Smith	123-98-4567	Daughter	☒
Clara Smith	551-12-5214	Daughter	☒

If more than four dependents, see instructions and check here ▶☐

No. of children on 6c who:
• lived with you **3**
• did not live with you due to divorce or separation (see instructions) **0**
Dependents on 6c not entered above **0**
Add numbers on lines above ▶ **5**

d Total number of exemptions claimed

Income

Attach Form(s) W-2 here. Also attach Forms W-2G and 1099-R if tax was withheld.

If you did not get a W-2, see instructions.

7	Wages, salaries, tips, etc. Attach Form(s) W-2	7	178,966.
8a	**Taxable** interest. Attach Schedule B if required	8a	
b	Tax-exempt interest. **Do not** include on line 8a	8b	
9a	Ordinary dividends. Attach Schedule B if required	9a	395.
b	Qualified dividends	9b	395.
10	Taxable refunds, credits, or offsets of state and local income taxes	10	
11	Alimony received	11	
12	Business income or (loss). Attach Schedule C or C-EZ	12	
13	Capital gain or (loss). Attach Schedule D if required. If not required, check here ▶☐	13	8,666.
14	Other gains or (losses). Attach Form 4797	14	
15a	IRA distributions	15a	b Taxable amount	15b	
16a	Pensions and annuities	16a	b Taxable amount	16b	
17	Rental real estate, royalties, partnerships, S corporations, trusts, etc. Attach Schedule E	17	
18	Farm income or (loss). Attach Schedule F	18	
19	Unemployment compensation	19	
20a	Social security benefits	20a	b Taxable amount	20b	
21	Other income. List type and amount	21	
22	Combine the amounts in the far right column for lines 7 through 21. This is your **total income** ▶	22	188,027.

Adjusted Gross Income

23	Educator expenses	23	
24	Certain business expenses of reservists, performing artists, and fee-basis government officials. Attach Form 2106 or 2106-EZ	24	
25	Health savings account deduction. Attach Form 8889	25	
26	Moving expenses. Attach Form 3903	26	
27	Deductible part of self-employment tax. Attach Schedule SE	27	
28	Self-employed SEP, SIMPLE, and qualified plans	28	
29	Self-employed health insurance deduction	29	
30	Penalty on early withdrawal of savings	30	
31a	Alimony paid b Recipient's SSN ▶	31a	
32	IRA deduction	32	
33	Student loan interest deduction	33	
34	Tuition and fees. Attach Form 8917	34	
35	Domestic production activities deduction. Attach Form 8903	35	
36	Add lines 23 through 35	36	0.
37	Subtract line 36 from line 22. This is your **adjusted gross income** ▶	37	188,027.

For Disclosure, Privacy Act, and Paperwork Reduction Act Notice, see separate instructions.
UYA

Form **1040** (2014)

513

Bob T and Debbie Smith   123-45-6789   Page **2**

Tax and Credits	38	Amount from line 37 (adjusted gross income)		38	188,027.

39a Check if: { You were born before January 2, 1950, □   Blind. } { Spouse was born before January 2, 1950, □   Blind. } Total boxes checked ▶ 39a **0**

b If your spouse itemizes on a separate return or you were a dual-status alien, check here ▶ 39b □

Standard Deduction for-

- People who check any box on line 39a or 39b **or** who can be claimed as a dependent, see instructions.
- All others: Single or Married filing separately, $6,200
Married filing jointly or Qualifying widow(er), $12,400
Head of household, $9,100

	40	**Itemized deductions** (from Schedule A) **or** your **standard deduction** (see left margin)		40	34,676.
	41	Subtract line 40 from line 38		41	153,351.
	42	**Exemptions.** If line 38 is $152,525 or less, multiply $3,950 by the number on line 6d. Otherwise, see instructions.		42	19,750.
	43	**Taxable income.** Subtract line 42 from line 41. If line 42 is more than line 41, enter -0-		43	133,601.
	44	**Tax** (see instructions). Check if any from: **a** □ Form(s) 8814 **b** □ Form 4972 **c** □ ___		44	24,218.
	45	**Alternative minimum tax** (see instructions). Attach Form 6251		45	1,457.
	46	Excess advance premium tax credit repayment. Attach Form 8962		46	
	47	Add lines 44, 45, and 46 . . . . ▶		47	25,675.
	48	Foreign tax credit. Attach Form 1116 if required	48	25.	
	49	Credit for child and dependent care expenses. Attach Form 2441 .	49		
	50	Education credits from Form 8863, line 19	50		
	51	Retirement savings contributions credit. Attach Form 8880 . . .	51		
	52	Child tax credit. Attach Schedule 8812, if required	52		
	53	Residential energy credits. Attach Form 5695	53		
	54	Other credits from Form: **a** □ 3800 **b** □ 8801 **c** □ ___	54		
	55	Add lines 48 through 54. These are your **total credits**		55	25.
	56	Subtract line 55 from line 47. If line 55 is more than line 47, enter -0- . . . . ▶		56	25,650.
Other Taxes	57	Self-employment tax. Attach Schedule SE		57	
	58	Unreported social security and Medicare tax from Form: **a** □ 4137 **b** □ 8919		58	
	59	Additional tax on IRAs, other qualified retirement plans, etc. Attach Form 5329 if required		59	
	60a	Household employment taxes from Schedule H		60a	
	b	First-time homebuyer credit repayment. Attach Form 5405 if required		60b	
	61	Health care: individual responsibility (see instructions) Full-year coverage ☒		61	
	62	Taxes from: **a** □ Form 8959 **b** □ Form 8960 **c** □ Instructions; enter code(s)		62	
	63	Add lines 56 through 62. This is your **total tax** . . . . ▶		63	25,650.
Payments	64	Federal income tax withheld from Forms W-2 and 1099	64	33,474.	
	65	2014 estimated tax payments and amount applied from 2013 return	65		

If you have a qualifying child, attach Schedule EIC.

	66a	**Earned income credit (EIC)** . . . . **NO** . .	66a		
	b	Nontaxable combat pay election. . . 66b			
	67	Additional child tax credit. Attach Schedule 8812	67		
	68	American opportunity credit from Form 8863, line 8	68		
	69	Net premium tax credit. Attach Form 8962	69		
	70	Amount paid with request for extension to file	70		
	71	Excess social security and tier 1 RRTA tax withheld	71		
	72	Credit for federal tax on fuels. Attach Form 4136	72		
	73	Credits from Form: **a** □ 2439 **b** □ Reserved **c** □ Reserved **d** □	73		
	74	Add lines 64, 65, 66a, and 67 through 73. These are your **total payments** . . . . ▶		74	33,474.
Refund	75	If line 74 is more than line 63, subtract line 63 from line 74. This is the amount you **overpaid**		75	7,824.
	76a	Amount of line 75 you want **refunded to you**. If Form 8888 is attached, check here . . . ▶ □		76a	7,824.

Direct deposit? See instructions.

▶ **b** Routing number _____ ▶ **c** Type: □ Checking □ Savings
▶ **d** Account number _____

	77	Amount of line 75 you want **applied to your 2015 estimated tax** ▶	77		
Amount You Owe	78	**Amount you owe.** Subtract line 74 from line 63. For details on how to pay, see instructions ▶		78	0.
	79	Estimated tax penalty (see instructions)	79		

Third Party Designee

Do you want to allow another person to discuss this return with the IRS (see instructions)? □ **Yes.** Complete below. ☒ **No**

Designee's name ▶ ___ Phone no. ▶ ___ Personal identification number (PIN) ▶ ___

Sign Here

Under penalties of perjury, I declare that I have examined this return and accompanying schedules and statements, and to the best of my knowledge and belief, they are true, correct, and complete. Declaration of preparer (other than taxpayer) is based on all information of which preparer has any knowledge.

Joint return? See instr. Keep a copy for your records.

Your signature	Date	Your occupation	Daytime phone number
			(260) 982-1904
Spouse's signature. If a joint return, **both** must sign.	Date	Spouse's occupation	If the IRS sent you an Identity Protection PIN, enter it here (see inst.)

Paid Preparer Use Only

Print/Type preparer's name	Preparer's signature	Date	Check □ if self-employed	PTIN
Matthew J Mize				P00588393

Firm's name ▶ Law Offices of Matthew J. Mize,   Firm's EIN ▶

Firm's address ▶   Phone no.

UYA   Form **1040** (2014)

SCHEDULE A
(Form 1040)

Department of the Treasury
Internal Revenue Service (99)

Itemized Deductions

▶ Information about Schedule A and its separate instructions is at *www.irs.gov/schedulea*.
▶ **Attach to Form 1040.**

OMB No. 1545-0074

2014

Attachment
Sequence No. 07

Name(s) shown on Form 1040

Bob T and Debbie Smith

Your social security number

123-45-6789

Medical and Dental Expenses		**Caution.** Do not include expenses reimbursed or paid by others.			
	1	Medical and dental expenses (see instructions).....................1			
	2	Enter amount from Form 1040, line 38 | 2 |			
	3	Multiply line 2 by 10% (.10). But if either you or your spouse was born before January 2, 1950, multiply line 2 by 7.5% (.075) instead . 3			
	4	Subtract line 3 from line 1. If line 3 is more than line 1, enter -0-	4		0.
Taxes You Paid	5	State and local (**check only one box**):			
		a ☒ Income taxes, **or** ⎫	5	11,194.	
		b ☐ General sales taxes ⎭			
	6	Real estate taxes (see instructions).....................6		13,845.	
	7	Personal property taxes................................7		432.	
	8	Other taxes. List type and amount ▶ _____			
		Excise Tax	8	184.	
	9	Add lines 5 through 8 9			25,655.
Interest You Paid	10	Home mortgage interest and points reported to you on Form 1098	10	4,041.	
	11	Home mortgage interest not reported to you on Form 1098. If paid to the person from whom you bought the home, see instructions and show that person's name, identifying no., and address ▶			
Note. Your mortgage interest deduction may be limited (see instructions).		_____			
		_____	11		
	12	Points not reported to you on Form 1098. See instructions for special rules . .	12		
	13	Mortgage insurance premiums (see instructions) 13	13		
	14	Investment interest. Attach Form 4952 if required. (See instructions.)	14		
	15	Add lines 10 through 14 15			4,041.
Gifts to Charity	16	Gifts by cash or check. If you made any gift of $250 or more, see instructions 16		4,980.	
If you made a gift and got a benefit for it, see instructions.	17	Other than by cash or check. If any gift of $250 or more, see instructions. You **must** attach Form 8283 if over $500.................17			
	18	Carryover from prior year	18		
	19	Add lines 16 through 18 .	19		4,980.
Casualty and Theft Losses	20	Casualty or theft loss(es). Attach Form 4684. (See instructions.)	20		0.
Job Expenses and Certain Miscellaneous Deductions	21	Unreimbursed employee expenses - job travel, union dues, job education, etc. Attach Form 2106 or 2106-EZ if required. (See instructions.) ▶ _____	21		
		_____			
	22	Tax preparation fees	22		
	23	Other expenses - investment, safe deposit box, etc. List type and amount ▶ _____			
		_____	23		
	24	Add lines 21 through 23 24			
	25	Enter amount from Form 1040, line 38 | 25 |			
	26	Multiply line 25 by 2% (.02)	26		
	27	Subtract line 26 from line 24. If line 26 is more than line 24, enter -0-	27		0.
Other Miscellaneous Deductions	28	Other - from list in instructions. List type and amount ▶ _____			
		_____	28		0.
Total Itemized Deductions	29	Is Form 1040, line 38, over $152,525?			
		☐ **No.** Your deduction is not limited. Add the amounts in the far right column for lines 4 through 28. Also, enter this amount on Form 1040, line 40. ⎫	29		34,676.
		☒ **Yes.** Your deduction may be limited. See the Itemized Deductions Worksheet in the instructions to figure the amount to enter. ⎭			
	30	If you elect to itemize deductions even though they are less than your standard deduction, check here . . . . ▶ ☐			

For Paperwork Reduction Act Notice, see Form 1040 instructions.

Schedule A (Form 1040) 2014

UYA

Details for Schedule A, Line 16

Bob T and Debbie Smith

123-45-6789 - 987-65-4321

Date	Description	Amount
	Annual Shop With cop Program	50.00
	Lovington Community Church	4,930.00
	Total	4,980.00

This W-2 belongs to: [X] Bob   [ ] Debbie

a Employee's social security number		OMB No. 1545-0008
123-45- 6789	[X] Standard W-2 (Typed or computer generated) [ ] Non-Standard W-2 (Altered or hand written) [ ] Form W- 2c, Corrected Wage and Tax Stmt.	

b Employer identification number	1 Wages, tips, other comp	2 Federal inc tax withheld
12-3456789	178,965 .63	33,474. 24

c Employer's name

Lextin Oil Supply

Employer's address
123 Industrial Blvd

	State	Zip Code
Employer's city **Lovington**	**NM**	**46581**

Employer's foreign country

Foreign province/county   Foreign postal code

3 Social security wages	4 Social Sec tax withheld
117,000 .00	7,254.00
5 Medicare wages and tips	6 Medicare tax withheld
182,921 .06	2,652.36
7 Social security tips	8 Allocated tips
0.00	0.00
9	10 Dependent care benefits
	0.00
11 Nonqualified plans	12 Code Amount
0.00	D 3,955.43

e Employee's first name

Bob T

Employee's last name	Suff.
Smith	

f Employee's address

1000 Residential Lane

	State	Zip Code
Employee's city **Lovington**	**NM**	**11111**

Employee's foreign country

Foreign province/county   Foreign postal code

13 Statutory employee [ ]	W 3,000.00
Retirement plan [X]	C 205.14
Third-party sick pay [ ]	V 16,139. 17
	AA 4,290.05
14 See expanded section below.	BB 18,207. 28
	0.00
	0.00

15 State	State ID No.	16 State wages	17 State inc tax	18 Local wages	19 Local W/H	20 Local name
NM	0001041851	178,965 .63	6,041.15	178,965 .63	5,152.81	OTHER
		0.00	0.00	0.00	0.00	
		0.00	0.00	0.00	0.00	
		0.00	0.00	0.00	0.00	
		0.00	0.00	0.00	0.00	
		0.00	0.00	0.00	0.00	
		0.00	0.00	0.00	0.00	
		0.00	0.00	0.00	0.00	

W-2 Wage and Tax Statement **2014** Department of the Treasury Internal Revenue Service

Other Items reported on this copy of Form W-2

10/12/15 01:47PM

If an ITIN was entered on Form 1040, Form 1040NR, or Form 1041 enter the social security number shown on Form W-2 _____

Check here if a minister or member of the clergy and wages are subject to self-employment taxes but no FICA taxes withheld (do not check if church employee income)	☐
Check here if you received more than one W-2 from this employer and this W-2 should not be included in the Excess FICA withholding calculations	☐
Check here if the dependent care benefits in box 10 above are provided at an employer provided facility	☐

Disability and Unemployment Insurance:

Mandatory contributions made for Disability Insurance (SDI) (CA, NJ, NY, WA)	0.00
Mandatory contributions to Rhode Island Temporary Disability Insurance (RI TDI) (RI)	0.00
Mandatory contributions made for Unemployment Insurance (AK, CA, NJ, PA)	0.00
Voluntary Plan for Disability Insurance contributions (VPDI) (CA)	0.00

IRC Section 125 Flexible Benefit Contributions Flexible Spending Account (FSA): 0.00
(For NY only enter the amount from a NYC established plan.)

Employees covered by the Railroad Retirement Tax Act (RRTA):

Railroad Tier 1 Compensation (RRTA compensation)	0.00
Railroad Tier 1 Compensation subject to Tier 1 Medicare tax	0.00

Tier I railroad retirement contributions (Tier 1 tax) .   0.00

Tier II railroad retirement contributions (Tier 2 tax)   0.00   **Total Railroad contributions** . . .   0.00

Medicare tax withheld (Medicare tax)	0.00
Additional Medicare tax withheld (Additional Medicare Tax)	0.00
Check here if you are a Railroad Employee Representative . . . . ☐	

Maryland State Retirement Pickup:	0.00
California mandatory contributions for Paid Family Leave:	0.00
New Jersey mandatory contributions for Family Leave Insurance (FLI):	0.00
New York Public Employee 414(h) retirement contributions:	0.00
New York START-UP NY wages	0.00
Union dues	0.00

Other Box 14 Entries NOT previously entered above

Description	Amount
RSUII	12,715.09
	0.00
	0.00
	0.00

10/12/15 01:47PM

Tip Income Information	
Tips under $20 per month you were not required to report	0.00
Other unreported tips received	0.00

Community Property Allocation	
This section is used for taxpayers who are currently filing a married filing separate return in a community property state. Income must be allocated between spouses. Community property states are: Arizona, California, Idaho, Louisiana, Nevada, New Mexico, Texas, Washington, and Wisconsin.	
Wages allocated to spouse	0.00

10/12/15 01:47PM

This information will transfer to Federal Schedule A, Line 10. If the mortgage interest is for rental, business, farm, or farm rental, do not enter the amount on this form; instead enter the deductible amount directly on the applicable form or schedule.

If the mortgage interest is for business use of the home, enter the **total** amount here. Schedule A, line 10 will be reduced by the indirect business portion.

The interest on this form belongs to:

- [X] Bob
- [ ] Debbie
- [ ] Bob and Debbie

Recipient's Federal Identification number	Payer's social security number		
35-1131741	123-45- 6789		

Recipient's/Lender's name **Mortgage Bank**	
Recipient's/Lender's address **1234 Money Lane**	

Recipient's/Lender's city	State	Zip Code
Lovington	**NM**	**11111**

Recipient's/Lender's foreign country

Lender foreign province/county   Foreign postal code

*Caution: The amount show n may not be fully deductible by you. Limits based on the loan amount and the cost and value of the secured property may apply. Also you may only deduct interest to the extent it w as incurred by you, actually paid by you, and not reimbursed by another person

OMB No.1545-0901

2014

Form **1098**

Mortgage Interest Statement

Recipient's/Lender's telephone number

1 Deductible mortgage interest received from payer(s)/borrow er(s)*
4,041.

Payer's/Borrow er's name
Bob T Smith

2 Points paid on purchase of principal residence
0.

Street address (including apt. no.)
1000 Residential Lane

3 Refund of overpaid interest (see instructions on w hether to report as Other Income on Form 1040.)
0.

City or tow n	State	Zip Code
Lovington	**NM**	**11111**

4 Mortgage insurance premiums
0.

Foreign country

5

Foreign province/county   Foreign postal code

Account number

[X] Check the box if all proceeds of the loan w ere used to buy, build, or improve your main or second home

[ ] Check the box if NOT all proceeds of the loan w ere used to buy, build, or improve your main or second home

If NOT all the proceeds of the loan were used to buy, build, or improve your main or second home, but some were used to pay off other debt such as car loans, credit cards, etc., enter the amount of mortgage interest paid that was NOT used towards the actual home.   0.

10/12/15 01:47PM

☐ Check the box to transfer the interest amount to Form 8396 if you w ere issued a qualified Mortgage Credit Certificate

Form **1098**   Department of the Treasury - Internal Revenue Service

10/12/15 01:47PM

FILER'S name			**2014** Form 1098-T Tuition Statement		

OMB No.1545-1574

FILER'S name **University**			**2014** Form 1098-T Tuition Statement		
FILER'S street address **University Address**			**1** Payments received for qualified tuition and related expenses*		**2** Amounts billed for qualified tuition and related expenses*
FILER'S city **Somewhere**	State **NM**	ZIP code **11111**		8,804.00	8,804.00
Foreign country			**Actual amount of tuition and fees paid in 2014***		
Foreign province/county		Postal code	☐		8,804.00
FILER'S telephone number			**3** If this box is checked, your educational institution has changed its reporting method for 2014		
FILER'S federal Identification number **35-6002041**	STUDENT'S social security number		**4** Adjustments made for a prior year		**5** Scholarships or grants**
STUDENT'S name				0.00	573.00
Street address (including apt. no.) **1000 Residential Lane**			**6** Adjustments to scholarships or grants for a prior year		**7** Checked if the amount in box 1 or 2 includes amounts for an academic period beginning January - March 2015 X
City **Lovington**	State **NM**	ZIP Code **11111**			
Foreign country				0.00	
Foreign province/county		Postal code	**8** Check if at least half-time student X		
Service Provider/Acct. No.			**9** Checked if a graduate student		**10** Ins. contract reimb/refund 0.00

Form**1098-T**
Internal Revenue Service

Department of the Treasury -

---

* The amount shown in box 1 or 2 may not represent the amount of tuition and fees actually paid in 2014. An education credit or deduction can only be claimed based on amounts that were actually paid during the year. Enter the amount of tuition and fees actually paid in the box below boxes 1 and 2.

The student's Statement of Account or similar statement should list the tuition and fees that were paid during 2014. The school may have attached this statement to the 1098-T. Keep these documents with your return so you can substantiate the amounts claimed.

** Do not enter the following types of payments in box 5:
    a. Veterans' education benefits (enter on Student Worksheet, Part IV, line 1)
    b. Employer-provided education benefits (enter on Student Worksheet, Part IV, line 2)
    c. Amounts also reported on Form W-2 as wages (enter on Form W-2)

10/12/15 01:47PM

The income on this form belongs to:

- [ ] Bob
- [ ] Debbie
- [X] Bob and Debbie equally

Copy 1 of 2000

Federal Form 1099-B/Capital Gain Transaction Details

(This document supports transactions being reported on the Federal Form 8949)

1a Description of property (Example 100 sh. XYZ Co.)			
FUNDAMENTAL INVESTORS FUND A / 360802102 / ANCFX - Sale 11.19500			

1b Date Acquired	1c Date Sold/Disposed	1d Proceeds	1e Cost or Other Basis
Various	02/10/2014	567.	452.

	1f Code, if any	1g Adjustments	Gain or Loss
		0.	115.
	4 Federal tax withheld	14 State	15 St. Identification no.	16 St. tax withheld

4 Federal tax withheld	14 State	15 St. Identification no.	16 St. tax withheld
0.00			0.00
			0.00

Select the Form 8949 category that describes this transaction. This indication will determine which copy of Form 8949 the transaction is reported on. See full reporting category descriptions below.

A- Short-term transaction in which basis was reported to the IRS
B - Short-term transaction in which basis was NOT reported to the IRS
C - Short-term transaction for which you did NOT receive a Form 1099-B
D - Long-term transaction in which basis was reported to the IRS
E - Long-term transaction in which basis was NOT reported to the IRS
F - Long-term transaction for which you did NOT receive a Form 1099-B

Form 8949 reporting category . . . . __A__

This property is to be taxed using the Schedule D 28% Rate Gain Worksheet . . . [ ]

Additional information that may be necessary to properly report this transaction:

Check here if you acquired property from a decedent who died in 2010 and whose executor made the election to file Form 8939 . . . . [ ]

Check here if this property is a security that became worthless during the tax year (Also enter 12/31 as the date sold) . . . . [ ]

Check here if this property is an option you purchased that has Expired . . . . [ ]

Check here if this property is an option that was granted (written) and has Expired . . . . [ ]

Check here if this property is from an Employee Stock Purchase Plan (ESPP) . . . . [ ]

Check here if this property is from an Incentive Stock Option Plan (ISO) . . . . [ ]

10/12/15 01:47PM

Check here if this property is from a Nonqualified Stock Option Plan (NQSO) .... ☐

Check here if none of the above apply .... ☒

If an ESPP or an ISO enter any Ordinary Income to be transferred to
Form 1040 line 7 or Form 1040NR line 8 .... 0.

(Normally the employer will include the ordinary income portion on your W-2 and no entry should
be made here. Make an entry here ONLY if you have determined you should report ordinary (wage)
income for this ESPP or ISO sale and NO amount was included on your W-2 by your employer)

* Do not enter withholdings that are being included on your W-2. Generally, if you had federal income
tax withheld on the sale of employee stock, your employer will include this withholding on your W-2.
Withholding on a 1099-B is generally only done for backup withholding - which would be done if you
did not furnish your taxpayer identification number to the payer.

Additional information to report Nonbusiness Bad Debts

Check here if this transaction is reporting a nonbusiness bad debt .... ☐

Nonbusiness bad debts are claimed as short-term capital losses. This are reported on Form 8949
with both C checked and therefore you should select reporting category C above for this transaction.
The IRS requires an additional statement to explain the nonbusiness bad debt being claimed.
Complete the additional information below and it will be included with your return.

Name of debtor ....

Description of bad debt ....

Date debt was due ....

Bad debt amount ....   0.

Your relationship (business or family) with debtor ....

Explain your efforts to collect this nonbusiness bad debt:

_____

_____

_____

_____

Explain why you decided the debt was worthless (For example, the borrower declared bankruptcy
or that legal action to collect would probably not result in payment of any part of the debt):

_____

_____

_____

10/12/15 01:47PM

The income on this form belongs to: ☐ Bob
                                      ☐ Debbie
                                      ☒ Bob and Debbie equally

Copy 2 of 2000

Federal Form 1099-B/Capital Gain Transaction Details

(This document supports transactions being reported on the Federal Form 8949)

1a Description of property (Example 100 sh. XYZ Co.)			
FUNDAMENTAL INVESTORS FUND A / 360802102 / ANCFX - Sale 21.12800			

1b Date Acquired	**1c** Date Sold/Disposed	**1d** Proceeds	**1e** Cost or Other Basis
Various	02/10/2014	1,070.	854.

	1f Code, if any	**1g** Adjustments	Gain or Loss
		0.	216.

	4 Federal tax withheld	**14** State	**15** St. Identification no.	**16** St. tax withheld
	0.00			0.00
				0.00
				0.00

Select the Form 8949 category that describes this transaction. This indication will determine which copy of Form 8949 the transaction is reported on. See full reporting category descriptions below.

A- Short-term transaction in which basis was reported to the IRS
B - Short-term transaction in which basis was NOT reported to the IRS
C - Short-term transaction for which you did NOT receive a Form 1099-B
D - Long-term transaction in which basis was reported to the IRS
E - Long-term transaction in which basis was NOT reported to the IRS
F - Long-term transaction for which you did NOT receive a Form 1099-B

Form 8949 reporting category . . . . _____D_____

This property is to be taxed using the Schedule D 28% Rate Gain Worksheet . . . ☐

Additional information that may be necessary to properly report this transaction:

Check here if you acquired property from a decedent who died in 2010 and whose executor made the election to file Form 8939 . . . . ☐

Check here if this property is a security that became worthless during the tax year (Also enter 12/31 as the date sold) . . . . ☐

Check here if this property is an option you purchased that has Expired . . . . ☐

Check here if this property is an option that was granted (written) and has Expired . . . . ☐

Check here if this property is from an Employee Stock Purchase Plan (ESPP) . . . . ☐

Check here if this property is from an Incentive Stock Option Plan (ISO) . . . . ☐

10/12/15 01:47PM

Check here if this property is from a Nonqualified Stock Option Plan (NQSO) .... ☐

Check here if none of the above apply .... ☒

If an ESPP or an ISO enter any Ordinary Income to be transferred to
Form 1040 line 7 or Form 1040NR line 8 .... _____0.___

(Normally the employer will include the ordinary income portion on your W-2 and no entry should
be made here. Make an entry here ONLY if you have determined you should report ordinary (wage)
income for this ESPP or ISO sale and NO amount was included on your W-2 by your employer)

* Do not enter withholdings that are being included on your W-2. Generally, if you had federal income
tax withheld on the sale of employee stock, your employer will include this withholding on your W-2.
Withholding on a 1099-B is generally only done for backup withholding - which would be done if you
did not furnish your taxpayer identification number to the payer.

Additional information to report Nonbusiness Bad Debts

Check here if this transaction is reporting a nonbusiness bad debt .... ☐

Nonbusiness bad debts are claimed as short-term capital losses. This are reported on Form 8949
with both C checked and therefore you should select reporting category C above for this transaction.
The IRS requires an additional statement to explain the nonbusiness bad debt being claimed.
Complete the additional information below and it will be included with your return.

Name of debtor .... _____

Description of bad debt .... _____

Date debt was due .... _____

Bad debt amount .... _____0.___

Your relationship (business or family) with debtor .... _____

Explain your efforts to collect this nonbusiness bad debt:

_____

_____

_____

_____

Explain why you decided the debt was worthless (For example, the borrower declared bankruptcy
or that legal action to collect would probably not result in payment of any part of the debt):

_____

_____

_____

10/12/15 01:47PM

The income on this form belongs to:

☐ Bob
☐ Debbie
☒ Bob and Debbie   equally

Copy 3 of 2000

Federal Form 1099-B/Capital Gain Transaction Details

(This document supports transactions being reported on the Federal Form 8949)

1a Description of property (Example 100 sh. XYZ Co.)			
GROWTH FUND OF AMERICA CL A / 339874106 / AGTHX - 170.82900			

1b Date Acquired	**1c** Date Sold/Disposed	**1d** Proceeds	**1e** Cost or Other Basis
Various	01/13/2014	7,250.	4,785.
	1f Code, if any	**1g** Adjustments	**Gain or Loss**
		0.	2,465.
	4 Federal tax withheld	**14** State **15** St. Identification no.	**16** St. tax withheld
	0.00		0.00
			0.00

Select the Form 8949 category that describes this transaction. This indication will determine which copy of Form 8949 the transaction is reported on. See full reporting category descriptions below.

    A- Short-term transaction in which basis was reported to the IRS
    B - Short-term transaction in which basis was NOT reported to the IRS
    C - Short-term transaction for which you did NOT receive a Form 1099-B
    D - Long-term transaction in which basis was reported to the IRS
    E - Long-term transaction in which basis was NOT reported to the IRS
    F - Long-term transaction for which you did NOT receive a Form 1099-B

       Form 8949 reporting category . . . . ___E___

   This property is to be taxed using the Schedule D 28% Rate Gain Worksheet . . . ☐

Additional information that may be necessary to properly report this transaction:

Check here if you acquired property from a decedent who died in 2010 and whose
    executor made the election to file Form 8939 . . . . ☐

Check here if this property is a security that became worthless during the tax year
    (Also enter 12/31 as the date sold) . . . . ☐

Check here if this property is an option you purchased that has Expired . . . . ☐

Check here if this property is an option that was granted (written) and has Expired . . . . ☐

Check here if this property is from an Employee Stock Purchase Plan (ESPP) . . . . ☐

Check here if this property is from an Incentive Stock Option Plan (ISO) . . . . ☐

10/12/15 01:47PM

Check here if this property is from a Nonqualified Stock Option Plan (NQSO) . . . . ☐

Check here if none of the above apply . . . . ☒

If an ESPP or an ISO enter any Ordinary Income to be transferred to
Form 1040 line 7 or Form 1040NR line 8 . . . .   0.

(Normally the employer will include the ordinary income portion on your W-2 and no entry should
be made here. Make an entry here ONLY if you have determined you should report ordinary (wage)
income for this ESPP or ISO sale and NO amount was included on your W-2 by your employer)

* Do not enter withholdings that are being included on your W-2. Generally, if you had federal income
tax withheld on the sale of employee stock, your employer will include this withholding on your W-2.
Withholding on a 1099-B is generally only done for backup withholding - which would be done if you
did not furnish your taxpayer identification number to the payer.

Additional information to report Nonbusiness Bad Debts

Check here if this transaction is reporting a nonbusiness bad debt . . . . ☐

Nonbusiness bad debts are claimed as short-term capital losses. This are reported on Form 8949
with both C checked and therefore you should select reporting category C above for this transaction.
The IRS requires an additional statement to explain the nonbusiness bad debt being claimed.
Complete the additional information below and it will be included with your return.

Name of debtor . . . .   _____

Description of bad debt . . . .   _____

Date debt was due . . . .   _____

Bad debt amount . . . .   _____ 0.

Your relationship (business or family) with debtor . . . .   _____

Explain your efforts to collect this nonbusiness bad debt:

_____

_____

_____

_____

Explain why you decided the debt was worthless (For example, the borrower declared bankruptcy
or that legal action to collect would probably not result in payment of any part of the debt):

_____

_____

_____

10/12/15 01:47PM

The income on this form belongs to:

☐ Bob
☐ Debbie
☒ Bob and Debbie equally

Federal Form 1099-B/Capital Gain Transaction Details

(This document supports transactions being reported on the Federal Form 8949)

1a Description of property (Example 100 sh. XYZ Co.)			
GROWTH FUND OF AMERICA CL A / 399874106 / AGTHX - Sale 116.98600			

1b Date Acquired	1c Date Sold/Disposed	1d Proceeds	1e Cost or Other Basis
Various	02/10/2014	5,000.	3,277.

	1f Code, if any	1g Adjustments	Gain or Loss
		0.	1,723.

	4 Federal tax withheld	14 State	15 St. Identification no.	16 St. tax withheld
	0.00			0.00
				0.00

Select the Form 8949 category that describes this transaction. This indication will determine which copy of Form 8949 the transaction is reported on. See full reporting category descriptions below.

    A - Short-term transaction in which basis was reported to the IRS
    B - Short-term transaction in which basis was NOT reported to the IRS
    C - Short-term transaction for which you did NOT receive a Form 1099-B
    D - Long-term transaction in which basis was reported to the IRS
    E - Long-term transaction in which basis was NOT reported to the IRS
    F - Long-term transaction for which you did NOT receive a Form 1099-B

      Form 8949 reporting category . . . . ___E___

    This property is to be taxed using the Schedule D 28% Rate Gain Worksheet . . . ☐

Additional information that may be necessary to properly report this transaction:

Check here if you acquired property from a decedent who died in 2010 and whose
    executor made the election to file Form 8939 . . . . ☐

Check here if this property is a security that became worthless during the tax year
    (Also enter 12/31 as the date sold) . . . . ☐

Check here if this property is an option you purchased that has Expired . . . . ☐

Check here if this property is an option that was granted (written) and has Expired . . . . ☐

Check here if this property is from an Employee Stock Purchase Plan (ESPP) . . . . ☐

Check here if this property is from an Incentive Stock Option Plan (ISO) . . . . ☐

10/12/15 01:47PM

Check here if this property is from a Nonqualified Stock Option Plan (NQSO) .... ☐

Check here if none of the above apply .... ☒

If an ESPP or an ISO enter any Ordinary Income to be transferred to
Form 1040 line 7 or Form 1040NR line 8 ....   0.

(Normally the employer will include the ordinary income portion on your W-2 and no entry should
be made here. Make an entry here ONLY if you have determined you should report ordinary (wage)
income for this ESPP or ISO sale and NO amount was included on your W-2 by your employer)

* Do not enter withholdings that are being included on your W-2. Generally, if you had federal income
tax withheld on the sale of employee stock, your employer will include this withholding on your W-2.
Withholding on a 1099-B is generally only done for backup withholding - which would be done if you
did not furnish your taxpayer identification number to the payer.

Additional information to report Nonbusiness Bad Debts

Check here if this transaction is reporting a nonbusiness bad debt .... ☐

Nonbusiness bad debts are claimed as short-term capital losses. This are reported on Form 8949
with both C checked and therefore you should select reporting category C above for this transaction.
The IRS requires an additional statement to explain the nonbusiness bad debt being claimed.
Complete the additional information below and it will be included with your return.

Name of debtor .... _____

Description of bad debt .... _____

Date debt was due .... _____

Bad debt amount ....   0.

Your relationship (business or family) with debtor .... _____

Explain your efforts to collect this nonbusiness bad debt:

_____

_____

_____

_____

Explain why you decided the debt was worthless (For example, the borrower declared bankruptcy
or that legal action to collect would probably not result in payment of any part of the debt):

_____

_____

_____

10/12/15 01:47PM

530   Taxes

The income on this form belongs to:

- ☐ Bob
- ☐ Debbie
- ☒ Bob and Debbie   equally

Copy 5 of 2000

Federal Form 1099-B/Capital Gain Transaction Details
(This document supports transactions being reported on the Federal Form 8949)

1a Description of property (Example 100 sh. XYZ Co.)

NEW PERSPECTIVE FUND CL A / 648018109 / ANWPX - Sale   149.66000

1b Date Acquired	**1c** Date Sold/Disposed	**1d** Proceeds	**1e** Cost or Other Basis
Various	02/10/2014	5,500.	3,911.

	1f Code, if any	**1g** Adjustments	**Gain or Loss**
		0.	1,589.

	4 Federal tax withheld	**14** State	**15** St. Identification no.	**16** St. tax withheld
	0.00			0.00
				0.00

Select the Form 8949 category that describes this transaction. This indication will determine which copy of Form 8949 the transaction is reported on. See full reporting category descriptions below.

A- Short-term transaction in which basis was reported to the IRS
B - Short-term transaction in which basis was NOT reported to the IRS
C - Short-term transaction for which you did NOT receive a Form 1099-B
D - Long-term transaction in which basis was reported to the IRS
E - Long-term transaction in which basis was NOT reported to the IRS
F - Long-term transaction for which you did NOT receive a Form 1099-B

Form 8949 reporting category . . . .   ___E___

This property is to be taxed using the Schedule D 28% Rate Gain Worksheet . . . ☐

Additional information that may be necessary to properly report this transaction:

Check here if you acquired property from a decedent who died in 2010 and whose executor made the election to file Form 8939 . . . . ☐

Check here if this property is a security that became worthless during the tax year (Also enter 12/31 as the date sold) . . . . ☐

Check here if this property is an option you purchased that has Expired . . . . ☐

Check here if this property is an option that was granted (written) and has Expired . . . . ☐

Check here if this property is from an Employee Stock Purchase Plan (ESPP) . . . . ☐

Check here if this property is from an Incentive Stock Option Plan (ISO) . . . . ☐

10/12/15 01:47PM

Check here if this property is from a Nonqualified Stock Option Plan (NQSO) .... ☐

Check here if none of the above apply .... ☒

If an ESPP or an ISO enter any Ordinary Income to be transferred to
Form 1040 line 7 or Form 1040NR line 8 .... _____ 0.

(Normally the employer will include the ordinary income portion on your W-2 and no entry should
be made here. Make an entry here ONLY if you have determined you should report ordinary (wage)
income for this ESPP or ISO sale and NO amount was included on your W-2 by your employer)

* Do not enter withholdings that are being included on your W-2. Generally, if you had federal income
tax withheld on the sale of employee stock, your employer will include this withholding on your W-2.
Withholding on a 1099-B is generally only done for backup withholding - which would be done if you
did not furnish your taxpayer identification number to the payer.

Additional information to report Nonbusiness Bad Debts

Check here if this transaction is reporting a nonbusiness bad debt .... ☐

Nonbusiness bad debts are claimed as short-term capital losses. This are reported on Form 8949
with both C checked and therefore you should select reporting category C above for this transaction.
The IRS requires an additional statement to explain the nonbusiness bad debt being claimed.
Complete the additional information below and it will be included with your return.

Name of debtor .... _____

Description of bad debt .... _____

Date debt was due .... _____

Bad debt amount .... _____ 0.

Your relationship (business or family) with debtor .... _____

Explain your efforts to collect this nonbusiness bad debt:

_____

_____

_____

_____

Explain why you decided the debt was worthless (For example, the borrower declared bankruptcy
or that legal action to collect would probably not result in payment of any part of the debt):

_____

_____

_____

10/12/15 01:47PM

The income on this form belongs to:

☐ Bob
☐ Debbie
☒ Bob and Debbie equally

Federal Form 1099-B/Capital Gain Transaction Details

(This document supports transactions being reported on the Federal Form 8949)

1a Description of property (Example 100 sh. XYZ Co.)				
NEW PERSPECTIVE FUND CL A / 648018109 / ANWPX - Sale 72.95000				

1b Date Acquired	**1c** Date Sold/Disposed	**1d** Proceeds		**1e** Cost or Other Basis
Various	10/24/2014	2,740.		1,921.

	1f Code, if any	**1g** Adjustments		**Gain or Loss**
		0.		819.

	4 Federal tax withheld	**14** State	**15** St. Identification no.	**16** St. tax withheld
	0.00			0.00
				0.00

Select the Form 8949 category that describes this transaction. This indication will determine which copy of Form 8949 the transaction is reported on. See full reporting category descriptions below.

   A- Short-term transaction in which basis was reported to the IRS
   B - Short-term transaction in which basis was NOT reported to the IRS
   C - Short-term transaction for which you did NOT receive a Form 1099-B
   D - Long-term transaction in which basis was reported to the IRS
   E - Long-term transaction in which basis was NOT reported to the IRS
   F - Long-term transaction for which you did NOT receive a Form 1099-B

            Form 8949 reporting category . . . .   E

   This property is to be taxed using the Schedule D 28% Rate Gain Worksheet . . . ☐

Additional information that may be necessary to properly report this transaction:

Check here if you acquired property from a decedent who died in 2010 and whose
   executor made the election to file Form 8939 . . . . ☐

Check here if this property is a security that became worthless during the tax year
   (Also enter 12/31 as the date sold) . . . . ☐

Check here if this property is an option you purchased that has Expired . . . . ☐

Check here if this property is an option that was granted (written) and has Expired . . . . ☐

Check here if this property is from an Employee Stock Purchase Plan (ESPP) . . . . ☐

Check here if this property is from an Incentive Stock Option Plan (ISO) . . . . ☐

10/12/15 01:47PM

Check here if this property is from a Nonqualified Stock Option Plan (NQSO) .... ☐

Check here if none of the above apply .... ☒

If an ESPP or an ISO enter any Ordinary Income to be transferred to
Form 1040 line 7 or Form 1040NR line 8 ....   0.

(Normally the employer will include the ordinary income portion on your W-2 and no entry should
be made here. Make an entry here ONLY if you have determined you should report ordinary (wage)
income for this ESPP or ISO sale and NO amount was included on your W-2 by your employer)

* Do not enter withholdings that are being included on your W-2. Generally, if you had federal income
tax withheld on the sale of employee stock, your employer will include this withholding on your W-2.
Withholding on a 1099-B is generally only done for backup withholding - which would be done if you
did not furnish your taxpayer identification number to the payer.

Additional information to report Nonbusiness Bad Debts

Check here if this transaction is reporting a nonbusiness bad debt .... ☐

Nonbusiness bad debts are claimed as short-term capital losses. This are reported on Form 8949
with both C checked and therefore you should select reporting category C above for this transaction.
The IRS requires an additional statement to explain the nonbusiness bad debt being claimed.
Complete the additional information below and it will be included with your return.

Name of debtor .... _____

Description of bad debt .... _____

Date debt was due .... _____

Bad debt amount .... _____0._____

Your relationship (business or family) with debtor .... _____

Explain your efforts to collect this nonbusiness bad debt:

_____

_____

_____

_____

Explain why you decided the debt was worthless (For example, the borrower declared bankruptcy
or that legal action to collect would probably not result in payment of any part of the debt):

_____

_____

_____

The income on this Form belongs to: ☐ Bob

☐ Debbie

☒ Bob and Debbie   equally

Form 1099-DIV - Dividends and Distributions

PAYER'S federal ID number 43-1591643	RECIPIENT'S ID number 123-45-6789	**1a** Total ordinary dividends 110.22	OMB No. 1545-0110
PAYER'S Name Investment Advisor 1		**1b** Qualified dividends* 110.22	**2014**
PAYER'S Street address		**2a** Total capital gain distrib. 1,380.69	**2b** Unrecap. Sec 1250 gain 0.00
City State Zip Code		**2c** Section 1202 gain	**2d** Collectibles (28%) gain 0.00
Foreign country name		**3** Nondividend distributions 0.00	**4** Federal income tax withheld 0.00
Foreign province/county Foreign postal code			**5** Investment expenses 0.00
RECIPIENT'S Name Bob Smith		**6** Foreign tax paid 13.29	**7** Foreign country Various
Street address (including apt. no.) 1000 Residential Lane		**8** Cash liquidation distributions 0.00	**9** Noncash liquidation distrib. 0.00
City State Zip Code Lovington NM 11111		**10** Exempt-interest dividends 0.00	**11** Specified private activity bond interest dividends 0.00
Foreign country name			
Foreign province/county Foreign postal code		**12** State **13** State ID no.	**14** State tax withheld 0.00
Account number**			0.00

Form **1099-DIV**   Department of the Treasury Internal Revenue Service

*Some dividends may be reported as qualified dividends in box 1b but are not qualified dividends. Highlight the amount above in box 1b and press the 'Form Instructions' button to review the instructions for when you will need to limit the amount you enter as qualified dividends.

** If you received multiple Form 1099-DIVs or a statement with multiple account numbers, and wish to list each account number separately, you will need to create a new Form 1099-DIV for each account number. It should also be noted that the account number(s) are not required to file your return.

Other information not reported on Form 1099-DIV

15	Income reported in Box 1a above that actually belongs to someone else	0.00
16	Income reported in Box 1b above that actually belongs to someone else	0.00
17	Income reported in Box 2a above that actually belongs to someone else	0.00
18	Income reported in Box 1a above that is exempt from state income tax.	0.00
19	Income reported in Box 10 that is also exempt from state income tax	0.00
20	Amount of restricted stock dividends reported as wages on Form 1040 or Form 1041 . . .	0.00

10/12/15 01:47PM

Foreign Tax Credit Information

21 ☐ Check here to include on Form 1116 even if no foreign tax paid in box 6.

22 ☒ Check here if these entries are for a mutual fund or other regulated investment company.

23 ☐ Check here if you did not actually receive a 1099-DIV.

24 Foreign source ordinary dividends . . . . | 110.22

25 Foreign source qualified dividends . . . . | 110.22

26 Foreign source capital gain distributions . . . . | 1,380.69

27 Foreign tax credit income category: ☒ Passive income   ☐ General income

Community Property Allocation
This section is used for taxpayers who are currently filing a married filing separate return in a community property state. Income must be allocated between spouses. Community property states are: Arizona, California, Idaho, Louisiana, Nevada, New Mexico, Texas, Washington, and Wisconsin.
Dividends allocated to spouse 0.00

The income on this Form belongs to:

- [ ] Bob
- [X] Debbie
- [ ] Bob and Debbie equally

Form 1099-DIV - Dividends and Distributions

PAYER'S federal ID number 43-1591643	RECIPIENT'S ID number 987-65-4321	**1a** Total ordinary dividends 284.83	OMB No. 1545-0110
PAYER'S Name Investment Advisor 1		**1b** Qualified dividends* 284.83	**2014**
PAYER'S Street address		**2a** Total capital gain distrib. 357.98	**2b** Unrecap. Sec 1250 gain 0.00
City State Zip Code		**2c** Section 1202 gain	**2d** Collectibles (28%) gain 0.00
Foreign country name		**3** Nondividend distributions 0.00	**4** Federal income tax withheld 0.00
Foreign province/county Foreign postal code			**5** Investment expenses 0.00
RECIPIENT'S Name Debbie Smith		**6** Foreign tax paid 12.02	**7** Foreign country Various
Street address (including apt. no.) 1000 Residential Lane		**8** Cash liquidation distributions 0.00	**9** Noncash liquidation distrib. 0.00
City State Zip Code Lovington NM 11111		**10** Exempt-interest dividends 0.00	**11** Specified private activity bond interest dividends 0.00
Foreign country name			
Foreign province/county Foreign postal code		**12** State	**13** State ID no.	**14** State tax withheld 0.00
Account number**			0.00

Form **1099-DIV**   Department of the Treasury Internal Revenue Service

*Some dividends may be reported as qualified dividends in box 1b but are not qualified dividends. Highlight the amount above in box 1b and press the 'Form Instructions' button to review the instructions for when you will need to limit the amount you enter as qualified dividends.

** If you received multiple Form 1099-DIVs or a statement with multiple account numbers, and wish to list each account number separately, you will need to create a new Form 1099-DIV for each account number. It should also be noted that the account number(s) are not required to file your return.

Other information not reported on Form 1099-DIV

15	Income reported in Box 1a above that actually belongs to someone else	0.00
16	Income reported in Box 1b above that actually belongs to someone else	0.00
17	Income reported in Box 2a above that actually belongs to someone else	0.00
18	Income reported in Box 1a above that is exempt from state income tax.	0.00
19	Income reported in Box 10 that is also exempt from state income tax	0.00
20	Amount of restricted stock dividends reported as wages on Form 1040 or Form 1041 . . .	0.00

10/12/15 01:47PM

Foreign Tax Credit Information

21 ☐ Check here to include on Form 1116 even if no foreign tax paid in box 6.

22 ☒ Check here if these entries are for a mutual fund or other regulated investment company.

23 ☐ Check here if you did not actually receive a 1099-DIV.

24 Foreign source ordinary dividends .... | 284.83

25 Foreign source qualified dividends .... | 284.83

26 Foreign source capital gain distributions .... | 357.98

27 Foreign tax credit income category: ☒ Passive income ☐ General income

---

Community Property Allocation

This section is used for taxpayers who are currently filing a married filing separate return in a community property state. Income must be allocated between spouses. Community property states are: Arizona, California, Idaho, Louisiana, Nevada, New Mexico, Texas, Washington, and Wisconsin.

Dividends allocated to spouse .... | 0.00

The income on this Form belongs to:

☐ Bob
☐ Debbie
☒ Bob and Debbie equally

Form 1099-DIV - Dividends and Distributions

PAYER'S federal ID number 43-1591643	RECIPIENT'S ID number 123-45-6789	**1a** Total ordinary dividends 0.00	OMB No. 1545-0110
PAYER'S Name Investment Advisor 1		**1b** Qualified dividends* 0.00	**2014**
PAYER'S Street address		**2a** Total capital gain distrib. 0.00	**2b** Unrecap. Sec 1250 gain 0.00
City State Zip Code		**2c** Section 1202 gain	**2d** Collectibles (28%) gain 0.00
Foreign country name		**3** Nondividend distributions 0.00	**4** Federal income tax withheld 0.00
Foreign province/county Foreign postal code			**5** Investment expenses 0.00
RECIPIENT'S Name Bob Smith		**6** Foreign tax paid 0.00	**7** Foreign country
Street address (including apt. no.) 1000 Residential Lane		**8** Cash liquidation distributions 0.00	**9** Noncash liquidation distrib. 0.00
City State Zip Code Lovington NM 11111		**10** Exempt-interest dividends 0.00	**11** Specified private activity bond interest dividends 0.00
Foreign country name			
Foreign province/county Foreign postal code		**12** State	**13** State ID no.	**14** State tax withheld 0.00
Account number**			0.00

Form**1099-DIV**   Department of the Treasury Internal Revenue Service

*Some dividends may be reported as qualified dividends in box 1b but are not qualified dividends. Highlight the amount above in box 1b and press the 'Form Instructions' button to review the instructions for when you will need to limit the amount you enter as qualified dividends.

** If you received multiple Form 1099-DIVs or a statement with multiple account numbers, and wish to list each account number separately, you will need to create a new Form 1099-DIV for each account number. It should also be noted that the account number(s) are not required to file your return.

Other information not reported on Form 1099-DIV

15	Income reported in Box 1a above that actually belongs to someone else	0.00
16	Income reported in Box 1b above that actually belongs to someone else	0.00
17	Income reported in Box 2a above that actually belongs to someone else	0.00
18	Income reported in Box 1a above that is exempt from state income tax.	0.00
19	Income reported in Box 10 that is also exempt from state income tax	0.00
20	Amount of restricted stock dividends reported as wages on Form 1040 or Form 1041 . . .	0.00

10/12/15   01:47PM

Foreign Tax Credit Information

21 ☐ Check here to include on Form 1116 even if no foreign tax paid in box 6.

22 ☐ Check here if these entries are for a mutual fund or other regulated investment company.

23 ☐ Check here if you did not actually receive a 1099-DIV.

24 Foreign source ordinary dividends .... | 0.00

25 Foreign source qualified dividends .... | 0.00

26 Foreign source capital gain distributions .... | 0.00

27 Foreign tax credit income category: ☐ Passive income ☐ General income

Community Property Allocation
This section is used for taxpayers who are currently filing a married filing separate return in a community property state. Income must be allocated between spouses. Community property states are: Arizona, California, Idaho, Louisiana, Nevada, New Mexico, Texas, Washington, and Wisconsin.
Dividends allocated to spouse 0.00

The income on this Form belongs to:

- [ ] Bob
- [ ] Debbie
- [X] Bob and Debbie equally

Form 1099-INT - Interest Income

PAYER'S Federal ID number	RECIPIENT'S ID number 123-45-6789	PAYER'S RTN (optional)	OMB No.1545-0112
PAYER'S name		**1** Interest income 0.00	**2014**
PAYER'S street address		**2** Early withdrawal penalty 0.00	
City State Zip Code		**3** Interest on U.S. Savings Bonds and Treasury obligations 0.00	
Foreign country name		**4** Federal income tax withheld 0.00	**5** Investment Expenses 0.00
Foreign province/county Foreign postal code		**6** Foreign tax paid 0.00	**7** Foreign country
RECIPIENT'S name Bob Smith		**8** Tax-exempt interest 0.00	**9** Specified private activity bond interest 0.00
Street address (including apt. no.) 1000 Residential Lane			
City State Zip Code Lovington NM 11111		**10** Market discount 0.00	**11** Bond premium 0.00
RECIPIENT'S foreign country		**12** Tax-exempt bond CUSIP no.* (see instructions)	
Foreign province/county Foreign postal code		**13** State **14** State Identification no.	**15** State tax withheld 0.00
Account number*			0.00

Form **1099-INT**   Department of the Treasury Internal Revenue Service

*If you receive multiple Form 1099-INTs or a statement with multiple account numbers or CUSIP numbers, and wish to list each account number or CUSIP number separately, you will need to create a separate 1099-INT for each account number, being sure to include the CUSIP number when applicable. It should also be noted that the account number(s) and CUSIP number(s) are not required to file your return.

Other information not reported on Form 1099-INT

16 Income reported in Box 1 above that actually belongs to someone else 0.00

17 Income reported in Box 3 above that actually belongs to someone else 0.00

18 Interest reported in Box 3 above that was included as income on prior year returns 0.00

19 Accrued interest paid on the acquisition of this security between payment dates 0.00

20 Amount from Box 8 that is both federal and state exempt interest 0.00

21 Amount from Box 8 that is accrued exempt interest 0.00

10/12/15   01:47PM

22 Amount from Box 21 that is accrued state exempt interest 0.00

Foreign Tax Credit Information

23 ☐ Check here to include on Form 1116 even if no foreign tax paid in box 6.

24 ☐ Check here if these entries are for a mutual fund or other regulated investment company.

25 ☐ Check here if you did not actually receive a 1099-INT.

26 Foreign interest income included in Box 1 . . . .   0.00

Community Property Allocation
This section is used for taxpayers who are currently filing a married filing separate return in a community property state. Income must be allocated between spouses. Community property states are: Arizona, California, Idaho, Louisiana, Nevada, New Mexico, Texas, Washington and Wisconsin.

Taxable interest 0.00

Interest allocated to spouse 0.00

This 1099SA belongs to: [X] Bob   [ ] Debbie

PAYER'S Federal Identification number	RECIPIENT'S social security number	OMB No. 1545-1517	Distributions From an HSA, Archer MSA, or Medicare Advantage MSA
11-1111111	123-45-6789	**2014**	

PAYER'S/TRUSTEE'S Name
HSA Payor

PAYER'S/TRUSTEE'S Street Address
P.O. Box 535473

PAYER'S/TRUSTEE'S City	State	ZIP code
Lovington	NM	11111

Form **1099-SA**

PAYER'S/TRUSTEE'S foreign country

PAYER'S foreign province/county   Foreign postal code

1 Gross distribution	2 Earnings on excess contributions
3,171.76	0.00

RECIPIENT'S name
Bob T Smith

3 Distribution Code	4 FMV on date of death
1	0.00

Street address (including apt. no.)
1000 Residential Lane

City or town	State	ZIP code
Lovington	NM	11111

5   HSA   [X]
    Archer MSA   [ ]
    MA MSA   [ ]

Foreign country

Foreign province/county   Foreign postal code

Account number (see instructions)
95000153523010

Additional Information not reported on Form 1099-SA

1   Enter the amount of this distribution, if any, that you rolled over from one HSA to another HSA, or from a MSA to another MSA or HSA (Does not apply to MAMSAs) 0.00

2   Enter excess contributions you made with after-tax funds (including those made on your behalf) and the earnings on those excess contributions that were withdrawn by the due date of your return. Earnings are included in the gross amount shown in box 1. (Does not apply to MAMSAs) 0.00

3   Enter the medical expenses you paid with the funds received in this distribution. 3,171.76

4   Taxable distribution (portion of this distribution not rolled over, withdrawn or used to pay qualified medical expenses) 0.00

5   Enter any excess pre-tax employer contributions that were not included in income on Form W-2 and must be reported as Other Income on line 21 of Form

10/12/15   01:47PM

1040 or Form 1040NR. Confirm this amount with your employer if necessary. . . . . | 0.00

6 Generally, if you receive a taxable distribution, you must also pay an additional tax on the amount included in income.

   a The additional tax is:
   - 20% for HSAs
   - 20% for Archer MSAs
   - 50% for Medicare Advantage MSAs.

   b For HSAs and Archer MSAs the additional tax does not apply if the beneficiary:
   - Dies
   - Becomes disabled
   - Turns age 65.

   c For Medicare Advantage MSAs the additional tax does not apply if the beneficiary:
   - Dies
   - Becomes disabled.

   d If an exception applies to the additional tax, enter the amount
   not subject to the additional tax . . . . | 0.00

   ☐ Exception applies

7 Based on your entries, the tentative additional tax
relating to this 1099-SA is . . . . | 0.00

8 The actual additional tax is calculated on:
   - Form 8889 if this is an HSA distribution.
   - Form 8853 if this is an Archer MSA or Medicare Advantage MSA distribution.
   - Please review the form(s) that apply to your distribution(s).

Employee Benefits

Employee Benefits Guide

Lextin Oil Supply Employee Benefits

2016

January 1–December 31, 2016

Lextin Oil Supply

<table>
<tr><td rowspan="6">

</td></tr>
</table>

2016 TRADITIONAL MEDICAL PLAN EMPLOYEE MONTHLY CONTRIBUTION		2016 HIGH-DEDUCTIBLE (HDHP) MEDICAL PLAN EMPLOYEE MONTHLY CONTRIBUTION	
Employee only:	$135.00	Employee only:	$80.00
Employee + Spouse:	$422.00	Employee + Spouse:	$273.00
Employee + Child(ren):	$415.00	Employee + Child(ren):	$244.00
Family:	$702.00	Family:	$353.00
Effective 1/1/2016 thru 12/31/2016		*Effective 1/1/2016 thru 12/31/2016*	

Medical and Prescription Drugs Benefits are insured by: **Capstone Medical**

PPO Network: **In New Mexico: Capstone Access PPO**   **Outside of New Mexico:**
Provider Directory: www.capstonemedical.com   **National Capstone PPO**

Dual Option Medical Plan Effective January 1, 2016	TRADITIONAL PLAN		HDHP PLAN	
	Network Benefits	*Non-Network Benefits*	*Network Benefits*	*Non-Network Benefits*
Primary Care Visit Copay	$25 Co-pay; 100%	Deductible; then 40%	Deductible; then 20%	Deductible; then 40%
Specialist Care Visit Copay	$40 Co-pay; 100%	Deductible; then 40%	Deductible; then 20%	Deductible; then 40%
Deductible				
Individual	$1,000	$2,000	$2,000	$5,000
Family	$3,000	$4,000	$4,000	$10,000
Co-insurance	You Pay 20%	You Pay 40%	You pay 20%	You pays 40%
Out-of-Pocket Maximum				
Individual (Includes Deductible)	$3,500	$8,000	$3,500	$8,000
Family (Includes Deductible)	$7,000	$18,000	$6,850	$18,000
Retail Prescription Drugs				
Generic Formulary	$10		Deductible; then 20%	Deductible; then 40%
Brand Formulary	$35	50%, min. $30	Deductible; then 20%	Deductible; then 40%
Non-Formulary	$60		Deductible; then 20%	Deductible; then 40%
Mail Order Prescription Drugs				
Generic Formulary	$20		Deductible; then 20%	
Brand Formulary	$70	Not Covered	Deductible; then 20%	Not Covered
Non-Formulary	$120		Deductible; then 20%	
Preventive Care				
Physician Home and Office Visits (PCP/SCP) Other Outpatient Services	100% Coverage	Deductible; then 40%	100% Coverage	Deductible; then 40%
Hospital Services	Deductible; then 20%	Deductible; then 40%	Deductible; then 20%	Deductible; then 40%
Outpatient Services	Deductible; then 20%	Deductible; then 40%	Deductible; then 20%	Deductible; then 40%
Maternity Services	Deductible; then 20%	Deductible; then 40%	Deductible; then 20%	Deductible; then 40%
Emergency Room Services	Deductible; then 20%	Deductible; then 20%	Deductible; then 20%	Deductible; then 20%
Urgent Care Centers	$50 Co-pay, 100%	Deductible; then 40%	Deductible; then 20%	Deductible; then 40%

Health Savings Account (HSA)
2016 Annual Internal Revenue Service Limits

Employee	$3,350
Family	$6,750
Catch-Up Contributions Ages 55 and Older	$1,000

Health Savings Account (HSA)
2016
Employer Annual HSA Contribution

Employee	$500
Employee/Dependent(s)	$1,000

The above is a brief outline of the benefit programs. Please see the Summary Plan Description for complete plan information. In a case of a discrepancy, the plan document will prevail.

Dental Plan 2016 Monthly Contributions	
	Dental:
Employee Only:	$6.00
Employee + Child(ren):	$13.00
Employee + Spouse:	$10.00
Family:	$20.00

Vision Plan 2016 Monthly Contributions	
	Vision:
Employee Only:	$1.00
Employee + Child(ren):	$2.00
Employee + Spouse:	$2.00
Family:	$4.00

Dental Benefit Summary	
	In-Network/Non-Network
Deductible (Applies only to Major Services)	
Individual	$50
Family	$150
Annual Plan Maximum	$1,000
Preventive Services	
Diagnostic Services	100%
Preventive Services	100%
Emergency Palliative Treatment	100%
Basic Services	
X-rays	75%
Oral Surgery	75%
Periodontics	75%
Endodontics	75%
Major Services	
Prosthodontics	50%
Major Restorative	50%
Orthodontia	50%
Separate Ortho Deductible	No
Ortho Lifetime Max	$1,200
Ortho Eligibility	Child, to age 19

Non-network charges are subject to reasonable and customary fees. Charges above R&C are the patient's responsibility.

Provider Directory: www.NMdental.com

Vision Benefit Summary

-Employee must use member doctor to receive full benefits

-Employee can use non-member doctor with reduced benefits
-Benefits cover 1 exam every 12 months
-No deductibles
Exam Benefit
  In-Network: $10 co-pay
  Out-of-Network: Up to $34 reimbursed
Materials Benefit: after $25 co-pay
-Frames: every 24 months, see plan description for details
-Lenses: every 12 months, covered in full in-network
-Contacts: (in lieu of glasses): every 12 months; $120 allowance
Provider Directory: www.visioncorp.com

Life and Disability Insured by: NewMex Life & Disability Co

Benefits Provided for Employees:

Basic Life and Accidental Death and Dismemberment (AD&D) and Long-Term Disability are paid for by Lextin Oil Supply

Basic Life / AD&D	
Benefit Amount:	2x's Annual Salary
Benefit Maximum:	$200,000
Benefit rounded to the next $1,000	

Long-Term Disability	
Elimination Period:	90 Days
Benefit:	60% of earnings
Maximum Monthly Benefit:	$9,500

Flexible Spending Accounts	
Unreimbursed Medical	
Available to employees who do not participate in the HDHP Medical Plan	
Maximum Annual Contribution:	$2,550
Dependent Daycare Expenses	
Available to all full-time IWU employees	
Maximum Annual Contribution:	$5,000

Voluntary Life and AD&D	
Employee Benefit	
Benefit Increments:	$10,000
Benefit Maximum:	Lesser of $150,000 or 5x's salary
	Max is $50,000 age 70 and over
New Hire Guarantee Issue:	Lesser of $150,000 or 3x's salary
Spouse Benefit	
Benefit Increments:	$5,000
Benefit Maximum:	Lesser of $50,000 or 2.5x's salary
	Cannot exceed 50% of employee amt
Guarantee Issue:	$50,000
Child Benefit	
Benefit Amount:	$10,000

The above is a brief outline of the benefit programs. Please see the Summary Plan Description for complete plan information.
In a case of a discrepancy, the plan document will prevail.

Lextin Oil Supply

Your health and financial security are important to us. Our benefit program offers a variety of plans that can enhance the lives of you and your family both now and in the future. As an eligible employee, you will be asked to make decisions about the employee benefits described in this booklet. Please take the time to study the information about the benefit plan offerings and go to www.benefitsconnect.net/JOS to enroll in your benefits.

Highlights of Our Benefits

- Dual Option Comprehensive Medical Plans
- Dental Plan
- Vision Plan
- Basic Life/AD&D
- Long-Term Disability
- Voluntary Life and Dependent Life
- Flexible Spending Accounts

Eligibility

All full-time employees who work at least 30 hours per week are eligible to participate in the employee benefit plans. For Medical, Dental, and Vision plans, covered dependents include your spouse and children to age 26 even if the children have access to an employer's plan.

Medical

Lextin Oil Supply makes available two medical plans from which you can choose. By offering two plans, you have the choice in selecting the benefit program that best fits the needs of you and your family. The group medical program is administered by Capstone Medical with access through Capstone Network. To obtain the most current participating provider listing, log onto www.capstonemedical.com.

Dental

Dental benefits are provided through Delta Dental. The plan is designed to provide you and your dependent family members with Preventive, Basic and Major dental care. Delta Dental has two levels of providers—PPO or Premier. You may visit either type of participating provider. You can log onto www.NMdental.com for current provider information.

Vision

Vision benefits are provided through Superior Vision. The plan provides one exam every 12 months. When you utilize a network provider, your exam will be covered after a $10 co-pay. Plastic lenses will be covered after a $25 co-pay when you utilize a network provider. For the most current provider information, go to www.visioncorp.com.

Disability

Long-Term Disability insurance will be provided to all active, full-time employees at **no cost.** This important benefit provides you 60% of your monthly Wage Base not to exceed a total maximum benefit of $9,500 per month.

Life Insurance

Lextin Oil Supply pays 100% of the contribution for Basic Life and Accidental Death and Dismemberment. This benefit is twice your annual salary. Maximums do apply. These benefits are insured by Lincoln Financial.

Voluntary Life Insurance

Employees have the option to purchase additional life insurance for themselves and their dependents as follows:

Employees: You may elect increments of $10,000, to a maximum of $150,000. Cost is dependent on age and the amount of insurance elected.

Spouse: You may elect coverage for your spouse in increments of $5,000. Your spouse's coverage cannot exceed 50% of the employee's elected benefit amount. Cost is dependent on age and amount elected.

Children: You may elect coverage for your unmarried, dependent children in the amount of $10,000 until age 18. Between the ages of 19 and 25, children are eligible only if they are full-time students.

Flexible Spending Accounts

The Flexible Spending Accounts are administered through HrPro. Employees who do NOT enroll in the High Deductible Health Plan are eligible to participate in the Health Care Reimbursement Account. All employees are eligible to participate in the Dependent Care Reimbursement Account.

Investment Statements

Investment Statements

CAMELO†

Combined Value	Last Period 12-31-2015	This Period 01-31-2016
Securities	$116,838.57	$110,683.06
FDIC.Cash and FDIC.Plus	$0.00	$0.00
FDIC.Sweep	$6,730.87	$4,733.04
SIPC.Cash	$858.54	$338.53
Total:	$124,427.98	$115,754.63

List of Accounts

Account
Number

RA8636300J

RB13910001

Bob and Debbie Smith
1000 Residential Lane
Lovington, NM 11111

Account Summary
Jan 01, 2016 - Jan 31, 2016

Account Summary | Holdings Summary | Holdings Detail | Folio Order Summary | Folio Activity Detail | Cash Sweep Activity | FDIC Holdings

Firm

Camelot Portfolios, LLC.

(419) 794-0536

IRA Contribution Summary

	For Prior Year	For Current Year
Totals:	$0.00	$0.00

Account Value

	As Of 12-31-2015	As Of 01-31-2016
Securities	$92,597.53	$87,802.86
FDIC.Cash and FDIC.Plus	$0.00	$0.00
FDIC.Sweep	$4,155.76	$4,677.27
SIPC.Cash	$349.51	$44.53
Total:	$97,102.80	$92,524.66

Interest and Dividend Summary

	Month Ending 01-31-2016	Year To Date
Interest Actually Paid	$0.04	$0.04
Dividends Actually Paid	$544.21	$544.21
Total:	$544.25	$544.25

Summary of Cash (Sweep) Activity

Beginning Balance	$4,505.27
Deposits	$0.00
Securities Sold	$0.00
Interest Paid	$0.04
Dividends Paid	$544.21
Div. adjustments from prior period	$0.00
Pending Cash	$0.00
Other Miscellaneous	$0.00
Withdrawals	$0.00
Securities Bought	$0.00
Checks Written	$0.00
Debit Card Transactions	$0.00
Fee Transactions	($327.73)
Federal Tax Withholdings	$0.00
State Tax Withholdings	$0.00
Ending Balance	$4,721.79

Holdings Summary

Folios	Market Value As Of 12-31-2015	Market Value As Of 01-31-2016

Opportunities Income: Subscribed as Opportunities Income	$92,597.53	$87,802.87
Cash (Sweep)	$4,505.27	$4,721.80
Totals:	$97,102.80	$92,524.66

Holdings Detail

Symbol	Security	# of Shares / Units	Price Per Share / Unit	Market Value
Folio: Opportunities Income (RA8636300J03)				
APIIX	API Efficient Frontier Income Instl	527.57200	$9.38	$4,948.63
AINV	APOLLO INVT CORP	741.37142	$5.07	$3,758.75
CEXAX	CAMELOT EXCALIBUR SMALL CAL INCOME A	648.38000	$6.81	$4,415.47
RNP	COHEN & STEERS REIT & PFD INCM	421.57129	$17.65	$7,440.73
KMM	DEUTSCHE MULTI-MKT INCOME TR SHS	519.34805	$7.50	$3,895.11
DRA	DIVERSIFIED REAL ASSET INC FD COM SHS	479.88901	$14.95	$7,174.34
EVV	EATON VANCE LTD DUR INCM FD SB I	747.67608	$12.33	$9,218.85
FDIC.CASH	FDIC CASH NOT COVERED BY SIPC	0.00183	$1.00	$0.00
FSD	FIRST TR HIGH INCOME L/S FD COM	880.11148	$13.73	$12,083.93
HYLS	FIRST TRUST HIGH YIELD LONG/SHORT ETF	97.63096	$46.51	$4,540.82
GMLPX	GOLDMAN SACHS MLP ENERGY INFRAS INSTL	660.95900	$6.59	$4,355.72
ROOF	IQ US REAL ESTATE SMALL CAP ETF	92.72410	$22.75	$2,109.47
KYE	KAYNE ANDERSON ENRGY TTL RT FD COM	209.60347	$7.56	$1,584.60
LAHYX	Lord Abbett High Yield I	722.97900	$6.74	$4,872.88
CPRFX	MUTUAL FD SER TR CAMELT PRM RTN A	1,755.08500	$7.93	$13,917.82
PSEC	PROSPECT CAPITAL CORPORATION	574.25740	$6.07	$3,485.74
Totals: Opportunities Income				**$87,802.86**
Folio: Cash (Sweep) (RA8636300J01)				
FDIC.SWEEP	FDIC SWEEP NOT COVERED BY SIPC	4,677.27000	$1.00	$4,677.27
USD	U S Dollars	--------	--------	$44.53
Totals: Cash (Sweep)				**$4,721.80**
Totals:				**$92,524.66**

Folio Order Summary

Date	Order #	Order Type	Buy Amount	Sell Amount	Net Amount
No Folio Trades for Period					
Totals:			$0.00	$0.00	$0.00

Folio Activity Detail

Trans Date	Trans Type	Capacity	Symbol	Security	Order Number	Settle Date	# of Shares / Units	Price Per Share / Unit	Trading Service Fees	Comm	Net Amount
Folio: Opportunities Income (RA8636300J03)											
01/05	Cash Dividend Receipt	-----	AINV	APOLLO INVT CORP	--------	-----	741.37142	$0.20	$0.00	$0.00	$148.27
01/05	Cash Dividend Receipt	-----	ROOF	IQ US REAL ESTATE SMALL CAP ETF	--------	-----	92.72410	$0.47476	$0.00	$0.00	$44.02
01/05	Fund Dividend/Interest	-----	LAHYX	Lord Abbett High Yield I	--------	-----	0.00000	$0.00	$0.00	$0.00	$26.32
01/15	Cash Dividend Receipt	-----	FSD	FIRST TR HIGH INCOME L/S FD COM	--------	-----	880.11148	$0.10	$0.00	$0.00	$88.01
01/15	Cash Dividend Receipt	-----	KYE	KAYNE ANDERSON ENRGY TTL RT FD COM	--------	-----	209.60347	$0.33	$0.00	$0.00	$69.17

01/21	Cash Dividend Receipt	-----	PSEC	PROSPECT CAPITAL CORPORATION	--------	-----	574.25740	$0.08333	$0.00	$0.00	$47.85
01/21	Cash Dividend Receipt	-----	EVV	EATON VANCE LTD DUR INCM FD SB I	--------	-----	747.67608	$0.1017	$0.00	$0.00	$76.04
01/29	Cash Dividend Receipt	-----	KMM	DEUTSCHE MULTI-MKT INCOME TR SHS	--------	-----	519.34805	$0.0425	$0.00	$0.00	$22.07
01/29	Cash Dividend Receipt	-----	HYLS	FIRST TRUST HIGH YIELD LONG/SHORT ETF	--------	-----	97.63096	$0.23	$0.00	$0.00	$22.46
Totals: Opportunities Income									**$0.00**	**$0.00**	**$544.21**

Cash Sweep Activity

Date	Tran Type	Transaction Description	Additional Details	Amount
01/04	Buy	FDIC.SWEEP		($349.51)
01/05	Fee	USD	MANAGEMENT FEE (Munn Wealth Management)	($14.08)
01/05	Fee	USD	MANAGEMENT FEE (Munn Wealth Management)	($289.37)
01/06	Buy	FDIC.SWEEP		($192.29)
01/06	Sell	FDIC.SWEEP		$277.13
01/11	Fee	USD	Brokerage and Clearing Fee	($24.28)
01/12	Sell	FDIC.SWEEP		$24.27
01/19	Buy	FDIC.SWEEP		($157.18)
01/22	Buy	FDIC.SWEEP		($0.04)
01/22	Buy	FDIC.SWEEP		($123.89)
01/22	Fund Dividend/Interest	FDIC.SWEEP		$0.04

FDIC Holdings

Annual Percentage Yield (APY):
Jan 01, 2016 - Jan 31, 2016 (31 days).

FDIC.CASH - Opportunities Income (RA8636300J03)	0.01%
FDIC.SWEEP - Cash (Sweep) (RA8636300J01)	0.01%

Balance At FDIC Insured Banks (Month End)

Eagle Bank - Silver Spring, MD	$4,677.29
Total Balance	$4,677.29

Bob and Debbie Smith
1000 Residential Lane
Lovington, NM 11111

Account Summary
Jan 01, 2016 - Jan 31, 2016

Joint - Rights of Survivorship

Account Summary | Holdings Summary | Holdings Detail | Folio Order Summary | Folio Activity Detail | Cash Sweep Activity | FDIC Holdings

Firm

Camelot Portfolios, LLC.

(419) 794-0536

Account Value	As Of 12-31-2015	As Of 01-31-2016
Securities	$24,241.04	$22,880.20
FDIC.Cash and FDIC.Plus	$0.00	$0.00
FDIC.Sweep	$2,575.11	$55.77
SIPC.Cash	$509.03	$294.00
Total:	**$27,325.18**	**$23,229.97**

Interest and Dividend Summary	Month Ending 01-31-2016	Year To Date
Interest Actually Paid	$0.02	$0.02
Dividends Actually Paid	$472.44	$472.44
Total:	**$472.46**	**$472.46**

Summary of Cash (Sweep) Activity

Beginning Balance	$3,084.14
Deposits	$0.00
Securities Sold	$0.00
Interest Paid	$0.02
Dividends Paid	$472.44
Div. adjustments from prior period	$0.00
Pending Cash	$0.00
Other Miscellaneous	$0.00
Withdrawals	($3,200.00)
Securities Bought	$0.00
Checks Written	$0.00
Debit Card Transactions	$0.00
Fee Transactions	($6.83)
Federal Tax Withholdings	$0.00
State Tax Withholdings	$0.00
Ending Balance	$349.77

Holdings Summary

Folios	Market Value As Of 12-31-2015	Market Value As Of 01-31-2016
Client Managed	$24,241.04	$22,880.20
Cash (Sweep)	$3,084.14	$349.77
Totals:	**$27,325.18**	**$23,229.97**

Holdings Detail

Symbol	Security	# of Shares / Units	Price Per Share / Unit	Market Value
Folio: Client Managed (RB1391000103)				
AGNC	AMERICAN CAPITAL AGENCY CORP COM	300.00000	$17.07	$5,121.00
NLY	ANNALY MTG MGMT INC	500.00000	$9.50	$4,750.00
CIM	CHIMERA INVT CORP COM NEW	300.00000	$12.39	$3,717.00
CLF	CLIFFS NATURAL RESOURCES INC	400.00000	$1.61	$644.00
F	FORD MTR CO DEL COM PAR $0.01	200.00000	$11.94	$2,388.00
FTR	FRONTIER COMMUNICATIONS CORP COM CL B	500.00000	$4.55	$2,275.00
KYE	KAYNE ANDERSON ENRGY TTL RT FD COM	300.00000	$7.56	$2,268.00
VNR	VANGUARD NATURAL RESOURCES LLC COM UNIT	648.00000	$2.65	$1,717.20
Totals: Client Managed				**$22,880.20**
Folio: Cash (Sweep) (RB1391000101)				
FDIC.SWEEP	FDIC SWEEP NOT COVERED BY SIPC	55.77000	$1.00	$55.77
USD	U S Dollars	--------	--------	$294.00
Totals: Cash (Sweep)				**$349.77**
Totals:				**$23,229.97**

Folio Order Summary

Date	Order #	Order Type	Buy Amount	Sell Amount	Net Amount
No Folio Trades for Period					
Totals:			$0.00	$0.00	$0.00

Folio Activity Detail

Trans Date	Trans Type	Capacity	Symbol	Security	Order Number	Settle Date	# of Shares / Units	Price Per Share / Unit	Trading Service Fees	Comm	Net Amount
Folio: Client Managed (RB1391000103)											
01/08	Cash Dividend Receipt	-----	AGNC	AMERICAN CAPITAL AGENCY CORP COM	--------	-----	300.00000	$0.20	$0.00	$0.00	$60.00
01/14	Cash Dividend Receipt	-----	VNR	VANGUARD NATURAL RESOURCES LLC COM UNIT	--------	-----	648.00000	$0.03	$0.00	$0.00	$19.44
01/15	Cash Dividend Receipt	-----	KYE	KAYNE ANDERSON ENRGY TTL RT FD COM	--------	-----	300.00000	$0.33	$0.00	$0.00	$99.00
01/29	Cash Dividend Receipt	-----	NLY	ANNALY MTG MGMT INC	--------	-----	500.00000	$0.30	$0.00	$0.00	$150.00
01/29	Cash Dividend Receipt	-----	CIM	CHIMERA INVT CORP COM NEW	--------	-----	300.00000	$0.48	$0.00	$0.00	$144.00
Totals: Client Managed									$0.00	$0.00	$472.44

Cash Sweep Activity

Date	Tran Type	Transaction Description	Additional Details	Amount
01/04	Buy	FDIC.SWEEP		($52.50)
01/05	Buy	FDIC.SWEEP		($456.53)
01/05	Fee	USD	MANAGEMENT FEE (Munn Wealth Management)	$0.00
01/05	Fee	USD	MANAGEMENT FEE (Munn Wealth Management)	$0.00

01/11	Buy	FDIC.SWEEP		($60.00)
01/11	Fee	USD	Brokerage and Clearing Fee	($6.83)
01/12	Sell	FDIC.SWEEP		$6.83
01/15	Buy	FDIC.SWEEP		($19.44)
01/19	Buy	FDIC.SWEEP		($99.00)
01/20	Withdrawal	USD	ACH Withdrawal	($3,200.00)
01/20	Sell	FDIC.SWEEP		$3,200.00
01/22	Buy	FDIC.SWEEP		($0.02)
01/22	Fund Dividend/Interest	FDIC.SWEEP		$0.02

FDIC Holdings

Annual Percentage Yield (APY):
Jan 01, 2016 - Jan 31, 2016 (31 days).
FDIC.SWEEP - Cash (Sweep) (RB1391000101)   0.01%

Balance At FDIC Insured Banks (Month End)
Eagle Bank - Silver Spring, MD $55.77
Total Balance $55.77

Asset Class

As Of: Sunday, January 31, 2016

Allocation Breakdown

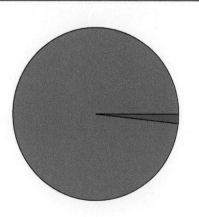

	Allocation	Market Value
■ Equities	98.24 %	$22,880.19
■ Cash	1.76 %	$409.77
Total:	**100 %**	**$23,289.96**

Bob and Debbie Smith JTROS
1000 Residential Lane
Lovington, NM 11111

Holdings

	Units	Price	Value
			$23,289.96
Cash			**$409.77**
CASH	354.00	$1.00	$354.00
MONEYFUND	55.77	$1.00	$55.77
Equities			**$22,880.19**
AMERICAN CAPITAL AGENCY CORP (AGNC)	300.00	$17.07	$5,121.00
ANNALY CAPITAL MANAGEMENT INC (NLY)	500.00	$9.50	$4,750.00
CHIMERA INVESTMENT CORP (CIM)	300.00	$12.39	$3,717.00
CLIFFS NATURAL RESOURCES INC (CLF)	400.00	$1.61	$644.00
FORD MOTOR CO (F)	200.00	$11.94	$2,388.00
FRONTIER COMMUNICATIONS CORP (FTR)	500.00	$4.55	$2,275.00
KAYNE ANDERSON ENERGY TOTAL RETURN (KYE)	300.00	$7.56	$2,268.00
VANGUARD NATURAL RESOURCES LLC (VNR)	648.00	$2.65	$1,717.19

Asset Class

As Of: Sunday, January 31, 2016

Allocation Breakdown

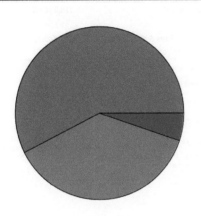

	Allocation	Market Value
■ Equities	57.45 %	$53,191.29
■ Fixed Income	37.38 %	$34,611.56
■ Cash	5.17 %	$4,788.50
Total:	**100 %**	**$92,591.35**

Debbie Smith
1000 Residential Lane
Lovington, NM 11111

Holdings

	Units	Price	Value
			$92,591.35
Cash			**$4,788.50**
CASH	111.23	$1.00	$111.23
MONEYFUND	4,677.27	$1.00	$4,677.27
Equities			**$53,191.29**
API EFFICIENT FRONTIER INCOME INSTL (APIIX)	527.57	$9.38	$4,948.63
APOLLO INVESTMENT CORP (AINV)	741.37	$5.07	$3,758.77
CAMELOT EXCALIBUR SMALL CAP INCOME A (CEXAX)	648.38	$6.81	$4,415.46
CAMELOT PREMIUM RETURN A (CPRFX)	1,755.09	$7.93	$13,917.83
COHEN & STEERS REIT & PREFERRED INCOME (RNP)	421.57	$17.65	$7,440.73
DIVERSIFIED REAL ASSET INCOME (XDRAX)	479.89	$14.95	$7,174.33
GOLDMAN SACHS MLP ENERGY INFRAS INSTL (GMLPX)	660.96	$6.59	$4,355.73
IQ US REAL ESTATE SMALL CAP ETF (ROOF)	92.72	$22.75	$2,109.47
KAYNE ANDERSON ENERGY TOTAL RETURN (KYE)	209.60	$7.56	$1,584.60
PROSPECT CAPITAL CORP (PSEC)	574.26	$6.07	$3,485.74
Fixed Income			**$34,611.56**
DEUTSCHE MULTI-MARKET INCOME (KMM)	519.35	$7.50	$3,895.10
EATON VANCE LTD DURATION INCOME FUND (EVV)	747.68	$12.33	$9,218.84
FIRST TRUST HIGH INCOME LONG/SHORT FUND (FSD)	880.11	$13.73	$12,083.93
FIRST TRUST TACTICAL HIGH YIELD ETF (HYLS)	97.63	$46.51	$4,540.81
LORD ABBETT HIGH YIELD I (LAHYX)	722.98	$6.74	$4,872.88

Envelope # BBQMZCBBBDFZR

CAMELOT PORTFOLIOS, LLC
1700 WOODLANDS DR
STE 100
MAUMEE OH 43537

Lextin Oil Supply 401k
Bob T Smith
1000 Residential Lane
Lovington, NM 11111

Your Account Value: **$1,170,036.15**

Change from Last Period: ▼ $46,359.90

	This Period	Year-to-Date
Beginning Account Value	**$1,216,396.05**	**$1,216,396.05**
Subtractions	-4,565.16	-4,565.16
Transaction Costs, Fees & Charges	*-4,565.16*	*-4,565.16*
Change in Investment Value *	-41,794.74	-41,794.74
**Ending Account Value ** **	**$1,170,036.15**	**$1,170,036.15**
Accrued Interest (AI)	0.00	
Ending Account Value Incl. AI	$1,170,036.15	

* Appreciation or depreciation of your holdings due to price changes plus any distribution and
  income earned during the statement period.
** Excludes unpriced securities.

Asset Class

As Of: Sunday, January 31, 2016

Allocation Breakdown

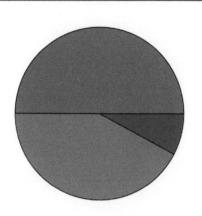

	Allocation	Market Value
■ Equities	49.93 %	$584,480.41
■ Fixed Income	42.33 %	$495,617.97
■ Cash	7.74 %	$90,618.49
Total:	100 %	$1,170,716.87

Lestin Oil Supply 401k
Bob T Smith
1000 Residential Lane
Lovington, NM 11111

Holdings

	Units	Price	Value
			$1,170,716.87
Cash			**$90,618.49**
CASH	680.66	$1.00	$680.66
MONEYFUND	89,937.83	$1.00	$89,937.83
Equities			**$584,480.41**
ABB LTD (ABB)	404.00	$17.30	$6,989.20
ALLIANZGI NFJ DIV INTEREST & PREM (NFJ)	375.00	$11.50	$4,312.50
AMERICAN CAPITAL AGENCY CORP (AGNC)	356.00	$17.07	$6,076.92
AMERICAN CAPITAL LTD (ACAS)	815.00	$14.02	$11,426.30
AMERICAN CAPITAL MORTGAGE INVESTMENT CORP (MTGE)	417.00	$13.03	$5,433.51
ANNALY CAPITAL MANAGEMENT INC (NLY)	1,126.00	$9.50	$10,697.00
API EFFICIENT FRONTIER INCOME INSTL (APIIX)	2,538.79	$9.38	$23,813.87
APOLLO INVESTMENT CORP (AINV)	3,898.00	$5.07	$19,762.86
APPLE INC (AAPL)	37.00	$97.34	$3,601.58
ARES CAPITAL CORPORATION (ARCC)	485.00	$13.90	$6,741.50
CALAMOS GLOBAL DYNAMIC INCOME (CHW)	645.00	$6.51	$4,198.95
CAMELOT EXCALIBUR SMALL CAP INCOME A (CEXAX)	6,020.70	$6.81	$41,000.95
CAMELOT PREMIUM RETURN A (CPRFX)	16,079.29	$7.93	$127,508.77
CATERPILLAR INC (CAT)	92.00	$62.24	$5,726.08
CHINA MOBILE LTD (CHL)	138.00	$54.53	$7,525.14
COACH INC (COH)	266.00	$37.05	$9,855.30
COHEN & STEERS INFRASTRUCTURE (UTF)	526.00	$18.18	$9,562.68
COHEN & STEERS REIT & PREFERRED INCOME (RNP)	2,495.00	$17.65	$44,036.75

Estate Planning

LAST WILL AND TESTAMENT

OF

Bob T. Smith

I, Bob T. Smith, a resident of LEA COUNTY, NEW MEXICO, being of sound and disposing mind and memory, declare that this is my Last Will and Testament, hereby revoking all previous wills and codicils.

I. Marital Status and Family

I am presently married to Debbie Smith who in this will is referred to as "[SPOUSE]". I have three children: __Sean Smith_____, __Chloe Smith_____, and _Clara Smith_____. I have no deceased children. All references in this Will to my "child" or "children" include not only the above children but also any child or children born to or adopted by me after the date of execution of this Will.

II. Executor

A. I hereby appoint Debbie Smith as the Independent Executor of this Will. If she is unable or unwilling to act or to continue to act in the capacity of Executor, then I appoint the following to serve as independent executor of this Will, in the order named:

1. _Sean Smith_____;

2. _Cathy Milborn_____;

3. _Ken R. Smith_____.

Whenever the word "executor" is used in this Will, it shall be deemed to refer to whoever of them is acting from time to time.

B. I direct that no action shall be had in the probate court in which this Will is probated in relation to the settlement of my estate, other than the probating and recording of this Will and the return of an inventory, appraisement, and list of claims. No bond or other security shall be required of any Executor appointed in this Will. As compensation for his services, I direct that my Executor receive such compensation as is fair, customary, and reasonable, taking into consideration the duties and responsibilities assumed and taking into consideration the value and nature of my estate and the time and work involved.

C. My Executor shall have, in extension and not in limitation of the powers given by law or by other provisions of this Will, the following powers with respect to the settlement and administration of my probate estate:

(a) To exercise with regard to the probate estate all of the powers and authority conferred by Article V of this Will on the Trustee over the trust estate.

(b) To employ any attorney, investment advisor, accountant, broker, tax specialist, or any other agent deemed necessary by my Executor; and to pay from my estate reasonable compensation for all services performed by any of them.

(c) When paying legacies or dividing or distributing my estate, to make such payments, division, or distribution wholly or partly in kind by allotting and transferring specific securities or other personal or real property in the manner deemed advisable by my Executor.

(d) To elect to treat all or any portion of any eligible property (including any trust I may have established during my life or under this Will) as qualified terminable interest property to the extent required to reduce the federal estate tax on my estate if my executor determines that it is in the best interests of all person interested in my estate taken as a whole.

(e) To make any elections allowed by the Internal Revenue Code or the tax laws of any state in order to take advantage of all tax savings that the law of any jurisdiction allows.

(f) To join with my spouse or her executor or administrator in filing any income tax return of the income of my spouse and myself for any period for which such a return may be permitted, and to agree with my spouse or her executor or administrator:

(a) As to how the burden of the liability for any income tax, or interest on that tax liability, arising out of the filing of a joint return by my Executor and my spouse or her executor or administrator, will be allocated between my estate and my spouse or her estate;

(b) As to who, as between my spouse or her estate and my estate, will be entitled:

(i) To any refund or credit of any income tax, or interest on that tax liability, based on the filing of a joint return by my spouse and myself or by my Executor and my spouse or her executor or administrator;

(ii) To any refund or credit of any amount paid on account of any joint declaration of any estimated income tax filed by my spouse and myself, and of the interest on any such refund; and

(iii) To the benefit of any payment made by my spouse and myself on account of any joint or separate declaration of any estimated income tax.

(g) When paying legacies or dividing or distributing my estate, to make such payments, division, or distribution wholly or partly in kind by allotting and transferring specific securities or other personal or real properties or undivided interests therein as a part of the whole of any one or more payments or shares at current values in the manner deemed advisable by my Executor.

All of the above powers may be exercised periodically in the discretion of my Executor without further court order or license.

III. Property Covered by Will

It is my intention by this Will to dispose of all of the separate property that I own and of one-half of the community property owned by Debbie Smith and myself at the time of my death. I elect not to exercise any power of appointment that I now have or that may be conferred on me after the date of execution of this will.

IV. Disposition of Estate

A. I devise all of my estate to Debbie Smith if she survives me for 180 days. If Debbie Smith disclaims this gift in whole or in part, I give the property so disclaimed to the Trustee of the Smith FAMILY TRUST as set forth in Article V of this Will.

B. If Debbie Smith does not survive me for 180 days, then I make the following gifts to the following persons:

I give all of my clothing, household furniture and furnishings, personal automobiles and other motor vehicles, boats, mementos, works of art, jewelry, and other tangible articles of a personal nature, or my interest in any such property, not otherwise specifically disposed of by this Will, and any insurance on any property described in this Paragraph, to my children who survive me for 180 days. The devise in this subparagraph is to be divided among my children in equal shares that they agree upon or, if they shall fail to agree, that my Executor shall determine. If any of my children fails to survive me for that period, then the share that would have gone to that child had he or she survived me for that period shall pass to the issue of that child per stirpes and not per capita.

V. Smith Family Trust

If Debbie Smith does not survive me for 180 days, then I give all of the rest and residue of my estate to Smith Family Trust, Law Office of Kern, Davis, and Jefferson, Trustees of *8000 Country Club Road, Lovington, NM, 11112* in trust, to be held, administered, and distributed in accordance with the following provisions:

A. <u>PAYMENT AND DISTRIBUTION OF INCOME AND PRINCIPAL</u>. The entire trust estate shall be administered as one trust until my youngest child then living reaches the age of 25 years. Until that time, the Trustee shall apply the net income and principal of the trust estate as follows:

(a) The Trustee shall pay to or apply for the benefit of each of my living children who are under the age of 25 years, in monthly or in other convenient installments but in no event less often than annually, as much of the net income and as much of the principal of the trust estate as the Trustee deems necessary for the proper care, support, and education of each child. No child who has attained the age of 25 years shall receive any of the payments specified in this subparagraph from the trust estate.

(b) The Trustee may pay more to or apply more for some beneficiaries than others and may omit some beneficiaries entirely, according to their particular needs for support.

(c) The Trustee, in exercising discretion with respect to the amount of payment of income or principal of the trust estate to any beneficiary, shall take into consideration any income or other resources available to the beneficiary from sources outside of this trust. The Trustee may consider any written statement of the beneficiary receiving payment as to other available income or resources. The determination of the Trustee with respect to the necessity of making payments out of income or principal to any beneficiary shall be conclusive on all persons interested in the trust.

(d) The Trustee shall accumulate and add to principal any net income of the trust not paid out in accordance with the discretion conferred on the Trustee.

B. In the event any of my children dies before the termination of the trust according to the terms of Paragraph C of this Article V and leaves surviving issue, then that child's share of the balance of the trust estate shall immediately be distributed to the issue of that child per stirpes. If any of my children dies before the termination of the trust and does not leave surviving issue, then that child's share of the balance of the trust shall be held in the trust for the benefit of my surviving children. If all of my children die before my youngest child reaches the age of 25 years, then the trust shall terminate, and the remaining trust balance shall be paid to the estate of the last surviving child.

C. When my youngest child then living reaches the age of 25 years, the trust shall terminate, and the Trustee shall immediately distribute the balance of the trust estate in equal shares to my children then living.

D. <u>Definitions.</u> As used in this Will, the terms set forth below have the following meanings:

(a) The term "children" includes adopted children and any children who may be born after the date of execution of this Will.

(b) The term "issue" means lineal blood descendants of those persons designated in this will, and includes legally adopted children of such persons.

(c) The term "education" includes both college and postgraduate study at any accredited institution of the beneficiary's choice for any period of time that, in the judgment of the Trustee, is advantageous to the beneficiary concerned. The Trustee shall provide adequate amounts for all related living and travel expenses of the beneficiary within reasonable limits.

E. No beneficiary or person with a remainder interest in this trust shall have any right to alienate, encumber, or pledge his or her interest in the principal or income of the trust in any manner, nor shall any interest of any beneficiary or remainder person be subject to claims of his or her creditors or liable to attachment, execution, or other process of law.

F. <u>GENERAL ADMINISTRATIVE POWERS OF TRUSTEE</u>. In order to carry out the purposes of any trust established by this Will, the Trustee, in addition to all other powers granted by this Will or by law, shall have the following powers over the trust estate, subject to any limitations specified elsewhere in this Will:

(a) To retain any property received by the trust estate for as long as the Trustee considers advisable.

(b) To invest and reinvest in every kind of property and investment that persons of prudence, discretion, and intelligence acquire for their own accounts.

(c) To manage, control, repair, and improve all trust property.

(d) To sell, for cash or on terms, and to exchange any trust property.

(e) To adjust or compromise any claims for or against the trust.

(f) To borrow money and to encumber or hypothecate any trust property.

G. The Trustee shall determine what is income and what is principal of the trust established under this Will. The Trustee shall further determine what expenses, costs, taxes, and charges of all kinds shall be charged against income and what shall be charged against principal in accordance with applicable statutes of the State of NEW MEXICO.

H. If Law Office of Kern, Davis, and Jefferson is unable or unwilling to act or to continue to act as the Trustee, then I appoint Cathy Milborn, *5111 Daisy Lane, Lovington, NM, 11112* as Trustee with the same powers, rights, discretions, obligations, and immunities. If Law Office of Kern, Davis, and Jefferson and Cathy Milborn are each unable or unwilling to act as the Trustee, then I appoint Ken R. Smith of *8514 Cat Tails Lane, Marion, IN 46953*, as Trustee with the same powers, rights, discretions, obligations, and immunities.

I. The Trustee shall receive a reasonable compensation for services as Trustee.

J. No Trustee appointed in this Will shall at any time be held liable for any action or default of that Trustee or of any other person in connection with the administration of the trust estate, unless caused by the Trustee's own gross negligence or willful commission of an act in breach of the trust.

K. The validity and administration of any trust established under this Will and the construction or interpretation of the Trust shall be governed by the laws of the State of NEW MEXICO.

VI. Guardianship

If my Debbie Smith predeceases me, I appoint as guardian of each child of mine for whom appointment of a guardian becomes necessary the individual or individuals designated in a separate writing signed by me in the presence of two witnesses.

If no such separate writing exists and Debbie Smith predeceases me, I appoint the following as guardian of the person of each child of mine for whom appointment of a guardian of a person becomes necessary:

Cathy Milborn, who resides at 5111 Daisy Lane, Lovington, NM, 11112

If no such separate writing exists and Debbie Smith predeceases me, I appoint the following, in the order named, as guardian of the estate of each child of mine for whom appointment of a guardian of the estate becomes necessary:

The trustee of any trust for the benefit of my children to serve as guardian of the estate the child of mine for which they are serving as trustee; then

Cathy Milborn, who resides at 5111 Daisy Lane, Lovington, NM, 11112

VII. No-Contest Clause

If any beneficiary under this Will, directly or indirectly, by legal proceedings or otherwise, challenges or contests this Will or any of its provisions or attempts in any manner to oppose or set aside the probate of this Will or impair or invalidate any of its provisions, any gift or other provision I have made to or for that person under this Will is revoked and shall be disposed of as if that contesting beneficiary had predeceased me without issue.

VIII. Payment of Estate Taxes

I direct that all estate, inheritance, transfer, or succession taxes imposed by reason of my death with respect to any interest in property that passes from me under this Will shall be paid from my residuary estate as an expense of administration, and shall not be apportioned from my entire estate.

IX. General Provisions

A. Debbie Smith and I are executing Wills at approximately the same time in which each of us is the primary beneficiary of the Will of the other. However, these Wills are not executed pursuant to any agreement between Debbie Smith and myself. Either Will may be revoked at any time at the sole discretion of the maker of the Will.

B. If any provision of this Will is held to be inoperative, invalid, or illegal, it is my intention that all of the remaining provisions of the Will continue to be fully operative and effective to the extent possible and reasonable.

C. All pronouns in this Will referring to an executor, and the term "Executor," shall be construed to mean any person acting as my executor or administrator, whether that person was originally appointed under this Will or is a successor of such person under the terms of this Will or according to law. All pronouns referring to a trustee, and the term "Trustee," shall be construed to mean any person acting as my trustee, whether that person was originally appointed under this Will or is a successor of such person under the terms of this Will or according to law.

D. All headings are used in this Will to describe the contents of each article, paragraph, or other division and are not be construed to be part of this Will.

E. This Will shall be construed in conformance with the law of the State of NEW MEXICO.

[SIGNATURE PAGE TO FOLLOW]

SIGNATURE CLAUSE

The Will set forth above is executed by me on this _____ day of _____, 2008, at _____, NEW MEXICO

_____

Bob T. Smith

ATTESTATION CLAUSE

We, _____ and _____, witnesses, sign our names to this instrument and declare that the testator, Bob T. Smith, signs and executes this instrument as his will and that each of us, in the presence and hearing of the testator, signs this Will as witness to the testator's signature. We are each 14 years of age or older, saw the testator sign the declaration, and the testator appears to be of sound mind to us.

_____

Name: _____

Address: _____

_____

_____

Name: _____

Address: _____

_____

SELF-PROVING AFFIDAVIT

STATE OF NEW MEXICO

COUNTY OF LEA COUNTY

Before me, the undersigned authority, on this day personally appeared Bob T. Smith, __Debbie Smith_____, and ___Cathy Milborn_____, known to me to be the testator and the witnesses, respectively, whose names are subscribed to the annexed or foregoing instrument in their respective capacities, and all of said individuals being by me duly sworn, Bob T. Smith, testator, declared to me and to the witnesses in my presence that said instrument is the last will and testament or a codicil to the last will and testament of the testator and that the testator had willingly made and executed it as a free act and deed for the purposes expressed therein. The witnesses, each on oath, stated to me in the presence and hearing of the testator that the testator had declared to them that the instrument is the testator's last will and testament or a codicil to the testator's last will and testament and that the testator executed the instrument as such and wished each of them to sign it as a witness; and under oath each witness stated further that the witness had signed the same as witness in the presence of the testator and at the testator's request; that the testator was 14 years of age or over and of sound mind; and that each of the witnesses was then at least 14 years of age.

_____

Bob T. Smith

_____

Debbie Smith

_____

Cathy Milborn

Sworn to and subscribed before me by Bob T. Smith, testator, sworn to and subscribed before me by _____ and _____, witnesses, this ____ day of _____, 20__.

(SEAL)

_____

(Signed)

_____

(Official Capacity of Officer)

LAST WILL AND TESTAMENT

OF

Debbie Smith

I, Debbie Smith, a resident of LEA COUNTY, NEW MEXICO being of sound and disposing mind and memory, declare that this is my Last Will and Testament, hereby revoking all previous wills and codicils.

I. Marital Status and Family

I am presently married to Bob T. Smith who in this will is referred to as "[SPOUSE]". I have three children: __Sean Smith_____, __Chloe Smith_____, and _Clara Smith_____. I have no deceased children. All references in this Will to my "child" or "children" include not only the above children but also any child or children born to or adopted by me after the date of execution of this Will.

II. Executor

A. I hereby appoint Debbie Smith as the Independent Executor of this Will. If she is unable or unwilling to act or to continue to act in the capacity of Executor, then I appoint the following to serve as independent executor of this Will, in the order named:

1. _Sean Smith_____;

2. _Cathy Milborn_____;

3. _Ken R. Smith_____.

Whenever the word "executor" is used in this Will, it shall be deemed to refer to whoever of them is acting from time to time.

B. I direct that no action shall be had in the probate court in which this Will is probated in relation to the settlement of my estate, other than the probating and recording of this Will and the return of an inventory, appraisement, and list of claims. No bond or other security shall be required of any Executor appointed in this Will. As compensation for his services, I direct that my Executor receive such compensation as is fair, customary, and reasonable, taking into consideration the duties and responsibilities assumed and taking into consideration the value and nature of my estate and the time and work involved.

C. My Executor shall have, in extension and not in limitation of the powers given by law or by other provisions of this Will, the following powers with respect to the settlement and administration of my probate estate:

(a) To exercise with regard to the probate estate all of the powers and authority conferred by Article V of this Will on the Trustee over the trust estate.

(b) To employ any attorney, investment advisor, accountant, broker, tax specialist, or any other agent deemed necessary by my Executor; and to pay from my estate reasonable compensation for all services performed by any of them.

(c) When paying legacies or dividing or distributing my estate, to make such payments, division, or distribution wholly or partly in kind by allotting and transferring specific securities or other personal or real property in the manner deemed advisable by my Executor.

(d) To elect to treat all or any portion of any eligible property (including any trust I may have established during my life or under this Will) as qualified terminable interest property to the extent required to reduce the federal estate tax on my estate if my executor determines that it is in the best interests of all person interested in my estate taken as a whole.

(e) To make any elections allowed by the Internal Revenue Code or the tax laws of any state in order to take advantage of all tax savings that the law of any jurisdiction allows.

(f) To join with my spouse or her executor or administrator in filing any income tax return of the income of my spouse and myself for any period for which such a return may be permitted, and to agree with my spouse or her executor or administrator:

(a) As to how the burden of the liability for any income tax, or interest on that tax liability, arising out of the filing of a joint return by my Executor and my spouse or her executor or administrator, will be allocated between my estate and my spouse or her estate;

(b) As to who, as between my spouse or his estate and my estate, will be entitled:

(i) To any refund or credit of any income tax, or interest on that tax liability, based on the filing of a joint return by my spouse and myself or by my Executor and my spouse or his executor or administrator;

(ii) To any refund or credit of any amount paid on account of any joint declaration of any estimated income tax filed by my spouse and myself, and of the interest on any such refund; and

(iii) To the benefit of any payment made by my spouse and myself on account of any joint or separate declaration of any estimated income tax.

(g) When paying legacies or dividing or distributing my estate, to make such payments, division, or distribution wholly or partly in kind by allotting and transferring specific securities or other personal or real properties or undivided interests therein as a part of the whole of any one or more payments or shares at current values in the manner deemed advisable by my Executor.

All of the above powers may be exercised periodically in the discretion of my Executor without further court order or license.

III. Property Covered by Will

It is my intention by this Will to dispose of all of the separate property that I own and of one-half of the community property owned by Bob T. Smith and myself at the time of my death. I elect not to exercise any power of appointment that I now have or that may be conferred on me after the date of execution of this will.

IV. Disposition of Estate

A. I devise all of my estate to Bob T. Smith if he survives me for 180 days. If Bob T. Smith disclaims this gift in whole or in part, I give the property so disclaimed to the Trustee of the SMITH FAMILY TRUST as set forth in Article V of this Will.

B. If Bob Smith does not survive me for 180 days, then I make the following gifts to the following persons:

I give all of my clothing, household furniture and furnishings, personal automobiles and other motor vehicles, boats, mementos, works of art, jewelry, and other tangible articles of a personal nature, or my interest in any such property, not otherwise specifically disposed of by this Will, and any insurance on any property described in this Paragraph, to my children who survive me for 180 days. The devise in this subparagraph is to be divided among my children in equal shares that they agree upon or, if they shall fail to agree, that my Executor shall determine. If any of my children fails to survive me for that period, then the share that would have gone to that child had he or she survived me for that period shall pass to the issue of that child per stirpes and not per capita.

V. Smith Family Trust

If Bob T. Smith does not survive me for 180 days, then I give all of the rest and residue of my estate to Smith Family Trust, Law Office of Kern, Davis, and Jefferson, Trustees of *8000 Country Club Road, Lovington, NM, 11112* in trust, to be held, administered, and distributed in accordance with the following provisions:

A. <u>PAYMENT AND DISTRIBUTION OF INCOME AND PRINCIPAL</u>. The entire trust estate shall be administered as one trust until my youngest child then living reaches the age of 25 years. Until that time, the Trustee shall apply the net income and principal of the trust estate as follows:

(a) The Trustee shall pay to or apply for the benefit of each of my living children who are under the age of 25 years, in monthly or in other convenient installments but in no event less often than annually, as much of the net income and as much of the principal of the trust estate as the Trustee deems necessary for the proper care, support, and education of each child. No child who has attained the age of 25 years shall receive any of the payments specified in this subparagraph from the trust estate.

(b) The Trustee may pay more to or apply more for some beneficiaries than others and may omit some beneficiaries entirely, according to their particular needs for support.

(c) The Trustee, in exercising discretion with respect to the amount of payment of income or principal of the trust estate to any beneficiary, shall take into consideration any income or other resources available to the beneficiary from sources outside of this trust. The Trustee may consider any written statement of the beneficiary receiving payment as to other available income or resources. The determination of the Trustee with respect to the necessity of making payments out of income or principal to any beneficiary shall be conclusive on all persons interested in the trust.

(d) The Trustee shall accumulate and add to principal any net income of the trust not paid out in accordance with the discretion conferred on the Trustee.

B. In the event any of my children dies before the termination of the trust according to the terms of Paragraph C of this Article V and leaves surviving issue, then that child's share of the balance of the trust estate shall immediately be distributed to the issue of that child per stirpes. If any of my children dies before the termination of the trust and does not leave surviving issue, then that child's share of the balance of the trust shall be held in the trust for the benefit of my surviving children. If all of my children die before my youngest child reaches the age of 25 years, then the trust shall terminate, and the remaining trust balance shall be paid to the estate of the last surviving child.

C. When my youngest child then living reaches the age of 25 years, the trust shall terminate, and the Trustee shall immediately distribute the balance of the trust estate in equal shares to my children then living.

D. <u>Definitions.</u> As used in this Will, the terms set forth below have the following meanings:

(a) The term "children" includes adopted children and any children who may be born after the date of execution of this Will.

(b) The term "issue" means lineal blood descendants of those persons designated in this will, and includes legally adopted children of such persons.

(c) The term "education" includes both college and postgraduate study at any accredited institution of the beneficiary's choice for any period of time that, in the judgment of the Trustee, is advantageous to the beneficiary concerned. The Trustee shall provide adequate amounts for all related living and travel expenses of the beneficiary within reasonable limits.

E. No beneficiary or person with a remainder interest in this trust shall have any right to alienate, encumber, or pledge his or her interest in the principal or income of the trust in any manner, nor shall any interest of any beneficiary or remainder person be subject to claims of his or her creditors or liable to attachment, execution, or other process of law.

F. <u>GENERAL ADMINISTRATIVE POWERS OF TRUSTEE</u>. In order to carry out the purposes of any trust established by this Will, the Trustee, in addition to all other powers granted by this Will or by law, shall have the following powers over the trust estate, subject to any limitations specified elsewhere in this Will:

(a) To retain any property received by the trust estate for as long as the Trustee considers advisable.

(b) To invest and reinvest in every kind of property and investment that persons of prudence, discretion, and intelligence acquire for their own accounts.

(c) To manage, control, repair, and improve all trust property.

(d) To sell, for cash or on terms, and to exchange any trust property.

(e) To adjust or compromise any claims for or against the trust.

(f) To borrow money and to encumber or hypothecate any trust property.

G. The Trustee shall determine what is income and what is principal of the trust established under this Will. The Trustee shall further determine what expenses, costs, taxes, and charges of all kinds shall be charged against income and what shall be charged against principal in accordance with applicable statutes of the State of NEW MEXICO.

H. If Law Office of Kern, Davis, and Jefferson is unable or unwilling to act or to continue to act as the Trustee, then I appoint Cathy Milborn, *5111 Daisy Lane, Lovington, NM, 11112* as Trustee with the same powers, rights, discretions, obligations, and immunities. If Law Office of Kern, Davis, and Jefferson and Cathy Milborn are each unable or unwilling to act as the Trustee, then I appoint Ken R. Smith of *8514 Cat Tails Lane, Marion, IN 46953*, as Trustee with the same powers, rights, discretions, obligations, and immunities.

I. The Trustee shall receive a reasonable compensation for services as Trustee.

J. No Trustee appointed in this Will shall at any time be held liable for any action or default of that Trustee or of any other person in connection with the administration of the trust estate, unless caused by the Trustee's own gross negligence or willful commission of an act in breach of the trust.

K. The validity and administration of any trust established under this Will and the construction or interpretation of the Trust shall be governed by the laws of the State of NEW MEXICO.

VI. Guardianship

If my Bob T. Smith predeceases me, I appoint as guardian of each child of mine for whom appointment of a guardian becomes necessary the individual or individuals designated in a separate writing signed by me in the presence of two witnesses.

If no such separate writing exists and Bob T. Smith predeceases me, I appoint the following as guardian of the person of each child of mine for whom appointment of a guardian of a person becomes necessary:

Cathy Milborn, who resides at 5111 Daisy Lane, Lovington, NM, 11112

If no such separate writing exists and Bob T. Smith predeceases me, I appoint the following, in the order named, as guardian of the estate of each child of mine for whom appointment of a guardian of the estate becomes necessary:

The trustee of any trust for the benefit of my children to serve as guardian of the estate the child of mine for which they are serving as trustee; then

Cathy Milborn, who resides at 5111 Daisy Lane, Lovington, NM, 11112

VII. No-Contest Clause

If any beneficiary under this Will, directly or indirectly, by legal proceedings or otherwise, challenges or contests this Will or any of its provisions or attempts in any manner to oppose or set aside the probate of this Will or impair or invalidate any of its provisions, any gift or other provision I have made to or for that person under this Will is revoked and shall be disposed of as if that contesting beneficiary had predeceased me without issue.

VIII. Payment of Estate Taxes

I direct that all estate, inheritance, transfer, or succession taxes imposed by reason of my death with respect to any interest in property that passes from me under this Will shall be paid from my residuary estate as an expense of administration, and shall not be apportioned from my entire estate.

IX. General Provisions

A. Bob T. Smith and I are executing Wills at approximately the same time in which each of us is the primary beneficiary of the Will of the other. However, these Wills are not executed pursuant to any agreement between Bob T. Smith and myself. Either Will may be revoked at any time at the sole discretion of the maker of the Will.

B. If any provision of this Will is held to be inoperative, invalid, or illegal, it is my intention that all of the remaining provisions of the Will continue to be fully operative and effective to the extent possible and reasonable.

C. All pronouns in this Will referring to an executor, and the term "Executor," shall be construed to mean any person acting as my executor or administrator, whether that person was originally appointed under this Will or is a successor of such person under the terms of this Will or according to law. All pronouns referring to a trustee, and the term "Trustee," shall be construed to mean any person acting as my trustee, whether that person was originally appointed under this Will or is a successor of such person under the terms of this Will or according to law.

D. All headings are used in this Will to describe the contents of each article, paragraph, or other division and are not be construed to be part of this Will.

E. This Will shall be construed in conformance with the law of the State of NEW MEXICO.

[SIGNATURE PAGE TO FOLLOW]

SIGNATURE CLAUSE

The Will set forth above is executed by me on this _____ day of _____, 2008, at _____, NEW MEXICO

_____

Debbie Smith

ATTESTATION CLAUSE

We, _____ and _____, witnesses, sign our names to this instrument and declare that the testator, Debbie Smith, signs and executes this instrument as his will and that each of us, in the presence and hearing of the testator, signs this Will as witness to the testator's signature. We are each 14 years of age or older, saw the testator sign the declaration, and the testator appears to be of sound mind to us.

_____

Name: _____

Address: _____

_____

_____

Name: _____

Address: _____

_____

SELF-PROVING AFFIDAVIT

STATE OF NEW MEXICO

COUNTY OF LEA COUNTY

    Before me, the undersigned authority, on this day personally appeared Debbie Smith, __Bob T. Smith_____, and ___Cathy Milborn_____, known to me to be the testator and the witnesses, respectively, whose names are subscribed to the annexed or foregoing instrument in their respective capacities, and all of said individuals being by me duly sworn, Debbie Smith, testator, declared to me and to the witnesses in my presence that said instrument is the last will and testament or a codicil to the last will and testament of the testator and that the testator had willingly made and executed it as a free act and deed for the purposes expressed therein. The witnesses, each on oath, stated to me in the presence and hearing of the testator that the testator had declared to them that the instrument is the testator's last will and testament or a codicil to the testator's last will and testament and that the testator executed the instrument as such and wished each of them to sign it as a witness; and under oath each witness stated further that the witness had signed the same as witness in the presence of the testator and at the testator's request; that the testator was 14 years of age or over and of sound mind; and that each of the witnesses was then at least 14 years of age.

_____

Debbie Smith

_____

Bob T. Smith

_____

Cathy Milborn

    Sworn to and subscribed before me by Debbie Smith, testator, sworn to and subscribed before me by _____ and _____, witnesses, this ____ day of _____, 20__.

(SEAL)

_____

(Signed)

_____

(Official Capacity of Officer)

Statutory Durable Power of Attorney

NOTICE: THE POWERS GRANTED BY THIS DOCUMENT ARE BROAD AND SWEEPING. THEY ARE EXPLAINED IN THE DURABLE POWER OF ATTORNEY ACT, CHAPTER XII, NEW MEXICO PROBATE CODE. IF YOU HAVE ANY QUESTIONS ABOUT THESE POWERS, OBTAIN COMPETENT LEGAL ADVICE. THIS DOCUMENT DOES NOT AUTHORIZE ANYONE TO MAKE MEDICAL AND OTHER HEALTH-CARE DECISIONS FOR YOU. YOU MAY REVOKE THIS POWER OF ATTORNEY IF YOU LATER WISH TO DO SO.

I, Bob T. Smith, who resides at 1000 Residential Lane, Lovington, NM, 11111 appoint:

Debbie Smith, who resides at 1000 Residential Lane, Lovington NM, 11111

as my agent (attorney-in-fact) to act for me in any lawful way with respect to all of the following powers except for a power that I have crossed out below.

TO WITHHOLD A POWER, YOU MUST CROSS OUT EACH POWER WITHHELD.

Real property transactions;

Tangible personal property transactions;

Stock and bond transactions;

Commodity and option transactions;

Banking and other financial institution transactions;

Business operating transactions;

Insurance and annuity transactions;

Estate, trust, and other beneficiary transactions;

Claims and litigation;

Personal and family maintenance;

Benefits from social security, Medicare, Medicaid, or other governmental programs or civil or military service;

Retirement plan transactions;

Tax matters.

IF NO POWER LISTED ABOVE IS CROSSED OUT, THIS DOCUMENT SHALL BE CONSTRUED AND INTERPRETED AS A GENERAL POWER OF ATTORNEY AND MY AGENT (ATTORNEY IN FACT) SHALL HAVE THE POWER AND AUTHORITY TO PERFORM OR UNDERTAKE ANY ACTION I COULD PERFORM OR UNDERTAKE IF I WERE PERSONALLY PRESENT.

New Mexico Statutory Durable Power of Attorney of Bob T. Smith

SPECIAL INSTRUCTIONS:

Special instructions applicable to gifts (initial in front of the following sentence to have it apply):

N/A I grant my agent (attorney in fact) the power to apply my property to make gifts, except that the amount of a gift to an individual may not exceed the amount of annual exclusions allowed from the federal gift tax for the calendar year of the gift.

ON THE FOLLOWING LINES YOU MAY GIVE SPECIAL INSTRUCTIONS LIMITING OR EXTENDING THE POWERS GRANTED TO YOUR AGENT.

None. _____
_____
_____
_____
_____

UNLESS YOU DIRECT OTHERWISE ABOVE, THIS POWER OF ATTORNEY IS EFFECTIVE IMMEDIATELY AND WILL CONTINUE UNTIL IT IS REVOKED.

CHOOSE ONE OF THE FOLLOWING ALTERNATIVES BY CROSSING OUT THE ALTERNATIVE NOT CHOSEN:

(A) This power of attorney is not affected by my subsequent disability or incapacity.

(B) This power of attorney becomes effective upon my disability or incapacity.

YOU SHOULD CHOOSE ALTERNATIVE (A) IF THIS POWER OF ATTORNEY IS TO BECOME EFFECTIVE ON THE DATE IT IS EXECUTED.

IF NEITHER (A) NOR (B) IS CROSSED OUT, IT WILL BE ASSUMED THAT YOU CHOSE ALTERNATIVE (A).

If Alternative (B) is chosen and a definition of my disability or incapacity is not contained in this power of attorney, I shall be considered disabled or incapacitated for purposes of this power of attorney if a physician certifies in writing at a date later than the date this power of attorney is executed that, based on the physician's medical examination of me, I am mentally incapable of managing my financial affairs. I authorize the physician who examines me for this purpose to disclose my physical or mental condition to another person for purposes of this power of attorney. A third party who accepts this power of attorney is fully protected from any action taken under this power of attorney that is based on the determination made by a physician of my disability or incapacity.

I agree that any third party who receives a copy of this document may act under it. Revocation of the durable power of attorney is not effective as to a third party until the third party receives actual notice of the revocation. I agree to indemnify the third party for any claims that arise against the third party because of reliance on this power of attorney.

If any agent named by me dies, becomes legally disabled, resigns, or refuses to act, I name the following (each to act alone and successively, in the order named) as successor(s) to that agent:

Sean Smith, who has permanent residence at 1000 Residential Lane, Lovington, NM, 11111

Signed this 2nd day of July 2015:

_____

Bob T. Smith

New Mexico Statutory Durable Power of Attorney of Bob T. Smith

STATE OF NEW MEXICO

COUNTY OF LEA COUNTY

This document was acknowledged before me on 2ND DAY OF JULY 2015 by Bob T. Smith

_____

Notary Public, State of New Mexico

THE ATTORNEY IN FACT OR AGENT, BY ACCEPTING OR ACTING UNDER THE APPOINTMENT, ASSUMES THE FIDUCIARY AND OTHER LEGAL RESPONSIBILITIES OF AN AGENT.

New Mexico Statutory Durable Power of Attorney of Bob T. Smith

Directive to Physicians and Family or Surrogates

Instructions for completing this document:

This is an important legal document known as an Advance Directive. It is designed to help you communicate your wishes about medical treatment at some time in the future when you are unable to make your wishes known because of illness or injury. These wishes are usually based on personal values. In particular, you may want to consider what burdens or hardships of treatment you would be willing to accept for a particular amount of benefit obtained if you were seriously ill.

You are encouraged to discuss your values and wishes with your family or chosen spokesperson, as well as your physician. Your physician, other health-care provider, or medical institution may provide you with various resources to assist you in completing your advance directive. Brief definitions are listed below and may aid you in your discussions and advance planning. Initial the treatment choices that best reflect your personal preferences. Provide a copy of your directive to your physician, usual hospital, and family or spokesperson. Consider a periodic review of this document. By periodic review, you can best assure that the directive reflects your preferences.

In addition to this advance directive, New Mexico law provides for two other types of directives that can be important during a serious illness. These are the Medical Power of Attorney and the Out-of-Hospital Do-Not-Resuscitate Order. You may wish to discuss these with your physician, family, hospital representative, or other advisors. You may also wish to complete a directive related to the donation of organs and tissues.

Directive to Physicians and Family or Surrogates of Bob T. Smith

DIRECTIVE

I, Bob T. Smith, recognize that the best health care is based upon a partnership of trust and communication with my physician. My physician and I will make health-care decisions together as long as I am of sound mind and able to make my wishes known. If there comes a time that I am unable to make medical decisions about myself because of illness or injury, I direct that the following treatment preferences be honored:

Terminal Condition: If, in the judgment of my physician, I am suffering with a terminal condition from which I am expected to die within 6 months, even with available life-sustaining treatment provided in accordance with prevailing standards of medical care:

    Option 1 __X__ I request that all treatments other than those needed to keep me comfortable be discontinued or withheld and my physician allow me to die as gently as possible; OR

    Option 2 _____ I request that I be kept alive in this terminal condition using available life-sustaining treatment. (THIS SELECTION DOES NOT APPLY TO HOSPICE CARE.)

Irreversible Condition: If, in the judgment of my physician, I am suffering with an irreversible condition so that I cannot care for myself or make decisions for myself and am expected to die without life-sustaining treatment provided in accordance with prevailing standards of care:

    Option 1 __X__ I request that all treatments other than those needed to keep me comfortable be discontinued or withheld and my physician allow me to die as gently as possible; OR

    Option 2 _____ I request that I be kept alive in this irreversible condition using available life-sustaining treatment. (THIS SELECTION DOES NOT APPLY TO HOSPICE CARE.)

Additional requests: (After discussion with your physician, you may wish to consider listing particular treatments in this space that you do or do not want in specific circumstances, such as artificial nutrition and fluids, intravenous antibiotics, etc. Be sure to state whether you do or do not want the particular treatment.)

    None. _____

    _____

    _____

    _____

After signing this directive, if my representative or I elect hospice care, I understand and agree that only those treatments needed to keep me comfortable would be provided and I would not be given available life-sustaining treatments.

If I do not have a Medical Power of Attorney, and I am unable to make my wishes known, I designate the following person(s) to make treatment decisions with my physician compatible with my personal values:

    1. N/A _____

    2. N/A _____

(If a Medical Power of Attorney has been executed, then an agent already has been named and you should not list additional names in this document.)

Directive to Physicians and Family or Surrogates of Bob T. Smith

If the above persons are not available, or if I have not designated a spokesperson, I understand that a spokesperson will be chosen for me following standards specified in the laws of New Mexico. If, in the judgment of my physician, my death is imminent within minutes to hours, even with the use of all available medical treatment provided within the prevailing standard of care, I acknowledge that all treatments may be withheld or removed except those needed to maintain my comfort. This directive will remain in effect until I revoke it. No other person may do so.

Signed: _____ Date: July 2, 2015

City, County, State of Residence: _____

STATE OF NEW MEXICO

COUNTY OF LEA COUNTY

This document was acknowledged before me on 2ND day of July 2015 by Bob T. Smith

_____

Notary Public, State of New Mexico

Definitions:

"Artificial nutrition and hydration" means the provision of nutrients or fluids by a tube inserted in a vein, under the skin in the subcutaneous tissues, or in the stomach (gastrointestinal tract).

"Irreversible condition" means a condition, injury, or illness:

(1) that may be treated, but is never cured or eliminated;

(2) that leaves a person unable to care for or make decisions for the person's own self; and

(3) that, without life-sustaining treatment provided in accordance with the prevailing standard of medical care, is fatal.

Explanation: Many serious illnesses such as cancer, failure of major organs (kidney, heart, liver, or lung), and serious brain disease such as Alzheimer's dementia may be considered irreversible early on. There is no cure, but the patient may be kept alive for prolonged periods of time if the patient receives life-sustaining treatments. Late in the course of the same illness, the disease may be considered terminal when, even with treatment, the patient is expected to die. You may wish to consider which burdens of treatment you would be willing to accept in an effort to achieve a particular outcome. This is a very personal decision that you may wish to discuss with your physician, family, or other important persons in your life.

"Life-sustaining treatment" means treatment that, based on reasonable medical judgment, sustains the life of a patient and without which the patient will die. The term includes both life-sustaining medications and artificial life support such as mechanical breathing machines, kidney dialysis treatment, and artificial hydration and nutrition. The term does not include the administration of pain management medication, the performance of a medical procedure necessary to provide comfort care, or any other medical care provided to alleviate a patient's pain.

"Terminal condition" means an incurable condition caused by injury, disease, or illness that according to reasonable medical judgment will produce death within six months, even with available life-sustaining treatment provided in accordance with the prevailing standard of medical care.

Explanation: Many serious illnesses may be considered irreversible early in the course of the illness, but they may not be considered terminal until the disease is fairly advanced. In thinking about terminal illness and its treatment, you again may wish to consider the relative benefits and burdens of treatment and discuss your wishes with your physician, family, or other important persons in your life.

Directive to Physicians and Family or Surrogates of Bob T. Smith

Information Concerning the Medical Power of Attorney

THIS IS AN IMPORTANT LEGAL DOCUMENT. BEFORE SIGNING THIS DOCUMENT, YOU SHOULD KNOW THESE IMPORTANT FACTS:

Except to the extent you state otherwise, this document gives the person you name as your agent the authority to make any and all health-care decisions for you in accordance with your wishes, including your religious and moral beliefs, when you are no longer capable of making them yourself. Because "health care" means any treatment, service, or procedure to maintain, diagnose, or treat your physical or mental condition, your agent has the power to make a broad range of health-care decisions for you. Your agent may consent, refuse to consent, or withdraw consent to medical treatment and may make decisions about withdrawing or withholding life-sustaining treatment. Your agent may not consent to voluntary inpatient mental health services, convulsive treatment, psychosurgery, or abortion. A physician must comply with your agent's instructions or allow you to be transferred to another physician.

Your agent's authority begins when your doctor certifies that you lack the competence to make health-care decisions.

Your agent is obligated to follow your instructions when making decisions on your behalf. Unless you state otherwise, your agent has the same authority to make decisions about your health care as you would have had.

It is important that you discuss this document with your physician or other health-care provider before you sign it to make sure that you understand the nature and range of decisions that may be made on your behalf. If you do not have a physician, you should talk with someone else who is knowledgeable about these issues and can answer your questions. You do not need a lawyer's assistance to complete this document, but if there is anything in this document that you do not understand, you should ask a lawyer to explain it to you.

The person you appoint as agent should be someone you know and trust. The person must be 18 years of age or older or a person under 18 years of age who has had the disabilities of minority removed. If you appoint your health or residential care provider (e.g., your physician or an employee of a home health agency, hospital, nursing home, or residential care home, other than a relative), that person has to choose between acting as your agent or as your health or residential care provider; the law does not permit a person to do both at the same time.

You should inform the person you appoint that you want the person to be your health-care agent. You should discuss this document with your agent and your physician and give each a signed copy. You should indicate on the document itself the people and institutions who have signed copies. Your agent is not liable for health-care decisions made in good faith on your behalf.

Even after you have signed this document, you have the right to make health-care decisions for yourself as long as you are able to do so and treatment cannot be given to you or stopped over your objection. You have the right to revoke the authority granted to your agent by informing your agent or your health or residential care provider orally or in writing or by your execution of a subsequent medical power of attorney. Unless you state otherwise, your appointment of a spouse dissolves on divorce.

This document may not be changed or modified. If you want to make changes in the document, you must make an entirely new one.

You may wish to designate an alternate agent in the event that your agent is unwilling, unable, or ineligible to act as your agent. Any alternate agent you designate has the same authority to make health-care decisions for you.

THIS POWER OF ATTORNEY IS NOT VALID UNLESS IT IS NOTARIZED OR SIGNED IN THE PRESENCE OF TWO COMPETENT ADULT WITNESSES. IF SIGNED BEFORE WITNESSES, THE FOLLOWING PERSONS MAY NOT ACT AS ONE OF THE WITNESSES:

> (1) the person you have designated as your agent;

> (2) a person related to you by blood or marriage;

Directive to Physicians and Family or Surrogates of Bob T. Smith

(3) a person entitled to any part of your estate after your death under a will or codicil executed by you or by operation of law;

(4) your attending physician;

(5) an employee of your attending physician;

(6) an employee of a health-care facility in which you are a patient if the employee is providing direct patient care to you or is an officer, director, partner, or business office employee of the health-care facility or of any parent organization of the health-care facility; or

(7) a person who, at the time this power of attorney is executed, has a claim against any part of your estate after your death.

I have been provided with this disclosure statement explaining the effect of the Medical Power of Attorney. I have read and understand the information contained in this disclosure statement prior to executing the Medical Power of Attorney itself.

Dated: July 2, 2015

_____
Bob T. Smith

Medical Power of Attorney

DESIGNATION OF HEALTH-CARE AGENT.

I, Bob T. Smith appoint:

Name: Debbie Smith

Address: 1000 Residential Lane, Lovington, NM, 11111

Phone: 936-695-0000

E-mail: Debbiesmith63@gmail.com

as my agent to make any and all health-care decisions for me, except to the extent I state otherwise in this document. This medical power of attorney takes effect if I become unable to make my own health-care decisions and this fact is certified in writing by my physician.

LIMITATIONS ON THE DECISION-MAKING AUTHORITY OF MY AGENT ARE AS FOLLOWS:

None.

DESIGNATION OF ALTERNATE AGENT.

(You are not required to designate an alternate agent but you may do so. An alternate agent may make the same health-care decisions as the designated agent if the designated agent is unable or unwilling to act as your agent. If the agent designated is your spouse, the designation is automatically revoked by law if your marriage is dissolved.)

If the person designated as my agent is unable or unwilling to make health-care decisions for me, I designate the following persons to serve as my agent to make health-care decisions for me as authorized by this document, who serve in the following order:

A. First Alternate Agent: Ken R. Smith

Address: 8514 Cat Tails Lane, Marion, IN 46953

Phone: 765-678-9912

B. Second Alternate Agent: Cathy Milborn

Address: 5111 Daisy Lane, Lovington, NM, 11112

Phone: 936-233-9876

The original of this document is kept at:

Law offices of Kern, Davis, and Jefferson

Lovington, NM, 11111

The following individuals or institutions have signed copies:

Name: Law Offices of Kern, Davis, and Jefferson

Address: 8000 Country Club Road, Lovington, NM, 11112

936-234-5567

Medical Power of Attorney of Bob T. Smith

DURATION.

I understand that this power of attorney exists indefinitely from the date I execute this document unless I establish a shorter time or revoke the power of attorney. If I am unable to make health-care decisions for myself when this power of attorney expires, the authority I have granted my agent continues to exist until the time I become able to make health-care decisions for myself.

(IF APPLICABLE) This power of attorney ends on the following date: **N/A**

PRIOR DESIGNATIONS REVOKED.

I revoke any prior medical power of attorney.

ACKNOWLEDGMENT OF DISCLOSURE STATEMENT.

I have been provided with a disclosure statement explaining the effect of this document. I have read and understand that information contained in the disclosure statement.

(YOU MUST DATE AND SIGN THIS POWER OF ATTORNEY.)

I sign my name to this medical power of attorney on 2nd Day of July 2015 at Lovington, New Mexico.

_____

Bob T. Smith

STATE OF NEW MEXICO

COUNTY OF LEA COUNTY

This document was acknowledged before me on 2ND DAY OF JULY 2015 by Bob T. Smith

_____

Notary Public, State of New Mexico

Medical Power of Attorney of Bob T. Smith

Declaration of Guardian in the Event of
Later Incapacity or Need of Guardian

I, Bob T. Smith, make this Declaration of Guardian, to operate if the need for a guardian for me later arises.

1. I designate Debbie Smith to serve as guardian of my person. In addition, I appoint Cathy Milborn to serve as first alternate guardian of my person and Ken R. Smith to serve as second alternate guardian of my person.

2. I designate Debbie Smith to serve as guardian of my estate. In addition, I appoint Cathy Milborn to serve as first alternate guardian of my estate and Ken R. Smith to serve as second alternate guardian of my estate.

3. If any guardian or alternate guardian dies, does not qualify, or resigns, the next named alternate guardian becomes my guardian.

4. I expressly disqualify the following person from serving as guardian of my person: NONE.

5. I expressly disqualify the following person from serving as guardian of my estate: NONE.

Signed: July 2, 2015

Declaration of Guardian for Bob T. Smith

I, Bob T. Smith, as Declarant, declare to the undersigned witnesses and to the undersigned authority that this instrument is my Declaration of Guardian, that I have willingly made and executed it for the purposes expressed in the Declaration in the presence of the undersigned witnesses, all of whom were present at the same time, as my free act and deed, and that I have requested each of the undersigned witnesses to sign this Declaration in my presence and in the presence of each other. I now sign this Declaration of Guardian in the presence of the attesting witnesses and the undersigned authority on this 2nd day of July 2015.

_____

Bob T. Smith

The undersigned, Cathy Milborn_____ and __Ken R. Smith_____, each being above fourteen years of age, after being duly sworn, declare to the Declarant and to the undersigned authority that the Declarant declared to us that this instrument is the Declarant's Declaration of Guardianship and that the Declarant requested us to act as witnesses to the Declarant's Declaration of Guardianship and signature. The Declarant then signed this Declaration of Guardianship in our presence, all of us being present at the same time. The Declarant is 18 years of age or over (or being under such age, is or has been lawfully married, or is a member of the armed forces of the United States or of an auxiliary thereof or of the Maritime Service), and we believe the Declarant to be of sound mind. We now sign our names as attesting witnesses in the presence of the Declarant, each other, and the undersigned authority on this 2nd day of July 2015.

_____

_____, Witness

_____

_____

_____

_____, Witness

_____

STATE OF NEW MEXICO

COUNTY OF LEA COUNTY

Subscribed and sworn before me by Bob T. Smith, the Declarant, and by _____, and _____, the witnesses, on 2nd day of July 2015.

_____

Notary Public, State of New Mexico

Declaration of Guardian for Bob T. Smith

Authorization for Release of
Bob T. Smith's
Protected Health Information

(Valid Authorization Under 45 CFR Chapter 164)

Statement of Intent: It is my understanding that Congress passed a law entitled the Health Insurance Portability and Accountability Act ("HIPAA") that limits use, disclosure or release of my "individually identifiable health information," as HIPAA and the supporting Regulations define that phrase. I am signing this Authorization because it is crucial that my health-care providers readily use, release or disclose my protected medical information to, or as directed by, that person or those persons designated in this Authorization to allow them to discuss with, and obtain advice from, others or to facilitate decisions regarding my health care when I otherwise may not be able to do so without regard to whether any health-care provider has certified in writing that I am incompetent for purposes of HIPAA.

1. Appointment of Authorized Recipients

Therefore, I, Bob T. Smith, an individual, hereby appoint the following persons or entities, or any of them, as Authorized Recipients for health-care disclosure under the Standards for Privacy of Individually Identifiable Health Care Information (45 CFR Parts 160 and 164) under the Health Insurance Portability and Accountability Act of 1996 ("HIPAA"):

Debbie Smith

Cathy Milborn—Sister-in-law

Ken R. Smith—Brother

the Trustee or Successor Trustee of any trust of which I am a beneficiary or a trustee, for the sole specific purpose of determining my capacity as defined in the trust agreement.

2. Grant of Authority

I authorize all covered entities as defined in HIPAA, including but not limited to a doctor (including but not limited to a physician, podiatrist, chiropractor, or osteopath), psychiatrist, psychologist, dentist, therapist, nurse, hospital, clinic, pharmacy, laboratory, ambulance service, assisted living facility, residential care facility, bed and board facility, nursing home, medical insurance company or any other health-care provider or affiliate (including but not limited to _____), to use, release and disclose my individually identifiable health information to my Authorized Recipients in accordance with and as authorized by 45 CFR Sec(s). 164.502(a)(1)(i) and (iv), 164.502(a)(2)(i), 164.524 and 164.528, including but not limited to, medical reports and/or records concerning my medical history, condition, diagnosis, testing, prognosis, treatment, billing information and identity of health-care providers, whether past, present or future and any other information which is in any way related to my health care except as specifically limited as to any Authorized Recipient named in Paragraph 1 above.

This disclosure includes the ability to ask questions and discuss my individually identifiable health information with the person or entity that has possession of my individually identifiable health information even if I am fully competent to ask questions and discuss this matter at the time.

It is my intention to give a full authorization for access to, disclosure, and release of ANY individually identifiable health information by or to the persons named in this Authorization as if each person were me.

3. Termination

My subsequent disability or incapacity will neither affect nor terminate this Authorization. This Authorization will terminate 1 year following my death or upon my written revocation expressly referring to this Authorization and the date it is actually received by the covered entity. Proof of receipt of my written revocation may be by certified mail, registered mail, facsimile, or any other receipt evidencing actual receipt by the covered entity. Such revocation is effective upon the actual receipt of the notice by the covered entity except to the extent that the covered entity has taken action in reliance on it.

HIPPA Authorization for Bob T. Smith

4. Re-disclosure

By signing this Authorization, I acknowledge that the information used, disclosed, or released pursuant to this Authorization may be subject to re-disclosure by an Authorized Recipient and the information once disclosed will no longer be protected by the rules created in HIPAA. No covered entity may require an Authorized Recipient to indemnify the covered entity or agree to perform any act in order for the covered entity to comply with this Authorization.

5. Instructions to the Authorized Recipient

An Authorized Recipient may bring a legal action in any applicable forum against any covered entity that refuses to recognize and accept this Authorization for the purposes that I have expressed. Additionally, an Authorized Recipient is authorized to sign any documents that the Authorized Recipient deems appropriate to obtain use, disclosure, or release of my individually identifiable health information.

6. Effect of Duplicate Originals or Copies

If I have executed this Authorization in multiple counterparts, each counterpart original will have equal force and effect. An Authorized Recipient may make photocopies (photocopies shall include: facsimiles and digital or other reproductions, hereafter referred to collectively as "photocopy") of this Authorization and each photocopy will have the same force and effect as the original.

7. My Waiver and Release

With regard to information disclosed pursuant to this Authorization, I waive any right of privacy that I may have under the authority of the Health Insurance Portability and Accountability Act of 1996, Public Law 104-191 (HIPAA), any amendment or successor to that Act, or any similar state or federal act, rule or regulation. In addition, I hereby release any covered entity that acts in reliance on this Authorization from any liability that may accrue from the use or disclosure of my individually identifiable health information in reliance upon this Authorization and for any actions taken by an Authorized Recipient.

8. Severability

I intend that this authorization conform to United States and New Mexico law. In the event that any provision of this document is invalid, the remaining provisions shall nonetheless remain in full force and effect.

I understand that I have the right to receive a copy of this authorization. I also understand that I have the right to revoke this authorization and that any revocation of this authorization must be in writing.

Dated: July 2, 2015

_____

Bob T. Smith, Principal

STATE OF NEW MEXICO

COUNTY OF LEA COUNTY

This document was acknowledged before me on 2nd day of July 2015 by Bob T. Smith, as Principal.

_____

Notary Public, State of New Mexico

HIPPA Authorization for Bob T. Smith

Declaration of Appointment of Guardian for
My Children in the Event of My Death or Incapacity

I, Bob T. Smith, make this Declaration of Guardian for my children, listed as follows, in the event of my death or incapacity and my spouse's inability to care for my children due to death or incapacity:

I designate Cathy Milborn as guardian of the person of my children. In addition, I designate Ken R. Smith as first alternate guardian of the person of my children.

I designate Cathy Milborn as guardian of the estate of my children. In addition, I designate Ken R. Smith as first alternate guardian of the estate of my children.

I direct that any guardian of the person of any child serve without bond.

If any guardian or alternate guardian dies, does not qualify, or resigns, the next named alternate guardian becomes guardian of my children.

If any person named as guardian is not a resident of the state I am a resident, it is my desire that any child of mine under legal disability move to the place where the guardian so named resides.

Signed: July 2, 2015

Declaration of Guardian for Children of Bob T. Smith

...Smith, as Declarant, declare to the undersigned witnesses and to the undersigned authority that this ...ment is my Declaration of Guardian for Children, that I have willingly made and executed it for the purposes ...pressed in the Declaration in the presence of the undersigned witnesses, all of whom were present at the same time, as my free act and deed, and that I have requested each of the undersigned witnesses to sign this Declaration in my presence and in the presence of each other. I now sign this Declaration of Guardian for Children in the presence of the attesting witnesses and the undersigned authority on this 2nd day of July 2015.

_____

Bob T. Smith

The undersigned, ___Cathy Milborn_____ and __Ken R. Smith_____, each being above fourteen years of age, after being duly sworn, declare to the Declarant and to the undersigned authority that the Declarant declared to us that this instrument is the Declarant's Declaration of Guardian for Children and that the Declarant requested us to act as witnesses to the Declarant's Declaration of Guardian for Children and signature. The Declarant then signed this Declaration of Guardian for Children in our presence, all of us being present at the same time. The Declarant is 18 years of age or over (or being under such age, is or has been lawfully married, or is a member of the armed forces of the United States or of an auxiliary thereof or of the Maritime Service), and we believe the Declarant to be of sound mind. We now sign our names as attesting witnesses in the presence of the Declarant, each other, and the undersigned authority on this 2nd day of July 2015.

_____

_____, Witness

_____

_____

_____

_____, Witness

_____

_____

STATE OF NEW MEXICO

COUNTY OF TRAVIS

Subscribed and sworn before me by Bob T. Smith, the Declarant, and by _____, and _____, the witnesses, on 2nd day of July 2015.

_____

Notary Public, State of New Mexico

Declaration of Guardian for Children of Bob T. Smith

Personal Property Memorandum
of Bob T. Smith

My Will refers to the disposition at my death of certain items of tangible personal property in accordance with a memorandum signed by me. I do hereby make this memorandum for that purpose.

If an item is marked with an (*) it is to be distributed to the person designated to receive the item only if my spouse predeceases me.

If the recipient of a particular item of personal property does not survive me, such item shall be disposed of as though it had not been listed in this memorandum.

Personal Property Distributions
for Bob T. Smith

Description of Tangible Personal Property	Person to Receive Property Address and Relationship	(*)
_____	_____	_____
_____	_____	_____
_____	_____	_____
_____	_____	_____
_____	_____	_____
_____	_____	_____
_____	_____	_____
_____	_____	_____
_____	_____	_____
_____	_____	_____

Dated: July 2, 2015 _____

_____
Bob T. Smith
Page _____

Personal Property Distributions
for Bob T. Smith

Description of Tangible Personal Property	Person to Receive Property Address and Relationship	(*)
_____	_____	_____
_____	_____	_____
_____	_____	_____
_____	_____	_____
_____	_____	_____
_____	_____	_____
_____	_____	_____
_____	_____	_____
_____	_____	_____
_____	_____	_____
_____	_____	_____
_____	_____	_____
_____	_____	_____
_____	_____	_____
_____	_____	_____
_____	_____	_____

Dated: July 2, 2015 _____

_____
Bob T. Smith
Page _____

Personal Property Distributions
for Bob T. Smith

Description of Tangible Personal Property	Person to Receive Property Address and Relationship	(*)
_____	_____	_____
_____	_____	_____
_____	_____	_____
_____	_____	_____
_____	_____	_____
_____	_____	_____
_____	_____	_____
_____	_____	_____
_____	_____	_____
_____	_____	_____
_____	_____	_____
_____	_____	_____
_____	_____	_____
_____	_____	_____
_____	_____	_____

Dated: July 2, 2015 _____

_____
Bob T. Smith
Page _____

Statutory Durable Power of Attorney

NOTICE: THE POWERS GRANTED BY THIS DOCUMENT ARE BROAD AND SWEEPING. THEY ARE EXPLAINED IN THE DURABLE POWER OF ATTORNEY ACT, CHAPTER XII, NEW MEXICO PROBATE CODE. IF YOU HAVE ANY QUESTIONS ABOUT THESE POWERS, OBTAIN COMPETENT LEGAL ADVICE. THIS DOCUMENT DOES NOT AUTHORIZE ANYONE TO MAKE MEDICAL AND OTHER HEALTH-CARE DECISIONS FOR YOU. YOU MAY REVOKE THIS POWER OF ATTORNEY IF YOU LATER WISH TO DO SO.

I, Debbie Smith, who resides at 1000 Residential Lane, Lovington, NM, 11111 appoint:

Bob T. Smith, who resides at 1000 Residential Lane, Lovington NM, 11111

as my agent (attorney-in-fact) to act for me in any lawful way with respect to all of the following powers except for a power that I have crossed out below.

TO WITHHOLD A POWER, YOU MUST CROSS OUT EACH POWER WITHHELD.

Real property transactions;

Tangible personal property transactions;

Stock and bond transactions;

Commodity and option transactions;

Banking and other financial institution transactions;

Business operating transactions;

Insurance and annuity transactions;

Estate, trust, and other beneficiary transactions;

Claims and litigation;

Personal and family maintenance;

Benefits from social security, Medicare, Medicaid, or other governmental programs or civil or military service;

Retirement plan transactions;

Tax matters.

IF NO POWER LISTED ABOVE IS CROSSED OUT, THIS DOCUMENT SHALL BE CONSTRUED AND INTERPRETED AS A GENERAL POWER OF ATTORNEY AND MY AGENT (ATTORNEY IN FACT) SHALL HAVE THE POWER AND AUTHORITY TO PERFORM OR UNDERTAKE ANY ACTION I COULD PERFORM OR UNDERTAKE IF I WERE PERSONALLY PRESENT.

New Mexico Statutory Durable Power of Attorney of Debbie Smith

SPECIAL INSTRUCTIONS:

Special instructions applicable to gifts (initial in front of the following sentence to have it apply):

N/A I grant my agent (attorney in fact) the power to apply my property to make gifts, except that the amount of a gift to an individual may not exceed the amount of annual exclusions allowed from the federal gift tax for the calendar year of the gift.

ON THE FOLLOWING LINES YOU MAY GIVE SPECIAL INSTRUCTIONS LIMITING OR EXTENDING THE POWERS GRANTED TO YOUR AGENT.

None. _____
_____
_____
_____
_____

UNLESS YOU DIRECT OTHERWISE ABOVE, THIS POWER OF ATTORNEY IS EFFECTIVE IMMEDIATELY AND WILL CONTINUE UNTIL IT IS REVOKED.

CHOOSE ONE OF THE FOLLOWING ALTERNATIVES BY CROSSING OUT THE ALTERNATIVE NOT CHOSEN:

(A) This power of attorney is not affected by my subsequent disability or incapacity.

(B) This power of attorney becomes effective upon my disability or incapacity.

YOU SHOULD CHOOSE ALTERNATIVE (A) IF THIS POWER OF ATTORNEY IS TO BECOME EFFECTIVE ON THE DATE IT IS EXECUTED.

IF NEITHER (A) NOR (B) IS CROSSED OUT, IT WILL BE ASSUMED THAT YOU CHOSE ALTERNATIVE (A).

If Alternative (B) is chosen and a definition of my disability or incapacity is not contained in this power of attorney, I shall be considered disabled or incapacitated for purposes of this power of attorney if a physician certifies in writing at a date later than the date this power of attorney is executed that, based on the physician's medical examination of me, I am mentally incapable of managing my financial affairs. I authorize the physician who examines me for this purpose to disclose my physical or mental condition to another person for purposes of this power of attorney. A third party who accepts this power of attorney is fully protected from any action taken under this power of attorney that is based on the determination made by a physician of my disability or incapacity.

I agree that any third party who receives a copy of this document may act under it. Revocation of the durable power of attorney is not effective as to a third party until the third party receives actual notice of the revocation. I agree to indemnify the third party for any claims that arise against the third party because of reliance on this power of attorney.

If any agent named by me dies, becomes legally disabled, resigns, or refuses to act, I name the following (each to act alone and successively, in the order named) as successor(s) to that agent:

Sean Smith, who has permanent residence at 1000 Residential Lane, Lovington, NM, 11111

Signed this 2nd day of July 2015:

_____

Debbie Smith

New Mexico Statutory Durable Power of Attorney of Debbie Smith

STATE OF NEW MEXICO

COUNTY OF LEA COUNTY

This document was acknowledged before me on 2ND DAY OF JULY 2015 by Debbie Smith

_____

Notary Public, State of New Mexico

THE ATTORNEY IN FACT OR AGENT, BY ACCEPTING OR ACTING UNDER THE APPOINTMENT, ASSUMES THE FIDUCIARY AND OTHER LEGAL RESPONSIBILITIES OF AN AGENT.

New Mexico Statutory Durable Power of Attorney of Debbie Smith

Directive to Physicians and Family or Surrogates

Instructions for completing this document:

This is an important legal document known as an Advance Directive. It is designed to help you communicate your wishes about medical treatment at some time in the future when you are unable to make your wishes known because of illness or injury. These wishes are usually based on personal values. In particular, you may want to consider what burdens or hardships of treatment you would be willing to accept for a particular amount of benefit obtained if you were seriously ill.

You are encouraged to discuss your values and wishes with your family or chosen spokesperson, as well as your physician. Your physician, other health-care provider, or medical institution may provide you with various resources to assist you in completing your advance directive. Brief definitions are listed below and may aid you in your discussions and advance planning. Initial the treatment choices that best reflect your personal preferences. Provide a copy of your directive to your physician, usual hospital, and family or spokesperson. Consider a periodic review of this document. By periodic review, you can best assure that the directive reflects your preferences.

In addition to this advance directive, New Mexico law provides for two other types of directives that can be important during a serious illness. These are the Medical Power of Attorney and the Out-of-Hospital Do-Not-Resuscitate Order. You may wish to discuss these with your physician, family, hospital representative, or other advisers. You may also wish to complete a directive related to the donation of organs and tissues.

Directive to Physicians and Family or Surrogates of Debbie Smith

DIRECTIVE

I, Debbie Smith recognize that the best health care is based upon a partnership of trust and communication with my physician. My physician and I will make health-care decisions together as long as I am of sound mind and able to make my wishes known. If there comes a time that I am unable to make medical decisions about myself because of illness or injury, I direct that the following treatment preferences be honored:

Terminal Condition: If, in the judgment of my physician, I am suffering with a terminal condition from which I am expected to die within 6 months, even with available life-sustaining treatment provided in accordance with prevailing standards of medical care:

> **Option 1**   __X__   I request that all treatments other than those needed to keep me comfortable be discontinued or withheld and my physician allow me to die as gently as possible; OR

> **Option 2**   _____   I request that I be kept alive in this terminal condition using available life-sustaining treatment. (THIS SELECTION DOES NOT APPLY TO HOSPICE CARE.)

Irreversible Condition: If, in the judgment of my physician, I am suffering with an irreversible condition so that I cannot care for myself or make decisions for myself and am expected to die without life-sustaining treatment provided in accordance with prevailing standards of care:

> **Option 1**   __X__   I request that all treatments other than those needed to keep me comfortable be discontinued or withheld and my physician allow me to die as gently as possible; OR

> **Option 2**   _____   I request that I be kept alive in this irreversible condition using available life-sustaining treatment. (THIS SELECTION DOES NOT APPLY TO HOSPICE CARE.)

Additional requests: (After discussion with your physician, you may wish to consider listing particular treatments in this space that you do or do not want in specific circumstances, such as artificial nutrition and fluids, intravenous antibiotics, etc. Be sure to state whether you do or do not want the particular treatment.)

None. _____

_____

_____

_____

After signing this directive, if my representative or I elect hospice care, I understand and agree that only those treatments needed to keep me comfortable would be provided and I would not be given available life-sustaining treatments.

If I do not have a Medical Power of Attorney, and I am unable to make my wishes known, I designate the following person(s) to make treatment decisions with my physician compatible with my personal values:

> 1. N/A _____

> 2. N/A _____

(If a Medical Power of Attorney has been executed, then an agent already has been named and you should not list additional names in this document.)

Directive to Physicians and Family or Surrogates of Debbie Smith

If the above persons are not available, or if I have not designated a spokesperson, I understand that a spokesperson will be chosen for me following standards specified in the laws of New Mexico. If, in the judgment of my physician, my death is imminent within minutes to hours, even with the use of all available medical treatment provided within the prevailing standard of care, I acknowledge that all treatments may be withheld or removed except those needed to maintain my comfort. This directive will remain in effect until I revoke it. No other person may do so.

Signed: _____ Date: July 2, 2015

City, County, State of Residence: _____

STATE OF NEW MEXICO

COUNTY OF LEA COUNTY

This document was acknowledged before me on 2ND day of July 2015 by Debbie Smith

_____

Notary Public, State of New Mexico

Definitions:

"Artificial nutrition and hydration" means the provision of nutrients or fluids by a tube inserted in a vein, under the skin in the subcutaneous tissues, or in the stomach (gastrointestinal tract).

"Irreversible condition" means a condition, injury, or illness:

(1) that may be treated, but is never cured or eliminated;

(2) that leaves a person unable to care for or make decisions for the person's own self; and

(3) that, without life-sustaining treatment provided in accordance with the prevailing standard of medical care, is fatal.

Explanation: Many serious illnesses such as cancer, failure of major organs (kidney, heart, liver, or lung), and serious brain disease such as Alzheimer's dementia may be considered irreversible early on. There is no cure, but the patient may be kept alive for prolonged periods of time if the patient receives life-sustaining treatments. Late in the course of the same illness, the disease may be considered terminal when, even with treatment, the patient is expected to die. You may wish to consider which burdens of treatment you would be willing to accept in an effort to achieve a particular outcome. This is a very personal decision that you may wish to discuss with your physician, family, or other important persons in your life.

"Life-sustaining treatment" means treatment that, based on reasonable medical judgment, sustains the life of a patient and without which the patient will die. The term includes both life-sustaining medications and artificial life support such as mechanical breathing machines, kidney dialysis treatment, and artificial hydration and nutrition. The term does not include the administration of pain management medication, the performance of a medical procedure necessary to provide comfort care, or any other medical care provided to alleviate a patient's pain.

"Terminal condition" means an incurable condition caused by injury, disease, or illness that according to reasonable medical judgment will produce death within six months, even with available life-sustaining treatment provided in accordance with the prevailing standard of medical care.

Explanation: Many serious illnesses may be considered irreversible early in the course of the illness, but they may not be considered terminal until the disease is fairly advanced. In thinking about terminal illness and its treatment, you again may wish to consider the relative benefits and burdens of treatment and discuss your wishes with your physician, family, or other important persons in your life.

Directive to Physicians and Family or Surrogates of Debbie Smith

Information Concerning the Medical Power of Attorney

THIS IS AN IMPORTANT LEGAL DOCUMENT. BEFORE SIGNING THIS DOCUMENT, YOU SHOULD KNOW THESE IMPORTANT FACTS:

Except to the extent you state otherwise, this document gives the person you name as your agent the authority to make any and all health-care decisions for you in accordance with your wishes, including your religious and moral beliefs, when you are no longer capable of making them yourself. Because "health care" means any treatment, service, or procedure to maintain, diagnose, or treat your physical or mental condition, your agent has the power to make a broad range of health-care decisions for you. Your agent may consent, refuse to consent, or withdraw consent to medical treatment and may make decisions about withdrawing or withholding life-sustaining treatment. Your agent may not consent to voluntary inpatient mental health services, convulsive treatment, psychosurgery, or abortion. A physician must comply with your agent's instructions or allow you to be transferred to another physician.

Your agent's authority begins when your doctor certifies that you lack the competence to make health-care decisions.

Your agent is obligated to follow your instructions when making decisions on your behalf. Unless you state otherwise, your agent has the same authority to make decisions about your health care as you would have had.

It is important that you discuss this document with your physician or other health-care provider before you sign it to make sure that you understand the nature and range of decisions that may be made on your behalf. If you do not have a physician, you should talk with someone else who is knowledgeable about these issues and can answer your questions. You do not need a lawyer's assistance to complete this document, but if there is anything in this document that you do not understand, you should ask a lawyer to explain it to you.

The person you appoint as agent should be someone you know and trust. The person must be 18 years of age or older or a person under 18 years of age who has had the disabilities of minority removed. If you appoint your health or residential care provider (e.g., your physician or an employee of a home health agency, hospital, nursing home, or residential care home, other than a relative), that person has to choose between acting as your agent or as your health or residential care provider; the law does not permit a person to do both at the same time.

You should inform the person you appoint that you want the person to be your health-care agent. You should discuss this document with your agent and your physician and give each a signed copy. You should indicate on the document itself the people and institutions who have signed copies. Your agent is not liable for health-care decisions made in good faith on your behalf.

Even after you have signed this document, you have the right to make health-care decisions for yourself as long as you are able to do so and treatment cannot be given to you or stopped over your objection. You have the right to revoke the authority granted to your agent by informing your agent or your health or residential care provider orally or in writing or by your execution of a subsequent medical power of attorney. Unless you state otherwise, your appointment of a spouse dissolves on divorce.

This document may not be changed or modified. If you want to make changes in the document, you must make an entirely new one.

You may wish to designate an alternate agent in the event that your agent is unwilling, unable, or ineligible to act as your agent. Any alternate agent you designate has the same authority to make health-care decisions for you.

THIS POWER OF ATTORNEY IS NOT VALID UNLESS IT IS NOTARIZED OR SIGNED IN THE PRESENCE OF TWO COMPETENT ADULT WITNESSES. IF SIGNED BEFORE WITNESSES, THE FOLLOWING PERSONS MAY NOT ACT AS ONE OF THE WITNESSES:

(1) the person you have designated as your agent;

(2) a person related to you by blood or marriage;

(3) a person entitled to any part of your estate after your death under a will or codicil executed by you or by operation of law;

(4) your attending physician;

(5) an employee of your attending physician;

(6) an employee of a health-care facility in which you are a patient if the employee is providing direct patient care to you or is an officer, director, partner, or business office employee of the health-care facility or of any parent organization of the health-care facility; or

(7) a person who, at the time this power of attorney is executed, has a claim against any part of your estate after your death.

I have been provided with this disclosure statement explaining the effect of the Medical Power of Attorney. I have read and understand the information contained in this disclosure statement prior to executing the Medical Power of Attorney itself.

Dated: July 2, 2015

_____

Debbie Smith

Medical Power of Attorney

DESIGNATION OF HEALTH-CARE AGENT.

I, Debbie Smith appoint:

Name: Bob T. Smith

Address: 1000 Residential Lane, Lovington, NM, 11111

Phone: 936-695-0000

E-mail: Bsmith@lextinoilsupply.com

as my agent to make any and all health-care decisions for me, except to the extent I state otherwise in this document. This medical power of attorney takes effect if I become unable to make my own health-care decisions and this fact is certified in writing by my physician.

LIMITATIONS ON THE DECISION-MAKING AUTHORITY OF MY AGENT ARE AS FOLLOWS:

None.

DESIGNATION OF ALTERNATE AGENT.

(You are not required to designate an alternate agent but you may do so. An alternate agent may make the same health-care decisions as the designated agent if the designated agent is unable or unwilling to act as your agent. If the agent designated is your spouse, the designation is automatically revoked by law if your marriage is dissolved.)

If the person designated as my agent is unable or unwilling to make health-care decisions for me, I designate the following persons to serve as my agent to make health-care decisions for me as authorized by this document, who serve in the following order:

A. First Alternate Agent: Ken R. Smith

   Address: 8514 Cat Tails Lane, Marion, IN 46953

   Phone: 765-678-9912

B. Second Alternate Agent: Cathy Milborn

   Address: 5111 Daisy Lane, Lovington, NM, 11112

   Phone: 936-233-9876

The original of this document is kept at:

Law offices of Kern, Davis, and Jefferson

Lovington, NM, 11111

The following individuals or institutions have signed copies:

Name: Law Offices of Kern, Davis, and Jefferson

Address: 8000 Country Club Road, Lovington, NM, 11112

   936-234-5567

Medical Power of Attorney of Debbie Smith

DURATION.

I understand that this power of attorney exists indefinitely from the date I execute this document unless I establish a shorter time or revoke the power of attorney. If I am unable to make health-care decisions for myself when this power of attorney expires, the authority I have granted my agent continues to exist until the time I become able to make health-care decisions for myself.

(IF APPLICABLE) This power of attorney ends on the following date: **N/A**

PRIOR DESIGNATIONS REVOKED.

I revoke any prior medical power of attorney.

ACKNOWLEDGMENT OF DISCLOSURE STATEMENT.

I have been provided with a disclosure statement explaining the effect of this document. I have read and understand that information contained in the disclosure statement.

(YOU MUST DATE AND SIGN THIS POWER OF ATTORNEY.)

I sign my name to this medical power of attorney on 2nd Day of July 2015 at Lovington, New Mexico.

_____

Debbie Smith

STATE OF NEW MEXICO

COUNTY OF LEA COUNTY

This document was acknowledged before me on 2ND DAY OF JULY 2015 by Debbie Smith

_____

Notary Public, State of New Mexico

Medical Power of Attorney of Debbie Smith

Declaration of Guardian in the Event of
Later Incapacity or Need of Guardian

I, Debbie Smith, make this Declaration of Guardian, to operate if the need for a guardian for me later arises.

1. I designate Bob T. Smith to serve as guardian of my person. In addition, I appoint Cathy Milborn to serve as first alternate guardian of my person and Ken R. Smith to serve as second alternate guardian of my person.

2. I designate Bob T. Smith to serve as guardian of my estate. In addition, I appoint Cathy Milborn to serve as first alternate guardian of my estate and Ken R. Smith to serve as second alternate guardian of my estate.

3. If any guardian or alternate guardian dies, does not qualify, or resigns, the next named alternate guardian becomes my guardian.

4. I expressly disqualify the following person from serving as guardian of my person: NONE.

5. I expressly disqualify the following person from serving as guardian of my estate: NONE.

Signed: July 2, 2015

Declaration of Guardian for Debbie Smith

I, Debbie Smith, as Declarant, declare to the undersigned witnesses and to the undersigned authority that this instrument is my Declaration of Guardian, that I have willingly made and executed it for the purposes expressed in the Declaration in the presence of the undersigned witnesses, all of whom were present at the same time, as my free act and deed, and that I have requested each of the undersigned witnesses to sign this Declaration in my presence and in the presence of each other. I now sign this Declaration of Guardian in the presence of the attesting witnesses and the undersigned authority on this 2nd day of July 2015.

_____

Debbie Smith

The undersigned, Cathy Milborn_____ and __Ken R. Smith_____, each being above fourteen years of age, after being duly sworn, declare to the Declarant and to the undersigned authority that the Declarant declared to us that this instrument is the Declarant's Declaration of Guardianship and that the Declarant requested us to act as witnesses to the Declarant's Declaration of Guardianship and signature. The Declarant then signed this Declaration of Guardianship in our presence, all of us being present at the same time. The Declarant is 18 years of age or over (or being under such age, is or has been lawfully married, or is a member of the armed forces of the United States or of an auxiliary thereof or of the Maritime Service), and we believe the Declarant to be of sound mind. We now sign our names as attesting witnesses in the presence of the Declarant, each other, and the undersigned authority on this 2nd day of July 2015.

_____ 　　　 _____

_____, Witness 　　 _____, Witness

_____ 　　　 _____

_____ 　　　 _____

STATE OF NEW MEXICO

COUNTY OF TRAVIS

Subscribed and sworn before me by Debbie Smith, the Declarant, and by _____, and _____, the witnesses, on 2nd day of July 2015.

_____

Notary Public, State of New Mexico

Declaration of Guardian for Debbie Smith

Authorization for Release of
Debbie Smith's
Protected Health Information

(Valid Authorization Under 45 CFR Chapter 164)

Statement of Intent: It is my understanding that Congress passed a law entitled the Health Insurance Portability and Accountability Act ("HIPAA") that limits use, disclosure or release of my "individually identifiable health information," as HIPAA and the supporting Regulations define that phrase. I am signing this Authorization because it is crucial that my health-care providers readily use, release or disclose my protected medical information to, or as directed by, that person or those persons designated in this Authorization to allow them to discuss with, and obtain advice from, others or to facilitate decisions regarding my health care when I otherwise may not be able to do so without regard to whether any health-care provider has certified in writing that I am incompetent for purposes of HIPAA.

1. Appointment of Authorized Recipients

Therefore, I, Debbie Smith, an individual, hereby appoint the following persons or entities, or any of them, as Authorized Recipients for health-care disclosure under the Standards for Privacy of Individually Identifiable Health Care Information (45 CFR Parts 160 and 164) under the Health Insurance Portability and Accountability Act of 1996 ("HIPAA"):

Bob T. Smith

Cathy Milborn – Sister

Ken R. Smith – Brother-in-law

the Trustee or Successor Trustee of any trust of which I am a beneficiary or a trustee, for the sole specific purpose of determining my capacity as defined in the trust agreement.

2. Grant of Authority

I authorize all covered entities as defined in HIPAA, including but not limited to a doctor (including but not limited to a physician, podiatrist, chiropractor, or osteopath), psychiatrist, psychologist, dentist, therapist, nurse, hospital, clinic, pharmacy, laboratory, ambulance service, assisted living facility, residential care facility, bed and board facility, nursing home, medical insurance company or any other health-care provider or affiliate (including but not limited to _____), to use, release and disclose my individually identifiable health information to my Authorized Recipients in accordance with and as authorized by 45 CFR Sec(s). 164.502(a)(1)(i) and (iv), 164.502(a)(2)(i), 164.524 and 164.528, including but not limited to, medical reports and/or records concerning my medical history, condition, diagnosis, testing, prognosis, treatment, billing information and identity of health-care providers, whether past, present or future and any other information which is in any way related to my health care except as specifically limited as to any Authorized Recipient named in Paragraph 1 above.

This disclosure includes the ability to ask questions and discuss my individually identifiable health information with the person or entity that has possession of my individually identifiable health information even if I am fully competent to ask questions and discuss this matter at the time.

It is my intention to give a full authorization for access to, disclosure, and release of ANY individually identifiable health information by or to the persons named in this Authorization as if each person were me.

3. Termination

My subsequent disability or incapacity will neither affect nor terminate this Authorization. This Authorization will terminate 1 year following my death or upon my written revocation expressly referring to this Authorization and the date it is actually received by the covered entity. Proof of receipt of my written revocation may be by certified mail, registered mail, facsimile, or any other receipt evidencing actual receipt by the covered entity. Such revocation is effective upon the actual receipt of the notice by the covered entity except to the extent that the covered entity has taken action in reliance on it.

HIPPA Authorization for Debbie Smith

4. Re-disclosure

By signing this Authorization, I acknowledge that the information used, disclosed, or released pursuant to this Authorization may be subject to re-disclosure by an Authorized Recipient and the information once disclosed will no longer be protected by the rules created in HIPAA. No covered entity may require an Authorized Recipient to indemnify the covered entity or agree to perform any act in order for the covered entity to comply with this Authorization.

5. Instructions to the Authorized Recipient

An Authorized Recipient may bring a legal action in any applicable forum against any covered entity that refuses to recognize and accept this Authorization for the purposes that I have expressed. Additionally, an Authorized Recipient is authorized to sign any documents that the Authorized Recipient deems appropriate to obtain use, disclosure, or release of my individually identifiable health information.

6. Effect of Duplicate Originals or Copies

If I have executed this Authorization in multiple counterparts, each counterpart original will have equal force and effect. An Authorized Recipient may make photocopies (photocopies shall include: facsimiles and digital or other reproductions, hereafter referred to collectively as "photocopy") of this Authorization and each photocopy will have the same force and effect as the original.

7. My Waiver and Release

With regard to information disclosed pursuant to this Authorization, I waive any right of privacy that I may have under the authority of the Health Insurance Portability and Accountability Act of 1996, Public Law 104-191 (HIPAA), any amendment or successor to that Act, or any similar state or federal act, rule or regulation. In addition, I hereby release any covered entity that acts in reliance on this Authorization from any liability that may accrue from the use or disclosure of my individually identifiable health information in reliance upon this Authorization and for any actions taken by an Authorized Recipient.

8. Severability

I intend that this authorization conform to United States and New Mexico law. In the event that any provision of this document is invalid, the remaining provisions shall nonetheless remain in full force and effect.

I understand that I have the right to receive a copy of this authorization. I also understand that I have the right to revoke this authorization and that any revocation of this authorization must be in writing.

Dated: July 2, 2015

_____

Debbie Smith, Principal

STATE OF NEW MEXICO

COUNTY OF LEA COUNTY

This document was acknowledged before me on 2nd day of July 2015 by Debbie Smith, as Principal.

_____

Notary Public, State of New Mexico

HIPPA Authorization for Debbie Smith

Declaration of Appointment of Guardian for
My Children in the Event of My Death or Incapacity

I, Debbie Smith, make this Declaration of Guardian for my children, listed as follows, in the event of my death or incapacity and my spouse's inability to care for my children due to death or incapacity:

I designate Cathy Milborn as guardian of the person of my children. In addition, I designate Ken R. Smith as first alternate guardian of the person of my children.

I designate Cathy Milborn as guardian of the estate of my children. In addition, I designate Ken R. Smith as first alternate guardian of the estate of my children.

I direct that any guardian of the person of any child serve without bond.

If any guardian or alternate guardian dies, does not qualify, or resigns, the next named alternate guardian becomes guardian of my children.

If any person named as guardian is not a resident of the state I am a resident, it is my desire that any child of mine under legal disability move to the place where the guardian so named resides.

Signed: July 2, 2015

Declaration of Guardian for Children of Debbie Smith

I, Debbie Smith, as Declarant, declare to the undersigned witnesses and to the undersigned authority that this instrument is my Declaration of Guardian for Children, that I have willingly made and executed it for the purposes expressed in the Declaration in the presence of the undersigned witnesses, all of whom were present at the same time, as my free act and deed, and that I have requested each of the undersigned witnesses to sign this Declaration in my presence and in the presence of each other. I now sign this Declaration of Guardian for Children in the presence of the attesting witnesses and the undersigned authority on this 2nd day of July 2015.

_____

Debbie Smith

The undersigned, ___Cathy Milborn_____ and __Ken R. Smith_____, each being above fourteen years of age, after being duly sworn, declare to the Declarant and to the undersigned authority that the Declarant declared to us that this instrument is the Declarant's Declaration of Guardian for Children and that the Declarant requested us to act as witnesses to the Declarant's Declaration of Guardian for Children and signature. The Declarant then signed this Declaration of Guardian for Children in our presence, all of us being present at the same time. The Declarant is 18 years of age or over (or being under such age, is or has been lawfully married, or is a member of the armed forces of the United States or of an auxiliary thereof or of the Maritime Service), and we believe the Declarant to be of sound mind. We now sign our names as attesting witnesses in the presence of the Declarant, each other, and the undersigned authority on this 2nd day of July 2015.

_____

_____, Witness   _____, Witness

_____   _____

_____   _____

STATE OF NEW MEXICO

COUNTY OF LEA COUNTY

Subscribed and sworn before me by Debbie Smith, the Declarant, and by _____, and _____, the witnesses, on 2nd day of July 2015.

_____

Notary Public, State of New Mexico

Declaration of Guardian for Children of Debbie Smith

Personal Property Memorandum
of Debbie Smith

My Will refers to the disposition at my death of certain items of tangible personal property in accordance with a memorandum signed by me. I do hereby make this memorandum for that purpose.

If an item is marked with an (*) it is to be distributed to the person designated to receive the item only if my spouse predeceases me.

If the recipient of a particular item of personal property does not survive me, such item shall be disposed of as though it had not been listed in this memorandum.

Personal Property Distributions
for Debbie Smith

Description of Tangible Personal Property	Person to Receive Property Address and Relationship	(*)
_____	_____	____
_____	_____	____
_____	_____	____
_____	_____	____
_____	_____	____
_____	_____	____
_____	_____	____
_____	_____	____
_____	_____	____
_____	_____	____

Dated: July 2, 2015 _____

_____

Debbie Smith

Page _____

Personal Property Distributions
for Debbie Smith

Description of Tangible Personal Property	Person to Receive Property Address and Relationship	(*)
_____	_____	_____
_____	_____	_____
_____	_____	_____
_____	_____	_____
_____	_____	_____
_____	_____	_____
_____	_____	_____
_____	_____	_____
_____	_____	_____
_____	_____	_____
_____	_____	_____
_____	_____	_____
_____	_____	_____
_____	_____	_____
_____	_____	_____
_____	_____	_____

Dated: July 2, 2015 _____

_____
Debbie Smith
Page _____

Personal Property Distributions
for Debbie Smith

Description of Tangible Personal Property	Person to Receive Property Address and Relationship	(*)
_____	_____	_____
_____	_____	_____
_____	_____	_____
_____	_____	_____
_____	_____	_____
_____	_____	_____
_____	_____	_____
_____	_____	_____
_____	_____	_____
_____	_____	_____
_____	_____	_____
_____	_____	_____
_____	_____	_____
_____	_____	_____
_____	_____	_____
_____	_____	_____

Dated: July 2, 2015 _____

_____
Debbie Smith
Page _____

Appendices

Appendices

Prevent identity theft—protect your Social Security number

Your Social Security Statement

January 2014

www.socialsecurity.gov

See inside for your personal information

What's inside...

Bob T. Smith
1000 Residential Lane
Lovington, NM 11111

What Social Security Means To You

This *Social Security Statement* will help you understand what Social Security means to you and your family. This *Statement* can help you better plan for your financial future. It gives you estimates of your Social Security benefits under current law. Each year, we will send you an updated *Statement* including your latest reported earnings.

Be sure to read this *Statement* carefully. If you think there may be a mistake, please let us know. That's important because your benefits will be based on our record of your lifetime earnings. We recommend you keep a copy of this *Statement* with your financial records.

Social Security is for people of all ages...
It can help you whether you're young or old, male or female, single or with a family. It's there for you when you retire, but it's more than a retirement program. Social Security also can provide benefits if you become disabled and help support your family when you die.

Work to build a secure future...
Social Security is the largest source of income for most elderly Americans today. It is very important to remember that Social Security was never intended to be your only source of income when you retire. Social Security can't do it all. You also will need other savings, investments, pensions or retirement accounts to make sure you have enough money to live comfortably when you retire.

About Social Security's future...
Social Security is a compact between generations. For more than 70 years, America has kept the promise of security for its workers and their families. But now, the Social Security system is facing serious future financial problems, and action is needed soon to make sure that the system is sound when today's younger workers are ready for retirement.

Today there are more than 37 million Americans age 65 or older. Their Social Security retirement benefits are funded by today's workers and their employers who jointly pay Social Security taxes — just as the money they paid into Social Security was used to pay benefits to those who retired before them. Unless action is taken soon to strengthen Social Security, in just 10 years we will begin paying more in benefits than we collect in taxes. Without changes, by 2040 the Social Security Trust Fund will be exhausted.* By then, the number of Americans 65 or older is expected to have doubled. There won't be enough younger people working to pay all of the benefits owed to those who are retiring. At that point, there will be enough money to pay only about 74 cents for each dollar of scheduled benefits. We will need to resolve these issues soon to make sure Social Security continues to provide a foundation of protection for future generations as it has done in the past.

Social Security on the Net...
Visit *www.socialsecurity.gov* on the Internet to learn more about Social Security. You can read our publications, use the *Social Security Benefit Calculators* to calculate future benefits, apply for retirement, spouse's or disability benefits, or subscribe to *eNews* for up-to-date information about Social Security.

Jo Anne B. Barnhart
Commissioner

* These estimates of the future financial status of the Social Security program were produced by the actuaries at the Social Security Administration based on the intermediate assumptions from the Social Security Trustees' Annual Report to the Congress.

Your Estimated Benefits

*Retirement   You have earned enough credits to qualify for benefits. At your current earnings rate, if you
stop working and start receiving benefits...

At age 62, your payment would be about .... $ 975 a month

If you continue working until...

your full retirement age (67 years), your payment would be about .... $ 1,412 a month

age 70, your payment would be about .... $ 1,761 a month

*Disability   You have earned enough credits to qualify for benefits. If you became disabled right now,
your payment would be about .... $ 1,293 a month

*Family   If you get retirement or disability benefits, your spouse and children also may qualify for benefits.

*Survivors   You have earned enough credits for your family to receive survivors benefits. If you die this
year, certain members of your family **may** qualify for the following benefits:

Your child .... $ 1,008 a month

Your spouse who is caring for your child .... $ 1,008 a month

Your spouse, if benefits start at full retirement age .... $ 1,344 a month

Total family benefits cannot be more than.. $ 2,473 a month

Your spouse or minor child may be eligible for a special one-time death benefit of $255.

Medicare   You have enough credits to qualify for Medicare at age 65. Even if you do not retire at age 65, be sure
to contact Social Security three months before your 65th birthday to enroll in Medicare.

> *** Your estimated benefits are based on current law. Congress has made changes to the law in the
> past and can do so at any time. The law governing benefit amounts may change because, by 2040,
> the payroll taxes collected will be enough to pay only about 74 percent of scheduled benefits.**

We based your benefit estimates on these facts:

Your date of birth ....April 5, 1966

Your estimated taxable earnings per year after 2006 ....$38,626

Your Social Security number (only the last four digits are shown to help prevent identity theft).............XXX-XX-1234

How Your Benefits Are Estimated

To qualify for benefits, you earn "credits" through your work — up to four each year. This year, for example, you earn one credit for each $1,000 of wages or self-employment income. When you've earned $4,000, you've earned your four credits for the year. Most people need 40 credits, earned over their working lifetime, to receive retirement benefits. For disability and survivors benefits, young people need fewer credits to be eligible.

We checked your records to see whether you have earned enough credits to qualify for benefits. If you haven't earned enough yet to qualify for any type of benefit, we can't give you a benefit estimate now. If you continue to work, we'll give you an estimate when you do qualify.

What we assumed — If you have enough work credits, we estimated your benefit amounts using your average earnings over your working lifetime. For 2007 and later (up to retirement age), we assumed you'll continue to work and make about the same as you did in 2005 or 2006. We also included credits we assumed you earned last year and this year.

Generally, estimates for older workers are more accurate than those for younger workers because they're based on a longer earnings history with fewer uncertainties such as earnings fluctuations and future law changes.

These estimates are in today's dollars. After you start receiving benefits, they will be adjusted for cost-of-living increases.

We can't provide your actual benefit amount until you apply for benefits. **And that amount may differ from the estimates stated above because:**

(1) Your earnings may increase or decrease in the future.

(2) Your estimated benefits are based on current law. **The law governing benefit amounts may change.**

(3) Your benefit amount may be affected by **military service, railroad employment or pensions earned through work on which you did not pay Social Security tax.** Following are two specific instances. You can also visit **www.socialsecurity.gov/mystatement** to see whether your Social Security benefit amount will be affected.

Windfall Elimination Provision (WEP) — In the future, if you receive a pension from employment in which you do not pay Social Security taxes, such as some federal, state or local government work, some nonprofit organizations or foreign employment, and you also qualify for your own Social Security retirement or disability benefit, your Social Security benefit may be reduced, but not eliminated, by WEP. The amount of the reduction, if any, depends on your earnings and number of years in jobs in which you paid Social Security taxes, and the year you are age 62 or become disabled. For more information, please see *Windfall Elimination Provision* (Publication No. 05-10045) at **www.socialsecurity.gov/WEP**.

Government Pension Offset (GPO) — If you receive a pension based on federal, state or local government work in which you did not pay Social Security taxes and you qualify, now or in the future, for Social Security benefits as a current or former spouse, widow or widower, you are likely to be affected by GPO. If GPO applies, your Social Security benefit will be reduced by an amount equal to two-thirds of your government pension, and could be reduced to zero. Even if your benefit is reduced to zero, you will be eligible for Medicare at age 65 on your spouse's record. To learn more, please see *Government Pension Offset* (Publication No. 05-10007) at **www.socialsecurity.gov/GPO**.

Your Earnings Record

Years You Worked	Your Taxed Social Security Earnings	Your Taxed Medicare Earnings
1982	550	550
1983	1,299	1,299
1984	2,254	2,254
1985	3,704	3,704
1986	4,962	4,962
1987	6,282	6,282
1988	7,827	7,827
1989	10,041	10,041
1990	12,297	12,297
1991	14,278	14,278
1992	16,399	16,399
1993	17,772	17,772
1994	19,346	19,346
1995	21,057	21,057
1996	22,946	22,946
1997	25,031	25,031
1998	26,991	26,991
1999	29,072	29,072
2000	31,251	31,251
2001	32,542	32,542
2002	33,380	33,380
2003	34,720	34,720
2004	36,756	36,756
2005	38,626	38,626
2006	Not yet recorded	Not yet recorded

Did you know... Social Security is more than just a retirement program? It's here to help you when you need it most.

You and your family may be eligible for valuable benefits:

When you die, your family may be eligible to receive survivors benefits.

Social Security may help you if you become disabled—even at a young age.

It is possible for a young person who has worked and paid Social Security taxes in as few as two years to become eligible for disability benefits.

Social Security credits you earn move with you from job to job throughout your career.

Total Social Security and Medicare taxes paid over your working career through the last year reported on the chart above:

Estimated taxes paid for Social Security:		Estimated taxes paid for Medicare:	
You paid:	$27,730	You paid:	$6,506
Your employers paid:	$27,730	Your employers paid:	$6,506

Note: You currently pay 6.2 percent of your salary, up to $97,500, in Social Security taxes and 1.45 percent in Medicare taxes on your entire salary. Your employer also pays 6.2 percent in Social Security taxes and 1.45 percent in Medicare taxes for you. If you are self-employed, you pay the combined employee and employer amount of 12.4 percent in Social Security taxes and 2.9 percent in Medicare taxes on your net earnings.

Help Us Keep Your Earnings Record Accurate

You, your employer and Social Security share responsibility for the accuracy of your earnings record. Since you began working, we recorded your reported earnings under your name and Social Security number. We have updated your record each time your employer (or you, if you're self-employed) reported your earnings.

Remember, it's your earnings, not the amount of taxes you paid or the number of credits you've earned, that determine your benefit amount. When we figure that amount, we base it on your average earnings over your lifetime. If our records are wrong, you may not receive all the benefits to which you're entitled.

Review this chart carefully using your own records to make sure our information is correct and that we've recorded each year you worked. You're the only person who can look at the earnings chart and know whether it is complete and correct.

Some or all of your earnings from **last year** may not be shown on your *Statement*. It could be that we still were processing last year's earnings reports when your *Statement* was prepared. Your complete earnings for last year will be shown on next year's *Statement*. **Note:** If you worked for more than one employer during any year, or if you had both earnings and self-employment income, we combined your earnings for the year.

There's a limit on the amount of earnings on which you pay Social Security taxes each year. The limit increases yearly. Earnings above the limit will not appear on your earnings chart as Social Security earnings. (For Medicare taxes, the maximum earnings amount began rising in 1991. Since 1994, **all** of your earnings are taxed for Medicare.)

Call us right away at **1-800-772-1213** (7 a.m.–7 p.m. your local time) if any earnings for years **before last year** are shown incorrectly. If possible, have your W-2 or tax return for those years available. (If you live outside the U.S., follow the directions at the bottom of page 4.)

3

Some Facts About Social Security

About Social Security and Medicare...

Social Security pays retirement, disability, family and survivors benefits. Medicare, a separate program run by the Centers for Medicare & Medicaid Services, helps pay for inpatient hospital care, nursing care, doctors' fees, and other medical services and supplies to people age 65 and older, or to people who have been receiving Social Security disability benefits for two years or more. Your Social Security covered earnings qualify you for both programs. For more information about Medicare, visit *www.medicare.gov* or call **1-800-633-4227** (TTY **1-877-486-2048** if you are deaf or hard of hearing).

Here are some facts about Social Security's benefits:

Retirement — If you were born before 1938, your full retirement age is 65. Because of a 1983 change in the law, the full retirement age will increase gradually to 67 for people born in 1960 and later.

Some people retire before their full retirement age. You can retire as early as age 62 and take your benefits at a reduced rate. If you continue working after your full retirement age, you can receive higher benefits because of additional earnings and special credits for delayed retirement.

Disability — If you become disabled before full retirement age, you can receive disability benefits after six months if you have:
- enough credits from earnings (depending on your age, you must have earned six to 20 of your credits in the three to 10 years before you became disabled); and
- a physical or mental impairment that's expected to prevent you from doing "substantial" work for a year or more *or* result in death.

Family — If you're eligible for disability or retirement benefits, your current or divorced spouse, minor children or adult children disabled before age 22 also may receive benefits. Each may qualify for up to about 50 percent of your benefit amount. The total amount depends on how many family members qualify.

Survivors — When you die, certain members of your family may be eligible for benefits:
- your spouse age 60 or older (50 or older if disabled, or any age if caring for your children younger than age 16); and
- your children if unmarried and younger than age 18, still in school and younger than 19 years old, or adult children disabled before age 22.

If you are divorced, your ex-spouse could be eligible for a widow's or widower's benefit on your record when you die.

Receive benefits and still work...

You can continue to work and still get retirement or survivors benefits. If you're younger than your full retirement age, there are limits on how much you can earn without affecting your benefit amount. The limits change each year. When you apply for benefits, we'll tell you what the limits are at that time and whether work would affect your monthly benefits. When you reach full retirement age, the earnings limits no longer apply.

Before you decide to retire...

Think about your benefits for the long term. Everyone's situation is different. For example, be sure to consider the advantages and disadvantages of early retirement. If you choose to receive benefits before you reach full retirement age, your benefits will be permanently reduced. However, you'll receive benefits for a longer period of time.

To help you decide when is the best time for you to retire, we offer a free booklet, *Social Security — Retirement Benefits* (Publication No. 05-10035), that provides specific information about retirement. You can calculate future retirement benefits on our website at *www.socialsecurity.gov* by using the *Social Security Benefit Calculators.*

There are other free publications that you may find helpful, including:

Understanding The Benefits (No. 05-10024) — a general explanation of all Social Security benefits;

Your Retirement Benefit: How It Is Figured (No. 05-10070) — an explanation of how you can calculate your benefit;

Windfall Elimination Provision (No. 05-10045) — how it affects your retirement or disability benefits;

Government Pension Offset (No. 05-10007) — an explanation of a law that affects spouse's or widow(er)'s benefits; and

Identity Theft And Your Social Security Number (No. 05-10064) — what to do if you're a victim of identity theft.

We also have other leaflets and fact sheets with information about specific topics such as military service, self-employment or foreign employment. You can request Social Security publications at *www.socialsecurity.gov* or by calling us at **1-800-772-1213**.

If you need more information—Visit *www.socialsecurity.gov/mystatement* on the Internet, contact any Social Security office, call **1–800-772-1213** or write to Social Security Administration, Office of Earnings Operations, P.O. Box 33026, Baltimore, MD 21290-3026. If you're deaf or hard of hearing, call TTY **1-800-325-0778**. If you have questions about your personal information, you must provide your complete Social Security number. If your address is incorrect on this *Statement*, ask the Internal Revenue Service to send you a Form 8822. We don't keep your address if you're not receiving Social Security benefits.

Para solicitar una *Declaración* en español, llame al 1-800-772-1213

Goal Setting and Decision Making

Goal and Action Plan Worksheet

INTERACTIVE ACTION LEARNING—GOAL AND ACTION PLAN #1

Goal Statement: What do you plan to accomplish?

Actions to Be Taken: What do you plan to do?	Who will do this?	By when?

List the benefits for you and others if you accomplish this goal. See and feel them.	List the obstacles you or the team will have to overcome to accomplish this goal. Are there actions you need to take in your goal plan?

Data to Measure Effectiveness: What will be different, and how will you know?

INTERACTIVE ACTION LEARNING—GOAL AND ACTION PLAN #2

Goal Statement: What do you plan to accomplish?

Actions to Be Taken: What do you plan to do?	Who will do this?	By when?

List the benefits for you and others if you accomplish this goal. See and feel them.	List the obstacles you or the team will have to overcome to accomplish this goal. Are there actions you need to take in your goal plan?

Data to Measure Effectiveness: What will be different, and how will you know?

Goal Statement: What do you plan to accomplish?

Actions to Be Taken: What do you plan to do?	Who will do this?	By when?

List the benefits for you and others if you accomplish this goal. See and feel them.	List the obstacles you or the team will have to overcome to accomplish this goal. Are there actions you need to take in your goal plan?

Data to Measure Effectiveness: What will be different, and how will you know?

Life Balance: Spiritual—Mental—Physical—Family—Career—Education—Financial

Print everything—it's easier to read. The concentration involved in writing implants your goal-directed initiatives for the week or day more firmly in your subconscious mind. NOTE: If you did nothing specific to reach any of your goals, write "Nothing" in red.

Week of: _____	Goal #1:	Goal #2:	Goal #3:
Monday			
Tuesday			
Wednesday			
Thursday			
Friday			
Saturday			
Sunday			

Highly Important: READ THE DAILY 7 EVERY DAY! To achieve your SMART goals and enjoy life balance, you need to do these on a **daily** basis:

1. Spiritually, mentally, emotionally, and physically prepare for each day in order to be fully engaged.
2. Greet people enthusiastically on the telephone, via e-mail, and in person.
3. Listen—really listen—to whomever you are with (EAr process).
4. Bring energy, values, and inspired ideas to your work every day.
5. Be a leader and learner by searching, listening, and expecting to find a better way every day.
6. Plan your work and work your plan by working on professional or project goals nearly every day.
7. Treat everyone as a VIP.

Time spent this week working toward my professional or project goals: _____

What was your most enriching goal directed action taken this week?

Achieving Your Goals Analysis Worksheet

DAILY PROGRESS NOTES AND CELEBRATIONS

Spiritual—Mental—Physical—Family—Career—Education—Financial

Print everything—it's easier to read. The concentration implants your goal-directed initiatives for the week or day more firmly in your subconscious mind.

NOTE: If you did nothing specific to reach any of your SMART goals write "Nothing" in red.

Week of: _____	Goal #1:	Goal #2:	Goal #3:
Monday			
Tuesday			
Wednesday			
Thursday			
Friday			
Saturday			
Sunday			

Highly Important: READ THE DAILY 7 EVERY DAY! To achieve your SMART goals and enjoy life balance, you need to do these on a **daily** basis:

1. Spiritually, mentally, emotionally, and physically prepare for each day in order to be fully engaged.
2. Greet people enthusiastically on the telephone, via e-mail, and in person.
3. Listen—really listen—to whomever you are with (EAr process).
4. Bring energy, values, and inspired ideas to your work every day.
5. Be a leader and learner by searching, listening, and expecting to find a better way every day.
6. Plan your work and work your plan by working on professional or project goals nearly every day.
7. Treat everyone as a VIP.

Time spent this week working toward my professional or project goals: _____

Most Life-Enriching Goal-Directed Learning Experience this Week

Goal-Setting Retreat Agenda

Friday Evening

Start your weekend with an unstructured evening. Make no attempt to start setting goals; instead, just enjoy talking with your spouse over a relaxing dinner, a leisurely walk, or some other communication-fostering activity.

Take time to pray together, even if praying with your husband or wife is a new or unfamiliar activity. The goal-setting process must be grounded in prayer; otherwise, it becomes merely an exercise in wishful thinking or selfish dreaming. Make this focus on prayer the backbone of the entire weekend.

Saturday Morning

Take time apart from one another to set goals as outlined in the "how-to" section of this chapter. Use the worksheets on pages 000–000 if you need help or direction. Do it all—from listing your hopes and dreams to categorizing and quantifying the goals. The only step you should omit is selecting your five top-priority goals; this is a step you and your spouse will work on together.

LONG LUNCH BREAK

Saturday Afternoon

With your lists in hand, get together with your spouse and compare notes. This can be a real eye-opening time. Judy and I usually agree on 70% to 80% of our goals; we tend to spend most of our time in this session discussing the other 20% to 30%. Remember, there are no right and wrong answers. Use this time as an opportunity to recognize and appreciate each other's priorities.

Saturday Evening

Relax. You have done a lot of work, and you may feel mentally or emotionally drained. Saturday evening should be a chance for the information you have garnered to "simmer," while you and your spouse take time simply to enjoy each other.

Sunday Morning

This is the fun—and challenging—part. Remembering that a goal-setting weekend is not a time to establish "my" or "your" goals, prepare to come up with a list of "our" goals. Pick no more than 10 objectives.

Next, be sure that these goals are well defined, and try to quantify them. Wherever possible, set times, dates, or amounts that will let you know when you've accomplished each goal.

Armed with a list of 5 to 10 goals you and your spouse have agreed to pursue together, you are now ready to establish a strategy for accomplishing them. Congratulations—you have already done the hardest part!

A Catalog of Ideas to Get You Started

Saving Goals

- How much do we need?
- How should we save? Weekly? Monthly? Annual bonus?
- Why? What are we saving for?

Debt Goals

- How much is okay?
- Should we avoid it completely?
- Should we get out of it?

Lifestyle Goals

- What kind of house do we need or want?
- Do we want to take a vacation? Where?
- What about areas such as entertainment, clothing, and so forth?

Education Goals for Children or Self

- Public or private schooling?
- College? University?
- Trade school?

Vacation Goals

- How many this year?
- Where to go?
- With kids? Without?

Insurance Goals

- Life, home, health, auto, other?
- How much do we need?
- What kind of policy suits our needs?

Giving Goals

- How much to give?
- Where to give?
- When to give? Weekly? Biweekly? Monthly?

Tax Goals

- Do we reduce our taxes?
- How can we manage them?
- Do we underwithhold?
- Overwithhold?

Family Goals

- Special needs for aging parents? Disabilities? A gifted child?
- Family time: When? What? How? Where? Why?
- One-on-one time with children?

Marriage Goals

- Date nights?
- Intimacy?
- Communication needs?

Career Goals

- Starting a business?
- Advancement?
- Job satisfaction? Location?

Children

- How many?
- Spacing?
- When to start a family?

Household Goals

- When, where, and what kind of home to buy/rent?
- Furniture needed?
- Special needs: room for guests, home office, and so forth?

Investment Goals

- Where to invest?
- Why invest?
- How much to invest?

Criteria Based Decision Model

1. Enter in the decision you are evaluating below:

2. List "Must-Haves" in the spaces below:

3. List "want to haves" in the spaces below:

4. Of the "want to haves" you listed above, please score them from 1–10 (10 being the best). Please score one as a 10 first, then score the remaining items relative to that one.

5. List alternatives in the spaces below:

6. Compare your "must haves" with your alternatives. If the alternative is in agreement with the "must have," select YES from the dropdown. If it is not in agreement, select NO. If you are not sure, select UNCERTAIN.

7. Compare your "want to haves" with your alternatives and score them from 1–10 (10 being best) based on how well the alternative meets the "want to have."

Example: Criteria Based Decision Model

Alternatives

Criteria		Retirement Account		Matham		Kitchen		Reserve: Parent Care		Equity Debt		Church		IPO	
Must-Haves	Priorities														
Biblical Support	Must Have	Yes		Yes		Yes		Yes		Yes		Yes		UNCERTAIN	
Bill Oliver Will (FP) agree	Must Have	Yes		UNCERTAIN		Yes		Yes		Yes		UNCERTAIN		UNCERTAIN	
	Must Have														
	Must Have														
Want-to-Haves	Priorities														
Honor Crown Commitment	10	10	100	10	100	10	100	10	100	10	100	10	100	5	50
Maximize Liquidity	6	5	30					7	42	10	60				
In Financial Plan	8	8	64	2	16	5	40	6	48	7	56	1	8	1	8
Unity re: decision	8	7	56	2	16	6	48	8	64	7	56	2	16	3	24
Maximize ROI	7	8	56	2	14	6	42	2	14	8	56			6	42
Totals		306		146		230		268		328		124		124	

Spending Plan

Spending Plan—Inputs

Spending Plan - Overview

Date: [ ]

Instructions for Use: Enter your marital status, number of children

Family Profile:

Marriage Status	Number of Kids

Instructions for Use: Enter your Annual Income and Cash on Hand

Income Profile:

Yearly Income	Amount of Cash on Hand

Instructions for Use: Select from the list your appropriate tax rate

Tax Profile:

Effective Tax Bracket (select from the drop down list)

Complete the following (sum all payments and balances for each category

Debt Profile:

Credit Card Payment	Credit Card Balance	Student Loan Payment	Student Loan Balance	Car Loan Payment	Car Loan Balance	Other Loan Payment	Other Loan Balance	Mortgage Payment	Mortgage Balance

Instructions: Provide the Interest rate for each debt

Interest Rates:	
Home Mortgage:	
Auto Loan:	
Student Loans:	
Credit Card:	
Other:	

Goal Setting:

Instructions: Create an initial base line for the following areas:

GIVING

Do you plan to give?	Yes
If so, what percentage of your income will you give?	

OWING

Extra payment goal on credit card debt:	
Extra payment goal on student loan debt	
Extra payment goal on car loan debt	
Extra payment goal on other loan debt	
Extra payment goal on your mortgage	

GROWING

How much do you plan on putting towards an emergency fund?	
How much do you want to save each month for college?	
How much do you want to save each month for retirement?	
Do you have any other savings goals?	

Spending Plan - Giving

GIVING	Goal
Do you plan to give?	Yes
If so, what percentage of your income will you give?	0%

	List the charities that you will give to and then describe why you want to support that charity, how you made your decision and how much you will give:
1	
2	
3	
4	
5	
6	

Spending Plan - Saving

	Goal
How much do you plan on putting towards an emergency fund each month?	$0.00
Explain your reasoning behind this goal, how long it will take you to accomplish the goal, and how you plan on accomplishing it:	
How much do you want to save each month for college?	$0.00
Explain your reasoning behind this goal, how long it will take you to accomplish the goal, and how you plan on accomplishing it:	
How much do you want to save each month for retirement?	$0.00
Explain your reasoning behind this goal, how long it will take you to accomplish the goal, and how you plan on accomplishing it:	
Do you have any other savings goals?	
Describe these goals and how you will accomplish them	
Stated as a percentage of income:	**#DIV/0!**	**#DIV/0!**

Spending Plan—Debts

Spending Plan–Debts

	Credit Card	Student Loan	Car Loan	Other Loan	Mortgage
Monthly Payment	$0.00	$0.00	$0.00	$0.00	$0.00
Balance	$0.00	$0.00	$0.00	$0.00	$0.00
Interest Rate	0.00%	0.00%	0.00%	0.00%	0
Remaining Months to Payoff	#DIV/0!	#DIV/0!	#DIV/0!	#DIV/0!	#DIV/0!
Original Goal					
Extra Monthly Payment	$0.00	$0.00	$0.00	$0.00	$0.00
New Remaining Term	#DIV/0!	#DIV/0!	#DIV/0!	#DIV/0!	#DIV/0!
Amount of Money Saved	#DIV/0!	#DIV/0!	#DIV/0!	#DIV/0!	#DIV/0!

Explain your reasoning behind your debt repayment goal, how long it will take you to accomplish the goal, and how you plan on accomplishing it:

Spending Plan—Lifestyle

Spending Plan—Lifestyle

Instructions for Use:
Only input data in cells that are shaded GREEN.

	Monthly	Yearly	
GROSS INCOME	$0.00	$0.00	
LESS EXPENSES			
Giving	$0.00	$0.00	
Taxes	$0.00	$0.00	
Debt	$0.00	$0.00	
Saving	$0.00	$0.00	
TOTAL EXPENSES	$0.00	$0.00	
NET SPENDABLE INCOME	$0.00	$0.00	
LESS LIVING EXPENSES			
Residence		$0.00	
Household Maintenance and Supplies	$0.00	$0.00	Equals 30% of housing cost
Children			
Daycare		$0.00	
Activities		$0.00	
Clothing		$0.00	
Food			
Groceries		$0.00	
Dining Out		$0.00	
Cell Phone		$0.00	
Health Insurance		$0.00	
Internet		$0.00	
Utilities			
Power		$0.00	
Water		$0.00	
Gas		$0.00	
Trash		$0.00	
Entertainment		$0.00	
Travel		$0.00	
Clothing		$0.00	
Car			
Gas	$0.00	$0.00	
Insurance		$0.00	
Repairs		$0.00	
TOTAL LIVING EXPENSES	$0.00	$0.00	
CASH FLOW MARGIN	$0.00	$0.00	

For each living expense, explain your options, final choice and thought process in a 2-3 sentence paragraph:

Residence

Household Maintenance and Supplies

Children

   Daycare

   Activities

   Clothing

Food

   Groceries

   Dining Out

Cell Phone

Health Insurance

Internet

Utilities

   Power

   Water

Gas	
Trash	
Entertainment	
Travel	
Clothing	
Car	
Gas	
Insurance	
Repairs	

Student Loan Repayment Options

Student Loan Repayment Options

Overview of Direct Loan and Federal Family Education Loan (FFEL) Program Repayment Plans

Repayment Plan	Eligible Loans	Monthly Payment and Time Frame	Eligibility and Other Information
Standard Repayment Plan	• Direct subsidized and unsubsidized loans • Subsidized and unsubsidized federal Stafford loans • All PLUS loans • All consolidation loans (direct or FFEL)	Payments are a fixed amount Up to 10 years (up to 30 years for consolidation loans)	All borrowers are eligible for this plan You'll pay less over time than under other plans
Graduated Repayment Plan	• Direct subsidized and unsubsidized loans • Subsidized and unsubsidized federal Stafford loans • All PLUS loans • All consolidation loans (direct or FFEL)	Payments are lower at first and then increase, usually every 2 years Up to 10 years (up to 30 years for consolidation loans)	All borrowers are eligible for this plan You'll pay more over time than under the 10-year Standard Plan
Extended Repayment Plan	• Direct subsidized and unsubsidized loans • Subsidized and unsubsidized federal Stafford loans • All PLUS loans • All consolidation loans (direct or FFEL)	Payments may be fixed or graduated Up to 25 years	• If you're a direct loan borrower, you must have more than $30,000 in outstanding direct loans • If you're a FFEL borrower, you must have more than $30,000 in outstanding FFEL program loans • Your monthly payments will be lower than under the 10-year Standard Plan or the Graduated Repayment Plan • You'll pay more over time than under the 10-year Standard Plan

Overview of Direct Loan and Federal Family Education Loan (FFEL) Program Repayment Plans

Repayment Plan	Eligible Loans	Monthly Payment and Time Frame	Eligibility and Other Information
Revised Pay-as-You Earn Repayment Plan (REPAYE)	• Direct subsidized and unsubsidized loans • Direct PLUS loans made to students • Direct consolidation loans that do not include PLUS loans (direct or FFEL) made to parents	• Your monthly payments will be 10% of *discretionary income* • Payments are recalculated each year and are based on your updated income and family size • If you're married, both your and your spouse's income or loan debt will be considered, whether taxes are filed jointly or separately (with limited exceptions) • Any outstanding balance on your loan will be forgiven if you haven't repaid your loan in full after 20 or 25 years	• Any DIRECT LOAN borrower with an eligible loan type may choose this plan • Your monthly payment can be more than the 10-year Standard Plan amount • You may have to pay income tax on any amount that is forgiven • Good option for those seeking *public service loan forgiveness* (PSLF).
Pay-as-You Earn Repayment Plan (PAYE)	• Direct subsidized and unsubsidized loans • Direct PLUS loans made to students • Direct consolidation loans that do not include (direct or FFEL) PLUS loans made to parents	• Your maximum monthly payments will be 10% of discretionary income • Payments are recalculated each year and are based on your updated income and family size • If you're married, your spouse's income or loan debt will be considered only if you file a joint tax return • Any outstanding balance on your loan will be forgiven if you haven't repaid your loan in full after 20 years	• You must be a *new borrower* on or after Oct. 1, 2007, and must have received a *disbursement* of a direct loan on or after Oct. 1, 2011 • You must have a high debt relative to your income • Your monthly payment will never be more than the 10-year Standard Plan amount • You'll pay more over time than under the 10-year Standard Plan • You may have to pay income tax on any amount that is forgiven • Good option for those seeking PSLF

Overview of Direct Loan and Federal Family Education Loan (FFEL) Program Repayment Plans

Repayment Plan	Eligible Loans	Monthly Payment and Time Frame	Eligibility and Other Information
Income-Based Repayment Plan (IBR)	• Direct subsidized and unsubsidized loans • Subsidized and unsubsidized federal Stafford loans • all PLUS loans made to students • Consolidation loans (direct or FFEL) that do not include direct or FFEL PLUS loans made to parents	• Your monthly payments will be 10% or 15% of discretionary income • Payments are recalculated each year and are based on your updated income and family size • If you're married, your spouse's income or loan debt will be considered only if you file a joint tax return • Any outstanding balance on your loan will be forgiven if you haven't repaid your loan in full after 20 or 25 years • You may have to pay income tax on any amount that is forgiven	• You must have a high debt relative to your income • Your monthly payment will never be more than the 10-year Standard Plan amount • You'll pay more over time than under the 10-year Standard Plan • Good option for those seeking PSLF

Income-Contingent Repayment Plan (ICR)	• Direct subsidized and unsubsidized loans
	• Direct PLUS loans made to students
	• Direct consolidation loans
		• Your monthly payment will be the lesser of
		  • 20% of discretionary income, or
		  • the amount you would pay on a repayment plan with a fixed payment over 12 years, adjusted according to your income
		• Payments are recalculated each year and are based on your updated income, family size, and the total amount of your direct loans
		• If you're married, your spouse's income or loan debt will be considered only if you file a joint tax return or you choose to repay your direct loans jointly with your spouse
		• Any outstanding balance will be forgiven if you haven't repaid your loan in full after 25 years
			• Any direct loan borrower with an eligible loan type may choose this plan
			• Your monthly payment can be more than the 10-year Standard Plan amount
			• You may have to pay income tax on the amount that is forgiven
			• Good option for those seeking PSLF
			• Parent borrowers can access this plan by consolidating their parent PLUS loans into a *direct consolidation loan*

Overview of Direct Loan and Federal Family Education Loan (FFEL) Program Repayment Plans

Repayment Plan	Eligible Loans	Monthly Payment and Time Frame	Eligibility and Other Information
Income-Sensitive Repayment Plan	• Subsidized and unsubsidized federal Stafford loans • FFEL PLUS loans • FFEL consolidation loans	Your monthly payment is based on annual income Up to 15 years	• You'll pay more over time than under the 10-year Standard Plan • The formula for determining the monthly payment amount can vary from lender to lender

Source: https://studentaid.ed.gov/sa/repay-loans/understand/plans.

Retirement Benefit

Your Retirement Benefit: How It's Figured

2016

As you make plans for your retirement, you may ask, "How much will I get from Social Security?" To find out, you can use the *Retirement Estimator* at **www.socialsecurity.gov/estimator**. Workers age 18 and older can also go online, create a personal account and request their *Social Security Statement*. To review your *Statement*, go to **www.socialsecurity.gov/myaccount**.

Many people wonder how we figure their Social Security retirement benefit. We base Social Security benefits on your lifetime earnings. We adjust or "index" your actual earnings to account for changes in average wages since the year the earnings were received. Then Social Security calculates your average indexed monthly earnings during the 35 years in which you earned the most. We apply a formula to these earnings and arrive at your basic benefit, or "primary insurance amount." This is how much you would receive at your full retirement age — 65 or older, depending on your date of birth.

On the back of this page is a worksheet you can use to estimate your retirement benefit if you were born in 1954. It's only an estimate; for specific information, talk with a Social Security representative.

Factors that can change the amount of your retirement benefit

- *You choose to get benefits before your full retirement age.* You can begin to receive Social Security benefits as early as age 62, but at a reduced rate. We reduce your basic benefit a certain percentage if you retire before reaching full retirement age.
- *You're eligible for cost-of-living benefit increases starting with the year you become age 62.* This is true even if you don't get benefits until your full retirement age or even age 70. We add cost-of-living increases to your benefit beginning with the year you reach 62, and up to the year you start receiving benefits.
- *You delay your retirement past your full retirement age.* We increase Social Security

benefits a certain percentage (depending on your date of birth) if you delay receiving benefits until after your full retirement age. If you do so, we'll increase your benefit amount until you start taking benefits, or until you reach age 70.

- *You're a government worker with a pension.* If you also get, or are eligible for, a pension from work for which you didn't pay Social Security taxes (usually a government job), we apply a different formula to your average indexed monthly earnings. To find out how the Windfall Elimination Provision (WEP) affects your benefits, go to **www.socialsecurity.gov/gpo-wep** and use the WEP online calculator. You can also review the WEP fact sheet to find out how we figure your benefit. Or, you can contact Social Security and ask for *Windfall Elimination Provision* (Publication No. 05-10045).

You can find a detailed explanation about how we calculate your retirement benefit in the *Annual Statistical Supplement, 2014, Appendix D*. The publication is available on the Internet at **www.socialsecurity.gov/policy/docs/statcomps/supplement**.

Contacting Social Security

Visit **www.socialsecurity.gov** anytime to apply for benefits, open a *my* **Social Security** account, find publications, and get answers to frequently asked questions. Or, call us toll-free at **1-800-772-1213** (for the deaf or hard of hearing, call our TTY number, **1-800-325-0778**). We can answer case-specific questions from 7 a.m. to 7 p.m., Monday through Friday. Generally, you'll have a shorter wait time if you call after Tuesday. We treat all calls confidentially. We also want to make sure you receive accurate and courteous service, so a second Social Security representative monitors some telephone calls. We can provide general information by automated phone service 24 hours a day. And, remember, our website, **www.socialsecurity.gov**, is available to you anytime and anywhere!

(over)

Your Retirement Benefit: How It's Figured

Estimating your Social Security retirement benefit

For workers born in 1954 (people born in 1954 become age 62 in 2016 and are eligible for a benefit)

This worksheet shows how to estimate the Social Security monthly retirement benefit you would be eligible for at age 62, if you were born in 1954. It also allows you to estimate what you would receive at age 66, your full retirement age, **excluding any cost-of-living adjustments for which you may be eligible**. If you continue working past age 62, your additional earnings could increase your benefit. People born after 1954 can use this worksheet, but their benefit may be higher because of additional earnings and benefit increases. If you were born before 1954, visit **www.socialsecurity.gov** and search for *Retirement Age Calculator*.

Step 1: Enter your earnings in Column B, but not more than the amount shown in Column A. If you have no earnings, enter "0."

Step 2: Multiply the amounts in Column B by the index factors in Column C, and enter the results in Column D. This gives you your indexed earnings, or the estimated value of your earnings in current dollars.

Step 3: Choose from Column D the 35 years with the highest amounts. Add these amounts. $_____

Step 4: Divide the result from Step 3 by 420 (the number of months in 35 years). Round down to the next lowest dollar. This will give you your average indexed monthly earnings. $_____

Step 5: a. Multiply the first $856 in Step 4 by 90%. $_____

b. Multiply the amount in Step 4 over $856 and less than or equal to $5,157 by 32%. $_____

c. Multiply the amount in Step 4 over $5,157 by 15%. $_____

Step 6: Add a, b, and c from Step 5. Round down to the next lowest dollar. This is your estimated monthly retirement benefit at age 66, your full retirement age. $_____

Step 7: Multiply the amount in Step 6 by 75%. This is your estimated monthly retirement benefit if you retire at age 62. $_____

Year	A. Maximum earnings	B. Actual earnings	C. Index factor	D. Indexed earnings
1955	$4,200		14.08	
1956	$4,200		13.16	
1957	$4,200		12.76	
1958	$4,200		12.65	
1959	$4,800		12.05	
1960	$4,800		11.60	
1961	$4,800		11.37	
1962	$4,800		10.83	
1963	$4,800		10.57	
1964	$4,800		10.16	
1965	$4,800		9.98	
1966	$6,600		9.41	
1967	$6,600		8.92	
1968	$7,800		8.34	
1969	$7,800		7.89	
1970	$7,800		7.51	
1971	$7,800		7.15	
1972	$9,000		6.52	
1973	$10,800		6.13	
1974	$13,200		5.79	
1975	$14,100		5.39	
1976	$15,300		5.04	
1977	$16,500		4.75	
1978	$17,700		4.40	
1979	$22,900		4.05	
1980	$25,900		3.71	
1981	$29,700		3.37	
1982	$32,400		3.20	
1983	$35,700		3.05	
1984	$37,800		2.88	
1985	$39,600		2.76	

Year	A. Maximum earnings	B. Actual earnings	C. Index factor	D. Indexed earnings
1986	$42,000		2.68	
1987	$43,800		2.52	
1988	$45,000		2.40	
1989	$48,000		2.31	
1990	$51,300		2.21	
1991	$53,400		2.13	
1992	$55,500		2.03	
1993	$57,600		2.01	
1994	$60,600		1.96	
1995	$61,200		1.88	
1996	$62,700		1.79	
1997	$65,400		1.69	
1998	$68,400		1.61	
1999	$72,600		1.53	
2000	$76,200		1.45	
2001	$80,400		1.41	
2002	$84,900		1.40	
2003	$87,000		1.36	
2004	$87,900		1.30	
2005	$90,000		1.26	
2006	$94,200		1.20	
2007	$97,500		1.15	
2008	$102,000		1.12	
2009	$106,800		1.14	
2010	$106,800		1.12	
2011	$106,800		1.08	
2012	$110,100		1.05	
2013	$113,700		1.04	
2014	$117,000		1.00	
2015	$118,500		1.00	

Social Security Administration
SSA Publication No. 05-10070
ICN 467100
Unit of Issue - HD (one hundred)
January 2016 (Recycle prior editions)

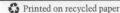

Discipleship Moments and Reflections

Discipleship Moments and Reflections

CHAPTER 1

DISCIPLESHIP MOMENT AND REFLECTION

Take some time to think through your personal convictions and reflect on the previous sections as it relates toon worldviews. Discuss the implications with your accountability and prayer partner.

DISCIPLESHIP MOMENT AND REFLECTION

If you own your own home, take a walk around your property to get a feel for the reality of this principle. Go barefoot if weather permits. Reflect on how long that dirt has been there and how long it will continue to be there. Then ask yourself if you really own it or whether you merely possess it. You may have the title to it in your fireproof file cabinet, but that title reflects your right to possess it temporarily, not forever. Only God literally owns it forever. Take a moment to contact your prayer and accountability partner and proclaim to him or her that everything belongs to God and that you understand that all possessions you manage are to be used for God's glory.

CHAPTER 2

DISCIPLESHIP MOMENT AND REFLECTION

Take a few moments and read the brief stories of Bernie Madoff and Allen Stanford. Then review the following verses. Talk to your prayer partner and accountability partner about ways you can protect yourself from falling into these traps. (**Proverbs 11:2, Proverbs 16:5, Proverbs 29:23, Proverbs 16:18, Galatians 6:3, Proverbs 27:2, Proverbs 26:12, James 4:6, Jeremiah 9:23, Philippians 2:3**)

DISCIPLESHIP MOMENT AND REFLECTION

Review the following verses, reflect, and pray that the Holy Spirit will provide you with insight into the practical application of these verses to your life. What areas of your life do you need to reassess and alter to become a better steward?

Time	Treasure	True Relationships
Genesis 1:28	2 Corinthians 9:6-7	1 Peter 4:10
Luke 12:42-46	Luke 16:11	1 Corinthians 4:1–21
		Titus 1:7

Talents
Colossians 3:23
Proverb 16:3

DISCIPLESHIP MOMENT AND REFLECTION

Answer the following lifestyle question: If God called you into full-time ministry tomorrow, could you go? Or are you in bondage to your lifestyle? Take some time to evaluate how your lifestyle is a reflection of your decision making. What changes in your decisions need to be made to begin to eliminate your debt bondage? Talk to your accountability and prayer partner about your decisions.

DISCIPLESHIP MOMENT AND REFLECTION

Take some time to come up with a list of questions you would like to ask about the way your spouse or the person you are in a relationship with thinks about money. You can use the questions listed here as a starting point. Get to know the person's thoughts and feelings about money. Find out where you agree and disagree. Talk to your accountability and prayer partner about the conversation, and pray together to see where the Holy Spirit leads you to go.

CHAPTER 3

DISCIPLESHIP MOMENT AND REFLECTION

Take a few minutes to review the scriptures just listed. As you review the verses, what common thread do you see in these verses? Do you have a true sense of contentment in your life? Pray through each of these verses and talk to your accountability and prayer partner on where the Holy Spirit is leading you.

As you look through these three explanations to society's lack of contentment, do you see yourself falling into any of these traps? Which of the three do you feel you struggle with the most? Talk to your accountability and prayer partner about the areas you struggle with, and pray together. What are ways that each of you can disciple each other to continually build your contentment?

DISCIPLESHIP MOMENT AND REFLECTION

What financial idols are in your life? Take a look at the previous list, or consider others that may come to mind. Write these down and seek guidance on how you can remove them from your worship. Talk to your accountability and prayer partner about your decisions, and have your partner help you by being holding you accountable.

CHAPTER 4

DISCIPLESHIP MOMENT AND REFLECTION

Make two columns on a piece of paper. In the first column, write commitments you have; in the second column, write down your priorities. As you look at the sheet, what thoughts come to mind? Are your priorities aligned with your commitments? Are there any commitments that are blocking you from your priorities? Talk to your accountability and prayer partner after your reflection. Pray that the Holy Spirit will help you begin to balance and align these two columns.

DISCIPLESHIP MOMENT AND REFLECTION

Take a few moments and reflect on this concept of consumptive versus productive uses of money. How would your life be different if you used your money in more productive ways (yielding more or resulting in more) than consumptive? Talk to your accountability and prayer partner about ways you can become more productive in your financial decision making.

DISCIPLESHIP MOMENT AND REFLECTION

Think back on the three main reasons for creating a financial plan. It takes you through a process of thinking through the plan, it establishes communication between spouses and family members, and it serves as a guide for financial decisions. How have you implemented a financial plan? What are the obstacles for you to begin the process? Talk to your accountability and prayer partner regarding your thoughts and feelings toward creating a financial plan.

DISCIPLESHIP MOMENT AND REFLECTION

Take a few minutes to determine what your number is; in other words, what's enough for you? We strongly encourage you to pray about this number, talk to your spouse or significant other, and then talk through this with your accountability and prayer partner. Make sure you can articulate why this is *the* number.

CHAPTER 5

DISCIPLESHIP MOMENT AND REFLECTION

Take a few minutes and begin to think about your goal-setting process. As you prepare, set some time to get in God's word (keeping a journal close by) and pray through Scripture as you begin to prepare your goals. Talk through your impressions, thoughts, and ideas with your accountability and prayer partner. Be intentional and start to write down your measurable goals.

DISCIPLESHIP MOMENT AND REFLECTION

Take this time to set some SMART goals, keeping the list of goals to three important and significant goals. If you are married, make sure they are mutually acceptable to your spouse. Write them down and share them with your accountability and prayer partner.

CHAPTER 6

DISCIPLESHIP MOMENT AND REFLECTION

Take a few minutes and pray for wisdom (James 1:5) as it relates to knowing and understanding how you personally will be affected by changes in inflation rates. To see the tremendous impact of a personal inflation rate that is less than the reported average annual inflation rate, review the chart above that reflects differences in the cost of goods over time. How do you see these differences impacting you personally? Talk to your accountability and prayer partner and see which ones impact them the most. What do you find the same? Different?

DISCIPLESHIP MOMENT AND REFLECTION (PART 1)

Have you admitted that there are areas of your financial life that cause you to be afraid? If so, what are they? Take a few moments to mentally catalog your financial fears. Do any of the following items threaten your sense of security? Review the list, marking any areas that reflect your individual concerns. Talk through these with your accountability and prayer partner.

DISCIPLESHIP MOMENT AND REFLECTION (PART 2)

Having pinpointed your specific fears, work through the following steps to deal with your concerns. (Hint: If you can't confidently answer all the questions in this section, come back and complete this page when you finish reading this book.)

DISCIPLESHIP MOMENT AND REFLECTION

This idea of confirmation bias is one of the main reasons why you should consider seeking professional objective advice from a financial advisor with a biblical worldview. As confirmation bias outlines, we can almost always confirm our decisions with supporting research. Take a moment and think about asking your accountability partner or prayer partner to be a sounding board in addition to your spouse, if married, when making purchasing decisions.

CHAPTER 7

DISCIPLESHIP MOMENT AND REFLECTION

Determine what financial life-cycle phase you are in (either self-preservation, accumulation, or distribution) and think about the idea that every dollar spent on short-term needs or wants takes away available income to meet long-term goals. If you are in the self-preservation phase, what can you do to move toward the accumulation phase more quickly? If you are already in the accumulation phase, what changes can you make to allocate more toward your accumulation goal? If you are in the distribution phase, reflect on where God wants you to reallocate His resources. Talk through these decisions with your accountability and prayer partner.

DISCIPLESHIP MOMENT AND REFLECTION

Think through this idea of God's calling verses our vocation. How have you understood the two? Do you need to pray for guidance and counsel regarding your vocation? What do you feel the Holy Spirit is leading you to pursue as a vocation? How does this differ from your call? Pray through these decisions with your accountability and prayer partner.

CHAPTER 8

DISCIPLESHIP MOMENT AND REFLECTION

Talk to your accountability partner and prayer partner, letting your partner know that you would like to track your expenses over the course of time (you decide—1 month, 3 months, 6 months, etc.). Have your partner encourage you and pray for you during this data-collection period. This can be a challenging task to complete, especially if you are married and both you and your spouse are seeking to track where your money goes. You might set up a reward for yourselves at the end of the time period. Once you are done, consider how the experience changed your perspective on spending money. Talk over the results with your accountability partner.

DISCIPLESHIP MOMENT AND REFLECTION

Take a few moments and pray. Recall that God has given you His provision (income/wealth) to manage on His behalf for the ultimate purpose of giving God the glory. As you pray and seek the Holy Spirit's leading on this process, keep in mind that God owns it all, and we are merely His managers. Pray through each category that you think is important to God and those that are not. The frame of reference is very important when setting up this budget. Talk to your accountability partner and prayer partner about the categories that the Spirit may be leading to you change or adjust.

CHAPTER 9

DISCIPLESHIP MOMENT AND REFLECTION

As you think about credit, do you use credit in the form of credit cards or other forms of lending? Why or why not? What personal convictions do you have about your use of credit? Talk to your prayer and accountability partner about your thoughts and discuss your partner's convictions about credit.

DISCIPLESHIP MOMENT AND REFLECTION

Review all the different types of loans. Which ones do you have or have you had in the past? Which types do you foresee using in the future? How do you think the use of credit will impact your life, either positively or negatively? Talk to your prayer and accountability partner about your thoughts.

DISCIPLESHIP MOMENT AND REFLECTION

The two biblical principles just listed show the significant effect that debt can have on our lives. Have you ever felt that God was leading you to do something but felt that your debt had created a barrier to allowing God to move in your life? Pray about this situation and seek God's grace and mercy. May the Spirit be your guiding light in eliminating the bondage debt can create!

DISCIPLESHIP MOMENT AND REFLECTION

Think back on two or three scenarios where you were affected by one of the common reasons for debt just presented. Describe the process that you used to take on debt and the outcome of that scenario. Spend time thinking about how this may have denied God an opportunity to work in your life.

DISCIPLESHIP MOMENT AND REFLECTION

Reflect on a decision you have made or are planning on making. How did or would you evaluate each of the considerations in that case? Talk through this with your accountability and prayer partner. What insights have you learned through this reflection?

CHAPTER 10

DISCIPLESHIP MOMENT AND REFLECTION

Take a moment to review your current financial standing. Compare your financial status with that of the American family financial statistics presented in Table 10.1. Talk to your prayer and accountability partner about any positive and negative feelings that surface during this process.

DISCIPLESHIP MOMENT AND REFLECTION

Review all of the short-term savings options. Are any of these viable options for you? Speak to your prayer and accountability partner for guidance or additional thoughts.

DISCIPLESHIP MOMENT AND REFLECTION

Consider the types of insurance you have and reflect on the following questions. If you don't pay your own insurance, ask those who are responsible for any insurance that you have the following questions.

- Why was the current insurance selected?
- Is there a type of insurance that you should have but do not?
- Is there a type of insurance that you have but perhaps may not need?

Use this time to review the information in this chapter to help determine the answers to these questions. Talk to your prayer and accountability partner about the answers.

CHAPTER 11

DISCIPLESHIP MOMENT AND REFLECTION

What are your initial thoughts as you think about home ownership and the "American dream"? When you purchased your home (if you own a home), can you recall your reasons for buying the house you chose? Did you feel you had the right, perhaps even an obligation, to buy? What would you tell members of the next generation if they were asking you about a decision to buy a home?

DISCIPLESHIP MOMENT AND REFLECTION

As you look on your financial and living situation, how much could you put toward a mortgage considering your debts? Would you be under the recommended 40% debt-to-income ratio?

DISCIPLESHIP MOMENT AND REFLECTION

Take a few minutes to read through some of these passages as you think about your home-buying experience. What prompting do you feel the Holy Spirit leading you to do? If you were to implement the 2.5 multiplier of income guideline, how much could you afford to pay for a home?

DISCIPLESHIP MOMENT AND REFLECTION

Reflecting back on the information presented in this chapter, what were your original goals regarding housing? How has your perspective changed since reading the chapter? Talk to your accountability and prayer partner about what you have learned thus far, and talk through any potential decisions you may need to make.

CHAPTER 12

DISCIPLESHIP MOMENT AND REFLECTION

As you think about a time when you replaced a car, what was your motivation to do so? Talk with your accountability and prayer partner and talk about how you can hold each other to staying with your current vehicle until one of the three reasons for replacing your car occurs.

DISCIPLESHIP MOMENT AND REFLECTION

Reflect back on any car-buying decisions you have made in the past. What would you do differently? If you have not bought a car, ask your accountability and prayer partner about his or her experiences. What would he or she have done differently? Talk about what you have learned thus far.

DISCIPLESHIP MOMENT AND REFLECTION

We hope that you have limited experience in filing auto insurance claims. Ask some of your mentors about their experiences, including your accountability and prayer partner. What types of claims did they file, what were the outcomes, and what advice could they give to you prior to filing an auto claim?

CHAPTER 13

DISCIPLESHIP MOMENT AND REFLECTION

Reflect back on your attitude toward paying taxes. Pray that God gives you the right attitude. Discuss your thoughts with your prayer and accountability partner.

DISCIPLESHIP MOMENT AND REFLECTION

Review your tax paperwork organization. Do you feel you need to make any changes to how you organize your tax documents to make your tax filing easier? Talk to your prayer and accountability partner how he or she organizes tax documents throughout the year.

CHAPTER 14

DISCIPLESHIP MOMENT AND REFLECTION

Take a moment to review your health insurance plan(s). Ask your prayer and accountability partner about his or her plan. Compare and contrast the differences and consider any changes you may want to make.

DISCIPLESHIP MOMENT AND REFLECTION

Take a moment to review your own life and disability insurance contracts or those of your parents. What type of insurance do they have, and what types of coverage do they have? Consider what you may need to change, and talk through these thoughts with your prayer and accountability partner.

CHAPTER 15

DISCIPLESHIP MOMENT AND REFLECTION

What future value goal to have $10,000 know what that amount will be in 20 years if saved at 8% annually. What other goals should you jot down for which it would be helpful to know the future value, such as an education or home value? Talk this through with your prayer and accountability partner.

DISCIPLESHIP MOMENT AND REFLECTION

If you had your choice, what types of investments would you feel comfortable investing in—stocks? bonds? CDs? What other types of investments make you uncomfortable? Talk to your prayer and accountability partner about each of these types of assets and get his or her opinion.

CHAPTER 16

DISCIPLESHIP MOMENT AND REFLECTION

Take a few minutes to think about the things you treasure most in the world. Write down where you think your treasure is currently and write down where you believe God wants it to be. Share these reflections with your prayer and accountability partner.

DISCIPLESHIP MOMENT AND REFLECTION

Take a few moments to reflect on the reasons we should give. Ask God to help turn your heart to becoming more generous, and ask Him to give you a bigger picture of heaven and eternity. Discuss with your accountability partner the challenges you face in giving and the barriers that you face when trying to be more generous.

DISCIPLESHIP MOMENT AND REFLECTION

Write down how much you think God wants you to give. Reflect on why we often look to find minimum requirements in giving. What does this reflect about our hearts?

CHAPTER 17

DISCIPLESHIP MOMENT AND REFLECTION

Take a moment to think about the statement that if you love your children equally, you will treat them uniquely. Do you think that this is sound advice for parenting? Did your parents treat you and your siblings this way? Reflect on what this statement means in our relationship with God and how He treats His children differently.

DISCIPLESHIP MOMENT AND REFLECTION

Think about reasons you may want to use a trust when leaving assets to another person. Think about how a trust works to protect assets, but may not work to protect legacy. Think about the best way to leave a legacy and how these tools and techniques fit into that plan.

CHAPTER 18

DISCIPLESHIP MOMENT AND REFLECTION

Social Security has probably been something you have thought about or perhaps you have heard discussed in conversations with others. What is your stance on Social Security? How do you plan to utilize this benefit? Talk these ideas through with an elder in your church regarding how he or she has utilized Social Security and the pros and cons of this decision. Ask the Holy Spirit to lead you to begin to think about how you may use this benefit now so that you can plan appropriately over your lifetime.

DISCIPLESHIP MOMENT AND REFLECTION

Eligibility for government housing programs, unemployment, SNAP (food stamps), and TANF generally isn't a life state that is dreamed of or sought after. How would you respond and how would you be challenged if you found yourself in need of one of these programs? Talk through this with your prayer and accountability partner.

CHAPTER 19

DISCIPLESHIP MOMENT AND REFLECTION

Find 10 individuals currently living in the same town as you who have financial advisors. Classify the advisors according to the descriptions just provided. Choose five advisors whom you might be interested in seeking financial advice from. Take one more step and research the company for whom each works to see if they continue to match up with your values.

DISCIPLESHIP MOMENT AND REFLECTION

In the previous Discipleship Moment, you gathered information on five financial advisors. Next, determine what certifications each advisor holds and reflect on which advisor would be most helpful in your circumstances.

DISCIPLESHIP MOMENT AND REFLECTION

Finally, take a third step in looking at the advisors you have chosen and examine whether they follow biblical principles.

Glossary of Terms

Accrued interest   All interest that has accumulated from an investment that has not been paid to the investor.

Actuaries   Mathematicians and statisticians who deal with risk and risk measurement.

Adjustable-rate mortgage   A mortgage loan type that includes an interest rate that can fluctuate or change during the loan period.

Adjusted gross income (AGI)   The amount used to compute various limitations imposed by the tax code.

Alimony   Payments to or for a spouse or former spouse under a separation or divorce decree.

Ambivalence   The exhibition of both positive and negative thoughts regarding something or someone, leading to some sort of psychological discomfort.

Amortization schedule   A payment table that will reflect the amount of principal and interest with each payment until all payments have been made.

Anchoring   The idea that we get "stuck" on an idea that we use in our decision even though that idea may be completely irrelevant.

Annual enrollment period   A period of time during which companies will allow employees to adjust their benefits.

Annual gift exclusion   The dollar amount of an asset that can be transferred every year from any person to any other person or persons free from any gift taxes and without using up any of your unified credit.

Automated clearing house (ACH)   An electronic network that allows an account holder to electronically approve a withdrawal of money from the account by providing the payee with the banking account number and routing number.

Automatic drafts   Money taken out of your account on regular intervals through an automatic process.

Bank statement   A collection of all transactions the bank has documented within the specific account, usually categorized by transaction type, first by deposits, then withdrawals.

Behavioral finance   Derived from a combination of disciplines—psychology, finance, and economics—and provides various explanations as to irrational financial decisions.

Beneficiary   The person or entity designated by the policy owner to receive the proceeds from the policy.

Biblical stewardship   The use of God-given gifts and resources (time, talent, treasure, truth, relationships, etc.) for the accomplishment of God-given goals and objectives.

Biblical wisdom   The quality of having experience, knowledge, and good judgment that is derived from knowing, understanding, and accepting the Scriptures as truth.

Business cycle   A repeatable pattern of growth (expansion) and decline (contraction) related to economic activity.

Business risk   The inherent risk that a company faces by being in business. Examples include poor management and unsuccessful products.

Capital gains   A gain from selling something at a higher price than what it was purchased for.

Capitalizes   The process by which accrued interest on a loan is added to the principal balance, thus increasing the total amount owed.

Cash management   The process of handling your cash and cash equivalents in order to meet your immediate obligations.

Check   A written item that gives the payee the ability to have funds withdrawn from the account.

Check register   A pamphlet where the depositor can write down all transactions, both deposits and withdrawals, related to the specific account.

Checking account   An account housed at a bank where a depositor can access his or her funds through the use of a various negotiable instruments, such as checks, debit cards, cashier's checks, or money orders.

Claim   A request for something to be considered.

Cleared   A term used in describing when the value of a negotiable item has been withdrawn from your account. An example is when a check you write to someone has been withdrawn from your account, which is then said to have cleared.

Closing costs   Costs that are associated with servicing a home purchase, such as attorney's fees, loan processing fees, and appraisal fees.

Co-insurance   The percentage of all claims, after the deductible has been met, that the policy holder is responsible for.

Collateral   Something of value that is pledged or assigned to a lender to hold in case the borrower is unable to repay the loan.

Commandments   Rules, typically given to us by God through His word.

Compounding   The process by which interest from savings earns additional interest and continues to do so until the money is withdrawn.

Confirmation bias   The claim that we will not use our research and understanding to make a decision or choice, but rather make a choice and then find the research/data to confirm our decision.

Consumer Price Index (CPI)   A measure of how the costs of goods and services change over a period of time.

Consumption   The use or using up of a resource.

Consumptive   To use or consume something.

Contentment   A state of being in which we are completely satisfied by our dependence on God's provision for our sustainment.

Convertible corporate bonds   Corporate bonds that have the ability to be converted into a specific number of equity shares by the issuer of the bond.

Correlation   The relationship (and strength of that relationship) between two investments.

Co-signer   Someone other than the borrower required to sign a promissory note, thus taking equal liability that the loan payments are made in agreement with the contract between the borrower and the lender.

Credit   An amount of money that a lender is willing to allow to be borrowed and then repaid.

Credit lines   The number of credit accounts established/opened on a credit report.

Credit report   A collection of information from lenders and other credit agencies that provides updates on existing credit accounts as well as a listing of recent inquiries by other potential lenders.

Credit score   A numerical score derived from a mathematical model that each credit reporting agency uses based on a wide variety of risk factors, such as length of credit history, amount of credit available, and number of credit lines opened.

Criteria   are defined as the principles or standards by which something can be decided.

Currency risk   The risk involved in the fluctuations of the global currencies as they relate to one another.

Death benefit   The amount of money the insurance company will pay the beneficiary of the policy.

Debit card   A plastic card with a magnetized strip on the back and a series of numbers on the front that provides any merchant electronic approval to remove the authorized amount from the account.

Debt   The amount of funds of a credit line that has been used and thus is owed back to the lender.

Debt-to-income ratio   This ratio is found by taking the sum of all your monthly debt payments (including your expected house payment) and dividing that by the household's combined gross income.

Decisions   The actions we take after consideration of all possible options.

Deductible   The total amount of claims that the policy holder is responsible for paying for prior to the insurance company making any payments on behalf of the policy holder.

Default   When a borrower does not meet his or her obligations in making payments on a loan.

Deficit   The amount by which our resources are not sufficient to meet a need.

Defined benefit plan   A retirement plan that provides a set benefit to employees when they retire, which usually lasts for their entire lives.

Defined contribution plan   A retirement plan in which employees direct their own contributions and fund selections for their retirement.

Disability benefit amount   The amount, usually established as a percentage, of replacement income a disability policy will pay out. The amount is often between 50% and 70% of the employee's salary.

Disability benefit level   The percentage of income that the policy holder is entitled to in the event he or she is unable to work.

Disability benefit period   The amount of time that a disability policy will provide benefits to the insured.

Disability insurance   A type of insurance that offers the insured income protection in the event that he or she becomes unable to work due to a qualified disability.

Discipline   A practice of training someone, to include yourself, to obey rules, or a code of conduct.

Discount programs   Voluntary benefits offered by employers that are established to offer reduced costs or discounts on products and services offered by other third parties.

Diversification   Owning a variety of different companies in different industries in your portfolio; spreading out among various different options.

Dividends   Cash payments from the excess earnings of a company to its shareholders.

Doctrine of constructive receipt   A tax concept that if one earns income and has the right to receive that income, he or she is in constructive receipt and must therefore pay tax on that amount of money.

Down payment   The upfront payment toward a purchase, usually for a home.

Effective tax rate   The ratio of total amount of taxes actually paid to total earned income.

Elimination period (waiting period)   A time period that must lapse prior to any benefits being paid out in a disability policy.

Enough   An inflow of money (either from wages or accumulated assets/investments) that will support four main objectives: (1) live, (2) give, (3) owe, and (4) grow.

Envy   An unpleasant, often painful emotion characterized by feelings of inferiority, hostility, and resentment produced by an awareness of another person or groups of people who enjoy a desired possession, position, attribute, or quality of being.

Escrow account   A designed account where a third party holds funds to be later used for specific purposes, mainly paying property taxes and annual homeowner's insurance.

Estate planning   The planning of how you want your possessions to be distributed and handled at your death.

Evidence of insurability   Proof of insurability or general health provided by a health-care professional.

Faith   The assurance of things hoped for; the conviction of things not seen (Hebrews 11:1).

Family life cycle   A concept that attempts to describe the effects of time on a family through marriage and child rearing, specifically in relation to income and expenses.

Fear of failure   A constant search for significance.

Fear of the future   A state of worry in an attempt to control or identify future events.

Federal Housing Administration   A home loan program in partnership with the Department of Housing and Urban Development and local lenders offering governmental guarantees to borrower loans.

Federal Reserve Fedwire system   A system that allows banks to transfer money from one Federal Reserve Bank to another, which can offer real-time settlement.

Financial capital   Owning assets that produce income.

Financial counselors   Those in a position to work with individual clients, usually one on one, to assist clients with establishing personal budgets, evaluating their current debts, helping set financial goals, and working to create an action plan to help reach those goals.

Financial independence   When one's income and assets are sufficient to meet short-term and long-term objectives.

Financial Industry Regulatory Authority (FINRA)   A self-regulatory organization whose role is to oversee those who conduct financial transactions on behalf of clients.

Financial life cycle   The process individuals go through in relation to their asset accumulation and distribution over their lifetime.

Financial planning   The continuing allocation of limited financial resources to changing and unlimited alternatives.

Fixed loans   Loans that have a fixed number of payments.

Fixed-rate mortgage A mortgage loan type in which the interest remains the same during the duration of the loan period.

Framing effect or framing bias The influence created based on the way or context in which information was presented.

Fully insured Having received the full 40 credits required to be eligible for Social Security retirement benefits and other Social Security benefits.

General obligation bonds (GO bonds) Bonds that do not have a revenue source and thus must be repaid through the ability of the municipality to tax its constituents (residents).

Giving Freely transferring ownership or possession of something to another, such as individuals, groups, or businesses.

Globalization The interconnectedness of companies across the globe that are involved in supply and demand of their products and services.

Goal A desired future outcome or expectation.

Goal setting Determining what future outcome or expectation is to be desired.

Gross earnings Total earnings, usually your annual salary amount or a calculation by which you take your hourly wage and multiply it by the number of hours you worked in a given pay period.

Group health plans Health plans that cover a group of individuals based on some common affiliation.

Growth investment Investments that are expected to grow quickly over a short period of time.

Health-care share ministries Health care in which members share in one another's health-care costs rather than relying on an insurance company.

High-deductible health plan (HDHP) An alternative to a traditional health insurance cost structure that enlists higher deductibles with lower premiums for the policy holder.

Hoarding Difficulty in discarding something or lack of control in accumulating possessions.

Home equity line of credit (HELOC) A revolving line of credit that uses the equity in one's home as collateral.

Hope Knowing what is not seen but believing it to exist.

Housing expense ratio A financial ratio that compares the amount of an anticipated house payment to include principle, interest, taxes, and insurance to that of the borrower's gross monthly income.

Human capital The skills, training, knowledge, and experiences that an individual can bring to his or her role in the labor force.

Identity risk (also known as identity theft) The risk associated with having one's identity compromised, such as having one's Social Security number stolen.

Identity theft See identity risk.

Indemnity plans A type of health insurance plan that allows the insured to pay for services as those services occur, usually requiring an annual deductible to be met.

Inflation The overall increase in the cost of goods and services over time.

Insurance   An agreement between two parties in which one party transfers a risk to another party for a fee.

Interest rate   The percentage rate charged for the use of money; the rate at which money earns interest.

Intestate   A person who dies without a will.

Intrinsic value   The difference between the market price of a company and the per-share value of its book value, or company assets less company liabilities.

Investment loan   The use of investments, such as a stock portfolio, as collateral to buy more investments.

Investment portfolio   A collection of different stocks (or other investments) that make up one's overall investment holdings.

Investment risk   The risk of buying financial investments such as stocks, bonds, art, collectibles, and so forth that have the potential to go down in value and become worth less than what was paid for them.

Irrevocable trust   A trust that cannot be revoked.

Itemized Deduction   An eligible expense that an individual taxpayer in the U.S. can potentially use as a deduction from their adjusted gross income. The sum of each itemized deduction will collectively be called one's total itemized deductions.

Liquidity   The amount of cash reserves a client has available.

Longevity risk   The risk that you may outlive your financial resources.

Long-term care insurance (LTC)   An insurance contract that is designed to cover expenses related to extended health-care services, such as living in a nursing home or the care required after being diagnosed with Alzheimer's disease.

Loss aversion   A concept implying that we are more heavily influenced by a loss than we are by a win.

Margin   The amount of excess from our required expenditures (cash inflow minus cash outflow = margin).

Marginal tax rate, also marginal tax bracket   The tax rate at which the next dollar of income will be taxed.

Marital deduction   Property that one spouse can transfer to the living spouse at his or her death without paying an estate tax.

Marital gift exclusion   Allows one spouse to transfer an unlimited amount to the other spouse before death without paying a gift transfer tax.

Market risk   The risk one takes by investing in the stock market as a whole.

Materialism   A tendency to consider material possessions as highly important.

Matrix   A collection of columns and rows that produce varying outcomes based on the rules applied to those columns and rows.

Medicaid   A health-care coverage program designed for low-income adults, children, and pregnant women and eligible people with disabilities.

Medicare   A social health-care program designed to supplement the cost of health care for those over the age of 65.

Medicare Advantage Plan   A third-party plan that offers Social Security Medicare plans to participants. Typically, these plans offer more benefits and generally lower costs to participants.

Medigap   Policies sold to Social Security beneficiaries that help to cover costs that are not covered by Medicare programs. You must be enrolled in Part A or Part B of Medicare to qualify for a Medigap policy.

Mental accounting   The tendency to mentally categorize our money into different conscious compartments based on certain criteria, mainly the origin of funds and purpose of funds.

Moral relativism   The idea that in a naturalistic worldview, moral laws are created by those who exist in society.

Mortality and expense (M&E) fee   A fee charged by the insurance company intended to cover the cost of death benefits to beneficiaries (mortality) and the expenses of the insurance carrier, such as administration and operation expenses.

Mortgage-payment-expense-to-income ratio (also known as mortgage-to-income ratio)   A ratio found by taking the total house payment (to include principal, interest, PMI, insurance, and taxes) and dividing that payment by the household's combined gross income.

Multiculturalism   The idea that all cultures are all equal and acceptable and are derived from their historical and continual evolution through their experiences.

Multiple Listing Service (MLS)   A database of property listings usually providing access to available homes within a geographical area and that is continuously updated. The MLS is accessed through real estate agents that subscribe to the MLS service.

Naturalism   The idea that nature has existed from the beginning and the world in which we live can and does explain everything.

Negative amortization   The process by which the amount you owe actually goes up rather than down due to adding interest to the balance of the loan.

Nonqualified account   Accounts that are not qualified, or eligible, to receive special tax considerations under the U.S. tax code.

Omnipotence   The phrase that describes God's experience. That fact that God has unlimited power.

Omnipresence   The phrase that describes God's perspective. The fact that God is everywhere.

Omniscience   The phrase that describes God's knowledge and understanding. The fact that God knows all things.

Opportunity cost   The value associated with any potential gain foregone by any other possible alternatives.

Opportunity cost of consumption   The foregone future value of money due to the use or using up of that money now.

Outpatient treatment   Medical services that are not conducted inside a hospital but in many cases a private doctor's office.

Overconfidence   The thought that we are above the averages.

Overdrafts   Items presented for payment on your account for which there are insufficient funds in your account to clear the items.

Par value   The initial value associated with each bond when issued.

Perspective   A point of view or attitude toward something.

Political risk   The risk associated with changes in the political arena, including changes in power or laws, that could negatively impact our daily lives.

Possessions   Items of property belonging to someone.

Posterity   Relating to all future generations of people.

Power of attorney   A written authorization appointing a person to act on your behalf in your personal or business matters.

Pragmatism   The idea that what is thought to work is thought to be best.

Premium   The amount paid annually to the insurance carrier for the transfer of risk.

Principle   A fundamental truth or proposition that serves as the foundation for a system of belief or behavior or for a chain of reasoning.

Private mortgage insurance   An insurance policy that is required by lenders when borrowers put down less than 20% of the purchase price in order to protect the lender from borrower default.

Probate   The process of proving up a will and transferring assets through the court system.

Productive   To yield or result in something more.

Prosperity   State of being prosperous; financially successful.

Protection   The act of keeping safe from an adverse even.

Provision   An amount to be provided.

Real interest rate   The stated interest rate adjusted for inflation.

Registered Investment Advisor (RIA)   A financial professional who is able to offer financial advice and charge an ongoing fee for that advice. The ongoing fee is usually established as a percentage of the assets managed or advised on for a client.

Relative deprivation   A theory suggesting that individuals do not look at their own realities, but rather base reality on comparison with others around them.

Responsibilities   A state of having a duty to deal with something or have control over something.

Revenue bonds   Bonds issued by cities in which the funds are used to improve or create a structure that will generate revenue.

Revocable trust   A trust that is able to be cancelled.

Revolving line of credit   A type of credit account that does not have a fixed number of payments.

Rights   Legal and contractual agreements of freedom of entitlement.

Risk   Hazard, or a potential loss; the idea that some event might occur that does not benefit you.

Risk tolerance   The level of risk a client is willing to take.

Savings   Resources, usually money, designated for a later use.

Single life annuity   A series of equal payments made to someone over their lifetime.

Small Business Association (SBA)　A governmental organization that helps small businesses and entrepreneurs by guaranteeing business loans offered by local banks.

SMART　Characteristics of goals: specific, measurable, attainable, realistic, and timely.

Social Security Administration　A governmental organization created in 1935 under the Old-Age and Survivors Insurance program (known as the Social Security Board until 1946) as part of the Social Security Act signed into law by President Roosevelt.

Social Security credits　Credits that are calculated using two components: your earnings (wages) and your work history (how long you have worked). One credit is earned for each $1,220 of income; no more than 4 credits can be earned in a given year.

Social Security disability benefits　Benefits received by those who meet the two criteria for being disabled: (1) being unable to work due to a medical condition lasting or expected to last at least 1 year or (2) having a condition that could lead to death.

Standard deduction　A fixed amount that a person can deduct from their adjusted gross income without having to itemize deductions.

Stewardship　The activities or job of protecting and being responsible for something.

Stock brokers　Originally, those who would buy and sell financial securities (stocks and bonds) and earn a commission on what they bought or sold for a client; more generally, those who receive compensation, usually in the form of commissions, for each transaction they help a client complete

Suitability　In regard to financial planning, investments that meet the objectives of an investor and that fall within the client's means.

Sunk costs　Time, money, or resources that have already been used and cannot be recaptured.

Supplemental Nutrition Assistance Program (SNAP)　A federally funded program that helps low-income families buy food. These programs are mainly run through state or county offices.

Supplemental Security Income　Governmental financial support for those adults who have a disability and children who have limited income and other resources for their support.

Sustainment　The act of being sustained; the required actions in order to meet our daily needs so that we may live.

Systematic risk　The risk of the overall market and economy.

Tax avoidance (see also Tax minimization)　The use of legitimate processes offered through the tax code that can reduce the amount of tax owed.

Tax evasion　The intentional act of preparing misleading tax documents and/or avoiding paying what is legitimately required.

Tax minimization (see also Tax avoidance)　The use of legitimate processes offered through the tax code that can reduce the amount of tax owed.

Taxable income　The portion of your earned income that is ultimately taxed after taking into account all deductions, exemptions, and other reductions of income.

Temporary Assistance for Needy Families (TANF)　A federal program that provides grant money to states in order to provide short-term financial support to low-income families who have dependents under the age of 18.

Testate   A person who dies with a will.

Testator   The person who is the writer of the will.

Theory   A system of ideas that, taken together, help explain something.

Time horizon   The length of time that an investor has before potentially needing to access the capital used to purchase an investment.

Tithe   A tenth; a portion of your income set aside for giving.

Trust   A fiduciary relationship that appoints a third party, a trustee, to hold assets for the benefit of a beneficiary.

Umbrella policy   An insurance policy that provides liability coverage over and above the coverage listed on one's auto and homeowner's insurance policies.

Unemployment   A benefit program that pays money to formerly employed workers who have become unemployed by no fault of their own and meet certain requirements determined by the state in which the worker lives.

Unsystematic risk   The risk associated with investing in a specific company or industry.

Utopianism   The idea that all humans are mostly good and that through the right governance (social structure) we can live in a perfect society.

Value investment   Investments sought after due to trading below their intrinsic value.

Values-based investing   The idea that investors can incorporate their values and personal convictions by aligning those values with the companies they invest in.

Volatility   The rate at which a stock will go up and down.

Warrants   Securities that allow the owner to buy the underlying stock at a specific price (known as the exercise price) for a certain period of time.

Worldview   The ultimate core beliefs that make up one's convictions about one's self and the world in which one lives.

Yield curve   The graphical representation in which interest rates are plotted against time, usually designed by a determined maturity.

Index

stock brokers, 457–458
stock option plans, 327–328
stocks
   investing in, 365–367
   overview, 361–363
Stoltmann, Andrew, 26
student loans, 193
suitability, 457
sunk costs, 133
Supplemental Nutrition Assistance Program (SNAP), 448
Supplemental Security Income, 444
survivor's benefits, 443–444
sustainment, 42
systematic risk, 363

T

Tada, Joni Eareckson, 130
Target Corporation, 406
Tax Act (2001), 427
tax avoidance, 300
tax evasion, 300
tax minimization, 300
taxable estate, 427–431
taxable income, 306
taxes. *See also* income taxes
   attitudes toward, 300–301
   behaviors, 301–302
   biblical insight on, 302–303
   calculating, 307–309
   filing status, 307
   investment strategies, 316–317
   paying, as stewardship indicator, 31–32
   perspective on, 300–301
   planning strategies, 313
   preparing and planning for, 309–311
   rates, 304–307
   shifting strategies, 315–316
   timing strategies, 313–315
   types of, 303–304
   withholding, 311–313
tax-sheltered annuities, 377
Temporary Assistance for Needy Families (TANF), 448
tenants in common, 425
term life insurance, 235–236
testamentary trusts, 426
testate, 423
testator, 423
theory, 154
Thinking Fast and Slow (Kahneman), 91
time, as decision-making barrier, 89
time horizon, 457
tithe, 398
titled assets, 425

tools principle, 422
traditional whole-life insurance, 236
transfer decision, in estate planning, 420–423
transitory income, 155
treasure principle
   estate planning and, 418–419
   giving and, 388–389
The Treasure Principle (Alcorn), 392, 418
Treasury securities, 231
trust principle, 422
trusts, 425–426
tuition assistance, 336–337

U

unemployment, 448
unequal cash flows
   future value of, 355–356
   present value of, 357–358
unified credit, 427
Uniform Small Loan Laws (USLL), 194
unitrusts (CRUT), 431
unity, borrowing and, 203
unity principle, 419–420
unsystematic risk, 363
U.S. savings bonds, 368–370
U.S. Treasuries, 370–371
use taxes, 304
utopianism, 2–3

V

value investment, 365
values-based investing, 377–378
variable life insurance, 237–238
Veterans Affairs (VA), 447–448
vision plans, 332
volatility, 362

W

waiting period, 335
warrants, 371
When Helping Hurts (Corbett & Fikkert), 396
Whyte, Liz Essley, 10, 11–13
wills, 423–424
Wills, David, 11, 12
worldview
   defined, 2
   other ideas, 2–4

Y

yield curve, 285, 286
young adult stage, 148
Your Living Expenses worksheet, 174–175